THE OXFORD HANDBOOK OF

MEGAPROJECT MANAGEMENT

The Oxford Handbook of Megaproject Management provides state-of-the art scholarship in the emerging field of megaproject management.

Megaprojects are large, complex projects which typically cost billions of dollars and impact millions of people, like building a high-speed rail line, a megadam, a national health or pensions IT system, a new wide-body aircraft, or staging the Olympics.

The book contains 25 chapters written especially for this volume, covering all aspects of megaproject management, from front-end planning to actual project delivery, including how to deal with stakeholders, risk, finance, complexity, innovation, governance, ethics, project breakdowns, and scale itself. Individual chapters cover the history of the field and relevant theory, from behavioral economics to lock-in and escalation to systems integration and theories of agency and power. All geographies are covered—from the US to China, Europe to Africa, South America to Australia—as are a wide range of project types, from "hard" infrastructure to "soft" change projects. In-depth case studies illustrate salient points.

The Handbook offers rigorous, research-oriented, up-to-date academic view of the discipline, based on high-quality data and strong theory. It will be an indispensible resource for students, academics, policy makers, and practitioners.

Bent Flyvbjerg is the first BT Professor and inaugural Chair of Major Programme Management at the University of Oxford. He is the author or editor of 10 books and more than 200 papers. His publications have been translated into 20 languages and are widely cited. His research has been covered by *Science*, *The Economist*, the *New York Times*, the *Wall Street Journal*, the *Financial Times*, *China Daily*, the BBC, CNN, and many other media sources. Flyvbjerg serves as advisor and consultant to governments and businesses around the world, including the UK and US governments and several Fortune 500 companies. He was twice a Fulbright Scholar and received a knighthood in 2002.

THE OXFORD HANDBOOK OF

MEGAPROJECT MANAGEMENT

Edited by

BENT FLYVBJERG

OXFORD

UNIVERSITY PRESS

Great Clarendon Street, Oxford, OX2 6DP,
United Kingdom

Oxford University Press is a department of the University of Oxford.
It furthers the University's objective of excellence in research, scholarship,
and education by publishing worldwide. Oxford is a registered trade mark of
Oxford University Press in the UK and in certain other countries

Published in the United States of America by Oxford University Press
198 Madison Avenue, New York, NY 10016, United States of America

British Library Cataloguing in Publication Data
Data available

Library of Congress Cataloging in Publication Data
Data available

ISBN 978–0–19–873224–2 (Hbk.)
ISBN 978–0–19–883110–5 (Pbk.)

Contents

PART III CURES

PART IV CASES

LIST OF ILLUSTRATIONS

List of Tables

LIST OF CONTRIBUTORS

Rhodante Ahlers is an Independent Researcher

Atif Ansar is Lecturer at the Blavatnik School of Government, University of Oxford

Robert A. Baade is the A. B. Dick Professor of Economics and Business at Lake Forest College in Lake Forest, Illinois

Karen Bakker is a Professor, Canada Research Chair, and Founding Director of the Program on Water Governance at the University of British Columbia

Chris Biesenthal is a Senior Lecturer at the School of the Built Environment at the University of Technology, Sydney

Alexander Budzier is a Business Development Manager at the Saïd Business School, University of Oxford

Demi Chung is a Senior Lecturer and Undergraduate Studies Coordinator at the University of New South Wales

Stewart R. Clegg is a Professor in the University of Technology Sydney Business School. He is also a Strategic Research Adviser, Newcastle University Business School, UK, and a Visiting Professor, School of Business and Economics, Universidade Nova, Lisbon, Portugal

Andrew Davies is Professor in the Management of Projects, The Bartlett Faculty of the Built Environment, University College London

Gerardo del Cerro Santamaría is Research Professor of Planning and Megaprojects at The Cooper Union for the Advancement of Science and Art in Manhattan

Mark Dodgson is Director of the Technology and Innovation Management Centre at the University of Queensland Business School

Helga Drummond is a Professor of Decision Sciences in University of Liverpool Management School and Visiting Professor of Business, Gresham College London

Bent Flyvbjerg is the BT Professor and inaugural Chair of Major Programme Management at the University of Oxford

David M. Gann is the Vice-President (Development and Innovation), Imperial College London

Nuno Gil is Academic Director at the Centre for Infrastructure Development, Manchester Business School

Carsten Greve is Professor of Public Management and Governance, Copenhagen Business School

Graeme Hodge is a professor of Public Policy in the Law Faculty at Monash University

Vered Holzmann Coller School of Management, Tel Aviv University

Sylvain Lenfle a professor of Innovation Management at the Conservatoire National des Arts et Métiers (CNAM) in Paris and associate researcher at the Centre de Recherche en Gestion (CRG), Ecole Polytechnique, France

Donald Lessard is the Epoch Foundation Professor of International Management, Emeritus at the MIT Sloan School of Management

Raymond E. Levitt is Professor of Civil and Environmental Engineering and Director of the Center for Global Projects (CGP) at Stanford University

Christoph Loch is a Professor and the Director of Cambridge Judge Business School at the University of Cambridge

Daniel Lunn is an Emeritus Fellow in the Department of Statistics, University of Oxford

Victor A. Matheson is Professor of Economics at the College of the Holy Cross

Benjamin Melamed is Distinguished Professor at Rutgers Business School

Roger Miller École EMD, Aix-Marseille

Julien Pollack is the Senior Lecturer at the School of the Built Environment, University of Technology

Hugo Priemus is Professor Emeritus System Innovation and Spatial Development, Delft University of Technology

Xuefei Ren is an Associate Professor of Sociology and Global Urban Studies, Michigan State University

Vivek Sakhrani is a PhD candidate and researcher at the Massachusetts Institute of Technology, and CPCS Transcom Inc

Knut Samset is Professor of Project Management at the Faculty of Engineering Science and Technology, Norwegian University of Science and Technology

Shankar Sankaran is Professor of Organizational Project Management at the School of the Built Environment, University of Technology Sydney

W. Richard Scott is Emeritus Professor of Sociology at Stanford University

Thayer Scudder is Emeritus Professor of Anthropology, California Institute of Technology

Aaron Shenhar is Professor of Project and Technology Management, CEO, The SPL Group and TLI

Matti Siemiatycki is an associate professor of Geography and Planning at the University of Toronto

Janis van der Westhuizen is an Associate Professor, Stellenbosch University

Bert van Wee is Professor in Transport Policy at Delft University of Technology

Roger Vickerman is the Dean for Europe and Professor of European Economics at the University of Kent

Gro Holst Volden is a Research Director for the Concept Research Program, Norwegian University of Science and Technology

Graham Winch is Professor of Project Management, Manchester Business School, University of Manchester

Yao Zhao is Professor and Department Vice Chair, Rutgers Business School, Rutgers University

Margreet Zwarteveen is Professor of Water Governance, UNESCO-IHE

CHAPTER 1

....

INTRODUCTION

The Iron Law of Megaproject Management

....

BENT FLYVBJERG

1.1 CLASSICS IN MEGAPROJECT MANAGEMENT

THE ambition for this inaugural edition of *The Oxford Handbook of Megaproject Management* is to become the ultimate source for state-of-the-art scholarship in the emerging field of megaproject management. The book offers a rigorous, research-oriented, up-to-date academic view of the discipline based on high-quality data and strong theory. Until lately, the literature in this new field was scattered over a large number of publications and disciplines, making it difficult to obtain an overview of the history, key issues, and core readings. *Megaproject Planning and Management: Essential Readings* (Flyvbjerg 2014a) assembled the central historical texts in the field. *The Oxford Handbook of Megaproject Management* has been designed to provide the most important contemporary readings. Taken together, the two books are intended to map out the best of what is worth reading in the megaproject management literature, past and present.

In a recent survey, the author asked 114 experts to identify the classics in megaproject management (Flyvbjerg 2014b: xxx–xxxi). The results show that if one defines a "classic" in the conventional sense—as a written work that is generally recognized as definitive in its field by a majority of experts in that field—then there are no classics in megaproject management. Remarkably, the publication proposed by the most respondents as a classic was proposed by only five respondents—several times less the required majority for a classic. In no less than 79% of cases, a publication put forward as a classic was proposed by one and only one respondent, indicating a huge spread in views regarding what the classics might be in this field.

Several explanations exist for this lack of consensus regarding classics in megaproject management. The field is young and unconsolidated as an academic discipline; therefore, perhaps more time is needed to develop and agree upon possible classics. Moreover, the field is multidisciplinary and fragmented, which makes consensus harder to come by. Whatever the explanation, Kuhn (2012) and other philosophers of science hold that classics are necessary to develop and strengthen an academic field, because classics serve as exemplars and reference points around which paradigmatic research may evolve and against which revolutionary research can pit itself. Following Kuhn and others, it is argued here that megaproject management, if it is to make progress as an academic field of inquiry and a professional field of practice, is very much in need of classics. *The Oxford Handbook of Megaproject Management* together with the previous book of historical texts have therefore been developed with the explicit purpose of contributing to the growth of such classics, and hopefully one or more papers in these books may one day become classics.

In addition to the print version of *The Oxford Handbook of Megaproject Management*, an electronic version is planned to ensure the widest possible dissemination and to allow updates as new research appears.[1] The primary audience for the book is the research academic community, professionals, doctoral students, master's programs, and executive education programs in management, strategy, planning, megaproject management, and project and program management. It is hoped that by providing the present set of cutting-edge contemporary readings in megaproject management the book will help progress the discipline, academically and professionally. It is also hoped that citizens and communities interested in and affected by megaprojects may find useful insights in this book.

1.2 What Are Megaprojects?

Megaprojects are large-scale, complex ventures that typically cost $1 billion or more, take many years to develop and build, involve multiple public and private stakeholders, are transformational, and impact millions of people.[2] Hirschman (1995: vii, xi) calls such projects "privileged particles of the development process" and points out that often they are "trait making;" that is, they are designed to ambitiously change the structure of society, as opposed to smaller and more conventional projects that are "trait taking"—they fit into and follow pre-existing structures and do not attempt to modify them. Megaprojects, therefore, are not just magnified versions of smaller projects. Megaprojects are a completely different breed of project in terms of their level of aspiration, stakeholder involvement, lead times, complexity, and impact. Consequently, they are also a very different type of project to lead. Conventional project managers should not lead megaprojects. Megaprojects require reflective practitioners (Schön 1983) as leaders who have developed deep domain experience in this specific field.

Megaprojects are increasingly used as the preferred delivery model for goods and services across a range of businesses and sectors, such as infrastructure, water and energy, information technology, industrial processing plants, mining, supply chains, enterprise systems, strategic corporate initiatives and change programs, mergers and acquisitions, government administrative systems, banking, defense, intelligence, air and space exploration, big science, urban regeneration, and major events (Chapter 2, Lenfle and Loch; Chapter 3, Siemiatycki). Examples of megaprojects are high-speed rail lines, airports, seaports, motorways, disease or poverty eradication programs, hospitals, national health or pension ICT systems, national border control, national broadband, the Olympics, large-scale signature architecture, dams, wind farms, server farms, offshore oil and gas extraction, aluminum smelters, the development of new aircrafts, the largest container and cruise ships, high-energy particle accelerators, and the logistics systems used to run large supply-chain-based companies such as Apple, Amazon, and Maersk.

To illustrate just how big megaprojects are, consider that in dollar terms some of the largest projects are as big as the GDP of many nations (Figure 1.1). Or take one of the largest dollar figures from public economic debate: the size of the US debt to China. This debt is just north of a US\$1 trillion and is considered so large that it may destabilize the world economy if it is not managed prudently. With this supersize measuring rod, now consider the fact that the combined cost of just two of the world's largest megaprojects— the Joint Strike Fighter aircraft program and China's high-speed rail project—is more than half of this figure. The cost of a mere handful of the world's largest megaprojects will dwarf almost any other economic figure, and certainly any investment figure. Finally, consider that in delivering a megaproject one has to—over a relatively short period of time—set up, run, and take down a temporary organization that is often the size of a billion-dollar corporation. The size of megaprojects is staggering no matter what the comparison, and is matched only by the challenges of managing one.

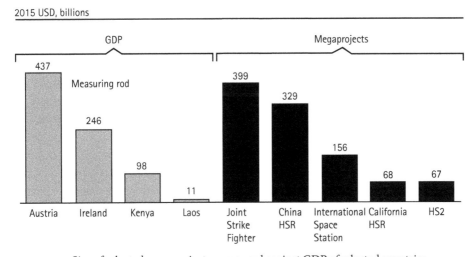

FIGURE 1.1 Size of selected megaprojects, measured against GDP of selected countries.

But megaprojects are not just large; they are constantly growing ever larger in a long historical trend with no end in sight. When New York's Chrysler Building opened in 1930 at 319 meters it was the tallest building in the world. The record has since been surpassed seven times, and from 1998 the tallest building has significantly been located in emerging economies, with Dubai's Burj Khalifa presently holding the record at 828 meters. That is a 160% increase in building height over eighty years. Similarly, the longest bridge span has grown even faster, by 260% over approximately the same period. Measured by value, the size of infrastructure projects has on average grown by 1.5–2.5% annually in real terms over the past century, which is equivalent to a doubling in project size two to three times per century (author's megaprojects database). The size of ICT projects, the new kid on the block, has grown much faster, as illustrated by a sixteen-fold increase from 1993 to 2009 in lines of code in Microsoft Windows, from five to eighty million lines. Other types of megaprojects, from the Olympics to industrial projects, have seen similar developments. Coping with increased scale is therefore a constant and pressing issue in megaproject management, as emphasized by Ansar et al. (Chapter 4). With increasing scale comes increasing globalization, and a set of institutional issues related to this (Chapter 5, Levitt and Scott).

"Mega" derives from the Greek word *megas* and means great, large, vast, big, high, tall, mighty, and important. As a scientific and technical unit of measurement, "mega" specifically means a million. If we were to use this unit of measurement in economic terms, then strictly speaking, megaprojects would be million-dollar (or euro, pound, or other) projects, and for more than a hundred years the largest projects in the world were indeed measured mostly in the millions. This changed with World War II, the Cold War, and the Space Race. Project costs now escalated to the billions, led by the Manhattan Project (1939–46), a research and development program that produced the first atomic bomb, and later the Apollo program (1961–72), which landed the first humans on the moon (Morris 1994; Flyvbjerg 2014b). According to Merriam-Webster, the first known use of the term "megaproject" was in 1976, but before that, from 1968, "mega" was used in "megacity" and later, from 1982, as a standalone adjective to indicate "very large."

Thus the term *megaproject* came into use just as the largest projects technically were megaprojects no more, but, to be accurate, "gigaprojects"—"giga" being the unit of measurement meaning a billion. However, the term *gigaproject* has not caught on. A Google search reveals that the word *megaproject* is used more frequently on the Web than the term *gigaproject*.[3] For the largest of this project type, costs of $50–100 billion are now common, as for the California and UK high-speed rail projects, and costs above $100 billion not uncommon, as for the International Space Station and the Joint Strike Fighter. If they were nations, projects of this size would rank among the world's top hundred countries measured by gross domestic product—larger than the economies of, for example, Kenya or Guatemala. When projects of this size go wrong, whole companies and national economies are affected.

"Tera" is the next unit up, as the measurement for a trillion (a thousand billion). To illustrate how the numbers scale, consider that one million seconds ago, compared with the present, is twelve days in the past; a billion seconds is thirty-two years in the past; and a trillion seconds is 31,710 years in the past, or the equivalent of several ice ages. Recent developments in the size of the very largest projects and programs indicate that we may presently be entering the "tera era" of large-scale project management. Owing to large cost overruns, the Joint Strike Fighter program looks to become the first stand-alone "teraproject" in human history, measured on life-cycle costs (United States Government Accountability Office 2012). Similarly, if we consider as projects the stimulus packages that were launched by the United States, Europe, and China to mitigate the effects of the 2008 financial and economic crises, then these are teraprojects too. Finally, if the major acquisition program portfolio of the United States Department of Defense—which was valued at $1.6 trillion in 2013—is considered a large-scale project, then this, again, would be a teraproject (United States Government Accountability Office 2013: 2). Projects of this size compare with the GDP of the world's top twenty nations, similar in size to the national economies of, for example, Australia or Canada. There is no indication that the relentless drive to scale is abating in megaproject development. Quite the opposite; scale seems to be accelerating. Megaprojects are growing ever larger.

1.3 How Big Is the Global Megaprojects Business?

Megaprojects are not only large and growing constantly larger; they are also being built in ever greater numbers at ever greater value. The McKinsey Global Institute (2013) estimates global infrastructure spending at US$3.4 trillion per year through 2013–2030, or approximately 4% of total global gross domestic product, mainly delivered as large-scale projects. *The Economist* (7 June 2008: 80) has similarly estimated infrastructure spending in emerging economies at US$ 2.2 trillion annually for the period 2009–2018.

To illustrate the accelerated pace at which spending is taking place, consider that China used more cement in the three years 2011–13 than the United States in the entire twentieth century. Similarly, in a recent five-year period China spent more on infrastructure in real terms than in the whole of the past century (Flyvbjerg 2014b). That is an increase in spending rate of a factor of twenty. Finally, in a recent four-year period China built as many kilometers of high-speed rail as Europe did in two decades, and Europe was extraordinarily busy building this type of rail during these years (Chapter 7, Ren). Not at any time in the history of mankind has infrastructure spending been this high measured as a share of world GDP, according to *The Economist*, who calls it "the biggest investment boom in history." And that is just infrastructure.

If we include the many other fields where megaprojects are a main delivery model—oil and gas, mining, aerospace, defense, ICT, supply chains, megaevents, and so on—then a conservative estimate for the global megaproject market is US$ 6–9 trillion per year, or approximately 8% of total global gross domestic product. For perspective, consider that this is equivalent to spending five to eight times the accumulated US debt to

China, *every year*. That is big business by any definition of the term. Moreover, mega-projects have proven remarkably recession-proof. In fact, the downturn from 2008 helped the megaprojects business to grow further by showering stimulus spending on everything from transportation infrastructure to ICT. From being a fringe activity—albeit a spectacular one—mainly reserved for rich, developed nations, megaprojects have recently transformed into a global multi-trillion-dollar business that affects all aspects of our lives, from our electricity bill to what we do on the Internet to how we work and shop and commute.

With so many resources tied up in ever larger and ever more megaprojects, at no time has the management of such projects been more important. The potential benefits of building the right projects in the right manner are enormous and are only equaled by the potential waste from building the wrong projects, or building projects wrongly. Never has it been more important to choose the most fitting projects and get their financial, economic, social, and environmental impacts right. Never has systematic and valid knowledge about megaprojects therefore been more important to inform policy, practice, and public debate in this very costly area of government and business. *The Oxford Handbook of Megaproject Management* is dedicated to delivering such knowledge.

1.4 TEN THINGS YOU MUST KNOW ABOUT MEGAPROJECTS

What drives the megaproject boom described above? Why are megaprojects so attractive to decision makers? The answer to these questions may be found in the so-called four sublimes of megaproject management (Table 1.1). The first of these,

Table 1.1 The "four sublimes" that drive megaproject development

Type of sublime	Characteristic
Technological	The excitement engineers and technologists get in pushing the envelope for what is possible in "longest–tallest–fastest" type of projects.
Political	The rapture politicians get from building monuments to themselves and their causes, and from the visibility this generates with the public and media.
Economic	The delight business people and trade unions get from making lots of money and jobs from megaprojects, including for contractors, workers in construction and transportation, consultants, bankers, investors, landowners, lawyers, and developers.
Aesthetic	The pleasure designers and people who love good design get from building and using something very large that is also iconic and beautiful, such as the Golden Gate bridge.

the "technological sublime," is a term variously attributed to Miller (1965) and Marx (1967) to describe the positive historical reception of technology in American culture during the nineteenth and early twentieth centuries. Frick (2008) introduced the term to the study of megaprojects and here describes the technological sublime as the rapture engineers and technologists obtain from building large and innovative projects, with their rich opportunities for pushing the boundaries for what technology can do, such as building the tallest building, the longest bridge, the fastest aircraft, the largest wind turbine, or the first of anything (see also Chapter 10, Miller et al.; Chapter 20, Holzmann et al.) Frick (2008) applied the concept in a case study of the multi-billion-dollar New San Francisco–Oakland Bay Bridge, concluding that "the technological sublime dramatically influenced bridge design, project outcomes, public debate, and the lack of accountability for its [the bridge's] excessive cost overruns" (239).

Flyvbjerg (2012, 2014b) proposed three additional sublimes, beginning with the "political sublime," which here is understood as the rapture politicians obtain from building monuments to themselves and their causes (Chapter 13, Baade and Matheson; Chapter 24, van der Westhuizen). Megaprojects are manifest; they garner attention and lend an air of proactiveness to their promoters. Moreover, they are media magnets, which appeals to politicians who seem to enjoy few things better than the visibility they get from starting megaprojects; except maybe cutting the ribbon of one in the company of royals or presidents who are likely to be present, lured by the unique monumentality and historical import of many such projects. This is the type of public exposure that helps politicians get re-elected. They therefore actively seek it out.

Next there is the "economic sublime," which is the delight financiers, business people, and trade unions get from making lots of money and jobs from megaprojects. Given the enormous budgets for megaprojects, there are ample funds to go around for all, including contractors, engineers, architects, consultants, construction and transportation workers, bankers, investors, landowners, lawyers, and developers. Finally, the "aesthetic sublime" is the pleasure designers and people who appreciate good design get from building, using, and looking at something very large that is also iconically beautiful, such as San Francisco's Golden Gate bridge or Sydney's Opera House.

All four sublimes are important drivers of the scale and frequency of megaprojects described above. Taken together they ensure that there exist strong coalitions of stakeholders who benefit from megaprojects and who will therefore work for more such projects to happen.

For policy makers, investment in infrastructure megaprojects seems particularly coveted, because, if done right, such investment (i) creates and sustains employment, (ii) contains a large element of domestic inputs relative to imports, (iii) improves productivity and competitiveness by lowering producer costs, (iv) benefits consumers through higher-quality services, and finally, (v) improves the environment when infrastructures that are environmentally sound replace infrastructures that are not (Helm 2008: 1; Chapter 11, Clegg et al.).

But there is a big "if" here, indicated previously with the words "if done right." Only if this is disregarded—as it often is by promoters and decision makers for megaprojects—can megaprojects be seen as an effective way to deliver infrastructure. In fact, conventional megaproject delivery—infrastructure and other—is highly problematic, with a dismal performance record in terms of actual costs and benefits, as we will see later. The following characteristics of megaprojects are typically overlooked or glossed over when the four sublimes are at play and the megaproject format is chosen for delivery of large-scale ventures:

1. Megaprojects are inherently risky because of long planning horizons and complex interfaces (Flyvbjerg 2006; Chapter 21, Davies).
2. Often projects are led by planners and managers without deep domain experience, who keep changing throughout the long project cycles that apply to megaprojects, leaving leadership weak.
3. Decision making, planning, and management are typically multi-actor processes involving multiple stakeholders, public and private, with conflicting interests (Chapter 6, van Wee and Priemus; Chapter 15, Winch; Aaltonen and Kujala 2010).
4. Technology and designs are often non-standard, leading to "uniqueness bias" among planners and managers, who tend to see their projects as singular, which impedes learning from other projects.[4]
5. Frequently there is overcommitment to a certain project concept at an early stage, resulting in "lock-in" or "capture," leaving alternatives analysis weak or absent, and leading to escalated commitment in later stages. "Fail fast" does not apply; "fail slow" does (Chapter 9, Drummond; Cantarelli et al. 2010; Ross and Staw 1993).
6. Because of the large sums of money involved, principal-agent problems and rent-seeking behavior are widespread, as is optimism bias (Eisenhardt 1989; Stiglitz 1989; Flyvbjerg et al. 2009).
7. The project scope or ambition level will typically change significantly over time.
8. Delivery is a high-risk, stochastic activity, with overexposure to so-called black swans; that is, extreme events with massively negative outcomes (Taleb 2010). Managers tend to ignore this, treating projects as if they exist largely in a deterministic Newtonian world of cause, effect, and control.
9. Statistical evidence shows that such complexity and unplanned events are often unaccounted for, leaving budget and time contingencies for projects inadequate.
10. As a consequence, misinformation about costs, schedules, benefits, and risks is the norm throughout project development and decision making. The result is cost overruns, delays, and benefit shortfalls that undermine project viability during project delivery and operations.

In Section 1.5, we will see just how big and frequent such cost overruns, delays, and benefit shortfalls are.

1.5 THE IRON LAW OF MEGAPROJECTS

Performance data for megaprojects speak their own language. Of such projects, 70–90% have cost overruns, depending on project type. For some projects, such as the Olympics, 100% have cost overruns. Overruns of up to 50% in real terms are common, and over 50% not uncommon. Cost overrun for London's Jubilee Line Underground extension was 80% in real terms; for Denver International Airport, 200%; Boston's Big Dig, 220%; the Canadian Firearms Registry, 590%; Sydney Opera House, 1,400%. Overrun is a problem in private, as well as public sector projects, and things are not improving; overruns have stayed high and constant for the 90-year period for which comparable data exist (Chapter 8, Flyvbjerg; Chapter 16, Hodge and Greve; Chapter 23, Chung). Geography also does not seem to matter; all 104 countries and six continents for which data are available suffer from overrun. Similarly, large benefit shortfalls are common, again with no signs of improvements over time and geographies (Flyvbjerg et al. 2002, 2005).

Combine the large cost overruns and benefit shortfalls with the fact that business cases, cost-benefit analyses, and social and environmental impact assessments are typically at the core of planning and decision making for megaprojects, and we see that such analyses can generally not be trusted. For instance, for dams an average cost overrun of 96% combines with an average demand shortfall of 11%, and for rail projects an average cost overrun of 40% combines with an average demand shortfall of 34%. With errors and biases of such magnitude in the forecasts that form the basis for business cases, cost–benefit analyses, and social and environmental impact assessments, such analyses will also, with a high degree of certainty, be strongly misleading. "Garbage in, garbage out," as the saying goes (Flyvbjerg 2009; for in-depth studies of dams, see Chapter 19, Scudder; Chapter 25, Ahlers et al.).

As a case in point, consider the Channel Tunnel, the longest underwater rail tunnel in Europe, connecting the United Kingdom and France. This project was originally promoted as highly beneficial both economically and financially. At the initial public offering, Eurotunnel, the private owner of the tunnel, tempted investors by telling them that 10% "would be a reasonable allowance for the possible impact of unforeseen circumstances on construction costs."[5] In fact, capital costs went 80% over budget, and financing costs 140%. Revenues started at a dismal 10% of those forecast, eventually growing to half of the forecast. As a consequence, the project has proved financially non-viable, with an internal rate of return on the investment that is negative, at –14.5%, with a total loss to Britain of US$17.8 billion. Thus the Channel Tunnel has detracted from the British economy instead of adding to it. This is difficult to believe when you use the service, which is fast, convenient, and competitive compared with alternative modes of travel. But in fact each passenger is heavily subsidized–not by the taxpayer, as is often the case for other megaprojects, but by the many private investors who lost billions when Eurotunnel went insolvent and was financially restructured. This drives home an important point. A megaproject may well be a technological success but a financial failure, and many are. An economic and financial *ex post* evaluation of the Channel Tunnel, which systematically compared actual with forecast costs and benefits, concluded that "the British Economy would have been better off had the Tunnel never been constructed" (Anguera 2006: 291). Other examples of financially non-viable mega-projects are Sydney's Lane Cove Tunnel, the high-speed rail connections at Stockholm and Oslo airports, the Copenhagen Metro, Denmark's Great Belt Tunnel—the second longest underwater rail tunnel in Europe after the Channel Tunnel, and the Chinese projects described in Ansar et al. (2016) (Table 1.2) (see also Chapter 17, Vickerman).

Large-scale ICT projects are even more risky. One in six such projects become a sta-tistical outlier in terms of cost overrun, with an average overrun for outliers of 200% in real terms. This is a 2,000% overincidence of outliers compared to normal, and a 200% overincidence compared with large construction projects, which are also plagued by cost outliers (Flyvbjerg and Budzier 2011). Given the central role of large-scale ICT proj-ects in many transforming organizations in both government and business, the preva-lence of ICT cost outliers are ticking time bombs under such transformations, waiting to go off. Total project waste from failed and underperforming ICT projects for the United States alone has been estimated at $55 billion annually by the Standish Group (2009).

Delays are a separate problem for megaprojects, and delays cause both cost over-runs and benefit shortfalls. For instance, results from a study undertaken at Oxford University, based on the largest database of its kind, shows that delays on dams are 45% on average (Ansar et al. 2014). Thus if a dam was planned to take ten years to execute, from the decision to build until the dam became operational, then it actually took 14½ years on average. Flyvbjerg et al. (2004) modeled the relationship between cost overrun and length of implementation phase based on a large dataset for major construction projects. They found that on average a one-year delay or other extension of the imple-mentation phase correlates with an increase in percentage cost overrun of 4.64%. To illustrate, for a project the size of London's $26-billion Crossrail project, a one-year delay would cost an additional $1.2 billion, or $3.3 million per day. The key lesson here is that in order to keep costs down, implementation phases should be kept short and delays small. This should not be seen as an excuse for fast-tracking projects; that is, rushing them through decision making for early construction start. All you do if you hit the ground running is fall, in the case of megaprojects. Front-end planning needs to be thorough before deciding whether to give the green light to a project or stop it (Williams and Samset 2010). You need to go slow at first (during project preparation) in order to run fast later (during delivery). But often the situation is the exact opposite. Front-end planning is rushed and deficient, bad projects are not stopped, implementation phases and delays are long, costs soar, and benefits and revenue realization diminishes and recedes into the future. For debt-financed projects this is a recipe for disaster, because project debt grows while there are no revenues to service interest payments, which are then added to the debt, and so forth. As a result, many projects end up in the so-called debt trap where a combination of escalating construction costs, delays, and increasing interest payments makes it impossible for project revenues to cover costs, rendering projects non-viable. That is what happened to the Channel Tunnel and Sydney's Lane Cove Tunnel, among many other projects.

Table 1.2 Large–scale projects have a calamitous history of cost overrun

Project	Cost overrun (%)
Suez Canal, Egypt	1,900
Scottish Parliament Building, Scotland	1,600
Sydney Opera House, Australia	1,400
Concord(e) Supersonic Aeroplane, UK, France	1,100
Troy and Greenfield Railroad, USA	900
Montreal Summer Olympics, Canada	720
Excalibur Smart Projectile, USA, Sweden	650
Canadian Firearms Registry, Canada	590
Medicare Transaction System, USA	560
National Health Service IT System, UK	550
Bank of Norway Headquarters, Norway	440
Lake Placid Winter Olympics, USA	320
Furka Base Tunnel, Switzerland	300
Verrazano Narrow Bridge, USA	280
Boston's Big Dig Artery/Tunnel Project, USA	220
Denver International Airport, USA	200
Panama Canal, Panama	200
Minneapolis Hiawatha Light Rail Line, USA	190
Humber Bridge, UK	180
Dublin Port Tunnel, Ireland	160
Montreal Metro Laval Extension, Canada	160
Copenhagen Metro, Denmark	150
Boston–New York–Washington Railway, USA	130
Great Belt Rail Tunnel, Denmark	120
London Limehouse Road Tunnel, UK	110
Brooklyn Bridge, USA	100
Shinkansen Joetsu High-Speed Rail Line, Japan	100
Channel Tunnel, UK, France	80
Karlsruhe–Bretten Light Rail, Germany	80
London Jubilee Line Extension, UK	80
Bangkok Metro, Thailand	70
Mexico City Metroline, Mexico	60
High-Speed Rail Line South, Netherlands	60
Great Belt East Bridge, Denmark	50

This is not to say that megaprojects do not exist that were built on budget and on time and delivered the promised benefits (Chapter 12, Gil; Chapter 14, Davies et al.). The Bilbao redevelopment project, with the Guggenheim Museum Bilbao, is an example of that rare breed of project (Chapter 22, del Cerro Santamaria). Similarly, recent metro extensions in Madrid were built on time and to budget (Flyvbjerg 2005), as were a number of industrial megaprojects (Merrow 2011). It is particularly important to study such projects to understand the causes of success and test whether success may be replicated elsewhere. It is far easier, however, to produce long lists of projects that have failed in terms of cost overruns and benefit shortfalls than it is to produce lists of projects that have succeeded. To illustrate, as part of ongoing research on success in megaproject management, the present author and his colleagues are trying to establish a sample of successful projects large enough to allow statistically valid answers. But so far they have failed. Why? Because success is so rare in megaproject management that at present, it can be studied only as small-sample research, whereas failure may be studied with large, reliable samples of projects.

Success in megaproject management is typically defined as projects delivering the promised benefits on budget and on time. If, as the evidence indicates, approximately 1–2 out of ten megaprojects are on budget, 1–2 out of ten are on schedule, and 1–2 out of ten are on benefits, then approximately 1–8 in a thousand projects is a success, defined as on target for all three. Even if the numbers were wrong by a large margin the success rate would still be dismal. This serves to illustrate what may be called the "iron law of megaprojects:" *Over budget, over time, under benefits, over and over again* (Flyvbjerg 2011). Best practice is an outlier, and average practice a disaster, in this interesting and very costly area of management.

1.6 THE MEGAPROJECTS PARADOX

This analysis leaves us with a genuine paradox: the so-called megaprojects paradox, first identified by Flyvbjerg et al. (2003: 1–10). On one side of the paradox, megaprojects as a delivery model for public and private ventures have never been more in demand, and the size and frequency of megaprojects have never been larger. On the other side, performance in megaproject management is strikingly poor and has not improved for the 90-year period for which comparable data are available, when measured in terms of cost overruns, schedule delays, and benefit shortfalls.

Today, megaproject planners and managers are stuck in this paradox because their main delivery method is what has been called the "break–fix model" for megaproject management.[6] Generally, megaproject managers—and their organizations—do not know how to deliver successful megaprojects, or do not have the incentives to do so. Therefore megaprojects tend to "break" sooner or later—for instance, when reality catches up with optimistic, or manipulated, estimates of schedule, costs, or benefits; and delays, cost overruns, and so on, follow. Projects are then often paused and reorganized—sometimes also refinanced—in an attempt to "fix" problems and deliver some version of the initially planned project with a semblance of success. Typically, lock-in and escalation make it impossible to drop projects altogether, which is why mega-projects have been called the "Vietnams" of policy and management: "easy to begin and difficult and expensive to stop" (White 2012; also Cantarelli et al. 2010; Ross and Staw 1993; Drummond 1998). The "fix" often takes place at great and unexpected cost to those stakeholders who were not in the know of what was going on and were unable to or lacked the foresight to pull out before the break.[7]

The break–fix model is wasteful and leads to a misallocation of resources, in both organizations and society, for the simple reason that under this model decisions to go ahead with projects are based on misinformation more than on information, with misinformation caused by a lack of realism at the outset. The degree of misinforma-tion varies significantly from project to project, as seen by the large standard devia-tions that apply to cost overruns and benefit shortfalls documented by Flyvbjerg et al. (2002, 2005). We may therefore *not* assume, as is often done, that on average all projects are misrepresented by approximately the same degree and that, therefore, we are still building the best projects, even if they are not as good as they appear on paper. The truth is, we do not know, and often projects turn out to bring a net loss, instead of a gain, to the government or company that promoted them. The root cure to the break–fix model is to get projects right from the outset so that they do not break, through proper front-end management, and then have competent teams deliver a realistic front end (Chapter 18, Volden and Samset; Williams and Samset 2010). But megaproject managers must also know how to fix projects once they break, for the simple reason that so many break. The present book deals with both types of situation: (i) getting projects right from the start, and (ii) fixing projects that break.

1.7 CHALLENGES, CAUSES, CURES

The chapters in the book have been selected to give readers a thorough, research-based understanding of (i) the *challenges* in megaproject management, (ii) the root *causes* of those challenges, and (iii) *cures* that may help meet the challenges. The book is thus sys-tematically focused on the *what*, the *why*, and the *how* of megaproject management. In addition, it contains a set of case studies to exemplify general points.

First, as regards the *what* of megaproject management—the *challenges*—Lenfle and Loch (Chapter 2) and Siemiatycki (Chapter 3) present the historical overview. Ansar et al. (Chapter 4) focus on the basic challenge of scale and attempt to theorize scale in terms of fragility. Levitt and Scott (Chapter 5) deal with institutional challenges, espe-cially as these pertain to global megaprojects; that is, projects that span activities in multiple countries, as is increasingly common for megaprojects. van Wee and Priemus (Chapter 6) spell out an important but often overlooked aspect of megaproject manage-ment: namely, the ethical and political issues involved; what is megaproject ethics, they ask? Finally, Ren (Chapter 7) poses a truly sobering question of current debt-financed megaproject investments in China: "Is this the biggest infrastructure bubble in the history of humankind?"

Second, for the *why* of megaproject management—the *causes*—Flyvbjerg (Chapter 8) explores a recent claim made by Cass Sunstein, professor at Harvard, that behavioral economics was pioneered by early research on large projects and that this research accounts well for behavior with megaproject planners and managers. Drummond (Chapter 9) updates and appraises key theories on escalation of commitment and lock-in, as they pertain to megaprojects. Miller et al. (Chapter 10) explain megaproject management in terms of games of innovation, and they explicate how the game is best played. Clegg et al. (Chapter 11) present an overview of how scholars and practitioners make sense of megaprojects and megaproject management, and how power is related to such sensemaking. Gil (Chapter 12) introduces a new collective-action perspective on the planning of megaprojects with a focus on dispute resolution, central to any megaproject. Baade and Matheson (Chapter 13) spell out the drivers of megaevents in emerging economies—an issue of growing importance as megaevents and other types of megaprojects have shifted in increasing numbers from developed to emerging economies, with the major part of investments now happening in the latter.

Third, concerning the *how* of megaproject management—the *cures*—Davies et al. (Chapter 14) describe a new delivery model for megaprojects aimed at securing innovation and flexibility in projects, and they illustrate how the model worked for three UK megaprojects. Winch (Chapter 15), drawing on developments in strategic management research, broadens the notion of stakeholder management to better take into account pressing issues of future generations and the natural environment. Hodge and Greve (Chapter 16) ask and answer the question of how well privatization works as a cure to the challenges of megaproject delivery. Vickerman (Chapter 17) identifies as dubious the common claim that the wider benefits of megaprojects are large and will often justify projects, even when direct benefits do not. Volden and Samset (Chapter 18) describe how Norway implemented a quality assurance program for megaprojects and how this has improved outcomes. Based on a lifetime of research, Scudder (Chapter 19) closes this part of the book by synoptically asking and answering the following question of the perhaps ultimate megaproject, the megadam: "Does the good megadam exist, all things considered?"

Fourth, and finally, Holzmann et al. (Chapter 20) launch the *case studies* with an in-depth inquiry into how the team on Boeing's 787 cracked the code of innovation in megaproject delivery—something high on the agenda for most megaprojects, irrespective of type. Davies (Chapter 21) spells out the lessons learned from the London 2012 Olympic Games in terms of systems integration—again a general concern in most megaprojects. del Cerro Santamaria (Chapter 22) updates and sets straight the record for perhaps the most iconic urban megaproject of the past generation, the $1.5-billion Strategic Plan for the Revitalization of Metropolitan Bilbao, spearheaded by what Philip Johnson, the godfather of architecture, called "the greatest building of our time:" Frank Gehry's Guggenheim Museum Bilbao. Chung (Chapter 23) navigates the maze of Australia's slightly dodgy experience with public–private partnerships in the provision of motorways, and identifies the challenges and opportunities for going forward. van der Westhuizen (Chapter 24) tells the story of megaprojects as mythical political symbols, focusing on Africa's first high-speed railway, the Gautrain, which was initially packaged with South Africa's bid to host the 2010 Soccer World Cup, another first for Africa. Lastly, Ahlers et al. (Chapter 25) study the Aswan High Dam on the Nile and the Nam Theun 2 on the Mekong to illustrate how dam development has changed recently to a situation where political power is more diffuse and where basic transparency and citizens' rights are therefore more difficult to secure; the authors suggest "dam democracy" as an organizing principle for addressing these issues.

In sum, the chapters for this book were selected to be strong on theory and to contain high-quality data, as an antidote to the weak theory and idiosyncratic data that characterize much scholarship in megaproject management (Flyvbjerg 2011). Strong theory is here understood as ideas with a high degree of explanatory power for phenomena in megaproject management. Good data are valid and reliable information that allows systematic comparison of important variables across projects, studies, geographies, and time, or make possible high-quality in-depth case studies. The focus on strong theory and good data is intended to help bring the field forward academically and professionally. As a further criterion, chapters were selected that are relevant not only to developed nations, but also to emerging economies, because at present the main part of investments in megaprojects is taking place here. Finally, chapters providing an historical overview of the field and good case studies have been included. The intention has been to produce a well-rounded book that is a must-read for anyone embarking on study, research, or practice in megaproject management, or who is impacted by megaprojects and wants to understand them better.

ACKNOWLEDGMENTS

I would like to thank the contributors to *The Oxford Handbook of Megaproject Management* for the quality of their contributions and for their patience with my requests for changes during the editing of the book. Special thanks are due to David Musson, former Business and Management Editor at Oxford University Press. David poked me seven years ago to do this book. I deferred, because at the time I did not think there was enough high-quality scholarship in the field of megaproject management to justify, let alone fill, a major volume like this. Today, this situation has happily changed. Megaproject management is rapidly establishing itself as a new field of academic inquiry. I would like to thank the University of Oxford and Saïd Business School for pioneering this development by having the foresight to establish the first permanent chair and the first degree program in the world in this budding area of scholarship, and for giving me the honor of being the first holder of the chair and academic director of the program. This gave me the ideal conditions for working on the *Handbook*. Finally, I wish to thank Clare Kennedy, Assistant Commissioning Editor of Business and Management at Oxford University Press, for excellently seeing the book through the production and printing process to become the handsome tome you are now holding in your hand or viewing on your screen.

Bent Flyvbjerg
Jericho, Oxford
July 2016

NOTES

1. See more at <http://www.oxfordhandbooks.com>.
2. "Megaprojects" are usually measured in billions of dollars; "major projects" in hundreds of millions; and "projects" in millions or tens of millions. Megaprojects are sometimes also called "major programs."
3. Google search, 17 January 2017.
4. "Uniqueness bias" is here defined as the tendency of planners and managers to see their projects as singular. This particular bias stems from the fact that new projects often use non-standard technologies and designs, leading managers to think their project is more different from other projects than it actually is. Uniqueness bias impedes managers' learning, because they think they have nothing to learn from other projects as their own project is unique. This lack of learning may explain why managers who see their projects as unique perform significantly worse than other managers (Budzier and Flyvbjerg 2013). Project managers who think their project is unique are therefore a liability for their project and organization. For megaprojects this would be a megaliability.
5. Quoted from "Under Water Over Budget," *The Economist*, 7 October 1989, 37–8.
6. The author owes the term "break–fix model" to Dr Patrick O'Connell, former Practitioner Director at the BT Centre for Major Programme Management, Saïd Business School, University of Oxford.
7. For a rare look behind the scenes of a break–fix project—to see in real time how a break happens and a fix is attempted—see Flyvbjerg et al. (2014), about Hong Kong's XRL high-speed rail line to mainland China, which broke in 2014, midway through construction.

REFERENCES

Aaltonen, K. and Kujala, J. (2010). "A project lifecycle perspective on stakeholder influence strategies in global projects," *Scandinavian Journal of Management*, 26: 381–97.

Anguera, R. (2006). "The Channel Tunnel: An ex post economic evaluation," *Transportation Research Part A*, 40: 291–315.

Ansar, A., Flyvbjerg, B., Budzier, A., and Lunn, D. (2014). "Should we build more large dams? The actual costs of hydropower megaproject development," *Energy Policy*, March: 43–56.

Ansar, A., Flyvbjerg, B., Budzier, A., and Lunn, D. (2016). "Does infrastructure investment lead to economic growth or economic fragility? Evidence from China," *Oxford Review of Economic Policy*, 32(3): 360–90.

Budzier, A. and Flyvbjerg, B. (2013). "Making sense of the impact and importance of outliers in project management through the use of power laws," *Proceedings of IRNOP (International Research Network on Organizing by Projects)*, vol. 11 (June), pp. 1–28.

Cantarelli, C. C., Flyvbjerg, B., van Wee, B., and Molin, E. J. E. (2010). "Lock-in and its influence on the project performance of large-scale transportation infrastructure projects: Investigating the way in which lock-in can emerge and affect cost overruns," *Environment and Planning B: Planning and Design*, 37: 792–807.

Drummond, H. (1998). "Is escalation always irrational?" *Organization Studies*, 19(6): 911–29.

Economist, The. (2008). "Building BRICs of growth," 7 June: 80.

Eisenhardt, K. M. (1989). "Agency theory: An assessment and review," *Academy of Management Review*, 14(1): 57–74.

Flyvbjerg, B. (2005). "Design by deception: The politics of megaproject approval," *Harvard Design Magazine*, no. 22, Spring/Summer: 50–9.

Flyvbjerg, B. (2006). "From Nobel Prize to project management: Getting risks right," *Project Management Journal*, 37(3): 5–15.

Flyvbjerg, B. (2009). "Survival of the unfittest: Why the worst infrastructure gets built, and what we can do about it," *Oxford Review of Economic Policy*, 25(3): 344–67.

Flyvbjerg, B. (2011). "Over budget, over time, over and over again: Managing major projects," in P. W. G. Morris, J. K. Pinto, and J. Söderlund (eds.), *The Oxford Handbook of Project Management*. Oxford: Oxford University Press, pp. 321–44.

Flyvbjerg, B. (2012). "Why mass media matter, and how to work with them: Phronesis and megaprojects," in B. Flyvbjerg, T. Landman, and S. Schram (eds.), *Real Social Science: Applied Phronesis*. Cambridge: Cambridge University Press, pp. 95–121.

Flyvbjerg, B. (ed.) (2014a). *Megaproject Planning and Management: Essential Readings*, vols. 1–2. Cheltenham, UK, and Northampton, MA: Edward Elgar.

Flyvbjerg, B. (2014b). "Introduction," in B. Flyvbjerg (ed.), *Megaproject Planning and Management: Essential Readings*, vols. 1–2. Cheltenham, UK, and Northampton, MA: Edward Elgar, pp. xiii–xxxiv.

Flyvbjerg, B., Bruzelius, N., and Rothengatter, W. (2003). *Megaprojects and Risk: An Anatomy of Ambition*. Cambridge: Cambridge University Press.

Flyvbjerg, B. and Budzier, A. (2011). "Why your IT project might be riskier than you think," *Harvard Business Review*, 89(9): 24–7.

Flyvbjerg, B., Garbuio, B., and Lovallo, D. (2009). "Delusion and deception in large infrastructure projects: Two models for explaining and preventing executive disaster," *California Management Review*, 51(2): 170–93.

Flyvbjerg, B., Holm, M. K. S., and Buhl, S. L. (2002). "Underestimating costs in public works projects: Error or lie?" *Journal of the American Planning Association*, 68(3): 279–95.

Flyvbjerg, B., Holm, M. K. S., and Buhl, S. L. (2004). "What causes cost overrun in transport infrastructure projects?" *Transport Reviews*, 24(1): 3–18.

Flyvbjerg, B., Holm, M. K. S., and Buhl, S. L. (2005). "How (in)accurate are demand forecasts in public works projects? The case of transportation," *Journal of the American Planning Association*, 71(2): 131–46.

Flyvbjerg, B., Kao, T.-C., and Budzier, A. (2014). "Report to the Independent Board Committee on the Express Rail Link Project," in *MTR Independent Board Committee: Second Report by the Independent Board Committee on the Express Rail Link Project*. Hong Kong: MTR, pp. A1–122.

Frick, K. T. (2008). "The cost of the technological sublime: Daring ingenuity and the new San Francisco–Oakland Bay Bridge," in H. Priemus, B. Flyvbjerg, B. van Wee (eds.), *Decision-Making on Mega-Projects: Cost–Benefit Analysis, Planning, and Innovation*. Cheltenham, UK, and Northampton, MA: Edward Elgar, pp. 239–62.

Helm, D. (2008). "Time to invest: Infrastructure, the credit crunch and the recession," *Monthly Commentary*, 18 December, <http://www.dieterhelm.co.uk>.

Hirschman, A. O. (1995). *Development Projects Observed*. Washington, DC: Brookings Institution. First published 1967.

Kuhn, T. S. (2012). *The Structure of Scientific Revolutions*, 4th edn. Chicago, IL: University of Chicago Press. First published in 1962.

Marx, L. (1967). *The Machine in the Garden: Technology and the Pastoral Ideal in America*. Oxford and New York: Oxford University Press.

McKinsey Global Institute. (2013). *Infrastructure Productivity: How to Save $1 Trillion a Year*. New York: McKinsey and Company.

Merrow, E. W. (2011). *Industrial Megaprojects: Concepts, Strategies, and Practices for Success*. Hoboken, NJ: Wiley.

Miller, P. (1965). *The Life of the Mind in America: From the Revolution to the Civil War*. New York: Harvest Books.

Morris, P. W. G. (1994). "The 1960s: Apollo and the decade of management systems," in *The Management of Projects*. Reston, VA: American Society of Civil Engineers, pp. 38–88.

Ross, J. and Staw, B. M. (1993). "Organizational escalation and exit: Lessons from the Shoreham nuclear power plant," *The Academy of Management Journal*, 36(4): 701–32.

Schön, D. A. (1991). *The Reflective Practitioner: How Professionals Think in Action*. New York: Basic Books. First published 1983.

Standish Group. (2009). *CHAOS Report*. West Yarmouth, MA.

Stiglitz, J. (1989). "Principal and agent," in J. Eatwell, M. Milgate, and P. Newman (eds.), *The New Palgrave: Allocation, Information and Markets*. New York: Norton, pp. 241–53.

Taleb, N. N. (2010). *The Black Swan: The Impact of the Highly Improbable*, 2nd edn. London and New York: Penguin.

United States Government Accountability Office (GAO). (2012). *Joint Strike Fighter: DOD Actions Needed to Further Enhance Restructuring and Address Affordability Risks*, Report GAO-12-437. Washington, DC: Government Accountability Office.

United States Government Accountability Office (GAO). (2013). *Defense Acquisitions: Assessments of Selected Weapon Programs*, Report GAO-13-294SP. Washington, DC: Government Accountability Office.

White, R. (2012). "A waste of money, for years to come," *The New York Times*, 27 January, <http://www.nytimes.com/roomfordebate/2012/01/26/does-california-need-high-speed-rail/high-speed-rail-is-a-waste-of-money-for-decades-to-come>.

Williams, T. and Samset, K. (2010). "Issues in front-end decision making on projects," *Project Management Journal*, 41(2): 38–49.

PART I

CHALLENGES

CHAPTER 2

HAS MEGAPROJECT MANAGEMENT LOST ITS WAY?

Lessons from History

SYLVAIN LENFLE AND CHRISTOPH LOCH

THE performance track record of megaprojects is dismal, even though the basic ingredients of successful large project management are not new. Put simply, the trick is to combine *uncertainty* in dealing with the difficulties of long time horizons and non-standard technologies with *stakeholder complexity* as expressed through the involvement of multiple powerful interested parties (Flyvbjerg and Cowi 2004). This challenge was conquered in the successful creation of the atomic bomb in the 1940s; but seventy years on, some of the lessons of the Manhattan Project are not being heeded, and modern megaprojects are the poorer because of it.

Take the nuclear reactor industry, a poster child for delays and budget overruns. The current generation II EPR reactors were announced as the future in 2003, and construction began on the first project in Finland in 2005 with plans to launch operation in 2009. But this project will (as of the status in August 2015) not start operating before 2018 and has already incurred a cost escalation from €3.3 billion to €8.5 billion (World Nuclear Association 2015). Another project using the EPR technology in Flamanville in France is now expected to take more than double the original timeframe and cost €9 billion rather than the initial estimate of €3.3 billion (*Le Monde*, 21 April 2015). The Hinkley Point C project in the United Kingdom is too early in its construction to show large overruns, but to reflect high risks, there are hefty price guarantees built into its building contract (Taylor 2016: ch. 12).

Nuclear power is not alone. Studies show that 90% of major projects are over budget, with overruns of above 50% being common (Flyvbjerg 2011). A country-specific study in Germany found that among 170 megaprojects, the average budget overrun was 73% (Kostka 2015). One study calls big cost overruns the "iron law of megaprojects" (Flyvbjerg 2014).

This chapter illustrates that it is possible to identify a few core management shortcomings that have significantly contributed to such systemic-like failures. We then show that knowledge of how to address these shortcomings existed and was partly applied as early as during the World War II. Thirdly, we will use this review of past knowledge in order to sketch some recommendations for managerial measures that might help improve performance of megaproject management today.

2.1 THREE COMMON CAUSES OF MEGAPROJECT FAILURES

When we describe the spectacular failures of large projects over the last decades, three overarching themes arise.

2.1.1 Underestimation of, or Refusal to Acknowledge, Uncertainty

Megaprojects are often started on the assumption that with enough planning, the design and project plan can be firmly designed at the beginning. But over long timeframes, with non-standard technology and multiple interested parties, it is impossible to plan for everything—and parties then slip into a damaging fight for control that results in multiple redesigns and additional costs.

A case in point is the Circored project, a pioneering iron ore reduction facility to produce pure iron briquettes, undertaken in Trinidad (Loch and Terwiesch 2002). The project began in 1995 with a target start of production in 1999, owned and run by the iron-ore company Cleveland Cliffs, using a new technology that Lurgi AG had developed and tested in a small prototype. An intensive risk analysis suggested that all problems could be anticipated and managed, but many unforeseen problems occurred in the scale-up, delaying the project by two years. Although the project ultimately succeeded technically, the delay made the facility vulnerable to the commodity price meltdown of 2002 and thus unprofitable. Ultimately, Cleveland Cliffs wrote off the plant and sold it at a steep discount to Mittal.

A key reason for the failure is that while Lurgi understood its technology's immaturity and technical risks, the plant owner rejected a longer testing phase on grounds that risks could be contained through proper planning and analysis. So ensuing problems had to be dealt with reactively, costing more in time and money than if properly addressed to begin with.

2.1.2 Stakeholder Neglect or Mismanagement

Megaprojects normally require coalitions of active partners in addition to the support or at least passive tolerance of external stakeholders who do not participate directly. Peril inevitably results when stakeholders are ignored, or when a false agreement is finessed, causing conflicts to fester, hidden behind wooly political statements.

A famous example is the Eurotunnel project (Bensen et al. 1989a and b), which between 1987 and 1994 dug a 50-km twin tunnel under the English Channel, through which passenger and freight trains now pass between Calais and Dover. The initial project had a seven-year duration and a (1987) budget of £4.8 billion, but ran over by 29% in schedule (after the original opening target of June 1993, freight operations started in May 1994, but full operations were not achieved until December 1994), and ran over budget by 65%, for a total cost of £8 billion. Also, some initial specifications were not achieved, with trains running through the tunnel at 80 km/h compared with the original target of 160 km/h—thus extending travel time and reducing tunnel capacity. But most importantly, the operator, Eurotunnel plc, came out of the project so debt-burdened that it could not turn a profit, and shareholders lost their investment twice (Garg et al. 2008), until finally the banks forgave a significant percentage of the debt in 2013.

The Eurotunnel troubles were *not* rooted in uncertainty: although some new tunneling machinery was used, related problems were quickly handled, and initial projections of revenues and operating profits turned out to be fairly close.

Instead, the root cause for Eurotunnel's woes was in the fraught relationships among the stakeholders: the construction consortium and the later operator Eurotunnel were in constant conflict and embroiled in lawsuits; the banks managed to transfer all risks, including inflation, to Eurotunnel, which resulted in a three-month work hold-up and an inflated debt burden.

Stakeholder conflicts are a major source of project problems and are especially dangerous for megaprojects, which by their very nature involve many parties with the power to exert influence. Whenever a party is ignored, or when an agreement forces one party into agreement or superficially glosses over differences in views or interests, then these agreements probably break apart when changes disrupt the equilibrium— at which point the parties then no longer collaborate but work against one another (Loch et al. 2015).

2.1.3 Inflexible Contractor Management (Prominently, Awarding Work to the Lowest Bidder)

Many parties have to collaborate in order to accomplish megaprojects owing to their sheer size and variety of expertise required. The well-known practice of "bid low and sue later" is caused by project owners awarding contracts on the basis of the lowest bid price, forcing contractors to bid aggressively and then work inflexibly—asking for more compensation with every change in the project.

This was already observed thirty years ago (McDonald and Evans 1998), and is still alive and well—and criticized by a German government commission that examined practices in large public works projects (Kammholz 2015). A globally visible specific example is in the $5.25-billion megaproject for the expansion of the Panama Canal, which invited bids in 2009 and was scheduled to open in 2014. A Spanish-led consortium of construction firms won the $3.2-billion bid for the locks of the fifty-mile waterway, underbidding a US-led rival consortium by $1 billion. But in 2014 the consortium demanded a $1.6-billion compensation from the Panama Canal Authority (PCA), the project owner, citing "breaches of contract" (for example, claiming they were misled about geological ground conditions). The dispute has already delayed the project to mid-2015. However, concerns were voiced right at the outset that the bid was too low, and that a cost increase would be required at some point (Kriel and Dowsett 2014). Although the PCA defends the original bid as reasonable, experts openly discuss the aggressive underbidding strategy used (*The Economist* 2014).

2.1.4 Interactions Among the Themes

These three root causes of problems are even more difficult to address because they strongly interact. For example, stakeholders in the Eurotunnel project had differing interests such as the short-term view of the constructor versus the long-term operator's view. In an atmosphere of mutual distrust, even moderate uncertainties are difficult to address, leading to disputes (such as over cost overruns) and even further distrust. As a result, collaboration becomes even harder.

Yet although these challenges are difficult to address, there are potential solutions that have been ignored. Relevant knowledge has been available for seven decades, but much of this knowledge has been disregarded and not used effectively in the project community—as we describe next.

2.2 WHAT PROJECT MANAGEMENT ALREADY KNEW IN THE 1940S

The irony is that, historically, there were projects where these three problems were in fact overcome. This is particularly true of the World War II and large post-war US military and space projects which, interestingly, are the roots of contemporary project management. Indeed, the Manhattan, Atlas, Polaris, and Apollo projects, to name the most famous ones, were managed very successfully, and on schedule. It is therefore interesting to draw lessons from these cases. At the conceptual level, these projects did two crucial things right.

First, on the organizational level, they created almost from scratch a dedicated organization to overcome the traditional bureaucratic fights that plagued major R&D projects. The development of Intercontinental Ballistic Missiles (ICBM) within the US Air Force and the US Navy is typical of this strategy. Consider briefly the Polaris case (Sapolsky 2003). The problem was to coordinate and integrate the functionally defined branches or bureaus and the dozens of firms involved. Moreover, as a new technology, ballistic missiles did not fit easily into the existing weapons acquisition structures: it was neither a bomber, nor a bomb, nor a guided missile. To overcome this problem, the Navy created the Special Project Office (SPO)—a new body that had complete autonomy and power to manage the Polaris project. It was supervised by a brilliant and powerful project manager, Admiral William F. Raborn, who infused a sense of dedication and urgency into the entire team. He said: "Our religion was to build Polaris" (Spinardi 1994: 35). The creation of this structure constitutes unquestionably one of the key success factors of the Polaris project (Sapolsky 1972). And we find a similar logic, a dedicated organization led by a brilliant project manager, in all the aforementioned projects (the Manhattan Engineer District and L. Groves, the Western Development Division of the USAF and B. Schriever, the Office of Manned Space Flight and S. Phillips). Therefore, the success of these projects rested on "doing what it took" with almost unlimited project management power, supported by almost complete autonomy to take the right actions in the interest of achieving the goals.

Second, concerning the management of uncertainty, these PMs developed brilliant insights. They understood, right from the outset, that one does not know what one does not know. This cannot be more clearly stated than by General Groves when he stated that, given the huge unforeseeable uncertainties of the design of the atomic bomb, they were "proceeding in the dark" (Groves 1962: 40) and, therefore "had to abandon completely all normal orderly procedures" (72).

What is fascinating is that they drew the right managerial conclusions: they combined experimentation (for example, in the form of pilots), parallel pursuit of alternatives, and dedicated (possibly costly) actions to gather information as part of the core project activities. The Manhattan Project forcefully demonstrates the relevance of this approach: acknowledging that it was impossible to define, at the outset, the right design of an atomic bomb, Groves and the steering committee decided to simultaneously explore different technical solutions both for the production of fissionable materials and for the design of the bomb. This explains why the two bombs dropped on Japan had completely different designs, and also how they succeeded in such a short time to overcome the tremendous scientific and engineering challenges (Lenfle 2011). This strategy was transferred directly to the ICBM Atlas project (and others) through discussions between Groves, Oppenheimer, and B. Schriever, chief of the Western Development Division of the USAF (Hughes 1998).

It is sobering for project management how these lessons have been lost in the course of the institutionalization of the discipline. Indeed, the principles of uncertainty management were theoretically well understood in the 1950s, especially the need for experimentation and adjustment, and the advantage of starting multiple parallel trials on subprojects in order to assure one successful outcome (Alchian and Kessel 1954; Arrow 1955; Klein and Meckling 1958). However, these principles had completely disappeared from PM textbooks and have only recently been rediscovered (from the view of multiple disciplines, for example, Leonard-Barton 1995; Loch et al. 2006). Lenfle and Loch (2010) show how flexible approaches to uncertainty were abandoned in favor of a more control-oriented view of PM as the accomplishment of a clearly defined goal through a phased/stage-gate logic.

This process unfolded in three dimensions (Lenfle and Loch 2010):

1. On the political side, the deployment of ballistic missiles completely changed the context. The fear of a "missile gap" disappeared, and the sense of utmost urgency of the military megaprojects faded away. This led to an important reorganization within the DoD in the form of the *Defense Reorganization Act* of 1958, which greatly increased the power of the Secretary of Defense over the armed services. It gave him the authority to "transfer, reassign, abolish, or consolidate" service functions, and control over the budget. This paved the way for the "McNamara revolution." Coming from the Ford Motor Company, Robert McNamara, named Secretary of Defense in 1961, started a complete reorganization of the planning process in the DoD. His objective was to consolidate planning and budgeting, which hitherto had been two separate processes. He pursued his objective with the implementation of the famous Program Planning and Budgeting System (PPBS). This process was antipodean with the logic of the early missile projects and prompted a complete reversal in project management. Indeed, it emphasized the complete definition of the system *before* its development in order to limit uncertainty and institutionalize a phased approach. This *de facto* eliminated parallel trials and concurrency. Therefore, the phased-planning approach (now called Stage-Gate) became the project management model of the DoD and the newly formed NASA (Johnson 2000). This was enforced by the diffusion of managerial tools such as PERT. In particular, a *NASA/DoD PERT/Cost Guide* was issued in 1962 and became part of the bidding process of both administrations, transforming these tools into *de facto* standards for project management. This limited the scope of project management for the ensuing decades. From now on, strategy was centralized at the DoD, and Project Management's role was to execute given missions.
2. This shift had a theoretical counterpart. Indeed, the McNamara revolution was theoretically grounded in RAND thinking and its faith in rational decision making.[1] This view was clearly expressed by Charles Hitch, an eminent RAND member who later became comptroller of the Department of Defense under McNamara. In 1960 he published *The Economics of Defense in the Nuclear Age*, which introduced a broad audience to a view of defense as an economic problem of resource allocation to achieve a desired objective. This view had major consequences for project management: the focus gradually changed from the "performance at all costs" attitude of the first missiles projects to one of optimizing the cost/performance ratio.

This new logic is clearly visible in the early literature on project management. For example, *Systems Analysis and Project Management* (1968) by Cleland and King became a classic. The book is typical of the phased logic. It consists of two parts that corresponded to the two key project phases. The first advocated the power of systems analysis to analyze complex strategic issues and define project missions. The second part dealt with project execution and emphasized the need to create a specific project organization to integrate stakeholder contributions, along with project planning and control using formal methods. The result of all of these events was that by the early 1970s the phased approach had become "natural."

3. The last stage of this standardization process was the creation, in 1969, of a professional organization: the US Project Management Institute. Indeed, the years following the success of Polaris saw a plethora of publications and an intense promotion of the PERT/CPM method by numerous consulting firms (Vaszonyi 1970). The planning method was viewed as synonymous with success in the management of large projects. The idea of a professional association arose in this context within the tight-knit community of PERT and CPM users (R. Archibald, E. Benett, J. Snyder, N. Engman, J. Gordon Davis, and S. Gallagher). Since all its founders were project control experts, it was natural for the PMI to focus on control tools, such as PERT/ CPM. Therefore, for the next two decades, "modern project management" became equated with PERT/CPM after Polaris and the MacNamara revolution (Snyder 1987).

This, as the reader will recognize, provides the basic principles of the dominant model of project management today: the stage-gate process. The problem is that this rational view of project management oversimplifies the processes at stake, particularly for innovative projects and for megaprojects with their inbuilt unforeseeability (because of long timeframes and stakeholder complexity). Moreover, this leads, as argued by Lenfle and Loch, to misinterpretations of the success factors of these projects. For example, Apollo is remembered in the project literature for the setting up of a complex project management system organized around a phased approach (Seamans 2005; Johnson 2002). While this unquestionably contributed to getting back on track during the project crisis of 1962–63, this narrow view neglects the upstream exploratory work and the fact that the phased approach was implemented quite late in the project. However, the fact is that this control-oriented approach of project management remains dominant today.

2.3 THE LIMITATIONS OF THE BREAKTHROUGH PROJECT MANAGEMENT STYLES OF THE 1950S

Based on the previous discussion, we might ask the question whether the issue is to "get some of the capability of the 1940s and 1950s back." But this, we think, would be too simple. Indeed, these projects unfolded in a very specific context and, therefore, were not exposed to the full spectrum of complications that face the megaprojects of today. One has to remember that, for all these projects, the context was the highest level of national urgency either because of World War II (Manhattan) or the Cold War with the USSR (Atlas, Polaris, and Apollo). This had two major consequences.

First, the project goals reflected the military nature of the missions and were, in a sense, "simple" (although technically impressive): build a nuclear bomb, build a missile that can hit a small target from a long distance, start the missile from a submarine, or go to the moon.[2] These do not reflect the goal complexity of projects that, today, inevitably have a societal component.

Second, the Cold War and the competition with the Soviets led to the suppression of any debate around the projects. It is useful here to remember John F. Kennedy's address to the Congress that formally launched the Moon project:

> If we are to win the battle that is going on around the world between freedom and tyr-
> anny, if we are to win the battle for men's minds, the dramatic achievements in space
> which occurred in recent weeks should have made clear to us all, as did the Sputnik
> in 1957, the impact of this adventure on the minds of men everywhere who are
> attempting to make a determination of which road they should take. (...) We go into
> space because whatever mankind must undertake, free men must fully share. (...)
> I believe this Nation should commit itself to achieving the goal, before this decade is
> out, of landing a man on the moon and returning him safely to earth. No single space
> project in this period will be more impressive to mankind, or more important for the
> long-range exploration of space; and none will be so difficult or expensive to accom-
> plish. (Special Message to the Congress on Urgent National Needs, 25 May 1961)

Indeed, if the stakes were "the battle between freedom and tyranny," there could be no debates around the project.[3] In other words, if we rely on contemporary concepts, stake-holder disagreements were absent or small. There were no parties that stopped support, or protesters that blocked further work, because they no longer agreed with changed outcomes, or external groups that demanded transparency and accountability.

This was also true for supplier management. These project teams had huge power over their suppliers—again, these were military projects where suppliers were paid well but had to unquestioningly carry out orders. In fact, the entire organization was designed to avoid politics. As demonstrated by Hughes (1998) for Atlas, and Sapolsky (1972) for Polaris, the main goal of the creation of the WDD and the SPO was explic-itly to avoid the bureaucratic fights and politicking that, traditionally, plagued large R&D projects. They were, in a sense, "closed" projects (Edwards 1996; Hughes 1998). Politics was reduced to the army and the government. There could be debates, but no protest outside likely to stop the project (Beard 1976). It was possible for Admiral Raborn to "build a fence to keep the rest of the Navy off of us" (Sapolsky 1972: 124) and to "engineer the politics of the program so as to provide resources without interfer-ence" (Spinardi 1994: 35–6). Therefore, the question of stakeholder management was literally out of the scope.

This very specific context disappeared with the end of the Cold War and the emergence of a networked world—it is no longer the case in megaprojects today. Now the challenge is to manage megaprojects in an "open" context in which no project team can hope to keep the outside world behind a fence. In this perspective, Hughes (1998) brilliantly demonstrates that the "system engineering" methods developed for military projects failed when confronted with civil megaprojects such as the famous Boston Central Artery Tunnel. Here, the challenge was to deal with the messy complexity of multiple stakeholders, each with different objectives and constraints. F. Salvucci, the Boston CA/T key figure, had to patiently negotiate his way through the maze of the Boston area, discussing with engineers, community groups, the City, the State of Massachussets, and so on, around to-be-defined criteria, such as the design of a bridge. Therefore, as argued by Lundin et al. (2015: 201–2), "The traditional view of the 'project client' as the single focal interlocutor of the project vanishes, giving place to a complex fuzzy system of diversified actors that has to be 'managed' in novel sophisticated governance and communication processes." The problem is all the more important because, they argue, there is an ever-growing demand of accountability for public and private megaprojects. General Groves never had to deal with this situation.

In other words, we cannot simply go back to the heyday of 1950s project management—what worked brilliantly then would be insufficient today. And yet, it is still worthwhile to repeat the lessons on uncertainty management from the 1950s, as some of the recent failed megaprojects simply violated what is known about uncertainty management. Moreover, knowledge on all three key drivers of megaproject failure has slowly accumulated over the last fifty years, not only on uncertainty management but also on stakeholder and contractor management. We will review the key lessons of this knowledge history in Section 2.4.

2.4 LESSONS AND RECOMMENDATIONS

2.4.1 Managing Uncertainty

Building on the work from the 1940s described earlier, project management theory has, since the stage-gate process became dominant, been able to articulate that many projects are characterized by variation (many small influences causing a possible range of duration and costs on a particular activity), which can be addressed by buffers, and foreseeable uncertainty or risk (identifiable and understood influences that the project team cannot be sure will occur, so different outcomes are possible), which can be addressed by planned and "programmed" risk management that "triggers" contingent actions depending on which risks occur (De Meyer et al. 2002). However, megaprojects suffer also from unforeseen uncertainty, which cannot be identified during project planning. The team either is unaware of the event's possibility or cannot create the contingencies. Unforeseeable uncertainty may be caused by large "unthinkable" events, or by many influences (including stakeholder actions) that interact through complexity. Unforeseeable uncertainty requires more flexible and "emergent" approaches than smaller uncertainty levels do (and than the stage-gate process has allowed for).

Still, the presence of unforeseeable uncertainty can be diagnosed. For example, discovery-driven planning (McGrath and MacMillan 1995, 2000) proposes to explicitly acknowledge that unknown unknowns exist and to uncover them with analyses such as assumptions checklists. Similarly, Loch et al. (2008) illustrated with the example of a start-up venture project, how the presence of unknown influences can be diagnosed by systematically probing for knowledge gaps in the project, building intuition about areas where unknown events may be looming. Two fundamental approaches exist for this level of unforeseeable uncertainty: trial-and-error learning and selectionism (Leonard-Barton 1995; Pich et al. 2002; Loch et al. 2006).

Under *trial-and-error learning*, the team starts moving toward one outcome (the best it can identify), but is prepared to repeatedly and fundamentally change both the outcome and the course of action as new information becomes available. Exploratory experiments, aimed at gaining information without necessarily contributing "progress," are an important part of this approach; failure of such experiments is a source of learning rather than a mistake. It is therefore important to track the learning and reduction in knowledge gaps rather than tracking only the progress toward a target. Well-known examples are pharmaceutical development projects, in which promising indications often emerge during large scale trials via unexpected (positive) side effects.

Alternatively, the team might choose to "hedge" and opt for *selectionism*, or pursuing multiple approaches in parallel, observing what works and what does not work (without necessarily having a full explanation why) and choosing the best approach *ex post facto*. Examples of this approach abound, including Microsoft's pursuit of several operating systems during the 1980s (Beinhocker 1999), or "product churning" by the Japanese consumer electronics companies in the early 1990s (Stalk and Webber 1993).

In a large-scale empirical study of sixty-five new venture projects, Sommer et al. (2009) showed that the best combination of learning and selectionism, as measured by their effect on project success, depends on the level of unforeseeable uncertainty in the project and the complexity of the project (Figure 2.1). When both uncertainty and complexity are low (lower left quadrant), planning and standard risk management are up to the task and the most efficient. When unforeseeable uncertainty looms large, be flexible and apply trial and error. When complexity is high, use parallel trials and narrow the field down to the best as soon as possible. The hardest situation is in the upper right quadrant, which is where megaprojects usually find themselves and where unforeseeable uncertainty and project complexity combine. It turned out that the highest success level was associated with parallel trials if they could be kept alive until uncertainty had been reduced to the point that all important risks were known. Otherwise, trial and error performed better. Of course, in any large project, trial and error and selectionism can be combined and applied differently across subprojects.

The largest challenge lies in the managerial structures and control-mindedness in large corporations, partially prompted by the stage-gate process revolution of the 1960s,

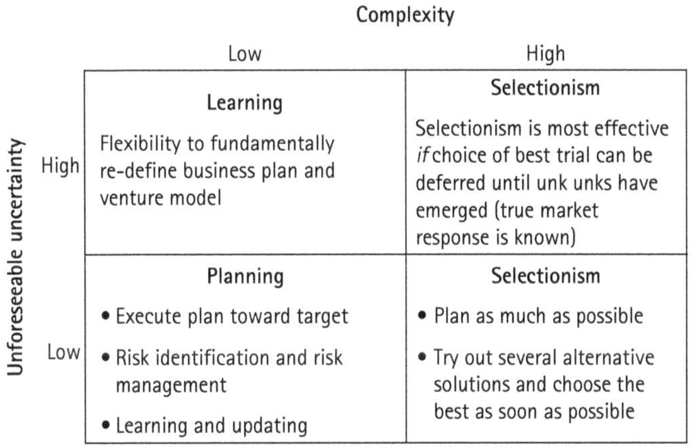

Complexity

	Low	High
High	**Learning** Flexibility to fundamentally re-define business plan and venture model	**Selectionism** Selectionism is most effective *if* choice of best trial can be deferred until unk unks have emerged (true market response is known)
Low	**Planning** • Execute plan toward target • Risk identification and risk management • Learning and updating	**Selectionism** • Plan as much as possible • Try out several alternative solutions and choose the best as soon as possible

Unforeseeable uncertainty (vertical axis label)

FIGURE 2.1 When to choose trial-and-error-learning or selectionism.

(From Sommer et al. 2009.)

discussed previously. It makes it very difficult for managers in large organizations to take on risks. For example, one study on "breakthrough innovation" in large companies shows that they use a stage-gate-like approach to selecting and executing large innovations, which pushes managers to conservativism and early termination of risky projects (He 2015). Similarly, Sehti and Iqbal (2008) demonstrated that the stage-gate process leads to project inflexibility, which, for innovative projects, is synonymous with failure. Even more fundamentally, the stage-gate process has shaped an "aesthetic" of eliminating uncertainty and experimentation through rigid up-front planning and control. For example, a study of relationships between startups and investors found that investors reacted with "punishment" (that is, by enforcing business reviews) to evidence of parallel trials and (to a lesser degree) trial-and-error iterations (Loch et al. 2011). Managers are, in principle, fully capable of intelligently responding to unforeseeable uncertainty, as R&D management and many experienced project management organizations amply demonstrate. However, much education is needed in order to equip management in many (particularly public) organizations, investors, and critically, the public with the flexibility required to deal with uncertainty.

2.4.2 Stakeholder Management and Project Governance

No universally agreed "national agenda" exists any longer, based on which the brilliant projects in the 1950s could successfully proceed, because megaprojects touch on too many interests and agendas to still be able to be pushed by any central will. Consultation and involvement of powerful interested parties has become a must. On the other hand, political compromises do not make good bases for decisions, and muddled goals and inconsistent decisions based on fluctuating agreements destroy projects. How can these two imperatives be reconciled? This is a question of project governance.

Project teams execute, but the scope and strategic positioning of a project is set at the level of project governance, typically at the level of the "steering committee" (SC). Loch et al. (2015) examined effective and non-effective SC practices in seventeen complex and uncertain projects (innovation, as well as organizational change), and found that the SC is the place where representation of interests (including consultation) needs to be combined with the production of a shared project vision and the translation of this vision into operational plans—in order to effectively identify conflicts and solutions as the environment of the project changes.

Several specific principles arise from the study:

- Stakeholder representation: the SC needs to represent the most important and powerful parties that have an interest in the megaproject (such as government, suppliers, or customers). At the same time, the size of the SC must not grow too large (by allowing "anyone with interest to participate") because large groups become too difficult to manage and keep together.
- Goal agreement. The SC has the critical responsibility to articulate a project vision that is at least acceptable to all parties, and then translate it into operational goals and targets that expose key conflicts. "Motherhood and apple pie" goals regularly get thrown out during later operational phases when conflicts inevitably do occur. Only if the conflicts are negotiated at the outset (in a way that maintains a shared project vision) can the goals evolve and change in negotiated ways that allow maintaining a shared vision.
- Staying informed and renegotiating during crises. The SC must invest enough time and effort to understand the key issues of the project (insisting on translation of technical language and issues into the strategic policy or business language that is needed to maintain the strategic positioning of the project). The SC must also invest the time and effort to stay informed, so when changes and crises occur (both inevitable over the time horizon of megaprojects), project modifications can be renegotiated in ways so that the parties maintain their agreement/support. If a party feels excluded or taken advantage of, projects fail, but if the SC can successfully manage one crisis together, it becomes stronger in managing the next.
- Keeping the project team aligned. The SC must maintain a position of control, which means in this context, understanding the key issues rather than maintaining and enforcing ("come what may") an initial project plan. Trust needs to be built with the project team that bad news and changes are treated reasonably, demanding solutions and accountability, but not looking for scapegoats to punish—otherwise, information about the true status of the project will not be forthcoming. This is necessary because changes *will* happen in a megaproject, and the SC needs to set up itself, as well as its project team, to be able to address these changes in ways that do not lead to the typical symptoms of megaproject disasters—such as mission creep, late mission changes because of political maneuvering, accumulated unaddressed problems, or the falling out with an important stakeholder.

Several key challenges exist that make these principles difficult to achieve. Interest conflicts and differences in thinking styles among stakeholders make the achievement of true alignment a long affair (leading to longer planning times) and consume significant managerial effort during a project. The temptations are ever present to not invest enough effort, or to exploit political circumstances of unbalanced power to one's own advantage.

This is also where the widely observed temptation of "low-balling early [on costs] and then present a fait-accompli to the stakeholders" (Flyvbjerg 2007) comes in. While this is certainly true in some cases, it is not inevitable. Evidence in Loch et al. (2015) suggests that if the SC represents stakeholders and seeks the dialog with them, and if it is sufficiently involved with the project team to be able to follow and evaluate progress, success overestimation can be avoided. Of course, this leaves out situations where a skeptical public (or political establishment) is simply not willing to accept a project under a realistic scenario, and the only way to get the project approved is by "lying" about it. But whoever engages in misrepresentations in order to get the project started ("they will learn and change their minds later") is running severe risks both for their own careers, as the project later runs into difficulties preprogrammed by the unrealistic initial estimates, and for the public, whose faith in project execution capabilities becomes undermined. Yes, it may be true that (for example) the Eurotunnel was a significant macro-economic success in hindsight, connecting London and Paris in ways that were previously unthinkable. But on the way there, many shareholders lost their money, and careers of good people involved were damaged, and so initial overpromising is perilous and not advisable, even if one might be able to construct a long-term justification for it.

2.4.3 Contractor Management

Contracts are core vehicles of governing partners and the subcontractors of pieces of work in projects, and they form a complex web of relationships in megaprojects. But contracts can handle only limited complexity (a contract can quickly run into thousands of pages, which means they become ineffective), and they are inflexible where flexibility is required to deal with the inevitable changes in megaprojects.

> A contract is a dangerous instrument and should always be approached with trepidation and caution ... Theoretically, the aim of a written contract is to achieve certainty of obligation of each party, the avoidance of ambiguities, and such definiteness of understanding as to preclude ultimate controversy. In practice, construction contracts are generally formed not to definitely fix obligations, but to avoid obligations. (MacDonald and Evans 1998: 1–2)

Specifically, contracts cause the temptation to explore gaps in the understanding of the counterparty to create obligations that one can then exploit—a fallacious expectation because the other side usually finds a way to sooner or later stall in their turn or to retaliate (von Branconi and Loch 2004). The well-known temptation to "bid low and sue later" falls in this context, but it often leads to protracted business and legal battles, victimizing the project.

Much evidence has been accumulated that contracts need to be designed with *flexibility*, and they need to be complemented with *relationships*. A good example is the celebrated Heathrow Terminal 5 project, which applied an integrated approach that incorporated careful strategic governance (accomplishing system integration) within diligent process management that included supplier selection by track record (rather than the lowest bid price) and flexible contracts that rewarded problem solving (Davies et al. 2009b). The project owner BAA "changed the rules of the game" by creating a new type of agreement based on two fundamental principles: the client bears the risk and works collaboratively with contractors in integrated project teams. BAA had to take responsibility for risks and uncertainties, while creating an environment within which suppliers could find solutions. Suppliers were repaid all the costs on a cost-transparent "open book" basis and incentivized to improve their performance and innovate by bonuses for exceeding previously agreed "target costs" and completion dates. If the performance of a project exceeds target costs, the profits are shared among team members. This contractual approach was underpinned by routines to expose and manage risks rather than transfer or bury them, and offered incentives for innovation and problem solving (Davies et al. 2009a: 24–5).

The Heathrow Terminal 5 project addressed one fundamental problem with contracts: they cannot specify all desired outcomes beforehand in the complex and uncertain environment of a megaproject, and fixing any outcomes (no matter with how many "contingencies) opens up incentive conflicts when contractors either cannot deliver or can deliver in unforeseen ways. The cost-reimbursement contracts with "innovation bonuses" offered a way out of this dilemma. But it is possible to go even further in turning contracts from fixed outcome descriptions into vehicles for collaborative problem solving. One example for this is the OSA Alliance between Orange (France Telecom's mobile telephone arm) with its partners in managing roaming, the complicated agreements that allow regional telecom operators to provide service for a customer from other regions and be reimbursed by the telecom operator who has a contract with the customer and charges this customer for the roaming (Van Der Heyden et al. 2006). The "contract" that partner operators in the alliance signed up for did not specify any specific collaboration procedures or outcomes, but was nothing but a specification of a *collaborative problem solving procedure*: how would the group make decisions in setting up a technical system, or a customer agreement, or a revenue sharing when it arose. Decisions were indeed made by voting, with safeguards that neither the large operators (with a revenue majority) nor the many small operators (with most votes) could force through agreements. Each specific agreement itself (what would normally be seen as a contract) became a mere technical description. This structure of agreements allowed the partners to keep collaborating flexibly and robustly in an environment of changing technologies and regulatory regimes. (The regulatory bodies tightened rules on roaming which had become very profitable.) However, when we discuss such collaboration structures with project and program managers, they usually are very uncomfortable because it feels to them like a "loss of control." This is another example of the control "aesthetics" that the dominance of the stage-gate process has created in project management.

And yet there are again large challenges in adopting these new methods that would allow addressing the systematic problems that have plagued megaprojects. The temptation to use "market forces" to depress prices to contractors, using unbalanced power to get one's way (if only for a short period), is ever present. As a case in point, the Heathrow Terminal 5 owner BAA was acquired in 2006 and, "in a complete reversal of strategy (and to the surprise of many in the UK construction industry) decided to revert back to the traditional role of client as procurer rather than project manager, relying on 'risk-shifting contracts,' detailed up-front specifications and inflexible routines" (Davies et al. 2016).

Similarly, the authors have discussed the OSA "framework contract" approach with managers from many companies, and have witnessed directly how deeply threatening managers find such an approach—it feels to them as if they are giving away control over their own fate. Yet another cultural and "aesthetic" influence that has been connected to the stage-gate process, which adds a specific definition of "professional standards" to the earlier-mentioned short-term temptations in making it very difficult to make the new methods in megaproject management enter the mainstream.

2.5 Conclusion

System engineering and technical complexity are well understood, but uncertainty and stakeholder complexity are still the big challenges for megaprojects. Avenues have been identified to address these challenges that require behavioral changes: these include resisting the temptation to press one's own advantage with contractors; accepting some loss of predictability and control; patience in bringing the multiple sides to the table that are always present in megaprojects; and the discipline to maintain a common direction that allows progress-directed decision making rather than merely conflict-avoiding compromises. Many of these techniques will require companies to learn new and potentially daunting behavior; but in fact many of these managerial mechanisms are tried and true techniques that worked wonders for megaprojects a few generations ago and could help point the way to a brighter future for huge projects in the future.

Notes

1. McNamara's thinking was rooted in, and had a major impact on, "cold war rationality"—the belief that one could find the optimal solution beforehand. Here, the reader may refer to Erickson et al. (2013).
2. Apollo is an ambiguous case, since it was a civil project largely managed by the military after 1963.

3. On the Manhattan Project, there was no debate simply because it was a "black," completely secret, project. Even Harry Truman, Roosevelt's Vice-President, ignored the existence of the project until he became President in April 1945.

REFERENCES

Arrow, K. (1955). *Economic Aspects of Military Research and Development*. Rand Corporation Document D-3142.

Alchian, A. A. and Kessel, R. A. (1954). *A Proper Role of Systems Analysis*. Rand Corporation Document D-2057: 16.

Beard, E. (1976). *Developing the ICBM. A Study in Bureaucratic Politics*. New York: Columbia University Press.

Beinhocker, E. (1999). "Robust adaptive strategies," *Sloan Management Review*, 40(3): 95–106.

Bensen, D., Thomas, H., Smith, R. C., and Walter, I. (1989a). *Eurotunnel-Background*. INSEAD-New York Stern School of Business, Case Study 08/95-2492.

Bensen, D., Thomas, H., Smith, R. C., and Walter, I. (1989b). *Eurotunnel-Equity*. INSEAD-New York Stern School of Business, Case Study 07/95-4528.

Davies, A., Dodgson, M., and Gann, D. (2009a). "From iconic design to lost luggage: Innovation at Heathrow Terminal 5," paper presented at the DRUID Summer Conference 2009, Copenhagen Business School.

Davies, A., Gann, D., and Douglas, T. (2009b). "Innovation in megaprojects: Systems integration at London Heathrow Terminal 5," *California Management Review*, 51(2): 101–25.

Davies, A., Dodgson, M., and Gann, D. (2016). "Dynamic capabilities for a complex project: The case of London Heathrow Terminal 5," *Project Management Journal*, 47(2): 26–46.

De Meyer, A., Loch, C. H., and Pich, M. T. (2002). "Managing project uncertainty: From variation to chaos," *MIT Sloan Management Review*, Winter: 60–7.

Economist, The (2014). "Your money or your locks," 3 January 2014.

Edwards, P. (1996). *The Closed World: Computers and the Politics of Discourse in Cold War America*. Cambridge, MA: MIT Press.

Erickson, P., Klein, J., Daston, L., Lemov, R., Sturm, T., and Gordin, M. (2013). *How Reason Almost Lost its Mind. The Strange Career of Cold War Rationality*. Chicago: University of Chicago Press.

Flyvbjerg, Bent and Cowi. (2004). *Procedures for Dealing with Optimism Bias in Transport Planning: Guidance Document*. London: Department for Transport.

Flyvbjerg, B. (2007). "Policy and planning for large infrastructure projects: Problems, causes and cures," *Environment and Planning B: Planning and Design*, 34: 578–97.

Flyvbjerg, B. (2011). "Over budget, over time, over and over again: Managing major projects," in P. W. G. Morris, J. K. Pinto, and J. Söderlund, *The Oxford Handbook of Project Management*. Oxford: Oxford University Press, pp. 321–44.

Flyvbjerg, B. (2014). "What you should know about megaprojects and why: An overview," *Project Management Journal*, 45(2): 6–19.

Garg, S., Loch, C. H., and De Meyer, A. (2008). *Eurotunnel: Eyes Wide Shut*. INSEAD Case Study 04/2008-5288.

Groves, L. (1962). *Now It Can Be Told: The Story of the Manhattan Project*. New York: Da Capo Press.

He, X. (2016). *Breakthrough Innovation in Large Companies*. PhD dissertation, Cambridge University Department of Engineering.

Hughes, T. (1998). *Rescuing Prometheus*. New York: Vintage Books.

Johnson, S. (2000). "From concurrency to phased planning: An episode in the history of systems management," in A. Hughes and T. Hughes, *Systems, Experts and Computers: The Systems Approach to Management and Engineering, World War II and After*. Cambridge, MA: MIT Press, pp. 93–112.

Johnson, S. (2002). *The Secret of Apollo: Systems Management in American and European Space Programs*. Baltimore, MD: John Hopkins University Press.

Kammholz, K. (2015). "Bericht rügt Deutschlands Vresagen als Bauherr," *Die Welt*, 29(6): Section *Politik*.

Klein, B. and Meckling, W. (1958). "Application of operations research to development decisions," *Operations Research*, 6(3): 352–63.

Kostka, G. (2015). *Grossprojekte in Deutschland-zwischen Ambition und Realität*. Study of the Hertie School of Governance.

Kriel, L. and Dowsett, S. (2014). "Insight: Lowball bid comes back to haunt Panama Canal expansion," *Reuters World*, 20 January.

Lenfle, S. (2011). "The strategy of parallel approaches in projects with unforeseeable uncertainty: The Manhattan case in retrospect," *International Journal of Project Management*, 29(4): 359–73.

Lenfle, S. and Loch, C. H. (2010). "Lost roots: How project management came to emphasize control over flexibility and novelty," *California Management Review*, 53(1): 32–55.

Leonard-Barton, D. (1995). *Wellsprings of Knowledge*. Cambridge, MA: HBS Press.

Loch, C. H., Pich, M. T., and De Meyer, A. (2006). *Managing the Unknown: A New Approach to Managing Projects Under High Uncertainty*. Hoboken, NJ: Wiley.

Loch, C. H., Solt, M. E., and Bailey, E. (2008). "Diagnosing unforeseeable uncertainty in a new venture," *Journal of Product Innovation Management*, 25(1): 28–46.

Loch, C. H., Sommer, S. C., Dong, J., Jokela, P., and Pich, M. T. (2011). "Managing risk and responding to uncertainty: How entrepreneurs and VCs can improve their effectiveness; a comparison of three countries," INSEAD Working Paper.

Loch, C. H., Sommer, S., and Mähring, M. (2015). "What project steering committees actually do: A framework for effective project governance," Working Paper, Cambridge Judge Business School/HEC Paris/Stockholm School of Economics.

Loch, C. H. and Terwiesch, C. (2002). *The Circored Project A, B and C*. INSEAD Case Study.

Lundin, R., Arvidsson, N., Brady, T., Ekstedt, E., Midler, C., and Sydow, J. (2015). *Managing and Working in Project Society: Institutional Challenges of Temporary Organizations*. Cambridge: Cambridge University Press.

McGrath, R. C. and MacMillan, I. (2000). *The Entrepreneurial Mindset: Strategies for Continuously Creating Opportunity in the Age of Uncertainty*. Cambridge, MA: Harvard Business Publishing.

McDonald, D. F. and Evans III, J. O. (1998). "Construction contracts: Shifting risk or generating a claim?" *AACE International Transactions*, LEG.01: 1–8.

McGrath, R. and McMillan, I. (1995). "Discovery-driven planning," *Harvard Business Review*, (July–August): 44–54.

Pich, M. T., Loch, C. H., and De Meyer, A. (2002). "On uncertainty, ambiguity and complexity in project management," *Management Science*, 48(8): 1008–23.

Sapolsky, H. (1972). *The Polaris System Development*. Cambridge, MA: Harvard University Press.

Sapolsky, H. (2003). "Inventing systems integration," in A. Prencipe, A. Davies, and M. Hobday, *The Business of Systems Integration*. Oxford: Oxford University Press, pp. 15–34.

Seamans, R. (2005). "Project Apollo: The tough decisions," *Monographs in Aerospace History Number 37*. Washington DC: NASA History Division.

Sehti, R. and Iqbal, Z. (2008). "Stage-gate controls, learning failure, and adverse effects on novel new products," *Journal of Marketing*, 72(1): 118–34.

Sommer, S. C., Loch, C. H., and Dong, J. (2009). "Managing complexity and unforeseeable uncertainty in startup companies: An empirical study," *Organization Science*, 20(1): 118–33.

Snyder, J. (1987). "Modern project management: How did we get there – Where do we go?" *Project Management Journal*, 18(1): 28–9.

Spinardi, G. (1994). *From Polaris to Trident: The Development of US Fleet Ballistic Missile Technology*. Cambridge: Cambridge University Press.

Stalk, G. and Webber, A. M. (1993). "Japan's dark side of time," *Harvard Business Review*, 71(4): 93–102.

Taylor, S. (2016). *The Fall and Rise of Nuclear Power in Britain*. Cambridge: UIT Cambridge.

Van Der Heyden, L., Doz, Y., and Vankatraman, V. (2006). *Orange Group's Open Seamless Alliance (OSA)*. INSEAD Case Study.

Vazsonyi, A. (1970). "L'histoire de Grandeur et de la Décadence de la Methode PERT," *Management Science*, 16(8): B449–55.

von Branconi, C. and Loch, C. H. (2004). "Contracting for major projects: Eight business levers for top management," *International Journal of Project Management*, 22(2): 119–30.

World Nuclear Association. (2015). "Nuclear power in Finland: Country profiles," 13 August, <http://www.world-nuclear.org/info/Country-Profiles/Countries-A-F/Finland/>.

CHAPTER 3

···

CYCLES IN MEGAPROJECT DEVELOPMENT

···

MATTI SIEMIATYCKI

3.1 INTRODUCTION

INFRASTRUCTURE megaprojects are an enduring feature of human civilizations. Throughout the world, the landscape is marked by the remnants of historic efforts to undertake construction initiatives on a massive scale, from the Egyptian pyramids to the Roman aqueducts, roads, and Coliseum, to the Greek Parthenon. While large-scale public works have been significant throughout history, it was with industrialization that megaprojects rose to prominence, as a strategic investment in productive capital and as ideology (Lehrer and Laidley 2008: 788). Today there are many different types of megaprojects, including immense transportation, energy, healthcare, office tower, justice, telecommunications, cultural, and information technology infrastructures that support the functioning of a modern society.

Megaprojects are defined by their large scale in terms of costs, which can range from $100 million to upwards of $1 billion, depending on the context in which they are being developed. They can be funded, built, and operated by public-sector, as well as private-sector institutions or some combination of the two. Megaprojects are also defined in terms of the scale of planning and engineering complexity, the high level of public and political interest that they attract, and their outsized impact on the surrounding economic, social, and natural environment. Indeed, megaprojects are identified as the largest-scale infrastructure and development projects that a given society undertakes, which attract the greatest amount of public interest, and have the most significant impacts and externalities on their surrounding communities.

One of the more puzzling aspects of megaprojects is that they tend to follow distinctive cycles or waves of innovation. It is quite common for the development of a new technology or type of infrastructure megaproject in one place to spark a wave of similar projects developed in a variety of other locations, before they are usurped by a subsequent wave of development of a new technology in the same asset class or a different type of infrastructure altogether. Put differently, new technologies or types of megaprojects appear to diffuse across space, from the place where an innovative idea emerges, through to a surge in popularity in many locations, before it declines in popularity either because the project type does not function as expected, has fulfilled the required goal, or has been replaced by a new technology that provides even better benefits.

To date, such patterns have often been identified and dismissed as one-off fads capturing the economic imperative or cultural *zeitgeist* of a specific moment in time. For instance, the "Bilbao effect" is a popular term to explain how the development of a new Guggenheim Museum with an iconic building design in the northern Spanish city in the late 1990s sparked a tidal wave of museum and cultural-institution developments around the world. And scholars have identified a dramatic recent upswing in the development of urban tram or streetcar systems globally, which reimagine the streetcars that were pervasive in the early 1900s but removed from most city streets because they were seen as outdated and inefficient. Yet a closer examination across a wide range of infrastructure asset types and time periods suggests that there is consistency in this wave-like pattern in the development of specific types of infrastructure, over fairly brief time periods. New infrastructure megaproject technologies often rise on the ashes of previous innovations, are developed in punctuated bunches, and then recede in popularity as they are superseded by the next big thing.

How pervasive are these cycles or waves of megaproject development? How do we explain the transfer of megaproject ideas and development from place to place? And how can this insight inform the decisions of infrastructure project planners, policy makers, and investors? It is these questions that are the focus of this chapter. But first, it is necessary to briefly examine where new ideas come from, and how they spread over time.

3.2 Riding the Wave

The cyclical nature of innovation development and diffusion is a topic of great interest for academics, policy makers, business leaders, and the general public. Over the years, extensive attention has been paid to documenting cycles in the way that new fashion styles, music, technologies, public policies, business management strategy, and nutrition emerge and spread. An important insight into the cyclical development of innovative new ideas or products is that they tend to follow a consistent "natural history" through different identifiable stages—most succinctly defined by Best (2006: 21) as "emerging, surging, and purging." This natural history is characterized by a standard "S" innovation curve, which is often depicted in a wave-like pattern to denote that a new innovation typically builds on the foundation of a previous product or idea that has run its course or is being improved upon (Figure 3.1).

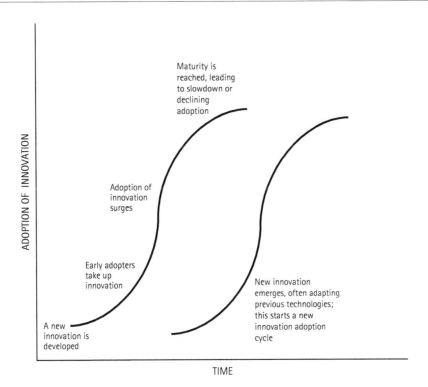

FIGURE 3.1 S-curve of innovation adoption.

To date, there has been limited examination of whether cycles of innovation diffusion may be an enduring part of the megaproject development process. However, when patterns of megaproject development are viewed at a global scale and tracked historically over time, it is clear that such dynamics are not just present, but are a driving force in determining which projects get built, where, and when. Table 3.1 provides an overview of seven types of megaproject dating back to the turn of the nineteenth century that have each displayed a similar emerge–surge–purge pattern in the way that they were developed, gained widespread adoption, and then subsequently declined in application. The following sections draw on illustrative examples of different types of megaproject to show the dynamics of infrastructure development cycles.

3.2.1 Riding the Wave, Again and Again

The century-long development of baseball stadiums in North America highlights the wave-like pattern of megaproject innovation. Baseball stadiums have been an enduring feature of the American landscape. However, the preferred design of these stadiums shifted abruptly when an innovator came along. As shown in Figure 3.2, baseball

Table 3.1 Selected waves of innovation in urban development, 1890–2007

Date	Description	Antecedents	Trendsetters	Surge	Decline
1890–1920	Electric tramways and streetcars	Animal-pulled omni-carts and trams in New York and New Orleans	Berlin electric demonstration tram in 1881	By the turn of the twentieth century, electrified trams were a common feature of the urban environment in cities on all six continents	Advances in bus and car technologies and spread of cities made trams less efficient, and they were removed from most cities by the 1960s
1900–1910	American city beautiful movement (redevelopment of city centers and parks using monumental designs)	Baron Haussmann's nineteenth-century redevelopment of Paris	Chicago 1893 "White City" Fair Grounds; Washington Mall redevelopment plan	City beautiful initiatives in Denver, New York, Seattle, Baltimore, Harrisburg, Philadelphia, and Chicago	Opposition to large expenses on urban aesthetics led to an increased emphasis on functionality of investments
1910–1935	Construction of British imperial capitals using city beautiful techniques	American city beautiful movement	Edwin Lutyens and Herbert Baker's design of New Delhi, begun in 1912	Imperial capitals initiatives in Lusaka, Salisbury (Harare), Nairobi, and Kampala	Beginning of decline of the British Empire, leading to independence following World War II
1935–1960	High-rise, single-use public housing megaprojects	Garden City; European Modernist movement, Le Corbusier	First Homes, New York City; Cabrini Green, Chicago; Boundary Estate, London; Stockholm Exhibition	St Louis, Chicago, Boston, Toronto, Birmingham, Paris, Stockholm, New Orleans, Glasgow, Sheffield, Atlanta, Detroit, Melbourne, and Sydney	Demolition of award-winning Pruitt-Igoe in St Louis sixteen years after it opened symbolized the failure of large housing projects; they have subsequently been demolished in many cities
1955–1970	Regional transportation planning and urban freeway construction	City beautiful movement, suburbanization following the end of World War II	Chicago Area Transport Study, 1955, which used regional traffic and economic modeling to emphasize new highway developments	Washington, Baltimore, Pittsburgh, Hartford, Philadelphia, San Francisco, Toronto, and Vancouver	High-profile protests opposing freeways in New York, led by urbanist Jane Jacobs, which spurred similar protests in other cities such as Toronto, San Francisco, and Vancouver

(continued)

Table 3.1 Continued

Date	Description	Antecedents	Trendsetters	Surge	Decline
1980– current	Light rail lines (adaptation of trams, either running on-street or on dedicated rights of way)	Nineteenth-century tramways; new urbanism emphasis on transit-oriented development	Rebranding and redesign of old trams as modern light rail in late 1970s: Gothenburg, San Francisco, Edmonton, and Portland	Between 1980 and 2000, more than sixty-five new light rail lines were constructed in cities around the world, and the construction of light rail lines continues to the present	n/a
1997– current	Iconic museums and cultural-led urban regeneration	City beautiful movement; Frank Lloyd Wright's 1959 Guggenheim Museum, New York	Bilbao Guggenheim Museum, designed by Frank Gehry	New York, London, Washington, Berlin, Milwaukee, Houston, Sheffield, and Hull	n/a

Source: Siemiatycki (2013).

stadium design has changed from the classic era of downtown brick, concrete, and steel stadiums with natural grass fields, to the modern period of large suburban municipal fields that were multipurpose and had artificial turf playing fields, to a more recent wave of "retro" ballparks that were located in downtown locations and reimagined the classic stadium design aesthetic.

The opening of the retro Camden Yards in Baltimore in 1992 sparked the most recent innovation wave of building retro baseball stadiums. Since that date, twenty-three of thirty teams have built new stadiums using the retro design style, meaning that this current wave of innovation has nearly reached its saturation point. Many of the current wave of retro ballpark projects cost hundreds of millions of dollars or even more than $1 billion as they incorporated increasingly complex features such as retractable roofs, and received public subsidies which were approved by both Democratic and Republican governments. In a number of instances, projects seeking to emulate the Camden Yards experience had large cost overruns and have failed to deliver on forecasted benefits in terms of economic development, local urban regeneration, or long-term increases in fan attendance. Nevertheless, Figure 3.2 shows the power of a wave of innovation across history: once a new ballpark design standard became in vogue, every single subsequent ballpark to be constructed over the subsequent two decades followed that style of design.

Intriguingly, this wave of retro stadium design at the turn of the twenty-first century has not extended beyond North American baseball parks. Globally, modern architecture and design has been the most common aesthetic for new stadiums constructed

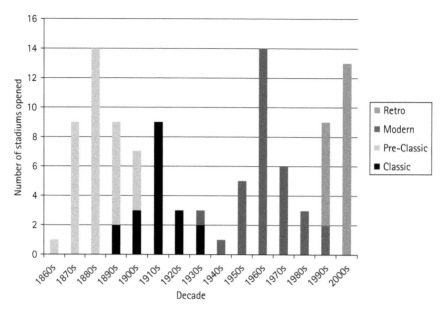

FIGURE 3.2 Number and type of Major League baseball stadiums constructed, 1860–2010.
(Source: http://www.ballparksofbaseball.com.)

during this period, even when they are designed by the same global architecture and design firms that worked on the retro baseball parks in North America. This suggest that the confluence of factors that has driven the retro stadium trend is particular to North America (and perhaps even more specifically baseball in America), and may be rooted in national economic and cultural conditions that are not necessarily transferrable elsewhere or to other sports.

3.2.2 Innovation Cycles Transcend Political Systems

The case of urban tram or streetcar systems provides an example of the diffusion of a technological innovation around the world to jurisdictions that have vastly different political systems, governance structures, and urban forms. This showcases how a single technology can serve to address a common global challenge, in this case the demand for mass urban mobility, in vastly different places. It also demonstrates the importance of symbolic messages. During a two-decade period at the turn of the twentieth century, urban trams were built in cities on five continents, including New York and Chicago (strong mayor, federalist democracy), Toronto (weak mayor, federalist democracy), London (unitary democracy with strong involvement of the national government in urban policy), Budapest and Sarajevo (Austro-Hungarian Empire), Calcutta and Alexandria (British rule of India and Egypt, respectively), and Rio de Janeiro (Portuguese colonial rule of Brazil). This rapid spread of trams was followed by the widespread abandonment of the technology in the mid-twentieth century. Streetcars were removed from the streets of almost every city in the world as they became increasingly unprofitable, viewed as part of the old urban order, and an impediment to the modern free flow of the private automobile. In the United States, the demise of streetcars was expedited by competition from urban buses, which was exacerbated by a conspiracy on the part of National City Lines corporation and its backers General Motors, Standard Oil, and Firestone Tire to create a bus monopoly in the urban transit industry (Mees 2010).

In the past quarter century, however, there has been a resurgence in the popularity of trams. Rebranded as light rail, tram systems costing hundreds of millions or billions of dollars have been built in dozens of cities globally. These tram systems are commonly promoted as a strategy to provide sustainable urban mobility alternatives to the private automobile, spur urban regeneration and smart growth, and attract creative industries and workers. Many of these new tram systems have faced significant challenges with construction cost overruns, delays, low ridership, and mixed evidence about whether they actually deliver development and environmental benefits (Pickrell 1992; Flyvbjerg 2007). Yet the wave of development has persisted despite the withering critiques. Light rail lines have been ascribed with a set of powerful symbolic meanings that transcend their tangible benefits, connoting messages of sustainable development, visionary leadership, and pride of place. The successful communication of these symbolic messages has enhanced the public popularity of light rail technology and lengthened the duration of this wave of investment.

3.2.3 New Technology Meets a Global Market

Super-tall skyscrapers provide an example of a class of megaproject that has surged in popularity as technology has evolved and it has been transposed to an eager market around the globe. As of 2015, there are ninety-two super-tall skyscrapers worldwide that are over 300 meters high—the common cutoff used to identify the tallest of the world's tall buildings (Council on Tall Buildings and Urban Habitat 2015). As shown in Figure 3.3, super-tall buildings are in the midst of a major surge of development. In the five years from 2010 to 2015, more super-tall buildings opened worldwide than in the previous eighty years, from the time that the first one was inaugurated. And super-tall buildings are growing taller than ever: between 1930 and 2000 the world's tallest building grew by 133 meters to 452 meters; and since 2000, the tallest building in the world grew by a further 377 meters to 828 meters. A closer examination of super-tall buildings illustrates how the confluence of technological, geographic, and economic factors has supported the boom in their development.

In their initial incarnation, super-tall skyscrapers were exclusively an American phenomenon. The first eight buildings over 300 meters tall were built between 1930 and 1989, and all were located in the United States. Until the 1980s, steel was the main structural material used, and super-tall skyscrapers were used for office towers. Classic buildings like the Chrysler Building and the Empire State Building in New York, and the Sears Tower (now Willis Tower) and the John Hancock Center in Chicago, came to be iconic

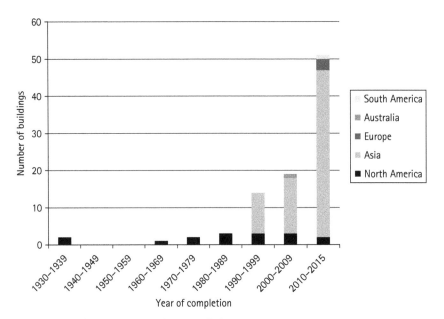

FIGURE 3.3 Global development of super-tall skyscrapers.

(From Council on Tall Buildings and Urban Habitat, 2015.)

features of their city skylines and important symbols of American engineering and business prowess. Thus while the technology existed to build super-tall buildings as early as the 1930s, very few were actually constructed, and there was not a market outside the United States.

The surge in super-tall building construction that began in the 1980s and really picked up in the 2000s coincided with three trends. First, new construction techniques have been developed to build super-tall buildings using concrete or composite structural materials. These materials allow the buildings to be built taller while maintaining a slender base, which makes them more economically viable, as there is not a very large podium that can be difficult to find tenants for. Innovative elevators have also been developed to move people more quickly through taller buildings. Second, super-tall buildings are now widely used for luxury residential or hotel uses, creating an entirely new market for tall buildings alongside offices. Third, super-tall buildings have become a global phenomenon, with the most rapid growth concentrated outside the United States in a handful of countries in East and Southeast Asia and the Middle East. In particular, the largest building boom has been in China and the Emirates of Dubai, which now are respectively home to 37% and 23% of all super-tall buildings. In these countries, super-tall buildings with iconic architecture have become important symbols of ascending global power and status—part of a luxury property-led economic development model, and a form of city marketing and branding. As such, the twenty-first-century boom in super-tall buildings globally reflects an adaptation of their American antecedents based on new building technologies and the construction of locally sensitive symbolic narratives in emerging markets.

3.2.4 Failure to Launch

Of course, not all new innovative technologies catch on and surge in popularity. One interesting question is what happens to new megaproject technologies or designs that run counter to a cycle of development? In cases where the type of infrastructure is targeted at a local user base and still provides benefit, it will continue to be operated. Monorails, for instance, a transit technology that was first developed in the nineteenth century, gained some level of popularity in Germany at the turn of the twentieth century and have been consistently touted by promoters as a solution to urban transit problems ever since. Yet with the exception of a few brief moments of interest and some application at amusement parks and airports, few monorails have been built as urban transit systems relative to other transit megaproject technologies. Those monorails that were built generally continue to operate and serve their local market, in places where they provide an effective transportation service. At a global scale, however, the monorail technology was widely surpassed in popularity by subways and light rail lines that became the urban rail technology of choice.

In other cases, missing a wave of innovation can be far more costly for project owners. In the case of emblematic sports stadiums, architecturally significant cultural facilities, large convention centers, and upscale waterfront redevelopments, the success of a megaproject is dependent on providing services to a local and international user base in a competitive market. For this type of asset, a megaproject that runs counter to a global wave of innovation and becomes uncompetitive may have diminished value to its owners and users, and thus require costly refurbishment or even complete replacement far earlier than the end of its technical lifespan. The experience with North American baseball stadiums highlights this point, as the last of the modern stadiums built just before the retro Camden Yards opened have become obsolete very quickly. In Toronto and Tampa Bay, large and expensive modern domed stadiums were considered technological wonders that would make their jurisdictions professional sporting hotspots when they first opened in the late 1980s and early 1990s. They are now seen as impediments to attracting the best players to play for the team and fans to attend games, as they lack the comfort of grass playing fields and the ambiance of the retro ballpark designs. In each city, the outdated stadiums have challenged the quality of the team on the field and the financial viability of the organization. Both teams are now exploring costly options to retrofit or build new stadiums to replace ballparks that are barely a quarter century old and still fully functional.

3.2.5 South to North Innovation Waves

Thus far, the examples provided have primarily showcased megaproject technologies that have diffused from the Global North to the Global South. This has been the predominant direction that the spread of new megaproject technologies have followed over the past two centuries. In the nineteenth century and early twentieth century,

European colonial systems provided a key channel through which new technologies were transferred from North to South. For instance, in Africa at the turn of the twentieth century, European empires undertook a punctuated burst of railway construction in their multiple colonies on the continent. This investment in infrastructure was meant to improve colonial command and control by enabling better exploitation of natural resources and improve connectivity into global flows of trade (Jedwab and Moradi 2012). More recently, international financial aid and technical assistance through multinational institutions such as the World Bank or national development agencies has been an important mechanism by which megaproject technologies and project funds have spread to the Global South. As the historic experience with North to South diffusion demonstrates, the adoption of new infrastructure megaprojects in the Global South has not always been voluntary. In some cases, colonial governments imposed the development of specific technologies; and more recently, bilateral aid or development agency funding has been made conditional on the development of specific types of megaproject. Many of these imposed megaprojects have had poor outcomes or exacerbated levels of social inequality in the host country.

While considerably less frequent, there are instances where megaproject innovations in the Global South have gained prominence and surged globally. The most prominent example is perhaps the wave of bus rapid transit systems (BRT). The first city to develop a BRT system on a large scale was Curitiba, Brazil, which in 1974 implemented an extensive network of high-capacity bus lines on fixed dedicated routes with high-quality stations. BRT provided a lower-cost, faster-construction, and more flexible alternative to urban rail technology. With high ridership and relatively low costs, Curitiba's bus rapid transit system inspired the implementation of similar projects across Brazil and parts of Latin America, and by a number of other cities in the Global North, including Ottawa and Pittsburgh. These projects grew in scale and became megaprojects costing hundreds of millions of dollars when the rights of way, stations, and vehicle costs were included. However, the technology never fully caught on at the time as a global wave, because there were concerns about capacity constraints for bus-based transit systems, and in many countries, buses had a reputation for being a mode of travel of last resort.

Then, in 2000, Bogota opened its TransMilenio BRT system, which changed the global paradigm regarding BRT. At $240 million, or $5.9 million per km for the 41-km first phase of the system, TransMilenio was far cheaper than a comparable metro system that was being considered at the time. Bogota's BRT also included passing lanes at each station and express services—innovations that altered perceptions about the capacity of BRT. And the boldly branded red articulated buses and modern station areas captured popular attention (UNDP 2012). In quick succession following the successful opening of the first TransMilenio BRT line, many other cities followed Bogota's lead and implemented similar BRT systems. In the 2000s, dozens of major cities in the Global South, including Jakarta, Delhi, Guangzhou, Johannesburg, Tehran, Istanbul, and Mexico City implemented bus rapid transit services. Bogota's experience also initiated a wave of BRT projects in North American and European cities.

In addition to innovative infrastructure technologies emerging in the Global South and spreading further afield, new patterns of South–South investing are spurring a wave of specific types of megaproject in developing countries. In particular, China has become a major infrastructure investor and builder of African infrastructure megaprojects. For African countries where the stock of infrastructure lags well behind the global norm, outside investment in infrastructure provides an opportunity to broaden their economic base. Meanwhile, for China, infrastructure investing in Africa is part of a strategic initiative to develop closer political ties and secure access to natural resources. This has led to a wave of major road and railway building, port construction, and energy projects across Africa that are financed and built by Chinese firms or state-owned enterprises. To date, more than thirty-five African countries are engaging with China for infrastructure deals, the largest being in Nigeria, Angola, Sudan, and Ethiopia. Following the Chinese lead, Brazil, India, and some Gulf States have also turned their interest to infrastructure investing in developing countries, particularly in their own local regions, thereby furthering the wave of megaproject construction in developing countries (Foster et al. 2008). As such, the pattern of South–South investing is not so much about the diffusion of a new technology, but rather in providing the financing, construction expertise, and motivation to initiate a surge in projects being built in places where infrastructure has tended not to be constructed previously.

3.2.6 Ending a Cycle

The case of nuclear power plant construction illustrates how abruptly a wave of innovation can be halted in the face of changing views on the effectiveness of technology and public concerns about safety. The construction of multi-billion-dollar nuclear power plants rode a wave of development in the 1970s and 1980s, with many projects built in both Western democracies and Eastern communist countries (Figure 3.4). These projects met ever-increasing global demand for power. Yet a confluence of factors contributed to a precipitous decline in new nuclear power plant development in the 1990s and 2000s, with relatively few new plants built in developed countries, and China being the primary market experiencing a mini-boom in reactor development. Accidents in close succession at Three Mile Island and Chernobyl and later Fukushima raised global concern about the safety of nuclear power plants, and highlighted worries about the risks of both the production of nuclear power and the radioactive waste disposal process. Nuclear power plants had become widely known for major construction cost overruns and delays. And the promise of scaling up renewable power sources provided the glimmer of the possibility of a viable alternative energy source.

While there has been a decline in the construction of new nuclear power plants, this has not led to a wholesale purging or shuttering of existing facilities. Most nuclear power plants constructed during the surge of popularity remain operational and provide an important source of electricity. Nuclear power accounts for around 12% of electricity produced globally, with thirteen countries deriving more than a third of their power

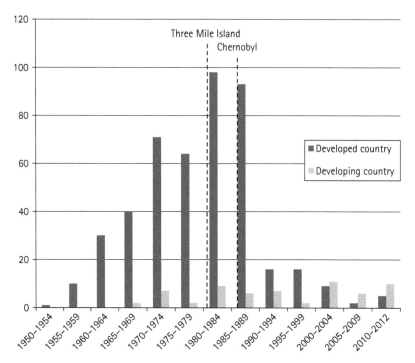

FIGURE 3.4 Boom and bust: Opening of new nuclear reactors worldwide.

(International Atomic Energy Commission 2016.)

from nuclear sources (Nuclear Energy Institute 2015). Nevertheless, since the 1990s, a number of developed countries such as Germany, Italy, and Switzerland have introduced plans to phase out the use of their existing nuclear power plants. In 2012, after the accident at Fukushima, China announced a moratorium on nuclear plant construction, but following plant safety inspections, the country has since renewed initiatives to develop new reactors as it seeks to find alternatives to producing power through coal. Against this backdrop, the future for nuclear power megaprojects remains highly uncertain.

3.2.7 An Enduring Feature of Infrastructure Development

Taken together, these examples show how waves of innovation are a common feature across a wide range of megaproject types, as new technologies are diffused from local initiatives, to national, regional, and even international cycles of development. The emerge–surge–purge (or at least decline) pattern of megaproject innovation and project development is a powerful enduring force that has been present for at least the past century. Cycles of project development transcend political ideology, economic systems, and governance structure, as new megaproject technologies have diffused between capitalist and communist countries—jurisdictions ruled by governments following liberal or conservative ideologies, as well as those taking nationalist or separatist perspectives. Each cycle appears to last for at least twenty years, reflecting the long time horizon over which megaproject planning and building occurs, and the time period that it may take to observe flaws in previous models of megaproject development that precipitate their declining popularity. Even some of the most successful megaproject technologies such as subways or urban metro railway systems that have endured for over a century have still seen waves where there were bursts of development followed by periods of less construction, or when development was more concentrated in certain regions of the world than in others.

To date, most cycles of megaproject development have been initiated in the Global North and have traveled south, but there are indications that this pattern may be beginning to change as countries in the Global South develop innovative solutions to problems that are widely applicable elsewhere. The inspiration for a wave of megaproject innovation can come from a place at the top of the global hierarchy of importance, such as London, New York, or Paris. Or a successful innovation may be initiated in a place that typically garners less global attention, such as Curitiba or Bogota in the case of BRT, Baltimore's Camden Yards for baseball stadiums, or Bilbao's Guggenheim in the case of the museum-building boom.

The duration of time and frequency with which the emerge–surge–purge pattern of megaproject development is observable suggests that it is not merely a function of corporate globalization, modern mass communication technologies, or increased ease of international travel, though these are all probable factors. There is something more fundamentally enduring about the way that infrastructure megaprojects fit into local and global political economies, and are promoted and consumed. Providing explanations for these cyclical patterns of infrastructure development is the topic of the next section.

3.3 Why Cycles of Megaproject Development?

Cycles of megaproject development, be they brief punctuated fads or longer-term trends, have multiple interrelated causes. They are driven by a complex mix of technological innovation, economics, social networks, ideologies, and interest groups that spur the diffusion of certain new megaproject approaches at punctuated moments in time. Moreover, the global diffusion of megaproject innovations is furthered by the political and policy lure of achieving major tangible benefits, as well as the potential to convey a powerful set of intangible symbolic messages that often get ascribed to certain megaproject technologies.

A fulsome explanation for the causes of megaproject cycles of development requires the blending of insights on innovation, policy mobility, and technology diffusion from three diverse disciplinary perspectives. For economists, waves of innovation and diffusion of new technologies are the result of a process of creative destruction, where new technologies that better meet demand at lower costs are constantly supplanting old ones. Political scientists observe that policy mobility results from the confluence of institutions, ideologies, and individuals that support the diffusion of certain technologies or policies at a given moment in time (Dolowitz and Marsh 2000). And geography and planning scholars have emphasized the importance of local cultures and unequal power dynamics in the policy transfer networks to explain how new ideas or technologies are reinterpreted and altered as they move from one place to another (McCann and Ward 2012). Examining each stage of the emerge–surge–purge innovation diffusion cycle that megaprojects pass through illustrates how certain actors, political economic interests, and ideologies come to predominate, thereby influencing which megaproject developments are transferred nationally or globally.

3.3.1 The Innovator

The infrastructure development cycle begins with an "innovator" creating a new item, product, or activity. When studying megaproject innovators and the novel ideas they create, it is necessary to identify the extent to which the innovation is truly new, where in the world it is being developed, the motivations for developing a new megaproject approach, and the way that different stakeholders from the private and public sectors are involved. Each of these factors provides insights into the types of innovation that are developed, and ultimately how transferable they will be to other jurisdictions.

As highlighted previously, the spark for a wave of innovation in the infrastructure sector can come from jurisdictions at the top of the global hierarchy that are well known, as well as less prominent locations. Importantly, both the public and private sectors are sources of megaproject innovations. Developing and implementing new technologies on a large scale carries significant risks that the private sector might not be willing or able to bear on their own. As such, it is quite common that some of the most audacious, innovative, daring, and risky megaprojects include a combination of government and private-sector involvement in terms of research and development, funding, ownership, and operations.

What is critical for an innovation to spark a cycle of development is that the novel approach addresses a common challenge being faced in a wide variety of jurisdictions. Some rare innovations, such as the motor vehicle, railway, airplane, computer, and Internet, are truly revolutionary in origin, in that they imagine a technology, entire product category, or idea that had never been tried before. These technologies have the capacity to entirely supplant previous infrastructural technologies and completely reorder spatial, social, and political relations. More often, an innovation is evolutionary in nature, reimagining or adapting technologies or ideas that existed for some time. These evolutionary innovations, like driverless trains or novel high-rise building techniques, make an incremental improvement to an existing technology, which might increase its utility, lower costs, diminish risk, or minimize the externalities.

There are diverse motivations for developing and implementing innovative infrastructure technologies at given times. Investments in novel megaprojects have the potential to deliver significant benefits by alleviating local problems and elevating the competitiveness of specific jurisdictions by tying them more closely into cross-border spaces of flows. Depending on the type of megaproject, it can make a place more accessible, safe, healthy, efficient, productive, learned, livable, beautiful, sustainable, or resilient, driving economic growth and prosperity. As such, there can be a considerable advantage for first movers that successfully harness a new type of megaproject. There are also significant political gains to be had: the local mayors of both Curitiba and Bogota used their high-profile leadership of successful pioneering BRT projects as a springboard to launch state-level and national political careers.

Another form of innovation is the construction of novel symbolic meanings for a megaproject. Infrastructure megaprojects become imbued with a wide set of powerful symbolic imageries that transcend their stated purpose, and are targeted at both a local and global audience. Official narratives developed by project planners and promoters tend to focus on themes of pride of place, an image of modernity and progress, optimism about the potential for collective action to deliver massive projects, and visionary leadership to execute plans on a large scale to solve pressing problems.

The Delhi Metro provides a case in point. In their promotional material and public discourse, project planners presented the new electric train system as a megaproject that would provide tangible benefits of combating traffic congestion and ameliorating air pollution. They also carefully constructed the image of the Metro also as a sleek, clean, and well-managed symbol of progress for modern Delhi that would put the city in line with the great capital cities of the world that all have extensive subway systems. On the day that the Delhi Metro opened, more than a million Delhiites lined up to ride the train that had become a point of pride in the city (see Siemiatycki 2006).

Outside the officially constructed narrative, megaprojects also have the potential to convey more negative symbolic associations, including wasteful spending, blatant rent-seeking, project management incompetence, and unchecked authority, power, and control. Against this backdrop, in many cases the construction of a lasting symbolic narrative to associate with a megaproject is hotly contested and evolves over time. In Boston, while the Big Dig to bury the central artery was initially viewed very negatively because of the high-profile construction cost overrun that the project experienced, years later a more positive narrative is emerging that recognizes the broader city-building benefits that have been achieved.

3.3.2 The Surge

Given the major tangible and symbolic benefits associated with the implementation of certain trendsetting megaprojects, it is not surprising that imitators of a successful idea would follow. A critical question is why some megaproject innovations surge in popularity to become global waves or longer-term trends, while others fail to catch on and achieve further adoption. Put differently, at any given moment many innovative mega-project technologies are being developed and experimented with around the globe—some revolutionary and others evolutionary. So how do we explain which ones surge in popularity to become part of a global wave of development? The answer to this question is multifaceted, influenced by the type of new technology and the benefits they deliver, the status, cache, and influence of the innovators and their promoters, and the political economy of who benefits from the new type of megaproject.

At the most basic level, megaproject innovations surge to wider uptake because they are superior to other alternatives in terms of the benefits they provide. These benefits can be diverse, including greater economic, environmental, or social benefits at lower costs than other alternatives, easier or lower risk to implement, and better adaptability to var-ied physical and governance contexts. Megaprojects that surge from local innovations to global phenomena are also those that fill a common pressing need faced by many societ-ies at a given time, be it for improved mobility and congestion relief, sanitation and clean drinking water, reliable energy, security, trade, tourism, livability, and so forth.

The type of megaproject and the need that it fulfills affects the rationales underlying a surge in popularity and implementation. Megaprojects providing hard infrastructural services such as public transit, urban road tunnels, water and waste-water treatment, and public housing tend to be focused on fulfilling the basic needs of local users, which can have the knock-on effect of making that place more externally competitive. And their success is not particularly impacted by different approaches taken elsewhere. The implementation of a novel BRT system in Bogota does not have a direct impact on the success of a subway system in Brussels. As such, the spread of these types of hard locally oriented infrastructures at any given time are largely driven by the availability of new technologies, governance capacity, the ability to mobilize the necessary resources, shift-ing priorities, and ideologies about the way to solve difficult collective problems, and the symbolic images associated with various technologies.

In contrast to hard local infrastructure, the success of other types of facilities are much more dependent on their interoperability and integration into national or global net-works of commerce or people to remain competitive. For this type of megaproject, a new wave of development can be quickly sparked if an innovative technology or design dis-places previous approaches and requires others to make similar investments to remain competitive. Ports, for instance, are a hard infrastructure that must be constantly kept up to date with the global technology standard for deep-water access, loading and unload-ing equipment, and surrounding ground transportation access, otherwise they will not be able to service the current types of ships or will become less efficient than competing facilities and ultimately lose market share to competitors. Some types of social infrastruc-ture such as convention centers also exist within a context of intense global competition. There are only so many conventions globally that require major meeting facilities for thousands of people. To tap into this lucrative market, cities have built ever more elabo-rate convention centers to attract globally footloose business activity to their jurisdiction, while antiquated facilities face the pressure of declining patronage.

In addition to the importance of the practical utility of an innovation, the rising tide of a cycle of infrastructure development is also part of a social, economic, and political process. Novel megaproject technologies or approaches are diffused through a series of interconnected networks and channels in such a way that they resonate with, and become adopted by, a wider following. With infrastructure megaprojects, an internationally connected group of prominent architects, designers, planners, consultants, and politicians has been central in uncovering novel technologies or project types, and communicating the merits of these infrastructures to a wider set of political and economic decision makers. There are various forums through which new megaproject ideas are disseminated, including media coverage of high-profile projects, policy conferences, World's Fairs and international sporting events, and international travel junkets.

The importance of the networks through which new ideas are disseminated should not be underestimated; some of the recent megaprojects that sparked international cycles of development were initiated or funded by prestigious and well-connected global organizations, even if they were located in less well-known locations. The Guggenheim in Bilbao that sparked a wave of museum megaprojects was designed by one of the world's most famous architects and was part of a well-established global museum franchise, which brought considerable international attention through their networks. Similarly, Bogota's BRT system was backed by the World Bank as a lower cost alternative to light rail. The World Bank subsequently trumpeted the success to other potential markets, raising awareness and ascribing legitimacy to the technology in other developed countries. And Camden Yards stadium in Baltimore was designed by the prominent international architecture firm HOK, which was subsequently hired to design sixteen new American baseball stadiums over the ensuing two decades, thus playing an important role in spreading the retro design innovation across the continent, and profiting from it. As illustrated by these examples, the connections of the originators of new technologies and the networks through which new ideas are disseminated influences which projects are most likely to spread widely.

Finally, there is a clear political economy to which megaprojects are diffused widely. Successfully diffused megaproject innovations are commonly those that appeal to individuals with elevated status, wealth, and prestige, and are part of local growth coalitions. The majority of megaproject technologies or approaches that have surged in popularity are those that provide the basis to make a jurisdiction more economically competitive, have the potential to generate large profits for key local interests such as property owners, developers, and industrialists, and project key messages of pride of place that appeal to important civic boosters and the mainstream media. To this end, megaprojects that surge in popularity are those that are consistent with the predominant ideology of the day, while making it possible for each jurisdiction to superimpose their own local symbolic narratives onto the megaproject.

3.3.3 The Cycle Ends

The decline of a cycle of innovation and megaproject development begins for a variety of reasons, including the reaching of a saturation point, the usurping of the old approach by a new technology, and emerging evidence of flaws in the original model of development. First, saturation may be reached, as the majority of markets where a specific type of technology is a viable option have taken it up and are benefiting from the original innovation. This applies most directly to globally oriented megaprojects that put facilities in one jurisdiction directly in competition with those in other places. Once every potential market has adopted the current state-of-the-art technology—for example, new stadiums or convention centers—there is no need for a continued wave of development until a major new innovation disrupts the status quo. Instead, we may see more minor renovations and expansions of existing facilities.

Second, the end of a megaproject development cycle may be initiated when a new technology emerges that provides greater tangible or symbolic benefits than the old approach. This is the classic case of creative destruction. It can be seen throughout the history of megaprojects: railways replaced canals for inland freight transportation in the nineteenth century; urban streetcars were largely replaced by the car and transit bus in the mid-twentieth century; and downtown retro baseball stadiums displaced modern suburban fields at the turn of the twenty-first century.

Third, flaws in the original megaproject approach might become more apparent than they were during the period of rapid uptake, when symbolic or political benefits ascribed to a megaproject obscure careful analysis of its tangible benefits and costs, or winners and losers. Megaprojects that are appropriate in one context or delivered great benefit for the original innovator may not be as effective elsewhere. While initial under-performance observed with a surging megaproject technology is often blamed on local political conditions or poor implementation processes, over time, expert and local community opposition has been instrumental in highlighting systemic flaws and ultimately halting waves of megaproject development.

Growing evidence of systemic cost overruns and benefit shortfalls on megaprojects such as light rail lines, iconic museum buildings, or power dams can lead to the cancelation of subsequent phases of existing projects, or halt adoption by other jurisdictions. Planning processes that lack transparency and accountability have been a source of community opposition. Changes in government or political power may halt waves of development by contributing to shifts in the types of project that are prioritized. And shifting economic conditions or public perceptions of a type of infrastructure can lead key megaproject supporters, such as local property developers and civic boosters that once supported a certain type of development, to switch their position if a technology comes to be seen as contradicting their interests. Indeed, opposition groups raising awareness about the negative externalities of megaprojects have been important in the decline of various technologies, especially the modernist transportation, public housing, and energy megaprojects of the mid-twentieth century.

Importantly, different types of megaproject are impacted differently by innovation and changing attitudes toward a specific technology, and therefore experience decline in different ways. Megaprojects are fixed capital, meant to last for generations. Yet some innovations impose complete creative destruction on the generation of infrastructure that came before, and the outdated technology is actively removed from the physical landscape. In the case of tramlines in the mid-twentieth century and baseball stadiums at the turn of the twenty-first century, at the end of their wave of development each was actively removed because they were no longer profitable, interfered with the technology that displaced them, and were symbolically representative of the old urban order.

Conversely in other cases, once a surge in megaproject development is over, that technology may continue to be used for decades to come, with money continuing to be spent on maintenance and upgrades. Nuclear power reactors provide a case where although few new facilities have been built in developed countries since the 1990s, most facilities have continued to be operated to provide a necessary energy source. Intriguingly, in the case of elevated urban freeways that were popularized in the 1950s and 1960s, after decades of use their future is now being hotly debated. While these facilities have continued to operate long after the wave of development ended in the 1970s, politicians and community groups in many cities are debating both their ongoing utility and symbolic meaning in an era where cities are focusing more than ever on sustainability, walkability, and livability. In fact, a growing number of cities, such as Boston, Seattle, Seoul, and San Francisco, have undertaken megaprojects to replace these aging artifacts of an old urban order. As the experience with freeways suggests, shifting utility and perceptions of one type of megaproject often initiates a feedback loop where opinion leaders are again out searching for and implementing the next big thing.

3.4 Conclusions: Where on the Innovation Curve Is Your Megaproject?

As demonstrated in this chapter, cycles of megaproject development are a common feature across a wide variety of locations, time periods, and infrastructure types. Over the past two centuries, new innovations in megaprojects have emerged in jurisdictions all around the world, have surged in popularity as they are adopted widely, and subsequently have seen declining implementation as they deliver on their promised benefits, fail to meet expectations in a large number of places, or are usurped by the next wave of development. The observation of the cyclical nature of megaproject development, as well as an understanding of the processes that drive them, provides powerful insights for public- and private-sector decision makers. Indeed, policy makers can learn about the probable success of a proposed project under review, and the risks involved, by studying three interrelated questions during the assessment phase of a project's development.

First, where in the cycle of development is a given type of infrastructure that is being considered, and how will it affect that particular type of megaproject? For some project types such as globally orientated cultural facilities, convention centers, or seaports, there is a significant first-mover advantage that accompanies being the innovator, which outweighs the high costs and risks of developing a new megaproject technology. In other cases, such as investments in correctly located urban rapid transit megaprojects, telecommunications initiatives, or green energy projects, large benefits continue to accrue from being a later adopter once the technology is perfected or a wave of development catches on. As megaproject technology reaches maturity with widespread adoption, project planners must consider the likelihood and impact on their project if a new wave of technology usurps the type of infrastructure they intend to develop.

Second, how comparable are the places where a megaproject idea is coming from and being transferred to? A surprising observation is that megaproject technologies such as bus rapid transit or high-tech bike-sharing systems that can cost hundreds of millions of dollars to implement have often been successfully transferred between jurisdictions with significantly different political systems, governance structures, or ideologies, provided that they are designed to solve similar tangible and symbolic problems. At the same time, a megaproject such as a new light railway line that delivered significant benefits in one place may fail elsewhere if it is inappropriately located, not accompanied by complementary policies that made the originator successful, does not consider the local cultural or economic conditions, or is unpopular with the surrounding community.

Third, what is the primary objective for the megaproject being developed? Is the project intended primarily to improve local conditions through the implementation of a hard piece of infrastructure, or is it mainly geared toward tying a region into global spaces of flows—be it for transportation, capital, trade, tourists, image and attention, and so on. Internationally orientated megaprojects tend to be especially sensitive to innovations elsewhere, whereas locally orientated infrastructures may still provide significant local benefit even if the global state-of-the-art has moved on. Taken together, answering these questions during the project assessment process will enable policy makers to take advantage of this understanding of the cycles of megaproject development. Decision makers can avoid the costly mistake of developing megaprojects that may be obsolete soon after construction is completed, or are inappropriate for the jurisdiction to where they are being transferred.

References

Best, J. (2006). *Flavor of the Month*. Berkeley: University of California Press.

Council on Tall Buildings and Urban Habitat. (2015). "100 tallest completed buildings in the world by height to architectural top," <http://skyscrapercenter.com/buildings>.

Dolowitz, D. P. and Marsh, D. (2000). "Learning from abroad: The role of policy transfer in contemporary policy-making," *Governance*, 13(1): 5–23.

Flyvbjerg, B. (2007). "Cost overruns and demand shortfalls in urban rail and other infrastructure," *Transportation Planning and Technology*, 30(1): 9–30.

Foster, V., Butterfield, W., Chen, C., and Pushak, N. (2008). "Building bridges: China's growing role as infrastructure financier for Sub-Saharan Africa," World Bank, <http://siteresources.worldbank.org/INTAFRICA/Resources/BB_Final_Exec_summary_English_July08_Wo-Embg.pdf>.

International Atomic Energy Commission. (2016). *Nuclear Power Reactors in the World*. Vienna: IAEC.

Jedwab, R. and Moradi, A. (2012). "Colonial investments and long-term development in Africa: Evidence from Ghanaian railroads," NEUDC Conference Working Paper, <https://www.dartmouth.edu/~neudc2012/docs/paper_34.pdf>.

Lehrer, U. and Laidley, J. (2008). "Old mega-projects newly packaged? Waterfront redevelopment in Toronto," *International Journal of Urban and Regional Research*, 32(4): 786–803.

McCann, E. J. and Ward, K. (2012). "Policy assemblages, mobilities and mutations: Toward a multidisciplinary conversation," *Political Studies Review*, 10: 325–32.

Mees, P. (2010). *Transport for Suburbia*. London: Earthscan.

Nuclear Energy Institute. (2015). "World statistics," <http://www.nei.org/Knowledge-Center/Nuclear-Statistics/World-Statistics>.

Pickrell, D. (1992). "A desire named streetcar: Fantasy and fact in rail transit planning," *Journal of the American Planning Association*, 58(2): 158–76.

Siemiatycki, M. (2006). Message in a metro: Building urban rail infrastructure and image in Delhi, India," *International Journal of Urban and Regional Research*, 30(2): 277–92.

UNDP. (2012). "Bogota, Colombia bus rapid transit project: Transmilenos," <http://www.esc-pau.fr/ppp/documents/featured_projects/colombia_bogota.pdf>.

CHAPTER 4

BIG IS FRAGILE

An Attempt at Theorizing Scale

ATIF ANSAR, BENT FLYVBJERG,
ALEXANDER BUDZIER, AND DANIEL LUNN

"There is nothing more deceptive than an obvious fact."

Sherlock Holmes in *The Boscombe Valley Mystery*, Sir Arthur
Conan Doyle

4.1 INTRODUCTION

THEORIES of big have advocated the proposition that "bigger is better" since the mid-nineteenth century, drawing especially on notions of economies of scale and scope (Stigler 1958; Silberston 1972; Chandler 1990), natural monopoly (Mill 1848; Mosca 2008), or preemptive capacity building (Porter 1980). Building big has traditionally been seen as necessary to secure efficient economies of scale and to lock competitors out of future rivalry (Ghemawat 1991; Ghemawat and der Sol 1998; Hayes and Garvin 1982: 78; Penrose [1959] 2009: 89–92; Wernerfelt and Karnani 1987). Economies of scale in the production of electricity, for example, assume declining average cost curve as output expands (Ansar and Pohlers 2014: Fig. 1).

Theories of big have held an enduring sway on management practice. Scaling is deemed necessary for survival and competitive advantage in many industries such as steel (Crompton and Lesourd 2008), shipping (Cullinane and Khanna 2000), banking (Cavallo and Rossi 2001), telecommunications (Majumdar and Venkataraman 1998; Foreman and Beauvais 1999), water, and electricity utilities (Kowka 2002; Pollitt and Steer 2012). Big ventures are witnessed when companies try to pursue new product or geographic markets: Motorola spent US$6 billion in technological rollout of its Iridium satellite constellation (Bhidé 2008); and the German steel company ThyssenKrupp spent over US$11 billion to enter the US and Brazilian markets (Ansar 2012). In the context of economic development, Sachs (2006) has popularized the view that big challenges—such as poverty alleviation, energy and water scarcity, or urbanization—can only be solved with "big push" solutions.

Theories of big are not universally accepted, needless to say. Schumacher (1973) championed "Small is beautiful." Easterly (2002, 2006) has argued against the big push "megareforms" that Sachs favors. Perhaps the most persistent attack on theories of big has come from Lindblom, who advanced the notions of "muddling through" (1959) and "disjointed incrementalism" (1979) as an alternative to "bigger is better." In the academic debate, a school of thought emerged around the notion of incrementalism, with concepts such as logical incrementalism (Quinn 1978), modularity (Baldwin and Clark 2000), real optionality (Copeland and Tufano 2004), and adaptive change (Heifetz et al. 2009). The key rationale for incrementalism is based on the well-documented limits of rationality in decision making under uncertainty (Atkinson 2011: 9).

Yet theories of big have maintained an enduring upper hand in mainstream business and government practice: megaprojects, justified on the bases of theories of big, are more ubiquitous and bigger than ever (Flyvbjerg 2014). A renewed enquiry into the validity of theories of big has become urgent because big capital investment decisions routinely fail in the real world. Motorola's Iridium went bankrupt within three years of its launch, wiping off nearly US$10 billion of equity (Kerzner 2009: 351). ThyssenKrupp's megaprojects in the Americas, initiated in 2005, suffered a worse fate. By June 2012, ThyssenKrupp's survival was in doubt, and the company's share price was a quarter of its May 2008 high. The company was forced to raise fresh capital in part by selling its ill-fated US steel plant at a steep discount to its archrivals ArcelorMittal and Nippon-Sumitomo. ThyssenKrupp's top management team, including the Chairman Gerhard Cromme, who initiated the big capital investments, was fired. Other cases of big bets gone awry abound. Losses from Boston's Big Dig or Citigroup's "bold bets" reach into the billions of dollars (Dash and Creswell 2008). Not only did the costs sunk into Japan's Fukushima nuclear power plant become unrecoverable; its clean-up costs rippled far into the economy. Beyond the financial calculus, even the reticent Chinese government is opening up to the profound and unforeseen human and environmental impacts of China's Three Gorges Dam (Qiu 2011; Stone 2008, 2011).

Over the last fifteen years, evidence from large datasets has mounted that the financial, social, and environmental performance of big capital investments, in the public and private sectors alike, is strikingly poor (see, for example, Nutt 1999, 2002; Flyvbjerg et al. 2002, 2003, 2005, 2009; Titman, Wei, and Xie 2004; Flyvbjerg and Budzier 2011; Van Oorschot et al. 2013; Ansar et al. 2014).

In this chapter we characterize the propensity of big capital investments to systematically deliver poor outcomes as "fragility"—a notion suggested by Taleb (2012). A thing or system that is easily harmed by randomness is fragile. We argue that, contrary to their appearance, big capital investments break easily—that is, they deliver negative net present value—owing to various sources of uncertainty that impact them during their long gestation, implementation, and operation. We do not refute the existence of economies of scale and scope. Instead, we argue that big capital investments have a disproportionate (non-linear) exposure to uncertainties that deliver poor or negative returns above and beyond their economies of scale and scope. We further argue that to succeed, leaders of capital projects need to carefully consider where scaling pays off and where it does not. To automatically assume that "bigger is better," which is common in megaproject management, is a recipe for failure.

In the following sections, we first develop and draw linkages between three theoretical concepts: Big, Fragility, and Scale versus Scalability. Building on the relevant literature, we advance twelve propositions about the sources and consequences of fragility, which we then apply to big capital investments. Specifically, we develop the construct of "investment fragility"—the threshold at which the cumulative losses from an investment exceeds the investment's cumulative gains. Second, we substantiate our propositions about the fragility of big capital investments using evidence from a dataset of 245 big dams. Our theoretical propositions and evidence from big dams suggests that big capital investments fail to achieve the aspirations of scalability and efficiency set for them at the outset. Once broken, these investments become stranded, causing long-term harm to the companies and countries that undertake them.

4.2 THEORY AND CONSTRUCTS

4.2.1 What Is Big?

Whether something is big seems obvious enough. Yet the construct of big and the related ideas of large, large-scale, major, mega, or huge, and so forth, prove deceptively elusive when subjected to scrutiny. A literature review of definitions of big and related words reveals a non-exhaustive list of multiple dimensions of the construct of big, such as:

- Physical proportions measured in height, length, mass, weight, area, or volume.
- Inputs required to build and run the thing measured in terms of quantities (and quality) of land, labor, or equipment required.
- Financial outlay measured in up-front capital expenditure (Flyvbjerg 2014), recurrent operational expenditure, or end-of-life costs (Clark and Wrigley 1995, 1997).
- Supply measured in the units of output that the thing can produce (Samuelson 1948; Stigler 1958) or the multiplicity of outputs (Chandler 1990).
- Demand being served, measured not only in terms of units of demand but also the quality, speed, and functionality (Weinstock and Goodenough 2006).
- Temporality measured in the time it takes to build the thing or the length of its life span (Gomez-Ibanez 2003).
- Spatial fixity or immobility and the cost of moving an asset—big tends to "spatial fixity" (Ansar 2012).
- Complexity measured, for example, with a focus on the technical aspects of the asset or its delivery (Simon 1962), or with a focus on the social and political complexity (Liu et al. 2007).

- Impact measured in the number of people who might benefit or be harmed, the number of functions enabled or disabled, or the magnitude and pace of change that the thing can cause in its environment.

The relationships among these multiple dimensions—and even the indicators within each dimension—are seldom straightforward. For instance, it is often taken for granted that in order to reduce the amount of time required to complete a venture, such as a software IT project, a manager would need to mobilize more programmers, which will also increase the capital expenditure of the venture (for a discussion, see Atkinson 1999; Williams 2005). Yet experienced managers report that such obvious relationships do not hold in practice. In contrast, Fred Brooks—the IBM executive responsible for development of IBM's System/360 family of computers in the 1960s, from which computers today have descended—formulated the famous "Brooks law:" "Adding manpower to a late software project makes it later" (Brooks 1995: 25).

Bigness entails multiple and unpredictable interactions across the dimensions we have listed with which theories of big—such as the notion of economies of scale—have not meaningfully engaged. The risk of big is reflected in these interactions, which we turn to now.

4.2.2 What Is Fragility?

Taleb (2012) proposes the construct of fragility, and its antonym antifragile, to capture the type of randomness and risk we talk about here. Taleb's inspiration for the concept came from his observation that there is no random event that can benefit a porcelain cup resting on a table, yet a wide range of uncertain events—such as earthquakes or human clumsiness—can pose harm (Taleb 2012: 268). Fragile things, like the porcelain cup, are vulnerable to members of the "disorder family," including, for example, randomness, uncertainty, volatility, variability, disturbance, or entropy—terms we use interchangeably below[1] to explore the fragility of big capital investments.

Fragility as a construct has found increasingly diverse use, regarding, for example, construction (Shinozuka et al. 2000; Choi et al. 2004); human bones (Seref-Ferlengez et al. 2015); global financial and banking crises (Davis 1995; Taleb et al. 2012; Klemkosky 2013; Calomiris and Haber 2014); mathematics (Taleb and Douady 2013); ecology and ecosystems (Nilsson and Grelsson 1995; Sole and Montoya 2001); interdependent networks (Callaway et al. 2000; Buldyrev et al. 2010; Vespignani 2010; Parshani et al. 2011; Gao et al. 2012; Morris and Barthelemy 2013); material sciences, such as in assessing properties of glass-forming liquids (Scopigno et al. 2003; Mauro et al. 2014; Martinez-Garcia et al. 2015); conflict-prone countries (USAID 2005; Ziaja 2012); democratic political systems (Mitchell 1995; Issacharoff 2007); and even personal ethics (Nussbaum 2001). Despite its diverse uses, *fragility* has certain common meanings across these fields. Taking our point of departure in Taleb's work, because this is the most comprehensive, and supplementing this with other sources, we first distill a general definition of *fragility*. Second, we use this to develop a more specific concept called "investment fragility," which we apply to big capital investments.

Fragility describes "how [a] system *suffers*" when it encounters disorder (Taleb and Douady 2013: 1677, italics in the original). The outcome of fragility is typically an irreversible loss of functionality. Our preliminary proposition, which we will refine below, is as follows:

> *Proposition 1.* Fragility is typically irreversible. Once broken, the fragile cannot be readily restored to its original function.

Fragility as a material property is signified by a material's breaking point (Scopigno et al. 2003; Martinez-Garcia et al. 2015). Mauro et al. (2014) call this unique intrinsic fragility threshold a "structural signature." Buldyrev et al. (2010) conducted similar structural analysis on networks such as electricity grids (also see Vespignani 2010). They find that intrinsic structural features of networks—such as number of nodes, whether a network is isolated or interdependent, and the number of interconnections with other networks—can help determine the "critical threshold" at which the various networks break down.[2] As a more generalizable proposition:

> *Proposition 2.* A thing (material, system, process, or network) has a unique "fragility threshold" which careful structural analysis and experimentation can reveal, at which it will break down under influence from stressor(s). All other things being equal, the lower the preset threshold the greater the fragility.

An assumed benefit of big is that the fragility threshold increases with size. However, Taleb (2012: 278–80) argues that larger organisms such as elephants tend to have a lower fragility threshold as a proportion of their size than do smaller organisms. Thus, for example, it might take a stone twice the body weight of a cat to cause a fatal outcome. But a boulder only half the bodyweight of an elephant might suffice for its fragility threshold. The source of this disproportionally greater fragility of bigger systems is to be found in the Nobel Prize-winning physicist P. W. Anderson's (1972) notion of "more is different." As a more generalizable proposition, we advance:

> *Proposition 3.* As a system grows bigger, the relative size of a stressor required to break it will decline disproportionately.

As suggested before, another source of fragility is the interconnectedness of systems. In other words, "inherited fragility." Inherited fragility helps to map out the diffusion of harm in the event of fragility in a corner of an interconnected system of systems. As a generalizable proposition:

> *Proposition 4.* In an interdependent system of systems with no redundancy, the threshold of fragility for the whole system of systems is the same as the threshold of the system's weakest component.

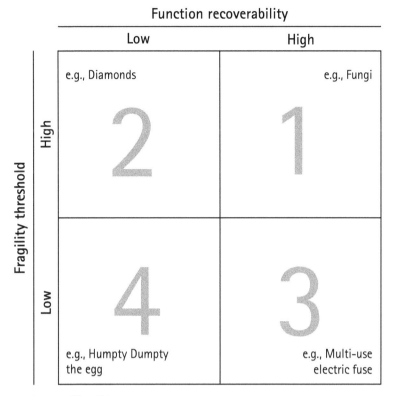

FIGURE 4.1 A map of fragility.

Figure 4.1 suggests a composite way to map different things on the spectrum of greater to lesser fragility. This constitutes two dimensions. First, the vertical axis shows how easily something breaks; that is, a high or low preset "fragility threshold." Second, the horizontal axis shows how easily the broken thing can be recovered to its self-same functional state once the fragility threshold is crossed; that is, high or low "function recoverability." Humpty Dumpty, the egg of the children's nursery rhyme, suffered from a double-whammy of fragility (Quadrant 4 in Figure 4.1): it broke easily; that is, it had a low threshold against fragility. And it could not be put together again.

However, not all things are as unlucky as Humpty Dumpty the egg. A multi-use electric fuse also breaks easily but can also be easily restored to perform its sacrificial function (Quadrant 3). In contrast, a diamond has a high fragility threshold but once broken the damage is irreversible (Quadrant 2). Finally, fungi—and many systems in nature (Taleb 2012)—do not break easily and easily recover (Quadrant 1). Incidentally, as our discussion on scalability in the next section shows, systems in Quadrant 1 share many properties with highly scalable systems.[3]

Proposition 5. Systems with a low fragility threshold and low function recoverability (Quadrant 4) require a great deal of cushioning to protect them from breaking.

Closely related to the distinction between "intrinsic" and "inherited" fragility is the distinction between "apparent" and "hidden" fragility. An egg's vulnerability to breaking is apparent. We thus handle eggs with care when bought at the grocery to cook for tomorrow's breakfast. We also do not act surprised when eggs break. Similarly, an electric fuse's fragility is apparent and in fact intended. In contrast, hidden vulnerability is insidious and entails surprise. Vespignani (2010: 985) finds that in cases of highly interconnected networks breakage is typically "abrupt" at a relatively low critical threshold, which introduces an element of surprise: "This makes complete system breakdown even more difficult to anticipate or control than in an isolated network."

Hidden fragility has an interaction effect with inherited fragility: an Achilles heel is a reminder of this phenomenon when a small hidden weakness is inherited by an otherwise mighty system.[4]

> *Proposition 6.* The information conditions necessary to make a system truly robust are very strong because some minor source of hidden fragility is likely to remain. In instances of hidden and inherited fragility, seemingly robust systems will break down abruptly at a surprisingly low critical threshold. Lack of preparedness in instances of hidden and inherited fragility will accentuate the consequent harm.

Although Taleb (2012: 270–1, for example) underplays the role of cumulative processes in creating fragility, hidden fragility is often created or exacerbated by them. Taleb typically focuses on fragility caused by one single blow. "Cumulative fragility," in contrast, is death by a thousand cuts. Keil and Montealegre (2000) liken such an ill-fated investment to a frog being boiled to death without knowing it (see also Keil 1995; Royer 2003).

Poorly understood dynamic changes often lower the fragility threshold without warning. Even a minor stressor, in such circumstances, leads to unexpected breakage. Seref-Ferlengez et al. (2015), for instance, find that human bones are constantly exposed to microdamage from routine stressors. As people age, microdamage from routine wear and tear begins to accumulate that contributes "additively to reduced fracture toughness"—that is, a lowering of the threshold at which the bone breaks (Seref-Ferlengez et al. 2015: 1). In technological systems, accumulation of small errors is often behind human-made disasters (Turner and Pidgeon 1997).

> *Proposition 7.* Cumulative hidden processes will increase the propensity of fragility of a system over time.

Hidden fragility also has sociological and psychological features. Scholars of power relationships suggest that organizations can tacitly choose to ignore the obvious (Flyvbjerg 1998) or people in organizations "know that we do not *want* to know" (Ansar 2015). Psychological biases such as overconfidence also "bring fragilities" owing to "expert problems (in which the expert knows a lot but less than he thinks he does)" (Taleb 2012: 215). Psychological theories predict that hidden fragilities in systems designed by experts will be the norm, not the exception (Kahneman 2011). NASA lost its $125-million Mars Climate Orbiter in September 1999 because one engineering team used metric units while another used imperial units for a spacecraft maneuver (Reichhardt 1999; see also Hodgkinson and Starbuck 2012: 2–5, for discussion of NASA's Space Shuttle disasters in light of theories of organizational decision making). "Our inability to recognize and correct this simple error has had major implications," said Edward Stone, the Director of the Jet Propulsion Laboratory (JPL) at NASA that oversaw the mission, according to CNN (30 September 1999). Also see *Proposition 6* on information conditions of correcting hidden fragility.

> *Proposition 8.* Behavioral and psychological biases will make the detection of hidden fragility more difficult. Hidden fragilities in systems designed by experts will be the norm, not the exception.

> *Proposition 9.* In sociological and organizational contexts, hidden fragility will be hidden in plain sight.

Although Taleb has tended to focus on external causes of disorder, ecologists working on fragility pay equal attention to internal changes that cause fragility (see Nilsson and Grelsson 1995). Theorists of "broken symmetry" have also noted that as internal complexity increases, the threat of internal sources of disturbance—often driven by entirely random processes—grows non-linearly, exposing a larger system to breakdown with no apparent cause (Anderson 2011). From a consequentialist perspective, the distinction between external and internal stressors is immaterial: it is the magnitude of the negative outcome that follows that matters. Taleb (2012: 136) argues:

> You can control fragility a lot more than you think … detecting (anti)fragility—or, actually, smelling it […]—is easier, much easier, than prediction and understanding the dynamics of events, the entire mission reduces to the central principle of what to do to minimize harm (and maximize gain) from forecasting errors, that is, to have things that don't fall apart, or even benefit, when we make a mistake … Not seeing a tsunami or an economic event coming is excusable; building something fragile to them is not.

From a consequentialist perspective, a generalizable proposition that can be advanced is as follows:

> *Proposition 10.* If a system or process is systematically delivering poor outcomes, it is an indicator of fragility. Discard or redesign the system.

> *Proposition 11.* It is easier to be robust against the magnitude of harm that fragility might bring than predict or control the sources of stressor(s).

4.2.3 The Special Case of "Investment Fragility"

So far we have analyzed general features of fragility. Now we turn to the special case of "investment fragility," which we define as *the vulnerability of a financial investment to becoming non-viable*; that is, *losing its ability to create net economic value*. When applied to physical assets such as roads, oil refineries, bridges, factories, real estate developments, and so on, investment fragility causes them to become "stranded assets"; that is, where "assets suffer from unanticipated or premature write-offs, downward revaluations, or are converted to liabilities" (Ansar et al. 2013a: 2). A broken or stranded asset is a net drag on the economy; that is, it consumes resources inefficiently that could have been put to alternative uses. An economy with too many assets prone to fragility is at a heightened risk of system-wide failure owing to the domino-like effect of inherited fragility that can spread from one corner of the system or systems to the whole.

4.2.3.1 *Benefit-to-Cost Ratio (BCR): A Rule of Thumb to Detect the Investment Fragility Threshold*

The fragility threshold of an investment can be located by modeling the investment's pay-off structure. Figure 4.2 illustrates such a pay-off structure graphically: the discounted stream of gain and the discounted stream of pain of a hypothetical investment is sorted in a descending order and then graphed. Since investments typically span long time horizons, it is imperative to incorporate the time value of money in the pay-off structure by introducing an appropriate discount rate (see Souder and Shaver 2010). The point of fragility in Figure 4.2 is where the cumulative pain—area "1"—just exceeds the

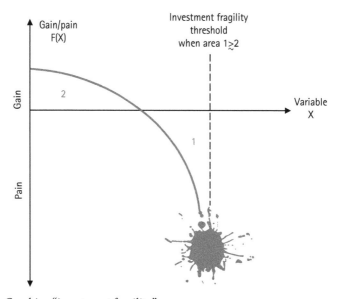

FIGURE 4.2 Graphing "investment fragility."

(Adapted from Taleb 2012: 273.)

cumulative gain—area "2." *In other words, an investment is broken when the cumulative gain-to-pain ratio falls below 1, less gain in the numerator than the pain in the denominator.* The gain-to-pain ratio, which is commonly thought of as *benefit-to-cost* ratio (BCR) in literature on capital budgeting, thus serves as a useful rule of thumb for detecting the fragility threshold of an investment.

Like the more general case of fragility, an asset suffers from greater *intrinsic* investment fragility when the absolute threshold of disturbance required to "break" it is low—for example, a low *ex ante* benefit-to-cost ratio—whereby a stressor easily pushes the benefit-to-cost ratio below 1. The stressor may be, for example, just one weather event in the sixty-year life of the asset that causes so much mess that costs of dealing with it spiral out of proportion. As with many fragile things, there is an element of surprise in investment fragility, as well—seemingly improbable, and often minor, stressor(s) can cause disproportionate harm.

An investment is more fragile when once broken it is difficult or nearly impossible to reposition it to make recovery possible via alternative uses. Less specific assets—for example, buildings that can change use—are less prone to becoming irreversibly broken than assets with a higher specificity (see Gómez-Ibáñez 2003 for a rich ground of interconnections between investment fragility and discussion on "hold up" in transaction cost economics).

Similarly, an asset has higher intrinsic investment fragility when its gain (anticipated benefits and any windfall) is capped but the pain (anticipated cost and any unforeseen losses) is uncapped. This propensity exhibits itself in the shape of Figure 4.2, where the top left part of the curve (gain) is bounded and finite but the bottom right part of the curve (pain) is unbounded and potentially an infinite pit. Based on this observation, Taleb (2012: 158, italics in the original) proposed: "*Fragility implies more to lose than to gain, equals more downside than upside, equals (unfavorable) asymmetry.*"

4.2.4 What Is Scalability?

The Oxford English Dictionary defines *scalable* and *scalability* in the following manner:

scalable, *adj.*
> Able to be changed in scale. *rare.*
> 1977 *Jrnl. Royal Soc. Arts* 125 770/1. Such lasers are scaleable since large volumes could be pumped uniformly.

scalability *n.* the property of being scalable.
> 1978 *Sci. Amer.* Nov. 44/2. It took demonstrations of the scalability of the technology and tests of improved beam focusing … to catalyze an effort that led to support by the AEC.

We note, in particular, the unsatisfactory definition of the word *scalable*. What does the ability to be changed (or equally change without external force) in scale mean? In practice, scalability is most commonly discussed in the field of computer science, system architecture, and software programming (Hill 1990; Gunther 2007). This is insufficeint for our purposes.

In academic literature, an understanding of whether, and under what conditions, something has the ability to be changed in scale has been deeply informed by advances in mathematics and particularly the field of fractal geometry. Mandelbrot's research identified two primary dimensions of scale: temporal and spatial. A grain of sand, a pebble, a rock, a cliff, and the coastline of, say, Britain represent a continuum of finer to coarser grades of the spatial scale (see Mandelbrot 1967). Similarly, the price movements of a stock price over a scale between five seconds to five years represents finer to coarser grades of a temporal scale. Finer and coarser grades of scale can also be thought of in terms of degrees of zoom-in (microscropic) and zoom-out (macroscopic). To Madelbrot's spatial and temporal scale, we introduce a third scale: "relational." The relational scale not only refers to the number of end-users (for example, few or many) but also to the heterogeneity of end-users and their tailored need (see Ansar 2010; Ansar 2012, for a more extensive discussion on a *spatial, temporal,* and *relational* multiscalar framework).[5]

Based on this understanding of scale, we define scalability as the ability of a thing (a system, system of systems, process, or network, for example) to *effortlessly* transition back *and* forth from the very micro to the very macro *spatial, temporal,* and *relational* scales. Effortlessness connotes minimum friction in terms of the time, cost, and so on, that it takes to build up or remove capacity. Over longer timescales, effortlessness implies ability to quickly upgrade without losing compatibility. However, if scalability is understood and practiced as mainly the ability to scale up, with scant attention to scaling down—which is the dominant approach today in both the academy and practice (Sutton and Rao 2014)—then this in and of itself adds fragility. Here we therefore understand scalability as the ability to change in both directions; that is, both up and down.[6]

In contrasting big and scale we arrive at a key insight. Big typically possesses a degree of slack, which Weinstock and Goodenough (2006) call the "ability to handle increased workload (without adding resources to a system)." A big power plant, for example, rarely operates at full capacity. If demand were to increase from one segment of the day to another, the power plant can be ramped up to meet some or all of the added demand. However, this limited slack is different from true scalability. Thus, although the big power plant might be able to meet some incremental demand in a spatially, temporally, and relationally narrow field, it cannot effortlessly be scaled up (or scaled back down) to resolve a national or global energy crisis. Linking big, scalability, and fragility, we therefore advance the following:

> *Proposition 12.* Fragility arises when big is forced into doing what was best left to the scalable.

4.3   FRAGILITY IN ACTION: EVIDENCE FROM LARGE DAMS

These twelve propositions about fragility are based on a literature study. We now test the propositions against evidence from capital investments in 245 large dams. Our study of large dams began as an inductive enquiry into an underresearched question: will the brisk building boom of hydropower megadams underway from China to Brazil yield a positive return? Our previous effort (Ansar et al. 2014) found strong evidence that most large dams were too costly and took too long to build to deliver a positive risk-adjusted return. Our empirical results motivated us to begin theory development that would help us answer why investments in large dams might be particularly prone to what we have called "investment fragility;" that is, for the benefit–cost ratio to fall below 1.

Figure 4.3 presents an overview of the dataset by regional location of the dams, wall height, project type, vintage, and actual project cost. With a total value of $353 billion (2010 prices) built between 1934 to 2007 on five continents in sixty-five different countries, our dataset on large dams is the largest of its kind. All large dams for which valid and reliable cost and schedule data could be found were included in the study. The data and the inductive study are described in Ansar et al. (2014).

4.3.1   Why Study Big Dams?

We find that large dams serve a particularly useful empirical setting to develop theory on investment fragility, for the following reasons.

First, big dams are archetypical megaprojects. Dams are bespoke, site-specific constructions that have large physical proportions, require mobilization of vast quantities of inputs (materials, land, labor, or physical equipment), entail huge up-front financial outlays, generate a large number of unit of outputs, take a long time to build, last a long time, are spatially fixated, and are highly complex not only in terms of number of constituent parts but also in terms of high interdependencies between constituent parts. Large dams typically also impact large numbers of people and the environment in their construction, operation, and eventual removal.

Second, dams are indivisible and discrete assets. A 90% complete dam is as valueless as a dam not built at all. For this reason, the physical scope and costs associated with a dam are methodologically well-defined and therefore particularly well-suited for like-for-like comparisons between planned and actual outcomes.

Third, the main part of the whole-life costs of a dam are rendered up front during the construction phase. Unlike thermal power plants, dams do not require large variable costs in subsequent time periods for feedstock. There is a degree of transparency possible with the cash flows (or streams of costs and benefits) associated with dams that is much more difficult to establish for other big capital investments.

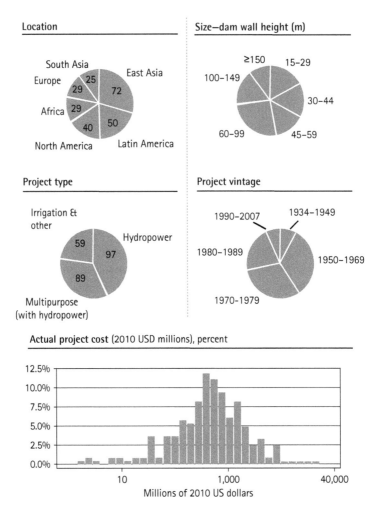

FIGURE 4.3 Sample distribution of 245 large dams across five continents (1934–2007), worth US$353 billion (2010 prices).

(From Ansar et al. 2014.)

Finally, results from large dams are generalizable to other big ventures. Large dams are a widely studied engineering problem, or what conventional theory might consider "a standardized production technology" (Sidak and Spulber 1997), generating basic services, such as electricity or water, as outputs with seemingly established demand trends. Intuition would suggest that the overall planning uncertainties ought to be more limited in large dams than, for example, big capital investments based on revolutionary new technologies. A discovery of systemic errors in the building of dams would be indicative that the problems of investment fragility will be even more severe for less standardized capital investments.

4.3.2 What Happens to Big Dams?

Proposition 10 suggested that if a system or process is systematically delivering poor outcomes it is an indicator of fragility. Specifically, we are interested in testing whether benefit–cost ratios fall below 1.

4.3.2.1 *Cost Performance*

With respect to cost overruns, we make the following observations:[7]

- Three out of every four large dams suffered a cost overrun in constant local currency terms.
- Actual costs were on average 96% higher than estimated costs (median 27%; *IQR* 0.86). The evidence is overwhelming that costs are systematically biased toward underestimation and overrun (Mann-Whitney-Wilcoxon $U = 29646$, $p < 0.01$); the magnitude of cost underestimation is larger than the error of cost overestimation ($p < 0.01$). The skew is towards adverse outcomes (that is, going over budget).
- Graphing the dams' cost overruns reveals a long tail, as shown in Figure 4.4; the actual costs more than double for two out of every ten large dams and more than triple for one out of every ten dams. The long tail suggests that planners have difficulty in establishing probabilities of events that happen far into the future. (Taleb [2007] 2010: 284)

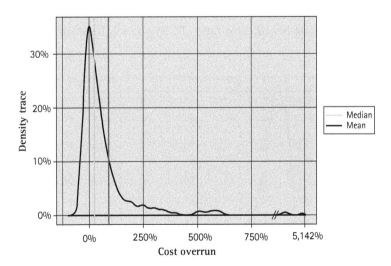

FIGURE 4.4 Density trace of actual/estimated cost (costs overruns) in constant local currency terms with the median and mean ($N = 245$).

(From Ansar et al. 2014.)

4.3.2.2 *Schedule Performance*

Not only are large dams costly and prone to systematic and severe budget overruns; they also take a long time to build.[8] Large dams on average take 8.6 years. With respect to schedule slippage, we make the following observations:

- Eight out of every ten large dams suffered a schedule overrun.
- Actual implementation schedule was on average 44% (or 2.3 years) higher than the estimate (median 27%, or 1.7 years) as shown in Figure 4.5. A schedule overrun is detrimental to the benefit–cost ratio, as it delays when much needed benefits come on line. This decreases the net present value of future benefits. Even without a cost overrun, a schedule delay in and of itself can cause investment fragility. As the bulk of the costs of a big dam are incurred up front they are not as sensitive to the discount rate as the benefits, which arrive farther in the future.
- Like cost overruns, the evidence is overwhelming that implementation schedules are systematically biased towards underestimation (Mann-Whitney-Wilcoxon $U = 29161$, $p < 0.01$); the magnitude of schedule underestimation (that is, schedule slippage) is larger than the error of schedule overestimation ($p < 0.01$).
- Graphing the dams' schedule overruns also reveals a long tail, as shown in Figure 4.5, albeit not as long as the tail of cost overruns. Costs are at a higher risk of spiraling out of control than schedules.

4.3.2.3 *Investment Fragility Threshold for Big Dams*

Proposition 2 advanced that different systems have different fragility thresholds. For big dams, the typical forecast benefit–cost ratio (BCR) was 1.4. In other words, planners

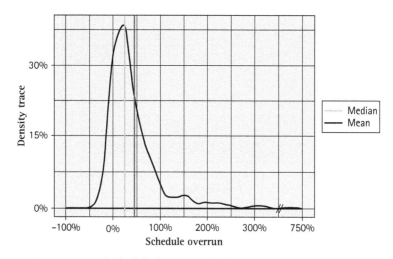

FIGURE 4.5 Density trace of schedule slippage with the median and mean ($N = 239$).

(From Ansar et al. 2014.)

expected the net present benefits to exceed the net present costs by about 40%. With no change in future benefits or operations and management costs, a project suffering a cost overrun ratio of 1.4 or greater would thus breach the fragility threshold—its BCR would fall below 1, and the broken asset's upfront sunk costs would become unrecoverable.

- The absolute threshold of 1.4 for big dams is broadly in line with many other physical infrastructure assets such as road, rail, bridge, or tunnel capital investments that too typically expect to generate a BCR of approximately 1.4 (NAO 2014).
- Using the BCR of 1.4 as the fragility threshold, we found that investments in big dams are more fragile than investments in road, bridge, or tunnel projects. Investments in big rail projects are, however, even more fragile than investments in big dams are. We arrived at this conclusion by comparing the evidence on 245 big dams with a sample of another 353 road, rail, and fixed-link (bridges and tunnels) projects (see Flyvbjerg et al. 2002, 2003, 2005; Ansar et al. 2013b).
- Investments in nearly half (47%) of the dams broke the fragility threshold; that is, a cost overrun ratio of 1.4 or greater, compared with 14% for roads ($n = 239$, $M_{Cost\ overrun} = 1.22$) and 25% for fixed links ($n = 39$, $M_{Cost\ overrun} = 1.37$). For rail projects ($n = 79$, $M_{Cost\ overrun} = 1.44$) just over 50% of the sample had a cost overrun ratio greater than 1.4.
- In terms of runaway cost overruns, however, investments in big dams have a poorer performance compared with rail projects. For big dams, the 80th percentile cost overrun is nearly double the original estimate ($P80_{Cost\ overrun} = 1.99$), and the 90th percentile is more than triple ($P90_{Cost\ overrun} = 3.07$), suggesting a long and fat tail. For rail, the skew toward runaway cost overruns is less pronounced ($P80_{Cost\ overrun} = 1.75$ and $P90_{Cost\ overrun} = 1.90$), suggesting a truncated tail compared to big dams, though still long and fat compared with a normal distribution.
- Our calculations of the fragility threshold of big dams have a conservative bias. We have assumed that dams' benefits did not also fall short of targets, even though there is strong evidence in the existing literature that this is the case (WCD 2000a; McCully 2001; Scudder 2005). We made this assumption because a comprehensive dataset of planned versus actual benefits of dams, like we have built for the cost and schedule of big dams, does not yet exist. Data which we have available on eighty-four hydroelectric large dam projects from our sample thus far suggest that they suffer a mean benefits shortfall of at least 11%.

Note that big dams suffer from the fundamental unfavorable asymmetry of fragile systems: the potential gain from big dams is capped, but the pain is uncapped (see Figure 4.2). For example, in years of extreme drought a big hydropower dam may produce next to no power, but in years of floods the dams' ability to generate electricity is capped at the maximum of its design limit. So the maximum benefits the dams can produce are bounded, but maximum losses—either from up-front cost overruns or subsequent operation and maintenance costs—are not. Factoring in benefit shortfalls and cost overruns on operation and maintenance costs, a bigger proportion of investments in big dams probably break than our conservative calculations suggest.

In summary, our conservative estimates suggest that investments in nearly half the dams break before the big dams even begin their operational life. This is due to outsized cost overruns on the upfront capital expenditure. Fragility at such an early stage of an investment's life cycle can be likened to an investment stillbirth. Subsequent discussion will show that the investment fragility risk only increases for durable and immobile big assets as their life progresses owing to "cumulative fragility."

4.3.3 Why Do Investments in Big Dams Break?

The explanation for why investments in big dams break can be found in the thought processes that lead to their construction. We reviewed previously confidential business cases (called *Staff Appraisal Report* or *Project Appraisal Document*) at the World Bank presented to the Bank's Board before a final decision to build big dams. A typical business case puts forth the following line of argumentation to justify financing for a dam:

- First, the business case outlines the massive electricity or water shortfall a country faces.
- Second, the business case argues that the country possesses large untapped hydropower resources.
- Third, the business case proposes that a big dam should be built on a site deemed by experts to be particularly advantageous. The business case goes on to argue that the proposed big dam will be a big increment in solving the electricity or water scarcity of the country.
- Fourth, the business case cites technical studies which show that the big dam will be capable of *quickly* filling the gap between current market need and market supply *and* offer slack to meet surging future demand.
- Fifth, the business case also cites studies by economists that the proposed big dam will be the "least costly expansion path that will adequately meet the projected demand" owing to its "economies of scale" (US Department of Energy 2009). Usually only one or two other alternatives are considered, such as a big dam against a big coal-fired power plant.
- Finally, detailed calculations are shown—sometimes spanning several appendices—that the present value of benefits of the proposed big dam, as of the date of the decision to build, will exceed the present value of the costs. In other words, that the benefit–cost ratio will exceed 1. Typically, little to no data on costs and benefits are shown for competing alternatives.

This thought process more resembles the rationalization of a pre-selected solution (a large dam) than the rational assessment of alternative ways to solve a given problem (provision of water and electricity). The process is rationalization presented as rationality (Flyvbjerg 1998). We identify several deep flaws.

First, although the typical business case correctly identifies the challenge as one of scalability—that is, to *effortlessly* turn on or off the supply of electricity and water any-where (*spatial*), at any time (*temporal*), and for anyone (*relational*)—instead of pro-posing a scalable solution the business case proceeds to propose a single-shot big fix. Recall *Proposition 12: Fragility arises when big is forced into doing what was best left to the scalable.*

Second, the number of alternatives considered against the preferred solution is few if any. Alternatives such as decentralized generation or improving energy productivity are ignored. As Priemus (2008: 105) illustrates, it is typical for planners to settle early on a big asset as the preferred solution, and then alternatives are "whittled down to nothing." This limits the option set presented to decision makers.

Third, by invoking the logic of purported economies of scale (by way of least cost expansion path), the business case then proposes building a staggeringly big dam, since the bigger the dam the more scalable and efficient it appears on paper. Even as a typical business case worries a great deal about efficiency that might arise out of big size, it fails to dwell on the non-linear risks that will arise from big commitments to durable and immobile assets.

4.3.3.1 *The Various Facets of Investment Fragility in Big Dams*

Thus far we have empirically substantiated the essential argument of this chapter that big capital investments are prone to fragility particularly when big is used as a blunt substitute for scalability. In particular we have looked at evidence for *Propositions 2, 10, and 12*. We now turn to finding empirical support for other propositions advanced in the theory section.

Proposition 1 advanced that fragility is typically irreversible. In the empirical setting of investments in big dams, this proposition takes on two facets. First, once the invest-ment is broken—typically because of an up-front cost overrun—it is nearly impossible to reposition the asset to generate a positive return; that is, increasing revenues to pay back the escalated up-front costs and debt financing on them proves elusive as best. The Yacyretá Hydroelectric Project—a joint venture between Argentina and Paraguay under the Yacyretá Treaty on the Parana River started in 1973 and only fully completed thirty-eight years later in 2011 according the treaty's intended proposal—is a telling case. The dam operated at 60% of its intended capacity from 1998 onward. In June 2001, the World Bank—one of the dam's financiers—published its *Implementation Completion Report* (ICR), which arrived at the following conclusion about the project's outcome (6, emphasis in the original):

> Based on the above, it is clear that the project has not met its goals as there is no solution on how to terminate the project, and operate at full capacity. As explained, the project has operated for a prolonged period of time at an unintended level [below intended capacity]. In addition, the project presents a poor ERR [Economic Rate of Return], negative NPV [Net Present Value] recalculated by this ICR, and uncertain project sustainability. As a result, the outcome of Loan 3520-AR is rated

unsatisfactory, and the outcome of the Yacyretá scheme as a whole is rated *unsatisfactory* mainly because of its big negative NPV.

The project's lower-than-expected volume of output was exacerbated by a lower-than-expected price of electricity. The World Bank (2001) report goes on to explain that the Yacyretá dam has a "big negative NPV" because "the spot price [of electricity sold] has been (and is estimated to remain so after year 2001) lower than US$30 per MWh [agreed in the forty-year 1973 treaty]." The ICR did not envision a scenario in which the dam would revert to a positive NPV owing to the sheer scale of costs sunk into the project.

Second, the breaking of an investment—unlike the porcelain cup at the beginning of this chapter—happens in slow motion. Yet decision makers appear unable to reverse commitment to the losing course of action. In the case of the Yacyretá Dam, the World Bank's *Project Performance Audit Report*, prepared by the World Bank's independent evaluation department, found:

> [World] Bank performance is rated as unsatisfactory. The appraisal overlooked the downside risk of a slower demand growth, which proved to be of paramount importance. Later, opportunities to reassess the project were wasted in spite of the recommendations made by a good quality and timely *Public Investment Review (PIR)* in 1985. The Bank also accepted non-compliance with financial covenants. (1996b: 14)

The Yacyretá Dam's *Project Performance Audit Report* (World Bank 1996b: 16) neatly summed up the insidious but irreversible fragility of big capital investments: "On several occasions the Bank had a good case for stopping the project before the major civil works were too advanced." But it did not. The phenomenon, whereby smart people and organizations are unable to stop themselves from throwing good money after bad, goes by many names in the academic literature, such as escalation of commitment or lock-in (McNamara et al. 2002). The financial magnitude of a big venture is so large that once started, the commitment turns into a binding, ruinous, codependence.

Proposition 3 suggested that proportionality matters when considering the impact of fragility. In the case of dams, an investment in a big dam built in a poor country plays out very differently when compared with an investment in a similar big dam built in a rich country. This position appears so obvious as to be trivial, but the real-life effects are striking.

Big dams built in North America ($n = 40$) have considerably lower cost overrun ($M = 11\%$) than big dams built elsewhere do ($M = 104\%$), as shown in Figure 4.6. Note, however, that three out of four dams in our reference class had a North American firm advising on the engineering and economic forecasts. Consistent with anchoring theories in psychology, we interpret this observation as an indication of an overreliance on the North American experience with large dams, which appears to be biasing cost estimates downward in the rest of the world. Experts may be "anchoring" their forecasts in familiar cases from North America and applying insufficient "adjustments" (Flyvbjerg et al.

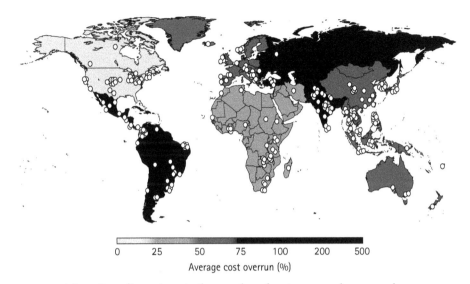

FIGURE 4.6 Location of large dams in the sample and cost overruns by geography.

(From Ansar et al. 2014.)

2009; Tversky and Kahneman 1974), for example, to adequately reflect the risk of a local currency depreciation or the quality of local project management teams. Proponents often hold up the Hoover Dam in the United States—finished in 1936—as a prime example for why similarly big dams ought to be built in poor countries. Evidence shows, however, that the likes of the Hoover Dam are false analogies. Instead, decision makers in developing countries should consider evidence for the entire dam record, and in the case of big dams, investment fragility is the most likely outcome in developing countries.

Similarly, with respect to construction schedule, we find that countries with a higher per capita income tend to have lower schedule overruns compared with countries with lower per capita income. We concur with the interpretation of Bacon and Besant-Jones (1998: 325) that "the best available proxy for most countries is [the] country-per-capita income ... [for] the general level of economic support that a country can provide for the construction of complex facilities." This result reinforces the argument that developing countries in particular, despite seemingly the most in need of complex facilities such as large dams, ought to stay away from bites bigger than they can chew.

Finally, when an investment in a big dam breaks in a poor country, the country's economy as a whole more readily inherits that fragility by way of accumulating debt. Brazil's Itaipu Dam was built in the 1970s. It cost nearly $20 billion—240% more in real terms than predicted—and it impaired Brazil's public finances for three decades. Similarly, the actual cost of the Tarbela Dam, the majority of which was borrowed from external sources, amounted to 23% of the increase in Pakistan's external public debt stock between 1968 and 1984, or 12% for Colombia's Chivor Dam (1970–77), as shown

Table 4.1 Total stock of public net external debt (US$ current, MM)

Year	Colombia	Pakistan
1968		3,252.4
1970	1,296.6	
1977	2,699.6	
1984		9,692.8
Debt increase over the implementation schedule	1,403.0	6,440.5
Cost of megadam over the relevant period (US$ current MM)	Chivor Dam	Tarbela Dam
	168.7	1,497.90
Cost of dam as percentage of debt increase	12.0%	23.2%

Source: Ansar et al. (2014).

in Table 4.1. Companies and countries with insufficiently large balance sheets to absorb adverse outcomes of big bets gone awry face financial ruin.

As the discussion leading to *Proposition 5* and *Proposition 6* showed, there is typically an aspiration to make a seemingly fragile system more robust. In investment fragility terms, this means building in a contingency as a buffer against cost overruns—the conventional logic being that if a project returns a BCR greater than 1 even after taking the contingency into account, then the investment can be considered robust; that is, it will not easily cross the fragility threshold. Evidence suggests, however, that standard contingencies are too low. For example, in providing a contingency against inflation for big dams in our sample, forecasters expected the annual inflation rate to be 2.5% on average, but it turned out to be 18.9% (averages for the entire sample). Had adequate contingencies been provided, the benefit–cost ratios would have been lower and investments would not have readily received the final go-ahead.

Sensitivity analysis is another mechanism by which an aspiration to robustness is formalized in business cases of big capital investments. But like contingencies, this exercise—as customarily conducted in business cases of big capital investments—is perfunctory. A typical *ex ante* sensitivity analysis stress tests for a very narrow range of variance around the base case, whereas the actual *ex post* evidence shows that a very wide range ought to have been tested. The difficulty is that when the sensitivity analysis range is widened from the narrowest confines to reflect real-life variance, the business case falls apart. The before-versus-after picture of Colombia's Guavio hydroelectric project is illustrative.

Figure 4.7 exhibits a facsimile of a representative section on benefit-to-cost analysis from the World Bank's 1981 *Staff Appraisal Report* of Colombia's Guavio hydroelectric project, which gave the final decision to build the dam. As the facsimile illustrates,

6.04   On this basis, the return on investment is about 15.0% (Annex 6.1), which compares favorably with the opportunity cost of capital for Colombia, estimated to be 11%.

6.05   A sensitively analysis was carried out to estimate the impact on the internal financial return of possible changes in cost and revenues. Thease are summarized below:

Rate of return on Investment Program (%)			
	Benefits		
Cost	85%	100%	11%
100%	11	15	17
115%	10	12	15

If the cost of the program increases by 15%, the rate of return would be about 12%. If the program costs do not increase but benefits are 15% lower than estimated, the return would be about 11%. If the program cost increase by 15% and the benefits decrease by 15% the return on the investment program would be about 10%. The equalizing rates obtained understate the real economic rate of return of EEEB's investment program since revenues from electricity sales do not fully reflect all benefits to society.

FIGURE 4.7 An aspiration to investment robustness in the Guavio hydroelectric project.

(From World Bank 1981: 42.)

planners of Guavio first conducted a base case scenario that showed that the dam had a positive economic rate of return (of 15%) greater than the opportunity cost of capital (11%). Planners then conducted a sensitivity analysis on the base case benefits and costs, but only subjected them to a stress test range of ±15%. The planners, despite acknowledging that their estimates were subject to uncertainty, appear reluctant to test for extreme events even if such events are characteristic for large dams, as we saw with the long, fat tails.

As it turned out, the Colombian utility that owned the Guavio Dam went bankrupt (World Bank 1996a: iii). The dam's actual outturn costs (in local currency constant prices) spiraled to six times their estimate. Instead of the +15% cost overrun that the *ex ante* sensitivity analysis allowed for, a +500% stress test would have been more appropriate! The investment in Guavio did not just break. It shattered.

The World Bank's *Implementation Completion Report*, which reported the *ex post* outcomes of the Guavio Dam, conceded that the investment in Guavio was broken even before the hydroelectric project began operational life. "Generally speaking the project's outcome has to be considered highly unsatisfactory ... this has been at a high cost, particularly in terms of the non-viability (financial and economic) of the project at completion" (World Bank 1996: iv).

Proposition 7 advanced that cumulative, and often hidden, processes increase a system's fragility over time. With respect to big dams, we have thus far focused on investment fragility that happens at the beginning of the life of a big dam because of a cost overrun that exceeds the expected future benefits. Now we turn to the "cumulative investment fragility" of big dams as they age. This occurs when large costs are incurred to repair, overhaul, or decommission the ageing big dam. These late-life costs can turn an ageing big dam into a liability in perpetuity. We review two case examples to elucidate cumulative fragility both from a material and an investment perspective.

Cumulative material fatigue from minor stressors, poor maintenance, and new demands placed on an infrastructure can cause physical collapse without warning. The sudden structural collapse of the Stava Dams in the Eastern Italian Alps on 19 July 1985, that resulted in 268 human fatalities, is a tragic case of physical fragility brought on as a result of years of neglect. The Stava Dams, even though visibly in a state of decay, had continued to perform their intended function. Since the cost of rehabilitating the dams was high, the owners—the Prealpi Mining Co of Bergamo[9]—felt little pressing need to act. The dams then collapsed with no apparent discreet cause—a hallmark of cumulative fragility (see Luino and Graff 2012: 1042). The physical fragility of the dams and the resulting casualties also caused investment fragility: financial liabilities for the clean-up exceeded €130 million and criminal sentences for many of the individuals involved in the operation of the dams.

A dramatic physical collapse is, however, not necessary to inflict cumulative investment fragility. The Kariba Dam, on the border between Zimbabwe and Zambia, presents a salient and current case.[10] The Kariba hydroelectric program was built in two phases. The first phase entailed the construction of the dam wall, which had a height of 128 meters and impounded Lake Kariba—the largest man-made lake in the world at the time. In contrast to the typical big dam, Kariba Phase 1 was built at breakneck speed. The civil works were completed in just four years, from 1955 to 1959. The first electricity was generated in January 1960 (WCD 2000b: 9). All six generators installed during the first phase were in operation by 1962, with a capacity of 666 MW, which exceeded the intended scope of 500 MW. Kariba's Phase 1, is also among the rare big dams that came in on budget, built within its then £80.8 million budget envelope (World Bank 1956; WCD 2000b).

Kariba's Phase 1 thus appears to have beaten the odds to a healthy birth. But cumulative processes have pushed Kariba toward investment fragility.[11] Outflows of water from the dam's sluice gates have, over time, eroded the plunge pool below the gates. The pool, which was initially 10 meters deep, has gradually worn down to over 80 meters, eroding toward the dam wall's foundations as shown in Figure 4.8. The structural integrity of Kariba Dam is now under a pressing threat.

The cumulative fatigue of Kariba Dam's structure has placed decision makers in an unenviable "squeeze:" either allow the dam to collapse and bear unthinkable human, environmental, and financial losses, or embrace huge outlays to maintain the dam in perpetuity. Now four institutions—the European Union, the Swedish Government, the African Development Bank, and the World Bank—have sprung into action to provide $295 million in loans to undertake repairs that are expected to take at least ten years (World Bank 2014). Although the scour in the plunge pool is the most pressing problem facing the Kariba, a number of other issues have begun to encroach, such as the swelling of the concrete and malfunctioning of flood gates. Kariba's maintenance bills are

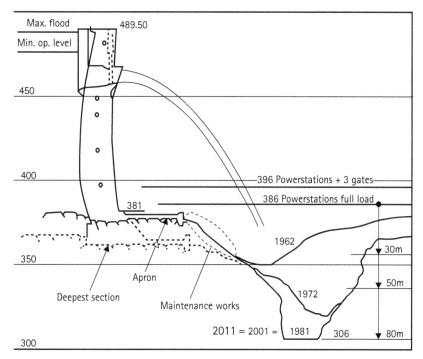

FIGURE 4.8 Cumulative fragility: Erosion near the foundation of Kariba Dam wall.

(From World Bank 2014: Fig. 2.)

unlikely to be a fixed predictable sum with a clear end date. Whether donors will find sources of finance in perpetuity to maintain the dam is an open question.

Kariba's material fatigue is a reminder that big dams have finite life spans. Even if not in the next decade or two, in foreseeable human history a big dam like Kariba will have to be removed (even if it were to be rebuilt) lest it were to accidentally collapse. No one has the remotest idea of how much will need to be spent on the end-of-life arrangements of a big dam like Kariba. Such rehabilitation and demise costs were not anticipated in Kariba's original BCR analysis. 95% of the world's big dams were built in the twentieth century, and many are approaching the stated end of their service lives (Lavigne 2005). Will dams less illustrious than the Kariba find resources for repairs in perpetuity? Or will the forgotten dams only be heard of when they collapse from cumulative fatigue, like the Stava Dams? There are more than 45,000 big dams in the world. Who will pay for their decommisoning or reconstruction?

Proposition 8 suggested that cognitive biases make it difficult for laypeople and experts alike to detect fragility. The Vajont Dam in Italy is perhaps a particularly unfortunate case illustrative of psychological and sociological dimensions of fragility. Located 100 km north of Venice, Vajont was the world's highest thin-arch dam, with a height exceeding 260 meters—equivalent to a sixty-story skyscraper—at its completion in 1960. The dam was built across the Vajont Valley—a deep, narrow gorge characterized by massive, near-vertical cliffs. On 9 October 1963, a giant landslide collapsed into the reservoir at an unanticipated speed, which generated a 250-meter tsunami that overtopped the dam, destroying villages downstream. Nearly 2,000 people died. Apart from levying exacting human loss, the dam also lost its economic function.

Although the proximate cause of Vajont's fragility appears to be an unexpected natural disaster, the root causes point to biases of human judgment under uncertainty (Tversky and Kahneman 1974; Kahneman and Lovallo 1993; Lovallo and Kahneman 2003; Kahneman 2011). The literature in psychology suggests that experts (such as statisticians, engineers, or economists) and laypersons are systematically and predictably prone to errors when forming judgments under uncertainty. Biases, such as overconfidence or overreliance on heuristics (rules-of-thumb) underpin these errors, which result in the underestimation of risk.

The behavior of the experts responsible for building Vajont is consistent with such cognitive biases. By November 1960 it had become clear that the rock mass sloping toward the reservoir behind the dam was severely fractured. Experts reached the conclusion that it was not possible to completely stop the landslide, but nonetheless "assumed that by elevating the level of the reservoir in a careful manner ... the rate of movement [of the sliding mass] could be controlled" (Petley 2008; see also Semenza and Ghirotti 2000; Kilburn and Petley 2003). Experts' psychological confidence that they could control the landslide is consistent with the notion of "illusion

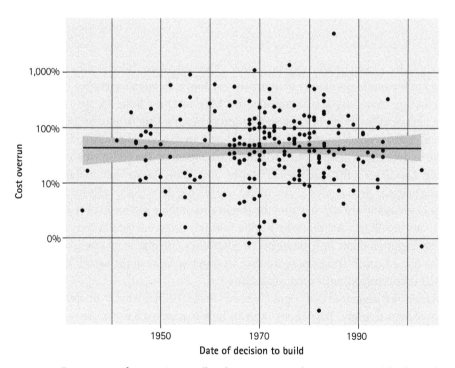

FIGURE 4.9 Inaccuracy of cost estimates (local currencies and constant prices) for large dams over time (1934–2007) (N = 245).

(From Ansar et al. 2014.)

of control"—a tendency for people to overestimate their ability to control outcomes (Kahneman and Riepe 1998).

Experts' illusion of control was exacerbated by a systematic underestimation of variance of the underlying risk factors they faced. Experts built several scale models to simulate the potential outcomes of a landslide into the reservoir behind the Vajont Dam wall. However, these models did not take account of the cumulative effect that a large mass might have if it slid at very high speed, which turned out to be the eventual outcome (Marco 2012: 145–6).

In line with *Proposition 9*, we find that at the organizational level such psychological biases appear not to be readily attenuated. For example, we analyzed whether cost estimates of big dams have become more accurate over time—the idea being that even if psychological causes led to errors in earlier projects, organizational factors would intervene over time to attenuate psychological biases. In contrast, our statistical analysis suggested that irrespective of the year or decade in which a dam was built there are no significant differences in forecasting errors ($F = 0.57$, $p = 0.78$). Similarly, we did not observe a trend indicating improvement or deterioration of forecasting errors ($F = 0.54$, $p = 0.46$), as also suggested by Figure 4.9. Organizations appear to not be learning from past mistakes. Why organizations fail to attenuate adverse outcomes of psychological biases continues to be a lively area of future research (see Durand 2003; Makadok 2011).

4.4 SUMMARY AND CONCLUSIONS

Megaprojects, in the private and public sectors alike, are more ubiquitous and bigger than ever before. These big capital investments are justified on the basis of theories of big that underpin two aspirations: an aspiration to efficiency from purported economies of size or scope; and an aspiration to scalability from building capacity ahead of demand. We found that big investments have a poor track record in delivering on either aspiration. Contrary to the conventional proposition of "bigger is better," we found big capital investments to have a propensity to fragility—vulnerability of the investments to become unrecoverable due to the impact of a random or random events. The notion of fragility has not been included in previous business and management theories. We propose its incorporation as an essential boundary condition on the theories of big.

Our theoretical argument can be summarized as follows: the emphasis of theories of big on efficiency and building capacity ahead of demand encourages managers to take "definitive, static bets" on big ventures (Klingebiel and Adner 2015: 222). What theories of big fail to incorporate in their logic is that oversizing a system increases its complexity disproportionately owing to the greater number of permutations of interactions now possible among more subcomponents, and this leads to fragility. Small errors in one or a few interactions of the bigger system magnify. All of this exerts a financial toll: propensity to cost overruns at construction, unexpectedly large bills in fixing new vulnerabilities when they become apparent as the system ages, and huge clean-up costs if the system has to be decommissioned or if it collapses. Despite their Goliath appearance, big capital investments break easily—that is, they deliver negative net present value—when faced with disturbances. A greater propensity to fragility is intrinsic to big investments.

We further argue that conventional theory has conflated big with scalability. Big entails being bespoke and complex with multiple attributes such as large upfront financial outlays, durable temporal horizons, spatial immobility, and the ability to produce large units of outputs. In contrast, scalability is independence from the constraints of space and time. For example, the hardbound printed *Encyclopaedia Britannica* in its totality is available only at a prescribed place (spatial), at a prescribed time (temporal), and to a limited audience (relational). Anyone can enjoy Wikipedia, anywhere, at any time. Wikipedia, unlike its printed rival, is scalable. Fragility arises when big is forced into doing what was best left to the scalable.

We substantiate our argument using evidence from a dataset of 245 big dams with a total value of $353 billion (2010 prices) built from 1934 to 2007 on five continents in sixty-five different countries. Our primary findings are:

- Nearly half the dams we studied suffered a cost overrun so large for the projects to be considered broken even before they began operations. That is, the capital sunk up front could not be recovered. Fragility at such an early stage of an investment's life cycle can be likened to an investment stillbirth.
- Cost risks for big dams have fat tails; the actual costs more than doubles for two out of ten dams, and triples for one out of every ten big dams.
- Managers do not seem to learn. Forecasts today are likely to be as wrong as they were between 1934 and 2007.
- Costs aside, big dams take a very long time to build—on average 8.6 years, which is a little late in coming to solve pressing energy and water needs.
- Investment fragility risk increases as the life of a big dam progresses, owing to cumulative processes—such as material fatigue and threat of catastrophic failure— that trigger the need for costly rehabilitation in perpetuity.
- Costs of maintaining or removing big dams past their intended service lives is a looming financial liability.
- The companies or countries that undertake big investments inherit their fragility. For example, the outsized costs of big dams and similar megaprojects have caused an explosive growth of debt in developing countries, hamstringing their economic potential. Developing countries, despite seemingly the most in need of complex facilities such as big dams, ought to stay away from projects that are big relative to the national economy.

Ought decision makers abandon all big ventures? Of course not. But they must carefully assess when bigger is better, instead of unthinkingly assuming that this is the case. Evidence suggests that on a risk-adjusted basis, more often than is assumed, big ventures are unlikely to present good value. Top decision makers responsible for giving the final green light to a big capital investment ought to remain skeptical of the numbers presented to them at appraisal. They should also seek to debias estimates of time to task completion, costs, and benefits by demanding more extreme stress tests, reflecting the full variance of phenomena, to determine the fragility threshold of the investment they are about to undertake. We would also advise against making big capital-investment decisions on razor-thin margins. Big investments need far more cushioning to avoid fragility than current management practice tends to assume.

If big is fragile, what is the alternative? We do not have the space here to answer this question. Elsewhere, we study managers who work by the heuristic "If big is fragile, then break it down" to deliver their projects successfully, and we study theories that support this approach, such as theories of modularization (Baldwin and Clark 2000; Schilling and Steensma 2001; Garud et al. 2003; Levinson 2006), real options in product innovation (Klingebiel and Adner 2015), and greater user–producer codevelopment (Grabher et al. 2008; Ansar 2012). We hope to report on this work later. For now, we conclude that before committing to a big venture, managers should rigorously consider possible alternatives. Scholars should similarly carefully re-evaluate theories of big. Our data indicate that the current tendency to accept theories of big at face value and lock in early in capital project decision making to a big "favorite solution," often erring toward the monumental, drives fragility and therefore incurs a high risk of failure.

Notes

1. Future efforts may require drawing more careful distinctions among the members of the disorder family (see also Goldstein and Taleb 2007, on volatility).
2. Buldyrev et al. (2010: 1025) report: "For an isolated single network, a significant number of the network nodes must be randomly removed before the network breaks down. However, when taking into account the dependencies between the networks, removal of only a small fraction of nodes can result in the complete fragmentation of the entire system."
3. Not all things fit neatly in the proposed 2 x 2 matrix in Figure 4.1. Although it is possible to glue back together a broken antique porcelain cup to restore the function of drinking tea, it is aesthetically displeasing. Similarly, Humpty the cannon could have been restored to its defensive function. But that proved unachievable in the time available despite the effort of "all the king's horses and all the king's men." The temporary fragility of the cannon, however, irreversibly spread to the Royalists forces. Thus even where a broken system is highly recoverable, three questions still remain relevant. (i) What effort (for ecample, cost or time) will the recovery take? (ii) What harm might occur to other things (such as inherited fragility) during the down time in which the recovery takes place? (iii) Will the recovery yield a functional inferior? What this suggests is that to make a system that has a high fragility threshold and is easily restored to its original function is incredibly difficult.
4. In Greek mythology, when Achilles was a baby, it was foretold that he would die young. To prevent his death, his mother Thetis took him to the River Styx, which was supposed to offer powers of invulnerability, and dipped his body into the water. But as Thetis held Achilles by the heel, his heel was not washed over by the water of the magical river.
5. Other academic fields such as geography and ecology have also taken a keen interest in scale, and typically use similar language—for example, finer or coarse/broader scale—as Mandelbrot (Wiens 1989; Wu and David 2002). Perhaps the noteworthy difference is that

whereas geometry tends to treat scale as a continuum, scholars in geography or ecology have preferred to conceptualize scale as a nested hierarchical structure such as Russian dolls. For example, a street, block, neighborhood, borough, city, province, country, region, continent, the planet, the solar system, and so on, are nested spatial structures. Although the nested hierarchical structure conceptualization is a blunt approximation, as long as the zoomed-out scales in a nested structure are not conflated with bigger, we are not against the use of such an approximation to aid understanding.

6. Our definition of *scalability* differs from the more popular conceptualizations, represented, for example, by Weinstock and Goodenough (2006). The differences are that Weinstock and Goodenough focus mainly on, first, relational scale concerns such as number of users or user-driven performance metric, whereas space and time cannot be ignored, and second, they focus almost entirely on the ability to scale up. Effortless scaling down is equally important, particularly when previous capacity becomes obsolete and needs to be removed. Thus it is not just important to meet increasing incremental demand but to know what to do if the demand disappears.

7. Actual outturn costs (also called actual CAPEX) are defined as real, accounted construction costs determined at the time of project completion. Estimated costs are defined as budgeted, or forecasted, construction costs at the time of decision to build. The actual outturn costs comprise the following elements: right-of-way acquisition and resettlement; design engineering and project management services; construction of all civil works and facilities related to completing a dam project; equipment purchases.

    Cost underrun or overrun is the actual outturn costs expressed as a ratio of estimated costs. The year of the date of the decision to build a project is the base year of prices in which all estimated and actual constant costs have been expressed in real (that is, with the effects of inflation removed) local currency terms of the country in which the project is located. Cost overruns can also be expressed as the actual outturn costs minus estimated costs in percent of estimated costs.

8. Actual implementation schedule of the project in months. The implementation start date (also known as the final decision to build) is the date of project approval by the main financiers and the key decision makers. The implementation completion date is the date of full commercial operation. Schedule slippage or schedule underrun or overrun is the actual implementation months expressed as a ratio of the estimated implementation schedule.

9. According to *The New York Times* (22 July 1985), the Montecatini Company had built the mine and Stava Dam complex in the early 1960s. It was taken over by the Italian state energy company, Enil, in 1979, and sold to Prealpi in 1981. Disaster struck in 1985.

10. Discussion of the Kariba case here benefited from personal communication with Jacques Leslie.

11. As part of its cumulative fragility, it is worth noting Kariba Dam's large and continuing negative social and environmental impacts, which were poorly mitigated. Thayer Scudder (2005: 1) writes, initially "considered a successful project even by affected people based on cost–benefit analysis, Kariba also involved unacceptable environmental and social impacts. The involuntary resettlement of 57,000 people within the reservoir basin and immediately downstream from the dam was responsible for serious environmental degradation which was one of a number of factors that left a majority of those resettled impoverished." Moreover, as an important aside, Phase 2 of the Kariba built 1970–77, constituting a 600 MW powerhouse, suffered a cost overrun 2.5 times its estimate, badly damaging the overall program's BCR (see World Bank 1983; WCD 2000b: 12–14).

References

Anderson, P. W. (1972). "More is different," *Science*, 177(4047): 393–6.

Anderson, P. W. (2011). *More And Different: Notes from a Thoughtful Curmudgeon*. Hackensack, NJ: World Scientific Publishing Company.

Ansar, A. (2010). *"New Departures" in Infrastructure Provision: An Ongoing Evolution away from Physical Assets to User Needs*. DPhil dissertation, Oxford University.

Ansar, A. (2012). "Location decisions of large firms: Analyzing the procurement of infrastructure services," *Journal of Economic Geography*, 13: 823–44, <http://doi.org/10.1093/jeg/lbs042>.

Ansar, A. (2015). *Transformational Leadership in the Public Sector: Lecture Delivered at the Major Projects Leadership Academy (MPLA)*. University of Oxford.

Ansar, A., Caldecott, B., and Tillbury, J. (2013a). *Stranded Assets and the Fossil Fuel Divestment Campaign: What Does Divestment Mean for the Valuation of Stranded Assets*. Oxford: University of Oxford.

Ansar, A., Flyvbjerg, B., and Budzier, A. (2013b). *The Time Bomb: Why Even the Best Companies Bet the Shop Without Knowing It*. Unpublished Working Paper, University of Oxford.

Ansar, A., Flyvbjerg, B., Budzier, A., and Lunn, D. (2014). "Should we build more dams?: The actual costs of mega-dam development," *Energy Policy*, 69: 43–56.

Ansar, A. and Pohlers, M. (2014). "Fluid populations, immobile assets: Synchronizing infrastructure investments with shifting demography," *International Area Studies Review*, 17(2): 222–48.

Atkinson, M. M. (2011). "Lindblom's lament: Incrementalism and the persistent pull of the status quo," *Policy and Society*, 30(1): 9–18, <http://doi.org/10.1016/j.polsoc.2010.12.002>.

Atkinson, R. (1999). "Project management: Cost, time and quality, two best guesses and a phenomenon, its time to accept other success criteria," *International Journal of Project Management*, 17(6): 337–42.

Bacon, R. W. and Besant-Jones, J. E. (1998). "Estimating construction costs and schedules: experience with power generation projects in developing countries," *Energy Policy*, 26(4): 317–33, <https://doi.org/10.1016/S0301-4215(97)00164-X>.

Baldwin, C. and Clark, K. (2000). *Design Rules: The Power of Modularity*. Cambridge. MA: MIT Press.

Bhidé, A. (2008). *The Venturesome Economy: How Innovation Sustains Prosperity in a More Connected World*. Princeton, NJ: Princeton University Press.

Brooks, F. P. (1995). *The Mythical Man-Month: Essays on Software Engineering*, 2nd edn. Reading, MA: Addison Wesley.

Buldyrev, S. V., Parshani, R., Paul, G., Stanley, H. E., and Havlin, S. (2010). "Catastrophic cascade of failures in interdependent networks," *Nature*, 464(7291): 1025–8, <http://doi.org/10.1038/nature08932>.

Callaway, D. S., Newman, M. E., Strogatz, S. H., and Watts, D. J. (2000). "Network robustness and fragility: Percolation on random graphs," *Physical Review Letters*, 85(25): 5468–71.

Calomiris, C. W. and Haber, S. H. (2014). *Fragile by Design: The Political Origins of Banking Crises and Scarce Credit*. Princeton, NJ: Princeton University Press.

Cavallo, L. and Rossi, S. P. (2001). "Scale and scope economies in the European banking systems," *Journal of Multinational Financial Management*, 11(4): 515–31.

Chandler, A. D. (1990). *Scale and Scope: Dynamics of Industrial Capitalism*, new edn. Cambridge, MA: Harvard University Press.

Choi, E., DesRoches, R., and Nielson, B. (2004). "Seismic fragility of typical bridges in moderate seismic zones," *Engineering Structures*, 26(2): 187–99.

Clark, G. L. and Wrigley, N. (1995). "Sunk costs: A framework for economic geography," *Transactions of the Institute of British Geographers*, 20(2): 204–23.

Clark, G. L. and Wrigley, N. (1997a). "Exit, the firm and sunk costs: Reconceptualizing the corporate geography of disinvestment and plant closure," *Progress in Human Geography*, 21(3): 338–58.

Clark, G. L. and Wrigley, N. (1997b). "The spatial configuration of the firm and the management of sunk costs," *Economic Geography*, 73(3): 285–304.

CNN. (1999). "NASA's metric confusion caused Mars Orbiter loss," 30 September, <http://edition.cnn.com/TECH/space/9909/30/mars.metric/>.

Copeland, T. and Tufano, P. (2004). "A real-world way to manage real options," *Harvard Business Review*, 82(3): 90–9.

Crompton, P. and Lesourd, J.-B. (2008). "Economies of scale in global iron-making," *Resources Policy*, 33(2): 74–82, <http://doi.org/10.1016/j.resourpol.2007.10.005>.

Cullinane, K. and Khanna, M. (2000). "Economies of scale in large containerships: Optimal size and geographical implications," *Journal of Transport Geography*, 8(3): 181–95, <http://doi.org/10.1016/S0966-6923(00)00010-7>.

Dash, E. and Creswell, J. (2008). "Citigroup saw no red flags even as it made bolder bets," *The New York Times*, 23: A1.

Davis, E. P. (1995). *Debt, Financial Fragility, and Systemic Risk*, new edn. Oxford: Clarendon Press.

Durand, R. (2003). "Predicting a firm's forecasting ability: The roles of organizational illusion of control and organizational attention," *Strategic Management Journal*, 24(9): 821–38.

Easterly, W. R. (2002). *The Elusive Quest for Growth: Economists' Adventures and Misadventures in the Tropics*. Cambridge, MA: MIT Press.

Easterly, W. R. (2006). "The big push déjà vu: A review of Jeffrey Sachs's *The End of Poverty: Economic Possibilities for Our Time*," *Journal of Economic Literature*, 44(1): 96–105.

Flyvbjerg, B. (1998). *Rationality and Power: Democracy in Practice*. Chicago: University of Chicago Press.

Flyvbjerg, B. (2009). "Survival of the unfittest: Why the worst infrastructure gets built, and what we can do about it," *Oxford Review of Economic Policy*, 25(3): 344–67.

Flyvbjerg, B. (2014). "What you should know about megaprojects and why: An overview," *Project Management Journal*, 45(2): 6–19, <http://doi.org/10.1002/pmj.21409>.

Flyvbjerg, B., Bruzelius, N., and Rothengatter, W. (2003). *Megaprojects and Risk: An Anatomy of Ambition*. Cambridge: Cambridge University Press.

Flyvbjerg, B. and Budzier, A. (2011). "Why your IT project may be riskier than you think," *Harvard Business Review*, September, <http://hbr.org/2011/09/why-your-it-project-may-be-riskier-than-you-think/ar>.

Flyvbjerg, B., Garbuio, M., and Lovallo, D. (2009). "Delusion and deception in large infrastructure projects," *California Management Review*, 51(2): 170–93.

Flyvbjerg, B., Holm, M., and Buhl, S. (2002). "Underestimating costs in public works projects: Error or lie?" *Journal of the American Planning Association*, 68(3): 279–95.

Flyvbjerg, B., Holm, M., and Buhl, S. (2005). "How (in)accurate are demand forecasts in public works projects? The case of transportation," *Journal of the American Planning Association*, 71(2): 131–46.

Flyvbjerg, B., Landman, T., and Schram, S. (eds.) (2012). *Real Social Science: Applied Phronesis*. Cambridge: Cambridge University Press.

Foreman, R. D. and Beauvais, E. (1999). "Scale economies in cellular telephony: Size matters," *Journal of Regulatory Economics*, 16(3): 297–306.

Gao, J., Buldyrev, S. V., Stanley, H. E., and Havlin, S. (2012). "Networks formed from interdependent networks," *Nature Physics*, 8(1): 40–8.

Garud, R., Kumaraswamy, A., and Langlois, R. N. (2003). *Managing in the Modular Age: Architectures, Networks, and Organizations*. Oxford: Blackwell.

Ghemawat, P. (1991). *Commitment: Dynamic of Strategy*, 2nd edn. New York: The Free Press.

Ghemawat, P. and Del Sol, P. (1998). "Commitment Versus Flexibility?" *California Management Review*, 40(4): 26–42.

Goldstein, D. and Taleb, N. (2007). "We don't quite know what we are talking about when we talk about volatility," *Journal of Portfolio Management*, 33(4): 84–6, <http://papers.ssrn.com/sol3/Papers.cfm?abstract_id=970480>.

Gómez-Ibáñez, J. A. (2003). *Regulating infrastructure: monopoly, contracts, and discretion*. Cambridge, MA: Harvard University Press.

Grabher, G., Ibert, O., and Flohr, S. (2008). "The neglected king: The customer in the new knowledge ecology of innovation," *Economic Geography*, 84(3): 253–80.

Gunther, N. (2007). *Guerrilla Capacity Planning: A Tactical Approach to Planning for Highly Scalable Applications and Services*. Berlin: Springer, <http://link.springer.com/10.1007/978-3-540-31010-5>.

Hayes, R. H. and Garvin, D. A. (1982). "Managing as if tomorrow mattered," *Harvard Business Review*, 60(3): 70–9.

Heifetz, R., Grashow, A., and Linsky, M. (2009). *The Practice of Adaptive Leadership*. Boston, MA: Harvard Business Press, <http://www.leadersthatlast.org/pdfs/the_practice_of_adaptive_leadership_review.pdf>.

Hill, M. D. (1990). What Is Scalability? *ACM SIGARCH Computer Architecture News*, 18(4), 18–21.

Hodgkinson, G. P., and Starbuck, W. H. (2012). *The Oxford Handbook of Organizational Decision Making* (Reprint edition). Oxford: Oxford University Press.

Issacharoff, S. (2007). Fragile Democracies. *Harvard Law Review*, 120(6), 1405–67.

Kahneman, D. and Lovallo, D. (1993). "Timid choices and bold forecasts: a cognitive perspective on risk taking," *Management Science*, 9(1): 17–31.

Kahneman, D. (2011). *Thinking, Fast and Slow*. New York: Farrar, Straus and Giroux.

Kahneman, D. and Riepe, M. W. (1998). "Aspects of investor psychology," *Journal of Portfolio Management*, 24(4): 52–65, <http://doi.org/10.3905/jpm.1998.409643>.

Keil, M. (1995). "Pulling the plug: software project management and the problem of project escalation," *MIS Quarterly*, 19(4): 421–47.

Keil, M. and Montealegre, R. (2000). "Cutting your losses: Extricating your organization when a big project goes awry," *Sloan Management Review*, 41(3), <http://sloanreview.mit.edu/article/cutting-your-losses-extricating-your-organization-when-a-big-project-goes-awry/>.

Kerzner, H. (2009). *Project Management Case Studies*. New York: Wiley.

Kilburn, C. R. and Petley, D. N. (2003). "Forecasting giant, catastrophic slope collapse: Lessons from Vajont, Northern Italy," *Geomorphology*, 54(1): 21–32.

Klemkosky, R. C. (2013). "Financial system fragility," *Business Horizons*, 56(6): 675–83, <http://doi.org/10.1016/j.bushor.2013.07.005>.

Klingebiel, R. and Adner, R. (2015). "Real options logic revisited: The performance effects of alternative resource allocation regimes," *Academy of Management Journal*, 58(1): 221–41, <http://doi.org/10.5465/amj.2012.0703>.

Kwoka, J. E. (2002). "Vertical economies in electric power: Evidence on integration and its alternatives," *International Journal of Industrial Organization*, 20(5): 653–71.

Lavigne, P. M. (2005). "Dam(n) how times have changed …," *William and Mary Environmental Law and Policy Review*, 29: 451.

Levinson, M. (2006). *The Box: How the Shipping Container Made the World Smaller and the World Economy Bigger*. Princeton, NJ: Princeton University Press.

Lindblom, C. E. (1959). "The science of 'muddling through,'" *Public Administration Review*, 19: 79–88.

Lindblom, C. E. (1979). "Still muddling, not yet through," *Public Administration Review*, 39(6): 517–26, <http://doi.org/10.2307/976178>.

Liu, J., Dietz, T., Carpenter, S. R., et al. (2007). "Complexity of coupled human and natural systems," *Science*, 317(5844): 1513–16.

Lovallo, D. and Kahneman, D. (2003). "Delusions of success," *Harvard Business Review*, 81(7): 56–63.

Luino, F. and De Graff, J. V. (2012). "The Stava mudflow of 19 July 1985 (northern Italy): A disaster that effective regulation might have prevented," *Natural Hazards and Earth System Sciences*, 12(4): 1029–44, <http://doi.org/10.5194/nhess-12-1029-2012>.

Majumdar, S. K. and Venkataraman, S. (1998). "Network effects and the adoption of new technology: Evidence from the U. S. telecommunications industry," *Strategic Management Journal*, 19(11): 1045–62.

Makadok, R. (2011). "Invited editorial: The four theories of profit and their joint effects," *Journal of Management*, 37(5): 1316–34, <http://doi.org/10.1177/0149206310385697>.

Mandelbrot, B. B. (1967). "How long is the coast of Britain," *Science*, 156(3775): 636–8.

Mandelbrot, B. B. and Hudson, R. L. (2008). *The (Mis)Behaviour of Markets: A Fractal View of Risk, Ruin and Reward*. London: Profile Books.

Marco, D. R. (2012). "Decision making errors and socio-political disputes over the Vajont Dam disaster," *Disaster Advances*, 5(3): 144–52.

Martinez-Garcia, J. C., Rzoska, S. J., Drozd-Rzoska, A., Starzonek, S., and Mauro, J. C. (2015). "Fragility and basic process energies in vitrifying systems," *Scientific Reports*, 5(8314), <http://doi.org/10.1038/srep08314>.

Mauro, N. A., Blodgett, M., Johnson, M. L., Vogt, A. J., and Kelton, K. F. (2014). "A structural signature of liquid fragility," *Nature Communications*, 5(4616), <http://doi.org/10.1038/ncomms5616>.

McCully, P. (2001). *Silenced Rivers: The Ecology and Politics of Large Dams*. London: Zed Books.

McNamara, G., Moon, H., and Bromiley, P. (2002). "Banking on commitment: Intended and unintended consequences of an organization's attempt to attenuate escalation of commitment," *Academy of Management Journal*, 45(2): 443–52, <http://doi.org/10.2307/3069358>.

Mill, J. S. (1848). *The Principles of Political Economy: With Some of Their Applications to Social Philosophy*. London: John W. Parker.

Mitchell, J. (1995). *The Fragility of Freedom: Tocqueville on Religion, Democracy, and the American Future*. Chicago: University of Chicago Press.

Morris, R. G. and Barthelemy, M. (2013). "Interdependent networks: The fragility of control," *Scientific Reports*, 3(2764), <http://doi.org/10.1038/srep02764>.

Mosca, M. (2008). "On the origins of the concept of natural monopoly: Economies of scale and competition," *European Journal of the History of Economic Thought*, 15(2): 317–53.

National Audit Office. (2014). *Lessons from Major Rail Infrastructure Programmes* (No. HC: 267, 14–15, p. 40). London: National Audit Office, <http://naodigitalchannels.polldaddy.com/s/site-feedback?st=1&iframe=1>.

Nilsson, C. and Grelsson, G. (1995). "The fragility of ecosystems: A review," *Journal of Applied Ecology*, 32(4), 677–92, <http://doi.org/10.2307/2404808>.

Nussbaum, Martha C. (2001). *The Fragility of Goodness: Luck and Ethics in Greek Tragedy and Philosophy*. Cambridge: Cambridge University Press.

Nutt, P. C. (1999). "Surprising but true: Half the decisions in organizations fail," *The Academy of Management Executive (1993–2005)*, 13(4): 75–90, <http://doi.org/10.2307/4165588>.

Nutt, P. C. (2002). *Why Decisions Fail: Avoiding the Blunders and Traps That Lead to Debacles*. Oakland, CA: Berrett-Koehler.

Parshani, R., Buldyrev, S. V., and Havlin, S. (2011). "Critical effect of dependency groups on the function of networks," *Proceedings of the National Academy of Sciences*, 108(3): 1007–10, <http://doi.org/10.1073/pnas.1008404108>.

Penrose, E. (2009). *The Theory of the Growth of the Firm*, 4th edn. Oxford: Oxford University Press.

Petley, D. N. (2008). "The Vaiont (Vajont) landslide of 1963," <http://www.landslideblog.org/2008/12/vaiont-vajont-landslide-of-1963.html>.

Pollitt, M. G. and Steer, S. J. (2012). "Economies of scale and scope in network industries: lessons for the UK water and sewerage sectors," *Utilities Policy*, 21: 17–31.

Porter, M. E. (1980). *Competitive Strategy: Techniques for Analyzing Industries and Competitors*. New York: Free Press.

Priemus, H., Flyvbjerg, B., and van Wee, B. (eds.) (2008). *Decision-Making on Mega-Projects: Cost–Benefit Analysis, Planning and Innovation*. Cheltenham, UK: Edward Elgar.

Qiu, J. (2011). "China admits problems with Three Gorges Dam," *Nature News*, <http://doi.org/10.1038/news.2011.315>.

Quinn, J. B. (1978). "Strategic change: 'Logical Incrementalism,'" *Sloan Management Review*, 20(1): 7–19.

Reichhardt, T. (1999). "NASA reworks its sums after Mars fiasco," *Nature*, 401(6753), 517, <http://doi.org/10.1038/43974>.

Royer, I. (2003). "Why bad projects are so hard to kill," *Harvard Business Review*, 81(2): 48–56.

Sachs, J. D. (2006). *The End of Poverty: Economic Possibilities for Our Time*. New York: Penguin.

Samuelson, P. A. (1948). *Economics*. New York: McGraw-Hill.

Schilling, M. A. and Steensma, H. K. (2001). "The use of modular organizational forms: an industry-level analysis," *The Academy of Management Journal*, 44(6): 1149–68, <https://doi.org/10.2307/3069394>.

Schumacher, E. F. (1973). *Small Is Beautiful: A Study of Economics as if People Mattered*, new edn. London: Vintage.

Scopigno, T., Ruocco, G., Sette, F., and Monaco, G. (2003). "Is the fragility of a liquid embedded in the properties of its glass?" *Science*, 302(5646): 849–52, <http://doi.org/10.1126/science.1089446>.

Scudder, T. (2005). *The future of large dams: dealing with social, environmental, institutional and political costs*. London: Earthscan.

Semenza, E. and Ghirotti, M. (2000). "History of the 1963 Vaiont slide: The importance of geological factors," *Bulletin of Engineering Geology and the Environment*, 59(2): 87–97, <http://doi.org/10.1007/s100640000067>.

Seref-Ferlengez, Z., Kennedy, O. D., and Schaffler, M. B. (2015). "Bone microdamage, remodeling and bone fragility: How much damage is too much damage? *BoneKEy Reports*, 4, <http://doi.org/10.1038/bonekey.2015.11>.

Shinozuka, M., Feng, M. Q., Lee, J., and Naganuma, T. (2000). "Statistical analysis of fragility curves," *Journal of Engineering Mechanics*, 126(12): 1224–31.

Sidak, J. G. and Spulber, D. F. (1997). *Deregulatory Takings and the Regulatory Contract: The Competitive Transformation of Network Industries in the United States*. Cambridge: Cambridge University Press.

Silberston, A. (1972). "Economies of scale in theory and practice," *The Economic Journal*, 82(325): 369–91, <http://doi.org/10.2307/2229943>.

Simon, H. A. (1962). "The architecture of complexity," *Proceedings of the American Philosophical Society*, 106(6): 467–82.

Sole, R. V. and Montoya, M. (2001). "Complexity and fragility in ecological networks," *Proceedings of the Royal Society of London B: Biological Sciences*, 268(1480): 2039–45.

Souder, D. and Shaver, J. M. (2010). "Constraints and incentives for making long horizon corporate investments," *Strategic Management Journal*, 31(12): 1316–36, <http://doi.org/10.1002/smj.862>.

Stigler, G. J. (1958). "The economies of scale," *Journal of Law and Economics*, 1: 54.

Stone, R. (2008). "Three Gorges Dam: Into the unknown," *Science*, 321(5889): 628–32, <http://doi.org/10.1126/science.321.5889.628>.

Stone, R. (2011). "The legacy of the Three Gorges Dam," *Science*, 333(6044): 817, <http://doi.org/10.1126/science.333.6044.817>.

Sutton, Robert I. and Huggy Rao (2014). *Scaling Up Excellence: Getting to More Without Settling for Less*. New York and London: Random House.

Taleb, N. N. (2010). *The Black Swan: The Impact of the Highly Improbable, with a New Section: "On Robustness and Fragility"* 2nd edn. New York: Random House.

Taleb, N. N. (2012). *Antifragile: Things That Gain from Disorder*. London: Allen Lane.

Taleb, N. N., Canetti, E. R., Kinda, T., Loukoianova, E., and Schmieder, C. (2012). *A New Heuristic Measure of Fragility and Tail Risks: Application to Stress Testing* (No. WP/12/216). Washington, DC: International Monetary Fund, <http://papers.ssrn.com/sol3/papers.cfm?abstract_id=2156095>.

Taleb, N. N. and Douady, R. (2012). "A map and simple heuristic to detect fragility, antifragility, and model error," *Quantitative Finance*, 1–21.

Taleb, N. N. and Douady, R. (2013). "Mathematical definition, mapping, and detection of (anti)fragility. *Quantitative Finance*, 13(11): 1677–89, <http://doi.org/10.1080/14697688.2013.800219>.

Titman, S., Wei, K. C. J., and Xie, F. (2004). "Capital investments and stock returns," *Journal of Financial and Quantitative Analysis*, 39(4): 677–700, <http://doi.org/10.2307/30031881>.

Turner, B. A. and Pidgeon, N. F. (1997). *Man-made Disasters*. Oxford: Butterworth-Heinemann.

Tversky, A. and Kahneman, D. (1974). "Judgment under uncertainty: heuristics and biases," *Science*, 185(4157): 1124–31.

USAID. (2005). "Measuring fragility: Indicators and methods for rating state performance."

US Department of Energy. (2009). *Center for Energy, Environmental, and Economic Systems Analysis (CEEESA)*, <http://www.dis.anl.gov/projects/PowerAnalysisTools.html>.

Van Oorschot, K. E., Akkermans, H., Sengupta, K., and Van Wassenhove, L. N. (2013). "Anatomy of a decision trap in complex new product development projects." *Academy of Management Journal*, 56(1): 285–307, <http://doi.org/10.5465/amj.2010.0742>.

Vespignani, A. (2010). "Complex networks: The fragility of interdependency," *Nature*, 464(7291): 984–5.

Weinstock, C. B. and Goodenough, J. B. (2006). *On System Scalability*. DTIC Document, <http://oai.dtic.mil/oai/oai?verb=getRecord&metadataPrefix=html&identifier=ADA457003>.

Wernerfelt, B. and Karnani, A. (1987). "Competitive strategy under uncertainty," *Strategic Management Journal*, 8(2): 187–94, <http://doi.org/10.1002/smj.4250080209>.

Wiens, J. A. (1989). "Spatial scaling in ecology," *Functional Ecology*, 3(4), 385–97, <http://doi.org/10.2307/2389612>.

Williams, T. (2005). "Assessing and moving on from the dominant project management discourse in the light of project overruns," *IEEE Transactions on Engineering Management*, 52(4): 497–508, <http://doi.org/10.1109/TEM.2005.856572>.

World Bank. (1956). *Appraisal of the Kariba Hydroelectric Project in the Federation of Rhodesia and Nyasaland* (No. T.O. 116-a). Washington, DC: World Bank.

World Bank. (1981). *Staff Appraisal Report: Colombia Guavio Hydro Power Project* (No. 3408-CO). Washington, DC: World Bank.

World Bank. (1983). *Project Performance Audit Report. Zambia: Kariba North Hydroelectric Project (Loan 701-ZA)* (No. 4661). Washington, DC: World Bank.

World Bank. (1996a). *Implementation Completion Report: Colombia Guavio Hydro Power Report (Loan 2008-CO)* (No. 15691). Washington, DC: World Bank.

World Bank. (1996b). *Performance Audit Report Argentina Yacyreta Hydroelectric Project (Loan 1761-AR) Electric Power Sector Project (Loan 2998-AR)* (No. 15801). Washington, DC: World Bank.

World Bank. (2001). *Implementation Completion Report (CPL-35200; SCL-3520A; SCPD-3520S) on a Loan in the Amount of 300 US$ Million to the Republic of Argentina for the Yacyreta Hydroelectric Project II* (No. 22489). Washington, DC: World Bank.

World Bank. (2014). *Environmental and Social Impact Assessment: Terms of Reference* (No. E4648) (pp. 1–29). World Bank, <http://documents.worldbank.org/curated/en/2014/09/20248277/zambia-kariba-dam-rehabilitation-project-environmental-assessment-environmental-social-impact-assessment-terms-reference>.

World Commission on Dams. (WCD). (2000a). *Cross-Check Survey: Final Report*. Cape Town, South Africa, <www.dams.org>.

World Commission on Dams. (WCD). (2000b). *Kariba Dam Zambia and Zimbabwe. WCD Case Study*.

Wu, J. and David, J. (2002). "A spatially explicit hierarchical approach to modeling complex ecological systems: Theory and applications," *Ecological Modelling*, 153(1–2): 7–26.

Ziaja, S. (2012). "What do fragility indices measure?" *Zeitschrift für Vergleichende Politikwissenschaft*, 6(1): 39–64, <http://doi.org/10.1007/s12286-012-0123-8>.

CHAPTER 5

INSTITUTIONAL CHALLENGES AND SOLUTIONS FOR GLOBAL MEGAPROJECTS

RAYMOND E. LEVITT AND W. RICHARD SCOTT

5.1 INTRODUCTION

MEGAPROJECTS are very large, complex projects requiring new, and often previously untested, management skills and techniques for their successful implementation. Multibillion-dollar projects have become the norm for many infrastructure and resource extraction facilities worldwide over the last decade. However, increased size and scope do not necessarily transform a large project into a "megaproject" in terms of coordination difficulty. Lessard et al. (2014) define project complexity in terms of a project's "difficulty, outcome variability and non-linearity, and (non) governability," and they propose a "House of Project Complexity"—a combined structural and process-based theoretical framework for understanding contributors to complexity. We agree with their characterization of the drivers of complexity. We distinguish "megaprojects" from other large projects in terms of the degree to which managers can reduce overall project coordination costs for handling overall project complexity through partitioning of the project into more or less autonomous subprojects. Further, "Global Megaprojects" also involve significant levels of cross-institutional complexity because they involve participants and outside groups from multiple countries with differing languages and institutions.

5.1.1 Spatial/Technical Configuration Complexity

The first key to the distinction between a large project and a megaproject (from a coordination standpoint) is the number and importance of intersubproject interdependencies that still remain between the most decomposable set of subprojects that can feasibly be conceived and executed. Large-scale, linear, "horizontal" projects such as roads, railroads, and pipelines with relatively few interconnected subsystems tend to be relatively easy to decompose into nearly independent geographical subprojects that face primarily local uncertainties, such as geological or climatic conditions. Such projects can be relatively autonomously coordinated as sets of subprojects, so they pose only a moderate need for central coordination. The $8-billion Trans-Alaska Pipeline System project was built in this way during the 1970s as a set of five separate pipeline subprojects (plus a number of pumping stations and other ancillary facilities), each of which was small enough to allow for competitive bidding by teams of constructors, and could be managed primarily as a standalone subproject. Large-scale road, railroad, power, and water transmission projects are also often procured and managed in this way.

In contrast, a large, spatially concentrated, "vertical" project that has many interconnected subsystems such as a nuclear power plant or large desalination facility is a megaproject because it cannot easily be subdivided, for management purposes, into any feasible configuration of "nearly decomposable [subprojects]" (Simon 1962). These projects exhibit both complexity and tight-coupling (Perrow 1984) among subprojects that have significant levels of the two most coordination-intensive kinds of interdependencies (Levitt 2015):

- *Compatible Interdependencies* that require intensive and continuous information sharing between the interdependent parties to ensure alignment of components' spatial and functional interfaces with each other.
- *Contentious Interdependencies* for which the interdependent parties have one or more conflicting subgoals; that is, where some values of a parameter that affects the conflicting subgoal are better for Party A but are worse for Party B, and vice versa. For example, the designer of a computer's screen prefers high levels of brightness and resolution, which require additional power; the power supply designer prefers to limit total power demand to keep the power supply as light as possible and extend the computer's battery life. Contentious interdependencies require negotiation between the parties to reach agreement on parameter choices (Levitt et al. 1999). In the event of deadlocks, they frequently trigger time-consuming escalation to higher levels of engineering and project management for resolution. So they remain difficult and costly to manage.

James Thompson's (1967) classic book, *Organizations in Action*, defines both of these types of interdependence somewhat tautologically to be "reciprocal interdependence"—the kind of interdependence that requires "mutual adjustment" to coordinate. However, he does not distinguish between these two kinds of "reciprocal" interdependence. For subtasks with "compatible interdependence," mutual adjustment by the interdependent parties requires only information sharing and updating between the interdependent parties to achieve coordination. In contrast, "contentious interdependence" is much more likely to lead to disagreement and conflict in the process of mutual adjustment, and escalation to resolve the deadlocks occurs more frequently.

5.1.2 Maturity of Involved Technologies

The maturity of the key technologies involved in a project also affects the project's divisibility into nearly decomposable subprojects. As complex technologies mature, the developers of subsystems comprising the technology evolve standard solutions for resolving interdependencies at subsystem interfaces through a combination of systematic analysis of remaining interdependencies and trial-and-error adjustment to coordination failures. The resulting standards for subsystem and interface specifications define an evolving "system architecture" for the technology.

A mature system architecture allows a product's multiple subsystems to be developed nearly autonomously. Moreover, it inevitably leads to supply chain fragmentation, as specialized providers of subsystems can produce and enhance their subsystems faster and more efficiently than a central provider, following principles of transaction cost economics (Williamson 1979). For example, IBM™ decided to standardize and publish the system architecture for its personal computer in the early 1980s. This spawned a large industry of component suppliers—for example, Seagate™ for disk drives, Logitech™ for mice and keyboards, and so on—and it turned the development of a new personal computer into a relatively simple project to manage, ultimately commoditizing the entire PC industry.

A complex project involving technologies that have matured to the level that formal or informal system architectures have become standardized and institutionalized thus lends itself to being subdivided more easily into nearly autonomous subprojects organized around its now modular subsystems. In contrast, a large project that incorporates multiple novel technologies whose subsystem performance and interface specifications has not yet been standardized and incorporated into the system architecture creates a large number of new compatible and contentious interdependencies to resolve. This adds substantial incremental coordination complexity for the system integrator to manage, and can transform a large project into a megaproject. Thus, from a coordination standpoint, a megaproject is a complex project whose scope, technologies, and system architectures are not yet well enough standardized and institutionalized to permit decomposition into nearly autonomous subprojects without incurring substantial additional central coordination costs; it must be centrally managed as an integrated whole.

In addition to project technical/spatial configuration and technology maturity, two additional complexity dimensions of large projects can make them exponentially more difficult to manage than equally large but less complex projects.

5.1.3 Scale of Project's Regional Economic and Political Impact

A large project based in or traversing through an uninhabited region in a country with low levels of environmental and social concerns and safeguards can be built without energizing or generating social movements that attempt to reshape the project or block it entirely. When a project has large enough impacts on valued natural environments or human populations, it begins to activate or spawn social movements attempting to reshape or block it. Managing the project then attains a level of political complexity that requires a completely different set of political and public relations skills to manage than a complex technical project for which there is an explicit or implicit social license to proceed—or no need for a social license in an autocratically governed country (McAdam et al. 2010). In this way, a project like the Alaska pipeline project described previously became a "megaproject" because of its regional economic and environmental impact and the resulting complexity of its relational external stakeholder management challenges, even though it was neatly divisible into nearly autonomous subprojects in terms of its spatial and technical configuration.

5.1.4 Cross-Institutional Complexity: "Global Megaprojects"

The fourth dimension of complexity that transforms a large project into a megaproject is its institutional complexity, arising from the participation of key project delivery partners coming from different national institutional frameworks who must find a way to resolve their differences so they can work effectively together to resolve multiple challenging technical, contractual, and political issues. We define a large project that has this dimension of complexity as a "Global Megaproject."

This chapter focuses on defining the unique complexity of global megaprojects, assessing the impact of cross-institutional differences, and identifying ways for its sponsors, managers, and other stakeholders to address these challenges. We adopt the formulation developed by Orr et al. (2011: 17) as our working definition of a "global megaproject:"

> A global project is defined as a temporary endeavor where multiple actors seek to optimize outcomes by combining resources from multiple sites, organizations, cultures, and geographies through a combination of contractual, hierarchical, and network-based modes of organization.

5.1.5 Chapter Outline

From this densely packed definition of global megaprojects, we abstract out those elements containing important institutional ingredients in this chapter. We embrace a broad conception of "institutions" to include symbolic frames, rules, and normative frameworks that provide guidance to, and justification for, varying modes of acting. These symbolic elements are often the source of misunderstandings, disagreements, and conflicts as actors interact across cultures, companies, professional specialties, and countries as they attempt to execute complex megaprojects. These elements are also the soil out of which solutions may be crafted as actors create a shared project identity and overriding objectives, relational contracts, shared governance arrangements, and a common conception of the work to be done and how it will be governed and coordinated.

The chapter is organized into three main sections. In the first, we unpack the notion of institutions to examine the varying elements and mechanisms involved in our conceptual framework. The second examines the distinctive institutional challenges posed by global megaprojects. And the third considers how the numerous project delivery participants and a variety of other stakeholders can craft institutional elements into a variety of contractual, relational, and psychological governance mechanisms to shape and influence project processes and outcomes.

5.2 THE MULTIFACETED NATURE OF INSTITUTIONS

Informed by the ideas generated from more than a century of scholarship (see Scott 2014: ch. 1), we embrace a broad, encompassing conception of institutions:

> Institutions comprise regulative, normative, and cultural-cognitive elements that, together with associated activities and resources, provide stability and meaning to social life. (Scott 2014: 56)

This definition stresses the centrality of symbolic elements in social life but insists that these be connected to the social behavior of actors and linked to resources: we focus on living institutions that are inhabited by actors and intertwined with the play of power. While the formulation privileges the capacity of institutions to guide and control behavior, it is equally important to recognize that institutions support and empower activities and actors. Also, acknowledging the reflexive dualism identified by Giddens (1979), we recognize the ongoing interplay of forces in which existing institutional structures provide a constraining context for actors and action while, at the same time, actors are busily working to harness their position and resources to reproduce, modify, and/or challenge these structures.

Our review of an extensive literature harking back at least to the middle of the nineteenth century persuades us that institutional theorists have devised and explored at least three different conceptions of the elements underlying institutions and the mechanisms that sustain them. Not surprisingly, these conceptions are broadly associated with disciplinary differences among the investigators. We briefly review each.

5.2.1 Diverse Institutional Elements

5.2.1.1 Legal–Administrative ("Regulative") Frameworks

From the "historical institutionalists" working at the turn of the last century conducting comparative studies of administrative systems, to the current rational-choice scholars investigating how rule systems emerge to regulate markets, political scientists stress *regulative* elements as the primary basis of institutions (for example, Burgess 1902; Moe 1984). Relatedly, economists emphasize these same elements as they examine ways in which the state regulates commerce or the types of governance systems that arise—or are designed—to manage exchanges within and between firms (for example, North 1990; Williamson 1979). Not surprisingly, their favored subjects of study are formalized administrative structures and legal systems created to manage political and economic behavior. In part because such systems operate to control strangers and/or adversaries, they rely heavily on the mechanism of coercion: surveillance machinery is created and sanctions are administered to encourage compliance. It is assumed that those subject to these systems are rational beings, calculating the costs and benefits of compliance or defiance and, in general, will behave instrumentally.

Global megaprojects are confronted with multiple forms of regulative frameworks, including the laws of home and host countries, legal agreements with financing firms, regulations of regional and local entities, and corporate hierarchies. On the "solution" side, project management units create rules and sanctions to buttress contractual agreements and to form the scaffolding for agreements between project and client entities.

5.2.1.2 *Normative Frameworks*

From the beginnings of their discipline, sociologists have embraced both a broader and more diffuse conception of institutions. Because they focus on arenas such as the stratification system and ethnic relations, religion, the family, the community, and voluntary associations, they stress the importance to social order of social obligations and binding expectations. They view social institutions as normative frameworks providing a moral order undergirding social life (for example, Durkheim 1912/1961; Selznick 1992).

Normative systems are made up of both values, providing conceptions of preferred or desired ends, and norms which specify how the valued states are to be pursued. The differing facets of society—for example, political, economic, family, religion—vary in terms of values they serve and the appropriate means for attaining them, giving rise to diverse *institutional logics* guiding behavior in these separate spheres (Davis 1949; Friedland and Alford 1991). Rather than assuming that individuals adopt an instrumental orientation, individuals are seen to be guided by a sense of appropriateness. Rather than asking "what are my interests?" individuals ask "what is my role in this system and how am I expected to behave in circumstances such as this?" (March and Olsen 1989). The mechanisms at work securing compliance are shared standards and internalized expectations that can incur severe social sanctions when violated.

Megaprojects operate in a sea of normative pressures ranging from the professional standards which undergird global construction practices to the moral standards evoked by NGOs overseeing the welfare of the environments and the rights of local communities. Normative frameworks also loom large in the kinds of mechanism that underlie relational contracting and the use of "soft" voluntary standards, such as the "Equator Principles" used by banks to indicate they are requiring that environmental and social safeguards be respected on projects that they finance.

5.2.1.3 *Cultural–Cognitive Frameworks*

For many decades, anthropologists have labored to examine and explain the extraordinary variation that exists over time and space among different tribes and peoples. The dominant explanation developed is that these groups embrace a shared conception of their social world, indeed a common notion of social reality itself (Kroeber and Kluckhohn 1952; Geertz 1973). Although emerging much later, a closely related conception has been devised by cognitive psychologists who stress the importance of cognitive frames, mental models, and related scripts as an explanation for individual behavior (for example, Lewin 1951; Shank and Abelson 1977). Linking these two views, Hofstede (1984) has suggested that individuals from different cultures are equipped with diverse "software" of their minds.

A cultural–cognitive conception of institutions stresses the extent to which social order relies on a shared understanding of the situation resting on deeply embedded, taken-for-granted assumptions that operate often beneath conscious awareness. The paring of cultural and cognitive stresses the bridge between subjective perceptions and interpretations on the one hand and wider shared semiotic systems of meaning on the other.

A hallmark of global megaprojects is the wide range of cultural differences they confront, ranging from varying economic and religious ideologies to differing ethnicities and languages. Cultural systems also support solutions, as ideas can be crafted to frame or reframe task conceptions, and shared identities can support cooperative behavior among participants (Swidler 1986).

In sum, over the centuries, scholars have identified and often selectively emphasized one or another type of institutional element based on their interest in varying chunks or types of social order. This work viewed as a whole underscores the multifaceted nature of institutional systems. In our view, it also suggests the wisdom of constructing an encompassing framework that can include all the elements providing the ingredients of rich and robust institutional systems.

5.2.2 Institutional Elements in Combination

While, as suggested, one type of element is dominant in some social orders, providing a distinctive "pillar" to support the structure, it is more common to observe the elements working in combination: the interaction of multiple "pillars." Any robust institutional arrangement is made up of varying combinations of regulative, normative, and cultural–cognitive elements. Part of the work of analyzing any institution is to parse the interplay of the several elements. In some cases they will be mutually supportive, as when informal work group norms emerge that are consistent with formal rules or broader ideologies; in other cases, rules may be enacted, but over time are redefined or transformed by ongoing work routines and belief systems; in still other cases the elements are misaligned, leading to instability, conflict, and change.

The mechanisms at work in sustaining and changing institutions also vary in their malleability. Formal rules and legal frameworks are more readily enacted or changed: they are "fast-moving" institutions compared to "slow-moving" normative and cultural systems, which more often evolve as the result of unintended, interdependent actions of collections of individuals over long periods of time (Roland 2004; Scott 2013: 114).

The challenges posed by analyzing institutions are rendered more transparent and understandable if we view them as working within a delimited social arena. One promising approach to defining these boundaries is provided by the concept of *organization field*.

5.3 ORGANIZATION FIELDS AND PROJECTS

Global megaprojects are usefully viewed as a distinctive type of organization field. Such an approach incorporates not only the full range of relevant relational elements (stakeholders), but also the salient symbolic elements that inform and motivate the actions of participants.

5.3.1 Organizational Fields

Following DiMaggio and Powell (1983: 148):

> By organization field, we mean those organizations that, in the aggregate, constitute a recognized area of institutional life: key suppliers, resource and product consumers, regulatory agencies, and other organizations that produce similar services or products.

Like the economists' notion of industry, an organization field usually highlights a category of similar organizations—for example, infrastructure construction projects—but also extends attention to other organizations providing crucial support or oversight. It allows us to treat as the focus of analysis a complex of diverse organizations operating in the same "small world"—organizations sharing the same or related institutional habits. "The notion of field connotes the existence of a community or organizations that partakes of a common meaning system and whose participants interact more frequently and fatefully with one another than with actors outside the field" (Scott 1994: 207–8).

As institutional systems, all organization fields contain actors—both individual and collective—who are supporting by varying amounts and types of capital—such as land, financial, social, and cultural—carry differing institutional logics, and are overseen by varying types of governance structures (Scott et al. 2000). Global megaprojects are a distinctive type of organization fields characterized by interactions among an extraordinarily diverse and shifting set of actors or stakeholders.

5.3.2 Multiple Levels

The examination of global megaprojects may be conducted at varying levels of analysis. For example, at the international level, Khagram (2004) chronicles the rise and fall of the construction of big dams, from its origins in the early twentith century in the United States, through its spread and eventual decline in the developing world. He parses the changes over times in stakeholders, institutional logics, and regulatory regimes in his rich institutional history. At a lower level, numerous studies examine project organizations conducting similar types of work within a given nation or region. For example, Jooste and colleagues (Jooste, Levitt, and Scott 2011; Jooste and Scott 2011) studied a sample of public–private partnership (PPP) construction programs, comparing field configurations in three areas: South Africa, the Province of British Columbia in Canada, and the Republic of Korea. They found varying program configurations involving differing sponsoring departments, company combinations and intermediaries, such as financial and legal advisers, auditors, advocacy groups, and consultants. More significantly, the approach allowed consideration of the broader political and societal environment affecting the conception and design of PPP programs. And we have many useful studies focusing on a single project organization as its work is affected by the surrounding support and control entities (for example, Mahalingam, Levitt, and Scott 2011; South, Levitt, and Dewulf 2015).

5.3.3 Distinctive Features of Global Megaprojects' Institutional Fields

As organization fields, global megaprojects exhibit a number of features which set them apart from other, less complex arenas.

5.3.3.1 A More Diverse Set of Participants

Megaprojects by their nature involve a diverse set of participants. The participants vary in terms of their professional roles: legislators, government agency executives, a range of private firms proving expertise from several planning disciplines, multiple engineering design disciplines, construction companies of multiple specialties, and their construction workers, who may be represented by up to fifteen separate craft-based unions in the United States.

During the twentieth century, governments or multilateral development agencies such as the World Bank or Asian Development Bank, typically took a leading role in financing megaprojects through the issuance and sale of government bonds. However, in the twenty-first century, governments worldwide are facing severe financial strictures so that many large infrastructure projects are being privately financed as long-term concessions of twenty-five to fifty years or even longer. This has brought a new set of financial participants into the megaprojects' fields, including infrastructure investment funds, and a variety of institutional investors who typically provide long-term debt for concession projects, such as pension funds, sovereign funds, family offices, and university endowments. Commercial banks provided megaproject debt in earlier times, but the stricter banking regulations that imposed higher capital reserves on banks worldwide based on their risk exposure have made it less attractive for them to lend money to long-term investments such as infrastructure concessions.

As projects proceed through the shaping phase into design and construction, a variety of NGOs and civic organizations will almost always be activated or even created to advocate for, or more often to oppose, some aspects of the project's scope, scale, and/or location, or even its *raison d'être*. Moreover, individuals with strong opinions regarding a given project can now disseminate their support for, or opposition to, aspects of a megaproject using both traditional and increasingly "viral" social media channels. In this sense, the entry of a megaproject into an existing organization field can transform the nature of the field, generating a very complex and heavily contested institutional field for the sponsors and managers of megaprojects to traverse.

Over the 30–50-year lifespan of a megaproject, local politics will often shift multiple times between local and national political parties that are more or less pro-development versus conservation, or pro-business versus pro-large government. Global geopolitics can change seismically as in the Arab Spring of the early 2000s; economic power can shift across continents as in the phenomenal economic rise of China during the 1990s and the fall of Europe's economic power following the 2007 financial crisis; and global demand for the commodities often associated with the inputs or outputs of megaprojects can rise or fall by orders of magnitude, as in the drastic fall in the price of crude oil, iron, copper, and gold in mid-2015 as China's economy declined abruptly from its decades-long, double-digit annual growth rate. Coping with all these risks poses huge governance challenges for global megaprojects, and can precipitously reshape their institutional fields.

5.3.3.2 *Varying Degrees of Local Embeddedness*

While some economic models assume that rational actors are unaffected by the social structures in which they are located, sociologists emphasize that all actors are embedded in and affected by concrete personal and social systems in which they operate (Granovetter 1985). However, particularly for global megaprojects, it is important to emphasize that the degree to which participants are embedded in the local context surrounding the project varies greatly. Defining "local embeddedness" as the "overall number of relationships and the level of interaction, coordination, or negotiation between an entrant" and other local entities involved in the project, (Orr and Levitt 2011: 185) document the substantial differences that exist among types of project participants. Based on interviews with more than fifty managers who had worked on global infrastructure projects, they found that general contractors exhibited the highest level of local embeddedness, while systems contractors, such as those who supply elevators in a building bioreactors for a water treatment system, exhibit lower levels. Developers and engineering, financial, or legal consultants show intermediate levels, but also greater variability depending on the nature of their services to the project.

Strategies for managing high levels of embeddedness vary from engaging in attempts to increase local knowledge (such as hiring locals) to decreasing the need for local knowledge (such as outsourcing to local contractors), to reducing the impact of a local knowledge deficit (buying political risk insurance, for example) (Orr and Levitt 2011).

5.3.3.3 *Long-Duration, Multiphase Project Life Cycle*

Megaprojects move through a predictable set of phases in their life cycle: shaping; design, and construction; startup and commissioning; operations and maintenance; and renovation, demolition, or recycling.

As Miller and Olleros (2000) point out, the project shaping phase is the crucible in which a megaproject is gestated and molded. During the project shaping phase, the lead stakeholder group promotes the project and shapes it through successive iterations to accommodate and/or overwhelm the economic, environmental, and social desires and constraints of other key stakeholders, including regulatory agencies, other legislators, and a variety of NGOs or community groups that become activated to support or oppose different versions of the project's scale, scope, and location. In most developed countries, the project is required to proceed through a lengthy environmental review process, which may also include a review of its social impacts. This phase can last from several years up to several decades. Projects like the Channel Tunnel from the United Kingdom to France, and the California High Speed Rail Project, were gestated over more than thirty years.

The proponents of a project during this phase typically include a group of local, state, and/or national politicians, a set of corporations that have an economic stake in the project's delivery or end use, one or more labor unions or trade associations whose members could benefit from the project, individuals or businesses that own real assets whose value would be enhanced by the project (such as the real estate tycoons who owned the orange orchards that would be irrigated by the proposed new aqueduct depicted in the movie, Chinatown), and multiple other individuals, media, and economically disinterested individuals who support the project for ideological reasons.

Projects sometimes advance through several iterations of the shaping phase, are abandoned by the original sponsors in the face of overwhelming opposition or a changed economic and political environment, and are then later rekindled by the same or new sponsors when conditions change. For example, satisfying the multiple state and federal regulatory agencies that had jurisdiction for environmental review of the Trans-Alaska Oil Pipeline System that was intended to ship crude oil from Prudhoe Bay on the North Slope of Alaska, to a marine terminal at the ice-free port of Valdez in the southern part of the state, made the project seem infeasible to both oil companies and regional politicians who supported this project during the 1960s. However, following the 1973 Arab oil embargo of the United States, oil prices rose dramatically and the national political mood shifted abruptly toward finding ways to address this "national petroleum emergency." Responding to the public outcry over gasoline scarcity and cost, the president and Congress of the United States took the unusual step of setting up an integrated environmental review process for this project by a single agency to simplify and obviate the tangle of legal and regulatory challenges that the project had previously faced. This made the project feasible to implement on a reasonable timescale, so a group of oil companies formed the Alyeska joint venture to deliver the project, five construction joint ventures were each contracted to deliver one segment of the pipeline, and this megaproject of enormous technical and logistical complexity moved ahead so rapidly that oil began flowing through the pipeline by 1977.

The shaping phase is arguably the most critical phase of a project and the most turbulent phase in terms of the development of its institutional field. The reason for this is that the conceptual planning and design decisions that are made during this phase of the project will typically lock in many aspects of what will be the final project configuration. Once the decision has been made by its proponents to commit more substantial investments to proceed with detailed design and construction, the steadily escalating investments by all parties in the agreed-upon scale, scope, and location, together with the incremental cost and time that would be involved in renegotiating and changing commitments and agreements that have been reached between the multiple stakeholders during this phase, make it increasingly unlikely that a project's fundamental shape will be significantly changed at the conclusion of the shaping phase.

Following the project-shaping phase, the level of investment in the project increases rapidly as detailed design, procurement of materials and components, and construction proceed, typically following an S-curve trajectory. At this phase, the project becomes very real to, and impactful upon, local communities. Megaprojects are large enough that they frequently drive local or even regional economic booms that create regional or even global scarcities of skilled labor and key commodities, components or construction equipment, and, in turn, drive up real estate and consumer prices for everything. In addition, they frequently generate significant amounts of vehicular traffic, noise, air pollution, pollution of waterways or groundwater, the importation of large numbers of construction workers, and all the "project camp followers" who can introduce alcohol abuse, drugs, prostitution, and other social ills that severely disrupt what were previously sleepy communities.

The operations and maintenance phase is the lengthiest phase of a megaproject's life cycle, and can extend for as long as 50–100 years. This phase is often the least challenging phase to manage. Nevertheless, governments worldwide have systematically undermaintained large infrastructure projects in favor of using government funds to launch more politically appealing new projects. When the old bridges literally collapse or the water system leaks so badly that it is beyond repair, local legislators then seek national assistance to build replacement projects in a crisis environment. Recent US examples include the clamor for federal assistance following the New Orleans flooding following levee collapses in the wake of hurricane Katrina, and the collapse of a bridge on an Interstate highway in Minnesota.

For infrastructure megaprojects such as water supply systems, bridges, or roads that charge tolls or fees to users, the level, rate of increase—or even very existence—of mandatory user fees can generate severe political challenges for the governmental or private project's owners and operators. New user fees and restrictions on groundwater pumping from the aquifer generated such an outcry from local urban water users and farmers, respectively, during the early operational phase of the Cochabamba water project in Bolivia, that it precipitated a mini-revolution regionally and ultimately a revolution that led to a new national government in the country.

In the final stage, when projects reach the end of their useful life for either technical or economic reasons, their assets must be renovated or demolished and their materials and components recycled to the extent feasible. This, too, can be a contentious process when powerful stakeholders disagree on the need or desirability of various options for expansion or renovation vs. demolition, as in the case of some older urban freeways in cities like San Francisco and Brooklyn. Because of lax oversight, companies often fail to take responsibility for clean-up or restoration activities. The phases identified for the life-course of megaprojects is reflected in a matching fragmentation of the supply chain that delivers them. As Lawrence and Lorsch (1967) explain, such fragmentation leads to a differentiation in skills, and more importantly, to a differentiation in goals. The separate firms or agencies that plan megaprojects, design them, build them, and operate them, develop local subgoals that increasingly diverge from those of the long-terms sponsors, investors, and users.

Flyvbjerg and his colleagues (2002; 2003) have persuasively argued and documented that megaproject planners—in explicit or implicit collusion with sponsoring agencies and firms—systematically underestimate the cost and time required to develop mega-projects and overestimate the demand for them. In a similar vein, Levitt et al. (1980) and Henisz et al. (2012) argue that design firms in a traditional design–bid–build mega-project delivery process have strong incentives to overdesign facilities, both to reduce the design effort required and to protect themselves against liability from failures. And the economic incentive for fixed price, competitively bid contractors in this delivery process is to bid just low enough to be selected, build at the lowest cost that can satisfy the specifications, and then seek additional compensation by negotiating change orders based on any perceived or defensible change, inconsistency, or incompleteness of the project design. This "broken agency" across project phases, detailed in Henisz et al. (2012) gravely complicates the management of megaprojects and can heavily impact their outcomes.

Global megaprojects thus have a very long life cycle, often exceeding the lives of companies, and almost always exceeding the tenure of particular legislators or political parties. They include a diverse set of participants with a variety of skills, different and frequently conflicting goals, different institutions, and dynamic levels of involvement. This creates a set of risks and associated management challenges for megaprojects that are very difficult to anticipate, even with the most diligent and thorough risk analysis.

5.3.3.4 *Shifting of Anchor Tenant*

As just described, major infrastructure projects pass through multiple life-cycle phases in which a variety of public, private, non-profit, and civic participants are activated and enter the project's institutional field, while others are deactivated and exit the field. At the same time, the central and most influential player in the institutional field that

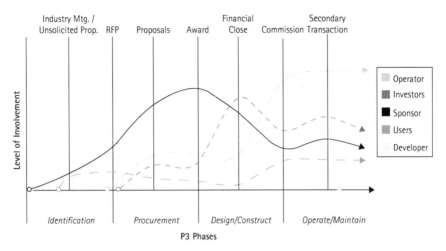

FIGURE 5.1 Involvement level of key actors in SR91X at critical events over the course of development.

(From South et al. 2015.)

primarily shapes the institutional logic and direction of the project—analogous to a stakeholder network's "anchor tenant" (Padgett and Powell 2012)—also changes by project phase.

For example, in a stakeholder network analysis of the California State Route 91 (SR91X) public–private infrastructure concession project, South et al. (2015) found that the levels of participation by key stakeholders in the project's institutional field rose and fell across project phases, as shown in Figure 5.1.

> As specific stakeholders interacted within the PPP and with each other, and in consequence with the critical events, the level of involvement changed dramatically. In the SR91X case, Caltrans took a dominant position at the beginning of the project, but upon concluding [the] award they became less involved with the PPP.
>
> [The California Private Transportation Company (CPTC)—a developer SPV consortium of three corporate organizations, including two US construction firms and one European toll-road operator] (and their parallel competition) were involved prior to the official RFP, and continued to participate as SR91X developed. As a result of a concession award to CPTC, the SPVs competition quickly diminished, but CPTC continued to develop a dominant place in the PPP. As financial close was achieved, CPTC had become the most involved stakeholder in SR91X. Then as the project was commissioned and early operations commenced, the majority ownership in the SPV consorti[um] recognized that the business model was not consistent with their operations. Daniel Hanson, a private executive closely involved with SR91X, noted, "It was lots of work, lots of friggin politics, so it didn't make sense to continue with equity in PPPs." Having derisked SR91X of construction and early development risks, CPTC sought opportunity to sell their equity in the concession. After an unsuccessful sale attempt to a newly formed nonprofit organization (established for the purpose of privately owning and managing SR91X), CPTC eventually

made an agreement with Orange County Transportation Agency (OCTA) to buy out their equity in the agreement. [OCTA] effectually become the new concessionaire. Although OCTA was interested in maintaining the existing business model and contracted with the previous SPV's operations equity partner who retained (and later expanded) their existing operations staff while OCTA dedicated less than two full-time equivalents to manage the asset. (South et al. 2015)

5.4 Responding to Megaprojects' Institutional Challenges: Mixing and Matching Governance Mechanisms

Global megaprojects are exceptionally challenging to manage, as has beeb explained. Their large and complex spatial and technical scope, their macroeconomic importance to regions and countries, their potential incorporation of novel embedded technologies, and their extended duration and institutionally diverse participants, all create huge coordination challenges. The attendant economic and political risks arising from these sources of managerial complexity have proven impossible to manage using strictly contractual means. As Williamson (1979) argues, the propagation of "contingent claims" clauses, which get incorporated into megaprojects' contracts in an attempt by lawyers to address every newly discovered or newly imagined risk, make the resulting multivolume contracts unwieldy and costly to create, negotiate, and administer. So, megaprojects inevitably incur huge claims and costly arbitration and litigation that can extend for decades. The current project to enlarge the Panama Canal is an excellent example of this tendency.

Fortunately, we have found that successful megaproject managers can and do augment their projects' necessarily incomplete contracts based on regulatory mechanisms, which have proven to be unable to fully address the management challenges of delivering global megaprojects, with "relational governance" mechanisms based on the other two institutional pillars: normative and cultural–cognitive elements. The final section of this chapter describes and explains some of the relational governance mechanisms that managers can employ to augment the contractual/legal governance of global megaprojects. A more detailed coverage of these mechanisms can be found in Henisz et al. (2012).

5.4.1 Enhanced Legal–Contractual Governance Mechanisms

Clauses can be embedded in megaprojects' contracts that "creat[e] a significant, long-term economic stake for the most influential counterparties—the 'selectorate' (Mesquita et al. 1999)—[to] align their interests" (Henisz et al. 2012). These include local hiring quotas, local procurement set-asides or investment in the project by local governments, and local pension funds or sovereign funds. By better aligning the interest of participants or incorporating those of potential project opponents, such clauses can reduce the tendency toward conflict or opposition. Similarly, if a multi-lateral bank, such as the World Bank or the Asian Development Bank, is brought in as a grantor or lender to the project, both the local government or private client and contractor must weigh the "shadow of the future"—the risk to their reputations that could potentially limit future business opportunities—when considering whether and how to deal with political, economic, geological, social, or other perceived changes in the project context that could be the basis for opportunistic claims or contractual renegotiations.

A second way to augment traditional contracts to align the interests of key members of the internal project delivery team is to set them up as a framework of alliance contracts. In the approach, the overall project management entity employs clauses in its contracts with supply chain partners that recreate many key elements of a uni-fied hierarchy (Stinchcombe 1986). This "virtually integrates" the geographically and functionally fragmented construction industry supply chain to reconstitute the proj-ect as a single "macrofirm" (Dioguardi 1983) or "quasi-firm" (Eccles 1981) in which the contractual terms attempt to create a framework in which all participants have more or less shared economic objectives (Gunnarson and Levitt 1982). This approach was employed in some North Sea oil projects, and was subsequently used to build Heathrow Terminal 5 (Gil 2009).

Sutter Health—a large US healthcare provider—is now using this form of contract to develop most of its new or refurbished multi-billion-dollar hospitals on the US West Coast, and the approach is gaining traction among other UK, US, and Australian cli-ents for delivering large, complex megaprojects. All the key parties to these so-called Integrated Project Delivery (IPD) contracts—the multiple design firms, the prime or general contractor, and the major specialty construction firms—sign a single integrated form of agreement (IFOA) in which they agree that each party's direct costs will be reim-bursed, liability claims against each other will be waived, and the parties' home office overhead costs and profits will be earned based on the degree to which a set of high-level project criteria and goals of the client are met, including budget, but also schedule, qual-ity, and other more subjective metrics.

However, even these legal mechanisms to augment project contracts can break down in the face of significant changes in any of the key project contextual dimensions, espe-cially when the potential fiscal or economic impact of changes reaches the level at which it poses significant political or business career risks to individuals—or profitably and even survival risks to their organizations—on either side of the contract. So how is it that global megaprojects are often successfully completed in spite of these challenges? We argue that successful clients and managers of project delivery teams employ addi-tional, relational governance mechanisms built on normative and cultural–cognitive institutions to encourage cooperative behavior and discourage opportunism by all par-ties in global megaprojects.

5.4.2 Normative and Cognitive–Cultural Governance Mechanisms

Normative and cognitive-cultural megaproject project governance mechanisms build on sociological and psychological processes that have by now been well studied and are broadly accepted. Social exchange in which parties exchange favors for obligations (Blau 1964; Homans 1958) and identity theory in which people augment or subsume their existing identities with identities based on perceived belongingness to new groups or communities (Armstrong 2002; Scott and Lane 2000) are two examples of this.

5.4.2.1 *Shared Identity Based on an Exciting Project Vision*

Managers of megaprojects have the opportunity to describe and continuously espouse the goals of their projects in ways that engage project participants' imaginations and passions. Unlike their peers in manufacturing, workers on construction projects build large and enduring "monuments" to their labor that offer a visible and "concrete" meaning for the work they do, and that they can proudly show off to their friends and families. Research by Borcherding (1972) on the motivation of construction workers illustrated this dramatically. Electrical workers on two very similar large coal-fired power plant megaprojects in the Four Corners area of the Southwestern United States were asked what they were doing by a researcher. A worker on the first project explained how he was connecting cables from a particular safety system to a gauge on a control panel. An electrical worker doing a virtually identical task on the second project said to the researcher: "I am lighting up the Southwestern United States!"

Fligstein (2001: 106, 112) points out that some skillful individuals can transform organization fields by "providing actors with collective identities as motives for action"—to "create new systems of meaning" that allow disparate groups to come together in the pursuit of goals that appeal to large numbers—to "find reasons to cooperate." Many megaprojects, especially social infrastructure projects such as hospitals or sports stadiums, and civil infrastructure projects such as water supply, roads, or power projects, produce not only concrete monuments to the labors of their participants, but also generate highly visible social economic or cultural benefits. Skillful managers can engage the imaginations and passions of workers and managers contributing to these benefits by making the project goals highly visible and by continuously reminding workers of the importance and societal value of the project in which they are engaged.

5.4.2.2 *Partnering and Colocation of Key Participants*

Several public and private organizations that are required by their charters or policies to employ traditional fixed-price, competitive bid contracting approaches attempt to use early engagement of participants in social settings that build trust to enhance their future cooperativeness. A "ropes course," with physical obstacles—such as high, smooth walls—that requires cooperation among participants for any individual to traverse them, is one example of this kind of trust-building exercise in which some megaproject clients engage. Early, all-hands, planning meetings in which the participants begin to define the conceptual design of the project collectively using teams made up of representatives from the client and multiple delivery firms are another example of a mechanism that can build trust and develop shared project identity. Managers will often make legally nonbinding pledges to one another in these settings to escalate issues for resolution by senior managers, for whom the shadow of the future may be more salient than the outcome of the current project. These and other "partnering" mechanisms that attempt to build shared project identity and trust between parties can help to advance project execution, but may break down in the face of changes that impact significantly on the project's perceived scope or schedule and the resulting cost implications for the various parties.

5.4.2.3 *Procedural Justice*

Research on procedural justice versus distributive justice has demonstrated that following "fair processes" in making controversial and highly contested decisions of all kinds will result in participants having a higher sense of ownership of the ultimate decision and a greater willingness to accept even outcomes that are suboptimal for them (Kim and Mauborgne 1991). The three elements that generate perceptions of procedural justice are: early *engagement of participants* in presenting and debating their points of view; clear and rational *explanation of the criteria and processes* used to make the final decision; and *setting out clear expectations* for what will occur next. All contribute to a sense of procedural justice and increase the level of cooperation by involved parties. When prior assumptions about the context of a project change, the extent to which managers employ processes that are perceived to be fair can significantly affect the degree of cooperation by and among other megaproject participants.

5.4.2.4 *Building a Strong Project Culture*

There is a large body of literature demonstrating that organization culture is set by the vision of organizational leaders as substantiated in their actions (Selznick 1957). Managers who assert that they care about the safety of workers on megaprojects above everything else, but focus only on cost and schedule when they visit projects that have recently experienced accidents, expose themselves as hypocritical and inauthentic. Successful megaproject managers immerse themselves in the local environments and the cultures of the various project participants and self-consciously act in ways that demonstrate sensitivity to the significant institutional differences among project participants. This allows them to avoid making a major cross-cultural *faux pas*, and to build bridges between their project's multiple sets of cultures and institutions. The Swedish manager of a successful major infrastructure project in Afghanistan (before the Russian occupation) wrote a book on the history and culture of Afghanistan at the end of the project. Other megaproject managers who have had success have studied the histories and religious texts of key groups on their projects and used this institutional contextual knowledge to govern their everyday practices.

5.5 Conclusions

Megaprojects pose political, institutional, macroeconomic, and fiscal challenges that create "wicked" problems for managers. Traditional legal–contractual governance mechanisms almost always break down in the face of the risks that these challenges create over their extended durations. We have identified some of the unique challenges of global megaprojects for which the cross-institutional differences create particular challenges. At the same time, we have shown how the three pillars of institutions can be used to shape governance mechanisms that render the legal–contractual mechanisms more supportive of long-term cooperation by the project's diverse participants, and to augment the legal–contractual mechanisms with relational contracting mechanisms sculpted from the normative and cognitive cultural pillars of institutions.

Readers interested in a more detailed description of the three pillars of institutions described in this chapter should refer to Scott (2014), and managers interested in harnessing these pillars of institutions to augment traditional governance approaches for global megaprojects can find additional detail and references about the bases and application of these mechanisms in Henisz et al. (2012).

References

Armstrong, E. A. (2002). *Forging Gay Identities: Organizing Sexuality in San Francisco, 1950–1994.* Chicago: University of Chicago Press.

Blau, P. M. (1964) *Exchange and Power in Social Life.* New York: Wiley.

Borcherding, J. D. (1972). *An Exploratory Study of Attitudes that Affect Human Resources in Building and Industrial Construction.* PhD dissertation, Department of Civil Engineering, Stanford University.

Burgess, W. (1902). *Political Science and Comparative Constitutional Law.* Boston, MA: Ginn.

Davis, K. (1949). *Human Society.* New York: Macmillan.

DiMaggio, P. and Powell, W. W. (1983). "The iron cage revisited: Collective rationality and institutional isomorphism in organizational fields," *American Sociological Review*, 48(2): 147–60.

Dioguardi, G. (1983). "Macrofirms: Construction firms for the computer age," *Journal of Construction Engineering and Management*, 109(1): 13–24.

Durkheim, E. (1912). *The Elementary Forms of the Religious Life.* New York: Collier.

Durkheim, E. (1961). *Moral Education: A Study in the Theory and Application of the Sociology of Education.* Glencoe, IL: Free Press of Glencoe.

Eccles, R. G. (1981). "The quasi-firm in the construction industry," *Journal of Economic Behavior and Organization*, 94 (Supplement): s17–s51.

Fligstein, N. (2001). "Social skill and the theory of fields," *Sociological Theory*, 19(2): 105–25.

Flyvbjerg, B., Bruzelius, N., and Rothengatter, W. (2003). *Megaprojects and Risk: An Anatomy of Ambition.* Cambridge: Cambridge University Press.

Flyvbjerg, B., Holm, M. S., and Buhl, S. (2002). "Underestimating costs in public works projects: Error or lie?" *Journal of the American Planning Association*, 68(3): 279–95.

Friedland, R. and Alford, R. R. (1991). "Bringing society back in: Symbols, practices and institutional contradictions," in W. W. Powell and P. J. DiMaggio (eds.), *The New Institutionalism in Organizational Analysis*. Chicago, IL: University of Chicago Press, pp. 232–63.

Geertz, C. (1973). "The Impact of the Concept of Culture on the Concept of Man," in *The Interpretation of Cultures*. New York: Basic Books, pp. 39–40.

Giddens, A. (1979). *Central Problems in Social Ttheory: Action, Structure, and Contradiction in Social Analysis*, Vol. 241. Berkeley, CA: University of California Press.

Gil, N. (2009). "Developing cooperative project client–supplier relationships: How much to expect from relational contracts," *California Management Review*, 51(2): 144–69.

Granovetter, M. (1985). "Economic action and social structure: The problem of embeddedness," *American Journal of Sociology*, 91: 481–510.

Gunnarson, S. and Levitt, R. E. (1982). "Is a building construction project a hierarchy or a market," *Proceedings of the Seventh INTERNET Congress, Copenhagen, Denmark*, 521–9.

Henisz, W. J., Levitt, R. E., and Scott, W. R. (2012). "Toward a unified theory of project governance: economic, sociological and psychological supports for relational contracting," *Engineering Project Organization Journal*, 2(1–2): 37–55.

Hofstede, G. (1984). *Culture's Consequences: International Differences in Work-Related Values*. Beverly Hills, CA: Sage.

Homans, G. (1958). "Social behavior as exchange," *American Journal of Sociology*, 63(6): 597–606.

Khagram, S. (2004). *Dams and Development: Transnational Struggles for Water and Power*. Ithaca, NY: Cornell University Press.

Jooste, S. F. and Scott, W. R. (2011). "Organizations enabling public–private partnerships: An organization field approach," in W. R. Scott, R. E. Levitt, and R. J. Orr (eds.), *Global Projects: Institutional and Political Challenges*. Cambridge University Press, pp. 377–402.

Jooste, S. F., Levitt, R., and Scott, D. (2011). "Beyond 'one size fits all': How local conditions shape PPP-enabling field development," *Engineering Project Organization Journal*, 1(1): 11–25.

Kim, W. C. and Mauborgne, R. A. (1991). "Implementing global strategies: The role of procedural justice," *Strategic Management Journal*, 12(S1): 125–43.

Kroeber, A. L. and Kluckhohn, C. (1952). "Culture: A critical review of concepts and definitions," *Papers: Peabody Museum of Archaeology and Ethnology, Harvard University*.

Lawrence, P. R. and Lorsch, J. W. (1967). *Organization and Environment: Managing Differentiation and Integration*. Boston: Graduate School of Business Administration, Harvard University.

Lessard, D., Sakhrani, V., and Miller, R. (2014). "House of Project Complexity: Understanding Complexity in Large Infrastructure Projects," *Engineering Project Organization Journal*, 4(4): 170–92.

Levitt, R. E. (2015). "An extended framework for coordinating interdependent tasks in a project or functional ecosystem," *Stanford University Global Projects Center Working Paper*.

Levitt, R. E., Logcher, R. D., and Ashley, D. B. (1980). "Allocating risk and incentive in construction," *Journal of the Construction Division*, 106(3): 297–305.

Levitt, R. E., Thomsen, J., Christiansen, T. R., Kunz, J. C., Jin, Y., and Nass, C. (1999). "Simulating project work processes and organizations: Toward a micro-contingency theory of organizational design." *Management Science* 45(11): 1479–95.

Lewin, K. (1951). *Field Theory in Social Science*. New York: Harper.

Mahalinam, A., Levitt, R. E., and Scott, W. R. (2011). "Rules versus results: Sources and resolution of institutional conflicts on Indian metro railway projects." In W. R. Scott, R. E. Levitt, and R. J. Orr (eds.), *Global Projects: Institutional and Political Challenges*. Cambridge: Cambridge University Press, pp. 113–34.

March, J. G. and Olsen, J. P. (2010). *Rediscovering Institutions*. New York: Simon and Schuster.

McAdam, D., Boudet, H. S., Davis, J., Orr, R. J., Scott, W.R., and Levitt, R. E. (2010). "'Site fights': Explaining opposition to pipeline projects in the developing world," *Sociological Forum*, 25(3): 410–27.

Mesquita, B. B. D., Morrow, J. D., Siverson, R. M., and Smith, A. (1999). "Policy failure and political survival: The contribution of political institutions," *Journal of Conflict Resolution*, 43(2): 147–61.

Miller, R. and Olleros, X. (2000). "Project shaping as a competitive advantage," in R. Miller and D. R. Lessard (eds.), *The Strategic Management of Large Engineering Projects: Shaping Institutions, Risks, and Governance*. Cambridge, MA: MIT Press.

Moe, T. M. (1984). "The new economics of organization," *American Journal of Political Science*, 28: 739–77.

North, D. C. (1990). *Institutions, Institutional Change and Economic Performance*. Cambridge: Cambridge University Press.

Orr, R. J. and Levitt, R. E. (2011). "Local embeddedness of firms and strategies for dealing with uncertainty in global projects," in W. R. Scott, R. E. Levitt, and R. J. Orr (eds.), *Global Projects: Institutional and Political Challenges*. Cambridge: Cambridge University Press, pp. 183–246.

Padgett, J. F., and Powell, W. W. (2012). *The Emergence of Organizations and Markets*. Princeton, NJ: Princeton University Press.

Perrow, C. (1984). *Normal Accidents: Living with High-Risk Technologies*. New York: Basic Books.

Roland, G. (2004). "Understanding institutional change: Fast-moving and slow-moving institutions," *Sudies in Comparative International Development*, 4: 109–31.

Scott, W. R. (1994). "Conceptualizing organizational fields: Linking organizations and societal systems," in H.-U. Derlien, U. Gerhardt, and F. W. Scharpf (eds.), *Systemrationalitat und Partialinteresse*. Baden-Baden: Nomos Verlagsgesellschaft, pp. 203–21.

Scott, W. R. (2013). *Institutions and Organizations: Ideas, Interests, and Identities*, 4th edn. Los Angeles, CA: Sage.

Scott, S. G. and Lane, V. R. (2000). "A stakeholder approach to organizational identity," *Academy of Management Review*, 25(1): 43–62.

Scott, W. R., Ruef, M., Mendel, P. J., and Caronna, C. A. (2000). *Institutional Change and Healthcare Organizations: From Professional Dominance to Managed Care*. Chicago, IL: University of Chicago Press.

Selznick, P. (1957). *Leadership in Administration*. New York: Harper and Row.

Selznick, P. (1992). *The Moral Commonwealth: Social Theory and the Promise of Community*. Berkeley: University of California Press.

Shank, R. C. and Abelson, R. P. (1977). *Scripts, Plans, Goals, and Understanding: An Inquiry into Human Knowledge Structures*. Hillsdale, NJ: Lawrence Erlbaum.

Simon, H. A. (1962). "The architecture of complexity," *Proceedings of the American Philosophical Society*, 106: 467–82.

Stinchcombe, A. L. (1986). "Contracts as hierarchical documents," in A. L. Stinchcombe and C. A. Heimer (eds), *Organizational Theory and Project Management: Administering Uncertainty in Norwegian Offshore Oil*. Oxford: Oxford University Press, pp. 121–71.

South, A. J., Levitt, R. E., and Dewulf, G. P. M. R. (2015). "Dynamic stakeholder networks and the governance of PPPs," *Proceedings of the 2nd International Conference on Public–Private Partnerships*, Austin, Texas, 26–29 May 2015.

Swidler, A. (1986). "Culture in action: Symbols and strategies," *American Sociological Review*, 51: 273–86.

Thompson, J. (1967). *Organizations in Action*. New York: McGraw-Hill.

Williamson, O. E. (1979). "Transaction-cost economics: The governance of contractual relations," *Journal of Law and Economics*, 22: 233–61.

CHAPTER 6

···

MEGAPROJECT DECISION MAKING AND MANAGEMENT

Ethical and Political Issues

···

BERT VAN WEE AND HUGO PRIEMUS

6.1 INTRODUCTION

TRANSPORT megaprojects have a huge impact on society. Not only do they cost a lot; they also have a big impact on accessibility, the landscape and the environment, and often on social cohesion and the spatial distribution of jobs, housing units, and other land uses. In addition, spending large sums of money on megaprojects results in high opportunity costs—the money could have been allocated to other, smaller projects (or to reducing government deficits). Decision making, contracting, the management of the building process, and the operation of the megaproject are therefore of high societal relevance. An important question therefore is how to provide decision makers with relevant input. Good projects are not only effective (they do what they should do) and efficient (often expressed as cost-effective), but they should also be fair. In many Western countries, megaprojects are evaluated *ex ante*, making use of cost–benefit analysis (CBA) (Hayashi and Morisugi 2000; Bristow and Nellthorp 2000; Grant-Muller et al. 2001). CBA covers efficiency and effectiveness (though effectiveness only implicitly) but not fairness, but it was never designed to do this. But that implies that if ethical issues are at stake a CBA alone is not sufficient in preparing decision making.

Ethical issues are not only related to the effects of a *specific* megaproject but also at a higher level, examples being feelings of fairness related to the distribution of expenditures regarding infrastructure for different regions; in many countries people think that there should be a balance in these expenditures.

Nevertheless, the ethical issues related to transport, transport infrastructure in general, and transport megaprojects in particular, have not been widely debated in the academic literature, although in recent years the attention paid to the topic has increased (for example, Martens 2006; Van Wee 2011; Harrison and Shepherd 2014). This chapter discusses these ethical issues insofar as they are important for the decision-making process and management of megaprojects. More specifically we discuss:

- Ethical aspects of the impacts of megaprojects on society.
- The ethics of doing research into the pros and cons of megaprojects.
- The quality of estimates of the costs and benefits of megaprojects.
- The democratic quality of the decision-making process.

These four topics are discussed in the next four sections respectively. The final section (6.6) explores avenues for future research and decision-making procedures to improve current weaknesses in ethics and political quality. This chapter focuses on *transport* megaprojects, but much of its content also applies to other types of megaproject. In what follows, the terms "megaprojects" and "infrastructure" refer to transport megaprojects and transport infrastructure.

6.2 ETHICAL ASPECTS OF THE IMPACTS OF MEGAPROJECTS ON SOCIETY

It is beyond the scope of this chapter to present a more or less complete overview of the (potential) ethically relevant impact of megaprojects. For a more comprehensive discussion we refer to Van Wee (2011). Here we limit ourselves to the main ethical aspects of megaprojects. These relate to:

- Distribution effects (for example, across regions, income groups), and via alternative resource allocations.
- Impacts on regional cohesion.
- Pricing.
- Discounting.
- The importance of irreversible effects on nature and the environment; these are crucial, because megaprojects often have a lifetime of many decades, and possibly more than a century.

Distribution effects have no impact on the overall results of a CBA and generally are at best reported. They can nevertheless be relevant for both society and politicians. For example, citizens and politicians generally prefer a relatively equal distribution of unemployment, income, access to opportunities, and so forth, and politicians are often willing to pay for a more equal distribution. The so-called Dutch Zuiderzeelijn—a potential new rail line connecting the sparsely populated and economically underperforming north of the Netherlands to the densely populated economically successful western part of the country (the Randstad)—was proposed partly to reduce economic inequalities. Reports underpinning the CBA showed that building the line could indeed result in additional jobs in the north, but at the cost of the eastern part of the country—a region that also underperforms economically—rather than the Randstad.

Of course, all large infrastructure projects can have distribution effects, but these are most likely to occur with megaprojects. Such projects can have relatively important effects on accessibility levels at a larger spatial scale. In addition to the impact on accessibility via changes in travel times (or Generalized Transport Costs; GTC), such projects can induce land-use changes: for example, they can make areas more attractive because of improved accessibility. If income levels vary between regions, megaprojects may, due to changes in accessibility and related economic effects (mainly redistribution of jobs), also have an impact on the distribution of income levels across regions.

The distribution effects of megaprojects are also indirectly relevant via the impacts on the selection of transport infrastructure projects to be made by politicians. Ministries of Transport generally have more or less fixed budgets. Megaprojects cost a lot of money—money that could have been spent on alternative, smaller projects—and it is very likely that the impact on regions or income groups of those alternative projects are not the same as those resulting from megaprojects. If those projects had not been built, the government deficit could have been reduced, or alternative governmental expenditures could have been made (so called "opportunity costs"). For most of the 1990s in the Netherlands the construction of two prestigious rail lines—the High-Speed Rail Line connecting Amsterdam via Rotterdam to Antwerp, Brussels and Paris, and the Betuweroute, a dedicated rail freight line connecting Rotterdam harbour to the German Ruhr area—had such an important claim on the budget for new infrastructure that less money was available for other projects.

Cohesion effects at the regional level can be politically important, at least at the EU level. Cohesion reasons are often used to legitimize EU infrastructure expenditures (Canaleta et al. 2002). Infrastructure can integrate economically less well performing regions such as southern Italy to wider economies. The Öresundsbrug between Denmark and Sweden and the Channel Tunnel between the United Kingdom and France aim to contribute to the integration of economies on both sides of the connection. The cohesion effects of megaprojects result from improvements in accessibility. These are again more obvious for megaprojects than are smaller transport infrastructure projects; megaprojects often improve connections between regions. In theory, improved accessibility can reduce barriers for interaction and consequently improve cohesion.

Pricing effects are a third ethically important topic. The pricing of units, such as travel times and emissions, are important for all transport infrastructure projects. We see no specific reason why these should be more important for megaprojects, so this relates to a more general discussion. A first potential ethical topic is the monetary valuation of travel-time changes. Most megaprojects aim to reduce travel times. An important question, therefore, is how these changes can be valued. The concept of the Value of Time (VOT) was developed for this reason. People with higher incomes have a higher VOT.

Introducing a toll on a motorway can result in benefits for a relatively small group of high-income people at the cost of a larger group of lower income people: for high-income people the travel-time savings due to a reduction in congestion are very valuable, but low-income people adapt their travel behavior (changing routes, mode of transport, or reducing travel). People with high incomes therefore have per person a higher impact on the outcomes of a CBA than people with a lower income (Mackie et al. 2003). In other words, decision making based on a welfare perspective (how to maximize welfare over a region or country) conflicts with the democratic principle of "one man one vote." To overcome this "problem" the so-called "equity value of time" was introduced in several countries, such as the United States. Its value is based on the VOT of people with an average income (Morisugi and Hayashi 2000, cited in Martens 2006).

A next potential problem with the calculation of welfare effects results from the CBA assumption that there is a linear relation between welfare and income. However, it seems plausible to assume that the increase in welfare that comes with a given income increase decreases the higher the income is. An increase in monthly income of €200 probably is of more importance for a person earning €1,000 per month than for a person earning €10,000 per month.

Thirdly, transport infrastructure can have an impact on safety levels. How should these be valued? Common practice is to value these based on the so called Value of a Statistical Life (VSL, VOSL) (see De Blaeij et al. 2003), based on the Willingness to Pay (WTP) of the traveler. A potential ethical problem is that the VOSL is higher for high-income groups than for low-income groups, raising equal "democratic" problems as in case of the VOT. Another problem is that in health economics decisions are often based on the costs per Quality Adjusted Life Year (QALY), which decreases with age, unlike the WTP-based VOSL which peaks at about the age of 40 (Shepard and Zeckhauser 1984). A study by Johansson-Stenman and Martinsson (2008) is an illustration of the fact that people do have ethical preferences with respect to safety. Their research on the ethical preferences of people of the value of life showed a decreasing value for older people and a lower value for car drivers than for pedestrians. (For a further discussion of the ethical aspects of valuing safety and risks see Van Wee and Rietveld 2013.)

Discounting is related to the fact that people value a certain amount of money now over the same amount of money in the future, even when corrected for inflation. In CBAs, future costs and benefits are discounted to express these in the units of a base year. The higher the discount rate and the further in the future costs and benefits are made, the less their value is expressed in the units of a base year. The importance of setting the discount rate is even more important for megaprojects than for smaller transport infrastructure projects, because megaprojects probably have more and stronger long-term effects than do smaller projects. One can think of related land-use effects, but also the impact on future CO_2 emissions may be relevant if megaprojects result in a substantial modal shift effect of large volumes of induced demand.

Irreversible or irreplaceable effects can easily occur in case of megaprojects because of their impacts on nature and the landscape. For example, several animal species cannot cross motorways or railway lines, reducing the size of their habitat, as a result of which they may not be able to survive. Of course, one can deconstruct such projects, but this very seldom happens. Van Wee (2011: 35–7) discusses this topic:

> ... some things are replaceable, others are not, and so irreplaceable things may be valued higher than replaceable things (Morton 1991). A mainstream economist supporting the welfare maximizing paradigm could argue that this distinction is not relevant: if things are irreplaceable and are valued positively, the fact that they are irreplaceable is expressed in the willingness to pay of consumers, or the values of decision makers. But let us link the concept of irreplaceable things to democracy in the sense of majority voting. Suppose in a country there is a debate about giving up an irreplaceable nature area to build a new motorway. For decades, a majority has voted against building the motorway. But after a certain election, 51% of members of parliament support the decision to build the motorway. Would it then matter if the nature area were to be an irreplaceable thing? One could argue that the choice to build the motorway is made democratically. But what if there is a fair chance that after (one of the) next election(s) a majority would regret the decision? From a longer-term perspective, one could also argue that it matters that the nature area is an irreplaceable thing.

6.3 THE ETHICS OF DOING RESEARCH INTO THE PROS AND CONS OF MEGAPROJECTS

In Western democracies, ministers can propose megaprojects for many reasons. Parliament, and preferably also the wider public, should be informed adequately and in time (see also Section 6.5). In many countries, misleading parliament—for example, by providing manipulated *ex ante* estimates of project alternatives—is considered to be a political sin or even unlawful. Ministers can even be forced to resign if they do not adequately inform parliament.

The role of a CBA is to support the decision making regarding megaprojects. But CBAs of megaprojects and studies that provide input for CBAs, such as travel demand forecasts, are often funded and supervised by one or multiple actors having a stake in the outcomes, such as civil servants acting in the interests of a minister. This raises questions about the independence of the CBA and related research. Of course, for a politician having an interest in the outcomes of research it is tempting to influence the researchers, even though providing biased information to parliament or the local/regional equivalents is considered unacceptable by both parliament and the general public. In addition, it can be tempting for researchers to adapt their results if they are placed under pressure. The Betuweroute, mentioned previously, is an important example: neither the demand forecasts nor the cost estimates were neutral, and they had to be adapted several times (Priemus 2005). Dissatisfaction led to the implementation of CBA guidelines for large national transport infrastructure projects (Eijgenraam et al. 1999).

However, hardly any research has been carried out studying the ethics of carrying out research. This section discusses the ethics of doing research into the pros and cons of megaprojects. It is based on a study of Van Wee and Molin (2012) (see Van Wee 2011 for a preliminary version). They interviewed eight Dutch researchers doing CBA and CBA-related research for large transport infrastructure projects (megaprojects and other large projects), and formulated fifty-four propositions based on those interviews. Next they sent the propositions to the interviewees and other researchers in the Dutch CBA community to score them on a seven-point Likert scale ranging from –3 (completely disagree) to +3 (fully agree) (or 9: not applicable). Table 6.1 presents the scores on

Table 6.1 Scores on statements related to the relationship between the researcher and client

	Completely disagree						Fully agree			
	-3	-2	-1	0	1	2	3	9	average	SD
A higher level of independence results in fewer assignments.	4	2	7	4	2	3	3	3	-0.2	1.9
Regions* have the tendency to ascribe overly positive scenarios in the *ex ante* evaluation of infrastructure projects.	0	2	1	2	4	11	4	4	1.4	1.4
Researchers sometimes act according to the tendency of regions, using overly positive scenarios for the *ex ante* evaluation of infrastructure projects.	1	3	3	5	7	5	1	3	0.3	1.5
Sometimes research results are adapted to make the outcomes more favorable for policy.	2	8	3	4	6	1	2	2	-0.4	1.7
In the Netherlands researchers hardly ever adapt calculations to support the results the client wishes to see.	1	7	7	5	4	1	1	2	-0.6	1.4
In the case of *ex ante* evaluations (such as CBAs), governmental bodies want to influence results by prescribing scenarios	1	0	4	3	7	7	2	4	0.8	1.5

(continued)

Table 6.1 Continued

	Completely disagree							Fully agree		
In the case of infrastructure projects the client often wants to influence the results.	0	1	3	2	12	7	1	2	0.9	1.2
Some CBAs are kept "low profile" because the client has no interest in disseminating the results.	0	2	1	5	5	7	6	2	1.2	1.5
A researcher can accept the points of departure of the client, even if he would prefer to make other choices, as long as he makes this explicit.	0	3	3	2	6	6	6	2	1.0	1.7
If research includes making an inventory of potential solutions, and one of the solutions is a solution the client does not want included, it is unacceptable to delete it.	0	0	1	3	4	10	8	2	1.8	1.1
I sometimes adapt formulations to the clients' wishes.	3	3	1	3	14	2	2	0	0.3	1.7
I have stopped an assignment for ethical reasons.	13	5	0	1	1	1	2	5	-1.7	2.0
I have threatened to stop an assignment for ethical reasons, as a result of which the client adapted his position.	9	4	1	2	2	2	3	5	-0.9	2.3
I accept that governmental bodies may prescribe scenarios which may influence results.	3	3	3	6	6	2	2	3	-0.1	1.8

* Regions can be provinces or regional sections of the Dutch road authority, or collaborations between multiple actors, including both previously mentioned and local municipalities.

a selection of propositions. Based on this Table and other analyses, the most important conclusions of their study are:

- Ethical codes (codes of conduct) do exist for Dutch universities, and several consultants, but the respondents hardly know about the content of these codes.

- The promoter of major infrastructure projects generally is the commissioning client (from now on, "client") of CBAs of those projects. This creates a conflict of interest, and therefore limits the usefulness of CBA.
- Consultants value the interests of the client more than those of society, whereas for researchers with a university background the opposite is true.
- The Netherlands has a guideline for CBAs for large national transport infrastructure projects. Respondents think that these increase the quality of CBAs for national projects in the Netherlands. At the same time they may reduce ethical dilemmas for researchers.

To summarize, the study confirms the pressure on researchers because the client has an interest in the outcomes of the CBA and related studies.

Van Wee and Molin (2012: 35–6) discuss the implications of their findings. They state that it is risky that clients commissioning CBAs and CBA-related research have an interest in the outcomes of the research, often wanting either a positive decision to build, or the alternative to be built. They consider this to be a conflict of interests, which they view as inherently problematic, and warn that it could reduce the (ethical) quality of CBA and related research. They further state that it would be better to have an independent client as the contact for research. This applies to all levels of governance—national, regional, and local. They emphasize the importance of the democratically chosen parliament and other bodies being neutrally informed. In addition, they propose codes of conduct, not only for researchers but also for the clients commissioning the research. They also suggest making use of independent second opinions, and of independent committees supervising research—not only for megaprojects or large projects, but also for smaller projects. The results of these second opinions or reports from independent committees should be included in the CBA and maybe also the research reports providing input for CBAs.

In addition to these implications, we think it important to realize that having a code of conduct is not enough. These codes must also be enforced to have effect. A case study by Flyvbjerg (2013b) shows that codes of conduct are not necessarily implemented—a conclusion that confirms the results of the study of Van Wee and Molin. We think that the best step is probably to institutionalize the enforcement of codes of conduct. For example, an independent committee could check the ethical behavior of researchers, or penalties could be incurred by researchers whose behavior conflicts with the code. There are thus many reasons for repeating what we have already stated: the client should be an independent contact.

To express it more generally: the role of the researcher and the role of politicians should not be mixed up. Researchers should carry out high-quality research useful for decision making, and politicians should decide, based on research but also on many other aspects, including political preferences. In addition to the importance of the independence of the research, we add that in the decision-making process actors can agree beforehand (before research is carried out) which research, which data, and which research institute they consider to be reliable and acceptable.

6.4 THE QUALITY OF ESTIMATES OF THE COSTS AND BENEFITS OF MEGAPROJECTS

The previous section discusses the ethics of carrying out research, concluding that it is cumbersome to have a client with an interest in the outcomes of research. But can such an impact be found empirically? *Ex ante* evaluations of the pros and cons of candidate options for a megaproject—CBAs, Multi-Criteria Analyses (MCAs)—assume "adequate" inputs. The most important inputs are cost estimates and demand forecasts. So, an important question is: how (un)biased are cost estimates and demand forecasts? And how can current practices with respect to assessing the demand and cost forecasts be improved? This section aims to answer these questions.

The questions raised are answered in a literature review by Van Wee (2007). He concludes that cost estimates are often biased: at the time of the formal decision to build, costs are more frequently underestimated than overestimated (for example, Flyvbjerg et al. 2003). The magnitude of cost overruns differs significantly within as well as between studies. CBAs are carried out to support decision making and therefore have to be carried out before the formal decision to build. Research into cost overruns generally takes the cost estimates at the formal decision to build as the point of departure, and compares those with the real-world costs of projects (Flyvbjerg et al. 2003). The preliminary cost estimates used for CBA can, however, be different from those at the time of the formal decision to build. Cantarelli et al. (2010) show that this was the case for two long-distance rail projects in the Netherlands opened in the 2000s: the Betuweroute, and the High-Speed Rail Line connecting Amsterdam to Belgium and France (see Section 6.2). The percentage increases of the cost estimates from the initial estimates to those when the formal decision to build was made was much more than between the decision to build and the project realization.

A second conclusion is that only a few papers pay attention to the quality of demand forecasts for infrastructure projects. Considering the huge costs of these projects, especially megaprojects, and the huge impacts, this seems strange. Van Wee (2007) concludes that overestimation of demand is more common than underestimation—more so for rail projects than for roads. Third, the most important reason for the flawed estimates of costs and demand seems to be the strategic behavior of those having an interest in a positive decision to build (for example, Flyvbjerg et al. 2003), although other interpretations of the results found are also possible. For example, Eliasson and Fosgerau (2013) conclude that cost overruns might result from selection bias. Assuming that selection bias does not fully explain the oft-found cost overruns, and that strategic behavior and optimism bias also occur, the question is: what should be done? Based on the literature, Van Wee (2007: 621) presents several ideas to improve the quality of demand forecasts, most of which can also be used to improve the quality of cost estimates:

- The application of state-of-the-art methods, data, and techniques.
- The introduction of "better" institutional arrangements.
- The introduction of clear targets and instruments to measure how targets can be realized and to reward good performance and punish bad performance.
- Improved transparency by making, for example, information publicly available.
- The inclusion of risk capital.
- The application of the method of "reference class forecasting," making use of an "outside view" (Flyvbjerg 2013a).
- The inclusion of an independent peer review.
- The introduction of measures to reduce or avoid strategic behavior, including manipulation; these measures can be clustered into (1) measures to improve public-sector accountability by transparency and public control, and (2) measures to improve private-sector accountability by competition and market control.

Flyvbjerg (2013a) goes one step further than proposing guidelines. He first discusses the concept of due diligence—a term "used for the performance of an investigation of a business, an investment, or person with a certain standard of care" (Flyvbjerg 2013a: 763). Although it may be a legal obligation, it commonly applies to activities carried out voluntarily. He states:

> The theory behind due diligence holds that performing this type of investigation contributes significantly to informed decision making by enhancing the amount and quality of information available to decision makers and by ensuring that this information is systematically used to deliberate in a reflexive manner on the decision at hand and all its costs, benefits, and risks.

Core questions relate to the expected value of the variable being forecast and its variance. He proposes a recipe for the forecast of a given cost or benefit:

1. Identification and description of the business case or forecast to be evaluated.
2. Establishing a benchmark that represents the outside view, against which performance may be measured.
3. Using the benchmark to evaluate performance in the forecast in question.
4. Checking the forecaster's track record from other, similar, forecasts.
5. Identifying further cost and benefit risks.
6. Establishing the expected outcome.
7. Soliciting comments from the forecaster.
8. Concluding as to whether the forecast is overestimated or underestimated, and by how much.

In an example, he demonstrates these steps. We agree with the potential of such a procedure. In addition, we repeat what we stated previously: not only should codes of conduct apply to researchers, but also to the clients commissioning research. Van Wee (2014) presents some first ideas about such a code of conduct:

1. Research is not contracted and supervised by an actor having an interest in the outcomes. It is an option to make use of an intermediate organization to contract the research.
2. Research is assessed by an independent party.
3. Researchers placed under pressure have the right or even the obligation to report this. This can have a preventive effect.
4. The clients commissioning the research may not prescribe models, tools, methods, or scenarios which may influence the results in such a way that the overview of the pros and cons of alternatives is not neutral.
5. In case of *ex ante* evaluations, clients should obligate researchers to use at least two contrasting scenarios.
6. Researchers have the right to report their findings in papers and to communicate these to the media.

6.5 The Democratic Quality of the Decision-Making Process

In many societies the democratic quality of decision making on megaprojects is considered to be very important. This section focuses on the democratic quality of decision making in general, and on two specific issues: (i) the underestimation by public authorities of the costs and risks of managing interfaces, and (ii) the impact of contracting fraud. These two aspects are selected because in recent evaluations of megaprojects in the Netherlands these aspects appeared to play an important role, and we believe this may also be relevant to other nations.

An important question is: what is the democratic quality of decision making? We think the democratic quality in this context depends on the way decision making on megaprojects is integrated into the general procedures of the democratic state, how the responsibilities of the different layers of government manifest themselves, and the way stakeholders and civic society are informed and involved. We discuss this further in what follows. Van Wee (2011: 20) provides a practical rule of thumb, suggesting that

> the quality of public decision making is higher, if the decision makers make the choice they would have made: (1) if they would have all (from their perspective) potentially relevant choice options available, (2) if they were fully informed, and (3) if they were able to evaluate different choice options.

We now elaborate in more detail on democratic quality.

6.5.1 Democratic Quality in General

Decision making on megaprojects is not only a matter of input from researchers, engineers, managers and other professionals, but is ultimately a matter of political decision making. In particular in the western world the democratic quality of the decision making process on megaprojects is considered to be very important. This democratic quality is higher when:

- Decision making is based on a valid problem analysis and when reliable information is available about the current situation and future trends and scenarios in terms of demography, economy, mobility, and costs.
- The public decision makers (arliament, regional authority, municipal council) can make a choice between different alternative solutions and the pros and cons (in the case of a CBA, the costs and benefits) have been calculated and analyzed per alternative, based on adequate methods and in a neutral, independent way, making clear what the impacts will be of each alternative.
- Citizens understand what problems are at stake, are informed appropriately about the decision-making process and about the (pros and cons of) competing alternatives. They must always have the possibility to give their input in an open process, for instance, about neglected aspects and alternatives. It is essential that there is broad societal support for the preferred alternative of the megaproject, and that those who will be confronted with damage as a result of the megaproject will be compensated properly.
- Stakeholders are identified, informed appropriately, able to participate in the decision-making process, and are invited to propose preferred alternatives. The background of public choices has to be explained to citizens in general and stakeholders in particular.

However, selecting alternatives and estimating pros and cons is often not a straightforward process. During the decision-making process, which usually takes years and sometimes even decades, there are many uncertainties, and expectations about future developments and political preferences may change. This may be a good reason to split a megaproject into parts, distinguishing "no regret" parts and other parts. No-regret decisions can be made in an earlier phase than other decisions. Both researchers and politicians have to make clear which factors are unknown or uncertain. This is mostly not the attitude of the politician responsible for the decision-making process. In general, such a politician wants to be considered as an achiever (*Macher* in German) who makes a strong impression, for example, to increase the chance of being re-elected, as explained by Public Choice theory (Buchanan and Tullock 1962). It is tempting for politicians to influence the process in such a way that it increases the chances of a positive decision (see also Section 6.3), for example, by assuming a scenario of high economic growth. As argued previously, this could endanger democratic values if parliament and the wider public are not informed adequately. Politicians can also try to obatin support for their plans at an early stage. Flyvbjerg et al. (2003) have shown that political decision making can often be characterized as an escalation of commitment, which leads to a mobilization of bias. As in a court of law, extreme objections and pleas are mobilized at the expense of finding the truth. This can reduce the open and democratic quality of decision making regarding megaprojects. Escalation of commitment very often leads to contested information, which supports strategic behaviour, sometimes even lying by public authorities.

6.5.2 Interface Management and Interface Risks

Megaprojects are mostly so big that the contracts are split into parts. This strengthens the competition between candidate contractors. An illustration from practice is the North–South Line for the underground in Amsterdam, where sixteen separate contracts were identified for individual metro stations and tunnels (Priemus 2009). The first seven contracts are specified in Table 6.2.

Another illustration is the civil engineering substructure of the High-Speed train connection between Amsterdam and the Belgian border, where seven parts were contracted

Table 6.2 Seven North–South Metro Line contracts

Contract	Date of contract	First round 12-12-2000	Second round 25-10-2001	Third round 1-5-2002	Contractor	Amount (x million euro)
Zinktunnel IJ	10/2001		0		Heijmans/ Strukton	54.2
Passage Central Station	5/2002		X	0	Strukton/ Van Oord	155.1
Caissons Damrak	5/2002		0		Heijmans	26.9
Drilling tunnels and mitigating measures	12/2000	0			Saturn	135.5
Rokin Station	10/2001	X	0		Max Bögl	
Vijzelgracht Station	5/2002	X	X	0	Max Bögl	223.2
Ceintuurbaan Station	5/2002	X	X	0	Max Bögl	
Total						594.9

X = unsuccessful contracting procedure

0 = successful contracting procedure

Source: Priemus (2009).

separately (see Table 6.3). A distinction was made between the substructure (design and construct: investment), the infra-provider (design, build, finance, and maintain for twenty-five years), and transport services (for fifteen years). The contractors for each component did not know who was going to realize the related parts.

The problem in these cases is that between the components which are contracted separately, many costs and risks in the interface of components play a role. This is important from an ethical point of view, because interface costs and risks are generally not made explicit beforehand and consequently are not included in the information provided to decision makers, and therefore interface costs and risks can reduce the basis needed for democratic decision making. Public authorities (as clients) tend to underestimate the

Table 6.3 HSL-South: contracts awarded for civil engineering substructure

Contract	Consortium	Participating companies	Date	Contracted sum (x million NLG)[1]
HSL-A4 Noordelijk Holland	Hollandse Meren	Ballast Nedam, Van Hattum, Vermer	16 July 2000	710
Zuid-Holland Midden	HSL-Consortium Zuid-Holland Midden	NBM-Amstelland, HBG, Heijmans	16 July 2000	866
Zuid-Holland Zuid	HSL-Drechtse Steden	Ballast Nedam, Van Hattum & Blankevoort, Strukton	16 July 2000	1105
HSL-A16 Brabant Noord	HSL-Brabant	Ballast Nedam, Volker Stevin, Strukton, Boskalis, Vermeer	16 July 2000	640
HSL-A16 Brabant Zuid	HSL-Consortium Brabant Zuid	HBG, NBM, Heijmans, Holsmann, HAM, Van Oord	16 July 2000	997
Total substructure	–	–	–	4318
Tunnel 'Green Heart'		Bouygues/Koop Tjuchem	17 December 1999	941
Connections to existing railway infrastructure	Aantakkingen Consortium	KWS, Ballast Nedam, NBM-Amstelland, HBG	25 January 2001	458
Total civil engineering works	–	–	–	5717

[1] 2.2 Dutch guilders (NLG) = €1 = US$1.4.

Source: Priemus (2009).

interface risks and do not accept extra costs to cover these risks. Contractors, however, tend to price these risks highly, sometimes even extremely highly—in particular, when their negotiating position is perceived as strong. In particular, in the case of megaprojects the costs of covering interface risks contributes strongly to the explanation of cost overruns (TCI 2004).

Where it is possible, the interface risks can be reduced by contracting infrastructure parts in different periods, as a result of which the contractors who come later can adapt to the parts which wer realized earlier, and more learning processes can be organized during the whole process.

6.5.3 Contracting Fraud

In many parts of the world the building industry has a long tradition in forming cartels and exchanging information before a contract is officially awarded. This is now labeled as contracting fraud, but was until recently considered by the contractors as a legally effective coordination mechanism to promote continuity (Doreé 2004; Priemus 2004). This gradually changed when competition policy was formulated by the European Commission in the last decade of the twentieth century, followed, step by step, by national governments.

In some megaprojects the consequences of these practices can still be observed, the High-Speed Rail Line south (see Section 6.2) being an example. The competition for this line's substructure contracts appeared to be fake. Each competing consortium consisted of building companies that were also part of one or more competing consortia (see Table 6.3, col. 2). It was very easy to exchange information between the consortia in the early stages. In the end, the official bids were about 40% higher than the budgets calculated by the Transport Ministry (TCI 2004).

In the first stages of the contracting procedure of the North–South Underground Line in Amsterdam, cartels appeared to have been active as well. The Dutch contractors tried to exclude foreign competitors. Nevertheless, some contracts were awarded to the experienced German contractor Max Bögl, who in the beginning could not contract Dutch subcontractors as a result of exclusionary policies by the Dutch main contractors which were discovered by accident and later condemned by Court (Priemus 2009).

In 2002 a Parliamentary Enquiry Committee into the Building Trade took place in the Netherlands (Parlementaire Enquêtecommissie Bouwnijverheid 2002). The Dutch parliament stressed the validity of both European and Dutch competition policy, which forbids cartels, including in the building industry. Since 2002 the situation seems to have improved, although, given the long tradition of cartels in the building industry and the high priority which contractors award to continuity of their business, it is still possible that in European countries and elsewhere contractors disturb the level playing field, having informal contracts with public officials (bribery) and among each other (cartel forming). External supervision by a public independent authority is crucial here.

Finally, experience has taught that the role of accountants must be made more critical, more professional, and more pro-active in preventing and correcting building fraud (Parlementaire Enquêtecommissie Bouwnijverheid 2002).

6.6 Avenues for Future Research and Decision-Making Procedures

We have argued that the ethical aspects of decision making and the management of megaprojects, as well as other transport projects, are potentially very important. Nevertheless, there is not much research in this area. In this section we present some avenues for future research related to decision-making procedures, but limit ourselves to research that is at least relevant for megaprojects, excluding research that is important for all transport (infrastructure) projects but not specifically for megaprojects.

Firstly, more research into the area of the distribution effects of megaprojects is needed. This deals with the distribution effects of regions and income groups, but many more distributions are relevant which are related to equity, including a level playing field and solidarity (see Thomopoulos et al. 2009). In addition, alternatives for government expenditures and their consequences need to be better understood. How would money be spent if it were not spent on megaprojects, and what then would be the impact? It might be better to include alternatives for governmental expenditures and their impacts in the decision making; CBAs normally do not include a comparison of alternative spending.

Secondly, research is needed in the area of discounting and irreversible effects. Which irreversible effects of megaprojects are relevant and when, what is the importance of long-term uncertainty for the estimates of effects, what is the importance of long-term effects and uncertainty in these effects on decision making and management?

Thirdly, more research is needed in the area of the ethics of doing research; as already explained, this area has hardly been explored. The impact on the estimates of effects can, however, be large, and consequently impact on the adequate functioning of decision-making procedures and democratic quality. We think that the impact of the commissioning client on the research is particularly relevant. Both research and related institutional rules can focus on the role of the researcher, the role of the client, and the interaction between the researcher and the client. For all three categories, incentives improve the independency and quality of the research and can aim to work either preventively or correctively, resulting in the categorization of Table 6.4.

Fourthly, more research is needed in the area of the quality of cost estimates and demand forecasts. During the past fifteen years or so, a tradition of such research has evolved, partly fueled by the influential work of Flyvbjerg et al. (2003). At the very least, research is needed into the institutional and managerial factors which have an impact on the quality of such estimates, including the impact of incentives that aim to improve the quality of these estimates.

Table 6.4 Categorization of incentives to improve the neutrality/independence of research, and some examples

	Preventive	Corrective
Client of research ("demand")	Code of conduct for clients (as far as we are aware these do not exist yet), rules for who can be the client	Political debate, parliamentary inquiries
Researcher ("supply")	Code of conduct, guidelines for CBAs	Second opinion
Interaction between the client and the researcher	Rules for selecting researchers/research institutes, guidelines for interaction between clients and researchers	Second opinion

Finally, more research is needed on the democratic quality of the decision-making processes for megaprojects, including research, consultancy, information gathering, and information processing. Core issues are the availability of information for all stakeholders at an early stage, the neutrality and reliability of information, data, and research, the openness, fairness, and flexibility of the process architecture, and the awareness of uncertainties and risks throughout the process (no briberies, no cartels, fair competition, a level playing field). In addition to institutional arrangements, the role of the press in informing the broader public about the dilemmas, alternatives, and priorities, is crucial.

References

Bristow, A. and Nellthorp, J. (2000). "Transport project appraisal in the European Union." *Transport Policy*, 7(1): 51–60.

Buchanan, J. M. and Tullock, G. (1962). *The Calculus of Consent*. Ann Arbor, MI: University of Michigan Press.

Canaleta, C. G., Arzoz, P. P., and Gárate, M. R. (2002). "Structural change, infrastructure and convergence in the regions of the European Union," *European Urban and Regional Studies*, 9(2):115–35.

Cantarelli, C. C., Flyvbjerg, B., van Wee, B., and Molin, E. J. E. (2010). "Lock-in and its influence on the project performance of large-scale transportation infrastructure projects: investigating the way in which lock-in can emerge and affect cost overruns," *Environment and Planning B: Planning and Design*, 37(5): 792–807.

De Blaeij, A., Florax, R. J. G. M., Rietveld, P., and Verhoef, E. (2003). "The value of statistical life in road safety: A meta-analysis," *Accident Analysis and Prevention*, 35(66): 973–86.

Doreé, A. G. (2004). "Collusion in the Dutch construction industry: An industrial organization perspective," *Building Research and Information*, 32(2): 146–56.

Eijgenraam, C. C. J., Koopmans, C. C., Tang, P. J. G., and Verster, A. C. P. (1999). *Evaluatie van infrastructuurprojecten. Leidraad voor kosten-batenanalyse. Deel I: Hoofdrapport.*

Onderzoeksprogramma Economische Effecten Infrastructuur [*Evaluation of infrastructure projects. Guideline for cost–benefit analysis. Part 1: Main report. Research program Economic Effects Infrastructure*]. Den Haag: Ministerie van V&W en EZ.

Eliasson, J. and Fosgerau, M. (2013). "Cost overruns and demand shortfalls: Deception or selection?" *Transportation Research Part B*, 57: 105–13.

Flyvbjerg, B. (2013a). "Quality control and due diligence in project management: Getting decisions right by taking the outside view," *International Journal of Project Management*, 31/5: 760–74.

Flyvbjerg, B. (2013b). "How planners deal with uncomfortable knowledge: The dubious ethics of the American Planning Association," *Cities*, 32: 157–63.

Flyvbjerg, B., Bruzelius, N., and Rothengatter, W. (2003). *Mega-Projects and Risk: An Anatomy of Ambition*. Cambridge: Cambridge University Press.

Grant-Muller, S. M., MacKie, P., Nellthorp, J., and Pearman, A. (2001). "Economic appraisal of European transport projects: The state-of-the-art revisited," *Transport Reviews*, 21(2): 237–61.

Harrison, G. and Shepherd, S. (2014). "An interdisciplinary study to explore impacts from policies for the introduction of low carbon vehicles," *Transportation Planning and Technology*, 37/2: 98–117.

Hayashi, Y. and Morisugi, H. (2000). "International comparison of background concept and methodology of transportation project appraisal," *Transport Policy*, 7(1): 73–88.

Johansson-Stenman, O. and Martinsson, P. (2008). "Are some lives more valuable? An ethical preferences approach," *Journal of Health Economics* 27(3): 739–52.

Mackie, P. J., Wardman, M., Fowkes, A. S., Whelan, G. A., Nellthorp, J., and Bates, J. J. (2003). *Value of Travel Time Savings in the UK. Prepared for the Department for Transport*. Leeds: Institute for Transport Studies, University of Leeds/John Bastes Services.

Martens, K. (2006), "Basing transport planning on principles of social justice", <http://www-dcrp.ced.berkeley.edu/bpj>.

Morisugi, H. and Hayashi, Y. (2000). "Editorial," *Transport Policy*, 7(1): 1–2.

Morton, A. (1991). *Disaster and Ddilemmas: Strategies for Real-Life Decision Making*. Oxford: Blackwell.

Parlementaire Enquêtecommissie Bouwnijverheid (2002). *De bouw uit de schaduw. Eindrapport Parlementaire Enquête Bouwnijverheid* [*Building industry out of the shadow. Final report*]," Tweede Kamer 2002–2003, 28.244, nrs. 5–6, The Hague: Sdu Uitgevers.

Priemus, H. (2004). "Dutch construction fraud and governance issues," *Building Research and Information*, 32(4): 306–12.

Priemus, H. (2005). "Centraal Planbureau en Betuweroute; schuivende panelen" ["National Bureau of Economic, Policy Analysis and Betuwe Line: shifting panels"] *Tijdschrift Vervoerwetenschap*, 41(3): 9–14.

Priemus, H. (2009). "Contracting public transport infrastructure: Recent experience with the Dutch High-Speed Line and the Amsterdam North–South Metro Line," presentation at the 11th International Thredbo Conference on Competition and Ownership in Land Passenger Transport, Delft University of Technology, 21 September.

Shepard, D. S. and Zeckhauser, R. J. (1984). "Survival versus consumption," *Management Science*, 30: 423–39.

Thomopoulos, N., Grant-Muller, S., and Tight, M. R. (2009). "Incorporating equity considerations in transport infrastructure evaluation: Current practice and a proposed methodology," *Evaluation and Program Planning*, 32(4): 351–9.

Tijdelijke Commissie Infrastructuurprojecten (TCI) (2004). "*Grote projecten uitvergroot. Een infrastructuur voor besluitvorming* [*Megaprojects scrutinized. An infrastructure for decision-making*]," Tweede Kamer 2004–2005, 29.283, nrs. 5–6, The Hague: Sdu Uitgevers.

van Wee, B. (2007). "Large infrastructure projects: A review of the quality of demand forecasts and cost estimations," *Environment and Planning B*, 34(4): 611–25.

van Wee, B. (2011). *Transport and Ethics: Ethics and the Evaluation of Transport Policies and Projects*. Cheltenham, UK, and Northampton, MA: Edward Elgar.

van Wee, B. (2014). "Naar een gedragscode voor opdrachtgevers? Een discussiepaper" ["Towards a code of conduct for clients of research. A discussion paper"]. *Colloquium Vervoersplanologisch Speurwerk*, 2014.

van Wee, B. and Molin, E. (2012). "Transport and ethics: Dilemmas for CBA researchers. An interview-based study from the Netherlands," *Transport Policy*, 24: 30–36.

van Wee, B. and Rietveld, P. (2013). "Using value of statistical life for the *ex ante* evaluation of transport policy options: A discussion based on ethical theory," *Transportation*, 40/2: 295–314.

CHAPTER 7

BIGGEST INFRASTRUCTURE BUBBLE EVER?

City and Nation Building with Debt-Financed Megaprojects in China

XUEFEI REN

7.1 INTRODUCTION

SINCE the early 1990s, China has built more megaprojects than any other country in the world. Local governments are the biggest investors for infrastructural megaprojects, and municipal governments across the country have invested massively in public utilities, roads, bridges, tunnels, parks, ports, airports, and subways. Private capital has also quickly flowed into the construction sector: private investment, often in partnership with local government, has spurred new megaprojects, especially in residential and commercial property development. Although the 2008 global recession may have led one to expect a significant decline in megaproject investment, in China, the economic downturn has given the central government a legitimizing tool in the form of a stimulus plan to direct investment into infrastructural megaprojects. The spending on fixed-asset investment—a measure that captures building activities such as real estate and infrastructure construction, among other things—reached an alarming 70% of the national GDP in 2013, and infrastructure spending has surpassed foreign trade as the biggest contributor to national economic growth.[1] China used 6.4 gigatons of cement in the three years of 2011, 2012, and 2013—more than the United States did in the entire twentieth century.[2] How can we explain this unprecedented level of investment in megaprojects in Chinese cities?

To date, the scholarship on urban megaprojects has focused mostly on postindustrial cities in North America and Europe. This literature has identified two major themes in the current wave of megaproject development since the early 2000s. First, many have pointed out the temporal variations of megaprojects: compared with the "great megaproject" era of the 1950s and 1960s, urban megaprojects today tend to be more inclusive, less disruptive, and more flexible for addressing different needs of local communities (Altshuler and Luberoff 2003; Diaz Orueta and Fainstein 2008). Second, several authors identify megaproject development as part of a broader strategy of entrepreneurial urban governance (Olds 2002; Flyvbjerg, Bruzelius, and Rothengatter 2003; del Cerro Santamaria 2013). Noting that economic restructuring over the past several decades has intensified intercity competitions for investment, they argue that urban construction has become increasingly dominated by high-profile projects that rely heavily upon private financial contributions.

These observations on urban megaprojects in the West, however, have limited explanatory power for China's megaproject boom. First, this shift from "great megaproject era" to "do no harm" (Altshuler and Luberoff 2003) is nowhere to be seen in Chinese cities, which since the early 1990s, have been experiencing their own phase of large-scale and highly disruptive urban renewal. Urban megaprojects significantly changed the textures of Chinese cities. Traditional neighborhoods were bulldozed to make way for new expressways, subway lines, and office and shopping complexes, and millions of residents were displaced from their homes in inner cities to the urban fringes. Second, the prevalence of megaprojects in Chinese city building calls into question whether they are an entrepreneurial strategy consciously pursued by local officials; that is, an inquiry that can be resolved only through empirical fieldwork. Different from Western cities, urban megaprojects have become the "rule" instead of "exceptions" for city builders in China.

Building on the literature on regional variations of urban megaprojects (Ren and Weinstein 2012; Lehrer and Laidley 2008; Haila 2008; Bezmez 2008), this chapter examines the economic and sociopolitical conditions that gave rise to China's megaproject era of the 1990s and 2000s. This chapter discusses both the deregulatory measures and financial innovations behind the massive boom of megaproject construction and the contestations and mixed legacies of China's megaproject boom. Megaprojects are conceived here broadly to include infrastructural projects (such as expressways, subways, sports stadiums, airports, utilities), as well as mixed-use commercial and residential projects. Instead of focusing on particular kinds of megaprojects, this chapter examines the common conditions that underlie the planning and implementation of megaprojects, such as the regulatory reforms in the land, housing, and finance sectors.

The chapter argues that a series of deregulatory reforms in land, housing, and finance have significantly empowered municipal governments in China, which are the largest undertakers of urban megaprojects. The land reform in the 1980s and 1990s separated the public land ownership from privatized land use rights, thus making land a commodity to be transacted in the market. The public land ownership gives municipal governments enormous power to acquire land for megaprojects with far below market-rate compensations to its current users. Since the early 1990s, the central government has also promulgated a series of regulations over housing demolitions and evictions, and these regulations paved the way for the large-scale residential displacement. Even with land acquired and resident populations evicted, megaproject construction would not be possible without financing. The rise of Local Investment Corporations (LICs)—a system of quasi-state enterprises set up by local governments—solved the problem by borrowing directly from the market, especially from state banks, on behalf of local governments. Thus, the various market-oriented regulatory reforms have created optimal conditions for the coming of China's great megaproject era.

7.2 SECURING LAND FOR MEGAPROJECTS

Urban megaprojects often require acquisition and consolidation of land parcels, and securing land for megaprojects is no easy task in many countries. In China, land acquisition for urban megaprojects has been facilitated by a number of major legal and regulatory changes in the land sector since the beginning of the market reform. These regulatory changes have significantly empowered municipal governments in land acquisitions, which in turn have triggered strong resistance and contestations across the country.

Land was not a commodity in socialist China between the 1950s and 1970s, and it was allocated by the state to *danwei* (state enterprises) for specific industrial projects. Article 10 of the 1982 Constitution specifies that no organization or individual may seize and sell land or make any other unlawful transfer of land (Yeh and Wu 1996). In the early days of the market reform in the 1980s, local governments lacked capital to build infrastructure and attract foreign investors, and some coastal cities such as Shenzhen began to experiment with privatization of land-use rights. In the early phase of the land reform, before the mid-1980s, the main agenda for local governments was providing cheap land to foreign investors to induce them to help build infrastructure. The experiment in the south went well, and investors from Hong Kong and Taiwan flocked to the Special Economic Zones in the Pearl River Delta to set up factories and take advantage of the cheap land.

To expand the land reform to other cities, the Constitution was amended in 1988 by the central government with the clause, "the right to use land may be transferred in accordance with the provisions of law" (Yeh and Wu 1996). Thus, the Constitution for the first time recognized market transactions of land-use rights. Privatized land-use rights were treated differently from land ownership, which remained public. Individual and institutional investors could obtain land-use rights for up to seventy years for residential property development, and fifty years for commercial property development.

The agenda of local governments for privatizing land-use rights has changed since the late 1990s, from giving incentives to investors to provide infrastructure, to generating local government revenues. Under current fiscal policies, revenues from land leasing are treated as "extrabudgetary" and do not have to be shared with the central government. As land is leased by local governments to private parties, and transacted among investors, land-leasing and transaction fees have become a major source of municipal government revenue. Governments use the revenue obtained from land leasing to improve urban infrastructure, which in turn can open up more land for development.

China's hybrid land market, comprising both public ownership and private use rights, has been operating within a multitrack system in which land is transacted through both public auctions and under-the-table negotiations between the government and private investors (Lin and Ho 2005; Lin 2009). Because local governments commonly transfer land-use rights through negotiations, the central government has sought to improve market transparency by urging that all commercial land be transferred publicly through auctions to the highest bidder. But as a practical matter, owing to the intertwined interests of local governments and investors, under-the-table negotiations remain the dominant method of land leasing. Many officials and their relatives are shareholders in real-estate companies and construction projects, and local governments commonly lease out land at prices far below market value to these well-connected enterprises. Local governments prefer negotiations to auctions because of the flexibility to lower land prices as a means of attracting investors (Xu, Yeh, and Wu 2009). Good connections with local governments are crucial for individuals and companies trying to obtain prime land at a fraction of its market price.

State expropriation of land takes many forms, from violent means such as mobilization of armed forces and forced demolitions, to administrative means such as manipulation of the *hukou* system. In China, urban land is owned by the state and rural land by village collectives. The state has the right, according to the current Constitution, to acquire rural land from farmers and urban land from its current users in the name of public interest. In most cases, farmers and urban residents are compensated by local governments at rates far below the market prices that investors would pay to acquire the same land, and local governments can easily pocket huge profits through land transactions—by acquiring land cheaply and then leasing it to investors.

Land grabs by city governments are widespread and have generated strong resistance from peasants. In 2005, for instance, in the small village of Dongzhou in Guangdong province, the local government decided to expropriate land from farmers and build a power plant. Dissatisfied with the compensation and distraught about environmental damage to crops, angry farmers took their grievance to the streets. The local government countered by mobilizing armed police, who opened fire on the protestors, killing a dozen villagers and wounding many more. This was the first time that armed forces had used deadly force against civilians since the 1989 Tian'anmen student movement.[3]

The protest over land acquisition in Wukan village in the Pearl River Delta marked a turning point in Chinese peasants' resistance against land grabs (Ren 2017). In 2011, villagers stormed into government offices, chased away local officials, and blocked the roads after they learned that the village government had leased out about a third of the village land to an outside investor. One of the representatives chosen by the villagers to negotiate with the village government had died in police custody. The stand-off between the villagers and security forces sent by local authorities continued for months. Finally, in 2012, the Guangdong provincial government intervened. The village officials were dismissed; the land deal was put on hold; and the villagers were allowed to hold elections to choose new leaders.[4]

Land expropriation can also be accomplished by changing the *hukou* status of farmers. *Hukou* is the system of national registration that divides the population into categories of urban and rural. Rural *hukou* holders, by law, are entitled to the land in the villages where they reside. In 2004, Shenzhen converted 235 square km of rural land to urban land in Bao'an and Longgang districts by reclassifying the *hukou* status of villagers from "agricultural" to "urban," or "non-agricultural." After becoming "non-agricultural" *hukou* holders, villagers no longer are entitled to rural land. Farmers are often compensated at rates far below market prices, and local governments apply most of the compensation to buying pensions and medical insurance for landless farmers, and the rest to building community facilities. The strategy of acquiring farmers' land by offering them urban *hukou* is widely pursued in many large cities (Xu, Yeh, and Wu 2009).

To summarize, the current land market in China—a legacy of both the Communist revolution and the market reform—is unique, and it makes land acquisition for megaprojects much faster, more disruptive, and undemocratic as compared to other countries. The public ownership over urban land gives municipal governments a monopoly to acquire land without having to offer adequate compensation to its current users, and the privatization of land use rights—in contrast to land ownership—has further strengthened municipal governments by channeling land-leasing revenues to municipal coffers. The ready availability of land has prepared the ground for the coming of China's megaproject era.

7.3 HOUSING DEMOLITIONS FOR MEGAPROJECTS

Public land ownership alone, however, cannot free up sufficient land for megaprojects, because most urban land parcels are used by communities and enterprises in the densely populated Chinese cities. Building urban megaprojects in China almost inevitably requires the demolition of existing housing stocks and evictions of residents. Large-scale urban renewal programs, designed to make inner-city land available for real-estate speculation and megaproject constructions, began in the early 1990s and peaked in the mid-2000s. As with regulatory reforms in the land sector, the central government has implemented a series of policies to legalize housing demolitions for profit-driven urban megaprojects.

Large-scale housing demolitions first began in the early 1990s in Beijing and Shanghai, as these two cities announced ambitious plans to remake themselves into China's global cities. For instance, in 1990 Beijing, municipal government launched the "Old and Dilapidated Housing Renewal Program" to redevelop 3 million square meters of old urban housing stock within fifteen years. The target of this first wave of redevelopment was inner-city neighborhoods. In 1993, the then-Xicheng district government began to develop a financial center within the second ring road—the heart of historic Beijing, razing many *hutongs*—traditional neighborhoods with courtyard houses and narrow alleys. Driven by interdistrict competition, other district governments soon followed suit to build their own flagship megaprojects. Oriental Plaza, a massive shopping and office complex invested by the Hong Kong business tycoon Li Ka-Shing, underwent construction in 1993, and more *hutong* neighborhoods vanished in spite of opposition from residents and preservationists (Wang 2003; Zhang and Fang 2004; Johnson 2005). The 2008 Beijing Olympics further fueled the machinery of urban renewal, and millions of residents were displaced from inner-city neighborhoods to outskirts without fair compensation (Ren 2011). By 2010 the work of urban renewal was mostly completed. Ordinary citizens, unable to afford the skyrocketing housing costs and rents, were relegated to the urban periphery of the continually sprawling Beijing. The "growth machine" of local governments and private developers was driving urban renewal programs, exacerbating the power imbalance that divided residents and the private–public growth coalition (Zhang 2002; He and Wu 2005; Chen 2009).

To understand the massive scale of forced housing demolitions in the 1990s and 2000s, one has to examine, again, the regulatory changes made by the state to enable such practices. Until 2011, forced demolitions were legalized with the Regulations on Urban Housing Demolitions enacted successively in 1991 and 2001 (State Council 1991, 2001). The two regulations formally legalized the practice of redeveloping neighborhoods without residents' consent, and also carrying out forced demolitions by administrative order. Residents could appeal to the People's Court, but the court could not issue an order to stop demolitions, and the regulations explicitly prohibit any delays in the demolitions during appeal if residents are provided some form of compensation or temporary housing. Mass demolitions in the 1990s led to widespread protests, and the central government eventually revised the demolition regulations in 2001. The 2001 Regulation tightened the control over developers, but the fundamental power relationships did not change: municipal governments were vested with great power to acquire housing from residents by administrative order, and residents were excluded from the decision-making process of urban renewal programs.

The State Council replaced the 2001 Regulation with a new legislation in 2011, and the most significant change was forbidding the eviction of residents through violence or otherwise forcing them out through practices such as cutting off water, heat, and electricity (State Council 2011). Departing from previous laws, the 2011 Regulation required consent from the majority of residents before any urban renewal project could proceed (Article 11). It specified the standard of compensation that includes the market value of the acquired property, relocation costs, and other losses incurred for the affected residents and businesses (Article 17). The 2011 Regulation required an independent third-party real-estate agency to assess the market value of the property, and these assessors will be fined between 50,000 and 200,000 *yuan* for flawed practices. It orders both monetary compensation and *in situ* resettlement, or a combination of two, to affected residents to choose from.

Aside from these more protective measures, the 2011 Regulation does not define what is "public interest." "Public interest" is broadly interpreted to encompass a variety of projects: from infrastructure; to facilities for education, culture, health, and environmental protection; and to affordable housing and renewal of old and dilapidated urban neighborhoods. It also reserves a last category of unspecified "other needs that serve public interest." Thus almost any public and private project can be interpreted as serving "public interest."

The 2011 Regulation introduced new measures to punish "nail households"—those who resist demolitions and refuse to be relocated with the compensation offered. If the resisting residents do not file an administrative litigation and refuse to relocate within the period specified by authorities in charge of demolitions, then municipal governments can file a case with the local court for a compulsory demolition order (Article 28). Also, the new regulation authorizes the police to punish resisting residents who use violence to stop demolitions, as well as developers who use violence to intimidate residents (Article 32). But as some have observed, the police is more likely to crack down on protesting residents than demolition crews hired by developers (Biddulph 2015: 120).

Overall, the 2011 Regulation reflects the changing power relations among the main stakeholders in redevelopment processes. Although municipal governments are the key decision makers over urban renewal programs, their power is no longer unchecked. Rights to housing are better protected today than in the 1990s and 2000s. Large-scale urban renewal programs can no longer be initiated without consents from residents, as the state is increasingly concerned with social unrest. The Shanghai bylaw of the 2011 Regulation, for example, requires 90% of residents' consent for any urban renewal project to proceed, after which 80% of the residents must agree with the compensation terms in order for demolition to take place (Shanghai Municipal Government 2011).

Housing demolitions in China, as in other countries, are highly contested, and forced demolitions have sparked widespread protests and demonstrations across the country, dating back to the early 1990s. The changes ushered in by the 2011 Regulation over housing demolitions, including majority-consent requirements and market-rate compensation for residents, can be interpreted as a response from the state to the two-decade-long housing-rights movements waged across the country. The pace of urban redevelopment and demolitions in China has clearly slowed down since 2010, partly because residents need to be compensated at the market rate for their housing, and developers and local governments no longer can afford megaprojects that involve relocating a large number of residents in central locations.

7.4 Financing Megaprojects: Local Investment Corporations

How local governments can invest so much in infrastructure often puzzles both specialists and casual observers of Chinese cities. The funding for local governments to invest in infrastructure megaprojects comes from a variety of sources, the most important of which is the LICs—quasi-state enterprises set up by municipal governments to borrow directly from the market to fund infrastructural megaprojects.

Municipal governments have long replaced *danwei* (state enterprises) as the main provider of infrastructure. Most municipalities do not have sufficient tax revenue—for example, they do not collect property taxes—to finance their ambitious infrastructure projects. Most properties are still owned by the public sector, and local governments are reluctant to tax their own assets and share the tax revenue with the central government. Moreover, the propertied middle class resists any policy experiments to impose property taxes. Given the limited local tax revenues and diminishing subsidies from the central government, extrabudgetary revenues and borrowing from the capital market have become major sources of infrastructure financing. Wu (2010) finds that the Shanghai city government charges more than twenty-eight kinds of fees to real-estate investors and that this extrabudgetary income accounts for up to 25% of infrastructure investment funds. Income from land leasing also counts as extrabudgetary revenue and has become the most significant source of revenue for local governments. In 2013, Shanghai city government pocketed more than 200 billion *yuan* from leasing land to developers—income that did not have to be shared with the central government, and land leasing revenues from the twenty largest cities in the country reached 1,500 billion *yuan*, increased by 63% than in the previous year.[5]

Moreover, borrowing from domestic and foreign capital markets through bonds, equities, loans from state-run banks, stock-market listings, and joint ventures has become a new way to raise funds, accounting for more than 30% of infrastructure investment capital (Wu 2010). Among these types of borrowing, loans from state-run banks have become the main method for municipal governments to finance their ambitious infrastructure projects. As the central government has tightened requirements for state-run banks' lending to municipal governments, special-purpose investment platforms such as LICs have been set up to evade these regulations. According to some estimates, by 2011 more than 10,000 LICs in capital markets had been set up by local governments to raise funds for investing in infrastructure (Wong 2011). Bank loans go not directly to municipalities, but instead to the accounts of these investment companies that finance the construction of roads, bridges, subways, and government offices. City-owned land valued at high prices serves as collateral for these loan deals. In this way, the debt incurred does not show up on the municipalities' balance sheets. As a result of using off-balance-sheet vehicles to raise funds, the size and structure of local government debt are opaque.

Most of the LICs set up by local governments are deeply in debt. For example, the Urban Construction Investment and Development Corporation of Wuhan—the capital city of Hubei province—has US$15 billion in registered assets and US$14 billion in debt. The total local-government debt in the country in 2014 was estimated to reach almost US$3 trillion, which was about 14% of China's GDP that year.[6] State-run banks are eager to lend to LICs set up by local governments because of high potential returns, in spite of warnings from financial regulators in Beijing about the increasing risks from these hefty infrastructure loans.

Build–Operate–Transfer (BOT) is a widely adopted model for building transport infrastructural megaprojects. The costs are shared between private investors and local governments and, after the initial investments are recovered through toll charges, the ownership rights are transferred to local governments. Although BOT has proved to be effective at tapping into the private market to finance infrastructure—by charging exorbitant fees to users—it has turned various infrastructure projects into profit-making machines for local governments and their private partners. For instance, in 2012, China boasted 100,000 km of the 140,000-km toll roads throughout the world, and by 2015, China had increased its toll roads to 162,600 km.[7] Owning and driving a car is a symbol of middle-class living in China, but it has also become costly with the endless toll road charges. The surge in toll charges for roads and bridges has also contributed to the inflation of food prices, as meat and vegetables have to be trucked into cities via toll roads on a daily basis. In June 2011, responding to public outcry over the country's toll system, the central government mobilized five ministries to launch a year-long campaign to eliminate unauthorized toll booths and legal booths that continue to operate beyond their authorization period. The campaign met strong resistance from local authorities.[8]

Chinese cities have made remarkable progress in building urban infrastructure by tapping into private capital from both domestic and foreign sources. The massive investment in infrastructure has been facilitated by public–private partnership and non-transparent LICs for fund-raising. Many infrastructure megaprojects are profit-making machines for both local governments and private investors. But the growing inability of local governments to repay their infrastructure loans threatens to derail the growth model based on infrastructure investment.

7.5 BEFORE 2008: THE ERA OF ARCHITECTURAL MEGAPROJECTS

Spectacular megaevents—and the construction of architectural megaprojects in preparation for these events—marked China's first decade of the twenty-first century. In 2001 Beijing won the hosting right for the 2008 Olympics, and two years later, Shanghai was chosen to be the hosting city for the 2010 World Expo. These two megaevents led to a construction boom in each of the hosting cities, used by municipal governments to legitimize large-scale demolitions and massive investments in megaprojects in the city. One of the dominant features of megaproject development in the 2000s is the use of prestigious international architects for promotion, and the highest-profile projects in the country were invariably commissioned to foreign architects. The symbolic capital of architectural design is transformed by local political elites into economic, political, and cultural capital in the process of megaproject constructions (Ren 2011). Private developers would commission well-known foreign architects to design luxury housing for branding and marketing, local officials would want to leave a landmark building designed by prestigious architects to advance their political careers, and the Chinese state sought "starchitects" to design national moments to symbolize the country's rise on the world stage. The National Stadium in Beijing, built for the 2008 Olympics, provides an example of nation building and place promotion by use of architectural megaprojects.

After Beijing won the hosting rights for the 2009 Olympic Games, the city government and the Olympic Organizing Committee sought a prestigious international firm to design the main stadium. In June 2002, the mayor of Beijing announced that the city would gather the best architectural designs from the world for Olympic stadiums. In October 2002, the city government and the Olympic Organizing Committee asked the Beijing Municipal Planning Commission to organize a competition of conceptual architecture designs for the stadium. The overwhelming number of international design teams and jury members reflected the preference for foreign architects among the city officials in Beijing. In April 2003, the Olympic Organizing Committee chose a Swiss architectural firm, Herzog & de Meuron Ltd, to design the National Stadium (Ren 2009).

While the design competition was underway, another separate bidding for ownership of the stadium took place. In August 2003, it was announced that a consortium of five firms led by CITIC (China International Trust and Investment Corp)—a large state bank with strong ties to the central government—was the winner of the ownership tender. Another firm in the consortium is Beijing Urban Construction Corp, the LIC discussed in the previous section. CITIC invested 42% of the total construction cost, with the remaining 58% provided by the city government, represented by Beijing State-Owned Assets Management Corp. The city government also provided subsidies by reducing land leasing fees and helping with demolitions. CITIC and the Beijing city government formed the National Stadium Ltd, which has thirty years of use rights for the stadium after the Olympic Games, after which, the ownership of the stadium will revert to the city. The "bird's nest"—nickname for the National Stadium—garnered significant international attention during the Olympic Games, but since then it has been left mostly empty in Beijing's Olympic Park.

7.6 AFTER 2008: RECESSION, STIMULUS PLAN, AND MUNICIPAL DEBT

Soon after the 2008 Olympics, the economic recession set in, but in China, the recession was used as a legitimizing tool to direct more investment in infrastructural megaprojects. The recession alarmed China's top leaders, who worried that the country would be dragged into economic stagnation, with adverse consequences in terms of political stability. In 2009 the central government responded by rolling out a stimulus plan of 4 trillion *yuan*—the world's largest, and three times larger than Obama's stimulus package—among which, 1.18 trillion would be provided by the central government and the rest matched by local governments through bank loans (Wong 2011). The stimulus package amounted to 12.5% of China's GDP in 2008, and was to be spread out over a period of twenty-seven months. The top three priority areas earmarked for the spending were transport and power infrastructure, post-earthquake construction, and affordable housing, with the rest extending to rural infrastructure, environmental protection, technology, health, and education. This large fiscal injection triggered deregulation in the financial sector, especially regarding bank lending, and also a relaxation of fiscal rules over local debt.

Local governments are the key players entrusted with implementing the 2009 stimulus program, and particularly with identifying particular infrastructure projects to be funded. To help local governments to raise capital and cofinance these projects, the central government made a series of deregulatory moves (Wong 2011). For example, the State Council approved a 200-billion *yuan* treasury bond on behalf of local governments, and the Ministry of Finance relaxed the standards on what counterpart funds could qualify for stimulus projects—basically, all sources at the discretion of local governments could be used for cofinancing.

One particular deregulatory measure has been the widespread use of LICs. Since local governments themselves are not allowed to borrow from the market, they set up LICs, to borrow from banks and raise funds through corporate bonds in order to invest in infrastructure and enhance city revenue in general. The LICs bundle together bank loans and other funds raised, and use municipal assets as equity and collateral. Owing to the public ownership of urban land, land has become the principal asset backing LICs, and city governments have used incomes from land leasing for servicing LICs' debt. No national agencies, not even the Ministry of Finance, can oversee the tens of thousands of LICs in the country set up by local governments. During the stimulus-spending period from 2008 to 2010, local governments borrowed massively through LICs and accrued a large amount of local debts. Servicing the debt has become a problem for many cities struggling with less robust economic growth and lesser tax revenues.

Because of the overinvestment in infrastructure brought about by the stimulus, Chinese city governments have accumulated a large amount of debts since 2008. The local government debt in the country doubled from 7 trillion *yuan* in 2009 to 14 trillion *yuan* at the end of 2010 (Wong 2011). These soaring municipal debts have to be explained by both long-term structural tendencies in municipal finance, such as the mismatch of revenues and responsibilities, and short-term policy programs, such as the 2009 stimulus program of the central government for which local governments were encouraged to borrow massively in order to match central subsidies and invest in infrastructures.

An urban fiscal crisis has been in the making in China since 2008. The rise of LICs has significantly enhanced the fiscal capacity and autonomy of local governments, but it has also created an unsustainable level of municipal debts because of binge borrowing of LICs from state banks. The deregulatory measures taken by the central government have significantly expanded the borrowing power of local governments and spawned an escalation of municipal debt. To rein in local debt, the central government is increasingly turning to the PPP (private–public partnership) model for financing. In May 2015, the central planning agency—the National Development and Reform Commission—announced a list of 1,043 projects totaling 1.97 trillion *yuan* (about US$317.75 billion), for which it invited private investors to help build and operate. But as long as the state banks continue to lend to local governments, it is questionable whether the shift to the PPP model can help to reduce local government debt.[9]

7.7 CONCLUSION

This chapter has examined the economic and sociopolitical conditions in China that have made the massive-scale construction of megaprojects possible. Since the beginning of the market reform in 1978, the government at all levels has initiated a series of market-oriented regulatory reforms in sectors of land, housing, and infrastructure financing. The separation of public land ownership from private land use rights with the 1988 Constitutional Amendment turned land into a commodity, and gave municipal governments a monopoly with which to lease out publicly owned land for earning revenues. Land acquisition for megaprojects was further eased with the 1991 and 2001 Regulations on housing demolitions, which legalized forced evictions and paved the way for urban renewal programs in the 1990s and 2000s. Furthermore, China's megaproject era also needs to be explained by the rise of LICs, which can borrow from state banks on behalf of local governments. These regulatory changes in land, housing, and municipal financing explain why China has been able to build more megaprojects in the past two decades than any other country in the world.

This article has also compared megaproject constructions before and after 2008, the beginning of the world economic recession. Before 2008, the hosting of megaevents often legitimized the construction of megaprojects, but after 2008 the world economic crisis became the new legitimizing tool, as in 2009 the Chinese government introduced a large-scale stimulus program to repel the recession, leading to another wave of investment in megaproject construction. As China's high-speed economic growth is coming to an end, many local governments today find themselves in deep debt from overinvestment in infrastructural megaprojects. Since the local government debt has reached about 40% of the GDP in 2015, it is unsustainable, and many local governments and investment vehicles will default on their debt without debt restructuring. In 2015, the Ministry of Finance finally introduced a refinancing program for local governments, which replaced about 3 trillion *yuan* (US$160 billion) of high-interest debt with lost-interest bonds. This can save local governments about 40–50 billion *yuan* of interest payment in a single year.[10]

This chapter has also highlighted the contested nature of megaproject development. Land acquisition and housing demolitions have led to widespread protests across the country, and the central government has responded by revising previous policies to extend better protection to people's rights to land and housing. The tightened regulations over land and housing acquisitions, together with the economic slowdown and the mounting municipal debt, signal the end of China's megaproject era.

NOTES

1. David Barboza, "Building boom in China stirs fears of debt overload," *The New York Times*, 7 July 2011, <http://www.nytimes.com/2011/07/07/business/global/building-binge-by-chinas-cities-threatens-countrys-economic-boom.html?_r=0>.
2. Ana Swanson, "How China used more cement in 3 years than the U.S. did in the entire 20th century?" Wonkblog, *The Washington Post*, 24 March 2015, <http://www.washingtonpost.com/news/wonkblog/wp/2015/03/24/how-china-used-more-cement-in-3-years-than-the-u-s-did-in-the-entire-20th-century/>.
3. "Chinese police shoot protesters," BBC News, 7 December 2005, <http://news.bbc.co.uk/2/hi/asia-pacific/4507130.stm>.
4. Andrew Jacobs, "Residents vote in Chinese village at center of protest," *The New York Times*, 1 February 2012, <http://www.nytimes.com/2012/02/02/world/asia/residents-vote-in-chinese-village-at-center-of-protest.html>.
5. "Land leasing revenues in 20 cities increased by more than 60 percent," *Xinhua Net*, 3 January 2014, <http://news.xinhuanet.com/fortune/2014-01/03/c_125954247.htm>.
6. Dexter Roberts, "A peek at China's local debt mess," *Bloomberg Business*, 9 January 2014, <http://www.bloomberg.com/bw/articles/2014-01-09/chinas-local-government-debt-is-almost-3-trillion>.
7. Yixue Wu, "Roads take an unbearable toll," *China Daily*, 25 April 2012, <http://usa.chinadaily.com.cn/business/2012-04/25/content_15137576.htm>; "China considers plan to bolster toll roads in search for growth," *Bloomberg Business*, 5 August 2015, <http://www.bloomberg.com/news/articles/2015-08-05/china-considers-plan-to-bolster-toll-roads-in-search-for-growth>.
8. "Trouble on the highway," *Caixin Online*, 29 June 2011, <http://english.caixin.com/2011-06-29/100274315.html>.
9. "China invites private investors to help build $318 billion of projects," *Reuters*, 25 May 2015, <http://www.reuters.com/article/2015/05/25/us-china-economy-infrastructure-idUSKBNoOA07R20150525>.
10. "China's local government debt: Defusing a bomb," *The Economist*, 11 March 2015, <http://www.economist.com/blogs/freeexchange/2015/03/china-s-local-government-debt>.

REFERENCES

Altshuler, A. and Luberodd, D. (2003). *Mega-Projects: The Changing Politics of Urban Public Investment*. Washington, DC: Brookings Institution Press.

Bezmez, D. (2008). "The politics of urban waterfront regeneration: The case of Halic (the Golden Horn), Istanbul," *International Journal of Urban and Regional Research*, 32(4): 815–40.

Biddulph, S. (2015). *The Stability Imperative: Human Rights and Law in China*. Vancouver: University of British Columbia Press.

Chen, X. (ed.) (2009). *Shanghai Rising: State Power and Local Transformations in a Global Megacity*. Minneapolis: University of Minnesota Press.

del Cerro Santamaria, G. (ed.) (2013). *Urban Megaprojects: A World View*. Bingley: Emerald Group Publishing.

Diaz Orueta, R., and Fainstein, S. (2008). "The new mega-projects: Genesis and impacts," *International Journal of Urban and Regional Research*, 32(4): 759–67.

Flyvbjerg, B., Bruzelius, N., and Rothengatter, W. (2003). *Megaprojects and Risk: An Anatomy of Ambition*. New York: Cambridge University Press.

Haila, A. (2008). "From Annankatu to Antinkatu: Contracts, development rights and partnerships in Kamppi, Helsinki," *International Journal of Urban and Regional Research*, 32(4): 804–14.

He, S. and Wu, F. (2005). "Property-led redevelopment in post-reform China: Aa case study of Xintiandi redevelopment project in Shanghai," *Journal of Urban Affairs* 27(1): 1–23.

Johnson, I. (2005). *Wild Grass: Three Stories of Change in Modern China*. New York: Pantheon Books.

Lehrer, U. and Laidley, J. (2008). "Old mega-projects newly packaged? Waterfront redevelopment in Toronto," *International Journal of Urban and Regional Research*, 32(4): 786–803.

Lin, G. (2009). *Developing China: Land, Politics and Social Conditions*. London: Routledge.

Lin, G., and Ho, S. (2005). "The state, land system, and land development processes in contemporary China," *Annals of the Association of American Geographer* 95(2): 411–36.

Olds, K. (2002). *Globalization and Urban Change: Capital, Culture, and Pacific Rim Mega-Projects*. New York: Oxford University Press.

Ren, X. (2009). "Architecture and nation building in the age of globalization: Construction of the National Stadium of Beijing for the 2008 Olympics," *Journal of Urban Affairs*, 30(2): 175–90.

Ren, X. (2011). *Building Globalization: Transnational Architecture Production in Urban China*. Chicago: University of Chicago Press.

Ren, X. (2017). "Land acquisition, rural protests, and the local state in China and India," *Environment and Planning C*, 35(1): 22–38.

Ren, X. and Weinstein, L. (2012) "Urban governance, megaprojects, and scalar transformations in China and India," in T. Samara, S. He, and G. Chen (eds,), *Right to the City in the Global South: Transnational Urban Governance and Socio-Spatial Transformations*. New York: Routledge.

Shanghai Municipal Government. (2011). *Shanghai Urban Housing Acquisition and Compensation Regulation*.

State Council. (1991). *Urban Housing Demolition Regulation*.

State Council. (2001). *Urban Housing Demolition Regulation*.

State Council. (2011). *Urban Housing Acquisition and Compensation Regulation*.

Wang, J. (2003). *Beijing Record*. Beijing: Sanlian Press.

Wong, C. (2011). "The fiscal stimulus program and public governance issues in China," *OECD Journal on Budgeting*, 11(3): 1–21.

Wu, W. (2010). "Urban infrastructure financing and economic performance in China," *Urban Geography*, 31(5): 648–67.

Xu, J., Yeh, A. and Wu, F. (2009). "Decoding urban land governance: State reconstruction in contemporary Chinese cities," *Urban Studies*, 46(3): 559–81.

Yeh, A. and Wu, F. (1996). "The new land development process and urban development in Chinese cities," *International Journal of Urban and Regional Research*, 20(2): 330–53.

Zhang, T. (2002). "Urban development and a socialist pro-growth coalition in Shanghai," *Urban Affairs Review*, 37(4): 475–99.

Zhang, Y. and Fang, K. (2004). "Is history repeating itself? From urban renewal in the United States to inner-city redevelopment in China," *Journal of Planning Education and Research*, 23(3): 286–98.

PART II

CAUSES

....

CHAPTER 8

DID MEGAPROJECT RESEARCH PIONEER BEHAVIORAL ECONOMICS?

The Case of Albert O. Hirschman

....

BENT FLYVBJERG

8.1 WHY HIRSCHMAN AND THE HIDING HAND MATTER

RECENTLY, when San Francisco's new Transbay Terminal megaproject—a multi-billion-dollar transit and real estate development scheme—incurred hundreds of millions of dollars in cost overruns, Willie Brown, former California State Assembly Speaker and Mayor of San Francisco, tried to calm the public with these words in his weekly column in the *San Francisco Chronicle*:

> News that the Transbay Terminal is something like $300 million over budget should not come as a shock to anyone. We always knew the initial estimate was way under the real cost. Just like we never had a real cost for the [San Francisco] Central Subway or the [San Francisco–Oakland] Bay Bridge or any other massive construction project. So get off it. In the world of civic projects, the first budget is really just a down payment. If people knew the real cost from the start, nothing would ever be approved. The idea is to get going. Start digging. (Brown 2013)

Willie Brown here expresses the essence of Albert O. Hirschman's famous principle of the Hiding Hand:

> If people knew the real costs and difficulties from the start, nothing would ever be approved. Therefore it is good they don't know, because we need to get things going, to start digging.

This point of view is also the oldest and most common justification of why low-balled cost estimates and optimistic business cases are often considered acceptable in large projects (Flyvbjerg 2009). Following this idea, a certain amount of ignorance—Hirschman originally called it "providential ignorance" (Alacevich 2014: 157)—is desirable when beginning new projects, because without it projects would not get started. And starting projects is good, according to both Hirschman and Brown.

It has been almost fifty years since Hirschman's (1967a) book about the principle of the Hiding Hand—*Development Projects Observed*—was first published, and both the book and principle today stand stronger than ever. The book was recently republished as a Brookings Classic (Hirschman 2015) and celebrated by people like Cass Sunstein (2015a), Harvard Professor and administrator in the Obama White House, and Malcolm Gladwell (2013), best-selling author and staff writer at *The New Yorker*. Hirschman (1967a: 1) was explicit that his purpose with *Development Projects Observed* and the principle of the Hiding Hand was to understand "project behavior in general." Based on this work, Sunstein (2015: 4) calls Hirschman an "early behavioral economist." In Hirschman we may therefore have something as rare as an early behavioral theorist in project management. If true, this is clearly something to treasure and to learn from. In what follows we will test this claim by testing Hirschman's principle of the Hiding Hand.

The impact of the principle of the Hiding Hand in the academy, policy, and practice is undisputed. And as more and bigger projects are built around the world in what has been dubbed the "biggest investment boom in history," the principle is becoming increasingly consequential in justifying rapidly growing project portfolios (Flyvbjerg 2014a).[1] Hirschman was that rare type of scholar who is as interested in practice as in theory, and he successfully sought influence on policy with his ideas, including the Hiding Hand. That makes the Hiding Hand principle particularly interesting, but also especially problematic, because it is the type of theory that for many policy makers and practitioners, even if wrong, is just too good to give up.[2]

The assessment below does not question the general giftedness of Hirschman's work or his status as "eminent 20th century intellectual" (Offe 2013: 584) and "one of the great heroes of economics" (Rodwin 1994: 36).[3] But it is time to rigorously test Hirschman's Hiding Hand principle, which has not been done before. Such test is the purpose of the present chapter. In a private comment made to his close friend and later Nobel laureate, the Harvard economist Thomas Schelling, Hirschman explained, at the time of writing up the principle of the Hiding Hand for publication, that this work was "an exploration, an experiment and I need [as] a critic someone who can understand that in the first place, and *then* tell me where I may have gone wrong" (Adelman 2013: 404, emphasis in original). In what follows I propose to be this critic, who Hirschman asked for but never had.[4] Specifically, as Hirschman's critic I will subject the principle of the Hiding Hand to the following three tests in escalating order of importance:

1. A test against a paradigmatic case, the Sydney Opera House, to which the principle has been assumed to apply in exemplary fashion.
2. A test for validity and reliability of Hirschman's sampling, data collection, and data analysis, on which the principle is based.

3. A statistical test against a sample of projects much larger, more representative, and with higher-quality data than the sample studied by Hirschman, in order to evaluate whether Hirschman's results may be replicated with more and better data.

All three tests will be carried out against Hirschman's (1967a: 1) own stated purpose for his work: namely, to understand "project behavior in general." Before carrying out the tests, however, let us first see in more depth what the principle of the Hiding Hand is and how it has been received by academics, policy makers, and practitioners.

8.2 What Is the Hiding Hand?

After having studied the outcomes of a number of large World Bank-financed development projects, Hirschman (1967a: 12) noticed, in *Development Projects Observed*:[5]

> If the project planners … had known in advance all the difficulties and troubles that were lying in store for the project, they probably would never have touched it … advance knowledge of these difficulties would therefore have been unfortunate.

As a case in point, Hirschman (1967a: 9–10) highlights East Pakistan's (now Bangladesh) Karnaphuli paper mill, the biggest in Asia at the time of its construction. The plan was to use vast, easily accessible bamboo forests as the main source for paper pulp. However, soon after the mill opened, as a freak incident of nature, 85% of the bamboo that supported production flowered and died. If the planners had known this, Hirschman argued, they probably would have never proposed and funded the mill. Instead, the managers were now forced to creatively find other sources of pulp, which they did from imports, collecting bamboo in other parts of the country, using lumber, and researching fast-growing bamboo species that might replace the unreliable original source, thus creatively diversifying the raw material base. To be sure, this was more costly and difficult than the original plan, but as a result the mill survived and created jobs for thousands of people, argued Hirschman.

Hirschman (1967a: 13) was quick to label what he saw a "general principle of action" and the Hiding Hand a "fairly general phenomenon." He explained that the reason he saw advance knowledge about costs and difficulties as unfortunate was that such knowledge was likely to result in a "gloomy view" (12) of the ability to meet the budget and overcome challenges, which might stop projects before they got started. Ignorance was better, Hirschman argued, because humans tend to also ignore or underestimate their ability in dealing with difficulties. Ignorance therefore "tricked" (13) people into doing projects they would not otherwise have done:

> [S]ince we necessarily underestimate our creativity, it is desirable that we underestimate to a roughly similar extent the difficulties of the tasks we face so as to be tricked by these two offsetting underestimates into undertaking tasks that we can,

but otherwise would not dare, tackle. The principle is important enough to deserve a name: since we are apparently on the trail here of some sort of invisible or hidden hand that beneficially hides difficulties from us, I propose the *Hiding Hand* ... The Hiding Hand is essentially a way of inducing action through error, the error being an underestimate of the project's costs or difficulties. (Hirschman 1967a: 13, 29; emphasis in original)

In coining the name for his newfound principle, Hirschman played on one of the most famous concepts in economic theory, Adam Smith's Invisible (Hidden) Hand. This indicates just how theoretically ambitious Hirschman was with the Hiding Hand and how significant he took it to be. He was explicit that he saw the principle as a theory, at first calling it the "theory of providential ignorance," only later changing this to the "principle of the Hiding Hand" (Alacevich 2014: 157). Hirschman (1967a: 1, 3, 7, 13) also emphasized that although his focus was on development projects he saw the principle-cum-theory as a "general" one that applies across project types and geographies in both developed and developing nations. This is not to say that Hirschman (1967a: 13) thought the Hiding Hand—with its characteristic "two offsetting underestimates" of costs and benefits—would apply to each and every project across all time and space. He was well aware that projects exist, "from bankruptcies and white elephants to lost or ruinously won wars," for which cost underestimates had not been offset by even larger benefit underestimates, but had instead been exacerbated by overestimated benefits followed by benefit shortfalls (Hirschman 1967a: 30). But Hirschman (1967a: 1, 13) theorized that the Hiding Hand "typically" applies—that is, in more cases than not—and that it was therefore the more overarching and more interesting principle for a general understanding of project behavior. Accordingly, he gave the Hiding Hand what he later called "pride of place" in *Development Projects Observed*, giving name to and taking up the first chapter of the book (Hirschman 1995a: ix). Sunstein (2015a: 1–2), in his foreword to the 2015 edition, rightly calls the Hiding Hand the "largest idea" in the volume and explains that "the result of the Hiding Hand is to produce an outcome that is as good as what the planner originally thought—or perhaps even better."

According to Hirschman's field notes, he stumbled on the idea for the Hiding Hand in Thailand, where he went to study a big irrigation project. He found that promoters of the project had overstated its benefits and understated its costs. Benefits were inflated by claims that the project would "make the desert bloom." Costs were low-balled to make the project attractive to investors. "[U]ndercosting" went hand in hand with "overselling" (Adelman 2013: 400–1). Given this observation, it is interesting to note that the project which inspired the Hiding Hand principle is atypical of the principle: According to the principle in its final and published form, the underestimation of costs and difficulties is non-intentional self-deception, whereas in the Thai irrigation project cost underestimation and overselling was intentional deception of others, according to Hirschman's notes. Hirschman apparently put a more innocent and optimistic spin on the Hiding Hand principle than warranted by the specific project that inspired it. This initial optimism would prove a sign of more to come.

The key mechanism driving the Hiding Hand is optimism caused by an ignorance of difficulties, including costs, which leads people to take on tasks they would not have taken up had they known the real challenges involved:

> The principle [of the Hiding Hand] suggests that far from seeking out and taking up challenges, people typically take on and plunge into new tasks because of the erroneously presumed absence of a challenge, because the task looks easier and more manageable than it will turn out to be. (Hirschman 1967a: 13)

Behavioral economists would later use terms like overconfidence bias, the planning fallacy, and optimism bias to describe and problematize the type of behavior Hirschman observed (Gilovich et al. 2002). Indeed, Sunstein (2015a: 4) thinks that Hirschman "can easily be seen as an early behavioral economist" and that *Development Projects Observed* "can plausibly be counted as a work in behavioral economics." In what follows we will see whether this is a reasonable interpretation and what may be learned from Hirschman and the Hiding Hand in terms of behavioral economics and project management. For now, we note that Hirschman (1967a: 12–13) concludes that "the difficulties [from starting a new project] and the ensuing search for solutions set in motion a train of events that not only rescued the project but often made it particularly valuable." Hirschman thus hypothesized that because of the Hiding Hand, the net benefits of plans end up as high as anticipated, or even higher, even if the costs turn out to be unexpectedly high. With the help of the Hiding Hand, projects turn out to be viable—to have positive net benefits. We therefore summarize the principle of the Hiding Hand—with its emphasis on "two offsetting" or "double" underestimates of costs and benefits—as follows (Hirschman 1967a: 13, 16):

> Higher-than-estimated project costs/difficulties will typically be outweighed by even higher-than-estimated project benefits/problem-solving abilities.

But Hirschman does not stop here. He further describes the functioning of the Hiding Hand as a learning process where the trickery of the Hand serves as a pair of "crutches" for the decision maker or planner,

> permitting him to go forward at a stage when he has not yet acquired enough confidence in his problem-solving ability to make a more candid appraisal of a project's prospective difficulties and of the risks he is assuming. The experience of meeting with these difficulties and risks and of being able to deal with them should then enable him to discard these crutches and to achieve a more mature appraisal of new projects ... The Hiding Hand is essentially a mechanism that makes the risk-averter take risks and in the process turns him into less of a risk-averter. (Hirschman 1967a: 26)

In this way, through "mechanisms of self-deception"—again a formulation that fits well with behavioral economics—the Hiding Hand tricks decision makers into taking risks they would not otherwise have taken and in the process teaches them (a) what the risks are, (b) that the risks are manageable, and (c) that it is therefore okay to be less risk averse for future projects (Hirschman 1967a: 34). "The Hiding Hand is thus essentially a transition mechanism through which decision makers learn to take risks, and *the shorter the transition and the faster the learning the better*," explains Hirschman (1967a: 28, 34; emphasis in original). Quick learning is desirable because it makes decision makers and planners "able to differentiate between acceptable and nonacceptable risk," thus bringing risks down over time with the help of the Hiding Hand. "You have to do all these fool things before you do the sensible things," Hirschman wrote in his field notes (Bianchi 2011: 18). However, there is a key assumption buried in this learning model of decision making, as indicated by Hirschman's use of the little word "should" in the main quote ("should then enable him to discard these crutches"). What happens if the "should" does not apply—that is, if learning does not take place and decision makers do not get better at identifying and managing risks for future projects? We will return to this question later. For now, we summarize this part of the Hiding Hand principle like this:

Project risks will tend to fall over time.

In sum, the Hiding Hand does its work through beneficial ignorance—or "ignorance of ignorance" as Hirschman (1967a: 35) put it. Beneficial ignorance hides two things from decision makers. First, the true costs and difficulties of projects remain obscure, which makes planners take up projects they would not have considered, had they known their true complications. Second, the Hiding Hand also conceals planners' problem-solving ability in dealing with costly and difficult projects, which makes planners able to successfully deal with such projects when the difficulties manifest themselves, at which time the planners' concealed abilities become overt and save the day. Overall, the Hiding Hand is therefore a good thing, according to Hirschman and his followers, because it makes projects go ahead and succeed—based on beneficial ignorance—that would not have done so had planners known at the outset the real costs and difficulties involved, exactly like Willie Brown argued recently (see Section 8.1).

8.3 HIRSCHMAN'S INSPIRATION FOR THE HIDING HAND

In developing the principle of the Hiding Hand, Hirschman (1967a: 16) was strongly influenced by a concept called "creative error," which he said was a close "approximation" to the Hiding Hand principle. This concept had been developed fifteen years previously by Sawyer (2014, first published 1952), who was then a 34-year old assistant professor at Harvard. Sawyer described creative error in the following manner:

> ... one cannot read far in the history of great economic undertakings ... without being struck by ... instances in which entrepreneurial error or misinformation not only is massively present *but where it appears to have been a condition of successful enterprise.* Cases, that is, in which *mis*calculation or sheer ignorance apparently was crucial to getting an enterprise launched at all. (Sawyer 2014: 143; emphasis in original)

Sawyer argued that creative error was key to the building of a number of large and historically important infrastructures, including the Welland Canal between Lake Erie and Lake Ontario, the Panama Canal, the Middlesex Canal, the Troy and Greenfield Railroad, and early Ohio roads. For these and other projects, Sawyer (2014: 144) found that "the error in estimating costs was at least offset by a corresponding error in the estimation of demand." Sawyer (2014: 145) writes of the Welland Canal, for instance:

> [W]e may very plausibly question whether the original capital would have come forward to start or later to complete the enterprise in the period in question had an accurate objective appraisal of final costs been offered. Once begun under benefit of error, however, ways were found gradually to finance the whole; and once completed the Welland Canal established itself beyond reasonable question.

Sawyer was at pains, however, to explain that he did not claim creative error to be a general phenomenon applying to all projects and enterprises. He was simply interested in this specific phenomenon and therefore sampled only projects for his study that had been subject to creative error; that is, projects that (a) had been begun owing to a cost underestimate that made the project look attractive to investors and (b) had actual benefits that outweighed costs making the project a success despite the initial cost underestimate and resulting cost overrun. Sawyer (2014: 147) explained about his sampling that the "only cases of interest" to him were

> a quite special kind of case within a category of investment in which unknowns as to both costs and returns necessarily bulk large; and within that category [I] neglected failures and select[ed] cases which were 'successful' ... despite an original gross miscalculation as to costs because that first error was happily offset by at least a corresponding underestimation of demand.

In fact, Sawyer uses more than a third of his text to explain this highly selective approach to sampling and to caution the reader that his results are an a priori consequence of the sampling and *not* an *ex post* empirical outcome. Sawyer is thus explicit he did not *find* creative error in a random sample of projects; he instead *describes* such error in a sample of projects where each project was selected non-randomly to show creative error. Hirschman completely ignores this aspect of Sawyer's work and presents it as if it supports the Hiding Hand principle and as if both phenomena were *ex post* empirical findings with close similarity:

> The resemblance between this idea [Sawyer's creative error] and the Hiding Hand principle is obvious. There is a double underestimate of both costs and benefits in Sawyer's scheme, while we have observed similarly, if more broadly, a double under-estimate of the various difficulties that lie across the project's path, on the one hand, and of the abilities to solve these difficulties, on the other. (Hirschman 1967a: 16–17)

By conflating his approach with that of Sawyer, and thereby presenting Sawyer's a priory sampling model as an *ex post* empirical result, Hirschman gets Sawyer exactly wrong. In what follows, we will explore the consequences of this for Hirschman's own sampling and for the validity of the Hiding Hand.

8.4 Impact of the Hiding Hand

Believing he had happened on a big idea, and pleased with his allusion to Adam Smith, Hirschman went looking for a large audience. He found it in the readership of *The Public Interest*—a magazine on political economy and culture, edited by Daniel Bell and Irwing Kristol, and aimed at policy makers, fellow scholars, and journalists. Kristol helped Hirschman revise into a more readable article the parts of *Development Projects Observed* about the Hiding Hand (Hirschman 1967b). The article had immediate influence, while the book at first was a bit of a flop, perhaps because the article initially cannibalized the book's market. But later the book gained traction, including with new editions, and it became a classic. Hirschman's ideas were picked up by policy makers and practitioners—from Washington's policy establishment to the United Nations, to the World Bank and development agencies around the world (Adelman 2013: 405). Göran Ohlin, a Swedish diplomat and professor of economics, wrote from the United Nations that he was applying the new concept to industrial development. Andy Kamarck, head of the World Bank's Economics Department, told Hirschman:

> You've helped in part to remove the unease that I have had in reflecting on the fact that if our modern project techniques had been used, much of the existing development in the world would never have been undertaken. It may be that with a further working out of the ideas that you explore in this chapter [chapter 1, "The Principle of the Hiding Hand"], we can avoid this future inhibitory role of economists. (Adelman 2013: 405)

Hirschman was mindful that even before he came along and gave the Hiding Hand principle a name and a theoretical rationale, promoters and developers seemed to be aware of the principle and how to use it to their advantage. In other words, you do not need to know Hirschman's theory to use it, or be subject to it, as is the case for most theory:

> Promoters and developers must long have been dimly aware of the Hiding Hand principle, for they have been remarkably adept at finding ways in which projects that would normally be discriminated against because they are too obviously replete with difficulties and uncertainties can be made to look more attractive to the decision maker. (Hirschman 1967a: 21)

Hirschman here talks about a type of rationalization used by promoters and developers to get projects started by making them look good on paper and in public discourse, typically by underestimating costs, risks, and difficulties while at the same time overestimating benefits and opportunities, so the *ex ante* benefit–cost ratio and general attractiveness of a project appear to be especially inviting. To many, Hirschman's Hiding Hand is appealing precisely because it seems to justify such rationalization. The message is the same as that delivered by Willie Brown for the San Francisco Transbay Terminal megaproject, and by promoters of the Sydney Opera House in the case study to be discussed: "Start digging."

It is easy to understand why this message is popular, especially with promoters and developers of projects. In general, developers like nothing better than to be allowed to proceed with their projects, since this is their job. And the principle of the Hiding Hand is a theory that encourages exactly that. It explains why decision makers should just go ahead and not worry too much about costs or other difficulties. It predicts that outcomes will be acceptable for them in doing so, because the Hiding Hand, with its emphasis on human problem-solving abilities in challenging situations, will overcome the difficulties. With such reasoning from a leading economist and founding father of project management scholarship, who would want to be the killjoy arguing against large projects by fretting about their challenges? Instead, the principle of the Hiding Hand justifies optimism and a propensity for action, both of which resonate deeply with the mentality of project promoters and other bullish people. This, more than anything else, explains why the mechanism of the Hiding Hand has had such deep and long-lasting influence. It also explains why lock-in and escalation of commitment are so pervasive in major project management, and why project abandonment rates are low (Cantarelli et al. 2014; Drummond 2014).[6] As said over and over—like a mantra—by Robert Moses, New York City's former construction coordinator, who probably initiated and led to completion more major projects than anybody else in human history and who is considered by many the ultimate master of lock-in and the Hiding Hand: "*Once you sink that first stake they'll never make you pull it up*" (Caro 1975: 218, 828–32, emphasis in original).

Robert Picciotto, who worked for the World Bank for forty years and who first met Hirschman in 1964, just before he embarked on the field work for *Development Projects Observed*, explained thirty years later, as vice president of the Bank, that the book "has long been an inspiration to project officers ... because it validates their day-to-day experience" (Picciotto 1994a: 341). Picciotto did not hesitate to call the book a "classic," as have many others, and to point out that Hirschman's ideas, which at first seemed subversive to some, including staff at the Bank, have become mainstream (Gasper 1986: 467; Rodwin 1994: 31–2; Alacevich 2014).

The article and the book also made their impact in academia, though more slowly at first. David Riesman, a fellow author from *The Public Interest*, was an early adopter, when he assigned Hirschman's article to his students at Harvard (Adelman 2013: 405). Later, the article and book became standard fare in university courses around the world in topics such as decision making, project management, development economics, planning, evaluation, and appraisal. Hirschman's work even received the rare honor of having a whole academic book dedicated to its exploration, with the Hiding Hand featuring prominently, and with contributions by scholars such as Nobel laureate Paul Krugman of Stanford, Karen Polenske and Donald Schön of MIT, and Jesse Ribot of Harvard (Rodwin and Schön 1994).

There was also critique, needless to say, from both practitioners and academics. When World Bank officials had the opportunity to read Hirschman's interim observations for the book, before publication, they dismissed many of them as "either fairly obvious or definitely wrong" (Alacevich 2014: 153). Hirschman made only minor changes to his manuscript, however, and initially the Bank was disappointed by the book, even if the critique died out after publication (Alacevitc 2014: 156, 163). The Bank was looking for clear, replicable appraisal standards, which Hirschman did not deliver. Academia, too, was more interested in project appraisal and cost–benefit analysis, following the trend of the day. With Hirschman being positively critical of cost–benefit analysis, promoters of this methodology tried not so much to critique Hirschman's book as to ignore it, but without luck in the longer term (Little and Mirrlees 1974; Reutlinger 1970; Squire and van der Tak 1975; Alacevich 2014: 161–4). In fact, Hirschman's ideas, including the Hiding Hand, would be used as an argument to not overemphasize the results of cost–benefit analyses in project appraisal, including by Bank officials, as witnessed by the quote from Andy Kamarck above. In academia, Lal (1983: 176) called the principle of the Hiding Hand "unconvincing" because, if true, it would eliminate the possibility of distinguishing *ex ante* between good and bad projects, which Lal found "absurd." Cracknell (1984: 17) observed that Hirschman's writings on the Hiding Hand made for "entertaining and provocative reading," but it did not fit Cracknell's experience with the UK Overseas Development Office.

Despite the critique, and sometimes probably because of it, today, a half-century after its initial publication, *Development Projects Observed* is still going strong, with a celebration of its ideas, including the Hiding Hand, by Malcolm Gladwell in *The New Yorker* (Gladwell 2013), a dedicated study by a professional historian of the genesis of the book calling it "groundbreaking" (Alacevich 2014: 139), and a new Brookings Classic edition with an enthusiastic preface by Sunstein (2015a) emphasizing the importance of the Hiding Hand.[7] The book is rightly considered among Hirschman's more influential, and the Hiding Hand among his most powerful ideas. Further securing the legacy of this and other work by Hirschman is Adelman's (2013) comprehensive intellectual biography, accompanied by an extensive review in *The New York Review of Books*, rightly calling Hirschman's work an "enduring achievement" (Sunstein 2013: 17).[8]

8.5 But Is It a Theory?

We have seen that Hirschman originally and explicitly used the term "theory" to describe the basic idea behind the principle of the Hiding Hand, namely that ignorance is good when making decisions about projects, because without ignorance, projects would not get started (Alacevich 2014: 157). We also saw that Hirschman insisted that the Hiding Hand is a principle of action aimed at understanding "project behavior *in general*," across project types, organizations, and geographies, including both developed and developing nations (Hirschman 1967a: 1, 13, emphasis added).

Nevertheless, several students of Hirschman claim that the principle of the Hiding Hand is not a theory and that Hirschman was averse to theorizing. Sunstein (2015: 1), for instance, writes that Hirschman "distrusted large claims and law-like generalizations." Adelman (2013: 115–6, 124, 145–6, 198, 236, 420–2, 503, 582, 620, 647) similarly emphasizes Hirschman's attraction to "*petites idées*" and dislike for "grand theory." Bish Sanyal directly calls Hirschman "antitheoretical" (Rodwin and Schön 1994: 320). In comments to an earlier version of the present chapter, Adelman (2015) expands on this line of argument:

> [Hirschman] was decidedly averse to "theory," as you know. And you keep insisting that he calls this a *theory* of the hiding hand. The key word is principle, much more in accord with the heuristic style of classical political economy. He does not seek a causal claim that travels across all time and place, and thus would fully appreciate that his "principle" does not apply in many cases. (Emphasis in original)

Similarly, Sunstein (2015: 1, 4) emphasizes that Hirschman is not a standard economist, as he "is not, in fact, offering a testable hypothesis, but instead a description of a mechanism," emphasizing "narrative descriptions" of actual practices over theory development.

Adelman is right that the key word Hirschman settled on—after first using "theory"— is "principle." But Adelman is wrong that the principle is not a theory and that Hirschman was averse to theory.[9] Hirschman (1994: 277–8) is himself direct and unambiguous on the latter point:

> I am not ... set against paradigms and theorizing. For I like to claim that I have come up with quite a few theoretical notions of my own ... from the ... "supply effect" ...

to ... "unbalanced growth" ... to ... my "tunnel effect." So I bristle a bit when I am
pigeonholed as "atheoretical" or "antitheoretical". (Hirschman 1994: 277–8)

In the same tenor, Hirschman talks explicitly about his "*theoretical* bent" and describes
his work as having "the hallmark of useful *theory* building," just as he is clear and self-
reflected regarding his "contribution to development *theory*" (Hirschman 1994: 278,
emphasis added). There can be no doubt, therefore, that Hirschman saw himself as
doing theory and that he was not against theorizing.

The misunderstanding that Hirschman was averse to theory seems to have arisen
from three sources. First, as observed by Offe (2013: 588–9), Hirschman accomplished
the paradoxical feat of making a "theory about the futility of theorizing," which seems
to have thrown people. Hirschman theorized that theories about the world may actually prove an obstacle to understanding and to effective action. In this sense Adelman
and others are correct that Hirschman is against theory. But he is against only a certain type of theory—the synoptic kind—not theory in general. And this does not make
Hirschman's own work atheoretical, as rightly noted by Offe.

Second, Hirschman's focus on *petites idées* appears to have led to the view that focusing on the particular would stand in opposition to focusing on the general and on theory, and especially grand theory (Adelman 2013). But Hirschman makes clear that for
him an opposition between the particular and the general does not exist: "Immersion
in the particular proved, as usual, essential for the catching of anything general," he
wrote in the Introduction to *Development Projects Observed*, dissolving the opposition
between the two (Hirschman 1967a: 3). Hirschman was too sophisticated a thinker to
operate in simple dichotomies of either/or. Instead he followed an old and fundamental phenomenological insight, that small questions often lead to big answers, and that
scholars therefore need to do work that is at the same time as detailed and as general
as possible. Such an approach voids the opposition of small and big, of *petites idées*
and theory. One leads to the other, instead of excluding it, according to this line of
thought, which is why Hirschman emphasized both *petites idées* and theory (Flyvbjerg
2001: 133–4).

Third, there is a confusion in the literature about Hirschman of two different uses
of theory: for explanation and for design. The use of theory for explanation is what
Hirschman talks about above, and he had no issue with this, not for himself nor for
other social scientists, except that some theories explain better than others, needless to
say. The use of theory for design, where law-like ideas are used to prescribe and plan
social action, or even the social order, is a different matter. Hirschman generally saw
such social engineering—whether driven by experts or revolutionaries—as highly
problematic and bound to fail. He was against theory used in this manner, especially in
development policy. However, in the present chapter we focus on theory as explanation,
and the principle of the Hiding Hand was very much developed by Hirschman to be
such a theory, with truth claims and causal mechanisms.

To illustrate, we have seen that in formulating the principle of the Hiding Hand,
Hirschman (1967a: 13, 15) made the statement that "people typically take on and plunge

into new tasks because of the erroneously presumed absence of a challenge, because the task looks easier and more manageable than it will turn out to be ... [T]otal costs are underestimated and investment decisions activated in consequence." This central statement is a truth claim about how people behave when starting new projects, and it explicates both causal mechanisms ("because," "in consequence") and assertions that may be tested. With the word "typically," Hirschman clearly asserts that the depicted behavior applies more often than not, which again is a specific claim that may be tested empirically, as discussed later. The same applies to the statement that "costs are underestimated" also discussed later. There is nothing in these truth claims that is alien to theorizing, explanation, and hypothesis testing, and in this sense the principle of the Hiding Hand is a theory. It explains, it predicts, it is testable. Adelman, Sunstein, and others are therefore wrong and patronizing when they deny Hirschman his explicit claims at theorizing. Whether his theories are valid is another question. Adelman and Sunstein are right, however, that Hirschman is not a conventional positivistic hypotheses-testing economist. He was too clever for that, understanding the power of phenomenology, case studies, thick description, and narrative.

Adelman and Sunstein are also wrong when they want to reduce the principle of the Hiding Hand to a "heuristic" or "mechanism," respectively. A heuristic is a rule of thumb or an educated guess that works under certain limited circumstances, but without claims of general applicability. This is much too modest an interpretation of the principle of the Hiding Hand. We have seen that Hirschman repeatedly emphasized that the principle is a general one, and that it applies across project types and geographies. Adelman is right, however, that Hirschman does not seek a causal claim that travels across "all" time and place. But few, if any, social science theories apply to all time and place (Flyvbjerg 2001), so this is hardly a useful criterion to identify the Hiding Hand as less of a theory than other work in the social sciences. Hirschman (1967a: 13, 16–17) explicitly says that the Hiding Hand "typically" applies—that is, more often than not—and he explains how it applies (by a "double underestimate" of costs/difficulties and benefits/problem-solving abilities). This is enough to qualify as theory, and it is much more than a heuristic.

Even if Adelman, Sunstein, and others are right when they say that Hirschman is not a standard economist, they are wrong when they describe him as mainly a "novelist" who uncovers and narrates stories that conventional economists overlooked or could not be bothered to tell (Krugman 1994: 287). Hirschman, too, would not agree with this. He explicitly rejects comments like these in the following manner:

> I ... cannot wholly agree when I am portrayed ... as someone who is primarily interested in noticing and underlining what more systematic-minded (theoretical) economists or social scientists have overlooked. (Hirschman 1994: 278; parentheses in original)

Such depiction of Hirschman is here also at odds with Sunstein's description of him as an early behavioral economist and of *Development Projects Observed* as a work in behavioral economics (Sunstein 2015a: 4). Behavioral economics is all about theorizing and the testing of hypotheses. So to claim Hirschman for this particular brand of economics and at the same time call him a "storyteller" not interested in hypotheses testing seems self-contradictory.

Finally, Adelman and Sunstein are wrong when they say the principle of the Hiding Hand is not testable. They might be right that such test was not a main concern for Hirschman; but that does not mean the truth claims of the Hiding Hand could or should not be tested. And perhaps Hirschman should have paid more attention to this, as we will see. In any case, in what follows we will see that such test is possible by returning to the three trials mentioned in the introduction to this chapter—the first of which is a test of the Hiding Hand against a paradigmatic case: Sydney Opera House.

8.6 SYDNEY OPERA HOUSE: A PARADIGMATIC CASE OF THE HIDING HAND

The principle of the Hiding Hand has been assumed to apply in exemplary fashion to the case of Sydney Opera House. The Opera House was inaugurated in 1973, and people are on record, then and now, stating that the Hiding Hand logic was crucial to making the project happen (for the full case see Flyvbjerg 2005a). New South Wales premier, Joe Cahill, who was up for re-election and fighting cancer, was as unapologetic as Willie Brown and Robert Moses above in low-balling the initial budget for the Opera House, to get it approved in Parliament. Cahill told his people: "I want you to go down to Bennelong Point [the location of the Opera House site] and make such progress that no one who succeeds me can stop this going through to completion."[10] Or in Willie Brown's words, again: "The idea is to get going. Start digging." Which they did in Sydney, literally, even before they had drawings of what they were building. Like Robert Moses, Cahill was a master of lock-in and escalation of commitment. People are also on record saying that this is a good thing (Skaburskis and Teitz 2003). The Opera House thus seems to be a paradigmatic case of the principle of the Hiding Hand—that is, a prototype proving Hirschman to be right about the benefits of the Hiding Hand. Here we test whether this interpretation is borne out by the facts of the matter.

Sydney Opera House was initially estimated to cost AU$ 7 million, but ended up actually costing AU$102 million and taking ten years longer to build than projected.[11] The 1,400% cost increase caused huge political and financial problems, but eventually the building was completed and it turned out to be a treasure to Sydney, New South Wales, Australia, and the world, with benefits seemingly far outweighing costs. In 2007, the Opera House was declared a UNESCO World Heritage Site—the youngest building in the world to achieve such status—on a par with the pyramids of Egypt and the Taj Mahal. Certainly this is a success story, a poster child of the Hiding Hand at work. And surely it is justified that the Opera House is often used to defend and confirm the logic of the Hiding Hand.

Skaburskis and Teitz (2003: 439) follow the Hiding Hand logic when—in a general debate over whether or not cost underestimates and overruns matter—they use Sydney Opera House as an example, and ask:

> Did people really think that the Sydney Opera House would come in on budget? Or did we all agree to accept the deception and engage in wishful thinking in order to make something that we really wanted happen? ... [D]o Australians really regret those dramatic sails in the harbour? Or would they have regretted more the deci-sion [not to build] that would most reasonably have been based on a fair prediction of costs?

This is the logic of the Hiding Hand at its most clear and most seductive. Who in their right mind would answer in the negative to these questions—especially anyone who has been to Sydney and witnessed the grace and magnificence of the Opera House? Let us stress test the rhetoric, however.

In retrospect, of course, Australians do not regret the Sydney Opera House. It has placed Australia on the world map like nothing else, helping the country move beyond the stigma of being known as a cultural backwater. In the process, a torrent of tour-ist dollars has followed, far outweighing the costs of the building, with more than seven million people visiting it each year. At first, though, the building was not called "dramatic sails in the harbour." This is an *ex post facto* rationalization of the aesthetic of the building. During design and construction, you would publicly see the aesthetic described as "copulating white turtles" or "something that is crawling out of the ocean with nothing good in mind," designed by an architect with "lousy taste" (Reichold and Graf 2004: 168).

Talking about the architect, only few people know his name, which is surprising given he designed arguably the most iconic building of the twentieth century.[12] And, if people know the name is Jørn Utzon, they can typically not name another building designed by him. The reason is that the cost overrun on the Sydney Opera House, and the contro-versy that followed, destroyed Utzon's reputation and career and kept him from build-ing more masterpieces. He was scapegoated for the problems on the Opera House and became that most tragic figure in architecture: the "one-building-architect."[13] This is the real "regret"—and real cost—of the Sydney Opera House (Flyvbjerg 2005a). To gauge the dimensions of this architectural and aesthetic tragedy, as a thought experiment con-sider the collected works of architect Frank Gehry, who is judged by his peers to be in the same league as Utzon. Then consider which Gehry building you would choose, if you could choose only one, and the rest would have to go. This illustrates the high price the government of New South Wales imposed on the world by deliberately playing the game of the Hiding Hand and thereby mismanaging the planning and construction of Sydney Opera House.

As observed by Picciotto (1994a: 221–2), the Hiding Hand all too easily turns into a sleight of hand used by people in powerful positions to get what they want. This is what happened in Sydney. Only on the surface of things does the Sydney Opera House look like a paradigmatic case of the Hiding Hand. Digging below the surface, we find that the Opera House is the exact opposite. It is a paradigmatic case of the disastrous consequences that may derive from managing by the Hiding Hand—here the destruction of the career and *oeuvre* of one of the most gifted architects of the twentieth century. Sydney drives home an important point: managing by the Hiding Hand is risky and disruptive, sometimes in drastic and unexpected ways, and the Hiding Hand is not big enough to hide all, or even most, difficulties. Some of the projects Hirschman studied incurred even more disastrous consequences than Sydney Opera House did, as we will see, though we would never know this from reading Hirschman.

8.7 Validity of the Hiding Hand

Besides not accounting well for cases it is supposed to explain, such as Sydney Opera House, the Hiding Hand is also flawed at a more fundamental level—that of sampling and data collection, with detrimental implications for scholarly validity. A close look reveals Hirschman's ideas to be based on an exceedingly small number of observations and biased data. Hirschman studied only eleven development projects, spread over four continents (Hirschman 1967a: 2–3).[14] That, as we will see, is much too limited a dataset to support the wide conclusions drawn. Yet Hirschman's small sample size has typically been ignored or papered over in the secondary literature, leaving the impression that the empirical foundations of the Hiding Hand are solid. This has become conventional wisdom, because, as often happens, the secondary literature has attracted more readers than the primary source. Elster (1983: 158), for instance, says that Hirschman did "numerous case studies" in support of the Hiding Hand; Catino (2013: 62) that Hirschman based the principle on "many projects analyzed." Other authors have glossed over the problem of sample size by euphemistically talking of "a number of" (Cracknell 1984: 17), "a series of" (Alacevich 2014: 139), or "various" (Lepenies 2008: 450) projects studied by Hirschman, or they have simply reported his results without reference to the sample size at all, like Klitgaard (1997: 1963). It is interesting to note that once a theory has become generally accepted and widely popular, apparently even highly regarded scholars do not bother to check and report on its empirical basis, not to speak of testing it. Based on such writings, which are typical of the literature on the Hiding Hand, readers have been led to believe that the empirical foundation of the Hiding Hand is sound. Only by going back and checking the primary source would a reader get an inkling that, in fact, a big question mark hovers over the principle of the Hiding Hand in terms of the most basic issue for any scholarly work: namely, that of validity and reliability.

It is not that Hirschman was unwarned regarding possible problems arising from his small sample of projects. As mentioned, the projects in the sample were all financed by the World Bank, and Hirschman collaborated with officials there in selecting the projects. The Bank initially had high hopes for the study, but when they saw the proposed sample, several Bank officials became skeptical. Robert F. Skillings, an economist with the Bank, explicitly warned against "the problems of random factors which unavoidably enter into a very small sample" (Adelman 2013: 388). Another officer similarly wondered "whether … such a small sample as a dozen projects out of about 300 [the relevant total at the time] will be sufficient to bring out valid general conclusions" (Alacevich 2014: 147). But Hirschman wanted to be able to personally visit each project and carry out his own interviews and observations on site, which made a large sample impractical. So he stuck to his eleven projects, despite the initial critique, which again was silenced by the popular appeal and positive reception of the work.

In addition to issues of sampling, a second problem with Hirschman's study of the Hiding Hand is biased data collection. Adelman (2013: 388) has systematically gone through the "abundance of field notes" behind the study. He found that the notes convey "a strong impression of basic confusion." Hirschman apparently "struggled to make sense of his observations" and "was having difficulty keeping his endeavor clear," because so many of the projects seemed idiosyncratic, whereas Hirschman wanted to ignore peculiarities in favor of "some broad brush strokes" (Adelman 2013: 388, 396). One might speculate that Hirschman's need for order and broad strokes became particularly strong exactly because of the confused state of his data collection. In any case, the principle of the Hiding Hand eventually became the main broad brush stroke.

According to Hirschman's notes, the "running theme" for the many project managers he interviewed was "that their projects had 'failed'" (Adelman 2013: 389). However, he "tended to be more hopeful than his witnesses," judging by his notes and his book, and he insisted on looking for things that worked despite the frustration of his informants. "Identifying silver linings was becoming an occupational habit" for Hirschman, according to Adelman (2013: 392)—and, one might add, an occupational *hazard*, because Hirschman's disordered approach meant that his biases ("silver linings") were never systematically problematized and tested for validity. Instead, Hirschman's optimism survived unproblematized through data collection; it "blinded him," and "his wish for surprising, positive effects overwhelmed what he saw and heard," according to Adelman's (2013: 393) detailed analysis of the archives.[15] Picciotto (1994b: 303) similarly observes that for Hirschman the reality of the development process, including principal-agent problems and other systemic difficulties, was "all cloaked in optimism and romanticism." In the present author's view, it might be completely legitimate—perhaps even ingenious—for a scholar to look for success where others see failure. But this would require the scholar to be open about his or her approach, so that others may test it. This is not what Hirschman did. For whatever reason, intentionally or not, Hirschman concealed his biased data collection, which made it appear that the Hiding Hand was an attribute of the projects he studied, when it was, in fact, an attribute of his biases and "the story he spun" to fit his data, which eventually became the story of the Hiding Hand (Adelman 2013: 394). The optimism of the Hiding Hand is that of its author and is not justified by the evidence—not even Hirschman's own evidence, as revealed in his field notes—according to this analysis. Offe (2013: 588) observes that Hirschman's optimistic model of development—where unforeseen challenges provide opportunities for creative solutions followed by success—is a "mirror image of his own life experience," from his escape from Nazi Germany to repeat immigrant experiences in France, England, Italy, Spain, and the United States. Offe speculates that this personal experience is the root cause of the pervasive optimism in Hirschman's scholarly work.[16] In Hirschman's (1971) own words, he had a "bias for hope" to a degree where this became the title of one of his later books.

Yale political scientist Charles Lindblom, who had earlier accompanied Hirschman on field research, warned him of the dangers of his approach (Adelman 2013: 396). So did Walter Salant of the Brookings Institution, who pointed out in a private note to Hirschman that his analysis was one-sided in the sense that it tackled only cases "where the difficulties and abilities to solve them were underestimated" (Adelman 2013: 404). What about cases where difficulties are underestimated and the ability to solve them overestimated, asked Salant? In his response, again private, Hirschman agreed that this was an issue, and he admitted that he had wanted "to emphasize unexpected successes," in order to show how the Hiding Hand might get risk averters to act (Adelman 2013: 405). Hirschman's emphasis on success is similar to Sawyer's selective sampling for creative error, described previously, with the important difference that Sawyer made it completely clear that he sampled for success, whereas Hirschman concealed this, both for Sawyer's work and for his own. Hirschman, in this manner, misrepresents his own and Sawyer's study. Given how emphatic Sawyer was regarding the issue of biased sampling, using a third of his text explaining it, it is difficult to see how Hirschman could have just overlooked this by accident. The omission seems to be by design. Nowhere in Hirschman (1967a, 1967b) is the biased data collection mentioned, leaving the illusion that Hirschman's Hiding Hand is an *ex post* empirical finding obtained from studying his data—an illusion that posterity has accepted—when in reality it is a methodological artifact of how the data were collected, including only observations that would affirm the Hiding Hand.

On this point, it is interesting to note a slight—almost imperceptible—difference between the way the Hiding Hand is presented in the original text, in *Development Projects Observed* (Hirschman 1967a), and in the edited text for *The Public Interest* (Hirschman 1967b). In the book, Hirschman (1967a: 7, 14) seems to hedge ever so slightly against some of the weaknesses identified previously, when, in passing, he calls the Hiding Hand "speculative" and useful only "[u]p to a point." The same applies to his private comment to Thomas Schelling (mentioned in Section 8.1) that the book was "an exploration, an experiment." It may seem somewhat disingenuous on the part of Hirschman, and methodologically unsound, that he would consider his work an experiment, but without telling his readers. He seems here to be aware, and was made aware by his colleagues, that the Hiding Hand may have weaknesses, even if, in his optimism, he never explored or even mentioned this. In the article for *The Public Interest*, however, the qualifiers in the book are edited out completely. Because of its initial wider circulation, the article came to dominate the reading of the Hiding Hand, and after its success, the reservations, which had been weak to begin with, were quickly ignored, both by Hirschman and his readers. Evidently the temptation to claim a general principle—an economic law in the tradition of Adam Smith and other great economists—was too big for Hirschman, despite the inadequate and biased data. Ironically, the scholar who would later become known for his devotion to *petites idées* and dislike for grand theory (Adelman 2013: 115–16), at this time unabashedly formulated and promoted a really Big Idea—the principle of the Hiding Hand.

Paul Krugman dismisses Hirschman as a "novelist" who "seduces people" by the "richness of plain English" (Krugman 1994: 287; Rodwin 1994: 11). This is a harsh assessment, and it has been countered by Tendler (1994: 289), who maintains that "Hirschman is more than a 'storyteller.'" Rodwin (1994: 11) has similarly, and rightly, identified Krugman's critique as self-defeating, because Krugman employs extensive storytelling to argue his point; in effect using storytelling to reject storytelling, which does not hold up in the court of methodological consistency, needless to say. But Krugman's and Tendler's viewpoints are both based on the false assumption that "storytelling" is a second-rate methodology in social science. To many, however, storytelling, or narrative, is one of the most powerful methods in the toolbox of social scientists, which is why even Krugman uses it, when it really counts. Witness the fact that many of the most treasured classics in each social science discipline are based on storytelling (Flyvbjerg 2001, 2011). But storytelling is just one method among many, and it may be done well or less well, like other methods. The problem with Hirschman is not storytelling as such; the problem is *bad* storytelling. If Hirschman had honored normal social science standards for validity and reliability in sampling, data collection, and analysis, he would have produced a valid and reliable narrative about his observations. Instead he violated basic rules of research and, as a consequence, produced an invalid and unreliable study. To this extent Krugman's critique is justified. But this has nothing to do with storytelling, even if Hirschman's is the type of work that gives storytelling a bad name. Instead it has everything to do with garbage-in-garbage-out, which applies to *any* methodology.

In his foreword to the 2015 edition of *Development Projects Observed*, Sunstein (2015a: 5) suggests that an "uncharitable reading" of Hirschman's book would indicate that he has committed the fallacy which statisticians call sampling on the dependent variable. Sunstein understandably has to be charitable to Hirschman in a foreword to his classic text. I would suggest, however, that pointing to Hirschman's fallacy is not an uncharitable reading but a precise and balanced one, and that this fallacy renders Hirschman's study invalid in scholarly terms. However, Sunstein's (2015a: 4) interpretation of Hirschman as an early behavioral economist, and of his publications on the Hiding Hand as works in behavioral economics, are a stretch. Hirschman's methodology is too non-rigorous and his data too low-quality, compared with mainstream behavioral economics. Moreover, contrary to behavioral economists, who tend to see overconfidence and bias as negative to outcomes, Hirschman emphasizes the positive aspects of biased behavior, because overconfidence and optimism are what trigger the Hiding Hand in his scheme of thought. Instead of seeing Hirschman as an example of an early behavioral economist we might therefore see him as a case for behavioral economists to study: a case of how damaging optimism bias can be, not only in policy and business, but in scholarship as well. Hirschman was more a victim than a student of bias.

One may well share Hirschman's view that the ability to problem-solve when unforeseen challenges arise is more important to success in large-scale ventures than even the best-laid strategies, synoptic planning, and cost–benefit analyses. But with the Hiding Hand Hirschman optimistically assumes that problem-solving abilities will be triggered when needed, instead of making this a question for empirical test. This is Hirschman's main error: he mistook, and misrepresented, his own optimistic view for empirical reality. All would have been well if he had claimed no more and no less than the following: (i) to have developed certain ideas—most importantly the Hiding Hand—based on studying a small sample of projects; (ii) that these ideas, in his view, might be useful for understanding economic development and the planning of large projects; and (iii) to warn that due to the small sample size, and because he deliberately collected data to emphasize success, it is impossible to know how often and where the ideas apply in the wider population of projects. Further study would need to clarify this. That would have been an honest and balanced way for Hirschman to present his study. Instead, he overextended his ideas, and especially the Hiding Hand, as a general principle of action. The fact is that neither Hirschman nor we know whether the Hiding Hand is in reality such a general principle, or just how general or local it is. Fifty years after the formulation of the principle, no-one has tested this in scholarly terms. Such test is the subject of the following two sections.

8.8 Does the Hiding Hand Save Failing Projects?

We have seen that Hirschman developed the principle of the Hiding Hand based on data from eleven large projects. Now we will test the principle against a bigger and better dataset, consisting of 2,062 such projects. We will see whether Hirschman's results are replicated with the greater sample.[17] The data are from the largest database of its kind, and cover the eight project types listed in Table 8.1. They are infrastructure projects like most of the projects in Hirschman's smaller sample.[18] For each project in the dataset, two datapoints were measured: namely, cost overrun and benefit overrun, respectively. Geographically, the dataset includes projects in 104 countries on six continents, covering both developed and developing nations. Historically, the data cover almost a century, from 1927 to 2013. Older projects were included to enable analyses of historical trends. The data were collected by the author and his colleagues over the past twenty years. Data collection systematically followed international standards—as opposed to Hirschman's idiosyncratic and biased data collection described previously—and the quality of the data is therefore correspondingly higher. Data collection and the database are described in detail in Flyvbjerg et al. (2002, 2005a) and Flyvbjerg (2005b).

As we have seen, the principle of the Hiding Hand may be summarized in the following two claims about project performance:

1. Higher-than-estimated project costs/difficulties will typically be outweighed by even higher-than-estimated project benefits/problem-solving abilities.
2. Project risks will tend to fall over time.

If the Hiding Hand principle is correct, then the two claims will, on average, be confirmed by actual project performance. If the principle is wrong, the claims will be rejected. We now test each of the two claims in turn.

Table 8.1 shows the results from a test of Hirschman's first claim, that higher-than-estimated project costs/difficulties (cost overrun) will be outweighed by even higher-than-estimated benefits/problem-solving abilities (benefit overrun); this is the situation where the problem-solving abilities of the Hiding Hand come to the rescue of projects that are failing due to unexpected difficulties and cost overruns. In Table 8.1, ideally

Table 8.1   Are higher-than-estimated costs outweighed by even higher-than-estimated benefits, as the Hiding Hand claims? The answer is a clear "no"; the Hiding Hand is rejected. (Cost and benefit overruns measured as actual divided by estimated costs and benefits A/E, respectively, in real terms.)

Project type	Cost overrun		Benefit overrun		p*
	N	Average cost overrun (A/E)	N	Average benefit overrun (A/E)	
Dams	243	1.96	84	0.89	<0.0001
BRT†	6	1.41	4	0.42	0.007
Rail	264	1.40	74	0.66	<0.0001
Tunnels	48	1.36	23	0.81	0.015
Power plants	100	1.36	23	0.94	0.0003
Buildings	24	1.36	20	0.99	0.01
Bridges	49	1.32	26	0.96	<0.0001
Roads	869	1.24	532	0.96	<0.0001
Total	1603	1.39 / 1.43‡	786	0.9 / 0.83‡	<0.0001

*) The p-value of the test with null hypothesis that benefit overrun is actually larger than cost overrun, using Mann–Whitney test (smaller p-values are better).

†) Bus rapid transit.

‡) Weighted and unweighted average, respectively.

costs and benefits would be measured over the full life cycle of a project. However, such data are rarely, if ever, available. International convention is therefore to measure costs/difficulties by the proxy of construction costs and benefits/problem-solving abilities by the proxy of first-year benefits. This convention is followed here. First-year benefits may seem a narrow proxy to use for overall benefits, and it has been criticized as such. But in fact, first-year benefits are a reliable measure, which is fortunate because the existence of benefits data for later years is so rare that benefits measurement would be rendered virtually impossible for large samples if we had to rely on later-year data. For a smaller sample of projects for which data are available on estimated and actual benefits covering more than one year after operations begin, it turns out that projects with lower-than-estimated benefits during the first year of operations also tend to have lower-than-estimated benefits in later years (Flyvbjerg 2013: 766–7). Using the first year as the basis for measuring benefits therefore appears not often to result in the error of identifying projects as underperforming in terms of benefits that would not be identified as such if a different time period were used as the basis for comparison.[19]

Cost overrun is measured as actual divided by estimated cost in real terms; that is, without inflation. Benefit overrun is measured as actual divided by estimated usage; for example, traffic for transportation infrastructure and power generation for energy infrastructure. Estimated costs and benefits are the estimates made at the time of decision to build (final business case). Actual costs are measured as recorded outturn costs; actual benefits as first-year benefits, or a later value as close to this as possible, if available and if first-year benefits were not available. Taking rail as an example, average cost overrun is listed in Table 8.1 as 1.40, which means that for rail projects actual costs turned out to be 40% higher than estimated costs on average and in real terms. Average benefit overrun for rail is listed as 0.66, which is evidence of a benefit shortfall of 34%, meaning that on average 34% of the estimated passengers never showed up on the actual trains.

If the basic idea of the Hiding Hand were correct, average benefit overrun would be larger than average cost overrun. We see that this is not the case for rail projects or for any of the eight project types in Table 8.1. Moreover, we see that for each and all project types on average there is no benefit overrun at all, but instead a benefit shortfall (benefit overrun < 1), which not only does not fit Hirschman's claim, but runs diametrically counter to it.[20] From the p-values in Table 8.1 we see that the rejection of the Hiding Hand applies at an overwhelmingly high level of statistical significance ($p<0.0001$, Mann–Whitney test)—a level that is rarely found in studies of social phenomena.[21]

To test the robustness of results, we ran the same tests for a subsample of 327 projects for which data were available for both cost overrun and benefit overrun for each project.[22] The results were similar. Average cost overrun for this subsample is 1.53, average benefit overrun 0.89 (compared with 1.39 and 0.9, respectively, for the larger sample). And again Hirschman's claim that benefit overrun is larger than cost overrun is rejected at an overwhelmingly high level of statistical significance ($p<0.0001$, paired Wilcoxon test). Finally, we tested results for the influence of project type and geography using Bayesian modeling.[23] We found only few significant differences across project type and geography and none of them ran counter to the main conclusion above that higher-than-estimated costs are *not* outweighed by even higher-than-estimated benefits. This is unsurprising, given the overwhelmingly high level of statistical significance at which the main claim was rejected.

It is particularly noteworthy for the tests above, that on average not only is benefit overrun not larger than cost overrun, as the Hiding Hand says it would be, but there is no benefit overrun at all. Instead we find the opposite, namely a benefit shortfall. This shows that Hirschman's idea of the Hiding Hand is wrong both by degree and by direction as it gets both the size and sign (minus instead of plus) wrong for benefit overrun. Instead of projects that generate benefits that compensate for cost overruns, as optimistically theorized by Hirschman (1967a: 13) with his "two offsetting underestimates," in reality the average project is impaired by a double whammy of substantial cost overruns compounded by substantial benefit shortfalls. This is bad for viability, needless to say, and if projects are large enough and the economies where they are built are fragile, just one major project gone wrong can negatively affect the national economy for decades, as Brazil and Pakistan have learned with their large-dams projects (Ansar et al. 2014), and Greece with the 2004 Olympics (Flyvbjerg and Stewart 2012). This problem is not limited to public-sector projects. Cost overruns, delays, and revenue shortfalls on the Airbus A380 jumbo jet put the company at risk and cost top management their jobs; K-Mart went bankrupt due to a billion-dollar IT project similarly gone wrong. Where is the Hiding Hand when you need it, the owners of these projects might rightly have asked Hirschman.

Sunstein (2015a: 4) adds an interesting and useful twist to the Hiding Hand, when he claims that the Hand has an "evil twin." Picciotto (1994b: 302) similarly observes that "[t]here might be two hiding hands." One is a Benevolent Hiding Hand, which is Hirschman's topic, the other a Malevolent Hiding Hand, "which also hides obstacles and difficulties, but in situations in which creativity does not emerge, or emerges too late, or cannot possibly save the day" (Sunstein 2015a: 4–5). For such situations, Streeten (1984: 116) talked about the "Principle of the Hiding Fist." Hirschman did not deny that circumstances like this may exist, but he never tested the obvious question as to which of the two Hiding Hands was the more common empirically—the benevolent or the malevolent one—and neither did anyone else. This question was not Hirschman's interest, and instead he optimistically claimed, based on the biased evidence from his eleven World Bank projects, that the Benevolent Hiding Hand is typical and thus the more common of the two. However, based on the data presented above we must reject this claim. According to the data, the "evil twin"—the Malevolent Hiding Hand, for which higher-than-estimated costs are *not* outweighed by even higher-than-estimated benefits—outnumbers the Benevolent Hiding Hand by a factor of 3.5:1. And again the rejection applies at an overwhelmingly high level of statistical significance, indicating just how wrong the claim of the Benevolent Hiding Hand is (p<0.0001, Mann–Whitney test, one-sided). Instead of Hirschman's Benevolent Hiding Hand being typical, as Hirschman theorized, the Malevolent Hiding Hand dominates by being present in 78% of projects.[24,25]

It should be stressed that the clear statistical rejection of the Hiding Hand does not mean that projects do not exist for which the Hiding Hand applies or that such projects may not be an interesting special case for study, as demonstrated by Sawyer (2014) and described previously.[26] Even in the dataset used to reject the Hiding Hand it would be easy to fish out projects that confirm its basic idea. For instance, the German Karlsruhe–Bretten light-rail line, which is in the dataset, had a cost overrun in real terms of 78% but an even larger benefit overrun of 158%, making the project viable, in accordance with the Hiding Hand. Similarly, the Danish Great Belt toll bridge—the longest suspension bridge in the world at the time of completion—had a cost overrun of 45% combined with a benefit overrun of 90%, again making the project fit Hirschman's principle. And so on. But to do data fishing like this and then call what you find a general principle of action, like Hirschman (1967a: 13) does, is more than a little disingenuous.[27] Data fishing is one of the oldest—and most unethical—tricks in the book of applied statistics. And while Hirschman did not directly fish data out of an existing dataset, we know from his notes and private correspondence that during data collection he deliberately emphasized success cases instead of representative ones, to the same effect and without telling his readers. The data fishing was done discreetly and was glossed over in Hirschman's writings, where it stayed concealed fifty years. In this instance, Krugman (1994: 287) is justified in criticizing Hirschman for seducing—and misleading—people by the "richness of plain English." To be generous to Hirschman, we may speculate that like any true optimist—and Hirschman was clearly an optimist, as argued earlier—he seduced not only his readers but also himself, which is what makes him more of an object for study by behavioral economists than a subject doing behavioral economics, as said.

8.9 Does the Hiding Hand Reduce Project Risk over Time?

Hirschman's second main claim is that project risks will come down over time because of learning from one project to the next. We saw that Hirschman depicts the Hiding Hand "essentially" as a "mechanism through which decision makers learn to take risks" and that, therefore, *"the faster the learning the better"* (Hirschman 1967a: 28; emphasis in original). Specifically, learning via the Hiding Hand makes decision makers better able to reduce risks over time as they find out how to distinguish between acceptable and nonacceptable risks, according to Hirschman. Schön (1994: 69) has studied Hirschman's theory of learning and rightly observes that: "A theory about learning must deal with performance that improves over time. Performance that deteriorates, regresses, or merely swings from one mode of action to another does not qualify as learning." In the context of the Hiding Hand, improved performance would mean a reduction of project risks over time, resulting in cost risks and benefit risks coming down, if not in the short term then in the medium and long term. If the data show such reduction, they support the Hiding Hand. If the data show no reduction, one would have to conclude that no learning takes place and that the Hiding Hand must be rejected on this count too.

Figure 8.1 shows the historical trend in cost and benefit risks, measured as cost and benefit overrun, for the projects in Table 8.1 for which data also exist for opening year. The data cover projects opened to service in the period from 1927 to 2011. If Hirschman's claims about learning were right, then cost overrun would come down

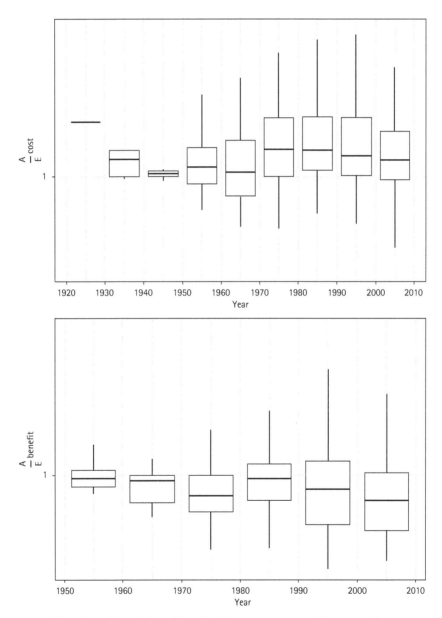

FIGURE 8.1 Box plots of cost risk and benefit risk 1920–2011; cost risk measured as cost overrun ($N = 1271$), benefit risk as benefit overrun ($N = 625$).

over time and benefit overrun would go up, both indicating reduced risks and better project performance. Considering Figure 8.1, no clear historical trends seem apparent. For cost overrun, statistical tests corroborate this impression as no significant relationship is found between cost overrun and time when using all 1,271 projects with information available for cost overrun and opening year (BF = 1.70, Bayesian test). When we analyze the 327 projects with available information for cost overrun, benefit overrun, and opening year, there appears to be a reduction in cost overrun over time of about 0.5% per year, which is statistically significant (BF = 134). The latter dataset includes data from 1952 to 2011.[28]

For benefit overrun, the tests show a statistically highly significant historical trend of declining performance of 0.5% per year, which again is the exact opposite of Hirschman's claim (BF = 799). This is when using the 625 projects with information about benefit overrun and opening year. When using the 327 projects with data for cost overrun, benefit overrun, and opening year, the significance disappears and we witness no movement over time, which again runs counter to Hirschman's claim. Moreover, the intercept is significantly less than one at 0.86 (BF = 17), indicating that instead of benefit overruns we actually find benefit shortfalls, opposite the claim.

For benefit overrun minus cost overrun, there is no significant movement over time, but the intercept stays highly significantly negative (BF = 2352), indicating that benefit overrun is consistently less than cost overrun, once more counter to Hirschman's claim. This is for the sample of 327 projects. For the period after 1980, the intercept is highly significantly negative at –1.031 (BF > 10000), but there is a significant movement over time: benefit overrun minus cost overrun is getting larger by 0.014 per year (BF = 90). This is not a percentage increase, but a nominal yearly increase. It is a positive development, to be sure, but unfortunately the increase is so small that, starting at the negative intercept, it would take seventy-four years for benefit overrun minus cost overrun to finally become positive; that is, before Hirschman's claim would become true that higher-than-estimated costs are outweighed by even higher-than-estimated benefits. Finally, the positive trend is not supported by the larger and thus more reliable samples of 1,271 projects (cost overrun) and 625 projects (benefit overrun), respectively.

Again, we tested for the influence of project type and geography using Bayesian modeling. Here we found statistical indication that cost overrun for dams have increased over time whereas cost overrun for rail has decreased; for the remaining six project types there was no statistically significant trend. For benefits, we found increasing overruns over time for power projects whereas overruns for roads were decreasing; again there was no statistically significant trend for the remaining six project types. Regarding geography, we found that cost overrun has increased over time in Latin America and North America, whereas cost overrun has decreased in Asia and Europe; for Africa and Oceania there were no statistically significant trends.[29] For benefit overrun, we found decreasing overruns (increasing benefit shortfalls) for Asia and Latin America; there was no statistically significant trend for Africa, Europe, North America, and Oceania. It should be mentioned that the differences between project types and geographies as regards change over time may be due to small numbers, especially for the early part of the period where observations are scant. Even if the dataset is the largest of its kind, when it is subdivided into eight project types, six regions, and up to nine time periods, some of the subsamples become quite small and results correspondingly less reliable. But even with the small subsamples, when splitting by country and project type there is still a clear effect, which confirms just how strong that effect is.

In sum, the statistical tests of the Hiding Hand carried out above falsify Hirschman's claims at an overwhelmingly high level of statistical significance. Not only do the data not support Hirschman's main claim—that higher-than-estimated project costs will typically be outweighed by even higher-than-estimated benefits—they show the exact opposite to be true. The typical (average) project is impeded by a double whammy of higher-than-estimated costs and lower-than-estimated benefits. This undermines project viability in a majority of cases instead of saving projects by the creative problem solving and benefit generation predicted by the Hiding Hand. In other words, Hirschman's Benevolent Hiding Hand is dominated by its "evil twin," Sunstein's Malevolent Hiding Hand. And not only do the data show this dominance to be remarkably consistent across all project types and geographies studied, it is also consistent over time, mainly due to deteriorating project performance on the benefit side, again in diametrical opposition to Hirschman's claims.

8.10 Hirschman Looking Back, Thirty Years Later

In 1994, thirty years after Hirschman began work on *Development Projects Observed*, he was writing the preface to a new edition of the book (Hirschman 1995a). Here he calls the original first chapter, about the Hiding Hand, "the most speculative chapter of the book" and "close to a provocation" (Hirschman 1995a: ix). He also admits, along the lines of the critique by Paul Krugman mentioned previously, that he had collected so many "fascinating stories" during his fieldwork that "storytelling came at times to overshadow analysis" (viii).[30] Finally, he now claimed that "[n]othing could be less 'operationally useful'" than the principle of the Hiding Hand, and that the "stories told in this first chapter of the book were of course not meant to hold any immediately applicable 'practical' lesson'" (Hirschman 1995a: ix). With these comments Hirschman set a very different tone from the self-assured tenor of the original text, with its claims of general applicability and lack of reservations about sampling, data, and analyses. To be sure, Hirschman did not reject the Hiding Hand in the new preface, or even suggest it should be revised. But thirty years after the fact he seemed more cautious, hedging against his earlier strong claim that the Hiding Hand denotes a general principle of action, but also against any responsibility for policy impact arising from the principle—impact he had actively sought to have earlier. However, Hirschman's reservations would be remembered much less than his principle, which had had thirty years to make its impact and would continue to do so. If anything, the Hiding Hand stood stronger after the 1995 edition of *Development Projects Observed*, and stands even stronger today with the 2015 edition, a half-century after its original publication.

Hirschman (1995a: ix) now also revealed a "hidden agenda" for his earlier grand claims for the Hiding Hand. He explained that he had wanted "to endow and surround the development story with a sense of wonder and mystery that would reveal it to have much in common with the highest quests undertaken by humankind" (ix). And further, "I came to see [my work] as having the latent, hidden, but overriding common intent to celebrate, to 'sing' the epic adventure of development—its challenge, drama, and grandeur" (viii). However well-received this agenda might have been with policy makers and development workers, it is safe to say it is an unusual motive for an academic work. This does not mean that the agenda could not be both interesting and legitimate, but it is unfortunate that Hirschman waited thirty years to tell his readers what the real intent of his study was, depriving them of the opportunity to judge for themselves its validity against this purpose. In any case, with an ambitious agenda like this, Hirschman had to come up with a really big idea, and this idea was the Hiding Hand. The loftiness and unacademic nature of the agenda may also help explain the lack of rigor and critical distance in Hirschman's data collection and analyses documented earlier in this chapter.

At the time of carrying out his research for *Development Projects Observed*, Hirschman had found the Hiding Hand and its supporting stories particularly well suited for pursuing his hidden agenda. Now, a generation later, he was in a different place. He presently subscribed to, and was widely known for, a type of self-critique which he called a "propensity to self-subversion," which he described as an intellectual activity involving himself "arguing against earlier propositions of mine because I noted that they were less general than I originally thought" (Hirschman 1995a: xi; 1995b). He also frankly acknowledged that when he was developing the Hiding Hand in the 1960s, in his own words: "I was busily building up my edifice of propositions about development and self-subversion was far from my mind" (Hirschman 1995a: xi–xii). It is interesting to note that although the Hiding Hand would have seemed an evident choice for self-subversion in 1995, Hirschman exempted this particular proposition from critique. The only self-criticism to be found is the few, brief comments, mentioned previously, from the preface to the 1995 new edition of *Development Projects Observed*.

Hirschman's lack of self-criticism is all the more striking, given the fact that a book like Rodwin and Schön's (1994) volume about his work contains extensive commentary on, and critique of, the Hiding Hand that may be read as an open invitation for Hirschman to respond and reconsider the idea. And although Hirschman (1994) answered other critique in this book, it is noteworthy that he does not mention the Hiding Hand with one word in his reply. He simply ignored this part of Rodwin and Schön's book. Add to this that some of the projects Hirschman had originally described as successes in *Development Projects Observed*—projects he claimed in the book to have been saved by the Hiding Hand—in the meantime had turned out to be disasters. For instance, his most prominent example in illustrating the Hiding Hand—East Pakistan's (now Bangladesh) Karnaphuli paper mill—turned a loss throughout the

1970s, becoming a drag on the national economy instead of the boost Hirschman had predicted; and Nigeria's 300-mile Bornu railway—another of Hirschman's projects—catalyzed ethnic conflict that led to secession and a tragic civil war with hunger and starvation and killings in breakaway Biafra throughout 1967–70 (Adelman 2013: 392).[31] According to Adelman (2013: 422), privately it disturbed Hirschman that he had failed to see a project he had just studied could have such disastrous consequences so shortly after. But, curiously, nowhere does this failure, or the fact that project outcomes seemed to run counter to the principle of the Hiding Hand, cause Hirschman to critically assess and revise the principle.

In sum, Hirschman's silence regarding the Hiding Hand is too striking to be overlooked, especially given his active engagement through self-subversion with reinterpreting and revising other parts of his work. It is difficult not to get the impression that Hirschman knew full well that the Hiding Hand was in need of self-subversion. But he also seemed to know that the Hiding Hand was so fraught with problems that it would disintegrate if it were subjected to critique. Hirschman's thinking about the Hiding Hand proved indeed to be an "experiment," as he had originally told Thomas Schelling but not his readers. Now, decades later, Hirschman seemed to conclude that the experiment had failed, or was beyond repair, but again without telling his readers. By this stage, perhaps his vested interest in the Hiding Hand was too strong. As mentioned in the introduction in this chapter, the principle of the Hiding Hand is the type of theory that, even if wrong, seems to many to be just too good to give up. Hirschman ultimately appears to have shared this view.

8.11 CONCLUSIONS

In this chapter we set out to test the claims that Albert O. Hirschman may be considered an early behavioral economist and that his main contribution to large-scale project management, *Development Projects Observed*, can be considered a work in behavioral economics. The focus has been on the book's key idea: the principle of the Hiding Hand. We reject the Hiding Hand for four reasons.

First, Hirschman's data collection was highly biased. He chose to focus on unexpected successes in his data collection, without telling his readers, who are therefore left with the impression that the Hiding Hand is an *ex post* empirical finding from balanced data collection, when in reality it is a methodological artifact of how the data were collected, including only observations that would affirm the Hiding Hand. Here, Hirschman came disturbingly close to outright data fishing, and committed the fallacy that statisticians call sampling on the dependent variable.

Second, with a sample of just eleven projects spread over four continents, Hirschman's dataset is much too limited to support the wide conclusions he drew. Unfortunately, the secondary literature on the Hiding Hand has ignored this—or glossed it over—giving the false impression that the empirical basis of the Hiding Hand is sound.

Third, Hirschman misrepresented his findings. In private, he called his study "an exploration, an experiment" (Adelman 2013: 404). But to his readers Hirschman (1967a: 13) claimed he had uncovered an economic law—a "general principle of action"— in the tradition of Adam Smith and other great economists. For thirty years Hirschman (1995a: viii) also kept silent about a hidden agenda he had for his study: namely, "to celebrate, to 'sing' the epic adventure of development—its challenge, drama, and grandeur." By not telling readers about the explorative and experimental nature of the study, by hiding his biased data collection and the hidden agenda that drove it, by ignoring issues arising from the smallness of his sample, and by claiming much more than his weak and biased data could support, Hirschman misrepresented his findings and misled his readers.

Fourth, statistical tests show that Hirschman's results may not be replicated with a larger and better dataset and must therefore be considered false. Using a sample almost two hundred times larger than Hirschman's original one, for which data were collected systematically following international standards, the following were found. (a) The main claim of the Hiding Hand principle—that higher-than-estimated project costs will be outweighed by even higher-than-estimated benefits—is rejected at an overwhelmingly high level of statistical significance ($p < 0.0001$). Not only is benefit overrun not larger than cost overrun, as the claim predicts, on average there is no benefit overrun at all, but the opposite—a benefit shortfall. Hirschman got both the size and sign (minus instead of plus) wrong for benefit overrun. In reality, instead of the "two offsetting underestimates" of costs and benefits claimed by Hirschman (1967a: 13), the average project is undermined by a double blow of substantial cost overruns compounded by substantial benefit shortfalls. (b) The second claim of the Hiding Hand principle—that project risks will tend to fall over time (due to learning)—is also rejected. For benefit risks we find a statistically highly significant historical trend of increasing benefit shortfalls of 0.5% per year (BF = 799). Again this is the opposite of what Hirschman claims. For cost risk, no significant relationship is found between such risk and time; that is, cost risk appears to be more or less constant over time (BF = 1.70). (c) Finally, testing Hirschman's claim that his Benevolent Hiding Hand (benefit overrun > cost overrun) would be more common than what Sunstein (2015a: 4) calls the "evil twin," the Malevolent Hiding Hand (benefit overrun < cost overrun), we find the opposite to be true. The Malevolent Hiding Hand is dominant in 78% of cases and outnumbers the Benevolent Hiding Hand by a factor 3.5:1, and again at an overwhelmingly high level of statistical significance ($p < 0.0001$).

To be fair to Hirschman, his biases and misrepresentations in developing the Hiding Hand seem to have been driven by a general optimism and not by deliberate deception, though there is a gray area between the two, which Hirschman entered from time to time. Nevertheless, each of these four points is enough to leave Hirschman's Hiding Hand significantly invalidated. Taken together, they form a devastating verdict. Nothing about the Hiding Hand is right for understanding "project behavior in general," as was Hirschman's (1967a: 1) stated purpose. The principle applies only to the special cases of success for which it was thought up, and some of those were imaginary, we now know, formed by Hirschman's optimism and hidden agenda more than by evidence on the ground. If there is a general principle of action at work in the type of behavior which Hirschman studied it is the opposite of that postulated by the Hiding Hand. In reality, instead of the success Hirschman (1967a: 16) promises through "creative error," project viability is undercut by a double whammy of substantial cost overruns compounded by substantial benefit shortfalls, as shown in Table 8.1. Finally, given the results of the present study, it might be a good idea to similarly test some of Hirschman's other work in order to decide which parts stand up to closer scrutiny and which do not.

The Hiding Hand resonates with romantics and cynics alike, which may well explain its lasting influence. Romantics are gratified by its intuitive appeal and its depiction of people as creative problem solvers who typically land their projects on their feet, despite initial difficulties. Hirschman was clearly a romantic. Cynics see the Hiding Hand as a means to justifying an end: getting projects started. Willie Brown, Joe Cahill, and Robert Moses belong to this category. But because the Hiding Hand is so fundamentally wrong, using it in policy and practice, as is commonly done, is likely to lead, at best, to the misallocation of scarce resources (Pareto inefficiency) and, at worst, to outright disasters, ranging from white elephants over destroyed careers and companies, to national crises and even war, as we have seen. Better concepts and theories than the Hiding Hand exist—theories of optimism bias, the planning fallacy, fragility, and strategic misrepresentation—and these theories should be used in preference to the Hiding Hand for explaining the data and for policy and practice (Kahneman 2011; Flyvbjerg et al. 2009).

The results discussed here therefore do not necessarily mean that the majority of projects that are subject to the Malevolent Hiding Hand should not have been attempted. They do mean, however, that the decisions and cost–benefit analyses for these and other projects should have been debiased before given the final go-ahead, instead of relying on the Hiding Hand. Well-tested methods exist for such debiasing, based on sound theory. Some of these methods have recently been made mandatory in project management the United Kingdom and Denmark for large transportation infrastructure projects, and the methods are also used ad hoc in many other countries, including the United States and China, as well as for many project types other than transportation (Flyvbjerg 2006, 2013; Batselier et al. 2016; Chang et al. 2016).

Regarding the question of whether Hirschman is an example of an early behavioral economist, and whether *Development Projects Observed* can be counted as a work in behavioral economics, as suggested by Sunstein, the answer is negative. The study and the data discussed here show that we need to see Hirschman as a case for behavioral economists to study—a case of how damaging optimism bias can be, not only in policy and business, but in scholarship as well. Hirschman was a victim, not a student, of bias. However, in rejecting Hirschman we must also—and more importantly—reject the Willie Browns of the world, with their self-interested tributes to beneficial ignorance and "start digging." Scholarship should test, not celebrate, such ideas.

ACKNOWLEDGMENTS

The author is grateful for the following important help. Dirk Bester carried out the statistical analyses for the chapter. Atif Ansar, Alexander Budzier, and Chantal Cantarelli each helped collect parts of the data used for the statistical analyses. Jeremy Adelman, Michele Alacevich, Alexander Budzier, Chantal Cantarelli, Jon Elster, Ole Jonny Klakegg, Claus Offe, and Cass Sunstein provided valuable comments on an earlier version of the chapter. Some of the data used in the chapter were previously used in Ansar et al. (2014) and Cantarelli et al. (2012).

NOTES

1. For a recent academic endorsement of the principle of the Hiding Hand, see Kriz (2015: 14–15), who says: "Hirschman was right when he identified a 'hiding hand' … interventions are … probably best undertaken by people naïve about the full consequences of the risk." Similarly Lepenies (2008: 450), who calls *Development Projects Observed* an "impressive analysis of development aid" with "explanations and analyses [that] are still valid today, including his 'Principle of the Hiding Hand' … the mere existence of the hiding hand is the reason why development projects are carried out in the first place."

2. The terms *principle* and *theory* are here used interchangeably. We shall return to the question of whether the principle of the Hiding Hand is indeed a theory.

3. Gladwell (2013: 2) similarly calls Hirschman "one of the twentieth century's most extraordinary intellectuals."

4. A new type of study of Hirschman's work by professional historians has begun to appear after the relevant archives have become accessible. Adelman (2013) is an example of this work as is Alacevich (2014). For the first time, such material and studies are available for developing a better understanding of Hirschman and his work. The present study makes extensive use of these to help assess the validity of Hirschman's data and analyses. It is the first time, to the knowledge of the author, that the newly available archival material has been used to systematically evaluate the Hiding Hand.

5. Two versions of Hirschman's classic text on the Hiding Hand exist (1967a, 1967b). The version cited here is the one published by the Brookings Institution in *Development Projects Observed* (Hirschman 1967a), which is the original text. The other version is an article published by *The Public Interest* as "The Principle of the Hiding Hand." The differences between the two texts are minor and consist mainly in the article being less technical and more readable than the book, thanks to editing by Irving Kristol, editor of *The Public Interest* at the time of publication (Adelman 2013: 405). *Development Projects Observed* was the third and culminating volume in a trilogy on development economics that also includes Hirschman (1958, 1963). The book was reissued in 1995 with a new preface by the author and reissued again in 2015 with a new foreword by Cass R. Sunstein and an afterword by Michele Alacevich. Sarah Hirschman—Albert O. Hirschman's wife—was a collaborator with her husband and did extensive work, in and out of the field, on the studies that led to the publications on the Hiding Hand (Adelman 2013: 388; Alacevich 2014: 149).

6. Even for IT projects, which are among the easiest type of project to abandon, and among the worst performing, the abandonment rate is estimated at only 9% (Sauer et al. 2007).

7. Similarly, Hirschman's (1967b) *Public Interest* article on the Hiding Hand was recently included in a collection of "Essential Readings" in megaproject planning and management edited by the present author (Flyvbjerg 2014b).

8. For recent uses of the Hiding Hand, see Waisberg (2014), Osimo and Codagnone (in progress), and Alston and Mueller (2015).

9. The term *theory* is used here to denote an idea, or a system of ideas, used to account for or explain a situation. This is similar to the way Hirschman uses the term.

10. Australian Broadcasting Corporation, "Lateline," 9 January 2003; television program transcript.

11. Actual outturn costs at AU$102 million are conservative and do not include AU$45 million allocated in 2002, in part to bring the building more in agreement with its original designs.

12. I have asked who the architect of Sydney Opera House is of more than a thousand people in lectures about the issues discussed in the main text, and rarely does anyone know—and if they do, they are usually of the same nationality as the architect or they are true architecture aficionados. When I similarly ask, as a control question, who the architect is of the Guggenheim Museum Bilbao or Los Angeles' Disney Concert Hall, many more know the answer.

13. Gehry (2009: 15) rightly observes that "winning the competition [for Sydney Opera House] was probably the worst thing that ever happened to him [Jørn Utzon]." Utzon did a few smaller and less well known buildings after Sydney—mainly two houses for his own family in Mallorca, Spain, Bagsværd Church in Denmark, and the Kuwait National Assembly—but nothing to fill the career of a master builder or to just keep a gifted architect busy (Flyvbjerg 2005a).

14. Hirschman (1967a: 3) used two criteria to select his small sample of World Bank projects: (a) the projects had to be well diversified as regards economic sector and geographical area, and (b) each project had to have an extended history, including several years of operations.

15. Adelman (2013: 392–3) further describes Hirschman's data collection as "hopeful;" it "resisted bleak conclusions, perhaps too obstinately," despite the fact that Hirschman's notes "are filled with the grouchy testimonies of his witnesses," and it amounted to a "personal failure [on Hirschman's part] to see the disasters of development and evaluate them," according to Adelman.

16. Lepenies (2008: 437) similarly observes that "work and life cannot be separated when discussing Hirschman."

17. Such test has not been done before, as said. The closest we get to tests of the Hiding Hand are Cracknell (1984) and Picciotto (1994a). Cracknell, who was an officer with the UK Overseas Development Administration (ODA), wrote that data from two hundred evaluations of ODA projects "lend little support" to the Hiding Hand (Cracknell 1984: 17–18), but unfortunately Cracknell did not present data or analyses to substantiate his claim. Picciotto, who was an officer with the World Bank, tried to evaluate the Hiding Hand, but the evaluation lacks rigor and good data, and concludes weakly that "the hiding hand has its advantages as well as disadvantages" (Picciotto 1994a: 223).

18. Only two of Hirschman's projects are non-infrastructure: namely, an industry project (the Karnaphuli paper mill discussed in the main text) and a livestock project.

19. Using first-year benefits has also been criticized for not taking into account positive development effects; for instance, increased real estate values following from improved transit

services. Such effects undoubtedly exist, but if transit has development benefits these must be expected to be roughly proportional to ridership, so that if ridership has been overestimated, so must have the development benefits, which means that the case for proceeding with the project was exaggerated. The difference between estimated and actual ridership, including first-year ridership, would therefore be a good proxy for assessing the extent of the problem. The same applies to types of infrastructure other than transit. For the full argument and further documentation, see Flyvbjerg (2005b; 2013). See also Vickerman, Chapter 17 in this volume.

20. It should be mentioned that results are probably conservative; that is, cost overruns and benefit shortfalls in the project population are most probably larger than in the sample. This is because availability of data is often an indication of better-than-average project management, and because data from badly performing projects are often not released. This must be kept in mind when interpreting the results from statistical analyses, and it means that the Hiding Hand is most probably even more false in the project population than in the sample. For the full argument, see Flyvbjerg et al. (2002, 2005a) and Flyvbjerg (2005b).

21. Significance is here defined in the conventional manner, with $p \leq 0.05$ being significant, $p \leq 0.01$ very significant, and $p \leq 0.001$ overwhelmingly significant.

22. Ideally, data would be available for both cost overrun and benefit overrun for each project included in the statistical tests. However, data availability is far from ideal in the measurement of major project performance. For only 327 projects out of the 2,062 in the sample were data available for both cost overrun and benefit overrun. Using this ideal criterion would therefore result in scrapping large amounts of useful information for the 1,735 other projects in the sample, which would clearly be unacceptable. We therefore decided to run the statistical tests twice—first for the 2,062 projects in the total sample, and second for the subsample of 327 projects with data available for both cost overrun and benefit overrun.

23. Parameters for the models were estimated using MCMC. The language JAGS was used for this, through the rjags interface to R (Plummer 2003, 2012; R Core Team 2012). Statistical significance for these tests was measured by the Bayes Factor (BF) instead of by p-values, where $12 < BF \leq 150$ indicates a statistically significant result and $BF > 150$ indicates a highly significant result.

24. One might speculate that conceivably the 22% of projects that complied with the Benevolent Hiding Hand may have generated more benefits in the aggregate than the 78% of projects that did not; that is, the projects subject to the Malevolent Hiding Hand. This would be an interpretation in line with Hirschman's general optimism and his "possibilism," which stresses "the possible rather than the probable" (Hirschman 1971: 28). A test shows, however, at an overwhelmingly high level of statistical significance, that (i) not only is this not the case, but (ii) in fact, the opposite happens, since the net effect of the Malevolent Hiding Hand is larger than the net effect of the Benevolent Hiding Hand ($p = 0.001$, two-sided Mann–Whitney test, H_o: the net effect on benefits of the Benevolent Hiding Hand is equal to the net effect on costs of the Malevolent Hiding Hand; tested for the 327 projects with data for both cost overrun and benefit overrun).

25. For a full analysis of the Malevolent Hiding Hand, see Flyvbjerg and Sunstein (2017).

26. Marseille (1994) describes a case where the Hiding Hand seems to apply.

27. Hirschman is not alone in doing data fishing to make major project performance look better than it actually is. More recently, Millar (2005) did the same (Flyvbjerg et al. 2005b).

28. This subsample is identical to the subsample of 327 projects used to test claim no. 1.
29. We used the United Nation's macrogeographical (continental) regions as the basis for our geographical analyses, <http://millenniumindicators.un.org/unsd/methods/m49/m49re-gin.htm>
30. Hirschman was writing the new preface for *Development Projects Observed* during the same period that a group of scholars and practitioners, including Paul Krugman, were systematically holding seminars and writing a book about Hirschman's work, celebrating and critiquing it (Rodwin and Schön 1994). Hirschman was sent the papers from the seminars and tapes and summaries of the discussions. He told the group that he had examined the extensive materials, and he returned his comments and a chapter for the book (Hirschman 1994; Rodwin and Schön 1994: 314). This exercise seems to have influenced Hirschman's new preface to *Development Projects Observed*.
31. Another example of a major project admired by Hirschman where the Hiding Hand triggered financial disaster instead of creative solutions is the Paz del Rio steel mill, Colombia (Alacevich 2007; Sandilands 2015).

REFERENCES

Adelman, J. (2013). *Worldly Philosopher: The Odyssey of Albert O. Hirschman*. Princeton, NJ, and Oxford: Princeton University Press.

Adelman, J. (2015). Personal communication, 12 and 13 March, author's archives.

Alacevich, M. (2007). "Early development economics debates revisited," *Policy Research Working Paper*, no. 4441. Washington, DC: World Bank.

Alacevich, M. (2014). "Visualizing uncertainties, or how Albert Hirschman and the World Bank disagreed on project appraisal and what this says about the end of 'High Development Theory'," *Journal of the History of Economic Thought*, 36: 137–68.

Ansar, A., Flyvbjerg, B., Budzier, A., and Lunn, S. (2014). "Should we build more large dams? The actual costs of hydropower megaproject development," *Energy Policy*, March: 43–56.

Batselier, J. and Vanhoucke, M. (2016). "Practical application and empirical evaluation of reference class forecasting for project management," *Project Management Journal*, 47(5): 36–51.

Bianchi, A. M. (2011). "Albert Hirschman and his controversial research report," SSRN, October, <http://papers.ssrn.com/sol3/papers.cfm?abstract_id=1945822>

Brown, W. (2013). "When warriors travel to China, Ed Lee will follow," *San Francisco Chronicle*, 27 July.

Cantarelli, C. C., Flyvbjerg, B., van Wee, B., and Molin, E. J. E. (2014). "Lock-in and its influence on the project performance of large-scale transportation infrastructure projects: Investigating the way in which lock-in can emerge and affect cost overruns," in B. Flyvbjerg (ed.), *Megaproject Planning and Management: Essential Readings*, vol. 1. Cheltenham, UK, and Northampton, MA: Edward Elgar, pp. 424–39. Originally published in *Environment and Planning B: Planning and Design*, 37 (2010), 792–807.

Cantarelli, C. C., Molin, E. J. E., van Wee, B., and Flyvbjerg, B (2012). "Different cost performance: Different determinants? The case of cost overruns in Dutch transport infrastructure projects," *Transport Policy*, 22: 88–95.

Caro, R. (1975). *The Power Broker*. New York: Vintage Books.

Catino, M. (2013). *Organizational Myopia: Problems of Rationality and Foresight in Organizations*. Cambridge: Cambridge University Press.

Chang, W., Chen, E., Mellera, B., and Tetlock, P. (2016). "Developing expert political judgment: The impact of training and practice on judgmental accuracy in geopolitical forecasting tournaments," *Judgment and Decision Making*, 11(5): 509–26.

Cracknell, B. (1984). "Learning lessons from experience: The role of evaluation in the administration of the U.K. aid programme," *Public Administration and Development*, 4: 15–20.

Drummond, H. (2014). "Is escalation always irrational?", in B. Flyvbjerg (ed.), *Megaproject Planning and Management: Essential Readings*, vol. 2. Cheltenham, UK, and Northampton, MA: Edward Elgar, pp. 291–309. Originally published in *Organization Studies*, 19(6) (1998).

Elster, J. (1983). *Sour Grapes: Studies in the Subversion of Rationality*. Cambridge: Cambridge University Press.

Flyvbjerg, B. (2001). *Making Social Science Matter: Why Social Inquiry Fails and How It Can Succeed Again*. Cambridge: Cambridge University Press.

Flyvbjerg, B. (2005a). "Design by deception: The politics of megaproject approval." *Harvard Design Magazine*, no. 22, Spring/Summer, pp. 50–59.

Flyvbjerg, B. (2005b). "Measuring inaccuracy in travel demand forecasting: Methodological considerations regarding ramp up and sampling," *Transportation Research A*, 39(6): 522–530.

Flyvbjerg, B. (2006). "From Nobel Prize to project management: Getting risks right," *Project Management Journal*, 37(3): 5–15.

Flyvbjerg, B. (2009). "Survival of the unfittest: Why the worst infrastructure gets built, and what we can do about it," *Oxford Review of Economic Policy*, 25(3): 344–67.

Flyvbjerg, B. (2011). "Case study," in N. K. Denzin and Y. S. Lincoln (eds.), *The Sage Handbook of Qualitative Research*, 4th edn. Thousand Oaks, CA: Sage, pp. 301–16.

Flyvbjerg, B. (2013). "Quality control and due diligence in project management: Getting decisions right by taking the outside view," *International Journal of Project Management*, 31(5): 760–74.

Flyvbjerg, B. (2014a). "What you should know about megaprojects and why: An overview," *Project Management Journal*, 45(2): 6–19.

Flyvbjerg, B. (ed.) (2014b). *Megaproject Planning and Management: Essential Readings*, vols. I–II. Cheltenham, UK, and Northampton, MA: Edward Elgar.

Flyvbjerg, B., Garbuio, M., and Lovallo, D. (2009). "Delusion and deception in large infrastructure projects: Two models for explaining and preventing executive disaster," *California Management Review*, 51(2): 170–93.

Flyvbjerg, B., Holm, M. S., and Buhl, S. (2002). "Underestimating costs in public works projects: Error or lie?" *Journal of the American Planning Association*, 68(3): 279–95.

Flyvbjerg, B., Holm, M. S., and Buhl, S. (2005a). "How (in)accurate are demand forecasts in public works projects? The case of transportation," *Journal of the American Planning Association*, 71(2): 131–46.

Flyvbjerg, B., Holm, M. S., and Buhl, S. (2005b). "Credibility problem for transit: Response to Millar," *Journal of the American Planning Association*, 71(4): 452.

Flyvbjerg, B. and Stewart, A. (2012). "Olympic proportions: Cost and cost overrun at the Olympics 1960–2012," Working Paper, Saïd Business School, University of Oxford.

Flyvbjerg, B. and Sunstein, C. R. (2017). "The principle of the malevolent Hiding Hand; or, the planning fallacy writ large," *Social Research*, 83(4): 979–1004.

Gasper, D. (1986). "Programme appraisal and evaluation: The Hiding Hand and other stories," *Public Administration and Development*, 6: 467–74.

Gehry, F. (2009). Interview carried out by Bent Flyvbjerg, author's archives.

Gilovich, T., Griffin, D., and Kahneman, D. (eds.) (2002). *Heuristics and Biases: The Psychology of Intuitive Judgment*. Cambridge: Cambridge University Press.

Gladwell, M. (2013). "The gift of doubt: Albert O. Hirschman and the power of failure," *The New Yorker*, 24 June.

Hirschman, A. O. (1958). *The Strategy of Economic Development*. New Haven, CT: Yale University Press.

Hirschman, A. O. (1963). *Journeys Toward Progress: Studies of Economic Policy-Making in Latin America*. New York: Twentieth Century Fund.

Hirschman, A. O. (1967a). *Development Projects Observed*. Washington, DC: Brookings Institution.

Hirschman, A. O. (1967b). "The principle of the Hiding Hand," *The Public Interest*, Winter: 10–23.

Hirschman, A. O. (1971). *A Bias for Hope: Essays on Development and Latin America*. New Haven, CT: Yale University Press.

Hirschman, A. O. (1994). "A propensity to self-subversion," in L. Rodwin and D. A. Schön (eds.), *Rethinking the Development Experience: Essays Provoked by the Work of Albert O. Hirschman*. Washington, DC, and Cambridge, MA: The Brookings Institution and the Lincoln Institute of Land Policy, pp. 277–83.

Hirschman, A. O. (1995a). "Preface," in *Development Projects Observed*, 2nd edn. Washington, DC: Brookings Institution.

Hirschman, A. O. (1995b). *A Propensity to Self-Subversion*. Cambridge, MA: Harvard University Press.

Hirschman, A. O. (2015). *Development Projects Observed*, 3rd edn. Washington, DC: Brookings Institution. Published as a Brookings Classic with a new foreword by Cass R. Sunstein and a new afterword by Michele Alacevich.

Kahneman, D. (2011). *Thinking, Fast and Slow*. New York: Farrar, Straus and Giroux.

Klitgaard, R, (1997). "'Unanticipated consequences' in anti-poverty programs," *World Development*, 25(12): 1963–72.

Krugman, P. (1994). "Krugman discussion: Modeling, learning, and policy," in L. Rodwin and D. A. Schön (eds.), *Rethinking the Development Experience: Essays Provoked by the Work of Albert O. Hirschman*. Washington, DC, and Cambridge, MA: The Brookings Institution and the Lincoln Institute of Land Policy, Appendix A, pp. 285–7.

Lal, D. (1983). *The Poverty of Development Economics*, 2nd edn. 1997, 3rd edn. 2002. London: Institute of Economic Affairs.

Lepenies, P. H. (2008). "Possibilism: An approach to problem-solving derived from the life and work of Albert O. Hirschman," *Development and Change*, 39(3): 437–59.

Little, I. M. D. and Mirrlees, J. A. (1968). *Manual of Industrial Project Analysis in Developing Countries*. Paris: Development Centre of the OECD.

Marseille, E. (1994). "Intraocular lenses, blindness control, and the Hiding Hand," in L. Rodwin and D. A. Schön (eds.), *Rethinking the Development Experience: Essays Provoked by the Work of Albert O. Hirschman*. Washington, DC, and Cambridge, MA: The Brookings Institution and the Lincoln Institute of Land Policy, pp. 147–75.

Millar, W. W. (2005). "Demand forecast article questionable," Letter to the Editor, *Journal of the American Planning Association*, 71(3): 334.

Offe, C. (2013). "'Getting ahead by trespassing,' review of Jeremy Adelman, *Worldly Philosopher: The Odyssey of Albert O. Hirschman*," *European Journal of Sociology*, 54: 583–91.

Osimo, D. and Codagnone, C. (in progress). "Open and evidence-based? Myths and reality of policy-making," draft available at <http://www.icpublicpolicy.org/conference/file/reponse/1435223271.pdf>

Picciotto, R. (1994a). "Visibility and disappointment: The new role of development evaluation," in L. Rodwin and D. A. Schön (eds.), *Rethinking the Development Experience: Essays Provoked by the Work of Albert O. Hirschman*. Washington, DC, and Cambridge, MA: The Brookings Institution and the Lincoln Institute of Land Policy, pp. 210–30, 341–2.

Picciotto, R. (1994b). "Marseille discussion: Learning via the Hiding Hand," in L. Rodwin and D. A. Schön (eds.), *Rethinking the Development Experience: Essays Provoked by the Work of Albert O. Hirschman*. Washington, DC, and Cambridge, MA: The Brookings Institution and the Lincoln Institute of Land Policy, Appendix A, pp. 301–4.

Plummer, M. (2003). "JAGS: A program for analysis of Bayesian graphical models using Gibbs sampling," in *Proceedings of the 3rd International Workshop on Distributed Statistical Computing, 20–22 March, Vienna, Austria*.

Plummer, M. (2012). "rjags: Bayesian graphical models using MCMC," R package version 3-7.

R Core Team (2012). *R: A Language and Environment for Statistical Computing*. Vienna: R Foundation for Statistical Computing.

Reichold, K. and Graf, B. (2004). *Buildings that Changed the World*. London: Prestel.

Reutlinger, S. (1970). *Techniques for Project Appraisal under Uncertainty*. Washington, DC: International Bank for Reconstruction and Development.

Rodwin, L. (1994). "Rethinking the development experience," in L. Rodwin and D. A. Schön (eds.), *Rethinking the Development Experience: Essays Provoked by the Work of Albert O. Hirschman*. Washington, DC, and Cambridge, MA: The Brookings Institution and the Lincoln Institute of Land Policy, pp. 3–36.

Rodwin, L. and Schön, D. A. (eds.) (1994). *Rethinking the Development Experience: Essays Provoked by the Work of Albert O. Hirschman*. Washington, DC, and Cambridge, MA: The Brookings Institution and the Lincoln Institute of Land Policy.

Sandilands, R. J. (2015). "The 1949 World Bank mission to Columbia and the competing visions of Lauchlin Currie (1902–93) and Albert Hirschman (1915–2012)," *History of Economic Thought and Policy*, 2015/1(1): 21–38.

Sauer, C., Gemino, A., and Reich, B. H. (2007). "The impact of size and volatility on IT project performance," *Communications of the ACM*, 50(11): 79–84.

Sawyer, J. E. (2014). "Entrepreneurial error and economic growth," in Flyvbjerg, B. (ed.), *Megaproject Planning and Management: Essential Readings*, vol. I. Cheltenham, UK, and Northampton, MA: Edward Elgar, pp. 143–48. Originally published in *Explorations in Entrepreneurial History*, 4(4) (1951–52): 199–204.

Schön, D. A. (1994). "Hirschman's elusive theory of social learning," in L. Rodwin and D. A. Schön (eds.), *Rethinking the Development Experience: Essays Provoked by the Work of Albert O. Hirschman*. Washington, DC, and Cambridge, MA: The Brookings Institution and the Lincoln Institute of Land Policy, pp. 67–95.

Skaburskis, A. and Teitz, M. (2003). "Forecasts and outcomes," *Planning Theory and Practice*, December: 429–42.

Squire, L. and Van der Tak, H. G. (1975). *Economic Analysis of Projects*. Baltimore: Johns Hopkins University Press.

Streeten, P. P. (1984). "Comment," in G. M. Meier and D. Seers (eds.), *Pioneers in Development*. New York: World Bank and Oxford University Press, pp. 115–18.

Sunstein, C. R. (2013). "An original thinker of our time," *The New York Review of Books*, 23 May, pp. 14–17.

Sunstein, C. R. (2015). "Albert Hirschman's Hiding Hand," Foreword to Albert O. Hirschman, *Development Projects Observed*, 3rd edn. Washington, DC: Brookings Institution.

Tendler, J. (1994). "Taylor discussion: Professional practice, modeling, lore, and prescription," in L. Rodwin and D. A. Schön (eds.), *Rethinking the Development Experience: Essays Provoked by the Work of Albert O. Hirschman*. Washington, DC, and Cambridge, MA: The Brookings Institution and the Lincoln Institute of Land Policy, Appendix A, pp. 288–9.

Waisberg, I. (2014). "Management consulting as Hiding Hand," *Academy of Management Proceedings*, January.

CHAPTER 9

MEGAPROJECT ESCALATION OF COMMITMENT

An Update and Appraisal

HELGA DRUMMOND

"The best laid schemes o' mice an' men, Gang aft a-gley."

Robert Burns

MEGAPROJECTS can be tortuous. Cost overruns of 50% happen regularly. Even overruns of 100% are not unusual (Flyvbjerg, Garbuio, and Lavallo 2009; Keil and Mähring 2010). For example, the estimated cost of the Sydney Opera House was AU$7 million. The building eventually opened in 1973, ten years late, at a cost of AU$102—a cost overrun of 1,400%—and this was for a scaled-down version of the original design (Flyvbjerg, Garbuio, and Lavallo 2009). The refurbishment of London's Savoy Hotel cost almost double what was forecast and took almost twice as long as expected (Biltz 2010). The Welsh Assembly building ended up 300% over budget. The Scottish Parliament building cost ten times more than expected. Edinburgh's tram system finally opened in 2014, three years late and £375 million over budget. The cost of Amsterdam's new underground metro almost doubled during construction (*Economist* 2009). The $5.3-billion expansion of the Panama Canal is well over budget and a year behind schedule (Webber 2015).

Some megaprojects become "black holes," forever consuming resources to no avail (Keil and Mähring 2010). Chicago's Deep Tunnel sewer project was derided as "money down the drain" (Staw and Ross 1987a, 1987b). The Shoreham nuclear power plant cost an estimated $6 billion, but was decommissioned without ever being used (Ross and Staw 1993). The US Air Force wasted six years and $1 billion on a new combat support system (Stross 2012). Berlin's Brandenburg airport was due to open in 2011; then it became late 2014, before slipping to 2016—at the earliest. Meanwhile, costs have spiraled from an initial forecast of €2.5 billion to over €4.3 billion. At least two out of three major IT projects fail (Nelson 2007).

Many of those that get finished never deliver anywhere near the promised benefits. Environmental impacts are frequently underestimated, while demand forecasts are often wrong by 20–70% (Flyvbjerg, Bruzelius, and Rothengatter 2009). For instance, the United Kingdom's M6 Toll Motorway has been open for over a decade, yet traffic levels are still well below what was anticipated. Likewise, traffic through the Channel Tunnel has been significantly less than forecast. The re-engineered Panama Canal can accommodate the world's biggest ships, but it remains to be seen if the investment will pay off, as industry experts believe that the boom in merchant shipping is over (Donnan 2015). Many more examples of "runaway" projects could be cited. Why do organizations never seem to learn?

Economics certainly offers clear guidance. That is, if important expectations are unlikely to be met, decision makers should review the project and reinvest scarce resources only if marginal benefits promise to exceed marginal costs of completion. Yet the history of megaprojects suggests that rather than cull duds, decision makers may reinvest only to end up "throwing good money after bad"—a phenomenon known as escalation of commitment (for example, Staw 1976; Brockner 1992; Drummond 1996). This chapter explores four main questions:

1. How does escalation start?
2. What drives decision makers to persist with economically poor megaprojects?
3. What can decision makers do to curb project run-aways?
4. What are the most promising directions for research?

9.1 How Does Escalation Start?

As the poet warns, in an uncertain world even best laid plans are apt to go awry. But megaprojects may be poorly planned to begin with. More precisely, human beings are thought to be innately overconfident (Langer 1975; Taylor 1980; Taylor and Brown 1988; Fischhoff, Slovic, and Lichtenstein 1977). Such delusional optimism means that planners may promise far more than can be delivered (see, for example, Flyvbjerg, Garbuio, and Lovallo 2009; Staw and Ross 1987a, 1987b; Ross and Staw 1993). For instance, the 2012 London Olympics promised huge long-term benefits to the United Kingdom that have yet to materialize. More recently, plans to build a 270-km canal in Nicaragua assume that the $50-billion project can be completed in five years. "That would entail doing $1 billion work per month, which in my view, as an engineer, is unthinkable," said an informed bystander (Webber 2015).

In theory, complex organizations are shielded from human foibles because they employ rigorous project planning and forecasting tools. Yet in practice those tools can make things worse. This is because they tend to be inward-looking, focused on the organization's capabilities, how executives propose to surmount challenges and address perceived risks, blind to the competition and market realities. Moreover, because comparable projects are frequently ignored, forecast costs and benefits may be rooted in fantasy (Lovallo and Kahneman 2003). For example, international trade fairs are notorious loss makers. Yet planners for the Canadian Trade Fair Expo 86 confidently expected to defy history by at least breaking even. But that assumed that every man, woman, and child in Canada would visit it at least once (Ross and Staw 1986). They did not. Moreover, although initial forecasts may be revised as they move up the organizational hierarchy, those revisions are rarely drastic enough, because the initial estimates tend to act as powerful anchors (see, for example, Kahneman, Lovallo, and Sibony 2011; Kahneman and Lovallo 1993).

Delusion may be compounded by deception. Planners competing for resources may deliberately underplay costs and project risk and overemphasize benefits to make the project seem attractive. Vested interests too propound the advantages of a project, but not the risks. For instance, in the 1950s UK architects, surveyors, construction firms, and politicians extolled the merits of high-rise living—poorly constructed buildings that soon became a byword for dampness, vandalism, and social isolation (see, for example, Kynaston 2015). Similarly, the Shoreham nuclear plant promised cheap, clean, and safe electricity (Ross and Staw 1993). Business-hungry contractors may submit artificially low bids, confident that overruns will be tolerated (Lovallo, Viguerie, Uhlaner, and Horn 2007; Flyvbjerg et al. 2009a, 2009b, 2009c). As poorly conceived projects take shape, wiser counsel gets drowned in a tidal wave of enthusiasm: "Go! Go! Go!"

Internal politics can create "camels." For instance, TAURUS—a £500 million (1993 figures) IT project commissioned by the London Stock Exchange—was canceled after three years of abortive effort because the design had become so complex that it could not be built to a sensible budget and timescale. A big mistake was in yielding to banks, brokers, custodians, and registrars—all wanting different designs and forever demanding changes (Drummond 1996).

Similarly, in the late 1990s the UK Ministry of Defence commissioned a £200 million IT platform known as Joint Personnel Administration (JPA) for paying the armed forces. Hitherto, the Army, Navy and Air Force ran separate systems. To save money, the Ministry opted for a civilian payroll software package. But military pay is extremely complex. Not only were there myriad and frequently changing allowances; the Army, the Navy, and the Air Force each had different rules. For example, a project manager said: '"You would have two families living next to each other in Cyprus, one of which was entitled to fly back to the UK, while the other wasn't" (Kelman et al. 2009: 9).

The only way to get the software to work was to harmonize and streamline—but that proved more difficult than senior management expected. In the end, only about 70% of pay and allowances were harmonized. Even so, the Ministry decided to proceed. A senior official said: ' "At the time we had gone absolutely as far as the market would bear" (Kelman et al. 2009: 12).

Expedience would return to haunt the project.

9.2 WHAT DRIVES ESCALATION?

Once poorly appraised projects meet the rocky road of reality, plans unravel. Costs start to overrun, deadlines slip, and doubts about whether promised benefits will materialize begin to circulate. It is thought that the overarching force for persistence is the sheer cost of quitting. Those costs may be psychological, social, economic, and organizational (for example, see Staw 1997: Whyte 1986; Rubin and Brockner 1975).

9.2.1 Psychological Drivers

Impending failure poses a profound ego threat. *Ego* refers to our sense of self, our innate desire to appear in a good light (see, for example, Crocker and Park 2004). More precisely, negative feedback is thought to trigger ego-defensive behavior, whereby decision makers lapse into denial in order to shield themselves from the gap between ambitions and reality. Denial can take many forms. For instance, decision makers may refuse to believe that problems are serious, or they may blame setbacks on chance factors beyond their control, such as freak weather conditions (Staw and Ross 1978). They also tend to focus more on feedback that seems to confirm preconceived views, while downplaying or even ignoring disconfirming data (Staw and Ross 1987a, 1987b; Zhang and Baumeister 2006). Moreover, they may actively root out supportive data in order to bolster their convictions (Nisbett and Ross 1980; Bazerman and Moore 2009: ch. 2). In addition, individuals with high self-efficacy (an individual's judgment about their ability to meet task demands successfully) may underestimate project risk (Jani 2011) and subsequently refuse to believe that the task is impossible (Whyte, Saks, and Hook 1997). For example, when TAURUS faltered a member of the monitoring group said, ' "I think they [the project team] … couldn't believe that it wouldn't work. They believed they knew how to make it work but it would just take longer and would cost a bit more" (Drummond 1996: 141).

Myopia may be particularly pronounced if decision makers like and value a project (affect bias). That is, they may be more aware of the strengths of "pet projects" than the weaknesses (Schultz-Hardt, Thurow-Kröning, and Frey 2009). Since these psychological traps tend to operate unconsciously, decision makers may genuinely believe that a success is close, when the reverse is true (Conlon and Parks 1987). For instance, an experiment by Boulding, Morgan, and Staelin (1997) found that 80% of participants persisted with a project even though feedback strongly suggested persistence would end in failure. Rather than quit, participants interpreted feedback so as to justify persistence.

As feedback becomes more consistently negative, beleaguered decision makers may experience pressure to justify all the time, money, and effort invested in the venture. Although these sunk costs are irrelevant because they cannot influence outcomes, decision makers may feel they have "too much invested to quit" (see, for example, Teger 1980; Arkes and Blumer 1985).

If so, decision makers may become risk-seeking. To be risk-seeking is to take a bigger risk than the situation warrants. Such behavior is thought to be prompted by negatively framed choices. That is, abandonment definitely means incurring a loss. Persistence offers the chance of avoiding that loss if the project pulls through, but risks seriously compounding it. Caught between a rock and a hard place, decision makers may take that risk (see, for example, Kahneman and Tversky 1979, 1982; Whyte 1986).

Persistence may eventually be driven by "goal substitution" effect. That is, as economically poor projects advance, the original success goal becomes forgotten as completion becomes all important (Conlon and Garland 1993; Fox and Hoffman 2002), particularly if the goal seems close and sunk costs are high (Moon 2001). For instance, the technical team realized that TAURUS would never work as envisaged. Latterly, all they cared about was finishing the task: '"Let's get the bloody thing done and behind us" (Drummond 1996: 140).

More recent research highlights additional dangers. Specifically, Ting (2011) found that when the goal seemed close, decision makers tended to exaggerate its value; while Jensen, Conlon, Humphrey, and Moon (2011) discovered unethical concealment of negative information.

9.3 Social Drivers

Most megaprojects are undertaken in a glare of publicity. Admitting failure publicly may be even more embarrassing than admitting it privately, as no one enjoys appearing incompetent. For example, Amsterdam is supported on stilts. When buildings along the new metro route suddenly sank by several centimetres, forcing people to escape from windows, Amsterdam's city insisted the project would go ahead even though there had been reports that construction might be less than perfect (*Economist* 2009). Besides, decision makers in the Western world are expected to keep their promises, to finish what they have started, and to appear resolute and generally "not for turning." Culturally, persistence in the face of adversity connotes strength, whereas withdrawal signifies weakness (see, for example, Staw and Ross 1987b).

9.4 Project and Economic Drivers

Ending a megaproject is likely to be expensive, particularly if salvage values are low (Staw and Ross 1987a). There may be penalty charges to contractors, redundancy payments, costs of ripping out partially completed works, obligations on leases, and so on. For example, planning for the London 2012 Olympics began in 2005. By the time the world financial crisis broke in 2008, decision makers were already committed, as hundreds of contracts had been let. Similarly, London's Cross-rail project is Europe's largest civil engineering project, involving a £15-billion investment and no less than 42 km of rail deep below the surface. At the halfway mark, the project had consumed 25 million working hours and produced around eight miles of tunnels. Moreover, almost 14,000 jobs depend on the project, directly and through the supply chain. Imagine the cost of removing miles of tunneling, restoring millions and millions of kilograms of clay, and dismantling all the part-built stations. Weighing exit costs in the balance, it may be nearly as expensive to quit as it is to continue.

9.4.1 Organizational Drivers

Ultimately, megaprojects may be driven by their own momentum (Drummond 1994). An elaborate administrative infrastructure may have been created to drive the project. Dismantling may be just too much trouble: "All the rules, procedures, and routines of an organization as well as the sheer trouble it takes for managers to give up day-to-day activities in favor of serious operational disruption can cause administrative inertia … Sometimes its easier not to rock the boat" (Staw and Ross 1987b: 71).

Besides, politically adroit executives may use their control over information to suppress the truth about the project if it is in their interests to do so (Harrison and Harrell 1993). Stakeholders who have invested in anticipation of completion may press for persistence regardless. For instance, the Channel Tunnel project survived mainly because banks had loaned so much money that they simply could not afford to "pull the plug." They too succumbed to escalation of commitment. Similarly, Airbus's A400M military aircraft is Europe's largest single defense contract. The A400M is designed to carry huge payloads over long distances and perform steep takeoffs in rough terrain. But the project has been dogged almost since its inception. Then, in May 2015, when the project was already four years behind schedule and billions of euros over budget, a plane crashed on a test flight near Seville, killing four members of the crew. The cause has yet to be determined. Ominously, engine failure cannot be ruled out. One reason why the seven nation-states sponsoring the A400M wait patiently, however, is their reluctance to see billions of euros in bailouts squandered (Hollinger and Vasager 2015).

9.4.2 Escalation as a Waiting Game: The Dynamics of "Lock-In"

Another reason why nation-states keep patience with the A400M is because they need the aircraft's capability. But how much longer should they wait? Moreover, there is no guarantee that the aircraft will live up to promises.

As those nation-states may have discovered, waiting begets waiting. More precisely, escalation theorists believe that "lock-in" to an economically suboptimal line of activity need not entail a deliberate decision to reinvest. It can happen through the simple passage of time—a phenomenon known as "entrapment."

The dynamics of entrapment were graphically demonstrated in a clever experiment by Jerry Rubin and Joel Brockner (1975). Participants were challenged to solve a crossword puzzle for an $8 cash prize. Thirteen minutes were allowed to complete the task, but after three minutes, the value of the prize dropped and continued to drop minute by minute. Alternatively, participants could simply take the $2.40 stake money and quit. After three minutes, however, the stake declined by 10% per minute. Crucially, participants were told that a dictionary was available to help solve the puzzle and that they were first, second, or third in line to receive it. Participants could either elect to wait for the dictionary or try to solve the puzzle. They could not work on the puzzle while waiting. In fact, there was no dictionary, and yet 87% of participants waited beyond the break-even point of three minutes. The longest waits were incurred where the jackpot declined slowly rather than more rapidly; where no pay-off chart was available, and when participants were "first in line." In other words, the longest waits are likely to be where the goal *seems* close and/or where the costs of persistence are hidden.

Lock-in can also result from "side-bets" (Becker 1960)—extraneous investments connected with the project that eventually make quitting too expensive. For example, organizations may be tempted to persist with an economically poor project rather than see a highly skilled and cohesive team dispersed.

9.5 Is Escalation Always Irrational?

Before discussing how to curb potentially project "runaway's" I should stress that persistence may be justified despite even severe setbacks. More specifically, in theory a project fails when it becomes clear that important expectations will not be met. In practice, however, things may not be clear-cut. Feedback may be patchy and unreliable, especially early on, and is almost invariably equivocal to some extent. So it may be wise to wait and see how things progress before abandoning a project. To a point, escalation is a normal business expense (Camerer and Weber 1999; Bowen 1987).

Even if a project is clearly going to be more expensive and/or deliver less than promised, persistence may still make economic sense. Ultimately, say Northcraft and Wolf (1984), decisions should reflect net gain. Net gain depends upon the size of the cost overrun and/or likely revenue or benefit shortfall, and the timing of expected returns. The so called "region of rationality," say Northcraft and Wolf (1984: 232), is the economically sustainable gap between intended and realized costs and revenues over time, allowing for future costs and the full range of future benefits. The wider the gap, the wiser it is to persist. Calculating the "region of rationality" is a job for an accountant. The principle, however, is easy to grasp. In a nutshell, assuming a part-finished project is worthless, if the expected marginal cost of completing the project is substantially less than the expected marginal revenues, persistence may be wise. Recall that the Savoy Hotel renovations cost a lot more than expected—but the additional investment may be worth it in the end.

Or will it? Uncertainty never goes away. Future costs may exceed expectations. Benefits may disappoint. Besides, beleaguered decision makers may be tempted to gild the lily. Indeed, research has shown that as projects fall behind schedule, decision makers became *more* optimistic about financial benefits (Meyer 2014). How much more sanguine are they likely to be about intangibles such as sustainable business growth, reputation, and employee wellbeing? In short, the revised case for continuance may be just as imbued with delusional optimism as the original, and perhaps even more so.

9.6 Managing Escalation

9.6.1 What Are You Getting Into?

Once megaprojects leave the drawing board, costs rise exponentially and the pressures to persist become well-nigh irresistible. The first prescription is that organizations should be extremely careful about what they get into. The National Health Service project was bound to become embroiled in controversy over medical ethics, patient confidentiality, information governance, and multisite—to say nothing of the technical challenges of integrating myriad legacy systems (Becker 2007; Whiney and Daniels 2013). By accepting "payment by results" contracts, Accenture and Fujitsu were storing trouble. Similarly, by allowing seven member states to dictate requirements, Airbus ended up building seven different aircraft. To make matters worse, Airbus wanted the US firm Pratt and Whitney to develop the novel turboprop engine powering the aircraft; but member states insisted on Rolls Royce. Moreover, Airbus agreed to absorb all cost overruns—even those resulting from customer changes (Hollinger and Vasager 2015): all in all, a recipe for trouble. The simple truth is that it is much easier to get into a mess than it is to get out of one.

9.6.2 Begin with Doubts

To paraphrase the philosopher Francis Bacon, it is better to begin with doubts and end in certainties than to start with certainties and end in doubt. It is a good mantra for evaluating megaprojects. What are projections based on? Even if reference class forecasting has been employed (Flyvbjerg 2008), how realistic is it? For instance, computations for the Channel Tunnel used data from small-scale projects such as tunneling under rivers or through mountains that bore no relation to the challenges of tunneling long-distance under the sea. Instead of confronting this issue, decision makers asserted that even if calculations proved wrong, revenues would handsomely compensate for any cost overruns (Drummond 2012). But that assumed that traffic would desert channel ferries. It has yet to do so.

Even if projections reflect realistic comparisons, they are only educated guesses—no matter how scientifically rigorous and authoritative they may seem. The trouble is that thick documents landing on desks with a thud can be hypnotic. This is because of their symbolic significance. A symbol is any artifact or gesture that embodies a deeper level of meaning than surface appearances suggest. For example, graphs and charts serve an instrumental purpose by condensing information, but they may also signify order and control (see, for example, Morgan, Frost, and Pondy 1983). To be more precise, symbols do three things. First, they condense information into a useable form; second, they structure how we think about things; and third, they affect how we react emotionally. They can also deceive, as they draw attention to certain facts and detract from others (Brown 1994; Barley 1983). Charts, graphs, computations, and all the other trappings of analysis signify scientific precision. Taking the information and appearing to analyze it signifies responsible and diligent management, and may make managers feel in control of uncertainty (for example, see Feldman and March 1981). Managers may think that everything is under control, but it is an illusion.

Any decision is only as good as the options considered. Before committing to a project, compare alternative investment opportunities side by side. It may seem obvious, yet research suggests that opportunity costs are easily neglected (Northcraft and Neale 1986). For instance, opponents of HS2—the putative high-speed rail link between London, Birmingham, Leeds, and Manchester—say that the money would be better spent upgrading existing railways. They may be right. But what else would that money buy? Another technique for identifying possibilities is to apply the so-called vanishing options test (Soll, Milkman, and Payne 2015: 70): that is, imagine that you cannot choose any of the options being considered. Now what?

9.6.3 Be Vigilant

The phantom-dictionary experiments imply that lock-in is inversely related to cost salience (Brockner, Shaw, and Rubin 1979). We may infer from this theory that decision makers are less likely to succumb to costly lock-in if they are vigilant. That means keeping the costs of persistence firmly in view; setting clear targets, and monitoring progress against them. Decision makers should also continure to revisit promised benefits. Recall the turn of fortune in merchant shipping and the Panama Canal, for example. Has the project been overtaken by events?

Budgets are a particularly important tool for recognizing cost overruns. In addition, it is thought that decision makers set so-called mental budgets—informal allocations of money, time, effort, and emotional energy—to a project (Heath 1995; Heath and Soll 1996). Budgets not only encourage vigilance; they also facilitate investigations into deviations from plans, making decision makers more accountable at every stage of the project (Tetlock 1985 discusses accountability).

There is, however, one caveat: budgets may induce decision makers to abandon an economically viable project. More specifically, experiments with sophisticated individuals have shown that as budget limits are reached, decision makers may decrease investment (Heath 1995). Yet by itself, budget depletion says nothing about the state of the project or whether it is worth completing on economic grounds. It is what accountants call a non-informative loss. That is, budget depletion merely states that a certain amount has been expended. Yet evidently, decision makers are not always able to distinguish between informative and non-informative losses. In addition, in a multistage project, projects that promise to generate net benefits tend to be abandoned even when additional expenditures at a particular stage would not threaten the project as a whole (Tan and Yates 1995). Budgets make a good servant but a bad master.

9.6.4 Do Not Let Persistence Become the Default Option

Once approved, it is usually assumed that megaprojects will be completed unless something utterly untoward happens (see, for example, Pan, Pan, Newman, and Flynn 2006b). Even so, it may be unwise to allow persistence to become the default option. More specifically, in a sequel to the phantom-dictionary experiments, Brockner, Shaw, and Rubin (1979) found that participants required to make an active decision to remain in a deteriorating situation tended to quit sooner rather than later—unlike participants for whom persistence was the default option.

It is thought that active decisions force us to consider past and future costs and attend to that information. In contrast, being able to decide passively may make decision makers oblivious to what persistence is costing—another reason to build in periodic "go/no go" reviews that include early and frequent project risk assessments and audits (Keil 1995). The alternative may be problems escalating into a crisis.

Yet even the most careful monitoring may not be foolproof. Research has shown that organizations can have all the requisite project management tools and protocols in place, and staff well trained and experienced in how to use them. Yet potentially ominous signals still get missed (Van Oorschot, Akkermans, Sengupta, and Van Wassenhove 2013). It is not clear why this happens. One possibility is that problems seldom emerge full blown. Another related possibility is that a single-minded drive to completion may result in decision makers losing sight of the bigger picture, so they end up forever firefighting, treating symptoms rather than the underlying malaise (Drummond 1996).

9.6.5 Set Limits (But Be Careful)

Setting limits can also help to curb project runaways (see, for example, Ross and Staw 1991). More specifically, Brockner, Rubin, and Lang (1981) conducted an experiment requiring some participants to publicly state limits on their involvement. Others set limits privately, and a control group set no limits at all. Unsurprisingly, perhaps, participants who set no limits invested most; an in contrast, participants who set limits publicly invested least. It is thought that limit setting curbs escalation by forcing decision makers to set expectations, enabling results to be compared against those expectations, and thus highlighting the gap. Making a public declaration also creates social pressures for consistency—another reason to apply the brakes.

But limits too can be double-edged. Brockner and colleagues also found that those who set limits in public tended to abandon projects when those limits were reached, even though their economic data said "persist." Public rectitude, it seems, can produce bizarre decisions.

9.6.6 Is the Project Viable?

As participants in the phantom-dictionary experiments discovered, it is unwise to assume that the mere passage of time will somehow bring us closer to our goal. Some megaprojects are like the phantom dictionary—destined never to arrive. If so, the sooner decision makers recognize it, the better.

Ideally, definitive evidence is required. For example, when the opening of Denver International Airport became severely delayed by problems with the promised fully automated baggage-handling system, a firm of consultant engineers conducted an experiment. They isolated a loop of track (a microcosm of the whole system), and tested it under a working load. Chaos ensued. Conveyor belts jammed and baggage cars crashed, showing conclusively that the design was unworkable (Monteagre and Keil 2000: 426).

Then what? Almost all projects are a means to an end. Denver airport authorities recognized that their goal was not to create a state-of-the-art baggage-handling system as such, but to get the airport up and running. A baggage system was vital, but that end could be achieved by building a standard semiautomated system using tried and tested technology (Monteagre and Keil 2000: 426). Similarly, Leeds recognized that the goal was not to build a tram line as such, but to provide a mass transit system. A trolley bus would suffice. Moral: solve the right problem.

9.6.7 Ask the Right Questions

Definitive evidence is not always obtainable. Moreover, when projects are in serious trouble, decision makers are likely to be told what they want to hear; that is, people are working very hard, that things are being brought under control, and that the project is "virtually finished." Such vacuous claims can be hard to disprove. But what are you *not* hearing? For instance, it is not what has been done that matters, but what *remains* to be done. A project may be 95% complete (virtually finished), but if the hardest part is at the end (for example, insertion of novel technology), that figure may be highly misleading.

Look beyond official information channels. For instance, one encouraging sign for London's Cross-rail has nothing to do with budgets and milestones. Rather, it is the rising house prices along the route—suggesting that long-term prospects are good, whatever short-term difficulties may arise. "Management by walking around" can redress problems of asymmetric information. Talk to people you would not normally meet. For example, former Chief Executive of the London Stock Exchange Peter Rawlins was moved by the refreshing candor of junior staff. When he asked them about TAURUS, he received straight answers that flatly contradicted his official information (Drummond 1996: 155).

9.6.8 Work with Uncertainty

Having established what remains to be done, the next question is how likely it is that it can and will be done within an acceptable timeframe and budget. Moreover, how likely is it that promised benefits will materialize?

Unlike tossing a coin, when the chance of it coming up "heads" is 50%; in a turbulent and ambiguous world, mathematical probabilities are hard to define. Bayesian statistics are beyond the scope of this chapter, but even a rough assessment can be helpful (Rubin and Weisberg 2004). For instance, when TAURUS fell seriously behind schedule a review concluded that the project could be finished in another eighteen months, provided there were no more delays. The Board quizzed the Chief Executive, Peter Rawlins:

> "Are you satisfied?" "I said that provided the Government enacted legislation within promised time-scale, provided there were no further changes to the project, and provided there were no more problems with the technology, then yes, I was content. But, big provisos." (Drummond 1996: 115)

In other words, "forget it." Indeed, in the event, the project never stood still. Legislation proved unimaginably complex. Moreover, for every technological problem solved, another one appeared. If the Board had weighed the probabilities they would have realized that there were too many critical and uncontrollable dependencies; nor was there anything in the history of the project to inspire confidence. The Board's mistake was in seeking certainty ("Are you satisfied?") where none existed.

9.6.9 Pay Attention to Symbols

Ultimately, a project only really fails when people will no longer support it (Sauer 1993; Baskerville and Land 2004). Mangers are more likely to succeed in maintaining support for a troubled (but not necessarily hopeless) project if they pay attention to symbols. Persistence signifies faith in a project (Elsbach 2003; Drummond 2014). For example, shortly after the fatal crash, Fernando Alonso—Airbus's flight test engineer—flew in an A400M as a gesture in tribute to those killed; but it also signified confidence in the aircraft *and* helped to deflect potentially awkward questions about its future (Hollinger and Vasager 2015). By the same token, sacking the project manager, cancelling leave, and consulting expert advice signifies that problems are being taken seriously and that something will be done (Pfeffer 1977, 1981).

Symbolic management rarely solves problems, but it buys time, which allows emotions and public fervor to subside. It also enables problem solvers to work without being constantly interrupted by demands for information. Given time, people also become accustomed to the possibility that expectations may not be met after all.

9.6.10 Removing Project Managers

Symbolism apart, if a manager has become so committed to a project and so personally identified with it as to have lost all sense of perspective, removing him may be wise. Again, health warnings apply. Escalation may be perpetuated if a new manger is determined to succeed where others have failed. The reverse error is also possible. That is, research has shown that supervisors tend to systematically underrate staff they did not appoint, while systematically overrating those they appointed personally (Bazerman, Beekun, and Schoorman 1982; Schoorman 1988). We may infer from these studies that managers who inherit a project may see things as worse than they really are (Drummond 2014).

9.6.11 Do Not Institute a Project "Death March"

Imagine a megaproject with no reviews, no audit, no milestones, and no limits. It would seem like the epitome of bad management. Yet decision makers should also be aware that these activities are symbolic. To be more precise, they are part of the ritual, so what may appear to be rigorous re-evaluation of a project or rigorous monitoring exercise may simply be managers going through the motions.

Such "death marches" may mask procrastination—to postpone necessary but painful action (Anderson 2003). The attraction is temporary psychological shelter at the expense of deeper entanglement. Incidentally, research suggests that culling a project does not always harm morale; quite the opposite. More specifically, Shepherd, Patzelt, Williams, and Warnecke (2014) found that engineers identified with their profession rather than individual projects. Culling duds was seen by engineers as an opportunity to redirect their professional skills to more promising possibilities.

9.7 REAL-OPTIONS THINKING

Recall that *failure* means only that a project cannot be delivered within specified criteria. This is not the same as *conclusive* evidence that with more time, more resources, and perhaps some changes, the project cannot succeed (Adner and Levinthal 2004).

What are the options? An option confers the right but not the obligation to take action in the future (Janney and Dess 2004): for example, to switch the project to another use, change the scale of the project, opt for staged implementation, or use the project as a springboard for future growth opportunities.

Again, conditions apply. Real options are seductive. This is because in theory, costs are fixed, while benefits are potentially unlimited (Leslie and Michaels 1997). But there are downsides. Not least, managers may be biased in how they value options. For instance, Tiwana et al. (2006) found that managers tended to most value springboard for growth options, probably because of fewest connotations of failure. Similarly, decision makers may not exercise abandonment options, seeing it as failure (Adner and Levinthal 2004). Besides, how much is flexibility worth? Real options are hard to value (Janney and Dess 2004). Then there is the question of when to exercise them. For example, a firm may purchase an oil field and acquire a licence but postpone drilling until oil reaches a certain price per barrel; but there are no guarantees that prices will remain at a given level for long (Zardkoohi 2004). Living with uncertainty may be cheaper than paying for options that may never be "in the money."

Even so, before abandoning a project, consider what potentially valuable options would be destroyed. For instance, if a troubled bespoke software project is abandoned in favor of an off-the-shelf product, the potentially lucrative option to licence the software is forfeit. If an oil field is sold off, all the options attached to it, such as gas exploration, or options to build on land, are destroyed. Likewise, by persisting with the A400M, Airbus is acquiring knowledge that may inform other ventures. Abandonment shuts off the flow of valuable information. In short, persistence may be justified when a project's option value is counted (Tiwana et al. 2006).

9.8 Issues for Research

Research should help organizations make better—that is, more economically wise—decisions and protect taxpayers and private investors. Although megaproject escalation has attracted significant research interest (see, for example, Keil and Mähring 2010; Mähring and Keil 2008; He and Mittal 2007; Pan et al. 2006a, 2006b; Keil et al. 2000; Keil 1995; Keil and Robey 1999; Drummond 1996), we also know that decision makers do not always respond to negative feedback by reinvesting (see, for example, Staw and Fox 1977; Singer and Singer 1985; Drummond 1995). Anecdotal evidence also tells us that megaproject escalation is by no means inevitable. When spectacular discoveries in East Africa failed to yield commercial quantities of oil, Tullow promptly capped dry wells and moved on. Accenture exited from the National Health Service contract despite a potential £1 billion penalty charge (later reduced to about £600 million). Two years later, after failing to renegotiate the contract, Fujitsu followed suit. Project leader Andrew Rollerson publicly declared: " 'It isn't working, and it isn't going to work" (Daft, Murphy, and Willmott 2010). Leeds abandoned its tram project for a cheaper trolleybus option, despite having invested more than £45 million. Why do some organizations manage a timely exit, whereas others become embroiled?

Research has been mainly experimental (for reviews, see Sleesman, Conlon, McNamara, and Miles 2012; Drummond 2014). The result is a long list of potential individual escalation drivers. But the fate of megaprojects is rarely decided by individuals acting alone. For instance, scholars continue to ask whether escalation requires personal responsibility (see, for example, Brockner 1992; Keil 1995; Whyte 1986; Sleesman et al. 2012). A more fruitful direction for megaproject research, however, may be to examine how *no* responsibility impacts. More specifically, research has shown that groups are less prone to escalation than are individuals. Moreover, groups with no responsibility whatsoever (that is, in experimental control conditions) are even less prone. But these studies have also shown that "no responsibility" groups are also least inclined to try to retrieve troubled projects (Whyte 1991; Leatherwood and Conlon 1987).

The distinction matters because megaprojects typically extend over ten to fifteen years. By the time that problems emerge, those responsible for authorizing the project may have long since moved on. For instance, the UK Ministry of Defence discovered that the contract with Boeing for the Chinook Mk3 helicopters precluded access to the software codes. Consequently, the helicopters could not be certified airworthy and ended up languishing in hangars for seven years, even though badly needed on operations (Ministry of Defence 2008). The Chinook story is one of the worst examples in project management history of escalating *in*decision where matters drift and decisions eventually get made and then unmade (Drummond 1994; Denis, Dompierre, Langley, and Rouleau 2011). For instance, it took thirty months just to agree an affordable program of work to modify the helicopters, enabling them to fly safely. That project was then abandoned, and the machines were converted back to Mk2s so that they would be available sooner rather than later. No one knows who drew up the contract (Ministry of Defence 2008). The question is whether ther would have been a greater sense of urgency if someone had been accountable. *Proposition*: no responsibility is more conducive to escalating indecision than individual or group responsibility.

Research should also explore whether responsibility is double-edged (Flyvbjerg et al. 2009a, discussing accountability). That is, initially it may prompt denial—particularly if decision makers careers are at stake (see, for example, Fox and Staw 1979). But once failure becomes well and truly apparent, responsibility (and therefore ego) may be a spur to action; to try to fix problems, to explore options, and above all, to act decisively.

Completion effects may also repay further study. Recall that as projects advance, completion may supplant other goals, including project quality (see, for example, Conlon and Garland 1993). But when does this substitution occur? The author experimented with extreme scenarios where projects were described as 10% complete and 90% complete. Clearly, in paper and pencil exercises, decision makers may be content to terminate projects that are only 10% complete. In reality, however, 10% complete could mean that planning consents are in place; contracts signed, staff and equipment hired, and a big hole in the ground has already been dug. By using more graphic experimental scenarios we may discover that substitution can occur much earlier in the project life cycle than previously thought.

If so, when it comes to explaining persistence with faltering megaprojects, goal substitution may be pivotal. By way of mental experiment (Platt 1964; Wicker 1985), what would a perfect correlation between goal substitution and escalation require? Intuitively we might think that high perceived efficacy (Whtye, Saks, and Hook 1997), moderate difficulty (Lee, Keil, and Wong 2015), and an attractive and seemingly proximate goal would act as accelerants. Yet the reverse dynamic is also plausible. That is, if completion becomes all-important (prompted perhaps driven by responsibility), perceived efficacy rises, and the goal seems more valuable, easier, and closer as decision makers steel themselves to meet the challenges. Indeed, we know that irrational influences can take an indirect path. For instance, research has shown that once funds are invested, decision makers tend to become more confident about the likelihood of success (Arkes and Hutzel 2000). Recall, too, that Ting (2011) found that more proximate goals seem more valuable. Conversely, Brehm and Wright (1983) found that persistence projects seem less valuable if the goal is difficult. Additionally, the relationship between goal substitution and escalation is likely to be intensified when giving up is costly and decision makers are oblivious to what persistence is costing and might eventually cost (Northcraft and Neale 1986). Significantly, Rubin and Brockner (1975) found that few participants in the phantom-dictionary experiment even requested a pay-off chart. *Proposition*: when goal substitution occurs, delusional optimism re-enters the equation.

Researchers have largely ignored contextual factors. Staw (1997) suggests that this is because they are not controversial. Yet a study by Hsieh, Tsai, and Chen (2015) found that if firms see larger, rival firms fail, it discourages escalation of commitment; but if smaller rivals succeed, that too acts as an accelerant. This might mean that megaproject escalation is more likely if comparable projects have succeeded—particularly if built by smaller and/or less experienced rivals.

Some projects get built because they are needed. Cost is immaterial, or is at least secondary (Northcraft and Wolf 1984). For example, the new road bridge over the Firth of Forth is vital to Scotland's economy, as the existing crossing (opened in 1964) is almost life-expired. At the time of writing (June 2015), the project is on schedule and slightly under budget. Things may yet unravel, but this yet-to-be-written case study suggests that not all megaprojects succumb to delusional optimism. Again, what makes the difference? Do essential projects tend to be more realistically appraised than non-essential projects, and if so, why? Speculatively, it may be precisely because everyone knows that they will be built, so there is no need to "game" the figures. This possibility might be tested by conducting field experiments examining how low, medium, and high competition for resources affects planners' estimates. Logically, we might expect that high competition produces the most optimistic predictions. Yet results may surprise. High competition may behove decision makers to be careful if they are to be taken seriously. In contrast, moderate competition may encourage a "free-for-all."

We also need new concepts. Concepts matter because they structure what we see, how we see, and how we think (see, for example, Morgan 1990). The notion of escalating indecision is useful because it throws the spotlight on the organizational pathologies that may produce costly inaction. Another possibility is escalating inevitability, which throws the spotlight on suboptimal decisions (compromises and concessions) made early in the project life cycle, and their potentially pernicious impact. Studying chains of events (such as Airbus ending up designing seven planes for seven customers) may show that the notion of ego-driven decision makers wilfully and recklessly reinvesting in doomed projects is partial. That is, escalating inevitability may highlight how persistence is driven less by human frailty and more by project factors playing themselves out as one suboptimal decision forces another suboptimal decision, and so on.

The notion of escalating inevitability has ramifications for practice. For example, when JPA faltered, public furore erupted with headline stories in the media of soldiers not being paid. As contractors, EDS worked with the Ministry of Defence to diagnose and fix problems without any assurances of what, if anything, they would be paid for all the additional work. Although EDS is thought to have incurred a significant loss as a result (Kelman et al. 2009), downing tools or issuing writs would almost *inevitably* have made things worse. Similarly, the Panama Canal authorities might have thought better than to sue contractors over who should pay for the overruns, as it only exacerbated the delay (Webber 2015). The concept of escalating inevitability encourages decision makers to consider what their decisions will *definitely* result in.

9.9 Conclusion

Most troubled megaprojects get finished eventually, though they usually end up costing a lot more than expected, and the promised benefits may be slow to materialize. London's Canary Wharf is now a thriving business district, but it was hardly an overnight success. Similarly, in the early years, orchestras in London's Barbican Centre played to an almost empty house. JPA works. But the clunky screens and limited functionality are a far cry from the streamlined system originally envisaged (Kelman et al. 2009). Amsterdam's new metro may well bring huge economic benefits to the city, but as the *The Economist* (2009) drily pointed out, only for those whose houses are still standing.

If I could make only one prescription I would urge organizations to be careful what they get into. Regardless of what drives escalation, the simple truth is that once megaprojects gain traction they are almost unstoppable. The first question concerns whether a megaproject is needed. Arguably, many are not (Flyvbjerg et al. 2009 discusses this point). For instance, a "no frills" version of TAURUS could have been built, using tried and tested technology, within six months (Drummond 1996). Health authorities in the United Kingdom have ended up building their own patient record systems—but they could have done that in the first place. Edinburgh's tram link to the airport seems redundant, as it takes longer than the bus. Does London really need another concert hall? The projected costs of HS2 have risen from around £35 billion to £50 billion, the result of accommodating objections to the proposed route. Is it worth the money (and waiting at least twenty years) to save half an hour between London and Birmingham? The real cost of any project is what we could have had instead.

Emphatically, I am not suggesting that decision makers shun risk or avoid ambitious but necessary projects—only that they pause for long enough to think about how they might unfold. This applies particularly to decisions made early on in the project that may have "knock-on" effects. Extant prescriptions for practice emphasize the need for vigilance (see, for example, Simonson and Staw 1992; Brockner, Shaw, and Rubin 1979; Keil, Rai, Mann, and Zhang 2003). But what good can that do if a project is already fatally compromised? Like politics, megaprojects may be the art of the possible. Even so, decision makers should think carefully about how expediency may return to haunt. For all the emphasis on uncertainty, some things *are* predictable. As the Tao counsels, only by avoiding the beginning of things can we escape their inevitable ends. Or as Peters (2010: 196) expresses it more positively: ultimately, success reflects what organizations *do not* do.

References

Adner, R. and Levinthal, D. A. (2004). "What is *not* a real option: Considering boundaries for the application of real options to business strategy," *Academy of Management Review*, 29: 74–85.

Anderson, C. J. (2003). "The psychology of doing nothing: Forms of decision avoidance result from reason and emotion," *Psychological Bulletin*, 129: 139–67.

Arkes, H. R. and Blumer, C. (1985). "The psychology of sunk costs," *Organizational Behavior and Human Performance*, 35: 124–40.

Arkes, H. R. and Hutzel, L. (2000). "The role of probability of success estimates in the sunk cost effect," *Journal of Behavioral Decision Making*, 13: 295–306.

Barley, S. R. (1983). "Semiotics and the study of occupational and organizational cultures," *Administrative Science Quarterly*, 28: 393–413.

Baskerville, R. L. and Land, F. (2004). "Socially self-destructing systems," in C. Avgerou, C. Ciborra and F. Land (eds.), *The Social Study of Information and Communication Technology*, Oxford: Oxford University, pp. 263–82.

Bazerman, M. H., Beekun, R. I., and Schoorman, F. D. (1982). "Performance evaluation in a dynamic context: A laboratory study of the impact of the prior commitment to the ratee," *Journal of Applied Psychology*, 67: 873–6.

Bazerman, M. H. and Moore, D. A. (2009). *Judgment in Managerial Decision-Making*. New York: Wiley.

Becker, H. (1960). "Notes on the concept of commitment," *American Journal of Sociology*, 66: 32–40.

Becker, M. Y. (2007). "Information governance in NHS's NPfIT: A case for policy specification," *International Journal of Medical Informatics*, 76: 432–7.

Biltz, R. (2010). "Savoy reopens after £220m revamp," *Financial Times*, 8 October, <http://www.ft.com>.

Boulding, W., Morgan, R., and Staelin, R. (1997). "Pulling the plug to stop new product drain," *Journal of Marketing Research*, 34: 164–76.

Bowen, M. G. (1987). "The escalation phenomenon reconsidered: Decision dilemmas or decision errors," *Academy of Management Review*, 12: 52–66.

Brehm, J. and Wright, R. A. (1983). "Perceived difficulty, energization, and the magnitude of goal valence," *Journal of Experimental Social Psychology*, 19: 21–48.

Brockner, J. (1992). "The escalation of commitment to a failing course of action: Toward theoretical progress," *Academy of Management Review*, 17: 39–61.

Brockner, J., Shaw, M. C., and Rubin J. Z. (1979). "Factors affecting withdrawal from an escalating conflict: Quitting before it's too late," *Journal of Experimental Social Psychology*, 17: 492–503.

Brockner, J., Rubin, J. Z., and Lang, E. (1981). "Face-saving and entrapment," *Journal of Experimental Social Psychology*, 17: 68–79.

Brown. A. D. (1994). "Politics, symbolic action and myth making in pursuit of legitimacy," *Organization Studies*, 15: 861–78.

Camerer, C. F., and Weber, R. A. (1999). "The econometrics and behavioral economics of commitment: A re-examination of Staw and Hoang's NBA data," *Journal of Economic Behavior and Organization*, 39: 59–82.

Conlon, E. J. and Parks, J. M. (1987). "Information requests in the context of escalation," *Journal of Applied Psychology*, 72: 344–50.

Conlon, E. J. and Garland, H. (1993). "The role of project completion information in resource allocation decisions," *Academy of Management Journal*, 36: 402–13.

Crocker, J. and Park, L. E. (2004). "The costly pursuit of self-esteem," *Psychological Bulletin*, 130: 392–414.

Daft, R. L., Murphy, J., and Willmott, H. (2010). *Organization Theory and Design*. Andover: Cengage.

Denis, J. L., Dompierre, G., Langley, A., and Rouleau, L. (2011). "Escalating indecision: Between reification and strategic ambiguity," *Organization Science*, 22: 225–44.

Donnan, S. (2015). "Frugal US consumers hit Panama Canal trade," *Financial Times*, 22 May, <http://www.ft.com>.

Drummond, H. (1994). "Too little too late: A case study of escalation in decision-making," *Organization Studies*, 15: 509–605.

Drummond, H. (1995). "De-escalation in decision-making: A case of a disastrous partnership," *Journal of Management Studies*, 32: 265–81.

Drummond, H. (1996). *Escalation in Decision-Making: The Tragedy of Taurus*. Oxford: Oxford University Press.

Drummond, H. (2012). *Economist guide to Decision-Making*. London: Economist Publications in association with Profile Books.

Drummond, H. (2014). "Escalation of commitment: When to stay the course?" *Academy of Management Perspectives*, 28: 430–46.

Economist, The (2009). "A big dig," 5 February, <http://www.Economist.com>.

Elsbach, K. D. (2003). "Organization perception management," in B. M Staw and L. L. Cumings (eds.), *Research in Organization Behavior*, vol. 25. Amsterdam: Elsevier, pp. 297–311.

Feldman, M. S. and March, J. G. (1981). "Information in organizations as signal and symbol," *Administrative Science Quarterly*, 26: 171–86.

Fischhoff, B., Slovic, P., and Lichtenstein, S. (1977). "Knowing with certainty: The appropriateness of extreme confidence," *Journal of Experimental Psychology: Human Perception and Performance*, 3: 552–664.

Flyvbjerg, B. (2008). "Curbing optimism bias and strategic misrepresentation in planning: Reference class forecasting in practice," *European Planning Studies*, 16: 3–21.

Flyvbjerg, B., Bruzelius, N., and Rothengatter, W. (2009). *Megaprojects and Risk: An Anatomy of Ambition*. Cambridge: Cambridge University.

Flyvbjerg, B., Garbuio, M., and Lavallo, D. (2009). "Delusion and deception in large infra-structure projects: Two models for explaining and preventing executive disaster," *California Management Review*, 51: 170–93.

Fox, F., and Staw, B. M. (1979). "The trapped administrator: the effects of job insecurity and policy resistance upon commitment to a course of action," *Administrative Science Quarterly*, 24: 449–71.

Fox, S. and Hoffman, M. (2002). "Escalation behavior as a specific case of goal-directed activity: A persistence paradigm," *Basic and Applied Psychology*, 24: 273–85.

Harrison, P. D. and Harrell, A. (1993). "Impact of 'adverse selection' on managers' project evaluation decisions," *Academy of Management Journal*, 36: 635–43.

He, X. and Mittal, V. (2007). "The effect of decision risk and project stage on escalation of commitment," *Organizational Behavior and Human Decision Processes*, 103: 225–37.

Heath, C. (1995). "Escalation and de-escalation of commitment in response to sunk costs: The role of budgeting in accounting," *Organization Behavior and Human Decision Processes*, 62: 38–54.

Heath, C. and Soll, B. (1996). "Mental budgeting and consumer decisions," *Journal of Consumer Research*, 23: 40–52.

Hollinger, P. and Vasager, J. (2015). "Crash casts shadow over Airbus' military transport aircraft," *Financial Times*, 11 May, <http://www.ft.com>.

Hsieh, K.-Y., Tsai, W., and Chen, M.-J. (2015). "If they can do it, why not us? Competitors as reference points for justifying escalation of commitment," *Academy of Management Journal*, 58: 38–58.

Jani, A. (2011). "Escalation of commitment in troubled IT projects: influence of project risk factors and self-efficacy on the perception of risk and the commitment to a failing project," *International Journal of Project Management*, 29: 934–45.

Janney, J. J. and Dess, G. G. (2004). "Can real-options analysis improve decision-making? Promises and pitfalls," *Academy of Management Executive*, 18: 60–75.

Jensen, J. M., Conlon, D. E., Humphrey, S. E., and Moon, H. (2011). "The consequences of completion: How level of completion influences information concealment by decision makers," *Journal of Applied Social Psychology*, 41: 401–28.

Kahneman, D. and Tversky, A. (1979). "Prospect theory: An analysis of decision under risk," *Econometrica*, 47: 263–91.

Kahneman, D., and Tversky, A. (1982). "The psychology of preferences," *Scientific American*, 246: 162–70.

Kahneman, D. and Lovallo, D. (1993). "Timid choices and bold forecasts: A cognitive perspective on risk taking," *Management Science*, 39: 17–31.

Kahneman, D., Lovallo, D., and Sibony, O. (2011). "Before you make that big decision," *Harvard Business Review*, June: 51–60.

Keil, M. (1995). "Pulling the plug: Software project management and the problem of escalation," *MIS Quarterly*, 19: 412–27.

Keil, M. and Mähring, M. (2010). "Is your project turning into a black hole?" *California Management Review*, 53: 6–28.

Keil, M. and Robey, D. (1999). "Turning around troubled software projects: an exploratory study of de-escalation of commitment to failing courses of action," *Journal of Management Information Systems*, 15: 63–87.

Keil, M., Rai, A., Mann, J. E. C., and Zhang, G. P., (2003). "Why software projects escalate: The importance of project management constructs," *IEEE Transactions on Engineering
Management*, 50: 251–61.

Keil, M., Tan, B. C. Y., Wei, K. K., Saarinen, T., Tuunainen, V., and Wassennar, A. (2000). "A
cross cultural study on escalation of commitment behaviour in software projects," *MIS
Quarterly*, 24: 299–325.

Kelman, S., Weatherhead III, A. J., and Weatherhead, R. W. (2009). "A different kind of partnership: The UK's Ministry of Defence and EDS develop the Joint Personnel Administration
program (JPA)," *Kennedy School of Government Case Program, CR16-09-1900-0*, pp. 1–22.

Kynaston, D. (2105). *Modernity Britain*. London: Bloomsbury.

Langer, E. J. (1975). "The illusion of control," *Journal of Personality and Social Psychology*, 32: 311–28.

Leatherwood, M. L. and Conlon, E. J. (1987). "Diffusibility of blame: Effects of persistence on a
project," *Academy of Management Journal*, 30: 836–847.

Lee, J. S., Keil, M., and Wong, K. F. E. (2015). "The effect of goal difficulty on escalation of commitment," *Journal of Behavioral Decision Making*, 28: 114–29.

Leslie, K. J. and Michaels, M. P. (1997). "The real power of real options," *The McKinsey Quarterly*,
3: 4–22.

Lovallo, D. and Kahneman, D. (2003). "Delusions of success: How optimism undermines executives' decisions," *Harvard Business Review*, July: 57–63.

Lovallo, D., Viguerie, P., Uhlaner, R., and Horn, J. (2007). "Deals without delusions," *Harvard
Business Review*, December: 92–9.

Mähring, M. and Keil, M. (2008). "Information technology project escalation: A processes
model," *Decision Sciences*, 39: 239–72.

Meyer, W. G. (2014). "The effect of optimism bias on the decision to terminate failing projects,"
Project Management Journal, 45: 7–20.

Ministry of Defence (2008). *Chinook Mk3 Helicopters*. London: TSO.

Monteagre, R. and Keil, M. (2000). "De-escalating information technology projects: Lessons
from the Denver international airport," *MIS Quarterly*, 24: 417–47.

Moon, H. (2001). "Looking forward and looking back: integrating completion and sunk-
cost effects within an escalation-of-commitment progress decision," *Journal of Applied
Psychology*, 86: 104–13.

Morgan, G. (1990). "Paradigm diversity in organizational research." in J. Hassard and D. Pym
(eds.), *The Theory and Philosophy of Organizations*. London: Routledge, pp. 13–29.

Morgan, G., Frost, P. J., and Pondy, L. R. (1983). "Organizational symbolism," in L. R. Pondy,
P. J. Frost, G. Morgan., T. C. Dandridge (eds.), *Organizational Symbolism*. London: JAI,
pp. 3–35.

Nelson, R. R. (2007). "IT project management: infamous failures, classic mistakes and best
practices," *MIS Quarterly Executive*, 6: 67–78.

Nisbett, R. E. and Ross, L. (1980). *Human Inference: Strategies and Shortcomings of Social
Judgment*. Englewood Cliffs: Prentice-Hall.

Northcraft, G. and Neale, M. A. (1986). "Opportunity costs and framing of resource decisions,"
Organizational Behaviour and Human Decision Processes, 37: 348–56.

Northcraft, G. and Wolf, G. (1984). "Dollars sense and sunk costs: A life cycle model of resource
allocation decisions," *Academy of Management Review*, 9: 225–34.

Pan, S. L., Pan, G. S. C., Newman, M., and Flynn, D. (2006a) "Escalation and de-escalation of
commitment to information systems projects: Insights from a project evaluation model,"
European Journal of Operational Research, 173: 1139–60.

Pan, S. L., Pan, G. S. C., Newman, M., and Flynn, D. (2006b). "Escalation and de-escalation of commitment: A commitment transformation analysis of an e-government project," *Information Systems Journal*, 16: 3–21.

Peters, T. (2010). *The Little Big Things: 136 Ways to Produce Excellence*. New York: Harper Collins.

Pfeffer, J. (1977). "The ambiguity of leadership," *Academy of Management Review*, 2: 104–12.

Pfeffer, J. (1981). "Management as symbolic action: the creation and maintenance of organizational paradigms," in L. L. Cumings and B. M. Staw (eds.), *Research in Organizational Behaviour*. Greenwich: JAI Press, pp. 1–52.

Platt, J. R. (1964). "Strong inference," *Science*, 146: 347–53.

Ross, J. and Staw, B. M. (1986). "Expo 86: An escalation prototype," *Administrative Science Quarterly*, 31: 379–91.

Ross, J. and Staw, B. M. (1991). "Managing escalation processes in organizations," *Journal of Managerial Issues*, 3: 15–30.

Ross, J. and Staw, B. M. (1993). "Organizational escalation and exit: Lessons from the Shoreham nuclear power plant." *Academy of Management Journal*, 36: 701–32.

Rubin J. Z. and Brockner, J. (1975). "Factors affecting entrapment in waiting situations: The Rosencrantz and Guildenstern effect," *Journal of Personality and Social Psychology*, 31: 1054–63.

Rubin, R. E. and Weisberg, J. (2004). *In An Uncertain World*. New York: Random House.

Sauer, C. (1993). *Why Information Systems Fail: A Case Study Approach*. Henley: Alfred Waller.

Schoorman, F. D. (1988). "Escalation bias in performance appraisals: An unintended consequence of supervisor participation in hiring decisions," *Journal of Applied Psychology*, 73: 58–62.

Schultz-Hardt, S., Thurow-Kröning, B., and Frey, D. (2009). "Preference-based escalation: A new interpretation for the responsibility effect in escalating commitment and entrapment," *Organizational Behavior and Human Decision Processes*, 108: 175–86.

Shepherd, D. A., Patzelt, H., Williams, T., and Warnecke, D. (2014). " How does project termination impact project team members? Rapid termination, 'creeping death', and learning from failure," *Journal of Management Studies*, 51: 513–46.

Simonson, I. and Staw, B. M. (1992). "Decision strategies: A comparison of techniques for reducing commitment to losing courses of action," *Journal of Applied Psychology*, 77: 419–26.

Singer, M. S. and Singer, A. E. (1985). "Is there always escalation of commitment?" *Psychological Reports*, 56: 816–18.

Sleesman, D. J., Conlon, D. E., McNamara, G., and Miles, J. E. (2012). "Cleaning up the big muddy: A meta-analytic review of the determinants of escalation of commitment," *Academy of Management Journal*, 55: 541–62.

Soll, J. B., Milkman, K. L., and Payne, J. W. (2015). "Outsmart your own biases," *Harvard Business Review*, May: 65–71.

Staw, B. M. (1976). "Knee-deep in the big muddy: A study of escalating commitment to a chosen course of action," *Organizational Behavior and Human Decision Processes*, 16: 27–44.

Staw, B. M. (1997). "Escalation research: An update and appraisal," in Z. Shapira (ed.), *Organizational Decision Making*. Cambridge: Cambridge University Press, pp. 191–215.

Staw, B. M. and Fox, F. V. (1977). "Escalation: the determinants of commitment to a chosen course of action," *Human Relations*, 30: 431–50.

Staw, B. M. and Ross, J. (1978). "Commitment to a policy decision: A multi-theoretical perspective," *Administrative Science Quarterly*, 23: 40–6.

Staw, B. M. and Ross, J. (1987a). "Behavior in escalation situations: Antecedents, prototypes and solutions," in L. L. Cummings and B. M. Staw (eds.), *Research in Organization Behavior*. London: JAI Press.

Staw, B. M. and Ross, J. (1987b). "Knowing when to pull the plug," *Harvard Business Review*, March/April: 65–72.

Stross, R. (2012). "Billion-dollar flop: Air Force stumbles on software plan," *The New York Times*, 8 December, <http://www.nytimes.com/20/12/09/tecnology/air-force-stumbles-over-software>.

Tan, H-T. and Yates, J. F. (1995). "Sunk cost effects: the influences of instruction and future return estimates," *Organizational Behavior and Human Decision Processes*, 63: 311–19.

Taylor, S. E. (1980). *Positive Illusions*. New York: Basic Books.

Taylor, S. E. and Brown, J. (1988). "Illusion and well-being: A social psychological perspective on mental health," *Psychological Bulletin*, 103: 193–210.

Teger, A. I. (1980). *Too Much Invested to Quit: The Psychology of the Escalation of Conflict*. New York: Pergamon.

Tetlock, P. E. (1985). "Accountability: The neglected social context of judgment and choice," in B. M. Staw and L. L. Cummings (eds.), *Research and Organizational Behaviour*, vol. 7. Greenwich CT: JAI Press, pp. 297–332.

Ting, H. (2011), "The effects of goal distance and value in escalation of commitment," *Current Psychology*, 30: 93–104.

Tiwana, A., Keil, M., and Fichman, R. G. (2006). "Information systems project continuation in escalation situations: A real options model," *Decision Sciences*, 37: 357–91.

Van Oorschot, K. E., Akkermans, H., Sengupta, K., and Van Wassenhove, L. K. (2013). "Anatomy of a decision trap in complex new product development projects," *Academy of Management Journal*, 56: 285–307.

Webber, J. (2015). "Lure of larger container ships fuels canal boom in central America," *Financial Times*, March 26, <http:www.ft.com>.

Whitney, K. M. and Daniels, C. B. (2013). "The root cause of failure in complex IT projects: Complexity itself," *Procedia Computer Science*, 20: 325–30.

Whyte, G. (1986). "Escalating commitment to a course of action: A reinterpretation," *Academy of Management Review*, 11: 311–21.

Whyte, G. (1991). "Diffusion of responsibility: Effects on the escalation tendency," *Journal of Applied Psychology*, 76: 408–15.

Whyte, G., Saks, A. M., and Hook, S. (1997). "When success breeds failure: The art of self-efficacy in escalating commitment to a losing course of action," *Journal of Organizational Behavior*, 18: 415–32.

Wicker, A. W. (1985). "Getting out of our conceptual ruts: Strategies for expanding conceptual frameworks," *American Psychologist*, 40, 1094–103.

Zardkoohi, A. (2004). "Do real options lead to escalation of commitment?" *Academy of Management Review*, 29: 111–19.

Zhang, L. and Baumeister, R. F. (2006). "Your money or your self-esteem: Threatened egotism promotes costly entrapment in losing endeavours," *Personality and Social-Psychology Bulletin*, 32: 881–93.

CHAPTER 10

···

MEGAPROJECTS AS GAMES OF INNOVATION

···

ROGER MILLER, DONALD LESSARD, AND VIVEK SAKHRANI

MEGAPROJECTS are intricate and customized solutions shaped over many years to fit specific contexts and market needs. Each project calls for multiple innovative choices to face wide ranges of foreseeable and emerging issues. Varying forms of risks are associated with the designing, financing, and building of the facilities that will deliver services.

This chapter focuses on megaprojects as games of innovation, where sponsors, experts, and potentially opposing stakeholders interact to shape opportunities into projects and to design and deliver these projects. The first part describes how projects are sponsored and shaped. The second part focuses on innovation spaces to create project value. The third part details the shaping process further and illustrates the dynamic capabilities necessary for clients, sponsors, and expert firms to shape projects using innovative solutions. The fourth part describes how the shaping of megaprojects is changing with the rise of public–private partnerships (PPPs). The fifth part concludes by examining how duos of sponsors and experts master the inherent complexity of megaprojects and develop architectures and processes that deliver with requisite complexity.

Our observations are based on extensive evidence from four sources. First we analyzed sixty large engineering projects in the fields of energy, transportation, oil, and gas. For each project, we interviewed sponsors, investors, contractors, opponents, legal advisers, and regulators (Miller and Lessard 2000). The second source of evidence is a modeling study calibrated on a large number of water projects globally (Sakhrani 2015). The third source of information is a number of oil and gas projects (Lessard, Sakhrani, and Miller 2014), including five MPs that have shaped petroleum development in Norway (Am and Hieberg 2014). Finally, we draw on a worldwide study of innovation practices (Miller and Côté 2012). In this chapter we focus on general patterns, and also provide examples of specific projects that illustrate salient points.[1]

10.1 SPONSORING AND SHAPING MEGAPROJECTS

The planning and management of large engineering projects can be viewed from two contrasting perspectives. The first is the *ex ante* rational view in which forecasts of revenues, costs associated with options, and risks are used to select the optimal project and implement it. However, decisions to plan megaprojects are rarely made in large-scale "once-and-for-all" analytical efforts by clients and sponsors. Grand decision-making sessions in which all options are considered to select the optimal path are rare. This rational approach relies on the rigor of analytical efforts and the perceived superiority of forecasting, or in the case of a formal options approach, the ability to model the principal dynamics. The second opposing perspective views megaproject management as an ongoing political process, which entails the exercise of power in moves and countermoves. Even technically complex projects can be subject to bargaining; sponsors, and stakeholders make trades to shape the alternatives. The final choice emerges over time out of the political process.

Our approach, based on the study of a large number of ventures, recognizes that the shaping of projects has a logic of its own. We argue that it is more productive to view megaprojects as **Games of Innovation** as defined by Miller and Côté (2012), than as linear engineering endeavors. Games are coherent patterns of interaction among actors that emerge as a response to contexts. The actors in megaprojects are a duo of a sponsor (coalition) and coalition of experts or, at times, a trio including a coalition of potentially opposing stakeholders.

Based on an analysis of 850 innovation projects, including but not limited to engineering megaprojects, Miller and Côté (2012) identify six distinct innovation patterns along two major dimensions: market and technical dynamism (moderate vs. turbulent) and innovation architectures ranging from stand-alone products, to open platforms, to tightly integrated closed systems.[2] The six resulting patterns are: (1) **Eureka** games that occur in highly turbulent technical and marketing contexts; they are based on discovery and entrepreneurship; (2) **New and Improved** games that take place in mature and moderately changing technical and marketing environments; such games focus on repeated incremental changes to products and processes to improve productivity; (3) **Breakthrough** games that involve novel scientific and engineering solutions designed to bring about new ways of doing things; sponsors work in collaboration with disciplinary experts; (4) **Battles of Architecture** that take place in highly dynamic environments and platforms, stressing competing and often mutually exclusive platform-based business models; 5) **Mass Customization** games that develop applications on platforms to deliver individual baskets of goods; (6) **Pushing the Envelope** games that take place in moderately turbulent environments in terms of technology and markets but where tight integration is required.

Pushing the Envelope games best characterize the shaping process we have observed (Miller et al. 2008) in megaprojects, as these projects not only involve moderate technical and market dynamism, but also have to form tightly integrated closed systems.[3] Megaprojects are rarely "built on spec"—developed in advance of demand as ready-to-market solutions for adoption. Instead, sponsors and expert firms respond to an articulated need, and jointly progress over many years through small-step innovations from an initial problem toward final commitment to an architecture. This contrasts with the conventional linear view of innovation often applied to projects in which the starting point is R&D, followed by product development and eventual market launch.

Innovations in megaprojects typically are not radical novelties, but contingent and adapted solutions to varied needs (Miller and Côté 2012). Clients, sponsors, and expert firms interact intensively to jointly develop solutions to revealed yet often evolving needs. Further, they often must interact with potentially opposing stakeholders to find acceptable solutions. Megaproject management is thus characterized by ambitious efforts and the integration of teams of experts, as well as of stakeholders, to bring closure to the system.

10.1.1   The Context of Megaprojects

Although most megaprojects seem to fall into well-scripted sectors—bridges, subways, highways, power dams, other large-scale energy and water projects, and integrated industrial and urban developments—each megaproject is different because of its particular technical and institutional context. Here are the key attributes of the contexts that characterizes megaprojects:

1. Megaprojects are large and technically complex engineering and financial ventures costing on average $1 billion dollars with a very wide variation in scale. Quite often, resistance and external pressures from many stakeholders accompany scale.
2. The technology behind megaprojects is not in continual and radical change. Instead, accumulated knowledge grows at a moderate pace. The engineering challenge is to build a tightly integrated closed system that delivers services, provides stable revenues, and is able to respond to risks.
3. Megaprojects involve large, lumpy, and irreversible financial commitments. Once built, projects become scope-specific; they are customized for the specific context, and are difficult to repackage and redeploy for any other than the original purpose.
4. Risks and turbulence emerge as major uncertainties in demand for services, technical solutions, and financial engineering play themselves out. When external and internal conditions change, projects are subject to conflicting pressures. In the absence of institutional buttresses to help structure decision processes, the shaping of megaprojects often plunges into a degenerating cycle of crises.
5. The performance of megaprojects can be measured along multiple dimensions such as functionality, transparency, delays, costs, contribution to economic development,

and so forth. Few projects score high on all dimensions. Cost overruns are common, but most megaprojects end up delivering the services sought by their sponsors. However, many authors stress the prevalence of disappointing results (Flyvbjerg et al. 2003). During the ramp-up period, initial market expectations are re-evaluated and the true worth of the project becomes apparent as revenues begin to flow in. Sponsors may find that revenues are much lower than expected.

6. Decision making in megaprojects takes place over many years. Front-end decision activities are spread over an average of approximately 6–7 years, while construction and ramp-up are much shorter (Miller and Lessard 2000). The journey from the initial idea proposed by a client-sponsor to commitment, construction, and ramp-up is unclear and tortuous. Progress requires resolving multiple issues over many years, through innovative steps until closure is reached and commitment to construct a specific well-defined project is possible.

10.1.2 Megaprojects Are Sponsored

Clients or sponsors of megaprojects such as network operators, public agencies, or industrial firms start by defining the bottlenecks, the problems, and the challenges they face. Examples of problems or bottlenecks are: (1) recurring traffic overload, suggesting that major investments are needed to build the missing links in highways systems; (2) low yields in the exploitation of oil and gas fields with established methods, thus calling for new ways of exploiting reserves; (3) frequent brown-outs in electric power networks, calling for reworking of the architecture. and so on. Natural resources also present megaproject opportunities. Many megaprojects aim not only at practical goals such as delivery of targeted services, but also involve high ambitions, lofty ideals, and economic development targets. Megaprojects are often tools to reach political objectives (Flyvbjerg et al. 2003).

Megaprojects are rarely built solely with in-house resources but involve the coordination by sponsors and institutions of external players, each playing distinct roles with different competences and often with different objectives. The processes for the coordination of players are strong leadership, extensive negotiations, and global contracts.

10.1.3 Duos of Complementary Organizations in Shaping Megaprojects

The shaping of megaprojects results from interactive decision making over many years within institutional and procedural frameworks between a duo of distinct types of organization: (1) the client-sponsor (sometimes called developer) with a major problem or bottleneck to solve;[4] (2) expert firms with engineering knowledge, financial resources, and experience that can design, finance, and build the project.

The driving member of the duo is usually the sponsor such as a public agency, a private operator, or a large industrial firm. The entity facing the problem or the bottleneck has a real need for a tailored solution to help it better serve its own clientele. The second part of the duo consists of groupings of expert firms that join in coalitions, form a project organization, and contract to bring expertise. Expert firms have developed the competencies and the experience to become credible partners and bidders. Expert firms have accumulated knowledge in the required disciplines and complementary engineering fields.

Shaping arises as sponsors, expert firms, and opponents confront perspectives and accumulated knowledge. The duo works until most issues are solved and until they arrive at some degree of final closure. Experts suggest novel approaches, redefine the problem, and seek best practices. Of course, clients or sponsors can always choose not to be innovative and stick to old ways.

Many paths for innovation may be pursued. The sponsors may decide to develop a solution internally using accumulated experience. However, sponsors rarely have all the expertise necessary to develop solutions of the problem at hand.

Instead, the sponsors rely on open sourcing and invite one or multiple groupings of complementary experts to sketch out and propose solutions. Quite often, the sponsor invites and pays competing groups of expert firms to ensure that he gets access to highly innovative solutions.

The duo can become a trio when affected parties are triggered to participate in order to reshape the proposed project. Most megaprojects, we have noted, meet resistance from environment groups, communities, or interest groups. The interests of these affected parties have to be integrated and taken into consideration.

10.1.4 Shaping as a Response to Issues

Clients or sponsors do not sit idle when challenged by risks and difficulties. On the contrary, they shape their projects according to the specific issues that need to be solved. In some cases, bundles of issues have to be resolved together. The institutional framework in which project shaping is embedded helps structure the allocation of shaping efforts to resolve issues. Table 10.1 lists a number of key interdependent issues for which solutions need to be developed.

Solutions to these issues emerge through an episodic shaping process, shown in Figure 10.1. At the starting point of each shaping episode, many futures are possible; solutions are not determined in advance but can be forged by the sponsoring group. Sponsors can develop many hypotheses about possible ways to sketch solutions to issues. Exploratory investments are made to elaborate strategies and gain momentum.

When opposition and counterforces are exerted, sponsors use rational arguments but also diplomacy to convince. After each shaping episode, sponsors start again if the value of the project is still acceptable. They can abandon if the project is likely to lead to

Table 10.1 Major issues around which megaprojects are shaped

- Definition of the problem and bottleneck by the sponsor
- Rough feasibility of project as an idea
- Demand forecast: reliability and long-term
- Frame agreement between sponsors
- Environmental challenges and actions
- Business and financial model for the long-term
- Variety of risks: market, technology, and institutions
- Access to world-class experts to suscitate partnerships
- Fairness, qualification, and bidding processes
- Gross contracts and procedures for dealing with changes
- Permits and regulatory decisions
- Commitment to final partnership agreement

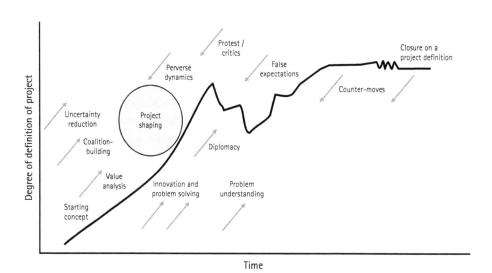

FIGURE 10.1 Project shaping.

irrational choices. For each shaping episode, efforts are made to grapple with a high level of uncertainties to achieve some degree of closure.

10.1.5 Shaping as an Active Sculpting of Project Elements

Interdependent issues cannot be resolved all at once. Instead, issues form bundles and prerequisites. Resolutions of key issues are often preconditions for proceeding to the resolution of other logically interlinked issues and problems. With the passage of time, previously resolved issues may re-emerge and become challenges that call for new shaping efforts. Even issues for which formal agreements had been made can be reopened as conditions and power shifts occur. Lessard et al. (2014) have divided the shaping of projects into four sets of activities:

1. **Adaptation to the inherent technical features** of the project. Projects are characterized by features such as location, size, systemic complexity, and extent of novelty (Dewar and Hage 1978; Shenhar and Dvir 2007). A wide diversity of scientific and engineering disciplines is required.
2. **Configuration of the project within the inherent institutional frameworks** that govern projects. Legislative, regulatory, and public finance frameworks eventually bind the parties (Scott 2013). The configuration is also influenced by stakeholders' reactions and power. Weak institutional frameworks lead to incomplete solutions. Highly structured institutional frameworks entail high shaping efforts but also higher governability.
3. **Project architecting of organizational arrangements** designed to respond to institutional features and realize the project (Burton and Obel 2004). Technical choices focus on design engineering, scale, logistical activities, and so on. Architectural strategies concern the viability of the project, business model, financing, partnership agreements, government participation, risk allocation, and crisis provisions (Anderson 1999).
4. **Fostering emergent properties to instil governability**. Emergent properties are outcomes in terms of performance (costs, delays, functionality) or attributes such as governability, flexibility, or quality. Emergent properties stem from the interdependencies and the interactions between technical or institutional features as well as project architecting (Lessard et al. 2014). For instance, projects can achieve governability through the built-in ability to face crisis or respond to turbulence. Sponsors use devices that instil the ability to respond to turbulence. Building governability is an art based on experience, judgment, and intuition.

Table 10.2 lists a few architectural devices for sculpting project elements. Sponsors study each device to provide responses in times of crises.

Table 10.2 Illustrative devices to shape and sculpt projects

▪ Framing agreement	▪ Concessions
▪ Public–Private-Partnership	▪ BOT Build Own and Operate
▪ Project financing	▪ Purchase contract
▪ Design build contract	▪ Rendezvous clauses
▪ Public consultation	▪ Callable funds

10.1.6. Shaping as an Episodic Process

Analyzing many projects, we noted that shaping occurs through progressive problem solving over multiple episodes:

1. **Shaping the opportunity**: This first episode lasts a few years as the client or sponsor, with the help of advisers, develops the project concept, imagines the coalition of partners, and signals its readiness to act. The sponsor positions itself as a credible party that has the resources to shape the opportunity. Debates as to the appropriate ways and means of shaping and financing the idea take place. When the opportunity becomes public, challenges by stakeholders often emerge. The opportunity has to be recycled and redefined to include these interests. Without a credible vision put forward by the leading sponsor, the project remains in an infancy trap. Resources of a few million dollars are allocated initially to explore and develop the concept. Engineering, financial, and marketing feasibility studies are undertaken to understand risks and identify options. Closure is achieved after much iteration if the viability of the concept is established. A Memorandum of Agreement sketches out the agreements. Yet the project is still only a multidimensional idea. The sponsor may decide to drop the project or embark on further iterations to refine the concept, solve a few interdependent issues, and solidify the coalition of partners. Typically, sponsors will allocate moderate sums (even up to few dozen million dollars) to develop a complete conceptual solution.

2. **Shaping the project:** This episode involves the building of investment scenarios, as well as the writing of a business case (financial model) for investors. Negotiations are held to ensure that eventual investments are protected against opportunistic behaviors by focusing on devices such as long-term contracts, frame agreements, and so on. Specialized experts join with the intent to contribute to overall value creation but also hope to capture "more than their fair share." The process is a seesaw between positive-sum collaboration and zero-sum gaming. Eventually, the balance becomes acceptable

3. **Reshaping the project:** Once it becomes clear that the project is likely to go ahead, fears resurface and affected interests mobilize. The sponsor tries to regains the consent of affected parties by recognizing their rights, negotiating compensations, and otherwise engaging in proactive strategies with communities. Gaining the right to build a project often requires the leading sponsor to demonstrate its credible commitments by incurring substantial expenditures for cleaning up polluted sites, organizing economic development initiatives, building complementary facilities, and so on. Unresolved issues that were skipped in previous episodes may reappear as the project is being developed. If parties are unable to forge new agreements, they must wait for judicial, political, or government decisions. The presence of institutional and environmental-assessment frameworks is extremely important here to help solve these dilemmas. Delays are the inevitable

consequences of such formal assessments. Institutional frameworks induce parties to either make trade-offs or kill the project.

4. **Engineering the project:** The concept of the project in financial and engineering terms is now clearer. Furthermore, the necessary coalitions have now been firmed up. Detailed engineering is now possible. Commitment to a final package takes place when all major issues have been resolved. In this episode, detailed designs are produced, and roles for execution are defined.

5. **Sprinting to build the project:** This episode, which is the focus of most formal tools for project management, usually takes place in a context of relative stability. The construction sprint period begins once full shaping has been achieved. Sprinting adds economic value to projects as it influences how quickly revenues can arrive. The major constraint is the time required to perform adequately the various tasks along the critical path without incurring undue risks. Turbulence at this stage is usually much lower, as major issues have been resolved.

6. **Ramping and operating the project:** Once the project is built, it enters into a ramp-up period. It is here that expectations about markets, technical functionality, and social acceptability are tested. In extreme cases the "teething problems" are so serious that the project is recycled into project reshaping. If no adequate (re) definition is possible, the project dies.

Table 10.3 summarizes the states of the contextual conditions, concept, coalition(s), form of commitment, process, and closure in each of these six phases for a typical megaproject (Lessard and Miller 2013). Figure 10.2 illustrates the progressive shaping and sculpting of a representative project as a sequence of options. Cycling back to agreements made in earlier episodes is often necessary. The path taken by each episode depends on the extent of closure in the previous ones.

10.2 CREATING PROJECT VALUE THROUGH INNOVATION

The prize in the Game of Innovation in megaprojects is value. The quest for value involves a dual effort of value creation and capture. The shaping process relies on innovation to unlock value. Value in megaprojects is closely tied to the multiple objectives of the duos—both the client sponsors and (leaders of the coalition of) expert firms. This highlights the tension that value objectives may not be clearly known at the outset and must be discovered, refined, and articulated in the shaping process. The effort to "push the frontier" is one of balancing trade-offs across often-competing and noncommensurate value dimensions.

Megaprojects create value for society over their life cycle by enabling fundamental transformations. The transformation may be technical, institutional, or both. The Second Severn Crossing, for example, fundamentally transformed the transport and

Table 10.3 Episodes in the shaping of projects

	Shaping the opportunity	Shaping the project	Reshaping the project	Engineering the project	Sprinting to build the project	Ramping up to operations
Contextual conditions	Sponsor and experts shape key choices; many degrees of freedom	Blocks of basic interdependent issues need resolution	As project gets "real" fears and risks emerge and threaten	Period of stability as key choices are set	Linear world of project management	Irreversible lock-in with few degrees of freedom
Concept	Vision and sketches of key dimensions	Holistic solutions to interdependent issues in technology, markets, and politics	Concept adapted to powerful players as they mobilize as project becomes real	Multidimensional concept is clear and becomes a plan	Concept is fixed; fast construction to achieve revenue generation	Concept is locked: market, technology, and political agreements
Coalition	Credible sponsor recruits partners and stakeholders	Roles defined: champion, experts, supporters, and forbearers	Broad set of members and powerful stakeholders	Broad set of stakeholders gives license to proceed	Coalition is fixed, buttressed by formal agreements	Coalition is fixed; callable resources are made available
Form of commitment	Verbal, informal, often public, but open to further shaping	Credible sponsor announces intentions	Agreement with powerful opponents	Detailed business plan	Sets of contracts and specifications	Final commitments, ownership, and financial structure
Process	Multiple iterations around vision	Sponsor, partners, and stakeholders negotiate	Iteration to stress test concept and coalition	Formal contracts and partnership	Back to linear world	All relationships are stabilized
Closure	Memorandum of Agreement	Concrete frame agreement	Agreement working out consequences of real project	Detailed plans	Contracts	Stable contracts and irreversible choices

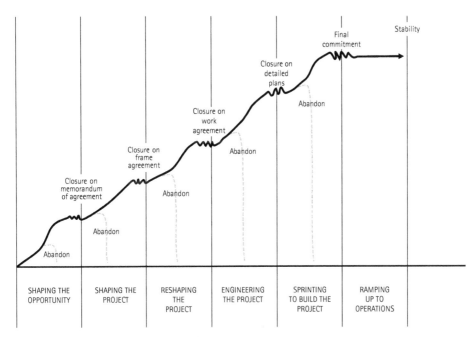

FIGURE 10.2 Shaping as a sequence of options.

economic integration possibilities in West Wales and England. Urban transport projects such as subways or Boston's Big Dig fundamentally change the potential of previously "stranded" districts (see Boston CA/T project in Hughes 2000). Large pumped storage projects such as Kazunogawa or the proposed Mirror of Tarapacá in northern Chile[5] allow grid balancing at much lower cost and with it, the greater integration of intermittent sources such as solar PV and wind. In contrast, the emergence of a Cofiroute as a private coalition to build highways through PPPs was an institutional transformation, as was the Confederation Bridge in linking public obligations and private financing.

The value of the project is intrinsic in the service it delivers; society benefits as many users consume electricity to drive economic and social endeavors, for example. Value of the service is made explicit, when it is priced using markets or tariffs. In services where unit pricing is a challenge (such as water, congestion, or reduced carbon emissions), value continues to be created, although the project organization and its architectural arrangements must embed mechanisms for value capture.

The shaping and delivery process installs the megaproject as an engine of value creation for society. Value is first realized during the initial ramp-up and during stable operations thereafter. The cost of different shaping stages is the price of subsequent options to secure value. Value is sometimes forgone when the megaproject is abandoned because the duo (or trio) cannot achieve closure in a compelling opportunity.

Players of the game seek to capture the prize of value by sculpting project arrangements in the front-end. The same devices (Table 10.2) that instil governance, such as frame agreements, concessions contracts, and one or more architectural models

(B-O-T), in conjunction with engineering and technological choices, safeguard the value potential of the project over its life cycle, and allocate it to the players of the game. These devices embed the terms of value exchange between the players.

The engineering literature on (systems) integration and architecture provides a useful lens for relating intentional design and platform choices to fostering intended value outcomes (Maier and Rechtin 2009). Changes in design lead to trades in value outcomes along competing value dimensions, which are aligned with the project's multiple objectives. The set of all possible project design and architectural choices is the **design tradespace**—so called because it comprehensively reveals trade-offs in value. The tradespace maps the landscape of design possibilities in relation to value. In the shaping process, however, members of the duo are "in" the landscape. They uncover possibilities by exploring changes in project architecture (for example, higher production capacity, phased investments, technological variants, pricing structures) to understand the resulting changes; that is, trade-offs in expected value. Much of this design exploration occurs before the (4) engineering stage of the project (see Table 10.3), because of the necessary and available flexibility. Members of the partnership lock-in project design and architecture in the detailed engineering stage to enable the subsequent sprint to build the project.

Figure 10.3 depicts the concept of value trade-offs across multiple objectives. Value dimensions are seen from the functional perspectives of the two members of the duo, the sponsor(s), and the (leader of the coalition of) experts—service levels that are valued by the sponsor and profits for the experts/contractors. There are a number of megaproject architectures and design configurations (A, E, B, C) that are interior to the achievable value frontier. As the duo explores these possibilities, they refine and reconfigure to identify efficient designs (D, G, F) and to make trade-offs along the value dimensions in order to come to a negotiated agreement about the final configuration.

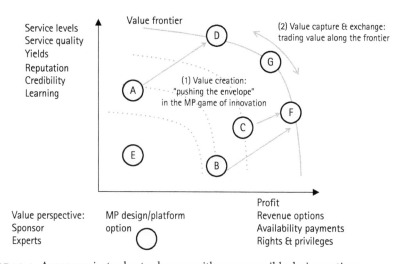

FIGURE 10.3 A megaproject value tradespace with many possible design options.

Value capture from the perspective of the public sector client-sponsor in the duo (trio) is intimately tied with the megaproject fulfilling its functional promise (reduced traffic congestion, reliable power supply, available passenger-lane-miles, and so on). In return, the sponsor trades either the monetized value of the service (ex. availability payments) or exclusive rights and privileges to the private experts (expansion options, toll collection rights, and right of first refusal on future projects) or some combination of these.

Expert firms in the coalition are driven by a near-term profit incentive, as well as the opportunity to establish credibility and reputation and internalize learning for long-term gains. Experts may trade away some share of profits to secure their role in the megaproject and demonstrate the "intangible" reputational and relational value they bring as credible partners.

Value creation and capture are interdependent. The players' multiple objectives in the Game of Innovation are to not only increase the size of the value pie as a whole but also their respective shares. Well-shaped projects may enable win–win situations. Players of the game (duos and trios) also sculpt the project arrangements to "push out the frontier" (creation) and then "move along the frontier" (capture).

Life-cycle value and other trade-offs exist in single-sponsor industrial megaprojects such as oil and gas projects as well (Merrow 2011). Here the sponsor must balance life-cycle economic gains (to the firm and community) with safety, legitimacy, and environmental impact. The sponsor may have to broaden the scope of the project to integrate the interests of an institutional partner and stakeholders (Freeman et al. 2007). The integration process may involve iterative exploration of the value tradespace.

Creating and capturing value in megaprojects thus intertwines the rational analytical process to assess the value of options with the political process of bargaining to balance value trade-offs. Duos and trios learn through exploration and articulate their interests in a refined voice. At its best, the Game of Innovation has the potential to evolve to a collaborative partnership.

10.3 Shaping as an Integration of Competencies, Capabilities, and Resources

Shaping megaprojects requires more than one competent actor. We have shown that it involves an iterative but nevertheless directed give and take among sponsors, experts, and contractors, and affected communities, regulators, and other stakeholders. Each must possess some of the complementary competencies required to shape, engineer, and deliver the project, but some parties must also develop the ability to bring these together and, at times, coshape them. In some instances, the orchestrator will be an individual sponsor or expert, but more often than not, some of the ability to bring the pieces together dynamically rests at the level of the ecosystem itself. Here we focus on the abilities of sponsors and of experts, paying special attention to the integrative dynamic capabilities that distinguish megaprojects.

10.3.1 Shaping Roles

Competent sponsors play the central role by behaving as responsible owners ready to analyze project concepts, engage in dialogue with competitive expert firms, and live with the consequences of their choices or omissions.

Effective sponsors need to have the skills to decide rapidly whether a project idea has value. Sponsors form task forces in which they join with lawyers, consultants, and investment bankers to decide with diligence whether project ideas are worth pursuing. Sponsors seek advice about market, technical, and geopolitical uncertainties before they start shaping.

Competent sponsors also have the relational abilities to interface with external partners, interact with government agencies, or collaborate with groups of expert firms. Effective sponsors have developed the ability to rapidly abandon projects that entail levels of investments that continue to escalate. Finally, effective sponsors have staying power when major downside risks materialize. In times of crisis, diversified sponsors can count on multiple revenue streams and call on networks of partners and coalition members to help a project survive.

In order to develop megaprojects, sponsors seek knowledge, advice, and services from organizations that have become experts in their relevant fields. Bankers and investors in infrastructure funds have learned the business of financial engineering and the forging of agreements between public and private parties. Bankers and investors not only bring access to equity funds; they also suggest best financial practices. Architects and engineers in their field of expertise can help provide best design and construction practices in their fields of knowledge. Experts, we have noted, accumulate extensive knowledge and relationships that puts them in a position to have substantial market share in their domain of expertise.

10.3.2 Capabilities Required for Shaping

Shaping megaprojects requires very different capabilities from those needed for selecting among or executing well-defined alternatives. While both require many individual competencies, as well as the ability to integrate complex sets of them, shaping requires a much larger and more robust set of integrative and dynamic capabilities.[6]

Operational capabilities are the discrete competencies required to perform a specific task or govern a particular process. These typically are best practices that start in one or two companies and then spread to the entire industry, thus providing limited differentiation. Integrative capabilities are the ability to design/orchestrate large numbers of activities in a structured pattern—being able to follow a recipe. This requires project management discipline, as well as stakeholder integration/management discipline. Dynamic capabilities are those that allow a sponsor, expert coalition, or the duo to create a new recipe. In some instances these are possessed by the sponsor or a specific expert, but in others, they lie directly with the coalition as opposed to any of its specific parties.

These integrative and dynamic capabilities are hard to develop, especially given the slow clock speed of megaprojects. As a result, a great deal of the potential for developing knowledge and capabilities comes from participating in multiple projects and coalitions that overlap in time, rather than in a sequence of projects over time. A large industrial sponsor typically will have a portfolio of programs that comprise many projects, but may only be executing a few of these at a time. A financial or legal expert, in contrast, may participate in many projects of a particular type that are being undertaken around the world at any point in time. Large contractors will fall somewhere in between. These different spans of capabilities-building experience are key to the competitive advantage of the various "shapers."

These levels of capability can be seen more sharply in the sculpting of project elements—technical, institutional, and architectural—described in Section 10.1.5 (Lessard et al. 2014).

Shaping the technical aspect of a megaproject typically requires bringing together many different components and drawing on many different disciplines. These must be integrated into alternative consistent overall designs. Further, they must be set in specific geographic and political contexts and different built environments. Examples of dynamic capabilities that we have observed in technical shaping, either by their presence or absence, include balancing which aspects of a project to replicate and which to adapt to particular circumstances; avoiding sequential suboptimization by discipline or project element; avoiding the extremes of premature lock-in or failure to commit to particular design principles early in the game; and keeping sight on key dimensions of value as the project goes through reshaping, engineering, or even during the sprint to completion as new developments trigger changes.

The institutional domain is more complex. Relational capabilities involve both knowledge and relationships—how particular interests relate to the overall values(s) being sought, and the credibility to engage in the required give and take. This is complex when it is only necessary to represent and bring together the various interests, but much more so if some of the interests, including those of the sponsor, need to be shaped in order for the project to develop. Examples of integrative dynamic capabilities we have observed include the ability to identify and engage those stakeholders who can either be most helpful or do most damage if not included, and how to separate or componentize those that need not be part of the central solution but require some level of attention in order to obtain forbearance for the project.

The architecture of project organization is perhaps the most challenging. It includes sequence, pace, integration, roles, and governance mechanisms for the project, and directly addresses the interdependence between the project as a technical artifact and a political deal. It must connect the internal routines of many organizations in ways that foster individual excellence, but also coherence and ultimately the completion of the project. It should be as simple as possible, but with governance that does not leave out important and potentially opposing stakeholders which if confronted down the line might trigger a "killer loop"—a return to an earlier stage of project shaping or design—entailing not only rework but also renegotiating with myriad parties.[7]

10.3.3 The Cost of Shaping and Competitive Advantage

The shaping of MPs is a costly, time-consuming business generally beyond the reach of smaller entrepreneurial firms. Shaping expenses can be very substantial. For standard projects with no exceptional difficulties, about 1% of total capital expenditures will be spent for framing, bidding, and legal expenditures. Shaping expenditures including competitive bidding costs represent on average 2–3% of the total cost for moderately difficult projects.

Shaping expenditures can shoot up to 30% when sponsors need to invest to demonstrate their willingness to solve environmental, political, or social problems. While many executives view shaping expenses as frivolous, effective sponsors view these as necessary for reasoned commitment. The costs incurred by bidders in competitive partnerships can also be surprisingly high. Bidding expenses reaching 4–5% of total capital expenditures are not uncommon. Sponsors with the ability to invest early at the front end are necessary.

The expense of shaping and the capabilities required limit the number of firms that can play. Furthermore, the slow clock speeds of megaprojects mean that requisite experience is accumulated only slowly, and only a few firms will develop the integrative dynamic capabilities required to accelerate learning by simultaneously participating in many projects in different institutional contexts.

As a result, sponsors, coalition leaders, and critical experts can bring great value to new opportunities, but can also capture some of that value.

10.4 SHIFT FROM THE TRADITIONAL TO THE PARTNERSHIP MODE OF SHAPING

The institutional conditions under which projects are shaped are themselves being modified. Shaping of projects and institutional frameworks coevolve. In the 1980s a new institutional model, PPPs, for sponsoring, building, and operating megaprojects emerged out of the Treasury Board of England. It was adopted in many countries to replace the traditional approach. The traditional approach is vertical in its emphasis. Sponsors define their solutions and decide upon what they see as their best option. Then, internal experts or engineering firms design projects to meet such solutions. Once detailed engineering is completed, projects are divided into work packages. Bids are then called from multiple contractors for each bundle of work packages.

Value is created in the traditional mode by the creative design choices developed by internal or external experts and by cost reductions achieved mostly through the bidding process. Unfortunately, sponsors in the traditional mode often work with outdated stocks of knowledge: they thus design inferior solutions. Furthermore, conflicts between sponsors and contractors eventually lead to increased costs and delays. Risks are eventually borne mostly by the sponsor.

Over the last decades, the public–private partnership approach has gradually been institutionalized to challenge the traditional mode of shaping megaprojects (Grimsey and Lewis 2007). The goal of the partnership approach is to open up the possibility of much higher rates of interactions that will increase innovative collaborations between sponsors and expert organizations. The goal is primarily to trigger innovations that enhance functionalities while at the same time giving rise to global contracts integrating design, construction, and life-cycle maintenance perspectives.

The major shift is from leadership by internal staff to leadership by external experts structured around a global contract. Three distinct forms of coalitions are established when using the partnership approach:

1. The first coalition builds on the readiness of the sponsor to officially declare that it is willing to use the PPP approach. The sponsor thus declares its intention to commit to a partnership mode with qualified experts and make space for the innovative approaches. The sponsor makes public the levels and characteristics of the demand he is ready to pay for over the long term. The technical and financial solutions to be used in designing and building the project are not spelled out.

2. The second level is the partnership between the sponsor and (a coalition of) competitively chosen experts. To build the partnership coalition, qualified expert firms in financing, engineering, procurement, and construction, as well as maintenance, are invited directly by the sponsor, or in many cases by an emergent leader of the coalition of experts to engage in the development of competitive proposals that meet the declared demand. These proposals cover issues such as performance, revenues, financing model, contributions, and toll revenues when applicable. The bearing of delivery risks is also allocated between the parties. Once the winning proposal has been selected by the sponsor, a global contract is then developed. The client or sponsor and the winning partnership coalition sign a comprehensive partnership agreement.

3. The third level of coalition is a project organization (often called special purpose vehicle) created under the leadership of the expert firm chosen by the winning coalition for the purpose of final design and construction of the project. To make room for innovations, a Design Build Finance Operate contract or a variant is used to provide the necessary incentives. Centralized decision procedures in the project organization are put in place to allocate responsibilities to respond to risks, develop solutions, and calculate trade-offs in the face of ongoing changes, many of

which are required by potentially opposing stakeholders. The project organization is usually coordinated by the leading expert firm.

Debates rage as to the alleged superiority of the partnership approach over the traditional mode. The argument in favor of the partnership approach is that incentives for performance and innovation can be built in early. Sponsors in the partnership mode can reduce costs and introduce new designs by centralizing major trade-offs and fostering the emergence of creative solutions (Lamman et al. 2013). The counter-argument is that in the end, subcontractors do not participate in the innovation process and are forced by sponsors to reduce costs by shrinking their margins.

While PPPs by definition involve a public sponsor and a private partner/coalition, similar solutions have been employed in industrial projects such and oil and gas, where the sponsor is typically a private oil company (or a set of companies as a working partnership), together with the public regulatory/fiscal authority, who in a sense is also a sponsor, as well as private experts/contractors. Am and Hieberg (2014) recount the history of the Ecofisk project in Norway, where a partnership including the government—though its regulator NPD and the state-owned oil company Statoil—"reshaped" the production technology and plan through partnership including private oil companies and contractors over a number of years. The partnership among other things included government support for research on new drilling technologies, as well as an adjustment in fiscal terms to recognize the costs associated with the higher recovery option. However, the majority of oil and gas projects are vertical in the sense that the fiscal arrangements, other regulations, and technical solutions are determined sequentially and "vertically" rather than through an iterative partnership.

10.5 Conclusion: Shaping as the Mastery of Complexity

It goes without saying that megaprojects are complex. Over a period of twenty years, we have observed in our studies that complexity emerges as a result of the interaction between the sculpted elements of megaprojects. While some technical challenges and institutional conditions are "inherent" in the megaproject opportunity, sponsors and experts lay in technical choices and organizational arrangements during the shaping and reshaping stages. These duos have their sights set on the prize of value(s), and they design projects to create and capture it. The extent to which players can push the value envelope depends on their dynamic capabilities for integrating the many essential disciplines and processes, sometimes within shifting institutional environments, as in the case with a move to PPPs.

Duos pursuing megaprojects must **embrace complexity** with requisite variety inherent in the project opportunity. Some opportunities may be more or less complex than the duo's previous ventures. In turn, the technical, organizational, and architectural choices they make while shaping the project, may further compound its complexity. The art of shaping megaprojects then also becomes one of making a series of proactive and conscious choices to address complexity. In some instances this can be accomplished by pursuing a series of smaller projects within an overall scheme rather than a single mega-project (Ansar et al. 2014; Flyvbjerg and Ansar 2015). In others, where technical and institutional considerations require a very extensive scope, architectures that decouple various elements such as engaging stakeholders early in the process before major capital outlays are made, or hedging against exchange rate and commodity price contingencies, will be the key to attaining a manageable degree of complexity.

Duos must **identify the mechanisms** necessary for instilling governance in an mega-project. The complexity resulting from architecting in these arrangements is necessary to safeguard the potential for value. The idea of requisite complexity—the degree of complexity necessary for unlocking value—goes against the popular grain that com-plexity should be minimized. In fact, capable sponsors incur the cost of shaping pre-cisely because this enables them to manage complexity in relation to value. For example, the sponsor in the Nanko power project in Osaka worked hard to integrate local stake-holder interests. The local community placed a high premium on a site design that was benign and aesthetically pleasing. Only by bringing them along could the sponsor deliver the project. While involving local interests in the shaping process from the start increased the complexity of the project, this was a requisite to both create and capture value. A counter-example was the Orlyval project in Paris, where excluding a key set of stakeholders from the shaping process allowed the project to be fast-tracked with a clean technological solution; but it turned out to be a white elephant, since it did not draw suf-ficiently wide "value boundaries."

Duos must **keep value trade-offs alive**. The initial aspirations of a megaproject rarely materialize as expected. Sponsors and experts must therefore play the megapro-ject Game of Innovation as a sequence of rounds, instead of a one-off gamble, to keep the megaproject "on the rails." This is critical in megaprojects because value accrues to members of the duo (or trio) over a long horizon, perhaps even carrying through to future projects through expertise and reputation. Even industrial sponsors with a high degree of vertical integration in project must balance trade-offs among cost, profit, safety, and environmental impact. They must also safeguard their credibility as dynamic integrators and relationships with peripheral stakeholders.

An interesting example is the evolution of PPP arrangements for different phases of Ontario's Highway 407. In the first round, the PPP sought primarily to bring lifetime (Capex vs. Opex) trade-offs into the project—something that the public sector has a very hard time doing, but also incorporating toll policy because this was viewed as key way not only to capture value but also to manage congestion. Over time, toll policy was separated out and retained by the province, with PPP being refocused on cost, availabil-ity, and congestion through fines imposed on the builder/operator.

Megaprojects present a conundrum. Their size and complexity invite cost overruns, schedule delays, and underdelivery on other key dimensions of value (Ansar et al. 2014). However, their size and scope often allow the internalization of costs and benefits that could not be obtained otherwise. Success depends more on the dynamic engagement of the duos (or trios) than on one-off grand designs.

NOTES

1. Examples are from Miller and Lessard (2000) and/or Lessard, Sakhrani, and Miller (2014) unless otherwise noted.
2. Baldwin and von Hippel (2011) show the conditions under which the innovation platform will be stand alone, integral, or an open platform when the elements are modular. Further work is required to combine these two perspectives to cover modular and integral systems.
3. This generalization is based on the physical megaprojects in our samples. Large IT projects often are more radical in nature, at times better characterized as Battles of Architecture.
4. The client-sponsor may be unitary such as the case of a large vertically integrated national water or energy company or may itself be a duo or even trio (ring-fenced business units), with one party typically taking the more dynamic entrepreneurial role. Examples of client-led collaborations include the Thames Water Ring and the Province of Ontario's Highway 407. Examples of sponsor-led collaborations include the ITA Dam and Hub Power. Gardermoen is an example of a project with a unified client-sponsor.
5. <http://www.pv-tech.org/news/chilean_developer_submits_plan_for_24_7_pv_plus_pumped_storage_plant>.
6. The concept of dynamic capabilities is developed most notably by Teece et al. (1997). See Garcia et al. (2014) for more extensive references and greater elaboration of these "levels" of capabilities.
7. See Eppinger (2001) for a discussion of "unplanned iterations" within a design structure matrix (DSM) characterization of project task interdependencies.

REFERENCES

Am, K. and Heiberg, S. (2014). "Public–private partnership for improved hydrocarbon recovery: Lessons from Norway's major development programs," *Energy Strategy Reviews*, 3: 30–48.

Ansar, A., Flyvbjerg, B., Budzier, A., and Lunn, D. (2014). "Should we build more large dams? The actual cost of megaproject development," *Energy Policy*, 69: 43–56.

Anderson, P. (1999). "Perspective: Complexity theory and organization science," *Organization Science*, 10(3): 216–32.

Baldwin, C. and von Hippel, E. (2011). "Modeling a paradigm shift: From producer innovation to user and open collaborative innovation," *Organization Science*, 22(6): 1399–417.

Burton, R. M. and Obel, B. (2004). *Strategic Organizational Diagnosis and Design: The Dynamics of Fit*. Boston: Kluwer.

Dewar, R. and Hage, J. (1978). "Size, technology, complexity, and structural differentiation: Toward a theoretical synthesis," *Administrative Science Quarterly*, 23(1): 111–36.

Eppinger, S. (2001). "Innovation at the speed of information," *Harvard Business Review*, 79(1): 149–58.

Flyvbjerg, B. and Ansar, A. (2015). "Should we build more megadams?," <https://www.linkedin.com/pulse/why-more-megadams-bad-idea-bent-flyvbjerg>.

Flyvbjerg, B., Bruzelius, N., and Rothengatter, W. (2003). *Megaprojects and Risk: An Anatomy of Ambition*. Cambridge: Cambridge University Press.

Freeman, R. E., Harrison, J. S., and Wicks, A. C. (2007). *Managing for Stakeholders: Survival, Reputation, and Success*. New Haven, CT: Yale University Press.

Garcia, R., Lessard, D., and Singh, A. (2014). "Strategic partnering in oil and gas: A capabilities perspective," *Energy Strategy Reviews*, 3C: 21–29.

Grimsey, D. and Lewis, M. K. (2007). *Public Private Partnerships: The Worldwide Revolution in Infrastructure Provision and Project Finance*. Cheltenham: Edward Elgar.

Hughes, T. P. (2000). *Rescuing Prometheus*. New York: Vintage Books.

Lamman, C., MacIntyre, H., and Berechman, J. (2013). *Using Public–Private Partnerships to Improve Transportation Infrastructure in Canada*. Vancouver, BC: Fraser Institute Research Studies.

Lessard, D. and Miller, R. (2013). "The shaping of large engineering projects," in H. Priemus and B. van Wee (eds.), *International Handbook on Mega-Projects*. Cheltenham: Edward Elgar.

Lessard, D., Sakhrani, V., and Miller, R. (2014). "House of project complexity: Understanding complexity in large infrastructure Projects," *Engineering Project Organization Journal*, 4(4): 170–92.

Maier, M. and Rechtin, E. (2009). *The Art of Systems Architecting*, 3rd edn. Boca Raton, FL: CRC Press.

Merrow, E. W. (2011). *Industrial Megaprojects: Concepts, Strategies, and Practices for Success*. Hoboken, NJ: Wiley.

Miller R. and Côté M. (2012). *Innovation Re-invented: Six Games that Drive Growth*. Toronto: University of Toronto Press.

Miller, R. and Hobbs, R. (2005). "Governance regimes for large complex projects," *Project Management Journal*, 36: 42–50.

Miller R. and Lessard D. (2000). *The Strategic Management of Large Engineering Projects: Shaping Institutions, Risks and Governance*. Cambridge, MA: MIT Press.

Miller, R, Olleros, X., and Molinié, L. (2008). "Innovation games: A new approach to the competitive challenge," *Long Range Planning*, 41: 378–94.

Sakhrani, V. (2015). *Negotiated Collaboration: A Study in Flexible Infrastructure Design*, PhD dissertation, MIT.

Scott, W. R. (2013). *Institutions and Organizations: Ideas, Interests, and Identities*. 4th edn. Thousand Oaks, CA: Sage.

Shenhar, A. J. and Dvir, D. (2007). *Reinventing Project Management: The Diamond Approach to Successful Growth and Innovation*. Cambridge, MA: Harvard Business Press.

Teece, D. J., Pisano, G., and Shuen, A. (1997). "Dynamic capabilities and strategic management," *Strategic Management Journal*, 18(7): 509–33.

Williams, T. M. (2005). "Assessing and moving on from the dominant project management discourse in the light of project overruns," *IEEE Transactions on Engineering Management*, 52(4): 497–508.

CHAPTER 11

....

POWER AND SENSEMAKING IN MEGAPROJECTS

....

STEWART R. CLEGG, SHANKAR SANKARAN, CHRIS BIESENTHAL, AND JULIEN POLLACK

11.1 INTRODUCTION

By conventional account, megaprojects are large, transformational, and complex under-takings with a long duration. Typically, their estimated cost is more than US$1 billion (Aaltonen and Kujala 2010; Flyvbjerg 2014), though we agree with Van Marrewijk (2015) that it is less the money involved and more the substantive features of the large-scale project that are significant. Above all, megaprojects are complex: complex in design, technologies, innovation, ambiguity, uncertainty, management, finance, budgeting, environmental impact, and mobilization of social movement and citizen opposition; in their temporality and temporal impact, public scrutiny and accountability; in their interorganizational relations, in collaborations between public and private sectors, and in their multiphasing and nonlinearity.

The large number of influential and critical stakeholders assures complexity from both the public and private sectors; often they are of such significance that they have a great impact on the society (affecting millions of people) and are an object of consid-erable scrutiny. The most visible megaprojects leave a spatial footprint as construction projects of one kind or another. However, they are not exclusively construction works; they can occur in IT, defense, innovation, disaster relief, and many other fields. With regard to their impact and the amount of resources dedicated to their delivery, mega-projects are not simply "magnified versions of smaller projects" (Flyvbjerg 2014: 6), but have distinctly different problems, power dynamics, and structures. Their size, duration, and complexity make them costly sites of complex processes of contested sensemaking and power relations.

Once upon a time, many such projects would have been public-sector initiatives. As a result of the *mega-costs* associated with megaprojects and cuts in government spending, an increasing number of megaprojects rely on private investments from banks, private investors, or capital funds. Investors have their own objectives, which may not be entirely aligned with the overall objectives of the project *per se*, making the megaproject arena an even more fertile ground for power dynamics to affect project progress. External involvement of private-sector capital means that continuation of vital project funding becomes partially contingent on third-party considerations of medium-term return on investment, which can affect important decisions throughout the project life cycle. These questions of financial calculation and related considerations dramatically change the nature of negotiations and the decision-making processes in megaprojects. In other words, megaprojects face major social, political, and cultural challenges, especially in the context of multiple stakeholders whose objectives, goals, and strategies will, in all probability, not be aligned.

Megaprojects are typically designed, organized, and delivered as mainly engineering-based (Giezen 2012); typically, the rational, linear, quantitative, and value-neutral (Çiçmil et al. 2006) aspects of project management are favored. The dominant scientific, normative, and dualist assumptions of traditional project management define these projects mainly in terms of project structure and prescriptive processes. Such assumptions ignore underlying power dynamics both in the start-up phase and in subsequent actions characterizing project practice (Çiçmil and Hodgson 2006; Clarke 1999; Clegg 1975).

Given the increasing number of megaprojects and the movement towards the professionalization of the discipline, project management practice has struggled to develop workable solutions and practices to address complexities that exceed the technical concerns of engineering. While there is a growing awareness that traditional project management approaches fail to meet the required standards of managing megaprojects, there is still a shortage of theoretical knowledge to draw on (for example, Flyvbjerg 2007; Holmes 2001; Maylor et al. 2008). Such knowledge exists but is rarely incorporated into the engineering discipline because it is embedded in social-science accounts of organizational politics. While successful project managers have to become adept at the "dark arts" of managing organizational politics, they often do so less through formal instruction in the discipline and more through embedded custom and practice learnt on the job. This chapter will examine current practices underlying the management of megaprojects and explore the role and importance of power relations in understanding them. To do so it must first address the ways in which the disciplines of management and engineering entered into a path-dependent alliance of disciplinary formation—one with an implicit set of power relations inherent in them, that constituted a rationalist bias in analysis ill-equipped to deal with the realpolitik of projects.

11.2 Evolution of (Mega) Project Management

11.2.1 Early Project Management

Project management as an explicit field of research began in the late twentieth century (Paton et al. 2010). However, significant interest in project management as a formal area of research started as early as the post-World War II era, with the significant growth of engineering-based disciplines such as construction, defense, chemical and aeronautics industries (Morris 1997: 19), and projects that could be described as megaprojects, even by today's standards. A preference for technical, scientific knowledge owing to the dominance of the engineering discipline led project management practice toward a focus on quantitative, positivist techniques and methods. Projects were researched in ways that aligned with existing engineering-based management methods as promoted by founders of modern "classical" management techniques, such as Frederick Taylor and Henry Fayol.

Engineering metaphors were readily acceptable in the work domains of projects and their management. The early formalization of project management was particularly influenced by the aerospace industry (Morris 2013: 13), drawing on hard systems thinking approaches, such as Systems Engineering and Systems Analysis (Morris 2002), cybernetics (Urli and Urli 2000: 33), emphasizing the quantitative use of techniques to control the budget, schedule, and quality of a delivered product (Yeo 1993: 115). Project management systems evolved, such as the program evaluation review technique (PERT) and critical path methods (CPM), building on the engineers' technical and scientific knowledge (Packendorff 1995; Winch 1998). These techniques tended to assume that the manager existed in a stable, closed, and uncontested world—one in which management control was a prerequisite, where it was possible to design solutions to problems clearly defined and blueprinted in advance, early in the project life cycle.

Contingencies always arise, of course. Increasingly, from the 1960s and 1970s, project management learning moved from drawing on the singularity and linearity of individual (organizational) experiences toward a theory of standardized rationalization (Paton et al. 2010). The standardization of rationalities embedded in engineering knowledge and local practice invariably meant the reassertion of the legitimacy of the former over the latter. By the 1980s the emergent discipline had advanced to become what we now know as "mainstream project management" (Ciçmil and Hodgson 2006). Innovations in technology enabled organizations to develop sophisticated project management tools (such as PRINCE2), and assisted the quest to professionalize the field, using the latest advancements drawn from the success of IT in the newly conquered computerized world. Those IT-based tools were used for planning and control as well as risk management (for example, Monte Carlo).

The use of IT systems satisfied clients' desires for the appearance of precise, robust, quantitative and complete budget, risk and performance estimations that seemingly provided objectively accurate projections through using logical algorithms. The use of IT-based project tools as a universal solution to addressing the complexity of the modern project environment was increasingly relied upon as the way to further professionalize project management. The world of standards beckoned (Higgins 2005; Higgins and Hallström 2008).

11.2.1.1 The Development of Standardized Models for Project Management

By the 1990s, project management was expanding as a field of study and practice. Increasingly, its engineering-based roots were applied in many different industries and sectors (Paton et al. 2010), projecting many of its early assumptions, such as the validity of early definition and a reductionist emphasis on simplicity and unitary expression, into new fields of endeavor. The subsequent prominence of projects and project management became described as a "projectification" (Lundin and Söderholm 1995; Midler 1995) of the business landscape, seen to reflect a post-bureaucratic form of organizing (Paton et al. 2010). While the organizational model of bureaucratic management required a stable authority structure, which the flux and temporal instability of project life tended to personify, rather than being attributed to structured authority relations, organizational stability in the post-bureaucratic form was embedded in standardized process, allowing structures to adapt to suit projects. Shifting toward a project-based approach of organizing has been a primary concern of organization studies since the 1990s (Whittington et al. 1999), as this 'new' structural form is characterized as being more dynamic, flexible, versatile, and predictable (Cicmil and Hodgson 2006). As such, Clarke (1999: 139) describes project management as a tool to address the changing world facing current business.

The implication of an increased reliance on projects as a universal solution to addressing the complexity of the modern environment and the increasing professional institutionalization of project management was to be achieved by introducing formal bodies of knowledge (such as PMBOK) that described the "generic nature" (Besner and Hobbs 2008) of a project and provided a universally applicable recipe for project management. The PMBOK was very prescriptive, much as a Delia Smith (2009) recipe might be, rather than theory applied in practice. Project management and its methodologies were still typically seen as rational, linear, and value-neutral, due to their natural evolution from an engineering-based discipline and their preference for quantifiable and objective project management tools (Cicmil et al. 2006). An underlying assumption is that project managers face an objective reality that can be represented consistently in a representative project life cycle—in a predictive model that serves as an exploratory tool for rational analysis. Implicit in this model is the assumption that the project can be managed and planned in advance. Because of the assumed objectivity of projects and their tools, traditional project management assumes that projects can be managed in a pre-given form by applying universal "best practices," where the strict, sequential, and linear application of project management processes in each stage of the life cycle will lead to a successful project outcome. Although there has been some acknowledgment that not all projects are alike, and that a variety of management approaches may be required (for example, Turner and Cochrane 1993), projects and their methods are typically assumed to be universally applicable in any given context and situation, and are able to provide simple solutions to achieve complex requirements (Winter et al. 2006). In this perspective, megaprojects would just be projects, writ large.

The assumptions inherent to hard systems thinking continue to influence the practice of mainstream project management, even though it is now being applied in a wide variety of industries where the assumption of simply definable and agreeable goals, and a stable context, are often not supported.

11.2.1.2 *The Development of an Interpersonal and Practice-Based Focus*

Although hard systems thinking remains a strong influence on mainstream project management, the debate within the systems thinking community has moved on. Starting in the early 1980s, a second broad group of approaches to systems thinking based on an interpretivist perspective started to emerge. These approaches, such as Soft Systems Methodology (Checkland 1981) and Strategic Assumption Surfacing and Testing (Mason and Mitroff 1981), emphasized the social and interpersonal aspects of a problem situation—that it is often necessary to facilitate the development of a mutually acceptable agreement on a way forward by structuring a problem situation, rather than exclusively focusing on the implementation of a technical solution. A variety of authors have argued for a greater emphasis on soft systems thinking in project management practice (for example, Winter and Checkland 2003; Yeo 1993). Although it does not appear that the use of soft systems thinking techniques will soon become mainstream project management practice, the field does appear to be responding to the need for a greater emphasis on the social and interpersonal aspects of project planning and implementation, as the inclusion of stakeholder management as a tenth knowledge area in the latest edition of the PMBOK Guide (PMI 2013) indicates.

A greater emphasis on the context-dependent aspects of project implementation is also apparent in another recent stream of project management research that tries to overcome the issues of rationality and objectivity. Instead of aiming toward the development of universal models for the abstracted conceptualization of project management, the emphasis is on the social science-based, process-oriented tradition of research (Blomquist et al. 2010; Blomquist and Packendorff 1998; Engwall 2003; Söderlund 2002). Practice-oriented studies emphasize that projects and their underlying processes are relational, evolving over time:

> People make sense as they act upon their world and, typically, accept new practices insofar as they do not contradict their taken-for-granted knowing of what constitutes appropriate practice. The forming of a practice coming-into-being is always constituting and reconstituting itself: it is becoming *per se*. (Bjørkeng et al. 2009: 156)

Practice-oriented project management studies view projects as a "social and organized setting in which numerous conceptual organizational theories and organizational behaviour frameworks can be applied and developed" (Blomquist et al. 2010: 6). The major contribution of the practice perspective is that projects must also be understood as social processes incorporating the complexities of social life (Ciçmil and Hodgson 2006). Traditional assumptions about projects as objective realities are challenged. The project manager is seen as a reflective practitioner who resolves issues in a context-dependent, pragmatic, and political fashion (Ciçmil and Hodgson 2006), since "there is considerable agreement that conventional, universal statements of what management is about and what managers do—planning, organizing, coordinating, and controlling—do not tell us much about organizational reality, which is often messy, ambiguous, fragmented, and political in character" (Alvesson and Deetz 2000: 60).

Practice-oriented project studies thus provide a much broader canvas—one that requires the researcher to focus on the microactivities performed by the individual situated within an organizational context that influences the ways in which the project is being conceived, interpreted, and delivered. The broader context entails not just the diverse spaces of the project occupied by the many formal and informal stakeholders, but also the temporalities and political issues through which these spaces evolve, engage, and entangle.

Although these practice perspectives have not been explicitly developed in relation to megaprojects, they have an evident affinity with analysis of them. Megaproject research, from this perspective, would need to focus on the context-dependent, interpersonal, and lived experience of management, rather than universal models, early definition, and quantification. However, there has traditionally been little evidence of the incorporation of power relation or politics in project management research (for example, Hodgson and Ciçmil 2008; Ciçmil and Hodgson 2006). This is of particular concern when the potential for power to affect the progress of megaprojects is considered. An initial way in which this incorporation might occur is through the sensemaking literature.

11.2.2 Sensemaking

Megaprojects have particular characteristics that highlight the need to incorporate power relations in the picture. Probably the first to recognize this explicitly in relation to project management was Clegg (1975). Using ethnographic techniques that entailed audio recording the proceedings on a construction site, largely in a project office, over a three-month period, Clegg analyzed his data in an innovative manner. At the core of his analysis was a realization of the central role played by contracts in constituting project relations. The typical hard money contract attempted to stipulate almost every aspect of the project in a rationalistic and linear manner, through a vast quantity of documentary material: technical drawings, blueprints, plans, and consultant reports—the "'bill of works." Project managers have to be highly skilled and competent in managing to make sense of what they do—a key competency that has become known as sensemaking, defined by Weick (1993: 635) as "the ongoing retrospective development of plausible images that rationalize what people are doing."

The characteristic activities that constitute sensemaking are captured well in Weick's definition. First, sensemaking is ongoing: we are always making sense, and our sense of what we are experiencing is always of the moment—fleeting, experiential, changing, and contextual. Second, sensemaking is retrospective: we make sense of something as it is elapsing and we are constantly reviewing the sense we make in terms of additional sense data. Third, the sense we make is plausible, as we never make perfect sense but only make provisional sense—sense that is good enough for the matter and people at hand. It allows us to go on with what we are trying to do. While accuracy may be desirable, reasonable constructions that are continuously updated work to provide directional guides, especially when things are changing fast. Plausible sense is always provisional in another way as well: it depends on the interest that we have there and then in making *that* sense and not another. We shall return to this aspect in more detail. Fourth, sensemaking is a material practice: it is made using representations of things such as models, plans, and mental maps that are used to try and navigate meanings and actions, steering them in certain directions—directions that others may well resist. Our stock of knowledge is political, emergent, and likely to be contested by others with different interests in sensemaking. Fifth, when sensemaking we rationalize the meaning of things in terms of the interest we vest in them. Sixth, although organizations contain many actants that are not people—such as computers and keypads—it is people who do the sensemaking, but they do so using material things and devices that perform as actants. Seventh, it is through performing practices that actors construct and negotiate the sense of what they are doing that may be different between actors engaged in the same projects, even when they think they are dealing with the same cues and seek to collaborate, which is not always the case in negotiations around projects.

We make individual sense of what is happening around us. We use our sense data to assemble impressions of unfolding events, and then use our cognitive capacities to make a pattern from the data. Many cues are used to make sense: past experience; what others say they think is happening; likely stories that you are familiar with that seem to fit the pattern that appears to be forming, as well as the rationalities that project management disciplines provide. Actors will not use these cues in a uniform way because they have different interests vested in their sensemaking, and, as a result, people can make wildly different senses from the same set of cues.

Project organizations have a considerable interest in members making common sense. It is because common sensemaking is important for organizations that a vital part of the project management task is to try to produce cues for common sensemaking. An important part of the project manager's job is to create, adapt, and use common frames of meaning that characterize the organization and its members. We shall investigate ways in which this might be achieved. Making sensemaking common is no easy matter; the more mega the project, the more problematic it becomes, as there is a greater span of contractors, subcontractors, external authorities, stakeholders, and a longer timeframe for all of these to become more entangled and complex.

Megaproject managers can use tools to get things done and understood in common: accounting systems, resource planning models, PERT, and so on. These tools are designed to be rational instruments to aid managing; however, tools do nothing on their own—they have to be used; they have to be made sense of in terms of the specific context of their application, the time available to do something, the information that is at hand, and the skills and capabilities that are available. The important thing is the *use to which these tools are* put—not that they *merely exist*—and the distinct agencies making sense of the context and situations of use. A number of factors thus enter into sensemaking.

Sensemaking is a complex phenomenon. It involves *social context*: it is influenced by the actual, implied, or imagined presence of others. If other people think that a particular interpretation makes sense, then you are more likely to do so as well. *Personal identity* is important in sensemaking, particularly in terms of professional identities, of which a great variety will typically exist in any megaproject team. Certain situations may subvert or reinforce this sense of identity. What people notice in elapsed events, how far back they look, and how well they remember the past—in other words, *retrospective meaning*—all influence sensemaking as, above all, it has a temporal meaning, inscribed in memories of events past. Organizationally this is extremely important, because sometimes the most important decisions are often the least apparent: decisions made by minutes secretaries—what to keep and what to discard—can provide the basis for any later sense that can possibly be made by project members whose memories of these events might be quite distinctly different. While these are not strategic or conspicuous decisions, they construct the organizational past. Project managers derive *salient cues* from their past experiences; thus they project their pasts onto their futures. Given the temporality and fluidity of project experience, this is an especially important element in project managing, because most actors will have a great many distinct experiences to draw on when making sense. With megaprojects, which typically traverse more institutional fields (government, business, community politics, and so on) over longer periods of time, these issues intensify in complexity and intractability.

Project planning tools provide *structure* to divide the unfolding of events into different patterns. Sensemaking creates meaning that is sufficiently *plausible* to carry on with current projects; such meaning is always enacted here-and-now and thus is always subject to revision as new data emerge or new interpretations are made of old data (Weick 1995: 2008). Hence, the story that emerges around megaprojects can be expected to be fragmentary, discontinuous, and subject to much subtle and sometimes not so subtle respecification. Megaprojects are complex stories; they typically have many narrators and many narratives—some well rehearsed and polished, others more fragmentary antenarratives (Löfgren 2015)—linking retrospective narrative to emergent stories, often in significantly ambiguous contexts (Alderman and Ivory 2015). Antenarratives may exist as a story turned into a formal narrative; they may be a bet, placed in hopes that something will become a retrospective narrative, a likely story in forecasting megaproject benefits. Sensemaking and antenarrative are endemic in project life. They contribute to the complexity of megaproject cultures, especially where people with different languages must work together (Smits, Van Marrewijk, and

Veenswijk 2015) and where there are multiple sites with distinct cultures (Smits et al. 2015; Bektaş, Lauche, and Wamelik 2015). Projects are full of plausible stories—rumor, gossip, official statements, business plans, and websites—each sensible in its own way, but none necessarily coherent with the others. Project organizations often have multiple sources of meaning.

Project managers often regard unions with hostility. Nonetheless, they achieve many positive things, such as legitimate grievance resolution and obliging more innovation in the use of capital and technology because the price of labor cannot be pushed lower. Civil society stakeholder groups are often viewed as potentially obstructive forces. When stakeholders are seen as the recipient of the outputs of a megaproject, they are often seen as passive beneficiaries rather than as actors who will engage with and transform the project outputs. This is problematic, given the high social costs that can often result from poorly managed megaprojects. For example, Jennings (2012) has identified that government funding was required to support the construction of the Millennium Dome after private equity could not be secured; the public sector was again asked to step in during the London 2012 Olympics to construct the Olympic Village after private developers withdrew. In Canada, real estate taxes were raised to pay the C$1-billion deficit that resulted from the Montreal Olympics development. The debt was paid off only thirty years later—significantly longer than the six to seven years originally projected.

In many ways, managerial claims to rationality are foundational for project management.[1] They have a significant function to play: it is unlikely that any megaproject could get off the ground without these claims to expertise being vested in its management. Nonetheless, most megaprojects, as they unfold, will test the bounds of rationality owing to the extreme complexity of the many actors and actants, the number of spaces traversed, and the lengthy elapsed time taken to achieve completion, as well as the very high degree of differentiated knowledge that must make sense together. How project relations actually pan out will always depend on the specific sensemaking that we find in local situations, discourses, and practices. Managerialism assumes that the decisions that management make can always be rationalized. In such a conception of the organization, resistance to project management decisions, wherever it comes from, is regarded as illegitimate and irrational.

Sensemaking traces a frame, enabling us to connect things together and make a coherent and connected picture, a metaphor (Grant 2008: 896). Once we have the frame, then we can make sense. Metaphors frame understanding to produce rationality. As we have said, one metaphor has long been dominant where project management is concerned: the metaphor of engineering. Metaphors influence the way we describe, analyze, and think about things. The metaphors of mainstream project management imply a unitary and objectivist view of the world, and suggest that commitment to early definition is both valid and desirable for megaprojects. The results of this can be seen in pressure for early progress and commitment to poor estimates. Jennings (2012) has noted that political acceleration of the Sydney Opera House project led to scope creep and uncertainty. Pressure from the New South Wales government in 1959 resulted in the project starting ahead of schedule while engineering design was still incomplete. The technical problems that resulted from this have been compared with the project management problems experienced during the Concord(e) development, the Montreal Olympics, the Millennium Dome, the Scottish Parliament project, and the Aquatics Centre for the London 2012 Olympics.

Unjustified belief in the need for megaprojects also appears to be common sensemaking, and has led to the commitment of funds to projects that may otherwise never have been initiated. Hall (1980) identified that the Bay Area Rapid Transit System carried only 51% of forecast riders. Phillips (2008) noted that usage estimates of the Sydney Cross City Tunnel prior to construction were 90,000 cars per day. After completion, the financing costs could not be met by tolls from the 26,500 cars that used the tunnel each day. Prior to construction the Sydney Lane Cove Tunnel was estimated to achieve between 90,000 and 110,000 cars per day, but achieved only 50,000 cars per day when the toll was introduced to the newly completed tunnel. The construction of the Sydney Airport Link provides a similar example. Ng and Loosemore (2007) identified that six months after the line was opened, passenger rates were only 12,000 per day, rather than the 46,000 predicted. The influence of the metaphors of mainstream project management on the sensemaking processes in megaprojects needs to be acknowledged, because many of the assumptions of engineering and hard systems thinking do not transfer to megaprojects, where interpersonal politics and power can play an exaggerated role.

11.2.3 Power

The size and complexity of megaprojects is a fertile ground for power dynamics, as multiple stakeholder groups with different and often competing objectives come together to deliver a project of monumental size and impact. The collaborations that ensue are constituted through complex contracting arrangements reinforced and legitimated by contract law. It is the documentation that these arrangements produce that constitutes the relations between parties. The ties that bind the collaboration together, at their most fragile, are ones of financial interest. More robustly, they can be multistranded, drawing various normative and cultural considerations into the web of alliances and relations. Essentially, megaprojects should be considered as arenas in which players from various fields, such as government, private sector contractors, subcontractors, architects, unions, community groups, regulatory authorities, and so on, are engaged. Each of these players has its own interests as stakeholders in the project—interests that shift in terms and alignments as projects and sensemaking unfold.

At the project outset, as Flyvbjerg (2014) suggests, there may well be good organizational reasons for bad organizational projections of costs and benefits. These projections, of course, are a kind of power: they are productive in gaining commitments, harnessing resources, and persuading key actors and constituencies that the projects are viable. An essential element of positive power—which the cynical might call "spin"—is often necessary to make projects happen. As megaprojects unfold, many other practices of power come into play: variation orders will be submitted where there are elements of indexicality in interpreting project plans—and there always will be such indexicality where there are different interests being brought to bear on documentary and other materials (Clegg 1975).

The most important thing to understand about megaprojects is that they are constituted by many documents produced by many hands in many different places, all of which are saturated with meaning. Hence, when these documents are used in context, their meaning is always subject to indexical interpretation (Garfinkel 1967). Differentially interested actors in the project processes will have differential interests in different aspects of the sensemaking associated with the project. For instance, Clegg (1975) found that a common sensemaking pattern in project management is for different actors to try to exploit different indexical meanings of documents that constitute the project. They interpret ellipses, ambiguities, and contradictions in the documents in terms of the specific interests that, organizationally, they strive to achieve; hence, they index meaning and do sensemaking in different ways that are politically and organizationally interested. The contractual particulars thus become an arena for politicking.

There is always an explicitly manifest power function in megaprojects, which is for the client organization to seek to ensure that the delivery is done in accord with contractual specifications. The organizational self-interest of the various parties contracted brings many power agendas into play. These agendas are not only concerned with the technical objectives of the project (such as time, cost, and scope), but also with the financial interests of the various organizations involved as well as political, economic, and aesthetic objectives (Flyvbjerg 2014). Communities will find that projects that proceed with a minimum of consultation can have hugely deleterious effects on everyday life and the community, often rendering them asunder (Paine and Burgess 2015). For megaproject managers, power relations play out in terms of accountabilities, in terms of targets set, met, and missed; milestones achieved, shifted, and slipped; industrial relations managed ill or well; communities' concerns considered and dealt with or not; and ecologies degraded or improved. The impact of megaprojects will always be multifaceted, and every facet is an exercise in managing with power.

Typically, in the tough world of megaproject construction, the power relations are not particularly positive. Employee relations will be often confrontational, drawing on traditions of militancy and anti-unionism, respectively, on the part of the respective parties. Where they are made more positive, this will often be because of "standover" tactics that contractors accede to by bribing the union for good behavior; that is, not disrupting the project (Doran 2015). "Public works contracts and construction" is the most corrupt sector of activity surveyed by Transparency International in its 2011 Index. An absence of explicitly conflictual power relations does not necessarily signal an absence of negative power relations nor indicate that the power relations are entirely positive.

Positive power relations, premised on the exercise of power with others rather than power over them are possible, and they do occur, perhaps more rarely than one would desire. To the extent that contractors and subcontractors interest can be aligned, client interests negotiated and brought into accord with those of contractors, employee interests aligned with those of employers, community concerns met, ecologies respected or improved—if all these elements of the project can be managed well, then the power relations will be less obtrusive, more subtle, *pianissimo*, in a low key.

It is only where specific forms of collaborative contracting, such as Alliance contracting, are in process, that would one expect to find positive power in abundance. Under such conditions, a common will, framed by an encompassing and designed project culture for governmentality (Clegg et al. 2002) rather than sectional interests in interpreting documents, topography, hydrography, and so on, organized around future perfect strategies (Pitsis et al. 2003), is more likely. Most projects will not conform to these conditions, which are usually signaled up-front through the form of contracting that occurs. The contracting tends not to be competitive based on the lowest tender, but is based on an indicative price prepared by third-party audit for the client organization in which interested parties are invited to express interest in contracting.

The contract, once assigned, usually on the basis of a goodness of fit between client and lead contracting organization, is then subject to a risk/reward ratio that makes it favorable for all major parties concerned to be innovative in finding savings, coming in below budget, on time, and perhaps also having to meet other performance indicators in respect of ecology, community, and health and safety. Where this type of contracting is deployed, the conditions that it creates, while highly positive in power terms for the parties to the contract, are not immune to subsequent power games where the projects are government initiated and subject to subsequent audit requirements that unfailingly find that a competitive tender was not used. On this basis, it can be, and frequently is, argued that the contract was too "slack," that it contained too much leeway, and so the usual power games over indexical detail were, of course, not necessary.

The more usual form of project process is one of messy muddling through, in which various bounded rationalities clash over project specifications, process, and outcomes, using various practices of pooled, sequential, and reciprocal interdependencies (Thompson 1967) to secure interests, outflank those whose interests do not align over whatever is at issue at the time, and gain small wins in specific episodes of power. Megaproject managers must be adept at managing with power; if not, they can expect to be done over, losing money, time, and professional face.

Megaproject management must deal with many forms of professional and occupational practice, bringing many different forms of power/knowledge into play. To the extent that each profession and occupation has its own ways of coding knowledge these do not always translate effortlessly. The classic examples have to do with the different trades and professions' capacity and propensity to read the same set of three-dimensional plans or models differently, with different relevancies. Small matters of interpretation can blow out into big matters of cost, time, design, and function. As megaprojects entail a degree of complexity that is greatly in excess of more standard projects, the opportunities for these different forms of sensemaking to spark confrontational power relations related to matters of responsibility (Lukes 2005) is high. Where the usual trades and professions are joined by esoteric knowledges embodied in social science, ecological, community, and political and economic expertise, the opportunities for conflictual power relations between people secure in their own knowledge areas but unfamiliar with that of those with whom they are obliged to collaborate escalates the potential for conflictual relations in which negative power comes into play.

One of the most detailed accounts of the processes alluded to as normal competencies for project managers are evident in *Rationality and Power: Democracy in Practice* (Flyvbjerg 1998)—a detailed case study of planning intended to limit the use of cars in the city center of Aalborg in Denmark. Although this case was not developed as an example of a megaproject, it illustrates ways in which projects entail highly fluid power processes in which power relations between actors involved in projects (not all of whom are necessarily direct stakeholders in the implementation process) shift and shape the project reality—a process that is exacerbated in megaprojects due to their visibility and the number of stakeholders typically involved.

Flyvbjerg's (1998) main theme is that power shapes rationality. At various stages, the different political actors sought to steer the project through their sensemaking preferences; they sought to structure obligatory passage points through which sensemaking would flow (Clegg 1989). Different claims were made for participation in different committees, and differential participation produced different outcomes at different times, favoring different preferences. Small battles were fought over who, and what, could be introduced in which arenas and meetings. In this way, the relations of meaning and membership in the various locales were contested, reproduced, or transformed. As these changed, then the obligatory passage points shifted, as these shifted the relations of power that had prevailed also changed. Small wins in specific episodes of power had the capacity to shift the configuration of the overall circuitry through which power relations flowed. The actors engaged in the plans were constantly seeking to fix and refix specific schemes, and although the play of power was very fluid, the underlying social integration of the small business people with each other, the Chamber of Industry and Commerce, and the editorial views of the local newspaper, seemed to mean that the small business people prevailed in the many struggles. The attempts to respecify the system integration of the traffic plan in Aalborg continually foundered on the reef of social integration. How Aalborg was planned, designed, and looked, as well as how it was not planned, not designed, and did not look, was an effect of power relations.

Flyvbjerg (1998) alerts us to a very important fact of power relations and rationalities: that when power and knowledge are entwined then the greater the power the less the need for rationality, in the sense of rational means–end justifications. The relation between rationality and power was an uneven relation: power clearly dominated rationality. That is, those who presently configured power sought to continue doing so and were quite ready to define the reality of the project in any way that seemed to them to further their preferences, using whatever strategies and tactics were available to them. In this sense, what was defined as rationality and reality was an effect of power, as it defined and created "concrete physical, economic, ecological, and social realities" (Flyvbjerg 1998: 227). What was advanced and argued as rationality depended wholly on power relations; the more disadvantaged in these the agents were, the more they were liable to have recourse to conceptions of rationality that downplayed power, and sought to position themselves through factual, objective, reasoned knowledge. The most powerful rationalities took the form of rationalizations rather than authoritatively grounded accounts. Often these were public performances of rationality which other agents who were witness to the rationalizations felt compelled not to reveal because they lacked the powers to do so; they anticipated and feared the reaction that their actions would in all probability produce should they move; dangers lurked in open conflict and identification of differences. The greater the facility with which agencies could have recourse to power relations, the less concerned they were with reason, and the less they were held accountable to it. Access to more power produced less reason. Mostly, power relations were both stable and inequitable. Where power relations could be maintained as stable and characterized by consensus and negotiations, rationality could gain a greater toehold; the more power relations became antagonistic, the easier it was to deploy arguments and strategies that elided it. Thus, rationality must remain within the existing circuits of power if it is to influence them. To challenge them is to play a losing hand.

Reading Flyvbjerg is important, because it takes us into the heart of projects as political processes as well as into the contexts in which their design is brought into being through processes of *becoming*: how dreams become designs, designs become concrete, and interests become embedded in the processes that surround these acts of becoming. The further utility of the general approach that scholars such as Clegg and Flyvbjerg have pioneered is evident when we consider one of the most contentious and successful dreams made concrete in the twentieth century: Sydney Opera House. Jennings (2012) investigated the executive political issues and consequent risks surrounding numerous megaprojects, and concludes as follows:

> While the sorts of formal controls favored by the regulatory state seem to have been all but missing from the case of the Sydney Opera House, its combination of over-optimistic planning and scope creep, fueled by political pressure to get the project started as soon as possible, seem to be the principal causes of under-performance of the project much like most of the other projects. (Jennings 2012: 250)

Flyvbjerg (2014) notes that one of the major reasons why megaprojects rarely come in on time and on budget, and with design integrity, is because they can often only be launched with an implicit optimism bias inherent and political support of the project from powerful stakeholders (such as federal or state government).

11.3 POLITICAL INFLUENCES IN MEGAPROJECTS

Megaproject are subject to enormous political constraints and mood swings throughout the project life cycle, since they are often part of election promises, political agendas, or other political decision-making processes, albeit there is rarely public acknowledgment of this fact. Hence, the support for or opposition to megaprojects often depends on the current political climate in which such a major undertaking takes place. Leijten (2013) argues that certain (often undisclosed) information has a great impact on decision making, which subsequently leads to strategic behaviour by interested parties. Politicians often need figures to justify their policies but realize that any estimate is likely to be wrong, and the more likely it is to be accurate, the greater the figure will be. Consequently, one issue with megaprojects is that they are often justified by forecasts of benefits that are biased in terms of political sensemaking. Figures are often used to rationalize political decisions based on the ideology of the political decision maker involved. As an example, a political party conscious of environmental impact may use figures on environmental deterioration as a factor to reject certain alternatives. "Soft" subjective figures can often be proposed in sensemaking as "hard," and have a substantial effect in anchoring a decision around a subjective estimate. Figures can often become a vehicle to contest policies, asking for more and more reports as a way of challenging project progress, as in the case of the Australian National Broadband Network. This could lead to "paralysis by analysis." Contestability of information could also have an opposite effect in rendering decisions to be intuitive, making them redundant. When projects are deliberately underestimated to gain approval they often result in lock-in (Cantarelli and Flyvbjerg 2013), resulting in holding on to projects longer than desired due to the complex power relations and interests at stake.

Ownership of a megaproject can shift gradually during implementation, eroding the values that the project owner presumed—something especially likely when an entrepreneurial actor influences public policy through the provision of private finance. An example is the Betuweroute freight railway line between the Port of Rotterdam and the German hinterland that was conceived by two entrepreneurial branches of public organizations (Leijten 2013: 72). The Dutch government became dragged into financing the project when the original plans became problematic.

Comparators that are used for decision making for private investment cannot predict how strategic behaviour will evolve during the project, which may affect public interest. Hard systems thinking and engineering assumptions persist in project management practice, particularly during the early stages of a megaproject where false confidence commonly pervades. Early definitions in megaprojects are often problematic due to the uncertainties involved. Private investors may also not share valuable information that will help define the project at an early stage when they are in competition with others who might benefit from that information. The decision makers may then start from a suboptimal outset. The motives of the public owner and private actor may also differ. The private actors may be interested in trying a new untested technology for their own benefit, or may require to use untested technologies because of commitments made during the formative stages of the project.

Grün (2004) argues that political influences have become more prevalent as the public sector becomes increasingly dependent on the private sector for delivering projects. Grün compares the sociopolitical influences on the Munich and Vienna hospital projects, and concludes that one characteristic sociopolitical influence is the ad hoc intervention by the owners. Political influences did not affect the technical goals of the

Munich project. Failures to achieve key goals, and significant cost overruns, did not pro-voke public attention, as they were eclipsed by the public focus on the Olympic Games being organized in Munich at that time. In contrast, the Vienna hospital was a disaster due to intensive political interference. When it was affected by a corruption scandal, the opposition parties forced the ruling party to establish "special internal control pro-cedures", which increased political interference, similar to Sydney Opera House. The influence of public perception on megaproject progress can also be seen in the London Ringway and Covent Garden developments, both of which were canceled due to pub-lic opinion (Ng and Loosemore 2007). Dewey and Davis (2013) also identified public involvement in planning decisions as a factor that contributed to the perceived failure of the Mexico City airport. In this case there was a significant division between the political class and citizens, and conflicts arose between the local and national authorities over the relevance of citizen participation in project development. A strong coalition of local, national, and international allies developed, using cultural identity, historical allegiances, and geographic location to build and expand struggle against the airport.

Interested contractors may also create pressure to start megaprojects that are attrac-tive to them for sustaining their business. An example is the influence of the British and French aircraft industry in promoting the Concord(e) project. Contractors may also try to enlarge the project by offering advanced technical systems that would need more assistance in the operational phase. Political influence may also affect the choice of contractors. Project owners may be forced to employ local contractors. Barriers such as "national security" can be used to justify the elimination of contractors who are bidding.

The number and variety of megaprojects is rising, such are the underlying political drivers. For instance, the desire of countries vying to host large sports events, such as the Olympic Games—events whose benefits for the country in question may not be as obvious as political sensemaking promotes but which are used as a global platform to promote local political actors. Boosting a particular industry sector—one that is closely linked to government spending and income—might be another reason for making the decision to undertake a megaproject. For instance, one of the reasons why Britain built Terminal 5 at Heathrow was to increase the aviation industry's contribution to Britain's GDP. Heathrow is expected to contribute £80 billion in 2030, rising from £11.4 billion in 2004 (Doherty 2008). To contextualize this, Singapore Changi airport contributes 5.6% to Singapore's GDP (Oxford Economics 2009).

11.4 CONCLUSION

Power relations are integral to the social construction of social reality; they are equally integral to the sensemaking that socially constructs material reality. Yet despite the abundant evidence of this reality that we have presented in this chapter there is a marked reluctance on the part of Classical Project Management (Winter et al. 2006) to recognize the pervasive reality of power relations in and around project relations. As we have been at pains to point out, power relations are not necessarily bad; power is not a dirty word. While much power in the megaproject world consists of parties seeking to exercise power over other parties in pursuit of specific sectional interests, it need not always be the case. Genuinely positive power practices can be contracted—but these are not the norm, and where they exist they will often be regarded as violations of the norm. In fact, the norms of competitive contracting do much to encourage negative power relations as, once a bid is won, the onus is on the contracting organization to ensure the profitability of the project by exercising power over all stakeholders. Doing this can start with inflated projections of the metrics of project success and deflated projections of project costs—costs that have to increase if profitability targets are to be met. It can continue with practices of bribery and corruption to ensure industrial peace and an attitude to communities and civil society organizations that regard them as obstacles to be bulldozed in the achievement of the planned project outcomes. Sucked into these negative power dynamics are the vanities and ambitions of politicians for whom a megaproject is often more important as a photo-opportunity and a hopeful vote-winner than as a complex undertaking launched in a spirit of informed openness.

Discussion of the power relations of those who actually determine the meanings behind the facts of project progress, as well as the ways in which rationalities are systematically skewed by powerful interest, is suppressed. Rationality cannot provide the ultimate warrant for project performativity (Spender and Scherer 2007); this much is evident from the work of Flyvbjerg (1998). Megaprojects usually require political sponsorship; political sponsors bask in the glow of publicity entailed in launching projects, but when the stories told to gain sponsorship and support run up against the realities of project performance, it is often the case that sponsors have vacated the scene, as the duration of megaprojects invariably exceeds that of the political figures who benefit from their initiation. In this case, the Sydney Opera House may be an outlier in terms of budget overrun (1,000%), but it is not an outlier in terms of its politics; rather, it is an exemplar.

ACKNOWLEDGMENTS

Thanks are due to Gita Shankar for proofreading and Lisa Adiprodjo for preparing the list of references.

NOTE

1. Managerialism involves the attempt to remake organizations in an idealized image revolving around a strong corporate culture, entrepreneurialism, quality, and leadership, and focused on achieving targets. The targets are often measured through audits—of culture, quality, job satisfaction, customer satisfaction, and so forth. These can be used to rank organizations according to a range of criteria. Power (1997) has argued that this is a sign that we

live in an "Audit Society," in which rankings of organizations are increasingly common, and where league tables determine the sense that is made of organizational performance. On this basis, as Flyvbjerg et al. (2003) conclude, most megaprojects are managerial failures.

REFERENCES

Aaltonen, K. and Kujala, J. (2010). "A project lifecycle perspective on stakeholder influence strategies in global projects," *Scandinavian Journal of Management*, 26(4): 381–97.

Alderman, N. and Ivory, C. "Dealing with ambiguity in complex projects: Planned or emergent practices?" in A. Van Marrewijk (ed.), *Inside Megaprojects: Understanding Cultural Practices in Project Management*. Copenhagen: CBS Press, pp. 175–209.

Alvesson, M. and Deetz, S., (2000). *Doing Critical Management Research*. London: Sage.

Besner, C. and Hobbs, B. (2008). "Project management practice, generic or contextual: A reality check," *Project Management Journal*, 39(1): 16–33.

Bektaş, E., Lauche, K., and Wamelik, H. (2015). "Knowledge sharing in megaprojects: A case study of as co-location approach," in A. Van Marrewijk (ed.), *Inside Megaprojects: Understanding Cultural Practices in Project Management*. Copenhagen: CBS Press, pp. 137–74.

Bjørkeng, K., Clegg, S., and Pitsis, T. (2009). "Becoming (a) practice," *Management Learning*, 40(2): 145–59.

Blomquist, T., Hällgren, M., Nilsson, A., and Soderholm, A. (2010). "Project-as-practice: In search of project management research that matters," *Project Management Journal*, 41(1): 5–16.

Blomquist, T. and Packendorff, J. (1998). "Learning from renewal projects: Content, context and embeddedness," in R. A. Lundin and C. Midler (eds.), *Projects as Arenas for Renewal and Learning Processes*. Dordrecht: Kluwer Academic Publishers, pp. 37–46.

Cantarelli C. C. and Flyvbjerg, B. (2013). "Mega-projects' cost performance and lock-in: Problems and solutions," in H. Priemus and B. Van Wee (eds.), *International Handbook on Mega-Projects*. Cheltenham: Edward Elgar, pp. 333–55.

Checkland, P. (1981). *Systems Thinking, Systems Practice*. Chichester: Wiley.

Ciçmil, S. and Hodgson, D. (2006). "New possibilities for project management theory: A critical engagement," *Project Management Journal*, 37(3): 111–22, <http://eprints.uwe.ac.uk/16783>.

Ciçmil, S., Williams, T., Thomas, J., and Hodgson, D. (2006). "Rethinking project management: Researching the actuality of projects," *International Journal of Project Management*, 24(8): 675–86.

Clarke, A. (1999). "A practical use of key success factors to improve the effectiveness of project management," *International Journal of Project Management*, 17(3): 139–45.

Clegg, S. R. (1975). *Power, Rule and Domination*. London: Routledge and Kegan Paul.

Clegg, S. R. (1989). *Frameworks of Power*. London: Sage.

Clegg, S. R., Pitsis, T., Rura-Polley, T., and Marosszeky, M. (2002). "Governmentality matters: Designing an alliance culture of inter-organizational collaboration for managing projects," *Organization Studies*, 23(3): 317–37.

Dewey, O. and Davis, D. (2013). "Planning, politics and urban mega-projects: Lessons from Mexico City's airport controversy," *Journal of Urban Affairs* 35(5): 531–51.

Doherty, S. (2008). *Heathrow's Terminal 5: History in the Making*. Chichester: Wiley.

Doran, M. (2015). "Trade union royal commission: Contractor felt he had no choice but to pay CFMEU ACT official $135k, inquiry hears," <http://www.abc.net.au/news/2015-07-13/royal-commission-into-trade-unions-begins-cfmeu-probe/6613916>.

Engwall, M. (2003). "No project is an island: Linking projects to history and context," *Research Policy*, 32(5): 789–808.

Flyvbjerg, B. (1998). *Rationality and Power: Democracy in Practice*. Chicago: University of Chicago Press.

Flyvbjerg, B. (2007). *Megaproject Policy and Planning: Problems Causes, Cures*. Aalborg, Denmark: Institut for Samfundsudvikling og Planlaegning.

Flyvbjerg, B. (2014). "What you should know about megaprojects and why: An overview," *Project Management Journal*, 45(2): 6–19.

Flyvbjerg, B., Bruzelius, N., and Rothengatter, W. (2003). *Megaprojects and Risk: An Anatomy of Ambition*. Cambridge: Cambridge University Press

Garfinkel, H. (1967). *Studies in Ethomethodology*. Englewood Cliffs, NJ: Prentice Hall.

Giezen, M. (2012). "Keeping it simple? A case study into the advantages and disadvantages of reducing complexity in megaproject planning," *International Journal of Project Management*, 30(7): 781–90.

Grant, D. (2008). "Metaphor and organization," in S. R. Clegg and J. R. Bailey (eds.), *The Sage International Encyclopedia of Organization Studies*. Thousand Oaks, CA: Sage, pp. 896–900.

Grün, O. (2004). *Taming Giant Projects: Management of Multi-Organizational Enterprises*. Berlin: Springer.

Hall, P. (1980). *Great Planning Disasters*. London: Weidenfeld & Nicholson.

Higgins, W. (2005). *Engine of Change: Standards Australia Since 1922*. Blackheath, NSW: Brandl and Schlesinger.

Higgins, W. and Hallström, K. T. (2008). "Technical standardization," in A. Iriye and P. Y Saunier (eds.), *The Palgrave Dictionary of Transnational History*. London: Palgrave Macmillan, 2008, pp. 1–7.

Hodgson, D. and Ciçmil, S. (2008). "The other side of projects: The case for critical project studies," *International Journal of Managing Projects in Business*, 1(1):142–52.

Holmes, A. (2001). *Failsafe Is Project Delivery*. London: Gower Publishing.

Jennings, W. (2012). "Executive politics, risk and the mega-project paradox," in M. Lodge and K. Wegrich (eds.), *Executive Politics and Governance*. London: Palgrave Macmillan, pp. 236–63.

Leijten, M. (2013). "Real-world decision-making on mega-projects: Politics, bias and strategic behaviour," in H. Priemus and B. Van Wee (eds.), *International Handbook on Mega-Projects*. Cheltenham: Edward Elgar, pp. 57–82, <http://books.google.com/books?hl=en&lr=&id=iH otAgAAQBAJ&oi=fnd&pg=PA57&dq=info:xOASd8Gpve4J:scholar.google.com&ots=PC6 50GTYLO&sig=NbnLinp7csQtLvJSuCTIaQBSZFU"\t"_blank">>.

Löfgren, O. (2015). "Catwalking a bridge: SA longitudinal study of a transnational megaproject and its ritual life," in A. Van Marrewijk (ed.), *Understanding Cultural Practices in Project Management*. Copenhagen: CBS Press, pp. 33–68.

Lukes, S. (2005). *Power: A Radical View*, 2nd edn. London: Palgrave Macmillan.

Lundin, R. A. and Söderholm, A. (1995). "A theory of the temporary organization," *Scandinavian Journal of Management*, 11(4): 437–55.

Mason, R. and Mitroff, I. (1981). *Challenging Strategic Planning Assumptions: Theory, Cases and Techniques*. New York: Wiley.

Maylor, H., Vidgen, R., and Carver, S. (2008). "Managerial complexity in project-based opera-tions: A grounded model and its implications for practice," *Project Management Journal*, 39(S1): S15–26.

Midler, C. (1995). "'Projectification' of the firm: The Renault case," *Scandinavian Journal of Management*, 11(4): 363–75.

Morris, P. (1997). *The Management of Projects*. London: Thomas Telford.

Morris, P. (2002). "Science, objective knowledge and the theory of project management," *Civil Engineering*, 150(2): 82–90.

Morris, P. (2013). "Reconstructing project management reprised: A knowledge perspective," *Project Management Journal*, 44(5): 6–23.

Ng, A. and Loosemore, M. (2007). "Risk allocation in the private provision of public infra-structure," *International Journal of Project Management*, 25(1): 66–76.

Oxford Economics (2009). *Economic Benefits of Air Transport in Singapore*, Singapore Country Report, <https://www.iata.org/policy/Documents/Benefits-of-Aviation-Singapore-2011.pdf>.

Packendorff, J. (1995). "Inquiring into the temporary organization: New directions for project management research," *Scandinavian Journal of Management*, 11(4): 319–33.

Pain, H. and Burgess, M. (2015). "WestConnex protest brings 1500 Newtown locals out to voice their objections," <http://www.smh.com.au/nsw/westconnex-protest-brings-1500-newtown-locals-out-to-voice-their-objections-20150201-13322y#ixzz30VfCQrfJ>

Paton, S., Hodgson, D., and Cicmil, S. (2010). "Who am I and what am I doing here?: Becoming and being a project manager," *Journal of Management Development*, 29(2): 157–66.

Phillips, G. (2008). *Analysis of Sydney Public–Private Partnership Road Tunnels*, Mathematics Learning Centre, Sydney University, <http://www.maths.usyd.edu.au/u/geoffp/melfin2.pdf>.

Pitsis, T., Clegg, S. R., Marosszeky, M., and Rura-Polley, T. (2003) "Constructing the Olympic Dream: Managing innovation through the future perfect," *Organization Science*, 14:5, 574–90.

Power, M. (1997). *The Audit Society: Rituals of Verification*. Oxford: Oxford University Press.

Project Management Institute (PMI). (2013). *A Guide to the Project Management Body of Knowledge (PMBOK Guide)*. 5th edn. Newtown Square, PA: Project Management Institute.

Smith, D. (2009). *Delia's Complete How To Cook: Both a Guide for Beginners and a Tried and Tested Recipe Collection for Life*. London: BBC Books.

Smits, K., Van Marrewijk, A., and Veenswijk, M. (2015). "The collabyrinth of cross-cultural collaboration in the Panama Canal megaproject," in A. Van Marrewijk (ed.), *Inside Megaprojects: Understanding Cultural Practices in Project Management*. Copenhagen: CBS Press, pp. 103–36.

Söderlund, J. (2002). "Managing complex development projects: Arenas, knowledge processes and time," *R&D Management*, 32(5): 419–30.

Spender, J. C. and Scherer, A. G. (2007). "The philosophical foundations of knowledge man-agement: Editors' introduction," *Organization*, 14(1): 5–28.

Thompson, J. D. (1967). *Organizations in Action*. New York: McGraw-Hill.

Turner, J. R. and Cochrane, R. (1993). "Goals-and-methods matrix: Coping with projects with ill-defined goals and/or methods of achieving them," *International Journal of Project Management*, 11(2): 93–101.

Urli, B. and Urli, D. (2000). "Project management in North America: Stability of the concepts," *Project Management Journal*, 31(3): 33–43.

Van Marrewijk, A. (ed.) (2015). *Inside Megaprojects: Understanding Cultural Practices in Project Management*. Copenhagen: CBS Press, pp. 16–17.

Weick, K. E. (1993). "The collapse of sensemaking in organizations: The Mann Gulf disaster," *Administrative Science Quarterly*, 38(4): 628–52.

Weick, K. E. (1995). *Sensemaking*. Thousand Oaks, CA: Sage.

Weick, K. E. (2008). "Sensemaking," in S. R. Clegg and J. Bailey (eds.), *International Encyclopeadia of Organization Studies*. Thousand Oaks, CA: Sage, pp. 1403–6.

Whittington, R., Pettigrew, A., Peck, S., Fenton, E., and Conyon, M. (1999). "Change and complementarities in the new competitive landscape: A European panel study, 1992–1996," *Organization Science*, 10(5): 583–600.

Winch, G. M. (1998). "The Channel Fixed Link: le projet du siècle," unpublished case study, Manchester University.

Winter, M. and Checkland P. (2003). "Soft systems: A fresh Perspective for project management," *ICE Proceedings of Civil Engineering*, 156(4): 187–92.

Winter, M., Smith, C., Morris, P., and Çiçmil, S. (2006). "Directions for future research in project management: The main findings of a UK government-funded research network," *International Journal of Project Management*, 24(8): 638–49.

Yeo, K. (1993). "Systems thinking and project management: Time to reunite." *International Journal of Project Management*, 11(2): 111–17.

....

CHAPTER 12

A COLLECTIVE-ACTION PERSPECTIVE ON THE PLANNING OF MEGAPROJECTS

....

NUNO GIL

12.1 INTRODUCTION

....

PREVAILING perceptions that capital-intensive developments of long-lived infrastructure such as railways and airports and recreation facilities such as Olympic parks, the so-called megaprojects, underperform have fueled two views. One view claims that promoters underestimate cost and schedule targets because of strategic misrepresentation and optimism bias (Wachs 1989; Flyvbjerg et al. 2003), lack of planning (Merrow et al. 1988; Morris 1994), or the use of rigid buyer–supplier contracts (Stinchcombe and Heimer 1985). Another view is common too—that megaprojects cannot be planned because the promoters are hostage to scope creep (Hall 1982; Shapiro and Lorenz 2000), escalation of commitment to losing courses of action (Ross and Staw 1986), and external events that they do not control (Altshuler and Luberoff 2003; Szyliowicz and Goetz 1995; Miller and Lessard 2000).

This chapter aims to move the debate forward using a collective action perspective. We argue that megaprojects are vast actor-networks formed to develop a new large-scale designed artefact: the infrastructure system. We also argue that high-order decision-making within these neworks is driven by the need to build interorganizational consensus at the core of the network. Consensus refers to the degree to which the collective goals and plans are agreed upon by all involved (Van de Ven 1976). The need to strike a consensus on high-order development decisions results from the distribution of the direct control over the interdependent resources that are critical to develop the new infrastructure, including land, finance, planning consent, political support, and knowledge of needs-in-use. The promoter of the megaproject can expect resource-rich actors to volunteer their resources only if the promoter shares the rights to directly influence high-order development decisions. Hence the development process is, per-force, consensus-oriented. As a result, the searches for mutually acceptable design solutions are ridden with interorganizational controversies. In other words, the core of the megaproject network, where high-order development decisions take place, is a consensus-oriented collective action or "pluralistic" setting (Denis et al. 2011).

In these settings, managers cannot rely on authority hierarchies (March and Simon 1958), markets (Ouchi 1980), or system integrators (Brusoni et al. 2001) to get things done. Rather, when authority to make interdependent decisions is distributed across legally independent actors, and thus the governance structure is relatively "flat," top managers must attend to the concerns of different actors so as to preserve a democratic decision-making process (Rothschild and Russell 1986). In other words, top managers have agency but cannot exercise it fully and must negotiate (Pfeffer and Salancik 1978).

The difficulties in reaching consensus when planning a megaproject are exacerbated because the planning decisions impair property rights under ambiguous pay-offs. Megaproject networks thus do not meet the known antecedents of cooperation, including a history of positive working relationships and mutual trust, a unifying higher-order goal, and the presence of a legitimate convener to draw together autonomous actors (Gray 1989; Ring and Van de Ven 1992; Thomson and Perry 2006). Another factor that makes it hard to strike consensus is the scarcity of resources to resolve disputes owing to rigid deadlines and tight budgets. Complicating matters, the actor-networks formed to plan megaprojects are highly institutionalized and interdependent with the environment; as Rittel and Webber (1973) put it, "planning problems are wicked problems." And yet, the participants in a megaproject network need to be governed and action needs to be coordinated to achieve a system goal. Hence the two core research questions motivating this study are: (i) what is the structure governing the planning stage of a megaproject? and (ii) what coordination mechanisms are available to carry the participating actors along and thus to sustain the planning stage?

This research adopts a multiple case-study approach with embedded units of analysis (Eisenhardt 1989; Yin 1984). Case studies allow researchers to incorporate contextual and temporal dimensions, and thus are suitable to explore novel ideas (Eisenhardt and Graebner 2007). The research site consists of four megaprojects in the United Kingdom—a pluralistic society with a strong regime of property rights and institutionalized mechanisms to enable any actor to contest the promoter's plans for a new infrastructure. The units of analysis are controversies between the megaproject promoter and resource-rich actors unified by the system goal.

The analysis reveals that the source of the interorganizational controversies is a conflation of three factors: (i) differing preferences for one-off planning decisions; (ii) scarcity of resources to resolve conflict; and (iii) the promoter's reluctance to let the performance targets slip to preserve legitimacy to operate in the eyes of third parties. The juxtaposition of cooperation efforts with tough bargaining and political activity creates a real risk of actors defecting. This in turn leads to inefficient processes and ambiguous outcomes. The central contribution of this study is a model that proposes how the interplay between the four mechanisms to coordinate sustain the highly fragile developments.

The rest of this chapter is organized as follows. First, it reviews literature on consensus-oriented developments. Then it introduces the research methods and the analysis. It concludes with a discussion that puts the sustainability of a highly fragile consensus-oriented community of production at the center of the performance debate on megaprojects.

12.2 BACKGROUND: CONSENSUS-ORIENTED DEVELOPMENTS

Interorganizational collaborations are central to management scholarship because they are critical to find solutions to complex problems wherein a single actor does not have all the information-processing capacity and resources to solve the problem (Van de Ven 1976; Gray 1989). One stream within this large body of literature relates to consensus-oriented developments of new products. This literature is informed by studies of communities of production that emerge voluntarily to produce open-source software and science. In these settings, known coordination mechanisms include boundary organizations (O'Mahony and Bechky 2008), boundary infrastructures such as models, prototypes, working groups (Tuertscher et al. 2014), and meritocracy-based authorities (O'Mahony and Ferraro 2007).

The planning stage of a new megaproject differs, however, from the aforementioned settings in important ways, and thus create opportunities for advancing organization and management theory. First, goal congruence among the claimants to planning decisions is dubious. The institutional environment forces the promoter to work with actors fully supportive of the goal, as well as with actors who demand a high price for their cooperation. This rules out the use of meritocracy-based authorities to resolve emerging disputes.

A second factor complicating the emergence of norms of cooperation is time pressure dictated by electoral and regulatory cycles.[1] Consensus building cannot be rushed, as holding lengthy talks is necessary to allow actors to make sense of complex problems and communicate to coordinate collective action. Hence time pressure amplifies risk perceptions and leads to bargaining and political activity (Ring and Van de Ven 1992; Gersick 1994).

Finally, large infrastructure developments cannot rely on modular design structures to circumvent difficulties in striking a consensus. Modularity reduces interdependency between design choices, which attenuates rivalry, encourages voluntary contributions of resources, and limits the impact of uncooperative behaviour (Baldwin and Clark 2000; Baldwin and von Hippel 2011). In contrast, when many independent actors share a right to directly influence the development of an *indivisible* asset, the design choices qualify as an Ostrom's (1990) shared resource; that is, they juxtapose low excludability (of participation in the decision-making process) with high rivalry (of preferences for the decision) (Gil and Baldwin 2013). Hence the risk is high that a collective development of an indivisible asset unravels if some of the claimants to planning decisions opt to free ride by refusing to compromise and cooperate.

Difficulties notwithstanding, large consensus-oriented collective action arenas can be sustainable if the governance structure is (i) polycentric—that is, decentralized across multiple centers of decision making and power with capacity for mutual adjustment—and (ii) robust for high-level authorities to respect local rule and for local claimants to respect high-level rules. This is the central argument in Ostrom's (1990) theory of self-governing natural shared resources, such as forestries and fisheries. Gil and Baldwin (2013) extend this argument to collective developments of capital-intensive assets for shared use. They do so through a study of a capital program to develop a fleet of state school buildings with limited resources (time and money) and multiple claimants (national and local governments and school teachers).

Developments of school buildings are, however, capital projects with benign goals which are amenable to unify hetereogenous actors. In contrast, megaprojects are capital-intensive enterprises with controversial and ambiguous system goals. And yet, the control of the resources necessary to achieve the goal is invariably distributed across independent actors. While these actors have hetereogeneous preferences and interests, they are unlikely to commit their resources unless they directly influence the planning decisions.

Complicating matters, megaprojects are hard to fully decompose. For example, a railway includes tracks, rolling stock, and stations; likewise, an airport includes concourses, runways, and walkways. These components are technologically coupled and draw finance from a central budget. Hence the decisions to plan each component are interdependent. Planning a megaproject thus involves building concurrently multiple interdependent consensuses albeit limited subgoal congruence. As local controversies surface when planning for one component, pressure mounts to relax local performance targets for that component. Because local slippages set tricky precedents and threaten global targets, governing bodies face a Catch-22 situation: if they govern by diktat, the risk of defection rises, whereas too much decentralization creates a risk of things spiraling out of control. This tension leads to what I term highly fragile developments, and I turn now to discuss their sustainability.

12.3 RESEARCH DESIGN, SAMPLE, AND METHODS

This research uses a comparative case study design (Eisenhardt 1989), in which cases are treated as independent experiments that confirm or disconfirm emerging theoretical insights in replication logic. To advance theory and yield more generalizable and robust insights (Yin 1984), I built a diverse and polarized sample as recommended for process-focused inductive studies (Siggelkow 2007). The sample includes four megaprojects: Heathrow airport's terminal two (T2); London Crossrail, a high-capacity underground railway; London 2012 Olympic park; and the United Kingdom's second high-speed railway (HS2). These cases are summarizsed in Table 12.1.

This sample allowed varying three fundamental attributes of the development process for a capital-intensive infrastructure. First, the cases differ in the level of technological decomposability of the infrastructure system. Figure 12.1 illustrates this in a stylized way.

An Olympic park is suggestive of a large decomposable system from a technological perspective. It comprises a set of stand-alone venues including a stadium, a pool, and a velodrome. Connecting the assets to one another are underground utilities. But the utility systems are "slaves" designed to pick up the effects of changes to the high-value venues.

In contrast, the technological structure of a railway system is far less decomposable. All stations connect to the same high-value functional components (tracks, control, and signaling systems), and must accommodate the same train cars. In turn, an airport suggests a hybrid technological system. Some components are physically integrated—for example, the tunnels that connect concourses—but other components, such as the car park and hotel, are not.

The sample also varies in the structure of participation of the planning process. The HS2 scheme is entirely publicly financed. Hence high-level development decisions mainly involve the central and local governments and public agencies that own interdependent assets. In contrast, Heathrow T2 is wholly financed by its private owner, BAA.[2] But as a monopolist, BAA must share the right to develop the new terminal with the regulator, and the main user in this case STAR Alliance, a global network of airlines. The other two cases involve public and private finance. The higher the number of claimants to the planning decisions, and the more diversified they were, the more difficulties we could expect in reaching consensus.

Third, the sample varies in the extent to which tight deadlines constrained the planning process and thus the development decisions. The London 2012 immovable deadline exerted massive pressure to make decisions. The other schemes faced no immovable deadlines, but pressure was still high, whether owing to politicians' will to see things done before general elections (the cases of Crossrail and HS2 first phase) or to the regulatory cycles in the case of BAA. Amplifying the pressure to make decisions was a history of three failed bids to win the Olympics contest and two failed attempts to get Crossrail off the ground.

12.3.1 Units of Analysis

The embedded units of analysis were incidences of salient controversies over high-level development decisions in the planning stage. Thirty-five controversies were cognitively filtered out by the respondents. Controversies trigger difficult questions. Should the parties search for a local design solution commensurate with the local performance targets set *ex ante*, or should they let the targets slip to facilitate the search for a consensual solution?

Table 12.1 High–level description of the sample of cases, interviewees, and archival database

Cases	London 2012	Heathrow T2	Crossrail	High–speed 2
Higher-order shared goal	Build an Olympic park and catalyze urban regeneration of east London	Build a new airport terminal for the STAR Alliance (STAR)	Connect east and west of London with a high-capacity train	Connect London to Birmingham (first phase); Birmingham to northern regions (second phase)
Key promoters	UK government; London governments; BOA; LOCOG[+]	BAA, Regulator, STAR Alliance	UK government, London Government	UK government
Time pressure during planning	Massive ~2 years (5–7) to totally redo planning after the victory of London's bid	High ~4 years (5–8) to plan before starting a new regulatory cycle (quinquennium)	High 4 years (1–5) to redo planning so as to start the Parliamentary process before the 2005 elections 2005–08 (Parliamentary process)	Massive (first phase) ~4 years (9–13) to plan so as to finish the Parliamentary process before 2015 elections Moderate (second phase) ~6–7 years to plan (2010–16/17)
Global target for the project budget	Gradually relaxed 2004, £4.2 billion (final prices, no VAT) 2007, £9.3 billion (final prices inc. VAT) 2013, £8.9–10.2 billion (different sources)	Gradually relaxed 2005, £1.0–1.5 billion (possibly 2005 prices) 2008, £2.0 billion (07/08 prices) 2014, £2.6 billion (cash prices)*	Gradually relaxed 2002, £9.8 billion (2002 prices) 2008, £15.9 billion (final prices)[+] 2014, £14.8 billion (cash prices)	Gradually relaxed 2010, ~ £30 billion (2009 prices) 2012, £32.7 billion (2011 prices) 2014, £42.6 billion (2011prices) + HS3, Crossrail2
Global target for the project timescale	Immovable Summer 2012	Relaxed and made "soft" 2005, open in 2012 2010, open "gradually" in 2014	Relaxed and made "soft" 2003, fully open in 2016 2012, 2017–19	Under pressure 2026, first phase 2030–33, second phase
Interviews (units of analysis)	Thirty-six (eleven controversies)	Nineteen (five controversies)	Thirty-three (nine controversies)	Thirty-five (twelve controversies)

Number and description of organizations interviewed	Eight: London2012 (bid company); ODA (promoters' agent); LOCOG (games operator); OPLC (park operator); Transport for London (TfL); CLM (programme manager); Land Lease (private developer); Network Rail (owner of UK rail infrastructure)	Five: STAR Alliance; Air Canada; BAA; HETCo and Balfour Beatty (private design and build companies)	8: CLRL (promoters' planning agent);Crossrail, (promoters' delivery agent); Network Rail; UK Treasury; Transport for London (TfL);Canary Wharf (private funder); Bechtel, Transcend (consultants)	11: HS2 Ltd (promoter's agent); Manchester City Council (MCC); Greater London Authority (GLA); Transport for London (TfL); Borough of Camden; Transport for Greater Manchester (TfGM); Network Rail; UK Treasury; Manchester Airport; CH2MHill, AECOM (consultants)
Archival data: Total number of documents (except news articles) organized by categories	Total number of documents: 469 Strategy and planning documents: 260 Financial reports: 6 Formal communication: 5 Newsletters and PR documents: 111 Design documents: 16 Meeting minutes: 71	Total number of documents: 114 Strategy and planning documents: 74 Financial reports: 6 Formal communication: 19 Newsletters and PR documents: 8 Design documents: 4 Meeting minutes: 3	Total number of documents: 122 Strategy and planning documents: 74 Financial reports: 2 Formal communication: 6 Newsletters and PR documents: 23 Design documents: 9 Meeting minutes: 8	Total number of documents: 66 Strategy and planning documents:22 Financial reports: 2 Formal communication: 20 Newsletters and PR documents:12 Design documents: 8 Meeting minutes: 2

* Inflation in construction prices was nil between 2008 and 2013.

† £15.9. billion (final prices for a completion date around 2016) is about £11.1 billion at 2002 prices (assuming 3.5% discount factor).

‡ British Olympic Association (BOA); London Organizing Committee of the Olympic and Paralympic Games (LOCOG) and International Olympic Committee (IOC)'s watchdog.

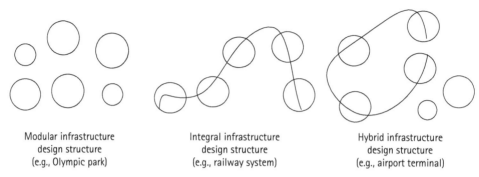

Modular infrastructure
design structure
(e.g., Olympic park)

Integral infrastructure
design structure
(e.g., railway system)

Hybrid infrastructure
design structure
(e.g., airport terminal)

FIGURE 12.1 Stylized representation of different infrastructure design structures.

Should the planning process proceed if the claimants cannot converge? Which actors have legitimacy to influence the local development decisions? Seeking answers for these questions was essential to understand the governance of these developments in the planning stage. The HS2 case allowed gathering data concurrently with the ongoing planning efforts.

12.3.2 Data Collection

Data collection started in 2011 when I obtained access to the top management team (chair, chief executive, and seven executive directors) of the Olympic Delivery Authority (ODA)—the public agency established to develop the Olympic park in 2005. This team reported to a top governing body formed by a four-party coalition: the national and London governments, the British Olympic Association (BOA), and LOCOG, the operator of the games and the International Olympic Committee (IOC) watchdog. The ODA attended the Olympic board meetings but had no power of veto.

Between 2011 and 2014 I leveraged the access granted to the ODA to, first, access top managers of other development partners for the Olympic park, and second, to negotiate access to the other schemes using the logic described previously. In a snowball fashion (Biernacki and Waldorf 1981), for all cases, I also interviewed directors of the suppliers contracted to produce a design, build, and manage the works.

In total, 121 formal interviews of up to two hours long were conducted by myself and doctoral students, and were tape-recorded. Non-disclosure agreements were not signed, but we always asked permission to use quotes and whether to keep the source anonymous. Some respondents gave us free rein to use the transcripts, whereas others occasionally asked us to stop the recorder and disallowed the use of particular quotes. Follow-up interviews were conducted to probe deeper into particular issues, double check a verbal account, and bridge gaps in the database.

To gather extra data and allow for member checks (Lincoln and Guba 1985), the emerging findings were shared with respondents, and a few were invited to give presentations and stay for lunch. We welcomed a total of thirteen guests, and for each visit, produced detailed hand-recorded notes of the seminar talks and lunch conversations.

To improve the accuracy of our data and the robustness of the conceptual insights (Jick 1979), the verbal accounts were triangulated against archival sources (Miles and

Huberman 1994). The planning process for any large infrastructure is well institutional-ized in the United Kingdom, and thus many planning documents are available online or become available through the Freedom of Information Act. Key documents included minutes of board meetings, formal communications, design change logs, and reports announcing performance targets and plans to achieve the goal. In the case of BAA, we examined annual corporate reports, master plans, and consultation documents. The controversies between BAA and STAR were documented in reports produced by the regulator and in letters between BAA, STAR, and the regulator.

Information on the internal project documents was played against reports produced by third parties. Hence we combed through reports produced by the National Audits Office, Parliamentary committees, government watchdogs, and other third parties. Other sources of data were articles and interviews with top managers in professional outlets, such as *New Civil Engineer, Construction News*, and articles in the national press, particularly for controversies that had fallen in the public domain.

12.3.3 Methods

I took a processual approach to theorization (Langley 1999) guided by the core ques-tion of how to sustain a fragile, consensus-oriented development. Subsidiary questions included: What is the governance structure? Where do interorganizational controver-sies come from? and How are they resolved? Following recommendations for inductive reasoning (Ketokivi and Mantere 2010), factual accounts were produced that provide a contextualized and chronologic understanding and guard against account bias (Miles and Huberman 1994) and tendencies for revisionism and self-aggrandizement (March and Sutton 1997).[3]

To first shed light on the governance structure, I used Design Structure Matrices (DSMs)—a tool from design theory that allows representing a complex system into a square matrix by capturing interdependencies between its constituent elements (Steward 1981). The cells along the diagonal of the DSMs represent high-order planning decisions (the names of the decisions are listed to the left of the rows to keep the matrix compact), whereas off-diagonal entries indicate the presence of interdependency between decisions. If the DSM has an entry in row i, column j, the decision concerning element i has a direct impact on the decision concerning element j. Hence the decisions represented in the diagonal cells have inputs entering from the top and bottom deci-sions, and outputs leaving from the left and right sides.

DSMs have been used to model the task structure to produce a detailed design but not the structure of the planning process for a capital-intensive development, and thus an original protocol for the content of the DSMs was required. The aim of the exercise was not, how-ever, to exhaustively model the planning process. Rather, it was to investigate the structure governing the high-level decisions. Hence, for the components that lodged the sampled controversies, the DSMs capture the interdependencies between decisions on the local goal, budget, and key requirements directly impacted by the controversy, including capacity, foot-print, and relevant subelements. For each DSM a companion matrix illustrates which actors directly influence the decisions and the forums where the issues are discussed.

The DSM analysis cannot, however, reveal how the issues are actually settled. Thus the DSM analysis was complemented with a qualitative analysis of the raw data using coding and tabular displays (Strauss and Corbin 1990). As I iterated between (i) reviewing transcripts and extracting quotes or "thought units" (Miles and Huberman 1994), (ii) using secondary data to verify the interview data, and (iii) developing the argument, I gradually discerned a high-level pattern to resolve interorganizational the controversies. I stopped iterating between data and theory when theoretical saturation was reached.

I proceed next to analyze the data before discussing the conceptual framework. Figure 12.2 illustrates the DSM and organizational matrices for two cases, whereas Table 12.2 illustrates a tabular display produced to analyze how controversies were resolved.

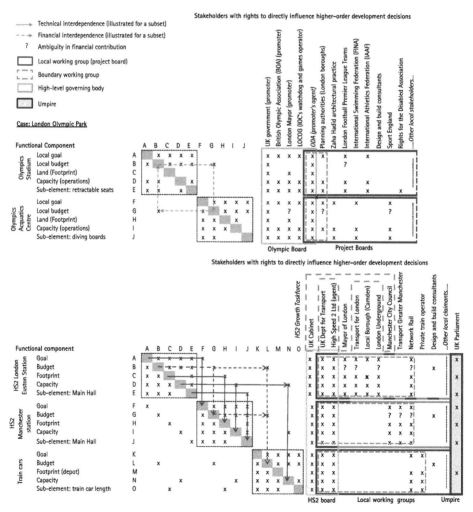

FIGURE 12.2 Excerpts of the design structure matrices and companion organizational matrices for the London Olympic Park and HS2 cases.

Table 12.2 Excerpt of tabular display analysing: Quality of the development environment and mechanisms used to resolve controversies

Case	Quality of the collaborative environment	Embedded controversy	Resolving the controversies				
			Quality of the negotiation talks	Locus of resolution	Problem solving	Design flexibility	Loosening targets
London Olympic Park	Plenty of evidence of intent to collaborate effectively; listen to stakeholders. A lot of it was listening to the communities, the grassroots...I Don't think anyone felt there was a hierarchy, there was a very healthy egalitarian challenge [ODA Official]. Reciprocity, I've never pushed to get that [need for greater flexibility] changed or to bypass that because I know exactly what is to sit in their chair [LOCOG Official]. Mutual trust This noble culture—sitting down on regularly, open, honest non-judgmental relationships, if something isn't going well stick it on the table—I think it's really important [ODA official].	Olympic Station	Lack of goal congruence	Tough: no willingness to seek compromise. What's wrong with leaving an athletics center ... Why do we have to publicly subside the richest clubs in the world? Why? It's public land ... it costs a fortune to accommodate ... Don't renege on your responsibility to public sport[ODA official].	Top governing body We went back to the Board 3 times... there were no credible [football club] bids–full stop [ODA official]	Mutual compromised under time pressure We needed to move ODA official]	Yes Foundations sized for worst-case scenario; retractable seats (in last round)	Yes 04,£282m (04 prices) 07,£422m (cash prices exc. VAT) 13,£537m (cash prices exc. VAT) 14, ~£600m (cash prices excl. VAT)
			Tough: efforts to leverage power imbalances. Broadcasters come to the party quite late ... and start saying things like we want this and that ... in a scheme of £7 billion, the retrofitting isn't a big thing [LOCOG Official].	Top governing body. They [IOC] aren't paying the bill [ODA official].	Unilateral concessions. We're having to embark on a fairly expensive change [ODA official].	No need for UK to be seen as leading on broadcast technology.	
		Divergences over sub-element (lighting)					
		Aquatics Centre	Sharp divergences over capacity budget, footprint.	Tough: efforts to leverage power imbalances. There was a lot of pressure to keep to the original budget ... the architects wouldn't compromise an inch ... it [budget] wasn't their problem ... they threatened to walk away ... they could have parted company from us .... and we parted company from them [ODA official].	Top governing body	Compromises and tough negotiation. Quid pro quos: for example, aesthetic stay, but venue must shrink to a third of original size.	Yes. Temporary 15,000 seats in modular wings.	Yes. 2004, £75 million [2004 prices], 2007, £182 million (cash price exc. VAT), 2013, £229 million (cash price exc. VAT).
		Divergences over sub-element (dividing boards)	Tough: no willingness to seek compromise. We [ODA] said we weren't going to change the diving boards ... they [FINA] sent an architect to prove they wouldn't work ... LOCOG was playing a political game telling FINA we can change ... they (LOCOG) wouldn't stand up to FINA, but we would [ODA Official].	Top governing body	Tough negotiation. Claimant (Aquatics Federation–FINA) caves in after much haggling, and new evidence.	No. Why buy this [roof] and don't buy the diving boards? ... I always saw it as a sculpture really [ODA official].	

(Continued)

Table 12.2 Continued

		Quality of the collaborative environment	Resolving the controversies				
Case	Embedded controversy		Quality of the negotiation talks	Locus of resolution	Problem solving	Design flexibility	Loosening targets
High-Speed 2	London Euston system. Lack of goal congruence, and sharp divergences over plans.	Plenty of evidence of intent to collaborate effectively; shared higher-level goal: the high-level principles, we've never had an issue with [TfL official] ... while I support the Government's aspiration ... the current proposal is inadequate [London of May or] willingness to meet face-to-face. I'm very happy to sit down ... want to reassure	Tough: people carrying cards close to the chest. We've asked can they [HS2 Ltd] share the cost data with us ... and they won't share that with us ... doubtless, they don't want us to be able to prepare ourselves to counter that [LGA official]. The process has worked somewhat like tennis. They [HS2 Ltd] will send us a proposal. We review it, pass it back, they look at it, pass it back [TfL official].	Umpire (or late deal). We'll petition because the design as it stands is awful [and] potentially unsafe ... it's not a failure to converge, just failure to agree with each other's visions [TfL official].	Ongoing negotiations. Original scheme was a fairy-godmother scheme [HS2 official]. Once bill is submitted ... there might be a story of we'd think about this a bit more if you drop that [LGA official].	Yes. We asked HS2 Ltd to make passive provision for Crossrail 2 ... so we can easily plug it into the development.	Yes. 2011, £1.1 billion, 2014, £2.1 billion. The principle that suggests that all the works at Euston are on the HS2 credit card has been accepted [TfL official].
	Manchester St. Goal congruence, but sharp divergences over plans.	Manchester supports about the plan [HS2 top official]. Mutual respect. They've [HS2 Ltd] got an idea of what they want to see and we too ... We're both respecting each other [Manchester Council official].	Moderate: genuine effort to seek consensus. We're engaged with the work that they [HS2] might be doing around station design ... they're engaged with us or the wider regeneration program ... our objective is always to try get consensus [Council elected leader]. They took our involvement very seriously ... it did feel like we were really part of the process [TfGM official].	Difficult to predict. We don't want to petition, we want to do it here [Council elected leader].	Ongoing negotiations. If government devolves tax return, the Council can consider to pay for investment [Council position].	Unlikely. They [HS2] came up with the option that it was one station next to another ... we see one integrated multi-model transport hub [Council official].	Yes (inevitable). 2011, £350m. But Council argues it will increase benefits. We aren't an open cheque book [HS2 official].

12.4 ANALYSIS

The analysis examines first the structure governing the high-level development decisions and then the sustainability of these highly fragile developments in the planning stage.

12.4.1 The Polycentric Structure Governing Megaproject Planning

Polycentricity is an intuitive approach to structure large arenas of consensus-oriented collective action. The idea is to decentralize governance across a nested structure of centers of decision-making and power and shared rules constraining and enabling action (Ostrom 1990, 2005). In agreement with this literature the DSM analysis reveals systematic efforts to decentralize governance. To substantiate this claim, I use the cases of the Olympics and HS2, which vary substantially in the technological decomposability of the infrastructure system. I first examine the decision-making structure as revealed by the DSM analysis, and then the governance structure as revealed by the organization matrices.

The DSM matrices for the two cases both show densely populated clusters of off-diagonals "x." These clusters show how the high-level development decisions for any particular component are closely interdependent to one another—a finding that is intuitive: the decision on the goal of a functional component whether it is a sports venue or a railway station is closely intertwined with the development decisions on the capital budget, the footprint (land needed), and the functional requirements for that component and vice versa.

As expected, the DSM matrices for the two cases differ in regards to the degree of interdependency across component clusters. In the case of the Olympics park, the high-level development decisions for one venue are independent of those decisions for another venue. Thus the Olympic park DSM is sparsely populated off the component clusters. The important exception is the interdependency between the local budget decisions, since increasing the capital budget for one venue potentially leaves less money available for the other venues. More interdependency exists between the components clusters in the HS2 case. First, the goals for each station need to be congruent; second, the budgets for the stations are also interdependent owing to equitability concerns and global constraints; and third, system-wide technological constraints create interdependency between the decisions on the local requirements. Hence the HS2 DSM is densely populated off the component clusters.

However, the organizational matrices for the two cases are remarkably similar. In both cases, the matrices show a decomposed structure of local working groups (so-called project boards), each one restricted to produce a mutually consensual design solution for the component of interest. Project board membership is open to the resource-rich local actors, including local governments and influential interest groups, but not to actors opposing the scheme or to resource-poor local actors (although consultation reaches all groups).

At the highest level, both organizational matrices show a top governing body restricted to the organizations that form the coalition of promoters; this governing body has direct influence over all the high-level development decisions. The omnipresence of the top governing body reflects the fact that the promoter of the project centrally controls the global targets (cost and schedule) that constrain all the local decisions. The agent of the promoter attends all the decision-making forums in a "boundary spanning" role (Tushman 1977).

Furthermore, both organizational matrices reveal middle-level decision-making forums created to help resolve the local issues. In the Olympics case, for example, a boundary organization was created, including the ODA, the executive agent of the coalition of promoters, and the four local governments with future jurisdiction over the Olympic park. The governance structure of the HS2 is also nested. Hence, in each city its leaders created boundary organizations open only to the officials of HS2 Ltd, the promoter's agent. And the promoter, the UK government, in turn created another boundary group, the HS2 Growth Taskforce, which reached out to the elected leaders of all cities with city-center stations.

12.4.2 Building Consensus

The analysis of the controversies reveals the difficulties in building local consensus within the design solution spaces constrained by the performance targets set *ex ante* of the collective development effort. The promoters' agent has a mandate to keep to the initial targets, whereas the local claimants insist that the budgets and/or timescales are too tight. This means that the top governing body has to constantly step in to resolve the issues with the local claimants.

The HS2 case is telling. The promoter and local claimants are unified by the goal of using the HS2 station developments to catalyze urban regeneration. But the local claimants argue that government is not supplying enough money to develop world-class stations integrated with public transit systems and the urban fabric. To make their case, the cities have commissioned masterplans. But under pressure to keep to the targets, HS2 Ltd recommended plans to government not fully endorsed by the cities. It was then up for Cabinet,[4] a level above, to decide the next move. One official explained: "HS2 Ltd, if you like, are the infantry out there; actually doing what they're told by [central] government. So HS2 Ltd get all the fights, appear to have all the fights, are the bad boys, but they're really only doing what they're instructed to do." Crucially, in all cases, the top governing bodies have less decision-making power than could be assumed *prima facie*. De jure, the promoters have power to impose a reasonable solution if a local group reaches impasse. But invariably the top governing bodies shy away from governing by diktat when local impasse surfaces. This was true for T2 ("if something gets talked, it gets changed," said a STAR person), and for the publicly financed schemes. Hence the

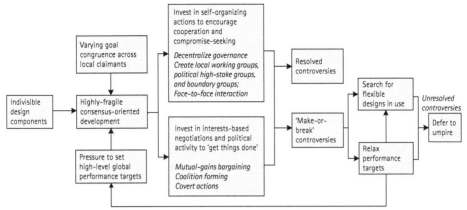

FIGURE 12.3 Sustaining highly fragile consensus-oriented developments.

search for possible solutions relies, on the one hand, on the willingness of all parties to compromise and reciprocate. On the other hand, it involves multi-gains bargaining and political activity until the claimants succeed to cut out a deal.

The coexistence of deliberative processes and interest-based negotiations makes these developments highly fragile. I turn now to discuss a pattern of four high-level coordination mechanisms that emerged to sustain them. Figure 12.3 illustrates the emerging logic.

12.4.3 Relaxing Performance Targets

Megaprojects are capital-intensive enterprises. The goals are controversial and trigger much opposition from actors in the environment. Other actors may be unified by the goal, but still disagree over the best way to achieve the goal. The ensuing disputes between the promoter, opponents, and others create ambiguity in the value of forging ahead and uncertainty in requirements. To attenuate ambiguity, the promoters invariably make commitments to performance targets at the onset of the planning effort. One non-elected official said that

> they [politicians] love announcing projects … our guidance is "no matter what your press people say … don't be drawn towards providing a spot figure; it's foolish, you've just created a hostage to fortune to yourself."

The analysis confirms claims that promoters suffer from optimism bias (Flyvbjerg et al. 2003); as one respondent put it, "early on, people's eyes are much bigger than their stomachs."[5] As working groups struggle to reach consensus, the promoters push back on requests from local actors for relaxing the performance targets (cost and time). Promoters dislike slippages because they compromise equity and potentially compromise the global targets. And yet, relaxing the performance targets is an invaluable mechanism to resolve the issues.

The Aquatics Center is a good example. The budget was set at £75 million in 2004 prices—a figure insufficient to deliver an iconic venue. One year in planning, the budget had duplicated and continued on a rise. Unilateral attempts by the ODA to bring the costs down infuriated local claimants who used political backchannels to force the ODA's hand. By 2008, a public outcry ensued after the budget spiraled to £242 million (final prices).

Throwing more resources into the "pot" (money, time, or both) relaxes the local solution space, but puts pressure on the global targets and affects the scheme's legitimacy in the eyes of the public. I turn now to analyze the value of buffers to mitigate the risk.

12.4.4 Global Buffers

Compiling registers of foreseeable events that can potentially cause overruns of the planning targets is an established practice (Cleland and King 1983). Once the potential impacts of the risky events are identified, simulations enable quantification of the best-case and worst-case scenarios at the onset of planning. The top governing body then faces a judgment call: either they set optimistic performance targets to increase the scheme attractiveness, or set more conservative targets that warrant more certainty to the targets. One respondent said:

> There's a bandwidth there ... if we push it [the budget] too far, we won't get the project at all ... so there's that game that goes on to try and find what the [UK] Treasury's real limits are, and how far can we really push it ... it's a political decision.

In the T2 case, for example, BAA ruled out the use of large buffers, confident in the firm's ability to neutralize the public backlash caused by any cost or schedule overruns during planning and later on in delivery. And indeed, both targets slipped multiple times during the development life cycle. In contrast, in the other cases, the elected leaders had no appetite to let the public see the performance targets slipping multiple times. The London 2012 case is a good example. The £4-billion[6] budget (final prices, no VAT) in the bid was wholly insufficient to leave a sustainable legacy. Complicating matters was uncertainty in the design requirements that could only be resolved after the 2008 Olympic games. But by mid-2006, public pressure mounted to re-fix the budget, and the Cabinet settled on a large buffer (£2.7 billion) on top of a £6.5-billion budget (final prices with VAT). One official said:

> Treasury were really, really clear ... big envelope and never knock on our door for money ... actually they were right ... we were then able to make decisions ... rather than being petrified because we didn't have enough money to do what we needed to do.

However, large buffers do not outrightly eliminate conflict. The findings show that promoters scrutinize the use of contingencies to mitigate the risk of running out of slack in the last stages of project delivery. Hence the decision-making process in planning still unfolds constrained by tight targets, especially when the promoter is reluctant to let another slippage occur. This does not mean that the promoter can succeed in avoiding self-fulfilling prophecies: London 2012 exhausted its contingency by the end of the delivery, and Crossrail follows the same path (NAO 2014). I turn now to discussion of the role of flexible design structures.

12.4.5 Flexible Design Structures

Modular design structures are the backbone of communities of production that rely on voluntary contributions of resources to achieve a collective goal (Baldwin and von Hippel 2011). But modularity costs time and money to achieve. It is also less complicated to develop modular digital systems than large physical infrastructure. Flexibility in integral physical assets can nonetheless be built in through investments in safeguards, such as redundancies. As a limited form of flexibility, investments in safeguards are bound to be controversial (Gil 2007; Gil and Tether 2011). Still, the analysis shows that many controversies in the sample were resolved after the performance targets were relaxed to safeguard integral designs.

The case of the Olympics Aquatics Center is telling. The bid proposed a massive venue with a wave-shaped roof. But as said, the cost forecasts quickly spiraled as the collective planning unfolded. To back down from the bid pledge was tricky, since the design concept had received worldwide acclaim. Complicating matters was a hard constraint on the minimum capacity of the venue. In the end the dispute was settled by using a safeguarded design, which consisted of building a small venue faithful to the original aesthetics and adding temporary modules to raise the capacity from 2,500 to 17,500 seats for the games.

The case of the Olympic stadium, in turn, illustrates the difficulties in negotiating flexible designs. From the onset of the planning stage the top governing body was divided over whether the stadium in legacy should host a football club or an athletics events. A football stadium was more viable in legacy, but would renege on the bid pledge. The alternative was to invest 20% more money into a dual-purpose venue with retractable seating. But football aficionados pushed back, calling it a "jack-of-all-trades." With time running out, the ODA proposed and the Olympic board endorsed a decision to forge ahead with a rigid design structure. The infighting between the dissenting parties continued until 2013, when an agreement was finally reached to invest £131 million to add retractable seating.[7]

In other incidences of controversies, an external party became involved in problem-solving— the mechanism discussed in the next section.

12.4.6 Arbitrating and Refereeing Disputes

In sports, an umpire is a person who acts as a referee and settles disputes between players competing to win. In planning megaprojects, autonomous actors also strive to win fights over the decisions that wil define the design. It turns out that the presence of a structure of nested umpires can put an end to emerging controversies that the claimants failed to self-resolve. Umpires can exist at different institutional levels. Some referees exist outside the project arena, whereas others can be a middle- or lower-level independent body created internally.

In the cases of Crossrail and HS2, the UK Parliament played the role of outside powerful referee. Every actor materially impacted by the plans was entitled to petition against the planning decisions of the promoter. Petitioners ranged from individuals and businesses unhappy with the outcome of the consultation, to resource-rich actors who shared the higher-order goal. These actors had in common disenchantment with the promoter's final plans, and trusted on Parliament to help them extract more concessions. One official said:

> HS2 didn't persuade us that our points were wrong nor did they persuade us that their points were right … [Petitioning] gives us the ability to correct what we feel is a mistake … that's ultimately about making your case that your vision is superior.

In the case of Heathrow T2, in turn, the industry regulator—an actor closer to the development process—played the role of umpire. The presence of the regulator was reassuring for both parties. As one BAA respondent said, "we're battling all the time … if the airlines don't like it, then they can bring in a formal dispute." And indeed, the airlines wrote several letters to the regulator complaining that the BAA was ignoring their needs—a claim which BAA contested. "Our job is to consult, not to get consensus … I can never get consensus on almost anything," said the BAA capital director. A level below, BAA recruited a retired director to play the role of arbitrator—the body which ruled that the design of T2 should allow for open and close gates at an additional cost for BAA of £4 million.

The presence of umpires brings advantages and disadvantages. Umpires resolve issues that deliberation and negotiation processes fail to resolve. But resorting to umpires is a source of late cycles of deliberation and knowledge creation that can lead to slippages in the performance targets, and is thus a source of much uncertainty in requirements during the planning process. The presence of umpires also fuels a lot of positional bargaining.

The Olympics case is the exception in that there was no powerful outside referee, since Parliament rushed to give the promoter planning powers immediately after London won the contest. To arbitrate emerging issues, the promoter set up an internal board with the local governments that had lost planning powers. But a level above there was no umpire. "You've got powerful figures all over the place … you can't govern," said one official (Norris et al. 2013). Facing a hard deadline, substantive slippages in the cost fore-casts ensued.

In summary, a megaproject creates a large consensus-oriented collective action prob-lem that is partially decomposable in different subproblems that matter to different local actors. I identify four high-level mechanisms to keep the development organization afloat. Slippages of targets facilitate local searches. Global buffers mask slippages. And flexible designs neutralize local conflict. Taken together, these mechanisms resolve most controversies. But there are limits to the amount and number of times that resources can be thrown in the pot to resolve controversies. Hence, as a safety net, unresolved issues can be deferred to an umpire.

12.5 DISCUSSION

I return now to the central question of how to sustain the highly fragile organizations formed to plan a capital-intensive infrastructure. In consensus-oriented developments, top management cannot unilaterally choose which decisions and tasks they central-ize at the top versus delegate to lower levels, and no "heavyweight managers" (Clark and Fujimoto 1991) exist empowered to overthrow local decisions. However, top man-agement cannot also work as a "rubberstamping hierarchy" (Rivkin and Siggelkow 2003) because only they have direct centralized control over the high-level resources that constrain all the local searches.

Polycentric governance attenuates the management complexity by limiting the membership of the local working group to the promoter and the local actors directly impacted by the solution to the local problem. Still, even in infrastructure systems that are technologically decomposable the subproblems remain interdependent because of the global performance targets set unilaterally by the promoter at the onset of the plan-ning process. As local groups tend to optimize locally because of self-interest (Knudsen and Levinthal 2007), pressure mounts to relax the local performance targets during planning. This creates a conundrum for the promoter's top management: if the pro-moter adheres to the performance targets it set upfront, it increases the risk of defection from the organization and of loss of critical resources during planning. In turn, if the promoter relaxes the local targets it threatens the legitimacy of the development in the eyes of the public and other third parties.

12.5.1 Relaxing Performance Targets and Flexible Designs

I discuss these two mechanisms together, as slippages in the performance targets were also a prerequisite to produce flexible design structures. Slippages in the performance targets "inject oxygen" that is critical to sustain a highly fragile development. If the ini-tial targets turn out unrealistic as planning unfolds, and promoters would still adhere to them, the local problems would remain intractable. In other cases, relaxing the performance targets is a prerequisite to allow for a risk-neutral flexible design solution with higher expected benefits for everyone.

Given that slippages in targets impair public legitimacy and fuel accusations of strategic misrepresentation, it is then reasonable to ask why the promoters make rigid commitments up front. Not doing so certainly sounds noble. But as Stone and Brush (1996) argue, when organizations plan in ambiguous contexts, the need to meet premature calls for commitments is a prerequisite to develop the legitimacy necessary to acquire the resources without which the plans cannot forge ahead. Put differently, the commitments up front (assuming that they are true to what bounded rational actors know at the time) dampen the ambiguity surrounding the value proposition and facilitate the ensuing resource acquisition process. Once the resources are acquired, a consensus-oriented search for local solutions ensues within a solution space constrained by those commitments. And yet, the analysis shows that it is hard to predict the outcome of consensus-oriented discussions when the decisions are long-lived and thus the stakes are high. Hence the initial commitments frequently turn out overly optimistic.

These insights suggest a need for a more nuanced conceptualization of performance in the context of the consensus-oriented arenas formed for megaproject planning. In extant studies of communities of production, homogeneity of logics and modularity dampen rilvary in the design preferences. This attenuates interorganizational conflict and the need for cooperative behavior. The problem is then one of coordinating work, and performance evaluation revolves around the efficiency of the process and the effectiveness of the solution. In contrast, if the consensus-oriented development is highly fragile, the development process is bound to be inefficient, as local searches will require much iteration and time-consuming negotiations. Bargaining will also create winners and losers, and will therefore lead to ambiguity on ensuing evaluations of the effectiveness of the outcomes (Lundrigan et al. 2015).

If process inefficiency and ambiguous outcomes are endemic to a consensus-oriented enterprise, this suggests that we cannot take for granted that these enterprises are sustainable. It thus seems fair to accept that it is legitimate for the promoter to relax the performance targets when it becomes clear that those same targets are creating intractable subproblems. Legitimizing slippages in the performance targets does not excuse promoters from being obliged to try to do a better job when setting the initial targets. But from the point of view of the actors participating in these consensus-oriented developments and unified by the system goal, positive performance revolves around the capability of sustaining the organization.

Hence what is new here is not that throwing more resources into the pot eliminates interorganizational conflict, but how to interpret this action. An organizational perspective suggests that a slippage of the initial cost and schedule targets—if it is commensurate with evolution in requirements during a consensus-oriented search for a design solution—is a legitimate mechanism to resolve emerging controversies. Thus an action to relax the performance targets does not express incompetence or Machiavellian misrepresentation. If relaxing the targets is necessary to carry the resource-rich actors along, this action results from optimism bias when the promoter unilaterally sets the targets up front. This optimism is not intended to masquerade dishonesty. Rather, it is rooted in a belief that it will not be that difficult for self-interested actors to figure out mutually consensual solutions for shared problems. This optimism in consensus-oriented collective action leads to fallibility in predicting the outcome of collective searches, as it skews the forecasting error towards underestimating the cost and time necessary to achieve consensus. But were it not for this same optimism bias, people would not even try to collectively resolve shared problems.

Crucially, the premise that a group of self-interested actors can self-organize to resolve a shared problem is not universal. Classical studies of collective action called for centralizing decision-making power in the hands of government or private firms (Hardin 1968; Olson 1965). Since then, scholars of consensus-oriented collective-action arenas have counterargued that there are reasons to be optimistic (Gray 1989; Ostrom 1990; Beck and Plowman 2014). Specifically in the world of consensus-oriented infrastructure developments, Gil and Baldwin (2013) show that if goal congruence is high, slippages in the performance targets are not a prerequisite to build consensus even if the initial solution space is constrained. In planning megaprojects, low goal congruence exerts more pressure to relax the performance targets. For the participants in the decision-making process, however, these slippages are a legitimate cost to pay for democratically resolving interorganizational conflict. The trick for the promoter is not to overuse this mechanism which, in the eyes of third parties, raises issues of accountability and undermines the promoter's legitimacy to use the resources.

The claim that the sustainability of a consensus-oriented development is per se a measure of performance is in agreement with extant literature in consensus-oriented collective action. These studies place the emphasis on the sustainability of shared resources and, as a corollary, on the sustainability of the self-organizing community that governs the resource (Ostrom 1990). A consensus-oriented development that is sustainable produces a final design that will fold into a physical artefact that the participating actors will happily to share in use. Therefore, in a consensus-oriented development, the shared resources are the design decisions "in-the-making." If the development process is sustainable this shared resource is sustainable too. But the form of this shared resource will later evolve from design decisions "in-the-making" into a physical artefact that independent actors share in use. This suggests that the community of design production is sustainable too. But it will evolve into a community in use.

12.5.2 Global Buffers

Built-in contingencies are buffers that create organizational slack—spare resources that allow an organization to adapt successfully to internal pressures for adjustment or external pressures for change (Bourgeois 1981). The effects of slack resources on how organizations perform are, however, contingent on the environment and the performance variable of interest (Voss et al. 2008). From an efficiency perspective, for example, Cyert and March (1963) argue that slack reduces political activity and bargaining, because with more resources available, there is less conflict. But Bourgeois (1981) notes that slack can also create opportunities for self-aggrandizing managers to engage in politics and sub-optimal behavior, and thus for self-fulfilling prophecies.

This study is inconclusive concerning whether global buffers are or are not a source of inefficiency, as we can only speculate about the outcomes had the buffers not been there. But in agreement with prior studies, the organizational slack created by the observed buffers was effective in facilitating local problem-solving. Indeed, many observed interoganizational controversies were resolved by letting the local performance targets slip. This would have been more difficult to do if management had no slack to absorb the slippages, and thus they would have no choice but to relax the publicly visible global performance targets.

Importantly, the slack created by global buffers is not a necessary mechanism to sustain a highly fragile development. The BAA case is a good example. This suggests a fundamental difference between private and publicly financed projects. Slippages in performance targets attract more public attention in the latter than in the former. This encourages elected leaders, their agents, and public policy to build in more slack resources in order to pre-empt bad news would the global resources not be enough to cope with the outcomes of consensus-oriented searches. Still there are limits to building slack, flexible designs, and letting the performance targets slip. This leads us to the role of structures empowered to settle disputes.

12.5.3 The Role of the Nested Umpires

In collective action literature, the absence of affordable conflict-resolution bodies is a source of fragility in governance (Ostrom 1990). An absence of an independent arbitrator increases the risks of impasse, power battles, and political manoeuvring; but the presence of an alternative forum to resolve conflicts also potentially creates a negative precondition for the parties to self-resolve their differences (Reilly 2001). Thus the umpire is also a source of inefficiency. Untangling the pros and cons of an umpire is further complicated because it is a source of noise in the negotiations.

Bargaining tactics aside, the analysis shows that in the large consensus-oriented collective action arenas that the planning of megaprojects create, some controversies cannot simply be self-resolved in a reasonable amount of time. The umpire is therefore a pragmatic mechanism to reassure all dissenting organizations that they will not get stuck into stalemate if they cannot bridge the differences. The findings suggest that the umpires exist at different levels, ranging from being a powerful outside referee imposed by the environment to a referee with power to settle disputes appointed by the participants of the planning process.

The need for internal umpires is in agreement with Ostrom's (1990) principle of robust governance that posits a need for affordable conflict-resolution mechanisms. More intriguing is the need for outside referees to sustain these consensus-oriented arenas. The idea goes against Ostrom's argument that polycentric governance structures are more robust if they trust on the ability of the participants to self-govern shared resources.

This suggests that the planning of megaprojects creates consensus-orientated collective-action arenas that are too fragile to be left to their own devices. The crux of the problem is that the planning process cannot get off the ground unless the promoter makes premature commitments to performance targets up front. But the chances are low of getting the targets right given the large number of subproblems that will ensue once the consensus-oriented planning process starts. The decisions have high stakes because they are hard to reverse and are long-lived. Congruence around the system goal may also be low. As a result, some claimants to the planning decisions demand a high price for cooperation and rule out the idea of losing without a fight. Hence, presupposing that consensus can emerge for all local problems is unrealistic. Resorting to an external umpire recognizes the limits of self-governance when goal congruence is low and the problem is interdependent with the environment.

12.6 CONCLUSION

The motivation for this study is a conundrum about megaprojects. Do these enterprises underperform or not when the performance targets slip during the planning process which is seemingly par for the course? To shed light on this question, I start by arguing that the planning of a megaproject creates a highly fragile consensus-oriented actor-network. The task of this actor-network is to develop a one-off infrastructure system. The members of the network are resource-rich autonomous actors which will share the infrastructure in use. These members want to influence the planning decisions in exchange for commiting their resources.

The study shows that large infrastructures can be invariably decomposed into a system of functional components, each one relevant to a different group of local actors. This high-level decomposability enables the creation of multiple decision-making groups to solve different local subproblems. While the governing structure shows a degree of polycentricity, the local subproblems remain interdependent. First, they are financially interdependent because the global performance targets constrain the solution spaces; and second, many technological decisions are interdependent because the components are hard to break apart into independent modules with clear, standard interfaces. The conflation of resource scarcity, low problem decomposability, and consensus-oriented decision making creates a wicked problem.

Evaluating the performance of a megaproject against the targets set at the onset of planning is therefore unduly harsh. It misses the point that the initial plans, insofar as they build upon assumptions that are true to what bounded rational actors know at the time and optimistic within reason, merely aim to get the ball rolling. These initial performance targets cannot, however, offer accurate forecasts as to the outcome of consensus-oriented searches for solutions. If the initial performance targets were to be too rigid, the planning process would not be democratic. Paradoxically, excessive slippages of the performance targets create the risk of a development becoming a political football and getting trashed in the court of public opinion. Hence the sustainability of any large infrastructure development in planning cannot be taken for granted, and indeed many schemes collapse after years of planning work.

This insight helps to move forward the debate on the performance of megaprojects. It suggests that it can be unfair to associate slippages in the performance targets to underperformance *when* slippages are commensurate with the outcomes of consensus-oriented collective searches. This insight matters in the context of publicly financed schemes in which elected leaders, agents, and policy lean toward very large contingencies. The organizational slack that contingencies build in is effective to dampen conflict, but creates a risk of inefficiency, suboptimal behavior, and a self-fulfilling prophecy. Large contingencies up front also shift the burden of resolving emerging controversies to one party: the promoter. A shared understanding of how slippages in performance targets come about has potential to contribute to creating an institutional environment where accountability for slippages can be shared. This then allows shrinkage of built-in contingencies to mitigate their downside risks.

The most important limitation to the generalizability of the findings is the environment surrounding the cases. The UK context offers a stringent regime of planning laws designed to protect property rights, and the country's political and legal system gives elected leaders incentives to heed local interests. Even societies modeled after the UK legal and political system will not have the same institutions and dimension. Hence differences can be expected in the forms of organizing to plan large infrastructure systems.

In conclusion, this study shows that to sustain a highly fragile consensus-oriented development, management needs to know when to resolve the make-or-break issues by relaxing rules, building slack and flexibility, or deferring problem-solving to umpires. Striking the right balance between these coordination mechanisms is necessary to preserve both the internal democratic decision-making processes and the legitimacy in the eyes of third parties—two prerequisites to sustain a fragile development in an ambiguous context.

Acknowledgments

I acknowledge the time and know-how of all respondents who contributed to this study. I give special thanks to Don Ward, chief executive of Constructing Excellence, for helping with access to top managers of the Olympic Delivery Authority and Crossrail. I am also grateful for insightful discussions and comments by Carliss Baldwin, Andrew Davies, Bent Flyvbjerg, Ray Levitt, Peter Love, Alan Penn, the participants in the 2015 Engineering Project Organizations conference, and reviewers of a draft submitted to the 2015 Academy of Management conference. I am solely responsible for any errors, omissions, or inaccuracies.

NOTES

1. In the United Kingdom, for example, the gap between general elections cannot exceed five years, and regulated monopolies tend to operate under obligations to produce a new capital plan every five years.
2. In 2012 the BAA changed its name to Heathrow Ltd, but here I have retained the BAA name for the sake of simplicity.
3. Four detailed factual narratives, one for each focal case, were produced using a Harvard-style teaching case presentation, and were circulated for comments.
4. The UK Cabinet is the collective decision-making body of the UK government, composed of the Prime Minister and the most senior ministers who head the government departments.
5. Wachs (1989) and later Flyvbjerg et al. (2003) go far to claim that promoters "lie" or "strategically misrepresent." The claim is hard to refute, as it plays to common conceptions, but supporting evidence is skin-deep. One respondent said: "If you weren't optimistic, you wouldn't get into this sort of job ... but in forty years of work I can't think of a single incident where people deliberately falsified the number."
6. This figure includes £971 million for venues, £89 million for conversion costs, £640 million for the Olympic infrastructure, £1,040 million for non-Olympic infrastructure, £700 million for local transport schemes, and £15 million bid costs. It excludes £766 million for land.
7. By October 2016, the costs of the stadium conversion had risen to £323 million, owing to difficulties encountered by the contractors in installing a roof to cover the athletics track and the retractable seating.

REFERENCES

Altshuler, A. A. and Luberoff, D. (2003). *Mega-Projects: The Changing Politics of Urban Public Investment*. Cambridge, MA: Brookings Institution Press.

Baldwin, C. Y. and Clark, K. B. (2000). *Design Rules: The Power of Modularity*, vol. I. Cambridge, MA: MIT Press.

Baldwin, C. Y. and von Hippel, E. (2011). "Modeling a paradigm shift: From producer innovation to user and open collaborative innovation," *Organization Science*, 22(6): 1399–417.

Beck, T. E. and Plowman, D. A. (2014). "Temporary, emergent interorganizational collaboration in unexpected circumstances: A study of the Columbia Space Shuttle response effort," *Organization Science*, 25(4): 1234–52.

Biernacki, P. and Waldorf, D. (1981). "Snowball sampling: Problems and techniques of chain referral sampling," *Sociological Methods and Research*, 10: 141–63.

Bourgeois III, L. J. (1981). "On the measurement of organizational slack," *The Academy of Management Review*, 6(1): 29–39.

Brusoni S., Prencipe A., and Pavitt K. (2001). "Knowledge specialization, organizational coupling, and the boundaries of the firm: Why do firms know more than they make? *Administrative Science Quarterly*, 46(4): 597–621.

Clark, K. B. and Fujimoto, T. (1991). *Product Development Performance*. Boston: Harvard Business School.

Cleland, D.I. and King, W. R. (1983). *Systems Analysis and Project Management*, 3rd edn. New York: McGraw-Hill.

Cyert, M.D. and March, J. G. (1963). *A Behavioral Theory of the Firm*. Englewood Cliffs, NJ: Prentice-Hall.

Denis, J., Dompierre, G., Langley, A., and Rouleau, L. (2011). "Escalating indecision: Between reification and strategic ambiguity," *Organization Science*, 22(1): 225–44.

Eisenhardt, K. M. (1989). "Building theories from case study research," *Academy of Management Review*, 14(4): 532–50.

Eisenhardt K. M. and Graebner M. (2007). "Theory building from cases: Opportunities and challenges," *Academy Management Journal*, 50(1): 25–32.

Flyvbjerg, B., Bruzelius, N., and Rothengatter, W. (2003). *Megaprojects and Risk: An Anatomy of Ambition*. Cambridge: Cambridge University Press.

Gersick, C. J. (1994). "Pacing strategic change: The case of a new venture," *Academy of Management Journal*, 37(1): 9–45.

Gil, N. (2007). "On the value of project safeguards: Embedding real options in complex products and systems," *Research Policy*, 36 (7): 980–99.

Gil, N. and Tether, B. (2011). "Project risk management and design flexibility: Analysing a case and conditions of complementarity," *Research Policy*, 40: 415–28.

Gil, N. and Baldwin, C. (2013). "Sharing design rights: A commons approach for developing infrastructure," Harvard Business School working paper, 14–025, January.

Gray B. (1989). "Conditions facilitating interorganizational collaboration," *Human Relations*, 38(10): 911–36.

Hall, P. (1982). *Great Planning Disasters*. Berkeley: University of California Press.

Hardin, G. (1968). "The tragedy of the commons," *Science*, 162(3859): 1243–8.

Jick, T. D. (1979). "Mixing qualitative and quantitative methods: Triangulation in action, *Administrative Science Quarterly*, 24(4): 602–11.

Ketokivi, M. and Mantere, S. (2010). "Two strategies for inductive reasoning in organizational research," *Academy of Management Review*, 35: 315–33.

Knudsen, T., and Levinthal, D. A. (2007). "Two faces of search: Alternative generation and alternative evaluation," *Organization Science*, 18(1): 39–54.

Langley, A. (1999). "Strategies for theorizing from process data," *Academy of Management Review*, 24: 691–710.

Lincoln, Y. S. and Guba, E. G. (1985). "But is it rigorous? Trustworthiness and authenticity in naturalistic evaluation," in D. D. Williams (ed.), *Naturalistic Evaluation*. San Francisco: Jossey-Bass.

Lundrigan, C., Gil, N., and Puranam, P. (2015). "The (under) performance of mega-projects: A meta-organizational approach," *Proceedings of the 75th Academy of Management Conference, Vancouver*.

March, J. G. and Simon, H. A. (1958). *Organizations*. New York: Wiley.

March, J. G. and Sutton, R. I. (1997). "Crossroads-organizational performance as a dependent variable." *Organization Science*, 8(6): 698–706.

Merrow, E.W., McDonwell, L.M., and Arguden, R.Y. (1988). *Understanding the Outcome of Megaprojects*. Santa Monica, CA: Rand Corporation.

Miles, M. B. and Huberman, A. M. (1994). *Qualitative Data Analysis: An Expanded Sourcebook*, 2nd edn. Thousand Oaks, CA: Sage.

Miller, R. and Lessard, D. (2000). *The Strategic Management of Large Engineering Projects*. Cambridge, MA: MIT Press.

Morris, P. W. (1994). *The Management of Projects*. London: Thomas Telford.

National Audit Office (2014). *Crossrail: Report by the Comptroller and Auditor General. Department for Transport*, 24 January. National Audit Office.

Norris, E., Rutler, J., and Medland, J. (2013). *Making the Games. What Government can Learn from London 2012*. London: Institute for Government.

O'Mahony, S. and Bechky, B. A. (2008). "Boundary organizations: Enabling collaboration among unexpected allies," *Administrative Science Quarterly*, 53(3): 422–59.

O'Mahony, S. and Ferraro, F. (2007). "The emergence of governance in an open source community," *Academy of Management Journal*, 50: 1079–106.

Olson, M. (1971) [1965]. *The Logic of Collective Action: Public Goods and the Theory of Groups*, revised edn. Cambridge, MA: Harvard University Press.

Ostrom, E. (1990). *Governing the Commons: The Evolution of Institutions for Collective Action*. Cambridge: Cambridge University Press.

Ostrom, E. (2005). *Understanding Institutional Diversity*. Princeton, NJ: Princeton University Press.

Ouchi, W. (1980). "Markets, bureaucracies, and clans," *Administrative Science Quarterly*, 25: 125–41.

Pfeffer J. and Salancik, G. R. (1978). *The External Control of Organizations*. New York: Harper & Row.

Reilly, T. (2001). "Collaboration in action: An uncertain process." *Administration in Social Work*, 25(1): 53–73.

Ring, P.S. and Van de Ven, A. H. (1992). "Structuring cooperative relationships between organizations," *Strategic Management Journal*, 13(7): 483–98.

Ross, J. and Staw, B. M. (1986). "Expo 86: An escalation prototype," *Administrative Science Quarterly*, 31(2): 274–97.

Rothschild, J. and Russell, R. (1986). "Alternatives to bureaucracy: Democratic participation in the economy," in J. F. Short (ed.), *Annual Review of Sociology*, vol. 12. Palo Alto, CA, pp. 307–28.

Rittel, H. W. J. and, Webber, M. (1973). "Dilemmas in a general theory of planning," *Policy Sciences*, 4: 155–69.

Rivkin, J. W. and Siggelkow, N. (2003). "Balancing search and stability: Interdependencies among elements of organizational design." *Management Science*, 49(3): 290–311.

Shapiro, A. and Lorenz, C. (2000). "Large-scale projects as complex systems: Managing scope creep," *The Systems Thinker*, 11(1): 1–5.

Siggelkow, N. (2007). "Persuasion with case studies," *Academy of Management Journal*, 50(1): 20–4.

Steward, D. (1981). "The design structure matrix: A method for man-aging the design of complex systems," *IEEE Transactions on Engineering Management*, 28(3): 71–4.

Stinchcombe, A. L. and Heimer, C. A. (1985). *Organization Theory and Project Management: Administering Uncertainty in Norwegian Offshore Oil*. London: Scandinavian University Press.

Stone, M. M. and Brush, C. G. (1996). "Planning in ambiguous contexts: The dilemma of meeting needs for commitment and demands for legitimacy," *Strategic Management Journal*, 17(8): 633–52.

Strauss, A. and Corbin, J. M. (1990). *Basics of Qualitative Research: Grounded Theory Procedures and Techniques*. Thousand Oaks, CA: Sage.

Szyliowicz, J. S. and Goetz, A. R. (1995). "Getting realistic about megaproject planning: The case of the new Denver International Airport," *Policy Sciences*, 28(4): 347–67.

Thomson, A. M. and Perry, J. L. (2006). "Collaboration processes: Inside the black box," *Public Administration Review*, 66(S1): 20–32.

Tuertscher, P., Garud, R., and Kumaraswamy, A. (2014). Justification and interlaced knowledge at ATLAS, CERN," *Organization Science*, 25(6): 1579–1608.

Tushman, M. (1977). "Special boundary roles in the innovation process," *Administrative Science Quarterly*, 22: 587–605.

Van de Ven, A. H. (1976). "On the nature, formation, and maintenance of relations among organizations," *Academy Management Review*, 1(4): 24–36.

Voss, G. B., Sirdeshmukh, D., and Voss, Z. G. (2008). "The effects of slack resources and environmental threat on product exploration and exploitation," *Academy of Management Journal*, 51(1): 147–64.

Wachs, M. (1989). "When planners lie with numbers," *Journal of the American Planning Association*, 55(4): 476–79.

Yin, R. K. (1984). *Case Study Research: Design and Methods* (3rd edn. 2003). *Applied Social Research Methods Series*, vol. 5. Thousand Oaks, CA: Sage Publications.

....

CHAPTER 13

UNDERSTANDING DRIVERS OF MEGAEVENTS IN EMERGING ECONOMIES

....

ROBERT A. BAADE AND VICTOR A. MATHESON

13.1 INTRODUCTION

ECONOMIC impact estimates from megasports events by some accounts have been, well, mega. The University of São Paulo and Ernst & Young estimated that the economic impact from the World Cup in June/July 2014 and the Summer Olympic Games in 2016 in Brazil together could total $100 billion and create 120,000 new jobs (Ernst & Young Terco 2011). Rather than joyous throngs filling Brazilian streets bestowing sainthood on the government savants who orchestrated the country's sport-induced economic windfall in June 2013, a reported million people mobbed the streets of Brazilian cities protesting the country's priorities as symbolized by hosting these hallmark events (Lundy 2013). How does one reconcile these extreme opposite positions? Why would citizens of the world's seventh largest economy vehemently and sometimes violently protest an increase in their GDP of 4.5% (World Bank 2014) and a reduction in the number of people unemployed by 10.62% (Trading Economics 2014).[1]

The wisdom of hosting sports megaevents has increasingly been questioned particularly for emerging economies. Independent scholars analyzing the economics of hallmark events almost unanimously share the angst of the Brazilian protestors primarily for two reasons. First, megasports events fail to deliver the economic bonanza promised by event organizers, boosters, and those who award the events. Second, the benefits and costs are disproportionately shared.

A mystery of sorts emerges in light of scholarly findings and recent practice. A reporter brought the puzzle into sharper profile recently when she asked the simple question: "If your analysis is right regarding the lack of any meaningful economic impact from mega-events, then why do cities and nations continue to compete so vigorously to host them?" Such practical questions do put scholars on their heels. The possibility exists that the majority of independent scholarship has missed the mark, and that it is prudent for developing countries to pursue hosting. The purpose of this article is to examine what motivates emerging economies to host, and to analyze whether those motives and outcomes associated with them do justify hosting.

The arguments for hosting relate primarily to the economics of doing so. The fundamental question is: do the costs and benefits justify developing countries hosting mega-sports events? If it can be demonstrated that the cost-benefit and risk-reward profiles for hosting as they currently exist do not justify doing so, then it is important to address the issue of what can be changed to improve the economic outcomes for the developing economies that have, with increasing frequency, so aggressively pursued them. Those who benefit, furthermore, often do not bear costs in proportion to the benefits derived. Independent scholarship began to surface in response to the obvious public finance issues involved, and the use of authoritative, "scientific" studies by boosters proposing that the benefits to the public in the final analysis far exceeded the costs, thereby justifying financial and moral support for hosting.

Emerging nations historically have hosted the FIFA World Cup more frequently than the Summer and/or Winter Olympic Games. Table 13.1 shows that during the period 1930 through 1966, developed and emerging countries hosted the World Cup on five and three occasions respectively. Historically, FIFA alternated the World Cup between the powerhouse soccer-playing countries in Latin America and Europe. If Russia and other BRIC (Brazil, Russia, India, and China) nations are categorized as emerging economies, then from 1970 through 2022, World Cup hosting has been divided equally between developed and emerging nations. Once again, if Russia is classified as an emerging economy, the last four World Cups have been awarded to developing countries. The trend appears to be toward emerging economies hosting the World Cup more frequently. This is explained, in part, by FIFA's more recent desire to expand the game into regions that have not typically embraced the sport in the same way that the traditional hotbed of the sport in Europe and Latin America have.

The Summer Olympic Games show a similar trend in that the frequency of hosting by emerging nations has increased over time. Specifically, the Summer Olympic Games were hosted exclusively by developed countries from 1928 through 1964. For the period 1968 through the present, developed and emerging nations have hosted twelve and four times respectively. The Winter Olympic Games has exhibited a similar increasing incidence of hosting by developing countries, but to a lesser degree. Developed countries were exclusive hosts for the Winter Olympic Games from 1928 through 1964. The period 1968 through the present has shown a 12:2 developed-to-emerging nation split if Russia (Sochi, Russia, in 2014) and the former Yugoslavia (Sarajevo, Yugoslavia, in 1984) are categorized as emerging economies.

Even simply bidding for the Olympics has become far more commonplace for developing nations. Between 1896 and 1996, 82% of all Summer Olympics bids came from industrialized countries, while 10% came from developing countries and another 8% came from Eastern Bloc or former Soviet states. Between 2000 and 2016, less than half of all bids came from industrialized nations. On the Winter Olympics side, 93% of bids

Table 13.1 Host cities for the World Cup since 1930

World Cup/year	Host country	Developed (D) or emerging (E)
1930	Uruguay	E
1934	Italy	D
1938	France	D
1950	Brazil	E
1954	Switzerland	D
1958	Sweden	D
1962	Chile	E
1966	England	D
1970	Mexico	E
1974	West Germany	D
1978	Argentina	E
1982	Spain	D
1986	Mexico	E
1990	Italy	D
1994	USA	D
1998	France	D
2002	South Korea	D
2006	Germany	D
2010	South Africa	E
2014	Brazil	E
2018	Russia	E
2022	Qatar	E

Source: "FIFA World Cup & Olympic Games Host Nations." 2015. *WorldFactsInc,* <https://sites.google.com/site/worldfactsinc/FIFA-World-Cup--Olympic-Games-Host-Nations>

between 1924 and 1998 came from the industrialized world, while only 57% of bidding cities from 2002 through 2024 came from the same regions.

13.2 DRIVERS FOR EMERGING ECONOMY HOSTING

Global developments beyond the world of commercial sport do explain to a significant extent the motivations for hosting hallmark events among both developed and emerging nations. The narrative in this portion of the article identifies the drivers in general and then discusses them more specifically. Painting with the broadest possible strokes, potential host nations/cities envision that hosting can be used to promote national unity and provide a clearer representation of the nation's personality and/or culture (Varrel and Kennedy 2011). Second, nations and cities seek to host in the expectation that it will significantly boost their economies. This particular motivation has assumed greater urgency given structural developments in the global economy. Some of the more important changes are identified and discussed in the remainder of this section.

First, the global economy has become more open. Economic competition has intensified across the world in the post-World War II era accelerating in the 1970s. The adoption of a system of floating exchange rates following the United States unilateral abrogation of the gold convertibility feature of the Bretton Woods International Monetary System in 1971 arguably contributed to an expansion of trade in goods, services, and assets globally. The increased international competition, in turn, arguably has contributed to economic instability, the global financial crisis of 2008 being one example. The collapse of oil prices as well as other commodity prices and currency instability, particularly in emerging economies in the late summer of 2015, represents another. The need to provide jobs, particularly for urban residents—always important—has become even more so in a world of growing economic instability. Social order and political sustainability would appear to have taken on greater urgency in light of terrorist movements that depend on an inability of governments to provide economic opportunity and distributive social justice for their citizens.

Second, urban populations have been growing at a stunning rate. 62.1% of the world's population lived in rural areas in 1975; that percentage fell to 53% by 2000 ("Urban Areas" 2002). It is estimated that 66% of the world's population will live in urban areas by 2050 (United Nations 2014). Most of this growth in urban populations has occurred in the developing world, with 5 million additional residents being absorbed by cities each month in emerging nations, which accounts for 95% of global urban growth ("Urban Areas" 2002). The migration to megacities has stressed those economies and social institutions, and governments have failed to keep pace in providing for many essentials. The provision of basic needs such as jobs, transportation, security, education, potable water, sewage treatment, and refuse disposal has languished. State, provincial, and federal governments have not been able to make up for the shortfall in funds to finance metropolitan infrastructure. Federal and state governments in some countries have, in fact, cut back on revenue sharing when cities have needed the funds most. This has occurred because governments at all levels have been experiencing financial stress.

The financial scissors crisis, cutting on both the revenue and cost side, for nations and cities has compelled a more entrepreneurial strategy by them in dealing with their financial woes.[2] Megaevents have the capacity to unify diverse and often adversarial political coalitions, and to accelerate the pace at which projects are conceived and completed. That coupled with the hope of a financial windfall from a megaevent, buoyed by event-booster studies, has proved too alluring to resist for many countries and cities in the developed and developing world. The emphasis on hosting sports teams, attracting political conventions, constructing museums, aquariums, and concert venues has reflected the broader metropolitan, entrepreneurial strategy for reinvigorating or sustaining urban economics, especially in the developed world. Emerging-economy municipal governments have not been able to provide consumer goods at the same level, but it appears that they have sought to imitate the success of the 1984 Los Angeles Summer Olympic Games, which turned a profit of approximately $225 million (in 1984 dollars) (Los Angeles Olympic Organizing Committee 1984).

Megaevent hosting has generally been viewed as one way of helping a city bolster its tourist trade. Tourism has the further advantage of being viewed as a clean industry that could give an urban economy a significant boost. The alleged transformation of Barcelona into a tourist destination following that City's hosting of the 1992 Summer Olympic Games lent currency to that proposition.

Third, with regard to tourism, that industry has grown at a rapid rate. Tourist arrivals numbered less than 20 million in 1950, reached 922 million by 2008, and are expected to reach 1.6 billion by 2020 ("The Global Growth of Tourism" 2014). Europe and the United States have been the most frequent travel destinations, but the extraordinary growth in tourism has occurred throughout the world to include Africa, the Middle East, and Asia. The trend is likely to continue as a result of advances in travel technology, holiday entitlement, increases in disposable income, availability and type of travel, and media coverage ("The Global Growth of Tourism" 2014). Tourism has been identified and emphasized by most countries as essential to increasing economic growth and creating jobs. The threat of terrorism, in the Middle East in particular, has provided powerful testimony to the importance of tourism, as terrorists have targeted the tourist industry in their attempts to undermine the economies of countries such as Tunisia and Egypt. Trends in the tourist industry imply that there are more potential visitors for any country, but at the same time there are more options available to tourists and a disinclination to visit countries that pose the most significant safety risks. A sports megaevent can provide an entrée into the potentially lucrative tourist trade.

Fourth, megasports events have evolved into significant, if not the most important and recognizable, global brands, and have been aggressively promoted to an international audience by those who "own" and "rent" them. A country is willing to pay handsomely for the opportunity to market themselves through occupying center stage on the planet for a fortnight or longer.

The marketing of megaevents has accelerated as a consequence of two historically distinct but intimately related developments: the first sale of television rights for the Olympic Games in 1956 in Melbourne, Australia,[3] and corporate sponsorships which fully emerged as a key part of the model for financing megaevents for and following the 1984 Summer Olympic Games in Los Angeles. Juan Antonio Samaranch, the late head of the IOC, identified the importance of television in 2001. Samaranch stated: "We need spectators at the Games, but the IOC does not insist on 100,000-seat stadiums. The Olympics are primarily put on for television" (Barney et al. 2004). The size of television audiences in particular has proved enormously seductive for developed and developing countries alike in vying for the right to host.

Corporate sponsors' *raison d'être* for their involvement in the financing of megasports events is to sell products. Advertising is critical to that effort. The broadcasts of the Olympic Games and the World Cup reach the largest potential market for any program on a consistent basis. The 2012 London Olympic Games set a television record for viewers in the United States, with 219.4 million tuned in for the event, breaking the 2008 Beijing Games record of 215 million US viewers alone ("London Olympics 2012 Ratings" 2012). The global audience for the Summer Olympic Games is approximately 3.2 billion people. No other event has as great an overall audience, but the finals of the FIFA World Cup typically have the greatest number of viewers for a single event: the World Cup Final. The championship match in 2010 between Spain and the Netherlands had an audience of 909 million people.

The media over the past several decades has developed a symbiotic relationship with megasports events. The integration of sports and the media within countries has been a development common to the commercial sports industry in most nations. Sports sell newspapers, beer, trucks, remedies for sexual dysfunction, and television sets. That growing intimacy between commercial sports and the media, a century in the making, arguably has to some extent muted media coverage of protests and other means through which hosting is criticized. If the media can benefit economically from hosting a megaevent, should it surprise anyone that the media is less willing and able to report objectively about the economic efficacy of doing so? There are those instances, however, where civil unrest as a consequence of hosting is sufficiently newsworthy to warrant media coverage—witness Brazilian unrest regarding their hosting the World Cup in 2014 and the upcoming Summer Olympic Games in 2016—but by and large, public criticism of hosting has either been underreported if not all together ignored by the media.

The corporate model and its emphasis on broadcast have been responsible for rewriting the *Olympic Charter* in several important ways as well. One of the more noteworthy was the 1986 revision of the *Charter* that allowed professional athletes to participate. This action, in part, was motivated by the desire to reinvigorate the US broadcast market, which had been flagging. Passing the torch from government to corporation sponsors as the primary means for funding megaevents has irrevocably changed them. Emerging economies could potentially benefit in numerous ways through their leaders rubbing elbows with sports celebrities as well as forging a more intimate relationship with corporate sponsors, which could generate greater foreign investment among other economic benefits.

Television has made event location less meaningful than in the time when live spectators drove revenues. The goal for the modern Games and their corporate sponsors is to reach as many viewers as possible. Megaevent sites are no longer confined to the developed, Western world. BRICs nations constitute the vanguard of emerging economies, and with their huge markets (BRICs had a population of 2.78 billion and accounted for 15% of global GDP in 2009), they are increasingly demanding equal access to center stage globally, social power, and economic opportunity. BRICs understands the symbolic importance of hosting megasports events, and have or will host the last three World Cups that have been awarded, two of the three Summer Olympic Games between 2008 and 2016, and the 2014 Winter Olympic Games. The IOC and FIFA interests and those of BRICs nations have neatly dovetailed. BRICs nations use hallmark sports events to achieve non-sports goals such as nation branding and social development; the IOC and FIFA want to bring their brands to the most populous countries in the world.

A final reason for hosting may well have something to do with the probability of a host country performing well on the global stage during the event. If hosting has proved too tantalizing for counties to resist for broadly defined marketing reasons, a virtuoso performance during the World Cup or the Olympic Games compounds the commercial promise. Twenty World Cups have been held since 1930, and the host country has won five times and placed second twice. A success rate of 25–35% makes hosting far more enticing.

It is fair to say that hosting a megasports event is driven to a significant degree by the promise of an economic windfall. While some groups in a society clearly will benefit more than others, a disproportionate sharing of benefits can be made more tolerable if it can be demonstrated that a city or country can be made better off overall through hosting, even if some constituencies are harmed by the event. And, of course, there is always the possibility, however remote, that an expansion of an economy can make everyone better off; "a rising tide raises all boats." The next section in this cahpter will review the literature with regard to the net benefits of hosting as promulgated by those who lead the charge to host.

13.3 REVIEW OF THE LITERATURE REGARDING HOSTING

Economists assume that economic actors are rational. Rationality implies that an action will be undertaken only if the economic benefits exceed the economic costs. Hosting a megasports event is rational if the benefits from so doing exceed the costs incurred where costs include both explicit and opportunity (implicit) costs. The litmus test for using public funds for hosting is not simply a positive accounting return from the event, but a positive economic return. Stated somewhat differently, the event must demonstrably provide the highest return from all the possible uses of public funds. Controversy about hosting has intensified arguably because of the seeming growing scarcity of public funds, and the need to ensure that those funds are put to the best possible use. A second fundamental public finance issue that looms large in the debate over using public funds to host hallmark events has to do with whether those who benefit from hosting assume costs in proportion to the benefits derived. Thomas Piketty's book *Capital in the Twenty-First Century* has brought into sharper focus the growing skewness in the distribution of wealth and income throughout the world. This growing inequality has heightened skepticism regarding projects that require significant public funding without substantial demonstrable benefits for the taxpaying public.

The literature on the subject of the efficacy of hosting megasports events historically has focused more on the issue of the rationality of hosting. That emphasis may have shifted somewhat, since emerging economies have exhibited a greater desire to host. It would appear to be the case that the prudent use of public funds is more imperative in emerging economies than in industrialized nations, since basic needs are less frequently met in the developing world. It is safe to say, however, that if there were no economic return from hosting, an inequitable distribution of benefits and costs would seem a virtual certainty. It is fair to say, furthermore, that much of the evolving debate about an economic return greater than zero has produced some creative and suspect representations of benefits while neglecting or underrepresenting important costs. All of these issues constitute the gist of scholarly criticism regarding the prudence of hosting.

Rather than reciting all the major scholarly research that has failed to find positive economic returns from hosting, it can simply be stated that scholars seem to be close to unanimous in their view that the benefits from hosting generally do not appear substantial enough (or that the costs are too great) to ensure an economic return. That view is based, to some extent at least, on the notion that whatever infrastructure that is constructed, other than sports facilities, is constructed to accommodate a hallmark event which could otherwise have been created without the huge and wasteful spending that constitutes the sports infrastructure specifically needed for the event. It would take benefits unique to a megaevent to argue for hosting on economic grounds.

A review of the literature has identified an article authored by economists that makes such a claim, albeit with some noteworthy caveats. Two authors proposed an outcome from hosting that, if true, would make hosting, or seeking to host, a seemingly rational act (Rose and Spiegel 2011). Rose and Spiegel found that hosting correlated with a 30% permanent increase in exports. If the Olympics or World Cup *caused* an increase in exports of that magnitude, it could be argued that any country with even a modestly sized export sector would be foolish not to host. Two important caveats have to be noted and were identified by Rose and Spiegel. First, hosting does not *cause* the increase in exports to any appreciable degree; the Olympics and World Cup rather signal the growing economic openness of the host nation. Second, "competing to host" is a signal sufficiently strong to induce the same outcome, as it relates to an expansion of the country's export sector. Would-be hosts, or applicant cities, experience the same or similar economic results without all the expenses and risks involved in hosting. This would appear to indicate that it is not hosting that matters, but a willingness to pursue a more liberal trade agenda that accounts for an increase in exports and an expansion of an economy. Indeed, further research on the topic by Maennig and Richter (2012) finds that when one compares bidding nations to otherwise similar non-bidding countries through an appropriate matching methodology, the supposed "Olympic Effect" disappears.

Other possible motivations for hosting revealed include instilling a sense of national pride or encouraging a nation to "feel good" about itself. A feel-good effect correlates with reduced crime rates and increased levels of physical activity that, in turn, lead to improved national health, according to some analysts. Health and happiness are difficult to measure, and there is the danger that values for qualitative impacts could be "measured" to ensure that hosting qualifies as a rational act.

It is noteworthy, once again, that the BRICs nations represent those emerging economies most inclined to host. There does appear to be agreement within this group of nations regarding a strategy for assuming a stronger voice in global affairs. Hosting a megaevent appears to be an important component of that strategy, as noted previously. The globe appears to be increasingly organized along regional lines, and it may well be that hosting a sports megaevent articulates a supranational or regional identity. It would be inaccurate, however, to think of BRICs as a single entity. Each of the four countries faces problems unique to them, and confronting their individual problems very likely trumps the pursuit of shared interests. Shared regional interests, however, do serve as a unifying force and have provided greater leverage in confronting the rest of the world. South Africa's 2010 World Cup was often referred to as the African World Cup when African leaders gathered prior to the event to promote and plan it.

13.4 ECONOMIC EXPECTATIONS AND OUTCOMES FROM HOSTING FOR EMERGING ECONOMIES

This section focuses on a comparison of economic outcomes expected from hosting to actual outcomes. The specific emerging-economy experiences analyzed are for the World Cup hosted by South Africa in 2010, the Commonwealth Games hosted by India in 2010, and the World Cup hosted by Brazil in 2014. South Africa is included in a group of countries referred to as the "next 11"—the eleven nations that are thought to be the most important emerging economies following the four BRICs countries. This three-country sample provides a good representation, therefore, of how hosting expectations compares with actual outcomes for emerging economies.

The most important driver for hosting arguably is the expected economic windfall which can be defined for either the short term or long term. The idea of nation branding has clear long-term commercial implications. Branding—the perception of what a country is and can do—involves the creation of a foundation for expanded commercial, political, and social interaction. A country that proves to be adept at organizing and performing all the tasks necessary to successfully host a sports megaevent, with its multitude of challenges, is more likely to be viewed as a trustworthy, competent partner in interactions going forward. Embellishing a nation's brand is clearly an important goal for a host city and/or nation; it is thought to be a means through which a significant economic legacy can be created.

Legacy benefits are difficult to assess. The short-term benefits from hosting—increased economic activity beginning with the construction phase in preparation for an event through the event itself—provides immediate feedback on the economic success of the event. If an economic windfall is to occur it should happen during the time building up to the event with a significant spike at economic ground zero, the time of the event. The focus in this portion of the article will be on employment, government finances, tourism, and the development of infrastructure vital to providing for an economic legacy. What do the experiences of South Africa, India, and Brazil provide in the way of feedback about the economic performance of sports megaevents? Table 13.2 provides statistics regarding key performance variables for the three sports megaevents hosted by South Africa, India, and Brazil for that which was expected and that which actually occurred.

The statistics in Table 13.2 indicate several noteworthy things. First, the actual costs of hosting are a significant multiple of the budget for hosting represented in the "Bid Book." The World Cup hosted by South Africa and the Commonwealth Games hosted

Table 13.2 Expected and actual outcomes for selected variables for megaevent hosting by South Africa, India, and Brazil

Statistic/country	South Africa: World Cup 2010, estimated value (actual value)	India (Delhi): Commonwealth Games (CWG) 2010, estimated value (actual value)	Brazil: World Cup 2014, estimated value(actual value)
Hosting costs	$343 million from Bid Book ($7.088 billion)	$265 million from Bid Book (approximately $4.1 billion)[a]	Approximately $13 billion (some estimates as high as $15 billion)[e]
Tourists attending the event	483,000 (between 220,000 to 310,000)	182,000 (75,606)	Approximately 600,000 (1 million)
Tourist overnight stays	14–18 days (10.3 days)		
Average tourist expenditure	$3,986 ($1,550)		
National financial accounting profit (loss)	(–$6.579 billion)	$145 million (–$3.7 billion). It was projected that CWG would add $4.94 billion to India's GDP.[b]	
Awarding entity profit	FIFA, $567 million		FIFA, $2.6 billion
Stadium expenditure amount	$1.544 billion	$1.02 billion	Bid Book cost = $1.1 billion ($3.6 billion, approximately 90% of which was public $)[c]
Stadium expenditure: % of total expenditures	37%	25%	27.7% ($3.6 billion/$13 billion)
Transportation expenditure	$1.716 billion	$1.983 billion	
Transportation expenditure as a % of overall expenditures	39%	48%	

(continued)

Table 13.2 Continued

Job creation	695,000 in 2009; 280,000 in 2010; and 174,000 in 2011[d]	It was projected that CWG would create 2.47 million "employment opportunities"[e]	3.63 million per one-year equivalent (25,383 net hires in June 2014)[f]

[a] Derived by taking the City of Delhi infrastructure expenditures other than those for sports facilities ($1.983 billion) and dividing that by the fraction of total expenditures to produce the Commonwealth Games (CG) represented by City of Delhi infrastructure expenditures (0.48). $1.983 billion/0.48 = 4.13 billion.

[b] The projected surplus was determined by subtracting the Bid Book cost of $265 million from the projected revenue of $410 million. The actual loss of $3.7 billion was determined by subtracting the actual cost of hosting of $4.1 billion from the actual net revenue of $40 million (revenue from CWG of $101.5 million minus the cost of generating that revenue of $61.5 million = $40 million in net revenue). The official position appeared to be that CWG would be "revenue neutral" or that it would generate a small surplus.

[c] FIFA (2007). *Brazil Bid: Inspection Report for the 2014 World Cup*, October 30, <http://www.fifa.com/mm/document/affederation/mission/62/24/78/inspectionreport_e_24841.pdf>.

Morpurgo, G. (2015). "Brazil and the World Cup's economic impact: A look back," *Perspectives: Student-Led Economics Journal*, 19 February, <http://kcleconomics.com/a-look-back-to-2014brazil-and-the-world-cups-economic-impact/>.

Associated Press (2015). "FIFA returns $100M to Brazil; World Cup cost $15 billion," *USA Today*, 20 January, <http://www.usatoday.com/story/sports/soccer/2015/01/20/fifa-returns-100m-to-brazil-world-cup-cost-15-billion/22050583/>.

[d] Identifying the number of jobs actually created is not possible because of the global recession that is popularly thought to have begun in the third quarter of 2008 with the implosion of global financial markets. South Africa appears to have lost approximately 1 million jobs due to the recession.

[e] Once again the onset of the recession of 2008 makes it virtually impossible to determine the number of jobs actually created. There was no post-CWG audit to determine this number, but all the evidence points to the fact that job opportunities were far below what had been projected.

[f] Mitra, A. (2014). "An Ethical Analysis of the 2014 FIFA World Cup in Brazil," *Seven Pillars Institute*, 8 September, <http://sevenpillarsinstitute.org/case-studies/ethical-analysis-of-the-2014-fifa-world-cup-brazil>.

Source: Konrad Adenauer Stiftung (2015). *Sustainable Mega-Events in Developing Countries*, <http://www.kas.de/wf/doc/kas_29583-1522-1-30.pdf?120124104515>.

by Delhi in 2010 resulted in actual costs that eclipsed the Bid-Book budget by 2,067 and 1,547% respectively. There was no Bid Book budget number identified for the World Cup in Brazil in 2014. Rather than specific numbers, the Bid Book provided the following information with regard to the cost of hosting the 2014 FIFA World Cup:

The bid LOC representatives were able to demonstrate that they had applied a sound methodology in preparing the preliminary budget that systematically addressed all of the requirements of the Hosting Agreement regarding the hosting and staging of the final competition of the 2014 FIFA World Cup™. The assumptions made in the preparation of the preliminary budget were well explained and

> documented and the level of supporting detail is sufficient to permit a detailed
> examination of the preliminary budget for the 2014 FIFA World Cup™ for all cost
> categories. (FIFA 2007)

The fact that the actual cost of hosting exceeded the Bid-Book cost by such a significant sum for the World Cup and South Africa and the Confederation Games in Delhi may be attributable to a perceived need to low-ball the cost estimates in bidding for an event and/or enormous cost overruns once the event is secured. Cost overruns may be the result of cost escalation clauses in construction contracts, legal challenges, unforeseen construction issues to include meeting environmental concerns, construction firms exercising monopoly power where it exists, and corruption.

Second, infrastructure costs relating to the construction of stadiums/arenas and training facilities for developing countries account for 25% or more of all costs of hosting. This percentage for emerging economies is likely to be considerably higher than it is for developed country hosts who already possess considerable stadium/arena infrastructure. For example, Los Angeles incurred relatively little in the way of infrastructure costs in hosting the 1984 Summer Olympic Games. Approximately 73% of the costs incurred for the Los Angeles Games were in fact administrative costs. Similarly, the United States spent just $5.3 million on stadium construction and refurbishment for the 1994 World Cup. This is a far different cost profile than what we see for emerging-country hosts (Zarnowski 2015). Stadium expenditures for the 2010 and 2014 World Cups in South Africa and Brazil totaled $2.1 *billion* and $3.6 billion, respectively. A misallocation of capital resources for stadiums will have long-term implications for growth and development.

Third, the number of additional visitors to South Africa and Delhi as a consequence of their events fell short of expectations. The number of additional tourists to visit South Africa in the June–July period was estimated to be 200,000, which was significantly below that which was expected, especially when compared to early claims following the announcement that South Africa had been selected to host the 2010 World Cup (South Africa's World Cup Warning to Brazil, 10 June 2014). Early indications are that incremental tourism in Brazil as a consequence of the World Cup exceeded expectations. That was the only case in which an outcome surprised in a positive way for all the data represented in Table 13.2. The evidence, however, with regard to the unexpected surprise as it relates to tourism in Brazil, was not consistently found. The Brazilian Airline Association reported a reduction in air traffic of 11–15% in June 2014 compared to June 2013 (Alves 2014). The reason for the decline in air travel apparently had to do with a significant reduction in the number of business people traveling within Brazil during the World Cup.

Job creation statistics are difficult to discern in the emerging country sample reviewed. The 2010 events job creation outcomes were clearly obscured by the 2008 global economic collapse due to the implosion of world financial markets. Based on the evidence that does exist, it appears that job creation that could be reasonably expected from an event based on the evidence from Brazil fell far below that which actually occurred. New hires in Brazil in June 2014 at the peak of World Cup activity amounted to only

25,383. Prorating the expected job creation outcome of 3.63 million implies that actual job creation was less than one tenth of that which was expected from the World Cup $(3.63/12 = 302,500; 302,500/25,583 = 11.82)$.

The important overall conclusion is that megasports events have not produced the economic outcomes that have motivated the emerging-country aggressive pursuit of them. The next section in this chapter will examine why actual outcomes have fallen short of that which is expected.

13.5 Reasons for Outcomes Falling Short of Expectations

This section of the chapter will identify and discuss why economic outcomes for sports megaevents have fallen short of expectations. The primary reasons are: (1) unreasonable expectations; (2) white-elephant stadiums; (3) monopoly rents appropriated by event owners; (4) poor event management; and (5) corruption. Each of these reasons will be discussed in the text that follows.

13.5.1 Unreasonable Expectations

The information recorded in Table 13.2 indicates that for the three-country sample of emerging economies hosting sports megaevents, the benefits are significantly exaggerated and the costs significantly underplayed. This reality for this sample of countries holds true for virtually all the countries, developing and emerging alike, that have hosted hallmark events (Matheson 2013). The reason for this economics chicanery very probably has to do with securing approval for using public funds to host in democracies. There is less of a need to do so in countries that are not democratic in practice. It should come as little surprise that among the original seven bidders for the 2022 Winter Olympics, all of the democratic nations dropped out of the race, citing cost concerns, leaving only Almaty, Kazakhstan, and Beijing, China—countries with little democratic tradition—as the only remaining potential hosts. Even in countries where the citizenry has little political voice, however, it is politically prudent to offer at least the pretense that megaevents can be catalysts for economic growth. Boosters would like the populace to believe that expenditures on megaevents should be viewed as investments and not as wasteful and ostentatious public consumption that benefit a few at the expense of the vast majority. Those who are asked to pay through the use of their taxes or diminished social services are tacitly asked to take pride in the very act of hosting and the knowledge that their country was capable of putting on such a grand spectacle.

Megaevent success can be measured through a comparison of what was promised relative to what was delivered. Perceived problems with the event are exacerbated (problems will always arise because megaevents by their very nature are socially disruptive) when outcomes from the event fail to match expectations. There are two ways to handle this problem: (1) improve outcomes, and/or (2) provide a more modest representation of that which can be expected. Management of expectations has apparently been excluded from consideration in selling megaevents to a public that is apparently becoming increasingly skeptical about their efficacy. A chief culprit in the realm of poorly managed expectations is the commissioned prospective economic-impact study for the event. The reality is that a model that enables a good understanding of what an event will do for a large, diverse urban economy has not yet been created. Input–output models, no matter how sophisticated, cannot by their nature account for the leakages and substantial substitution effects that ensue when an exogenous shock occurs. The sense that technical competence ensures correct outcomes very probably overwhelms the common sense of official decision makers, or they want to believe the "authoritative" findings of commissioned researchers for other reasons. It is arguably a better strategy to use *ex post* findings or audits of previous similar megaevents to forecast the probable impact of an event than to allow expectations to be formed by prospective booster studies. Properly developed and managed expectations are key to the perception of success of a megaevent.

Failure to manage expectations has both short-term and long-term consequences that may be serious. The protestations in the streets of Brazilian cities were prompted by the perception that the staging of the 2014 World Cup and the 2016 Summer Olympic exemplified misplaced priorities and catered to the interests of a financially privileged minority. These perceptions not only threatened the immediate political construct, but further frayed the social fabric in the long term through expanding the divide among social classes. Such costs can be huge, and difficult to undo. Any measure of the return-risk profile for megaevents should account for the increasing tension among classes that can be induced through hosting a megaevent, as opposed to using those substantial funds to achieve other social objectives.

13.5.2 White-Elephant Stadiums

The demands placed on applicant cities or nations for playing facilities to accommodate a sports megaevent most vividly illustrate the excesses of these social spectacles. The term "white elephant" in conjunction with stadiums and arenas has become a cliché in many languages. It is not just the cost of building the facilities that imposes a financial burden, but their maintenance can compromise budgets for the long term. Operation and maintenance (O&M) costs for stadiums run into millions of dollars annually once the event ends, and if the stadiums lie fallow or are underutilized, these costs represent a clear-cut and enduring burden. Greece and the City of Athens, which hosted the 2004 Summer Olympic Games, have incurred costs "estimated at $784 million simply to maintain this ghost town of Olympian extravagance" (Perryman 2012). Careful and creative thought needs to be devoted to reusing all components of infrastructure, and the harsh reality in the world of megasports events is the lack of synergy between venues for the games and other sectors of the host economy.

The construction of venues follows event-organizer mandates. International organizations that award megasports events, such as the IOC and FIFA, require venue construction to certain specifications that many would consider excessive. These excesses persist because they have become a feature, a budgetary line-item, in the bidding process and event implementation and accommodation. *The Economist* commented:

> The Olympic movement, a juggernaut controlled by an unaccountable sporting elite, is less flexible. The danger signs are in place, with newspapers reporting on the five-star hotel rooms reserved for foreign Olympic bigwigs and the miles of special traffic lanes that will be reserved for Olympic VIPs. Perhaps sporting success will neutralize public resentment, and the country will feel only pride at hosting a splendid games, fueling new confidence in Britain's future. But, for now, the Olympic debate revolves around material costs and benefits rather than glory. If you want certain cheer, bet on a celebration of Britain's past. (Bagehot 2011)

The need to impress the IOC and FIFA to win the increasingly intense competition to host is an accepted part of the process. As bidding costs mount, bribes, material excess, and a willingness to pay excessively to host, are more likely to occur. Salt Lake City provided a cautionary tale with regard to the lengths that cities are willing to go to secure an event. The bid-rigging scandal associated with the 2002 Salt Lake City Winter Games stained the previously squeaky-clean reputation of the area.

Facility construction extravagance is but one aspect of the excesses promoted by the current arrangements. The IOC Charter does not appear to be overly demanding as it relates to facilities, as the following provision indicates:

> … to create, where needed, simple, functional and economical sports facilities in cooperation with national or international bodies. (International Olympic Committee 2013)

In practice, simple and economical structures are not the norm in stadium construction for megaevents. "Where needed" does not comport with actual construction practice. Beijing's Bird Nest cost $478 million, and London's Wembley Stadium carries a 2014 price tag of £889 million ($1,475 billion in 2014 dollars). The elaborate structures for the opening ceremonies and some events could be attributable to an extreme example of branding or an edifice complex on the part of the host city or nation; but the other major culprit appears to be those entities that award the events. The IOC and FIFA demands clearly contribute to the ever-escalating stadium costs. The stadiums come at the expense of other social investments such as education, sanitation, and public transportations. Brazilians understood the nature of the trade-offs, and ordinary Brazilians were particularly irked by the special accommodations that were made for FIFA officials in moving them around their traffic-challenged cities. Brazilians protesting the recent 9% price increase in public transportation could be heard shouting "give us FIFA transportation."

FIFA has articulated eleven main points in their stadium manual for construction. FIFA requires host countries to have at least eight modern stadiums capable of seating at least 40,000 spectators, and one stadium with a capacity of 80,000 for the opening and final games. Some of the mandates are spectator-and environment-friendly; others clearly emphasize the branding and marketing of the event itself consonant with FIFA's economic interests presently and in the future ("Know the FIFA Requirements" 2009).

The upshot is that modifications based on FIFA and IOC requirements increase costs substantially. The opening match for the 2014 World Cup in Brazil required modifications on the Itaquerao Stadium original project from R$335 million ($137 million in 2014 dollars) to R$1.07 billion ($436 million in 2014 dollars) to accommodate FIFA's requirements. It has been reported that the stadium in Manaus in the Amazon which cost $319 million to build may well not be used again for a highly attended event. Brazilian officials are looking for a public–private partnership that will support the stadium, but the local soccer clubs hold no such promise in that they draw no more than 1,000 fans for a game. Manaus may well have a stadium shelf-life of only four games, all for the World Cup. Despite maintenance costs estimated at $250,000 per month, the stadium is currently used for birthday parties and as a bus depot (Ormiston 2014).

Other examples of excessive and wasteful stadium infrastructure mandated expenditures abound. South Africa's hosting of the 2010 World Cup followed an all too familiar pattern. The South African Premier Soccer League, ABSA Premiership, averages 7,500 fans per match, and has no need for stadiums of the size mandated by FIFA. The five new stadiums constructed for the World Cup cost approximately $1 billion. Two of the new stadiums built—Peter Mokaba and Mbombela—were built at a cost of $150 million and $140 million respectively. They are utilized on occasion for soccer and rugby matches. Mbombela Stadium, for example, hosted twelve soccer matches in 2013 with an average attendance of 7,606, representing on average 16.5% of stadium capacity. Mokaba stadium does not list any full-time or even part-time tenant (Fieno 2014).

The Helliniko Olympic Complex in Athens was supposed to be converted into the largest metropolitan park in Europe following the 2004 Summer Olympic Games. Today the complex is for all intents and purposes deserted (Sanburn 2012).

The Bird's Nest and Water Cube in Beijing—the iconic structures of the 2008 Beijing Summer Olympic Games—have failed to find regular continued use as sports competition venues (Lim 2012). The Bird's Nest has rarely hosted large events since the Olympics, and portions of the stadium have been converted to apartments. The Water Cube was opened for public swimming in 2009, making it the world's most expensive lap pool. It subsequently underwent significant renovations and reopened as a large, indoor water park. While this is a fine long-term use for an otherwise underutilized facility, it is also an extraordinarily expensive way to build a water park (Matheson 2013).

The Sydney Olympic Park was declared a white elephant shortly after the 2000 Games ended. In fact, the net cost of the 2000 Summer Games (costs in excess of benefits) has been estimated at $1.5 billion (*The Independent* 2008).

Risk appears inescapable for an event host or potential host, but it has not seemingly discouraged some applicant cities from aggressively pursuing megaevents. In fact, in the best gambling tradition, the question appears to be: do you bet a little or a lot? The British Culture Secretary, Jeremy Hunt, in reflecting on the Summer Olympic Games in London succinctly articulated the conundrum:

> You can take two attitudes to the Olympics. You can say, these are times of auster-ity, and therefore we should pare them down as much as possible. Or you can say, because these are times of austerity, we need to do everything we possibly can to har-ness the opportunity. (Clarke 2012)

Emerging economies simply cannot afford to devote a significant portion of their infra-structure budgets to the construction or renovation of underutilized capital that fails to have much of a synergistic relationship with other sectors of a growing economy. The social costs associated with stadium and arena construction and underutilization rep-resent a long-term problem in that they must be maintained. It is too often the case, fur-thermore, that sports stadiums are built in places for which the opportunity cost of the land is high. Increasingly, those who defend public funding for megaevents stress that the benefits from hosting occur over the long term. The positive legacy of a hallmark event, which arguably has evolved into the most important reason for hosting, could be muted, if not altogether negated, by the adverse effects on an economy induced by funding and building sports facilities, which crowd out investment in other forms of infrastructure that can provide an economic legacy. Those who advocate public fund-ing of hallmark events often opine that infrastructure investments that do provide an economic legacy would not occur as rapidly or at all if there were not an event around which diverse political groups could coalesce. Sports facilities infrastructure, nonethe-less, is a very high price to pay for an acceleration of socially necessary infrastructure that responsible, effective government in any event should be providing.

None of this is to deny the progress that some host cities have made. Brazil, for exam-ple, has made great strides in reducing poverty and expanding the middle class since 2005. There is no disputing the fact that spending on education, health, and transporta-tion in Brazil has dwarfed spending on stadiums, but the success of progressive legisla-tion in Brazil has not been the result of the World Cup (Flannery 2014). South Africa, India, and Brazil all provided something of an economic legacy through spending on infrastructure other than sports facilities in accommodating an event. The question is: could these emerging host nations have improved the lives of their citizens appre-ciably more without the egregiously wasteful spending on sports infrastructure that accompanies megasports events?

13.5.3 Monopoly Rents Appropriated by Awarding Organizations

Sports facilities do not represent the only significant misappropriation of funds associ-ated with sports megaevents. Those who award events, the monopolistic suppliers, have been criticized extensively for appropriating a disproportionate share of the revenues that the event generates. The information in Table 13.2 indicates that FIFA's profit from the 2010 World Cup in South Africa was $567 million, while a more recent figure provided by FIFA shows $631 million in profit on revenue of $3.65 billion (*Jamaica Observer* 2011). FIFA reported revenue for the 2014 World Cup of $4.8 billion, with profit equal to $2.6 billion (Manfred 2015). FIFA's records, as they relates to expenditures, indicated that they contributed "$453 million to the local organizing committee between 2011 and 2014, and, gave Brazil a $100 million 'legacy' payment after the tournament" (Manfred 2015). To provide some context, the profit that FIFA made is equal to approximately 72% of Brazil's stadium expenditures.

The risk–reward profile for FIFA is far different for that of the host nation. FIFA and the IOC require what amounts to a blank check to ensure that all costs from an event are covered to include the cost overruns that always accompany any sports megaevent. FIFA and its subsidiaries, to include any third-party organizations hired by or associated with FIFA to assist in producing the World Cup in Brazil, were granted tax-exempt status (Mitra 2014). FIFA assumes no risk in that its infrastructure is provided, and it appropriates all the revenue from tickets sold to the event. That is not the typical risk–reward profile for a business. It is certainly not that which applies to the nation hosting the World Cup, which assumes the risk of significant capital investment with a disproportionately small share of the immediate rewards.

13.5.4 Poor Management

One of the most important aspects of "nation branding" as it relates to hosting a megaevent is the display of managerial and organizational prowess necessary to produce spectacles of the size and scope of a World Cup, Commonwealth Games, or Olympic Games. The danger is that the message could be negative if the host displays incompetence. A host nation occupies center stage on the globe for a period of time leading up to the event, during the event, and following the event. The spotlight has become more intense over time with the growing sophistication and popularity of the Internet and social media. Any foul-up will be magnified, and the host country's brand tarnished. Display before play, and woe betide the country that does not organize and manage the event well.

Before the 2010 World Cup, the fear that South Africa's reputation for certain kinds of crime would further harm South Africa's reputation and undermine their attempts to advance tourism through hosting the World Cup. The fact that South Africa hired more than 40,000 additional police to ensure that World Cup spectators would be secure was probably critical for negating that fear and ensuring an expansion of the tourist industry following the event. It has been reported, however, that South Africa spent an estimated $13,000 for every additional visitor for the 2010 World Cup (Egan 2014). This sum will diminish, of course, if the favorable impression that South Africa made on first-time visitors to the World Cup translates into additional tourists. That remains to be seen.

Sochi, Russia, Brazil, and Qatar, most recently, arguably have not always fared well under the harsh glare of media lights. The extraordinary cost of the Sochi Winter Olympic Games (more than $50 billion), deficient hotels, and threats of terrorism appeared daily and cast Sochi and Russia in an unfavorable light. Brazil's vocal protestors, stadium disasters, the slow pace of construction, and the changing of government leadership in managing the many event-related crises in Brazil, may have damaged the Brazilian brand. Brazil's image had to suffer when IOC Vice President John Coates stated that Rio's preparations for the 2016 Summer Olympics Games are "the worst I have experienced" (Barnes 2014). An exposé regarding the toxic nature of the water in which certain Olympic sports will be held in Rio's environs has had an adverse impact on Brazil's image (*NPR* 2015). The well-publicized human rights abuses of guest workers in Qatar, coupled with the unprecedented costs of stadium construction for the 2022 World Cup there, may have done extraordinary harm to the "Qatar brand." The point is that branding through an event cuts both ways. The risk is great that hosting can tarnish a country's image if the event is poorly managed, as well as good organization and management enhancing it.

13.5.5 Corruption

The structure of the megasports events market provides ample opportunity for corruption. First, the awarding entities are the sole providers of a product: the event. Second, the size of the event necessitates public subsidies, and those who oversee spending are less attentive to the use of third-party funds. Third, the financial benefits of hosting an event are concentrated in the hands of a few industries; construction companies, banks, and the hospitality sector generally benefit. If these sectors are dominated by a few large firms, then the bidding process may well involve kickbacks, political contributions, and bribery to secure contracts. These forces allegedly have been manifest in Brazil in conjunction with preparations for the 2014 World Cup and the 2016 Summer Olympic Games. *The Economist* recently reported:

> However, in September a police investigation found that some of this growth was thanks to padded contracts that at least six of Brazil's biggest construction firms, with combined domestic revenues of 19 billion reals ($8.8 billion) in 2013, had for years been signing with Petrobas, the state-controlled oil giant in exchange for kickbacks to politicians. Around thirty construction executives are now awaiting trial on charges of corruption or money laundering, including the boss of UTC Engenhana, Brazil's seventh-biggest builder. (*The Economist* 2015)

Corruption has recently been alleged involving FIFA officials. Fourteen people, including nine FIFA and five corporate executives, were indicted on 27 May 2015, and face racketeering, conspiracy, and corruption charges in the United States. The forty-seven-count indictment alleges that those indicted engaged in illegal activities to enrich themselves over twenty-four years. The length of time over which illegal activity has been alleged suggests that corruption is systemic in the sports megaevent industry and includes developed as well as emerging nations.

13.6 CONCLUSIONS

The purpose of this chapter was to analyze the motivations for emerging nations to bid for sports megaevents. It first identified what the drivers were, and why. It also analyzed those motivations in an attempt to assess whether the drivers made sense in light of the outcomes versus the expectations regarding the benefits from hosting. The outcomes versus expectations suggest that it does not make sense for emerging nations to host hallmark sports spectacles if quantifiable benefits are compared to costs. What the outcomes do suggest is that emerging-nation hosting is most probably a signal that a developing country communicates to the rest of the world that it perceives itself as ascending, and possesses economic might that merits a larger voice in global affairs. Soft diplomacy appears to be a particular strategy of the BRICs nations, as most of the sports megaevents that have been hosted by emerging nations are members of that group, or what is referred to as the "next 11." The intensity of the message would appear to vary across the emerging nations, reflecting both their real and perceived economic and political strength.

It is clear that hosting has become an increasingly expensive gambit, and one with the potential to harm the economy of an emerging nation. There are clearly some things that need to be done to ensure that countries are not victimized through hosting. The most obvious thing is the mitigation of the power of the monopoly producers—FIFA and IOC in particular; they have to be regulated at the very least. Expensive stadiums, corruption, and the inequitable arrangement with regard to revenue sharing is a direct consequence of the exercise of monopoly power. Applicant cities and nations need to recognize their shared interests and join together to ensure that the sports megaevents that the world appears to want are provided, adhering to sound economic principles and practice. Most countries simply cannot afford the high risk and low returns that characterize hallmark events currently.

It is also important to use what is available in the way of information regarding economic outcomes and expectations to provide a realistic perception about how an event will affect a host nation's political economy. The "authoritative studies" commissioned and disseminated by those who stand to gain from an event have proved harmful in that they systematically raise expectations beyond that which is reasonable. Unmet expectations can undermine the political and social fabric and cause long-term harm to a host nation. As it currently stands, the entire structure of the sports megaevent market shouts "potential host beware." This needs to be changed to ensure that hosting provides benefits at least equal to costs, and that the benefits are shared in a way that includes ordinary citizens who fund the event through their tax dollars or a reduction in social services. In the current arrangement, gold is more scarce for hosts than it is for the athletes who actually compete.

Notes

1. There are, according to the latest reports, 1.13 million unemployed people in Brazil out of a workforce of 23.29 million. See <http://www.tradingeconomics.com/brazil/unemployment-rate>. Creating 120,000 new jobs would reduce the unemployed persons number by 10.62 %.
2. Federal revenue sharing in the United States, for example, was significantly reduced in 1987, and that created a financial crisis in many cities across the United States. See <http://www.nytimes.com/1987/01/31/us/end-of-federal-revenue-sharing-creating-financial-crises-in-many-cities.html?src=pm&pagewanted=2>.
3. Television rights generated a mere 4% of the revenues generated by the Games, but the die had been cast. It is also noteworthy that the 1956 Games were boycotted by newsreel and television networks across the world over the issue of free coverage. See Barney et al. (2004) for detailed information on these important developments.

References

Alves, L. (2014). "World Cup has not been good for Brazil Airlines," *Rio Times*, 1 July, <http://riotimesonline.com/brazil-news/rio-business/world-cup-has-not-been-good-for-brazil-airlines/>.

Associated Press. (2015). "FIFA returns $100m to Brazil; World Cup cost $15 billion," *USA Today*, 20 January, <http://www.usatoday.com/story/sports/soccer/2015/01/20/fifa-returns-100m-to-brazil-world-cup-cost-15-billion/22050583/>.

Bagehot [columnist]. (2011). "Olympic Britain v. Royal Britain," *The Economist*, 31 December, <http://www.economist.com/node/21542196>.

Barnes, T. (2014). "Preparations for Rio Olympics 'the Worst,' committee official says," *The New York Times*, 29 April, <http://nyti.ms/1hbV1Ci>.

Barney, R. K., Wenn, S. R., and Martyn, S. G. (2004). *Selling the Five Rings*. Salt Lake City: University of Utah Press.

Clarke, J. (2012). "How much will the London Olympics cost? Too much," *Forbes*, 28 March, <http://www.forbes.com/sites/johnclarke/2012/03/28/how-much-will-the-london-olympics-cost-too-much/>.

Economist, The. (2015). "Brazilian construction firms: Knock 'em down, build 'em up: Government cuts and a bribery scandal will prompt a shake-out in the industry," 23 May, <http://www.economist.com/sections/business-finance>.

Egan, M. (2014). "South Africa's World Cup warning to Brazil," *CNN Money*, 10 June, <http://money.cnn.com/2014/06/09/investing/world-cup-south-africa-brazil>.

Ernst & Young Terco. (2011). *Sustainable Brazil: Social and Economic Impacts of the 2014 World Cup*, <http://www.dohagoals.com/lang/content_en/downloads/copa_2014.pdf>.

Fieno, J. V. (2014). "Four years on, South Africa's World Cup has failed to live up to promises," *World SoccerTalk*, 12 June, <http://worldsoccertalk.com/2014/06/12/south-africa-four-years-later/>.

FIFA. (2007). *Brazil Bid: Inspection Report for the 2014 World Cup*, 30 October <http://www.fifa.com/mm/document/affederation/mission/62/24/78/inspectionreport_e_24841.pdf>.

FIFA World Cup & Olympic Games host nations. (2015). *WorldFactsInc*, <https://sites.google.com/site/worldfactsinc/FIFA-World-Cup--Olympic-Games-Host-Nations>.

Flannery, N. P. (2014). "World Cup economics: Why Brazil's bashers have got it wrong," *Forbes*, 23 June, <http://www.forbes.com/sites/nathanielparishflannery/2014/06/23/world-cup-economics-why-brazils-bashers-have-got-it-wrong/>.

Independent, The. (2008). "After the party: What happens when the Olympics leave town," 19 August, <http://www.independent.co.uk/sport/olympics/after-the-party-what-happens-when-the-olympics-leave-town-901629.html>.

International Olympic Committee (2013). *Olympic Charter*, 9 September, Bye-Law to Rule 5,7: 20.

Jamaica Observer. (2011). "FIFA reports $631-m profit on 2010 World Cup," 5 March, <http://www.jamaicaobserver.com/sport/FIFA-reports-631-m-profit-on-2010-World-Cup_8463347>.

Konrad Adenauer Stiftung. (2015). *Sustainable Mega-Events in Developing Countries.* <http://www.kas.de/wf/doc/kas_29583-1522-1-30.pdf?120124104515>.

Know the FIFA requirements for World Cup stadiums. (2009). *Portal 2014*, 9 September, <http://www.portal2014.org.br/noticias/2350/KNOW+THE+FIFA+REQUIREMENTS+FOR+WORLD+CUP+STADIUMS.html>.

Lim, L. (2012). "China's post-Olympic woe: Hot to fill an empty nest," *NPR*, 10 July, <http://www.npr.org/2012/07/10/156368611/chinas-post-olympic-woe-how-to-fill-an-empty-nest>.

London Olympics 2012 ratings: Most watched event in TV history. (2012). *The Huffington Post*, 13 August, <http://www.huffingtonpost.com/2012/08/13/london-olympics-2012-ratings-most-watched-ever_n_1774032.html>.

Los Angeles Olympic Organizing Committee. (1984). "Official report of the Games of the XXIIIrd Olympiad Los Angeles, 1984," <http://library.la84.org/6oic/OfficialReports/1984/1984v1pt3.pdf>.

Lundy, M. (2013). "Brazilians have reason to protest the cost of the Olympics and World Cup." *Globe and Mail*, 24 June, <http://www.theglobeandmail.com/globe-debate/brazilians-have-reason-to-protest-the-cost-of-olympics-and-world-cup/article12742114/>.

Maennig, W. and Richter, F. (2012). "Exports and Olympic Games: Is there a signal effect?" *Journal of Sports Economics*, 13(6): 635–41.

Manfred, T. (2015). "FIFA made an insane amount of money off of Brazil's $15 billion World Cup," *Business Insider: Sports*, 20 March, <http://www.businessinsider.com/fifa-brazil-world-cup-revenue-2015-3>.

Matheson, V. (2013). "Assessing the infrastructure impact of mega-events in emerging economies," in G. K. Ingram and K. L. Brandt (eds.), *Infrastructure and Land Policies*. Cambridge, MA: Lincoln Land Institute, pp. 215–32.

Mitra, A. (2014). "An ethical analysis of the 2014 FIFA World Cup in Brazil," *Seven Pillars Institute*, 8 September, <http://sevenpillarsinstitute.org/case-studies/ethical-analysis-of-tje-2014-fifa-world-cup-brazil>.

Morpurgo, G. (2015). "Brazil and the World Cup's economic impact: A look back," *Perspectives: Student-Led Economics Journal*, 19 February, <http://kcleconomics.com/a-look-back-to-2014brazil-and-the-world-cups-economic-impact/>.

NPR. (2015). "AP study finds viruses linked to raw sewage in Rio de Janeiro Olympics waters," 10 July, <http://www.npr.org/2015/07/30/427839942/ap-study-finds-viruses-linked-to-raw-sewage-in-rio-de-janeiro-olympic-waters>.

Ormiston, S. (2014). "In Amazon's Manaus, Brazil's dreamiest World Cup adventure," *CBS News: World*, 9 June, <http://www.cbc.ca/news/world/in-amazon-s-manaus-brazil-s-dreamiest-world-cup-adventure-1.2669024>.

Perryman, M. (2012). "Do the Olympics boost the economy? Studies show the impact is likely negative," *Daily Beast*, 30 July, <http://www.thedailybeast.com/articles/2012/07/30/do-the-olympics-boost-the-economy-studies-show-the-impact-is-likely-negative.html#url=/articles/2012/07/30/do-the-olympics-boost-the-economy-studies-show-the-impact-is-likely-negative.html>.

Piketty, T. (2014). *Capital in the Twenty-First Century*, transl. A. Goldhammer. Cambridge, MA: Belknap Press.

Rose, A. K. and Spiegel, M. M. (2011). "The Olympic effect," *The Economic Journal*, 1212(553): 652–77.

Sanburn, J. (2012). "Was it worth it? Debt-ridden Greeks question the cost of the 2004 Olympics," *Time*, 9 July, <http://olympics.time.com/2012/07/09/amid-economic-turmoil-some-greeks-look-back-at-2004-olympics-as-losing-proposition/>.

The Global Growth of Tourism. (2014). Coolgeography.co.uk, <http://www.coolgeography.co.uk/GCSE/AQA/Tourism/Tourism growth/Tourism Growth.htm#arrivals>.

Trading Economics. (2014). "Brazil unemployment rate," <http://www.tradingeconomics.com/brazil/unemployment-rate>.

Urban Areas: Global Overview. (2002). In *Global Environment Outlook 3: Past, Present and Future Perspectives*, <http://www.grida.no/geo/geo3/english/pdfs/chapter2-8_urban.pdf>.

Varrel, A. and Kennedy, L. (2011). "Mega-events and megaprojects." *Chance 2 Sustain: Policy Brief 3*, June, <http://www.chance2sustain.eu/fileadmin/Website/Dokumente/Dokumente/Publications/Chance2Sustain_-_Policy_Brief_No3___Mega-Events_and_Megaprojects_-_WP2.pdf>.

United Nations. (2014). "World urbanization prospects," <http://esa.un.org/unpd/wup/Highlights/WUP2014-Highlights.pdf>.

World Bank. (2014). "Countries: Brazil, overview," <http://www.worldbank.org/en/country/brazil/overview>.

Zarnowski, C. F. (2015). "A look at Olympic costs," <http://library.la84.org/SportsLibrary/JOH/JOHv1n1/JOHv1n1f.pdf>.

PART III

CURES

CHAPTER 14

INNOVATION AND FLEXIBILITY IN MEGAPROJECTS

A New Delivery Model

ANDREW DAVIES, MARK DODGSON, AND DAVID M. GANN

14.1 INTRODUCTION

MEGAPROJECTS are the delivery model used to produce large-scale, complex, and one-off capital investments in a variety of public and private sectors such as infrastructure, defense, mining, manufacturing plants, healthcare, big science, air and space exploration, and major sporting events. With a total capital cost of $1 billion or more, megaprojects are extremely risky ventures, notoriously difficult to manage, and often fail to achieve their original objectives (Flyvbjerg, Bruzelius, and Rothengatter 2003; Merrow 2011). Cost overruns, time slippages, and poor operational outcomes are common. According to one estimate, nine out of ten megaprojects are over budget, and overruns of more than 50% are not uncommon (Flyvbjerg 2014: 9). For example, the construction of the Channel Tunnel—the underwater rail tunnel connecting the United Kingdom and France—was 80% over budget.

As well as coping with their scale and complexity, dealing with uncertainty is a pressing and persistent challenge in megaproject management. Because megaprojects—such as airports, high-speed rail, or the Olympics—take many years to plan and deliver, it is difficult to know whether the eventual outcome will achieve goals that will have been established years or even decades earlier. Efforts are made to identify risks and uncertainties at the outset, but it is not possible to foresee all the eventualities and changes in technologies, markets, finance, and other conditions that may occur while the project is underway. Take, for example, the Terminal 5 project at London's Heathrow airport.

It went through the longest planning inquiry in UK planning history, and just as the design was being finalized, something completely unexpected happened: a terrorist attack on the Twin Towers in New York on 11 September 2001. The project received government approval in November 2001, but had to be redesigned to address new and more stringent airport security requirements.

Previous research emphasizes that project sponsors and clients systematically underestimate the costs and overestimate the benefits during the front-end development of a megaproject (Morris and Hough 1987; Miller and Lessard 2000; Flyvbjerg et al. 2003; Williams and Samset 2010; Merrow 2011; Flyvbjerg 2014; Edkins, Geraldi, Morris, and Smith 2013). This focus on front-end planning and optimistic behaviour identifies some of the important reasons why megaprojects have performed so badly, but megaprojects also fail because the model used to deliver them is unable to innovate and adapt plans to changing and unexpected conditions. Under the delivery model most commonly used, clients assume they can identify all the uncertainties that might impact the project at the outset, freeze the design at an early stage, and use fixed-price contracts that transfer risks and create adversarial relationships with contractors during the execution of a project.

This chapter examines how organizations responsible for three UK megaprojects— Heathrow Terminal 5, London 2012 Olympics, and Crossrail—have made significant efforts to create a more innovative and flexible delivery model. This new approach recognizes that over the life of a megaproject, new and unexpected options for delivering it will emerge, including opportunities to take advantage of innovative new practices, processes, and efficiencies made possible by new technology.

Drawing upon the strategy literature (Teece, Pisano, and Shuen 1997; Eisenhardt and Martin 2000; Zollo and Winter 2002) and our own empirical research, we argue that clients can develop the "dynamic capabilities" required to adapt plans, modify routines, and innovate when new opportunities arise or conditions change rapidly and unexpectedly. Our research conducted between 2005 and 2015 identified the dynamic capabilities associated with a new innovative and flexible project delivery model. The model consists of five strategic processes used by managers to address the risks and opportunities involved in megaproject management:

- Search capabilities: to identify, test, and combine components of the delivery model required to address the uncertainty and achieve the goals of the project.
- Adaptive problem-solving capabilities: by establishing project team structures and processes to deal with emergent problems and opportunities.
- Test and trial capabilities: to test novel and high-risk practices and conduct trials to ensure that new technology is proven prior to its introduction on the project.
- Strategic innovation capabilities: to create a formal and deliberate process to leverage the innovative resources and capabilities of the project supply chain and research partners.
- Balancing capabilities: to manage the trade-offs between performing planned routines and promoting innovation when unexpected events happen, new opportunities arise, or conditions change.

The rest of this chapter is divided into three main sections. The literature review in the next section identifies the innovative and flexible processes embodied in dynamic capabilities required to address the uncertainties surrounding megaprojects. Section 14.3 illustrates how dynamic capabilities were applied in our case-study projects, and Section 14.4 identifies the key features of a new flexible delivery model and considers how different types of clients, permanent and temporary, develop and deploy dynamic capabilities in megaprojects.

14.2 MANAGING UNCERTAINTY IN MEGAPROJECTS

A megaproject is a temporary organization and process established to design and build a unique product, system, or outcome (Davies, Gann, and Douglas 2009; Davies and Frederiksen 2010). Established as a standalone organization, megaprojects can be led by a client team, prime contractor, or some form of temporary alliance, joint venture or coalition of multiple parties (clients, contractors, suppliers, and other stakeholders) that work jointly on a shared activity for a limited period of time in an uncertain environment (Jones and Lichtenstein 2008; Merrow 2011). Each project is usually decomposed into many smaller interrelated projects and organized as a program. A systems integrator organization—the client, prime contractor, or delivery partner—is established to coordinate the efforts of numerous subgroups and suppliers involved in project activities (Davies et al. 2009; Merrow 2011; Davies and Mackenzie 2014). This organization manages the overall program and the interfaces between projects, and deals with external suppliers through separate contracts, and is accountable for meeting time, cost, and quality performance goals. A megaproject is also a temporary process extending over many years or even decades from front-end planning and design, through construction, integration, and testing to back-end handover to operations (Artto, Ahola, and Vartianinen 2016).

14.2.1 Delivery Model

Each megaproject has its own delivery model involving two basic stages. A front-end "planning" stage occurs when the sponsor and client define how the project will meet their overall strategic objectives, shape the governance structure, prepare the contracting approach, and devise a procurement strategy to consider alternative ideas and ways of stimulating innovation during the tendering phase. An "execution" stage occurs when the project receives approval to proceed and contractors design, construct, integrate, commission, test, and back-end handover the assets to an operator.

Several important studies argue that megaprojects often fail due to poor decisions made during the planning stage. Morris and Hough's (1987) study of major projects emphasized the key role of the owner or sponsor in shaping the front-end project definition stage (see also Morris 1994, 2013; Edkins et al. 2013). Miller and Lessard's (2000) study of large engineering projects also focused on the sponsor's shaping role, particularly in terms of developing new forms of contract and governance to deal with complex projects and turbulent external environments. Flyvbjerg et al. (2013) argue that the poor performance of megaprojects is due to either delusional optimism or deliberate deception in the knowledge that low costs promised early will turn out to be much higher, and expected benefits may not materialise (Flyvbjerg, Garbuio, and Lovallo 2009). Merrow (2011) maintains that success depends on the active engagement of the project sponsor in the front-end, but also emphasizes the importance of establishing the right execution approach for each megaproject, such as forming a strong and capable owner-led project team, selecting the right organizational structure, and building capabilities to manage the interfaces between different parts of the project.

Research identifies many factors that contribute to the successful delivery of large projects, such as a focus on value creation, strong project leadership, a high performance culture, and collaborative project teams (Dvir and Shenhar 2011). Some of the key dimensions that make megaprojects so difficult to manage include their size (Morris and Hough 1987; Flyvbjerg et al. 2003; Merrow 2011), uncertainty (Miller and Lessard 2000; Shenhar 1993, 2001; Shenhar and Dvir 1996; Floricel and Miller 2001; Flyvbjerg et al. 2003; Loch, De Meyer, and Pich 2006; Lenfle and Loch 2010; Brady, Davies, and Nightingale 2012), complexity (Shenhar and Dvir 2007; Davies and Mackenzie 2014; Brady and Davies 2014), urgency (Morris and Hough 1987; Shenhar and Dvir 2007) and institutional structure (Scott, Levitt, and Orr 2011). Sponsors and clients responsible for megaprojects need to address all of these dimensions, but research on the management of large UK infrastructure projects (Gil 2009; Davies et al. 2009; Davies, Dodgson, and Gann 2016) suggests that adapting to uncertainty is one of the most challenging aspects involved in delivering megaprojects.

14.2.2 Innovation and Uncertainty

Many uncertainties associated with megaprojects are foreseeable and can be addressed at the start using risk management and contingency planning. But these techniques encourage efforts to "get back to the plan" when unexpected events happen, rather than learn new things, change direction, and improvize to solve problems (Loch et al. 2006). Because megaprojects are highly uncertain, clients traditionally prefer to rely on existing routines, tried and tested practices, and proven technologies, rather than introduce additional risks associated with innovation (Van Marrewijk, Clegg, Pitsis, and Veenswijk 2008). This tendency to associate risk with "downside threats" ignores the "upside opportunities" that flow from innovation (Ward and Chapman 2003: 98). This is surprising, because classic studies of large, high-risk projects emphasized the role played by innovation in managing and mitigating uncertainty.

In his study for the World Bank, for example, Hirschman (1967) introduced the principle of the Hiding Hand to identify the creativity and innovation that is unleashed to deal with the many hidden uncertainties encountered during the execution of a large project—particularly those with long gestation periods when unexpected problems arise much later and require more serious efforts to resolve them. A challenging project is undertaken, Hirschman argued, because we present it "to ourselves as more routine, simple, and undemanding of genuine creativity than it will turn out to be" (1967: 13). However, the Hiding Hand mechanism has been criticized for being overly optimistic (Flyvbjerg 2014), and neglects to identify the specific processes fostering innovation when required.

The relationship between innovation and uncertainty is also considered in Stinchcombe and Heimer's (1985) study of large and complex North Sea oil and gas projects. These projects depend on a variety of planned project routines, schedules, and contingencies when conditions are stable and predictable, but unforeseen situations encountered during the execution of a project must be resolved by decisions to change plans, adapt processes, and promote innovation when conditions change or new opportunities arise.

The idea that managers of megaprojects need to strike a balance between executing planned routines and promoting innovation when conditions change is clearly established in early studies of defense systems projects. In their study of NASA's space program, for example, Sayles and Chandler (1971: 13) recognized that in all complex projects "there is a search for an adequate compromise between the need for frozen plans (to minimize costly changes) and the desire for flexible planning." NASA's ability to adapt and innovate during the execution of the Apollo program was supported by techniques developed in the 1950s (which are widely used today), such as systems integration, change control, configuration management, and progressive design fixity (Johnson 2002).

14.2.3 Dynamic Capabilities

This early research underlines the importance of performing routine and innovative action depending on the degree of uncertainty in a megaproject. The question is: how do organizations delivering such infrastructure develop the capabilities to achieve this balancing act? In this respect, the literature on dynamic capabilities is helpful in explaining how organizations develop the adaptive processes, simple rules, and routines required to solve emergent problems, explore innovative opportunities, and address uncertainty.

The concept of dynamic capabilities is primarily associated with the resource-based view of the firm (Teece et al. 1997; Teece 2007, 2010; Eisenhardt and Martin 2000) and evolutionary theory (Zollo and Winter 2002; Helfat and Peteraf 2003). The concept was introduced by strategy scholars to explain how firms in all types of industries, including project-based ones, adapt, integrate, and reconfigure their routines and resources to survive and grow successfully in rapidly changing and uncertain environments (Teece et al. 1997; Eisenhardt and Martin 2000; Eisenhardt and Sull 2001; Helfat 2000; Winter 2000, 2003, 2010; Zollo and Winter 2002; Helfat and Peteraf 2003, Teece 2007, 2012).

A dynamic capability is a purposeful activity, identifiable strategic process, and learned managerial routine (for example, new product development or portfolio management) for promoting innovation and adapting to uncertainty (Eisenhardt and Martin 2000; Dodgson, Gann, and Phillips 2014). It does not refer to ad hoc creativity and improvisation (Winter, 2003) or the leadership skills of executives or competence of a senior management team. Dynamic capabilities can be defined as a few simple rules and key processes. They provide the guidelines within which managers can pursue innovative opportunities and deal with rapidly changing and uncertain conditions (Eisenhardt and Sull 2001).

Whereas research has focused primarily on how firms extend their resource base and generate innovation in response to changing conditions, another stream of thinking about dynamic capabilities stresses the importance of balancing stability and change, efficiency and flexibility to keep pace with a range of environmental conditions (Adler, Goldoftas, and Levine 1999; O'Reilly and Tushman 2008; Eisenhardt, Furr, and Bingham 2010). O'Reilly and Tushman (2008) suggest that dynamic capabilities support ambidexterity by helping organizations adapt to rapidly changing and uncertain conditions, while at the same time knowing how and when to exploit existing operational routines in a stable and predictable environment.

The concept has been applied to understand how project-based firms deploy projects to maintain their existing customers, while launching innovative projects to enter, develop, and grow in new markets (Gann and Salter 2000; Davies and Brady 2000; Brady and Davies 2004; Ethiraj, Kale, Krishnan, and Singh 2005; Söderlund and Tell 2009; Cattini, Ferriani, Frederiksen, and Täube 2011; Davies and Brady 2016). However, scholars have only recently started to consider how dynamic capabilities are deployed to manage large and complex projects (Winch 2014; Davies and Brady 2016; Winch and Leinringer 2016; Davies et al. 2016). The balancing role of dynamic capabilities is addressed by Davies and Brady (2016), who show that clients and delivery partners can develop the dynamic capabilities to respond flexibly to the varying degrees of uncertainty found in complex projects. Winch and Leiringer (2016) develop the idea of "owner project capabilities" to identify the strategic, commercial, and governance capabilities required to deliver infrastructure projects. In their study of the Heathrow Terminal 5 project, Davies et al. (2016) identify how BAA built, codified, and mobilized a set of dynamic capabilities that became embodied in a flexible contract, collaborative integrated project team structures, and simple rules to promote innovation and flexibility.

14.2.4 Dynamic Capabilities in Megaprojects

The literature concerned with understanding how uncertainty is addressed in complex, novel, and fast-changing projects helps us to identify five specific dynamic capabilities enabling innovation and flexibility in megaprojects (see Table 14.1):

- Search capabilities.
- Adaptive problem-solving capabilities.

Table 14.1 Dynamic capabilities in megaprojects: Strategic processes
and core literature

Dynamic capabilities	Strategic processes and literature
Search capabilities	Calibrating uncertainty and reference-class forecasting (Lavallo and Kahneman 2003; Flyvbjerg 2014) Learning internally and externally from other projects and industries (Davies et al. 2009; Davies et al. 2016) Searching, testing, and selecting new combinations of ideas, technologies, and practices (Davies et al. 2009; Davies et al. 2016)
Adaptive problem-solving capabilities	Problem-solving teams (Mintzberg 1983; Edmondson, 2012a, 2012b) Flexible contracts (De Meyer et al. 2002; Gil 2009) Psychological safety (Edmondson 2012a, 2012b)
Test and trial capabilities	Learning and feedback from real-time performance (Eisenhardt and Tabrizi 1995) Learning, multiple trials, and selectionism (Loch et al. 2006)
Strategic innovation capabilities	Formal innovation strategy (Davies et al. 2014; Dodgson et al. 2015)
Balancing capabilities	Frozen vs. flexible planning (Sayles and Chandler 1971) Disciplined flexibility (Sapolsky 1972) Targeted flexibility (Lenfle and Loch 2010) Progressive design freeze, Change Control Board and Configuration Management (Johnson 2002)

- Test-and-trial capabilities.
- Strategic innovation capabilities.
- Balancing capabilities.

First, a dynamic capability is required during the front-end planning to search for new or successful ideas, practices, and technologies in other projects and industrial settings, create options and variety, and then select from within that variety to address future conditions facing the project (Davies et al. 2009; Davies et al. 2016). Selected ideas, practices, and technologies can be adapted, modified, and combined to create a delivery model that is designed to achieve the overall goals of the project, while adapting to changing and unforeseen conditions.

The search process is guided by up-front efforts to forecast the uncertainties involved in delivering the project, including technical, market, and social and institutional risks (Miller and Lessard 2001). As we have seen, most high-risk projects are late, over budget, and fail to achieve original specifications. In seeking to understand the uncertainties involved, managers can learn from their own capabilities and experiences with projects conducted in the past. But organizations inclined to adopt this intuitive "inside view" tend to be overly optimistic and fail to consider all the possible sequence of events that might delay or disrupt the project (Lavallo and Kahneman 2003). By using "reference-class forecasting" techniques to examine the experience of similar projects undertaken elsewhere, managers can gain a more accurate understanding of a project's probable outcome (Flyvbjerg 2014). Adopting this "outside view" is supported by recruiting managers and bringing in consultants providing comparative data on other projects and industries.

Clients, contractors, and delivery partners may decide to repeat previous routines, make incremental adjustments, or create entirely new delivery models. In the most radical type of "breaker project," clients experiment with new practices and technologies, create new governance structures, and transform existing institutions (Michaud and Lessard 2000).

Second, a dynamic capability based on adaptive problem-solving is required to innovate and solve emergent events and evolving client requirements during the execution of a megaproject (Dvir and Shenhar 2011; Davies et al. 2016). In a megaproject, this adaptive problem-solving process is underpinned by flexible contracts and project team structures.

Whereas fixed-price contracts may be adequate for dealing with predictable and stable conditions, some form of flexible contract is required to deal with unexpected and rapidly changing conditions (Shenhar and Dvir 2007; Pich, De Meyer, and Loch 2002; Loch, De Meyer, and Pich 2006; Gil 2009). In a cost-plus or cost-reimbursable contract, for example, the client and contractor enter into a relational agreement to build trust and collaboration and share risks and opportunities. Flexible contracts acknowledge the impossibility of "enumerating all possible contingencies and/or stipulating appropriate adaptations to them in advance" (Williamson 1985: 79). They support coordination by mutual adjustment (Thompson 1967) when planned project activities and schedules are modified in real time to address unforeseen circumstances. The client bears the risk and creates incentives encouraging project teams to expose rather than hide problems, recover costs and achieve agreed profit margins, exploit innovative possibilities, and build high-quality solutions to problems.

A megaproject is decomposed into numerous smaller projects, each executed by project teams. People with different knowledge and skills brought together in project teams are able to adapt and respond flexibly to rapidly changing conditions, unforeseen problems, and emergent opportunities (Mintzberg 1983; Söderholm 2008; Geraldi, Lee-Kelley, and Kutsch 2010; Edmondson 2012a, 2012b). These teams treat existing knowledge and skills as bases on which to break away from past routines and build new ones. Project teams rely on simple rules to scope out the challenge, identify interdependent tasks, and structure collective action (Edmondson 2012a, 2012b). Team working facilitates quick adaptation, often changing the direction and focus of a project. Working in a "psychologically safe" environment encourages members of project teams to take risks, overcome setbacks, and engage in collaborative learning and innovation.

Third, a dynamic capability is required to test novel or high-risk practices and ensure that new technology is proven in off-site trials, pilot studies, or other operational environments prior to its introduction on the project. Novel and uncertain projects have to adapt to many foreseen risks and unforeseen uncertainties by learning from the feed-back gained by conducting tests and multiple trials (Eisenhardt and Tabrizi 1995; Loch et al. 2006; Perminova, Gustafsson, and Wikström 2008). Tests can be undertaken to learn how to conduct a novel or complex project activity, identify the risks associated with it, and make the changes required to deal with them. Trials of new practices and unproven technologies ensure that risks and obstacles to efficient performance are identified, diagnosed, and solved. Projects developing radically new technologies may undertake multiple trials in parallel and independently of each other, before selecting the preferred one (Loch et al. 2006). For example, faced with considerable scientific and technical uncertainties and under considerable time constraints, the Manhattan proj-ect developed two bomb designs and three methods to create fissile material (Johnson 2002; Lenfle and Loch 2010; Lenfle 2011).

Fourth, a dynamic capability in strategic innovation identifies what challenges to pur-sue and establishes a formal innovation process that supports the goals of the mega-project, including the overall program and individual projects within it. Formulating and implementing an overall innovation strategy helps to plan, coordinate, and deploy the innovation resources and capabilities of the entire project supply chain and with research partners, such as universities (Davies et al. 2014; Dodgson et al. 2015). Supported by a digital infrastructure platform, an integrated innovation process can be put in place with the incentives and rewards, encouraging project contractors and sup-pliers to commit the resources and apply the capabilities required to address key innova-tion challenges, develop ideas, and exploit new opportunities.

Fifth, a dynamic capability is required to balance the need for routine and innovative action depending on the conditions encountered, stable or uncertain, during the execu-tion of a project. This is because a megaproject is a "conglomeration" of predictable, stan-dardized, and repetitive routines that been performed many times on previous projects as well as uncertain, novel, and innovative procedures applied for the first time (Engwall 2003). Efforts can be made to "freeze" the design, execute planned routines, and stabi-lize construction schedules at the outset, but some flexibility is required to explore new innovative possibilities and solve unexpected problems while the project is underway.

Several techniques providing the flexibility to manage the trade-off between stability and change in complex projects were originally developed in the 1950s and 1960s, such as the idea of progressively freezing the design in stages and using a "change control board" (Johnson 2002). The Polaris intercontinental ballistic missile program relied on the idea of "disciplined flexibility": the discipline to work within the predictable con-straints, the determination to meet schedules, and the flexibility to avoid premature commitment to any particular goal and keep options open to adapt to changing and emergent situations (Sapolsky 1972: 250).

A recent study of the Manhattan project suggests that "targeted flexibility" also pro-vides a solution to this balancing act (Lenfle and Loch 2010). As shown in Figure 14.1, the different pieces of uncertainty in a megaproject can be broken down into distinct projects, structures, and processes to address foreseeable risks (upfront planning, stan-dardized execution routines, and risk management) and unforeseeable uncertainty

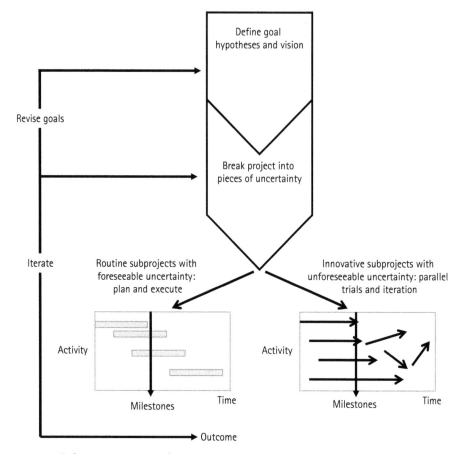

FIGURE 14.1 Balancing routines and innovation in megaprojects.

(Adapted from Lenfle and Loch, 2010.)

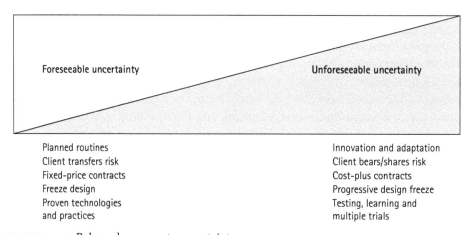

FIGURE 14.2 Balanced response to uncertainty.

(parallel trials and iterative learning to support innovation). Figure 14.2 identifies the types of contract, processes, and behaviours associated with routine and innovative action needed to balance foreseen and unforeseen uncertainty. Projects also use targeted flexibility to address different phases of the project life cycle: a cost-plus contract may be used in the early phase of development when uncertainty is high, and a fixed-price contract is more appropriate when the uncertainty gradually diminishes at a later stage (Shenhar and Dvir 2007: 94).

14.3 ILLUSTRATIVE RESEARCH FINDINGS

In this section we refer to our own published research focusing on how UK infrastructure clients have been developing dynamic capabilities to promote innovation and flexibility in megaprojects. We introduce the three projects and the role they have played in creating a new project delivery model, and include selected examples to describe how the five dynamic capabilities identified in our literature review were deployed in the case studies.

14.3.1 Context: UK Infrastructure Projects

The authors were involved in a long-term program of research during 2005–2015 examining how three large private and public clients have been exploring new ways of delivering large infrastructure projects. We focused on how the clients working with contractors and delivery partners developed dynamic capabilities to manage Heathrow Terminal 5 (T5), London 2012 Olympics construction, and Crossrail projects. We conducted more than a hundred interviews with CEOs, Project Directors, Project Managers, Directors, and project team members. A detailed description of our qualitative research methods can be found in the Davies et al. (2016); Davies and Mackenzie (2014); and Dodgson et al. (2015).

The T5 project was established to design and build a new £4.3-billion terminal for British Airways at Heathrow airport. At the time, BAA was the client organization responsible for delivering the project. BAA was a privately owned airport owner and operator, which was renamed Heathrow Airport Holdings in 2012. T5 was considered an extremely high-risk project. When construction started in 2002, investment was equivalent to approximately two thirds of BAA's capital value. The construction program consisted of sixteen major projects and 147 subprojects. The T5 project experienced significant problems when it opened for service on 27 March 2008. BA misplaced 20,000 bags and canceled 501 flights, incurring costs of around £16 million. The terminal achieved the first full schedule of operations twelve days after opening. Despite the chaotic opening, the project is considered to have achieved its goals of designing and building high-quality infrastructure exactly on schedule, within budget, and with a satisfactory safety record.

London was awarded the 2012 Olympic and Paralympic Games on 6 July 2005. The Olympic Delivery Authority (ODA) was set up in 2006 as a temporary client and public-sector organization responsible for overseeing the design and construction of the Olympic Park infrastructure, venues, Olympic Village, and transport systems. CLM—a temporary joint venture between CH2MHill, Laing O'Rourke and Mace— was formed specifically to act as the ODA's "delivery partner." The construction program consisted of more than seventy individual projects (planned, approved, and managed by principal contractors). The major venue projects were clustered on the Olympic Park (the Olympic Stadium, Aquatics Centre, Velodrome, the International Broadcast Centre/Press Media Centre, and the Athletes Village), many of which were individually large, high-cost, and complex. Unlike T5 and Crossrail, the pace, planning, and scheduling of the London Olympics project was dictated by an "immoveable deadline." The project was completed successfully, on time, in July 2011, thirteen months before the games started on 27 July 2012, providing the Games' organizing committee with sufficient time to test the venues and use the feedback from the trials to prepare for the Games. But the project was not delivered within the original budget of £4.2 billion for constructing and hosting the games submitted with the bid document in 2005. A revised total budget of £6.5 billion established in 2007 was increased to £9.3 billion in 2009 to provide a more realistic estimate of the costs involved. While the final cost of £6.8 billion was within the new £8.1-billion baseline allocated for construction, the project was significantly over budget when compared with the original baseline.

Crossrail is a £14.8-billion project established to design and build a new metro railway from Reading and Heathrow airport in the west through central London to Shenfield and Abbey Wood in the east. This 118-km route includes 21 km of rail tunnels running straight through the heart of central London. Crossrail Limited (CRL) was established in 2008 as a publicly owned and temporary client organization. CRL is the overall program manager and is accountable to the joint project sponsors: the Department for Transport (DfT) and Transport for London (TfL). Transcend, a temporary joint venture between AECOM, CH2MHill, and the Nichols Group, was employed to manage the overall program. Crossrail Central, a joint venture between Bechtel, Halcrow, and Systra, was employed to manage the delivery of the Central Section works. The overall program is divided into many projects, including tunneling, station platforms, signaling, and rolling stock. The largest individual project awarded to the Dragados Sisk joint venture was to construct the £500-million central tunnel section between Farringdon and the City of London. Construction started in 2009, and planned completion is 2018 when Crossrail will begin to transition to an operational railway.

These three megaprojects are part of the UK government's efforts to achieve radical improvements in performance by encouraging innovation in large infrastructure projects. In the 1990s, for example, the UK government commissioned two influential studies—the Latham (1994) and Egan (1998) reports—to investigate how the poor performance of construction projects could be overcome by developing new ideas and learning and by adopting innovative practices from other projects industries. Sir John Egan, one of the report's authors and CEO of BAA in the 1990s, used lessons learned from other projects and industries to develop the radically new model created to deliver the T5 project.

In many ways, T5 is now seen as a "breaker project" (Michaud and Lessard 2000) because it represented an effort to abandon traditional practices and create a radically new megaproject delivery model based on a collaborative, innovative, and flexible process (Davies et al. 2009). Lessons learned, good and bad (such as the need to avoid T5's badly handled opening), have been shared between T5 and London 2012 Olympics and subsequent projects, beginning an industry-wide narrative about the need for a far-reaching institutional transformation in the ways in which innovation in megaprojects is delivered in the United Kingdom. For example, a report by the Royal Academy of Engineering (2014) highlights how the transfer of lessons learned from the delivery of the London 2012 Olympics and have been applied on other megaprojects.

14.3.2 Dynamic Capabilities in UK Megaprojects

We now use examples from our research to illustrate how the five dynamic capabilities have been deployed to manage megaprojects in the United Kingdom.

14.3.2.1 *Search Capabilities*

The T5 case illustrates the search process involved in selecting and combining new ideas, practices, and technologies required to achieve the project's goals and deal with unexpected and changing conditions. BAA used the learning gained from other projects and industries, the results of in-house trials, and statistical studies of related projects to create a new project delivery model embodied in a contract and delivery document known as the "T5 Agreement" (Davies et al. 2009; Davies et al. 2016).

While planning for T5, BAA recruited a team of managers to bring in their experience of other megaprojects (for example, GSK's new UK research facility, oil and gas platforms, and Hong Kong International Airport) and industrial practices. Members of the team embarked on field trips to other firms, industries, and projects throughout the world to discover how successful practices, technologies, and ideas (such as digital models in the aerospace and just-in-time logistics in the car industry) worked and might be transferred to the T5 project. BAA's own capital projects provided a useful testing ground to experiment with elements of the T5 Agreement on a small scale, ensuring that obstacles to effective performance could be detected, diagnosed, and solved before the project began. BAA also applied the collaborative risk-bearing approach later used on T5 to resolve issues that had disrupted the Heathrow Express project connecting the airport with London's Paddington Station. As a result, the project met its new target date and opened for service in 1998. In the words of one BAA manager, the learning gained from the Heathrow Express project "was proof that the T5 Agreement could work" (BAA interview 2005).

BAA adopted an outside view to understand the uncertainties involved in delivering T5. A comparative study of related project cases was undertaken to identify the risks and uncertainties associated with T5, including every major UK construction project over £1 billion built over the previous decade, and every international airport opened during the previous fifteen years. Informed by these studies, BAA's Project Director recognized that "the fascinating thing about a megaproject like this is not to try and get certainty where certainty doesn't exist" (BAA interview 2009). They found that the poor performance of these megaproject was associated with fixed-price contracts and efforts to transfer risk to a prime contractor. These projects—such as the Channel Tunnel joining the United Kingdom and France, and the extension of London Underground's Jubilee Line—culminated in major cost, time, and quality overruns because of disputes and legal battles between clients and contractors over responsibility for scope changes. BAA predicted that without a radically different delivery strategy, T5 would be £1 billion over budget and one year late, and result in six fatalities.

Whereas BAA invested time and resources in the search to create a delivery model for T5 that could be reused on future projects, as temporary client organizations the search processes conducted by the ODA and CRL focused on dealing with the specific challenges and uncertainties associated with a one-time project. Both decided to appoint delivery partner organizations involving several firms with previous experience, capabilities, and successful track records in delivering megaprojects. Both projects learned lessons from other UK megaprojects, such as how to avoid the chaotic handover to operations experienced at T5.

14.3.2.2 *Adaptive Problem-Solving Capabilities*

The T5, London 2012 Olympics, and Crossrail projects have all made extensive use of adaptive problem-solving processes, involving a combination of flexible contracts and multidisciplinary project teams.

The T5 Agreement with BAA's first-tier contractors was based on a cost-reimbursable contract and integrated project teams (Gil 2009; Davies et al. 2009; Davies et al. 2016). The T5 Agreement reflected BAA's decision that the project's risk should not be transferred to a contractor because it was impossible to predict or control all eventualities from design through construction to operational handover. Under this relational contract, suppliers were repaid their costs on a transparent open-book basis and incentivized to improve performance by bonuses for exceeding previously agreed target costs and completion dates. The contract did not specify in detail the work to be undertaken, but rather was a commitment from suppliers to provide high-calibre people with the right combination of knowledge and skills required to perform specific project tasks at the right time, irrespective of their parent company's needs. The T5 Agreement specified that work would be conducted in integrated project teams involving BAA and first-tier suppliers. Teams were expected to work constructively towards achieving project goals by solving problems, responding to opportunities, and acting on any learning gained, rather than "allocating blame or exploiting the failure or difficulties of others for commercial advantage" (Wolstenholme, Fugeman, and Hammond 2008: 12). The delivery handbook provided a set of simple rules and procedures to help integrated project teams to deal with unexpected problems and opportunities:

> Conventional project logic seeks to predefine all requirements and banish change once the project has started. Yet flexibility and adaptability are key objectives for T5. Conventional processes and solutions are therefore not tenable. It will require flexibility of approach: flexibility of solutions; latest responsible decision making, etc. For this reason processes, practices and deliverables will be firmed up in stages. (BAA Delivery Handbook 1999)

The Olympics and Crossrail projects also used flexible forms of contract and colocated integrated project teams to manage the overall program and deliver individual projects within it (Davies and Mackenzie 2014). In the case of the Olympics, for example, CLM worked as the ODA's delivery partner under a contract with the incentives to meet schedule targets and support collaboration. In the start-up planning phase, when the ODA and CLM were established as standalone organizations, they were colocated in an off-site office in London's Canary Wharf to create the team and align their strategic objectives, processes, and culture. Building a relationship based on trust and openness was facilitated by holding joint team events and social activities. When the program moved from planning to construction, CLM worked with an ODA representative and the principal contractors in colocated and integrated project teams on the construction site.

The integrated team structure can also be used to forge collaboration and overcome tensions that arise when companies with differing interests, incentives, and objectives are expected to work together. For example, the Crossrail project established an "integrated program team" structure to resolve some of the problems it had encountered in building collaboration and trust among CRL and its two delivery partner organizations (Davies et al. 2014). A new colocated matrix organization was formed on one floor of CRL's Head Office, involving members of the client and two delivery partners.

14.3.2.3 *Test and Trial Capabilities*

The well-known risks of cost and time overruns associated with the adoption of new technology and innovative new practices were minimized on the T5, Olympics, and Crossrail projects by decisions to use proven technologies and reliable practices. Where new technologies and uncertain practices were introduced, they were first tested and proven in trials, dry runs, and other operational environments before being taken to the projects.

The T5 project conducted tests and trials to identify and address the risks associated with new technologies and potentially disruptive project activities such as rehearsals, pilot studies to model performance, running dedicated offsite test facilities, and training and familiarization of staff with new technology (Davies et al. 2009; Davies et al. 2016). For example, the "roof project" for the main terminal building was considered one of the most challenging and uncertain projects on T5. The integrated project team responsible for this project were encouraged to identify and expose the risks and safety concerns associated with the challenge of erecting roof abutment structures with spans of over 150 metres on site. Their solution was to test the erection of the pre-erected roof structure in advance, in an off-site location in the north of England. The pilot trial identified 140 lessons, each with a preemptive risk mitigation plan to enable rapid construction on site (National Audit Office 2005: 5). As one manager put it: "A key success factor on T5—enabled by early involvement with the suppliers and integrated working—is the first run studies and prototyping because getting people early allows you to plan your approach and one big success on that would be the roof" (BAA interview 2006). The project was delivered three months earlier than originally planned, enabling delays caused by the wet winter of 2001–2002 to be recovered.

Driven by an "immoveable deadline," the ODA deliberately maintained a limit on innovation to keep the project on track to completion. In seeking to avoid the costs and time overruns associated with other projects, such as the London Jubilee Line extension's overambitious plans for new technology, the ODA made extensive use of existing methods and tested processes. Learning lessons from the disrupted opening of T5 (Brady and Davies 2010), the ODA decided to complete the construction program in July 2011 to provide one year of testing on live events in the run-up to the Games, which opened on 27 July 2012.

14.3.2.4 *Strategic Innovation Capabilities*

Whereas innovation in the T5 and Olympics projects focused on tackling specific challenges and opportunities when they emerged during execution, Crossrail is significant because it introduced the radically new idea of establishing a deliberate and formal strategy for the project to exploit the innovative resources and capabilities of contractors and other members of the project supply chain (Davies et al. 2014; Dodgson et al. 2015).

The "Crossrail Innovation Strategy" was established in 2012 to develop, finance, and introduce innovations that would help to overcome strategic challenges and achieve the project's overall vision and time, cost, and quality objectives. Members of different projects and suppliers were encouraged to submit their ideas for innovation. If successful, they would gain the resources required to development, test, and implement them. An innovation team was responsible for identifying, evaluating, and developing new ideas, managing a portfolio of invested projects, and sharing successful innovations across the project. An online digital platform called "Innovate18" was developed for the organization to provide a mechanism to submit ideas (innovation portal), to manage, track, and report on the progress of ideas (Innovation Management System) and to communicate and share innovations across the Crossrail community (via the website). New ideas likely to be of benefit to Crossrail were developed after gaining the relevant sponsorship and commitment from interested parties. By mid-2014, the innovation program had completed three rounds of evaluation and provided funding to support thirty innovations.

The idea of developing innovation strategies for megaprojects is gaining support in the United Kingdom. When the CRL program director moved to become the CEO of

Thames Tideway Tunnel in 2014 he wanted to emulate Crossrail's strategic approach to innovation. The £4.2-billion project has developed an innovation strategy tailored to the challenges and requirements involved in constructing a 25-km tunnel to replace London's nineteenth-century sewer system. The project has developed its strategic innovation capabilities by consulting academics and practitioners involved in developing the CRL strategy, recruiting members of the CRL innovation team, replicating CRL's processes, and reusing the digital platform it had developed. More recently, HS2 Limited—the client organization responsible for developing the United Kingdom's new high-speed £50-billion railway line—has also developed an innovation strategy for the project.

14.3.2.5 *Balancing Capabilities*

Our research identified how balancing capabilities provided the disciplined flexibility required to maintain routines when conditions were stable, while responding adaptively to changes in technologies, user needs, and the operating environment. The process of "progressive design fixity" was used on T5 to avoid freezing designs too early and incurring costly revisions at a later stage (Gil and Tether 2011). The ODA had a highly effective change control process to uncover unexpected problems hindering progress and identify opportunities to promote innovation. Any significant change proposed by a contractor had to be approved by the Change Control Board chaired by the ODA. For example, an important innovation proposed by ISG (the contractor responsible for constructing the Velodrome) and approved by the Board was the decision to change from a steel roof to a cable net roof, resulting in signification reductions in time and cost (Davies and Mackenzie 2014). The ODA renegotiated ISG's contract, changing it from a pain/gain to a fixed-price contract to ensure that the risk associated with the innovative change was transferred to the contractor.

We also identified the balancing role of targeted flexibility. Whereas the T5 Agreement was an umbrella contract used by most of BAA's first tier contractors, the Olympics and Crossrail projects used a suite of New Engineering Contracts (NEC) to address the specific challenges and uncertainties of individual projects within the program (Davies and Mackenzie 2014). On the Olympics project, for example, the ODA used NEC Option A (fixed price) contracts to deal with known and predictable conditions associated with simple and less risky projects (such as the temporary venues), whereas NEC Option C risk-sharing target-cost contracts were used to promote the collaborative behaviour and flexibility needed to expose risks and solve unexpected problems associated with the largest and most challenging projects (Aquatics Centre, Velodrome, and Olympics Stadium). Under this approach, principal contractors were encouraged to exploit their own distinctive capabilities and prior experience to find their own way of meeting individual targets for their projects:

> We were given the freedom to determine how we were going to deliver targets that the ODA were setting. And we will do things slightly differently because of the circumstances we found ourselves in, it's driven by the nature of the venue and program issues. (Principal contractor interview 2011)

However, a balance had to be struck between stability and change:

> You can't have constant change, there have to be fixed points where things that have been completed … If you change after that date that then means that another contractor has to change what they're supplying to accommodate that. (CLM interview 2011)

While each individual project was planned and managed relatively independently by a principal contractor, the ODA and CLM ensured that discipline was maintained by applying standardized and consistent processes across the entire program, such as a monitoring and assurance process to provide detailed, regular, and accurate information on the progress of individual projects and increase the visibility of unexpected problems.

14.4 DYNAMIC CAPABILITIES AND THE FLEXIBLE DELIVERY MODEL

Our research has shown that some of the United Kingdom's largest and most important infrastructure clients and delivery partners have been exploring and creating new ways of delivering megaprojects. BAA led the way in creating an entirely new model for T5, departing radically from previous ways of planning and executing megaprojects. BAA's search during the preparation for T5 found that the poor performance of a megaproject project was associated with fixed-price contracts that pass on the risk and create adversarial relationships with contractors. Under this approach, clients select the lowest price bid, believing this to be the best route to remain within time and budget. Morris and Hough (1987) provide further historical evidence of the problems with fixed-price contracts in their studies of major projects such as the Thames Barrier, but more recent examples include the Channel Tunnel, the Jubilee Line Extension, the Swanwick Air Traffic Control system, and Wembley National Football Stadium.

The traditional model assumes that uncertainties and future conditions likely to impact on the project can be identified up front, and contingency plans can be put in place to deal with them should they arise during the execution of the project. Under this model, organizations involved in megaprojects (sponsors, clients, and contractors) are reluctant to introduce novel ideas and innovative approaches, preferring instead to rely on tried and tested techniques, established routines, and proven technologies. Efforts are made to freeze the design at an early stage, and the project is executed as planned, using contingencies funds to address risks that impact on the project. When unforeseen events happen in megaprojects using fixed-price contracts, clients and contractors often end up in disputes over responsibility for unforeseen changes, resulting in endless legal battles, cost overruns, and further delays.

14.4.1 Towards a Flexible Delivery Model

T5 initiated an institutional transformation in the management, governance, and structure of UK megaprojects and a move toward a radically new delivery model combining innovative and flexible processes, incentivizing the collaborative behaviors required to react swiftly to uncertain and rapidly changing conditions. As our research underlines, elements of the T5 delivery model are being shared and transferred from one project to the next. The Olympics and Crossrail projects emulated some of the key collaborative processes (such as risk-sharing contracts and integrated project teams) used to deliver T5, and added new ones supporting flexibility and innovation.

The flexible-delivery model is based on a set of strategic processes and simple rules for dealing with uncertainty in megaprojects. Clients use flexible risk-sharing or risk-bearing contracts, and work with contractors in integrated project teams to deal with rapidly changing and unpredictable conditions. Contractors are brought in early to help shape design and construction activities. Freezing the design progressively as the project evolves provides the flexibility required to deal with changing requirements or new opportunities. When unexpected things happens or new opportunities arise during execution, members of integrated project teams are incentivized to work collaboratively to identify problems, explore new opportunities, and find innovative solutions. However, there are some differences between the projects. For example, whereas BAA created a bespoke risk-bearing contract for T5, the ODA and CRL have made use of a variety of risk-sharing contracts targeted to deal with the different pieces of uncertainty associated with individual projects within the overall programs. CRL stands out as the first project to develop and implement an innovation strategy.

14.4.2 Dynamic Capabilities and Uncertainty

The traditional delivery model relies on the planning and execution routines of the client and its contractors to predict future conditions and manage uncertainties while the project is underway. It assumes that information about the future state of the world is adequate and that a project can be carefully optimized as a well-understood, predictable, and rational process (Pich et al. 2002; Brady, Davies, and Nightingale 2012). The processes established to deal with uncertainty during the execution of a project resemble the well-understood "standardized operating procedures" that firms rely on to deal with stable and predictable conditions. Project routines, task scheduling, and risk-management techniques are executed as originally planned, and prespecified instructions, contingencies, and actions are triggered when previously identified signals or risks occur during project delivery (Pich et al. 2002).

The flexible model, by contrast, depends on dynamic capabilities to deal with the uncertainty and the rapidly changing conditions during the planning and execution stages of a megaproject. This model assumes that information is inadequate at the outset because of our cognitive inability to predict future conditions and identify unforeseen events (Pich et al. 2002; Davies 2014). Dealing with information inadequacy and unforeseen uncertainty requires an ability to conduct new plans, adapt processes, and innovate while the project is underway (Stinchcombe and Heimer 1985; Eisenhardt and Tabrizi 1995; Loch et al. 2006; Shenhar and Dvir 2007). We identified a set of five strategic processes that managers of megaprojects are using to increase innovation and flexibility:

- Search capabilities applied in the planning stage to address information inadequacy by calibrating the uncertainty facing the project, identifying new ideas, practices, and technologies, and selecting the best of the combination for dealing with future conditions (such as reference-class forecasting, learning from in-house projects, and site visits to other projects and industries).
- Adaptive problem-solving capabilities are required to deal with unexpected events and opportunities while the project is underway (for example, T5 Agreement, collaborative contracts, integrated project teams, and integrated program teams).
- Test and trial capabilities are used to identify risks associated with novel or high-risk practices and to ensure that new technologies are reliable and proven prior to their introduction on the project (such as learning from prototype tests and operational handover trials on T5, and ODA testing on live events).
- Strategic innovation capabilities used to establish a deliberate, formal, and systematic process to exploit the innovative resources of the project supply chain and research partners, and implementing them on the project (for example, CRL's innovation strategy).
- Balancing capabilities are required to manage the trade-offs involved in performing routines as planned and responding flexibly by promoting innovation when conditions change rapidly and unexpectedly (for example, progressive design fixity, Change Control Board, and a tailored suite of contracts).

Although each project has capitalized on the learning and capabilities developed in previous ones, the main focus of dynamic capability development varies between projects. T5 concentrated on developing front-end search capabilities to create a radically new project delivery model. Innovation in the Olympics project emphasized the role of balancing capabilities to support innovation within a disciplined, stable, and consistent process focused on achieving a fixed deadline. The emphasis with Crossrail has been on developing and applying strategic innovation capabilities.

We recognize that megaprojects conducted in the past may have employed one or more of these capabilities, but our study of T5 and the Olympics and Crossrail projects suggests that an organization's ability to deal with uncertainty and rapidly changing conditions is significantly augmented when all five are deployed. The application of dynamic capabilities varies over the life cycle of a megaproject. Whereas search capabilities are applied in isolation during the front-end planning stage, the other four—adaptive problem-solving, test and trial, strategic innovation, and balancing capabilities—should be integrated and configured to work in unison when dealing with the conditions and challenges encountered during the execution stage.

Our research argued that two contrasting types of client organizations can develop the dynamic capabilities required to manage a megaproject (Davies et al. 2016). As an example of an enduring or permanent client organization, BAA was responsible for delivering a number of megaprojects over many years in a manner similar to, for example, BP, Shell, Network Rail, Highways England, and the London Underground. It had an opportunity and incentive to develop dynamic capabilities for T5 and apply the learning gained to improve the delivery of subsequent projects (such as Terminal 2).

As examples of temporary client organizations, the ODA and CRL were established as standalone entities and were designed to last for the duration of each project. The ODA was disbanded soon after the completion of the Olympics construction program, and CRL will be dismantled when Crossrail opens for service. Unlike BAA, the ODA and CRL understood that the dynamic capabilities required to manage their projects could not be developed entirely in-house on a temporary basis. They established delivery partners involving several contractors with prior capabilities and experience in managing megaprojects. In the case of the Olympics, the ODA's delivery partner brought together the knowledge and resources of three different firms, including two (Laing O'Rourke and Mace) that brought their prior experience gained on T5.

Temporary clients established to manage megaprojects are rarely, if ever, short-lived organizations. The long planning and execution periods of most megaprojects provide clients with an opportunity to prepare and develop dynamic capabilities that, while temporary, may be applied over many years or even decades. For example, HS2 Ltd will be in place for the duration of a construction project expected to last several decades. The longevity of each of these temporary organizations helps to explain how dynamic capabilities can be transferred from one megaproject to the next by deliberate learning, emulation, and cross-fertilization of ideas. This has been facilitated by the movement of individuals between projects. This can be illustrated with two examples. First, the approach to strategic innovation in Crossrail was informed by the CEO of CRL's previous experience as Project Director of T5. Second, when CRL's Program Director became CEO of the Thames Tideway Tunnel project he emulated the strategic innovation approach used on Crossrail. Both projects now use the same digital platform (Innovate18) to exchange innovative ideas. This illustrates the importance of project professionals as "carriers" of innovative practices and capabilities between projects (Scott et al. 2011; Grabher and Thiel 2015).

14.5 CONCLUSION

This chapter considered how infrastructure clients in collaboration with contractors and delivery partners in the United Kingdom have developed a new flexible delivery model to manage megaprojects. We showed how clients responsible for three projects—T5, the Olympics, and Crossrail—recognized that the traditional approach to megaproject management is no longer viable. They participated in efforts to experiment with and develop a radically new and highly adaptive model based on collaboration, flexible contracts, integrated project teams, and innovation. Referring to the dynamic capabilities literature (Teece et al. 1997; Eisenhardt and Martin 2000; Zollo and Winter 2002), we argued that managers rely on five strategic processes and simple rules to promote the innovation and flexibility required to deal with highly uncertain and rapidly changing conditions encountered in megaprojects. We identified how these dynamic capabilities have been applied in different ways on the three projects. Some scholars have recently examined dynamic capabilities in permanent organizations (Winch 2014; Winch and Leiringer 2016; Davies et al. 2016), but further research is needed to explore how temporary organizations can build and apply the dynamic capabilities needed to manage large, one-off projects when ostensibly there is little or no possibility for reusing these capabilities on future projects.

References

Adler, P. S., Goldoftas, B., and Levine, D. I. (1999). "Flexibility versus efficiency? A case study of model changeovers in the Toyota production system," *Organization Science* 10(1): 43–68.

Artto, K., Ahola, T., and Vartiainen, V. (2016). "From the front end of projects to the back end of operations: Managing projects from value creation throughout the system lifecycle," *International Journal of Project Management*, 35(2), 258–70.

BAA. (1999). *The T5 Agreement: Delivery Team Handbook*, BAA Company Document.

Brady, T. and Davies, A. (2004). "Building project capabilities: From exploratory to exploitative learning," *Organization Studies*, 25(9): 1601–21.

Brady, T. and Davies, A. (2010). "From hero to hubris: Reconsidering the project management of Heathrow's Terminal 5," *International Journal of Project Management*, 28, 151–7.

Brady, T. and Davies, A. (2014). "Managing structural and dynamic complexity: A tale of two projects," *Project Management Journal*, 45(2): 21–38.

Brady, T., Davies, A., and Nightingale, P. (2012). "Dealing with uncertainty in complex projects: Revisiting Klein and Meckling," *International Journal of Managing Projects in Business*, 5(4): 661–79.

Cattani, G., Ferriani, S., Frederiksen, L., and Täube, F. (2011). "Project-based organizing and strategic management: A long-term research agenda on temporary organizational forms," *Advances in Strategic Management*, 28: 3–26.

Davies, A. (2014). "Innovation and project management," in M. Dodgson, D. M. Gann, and N. Phillips (eds.), *The Oxford Handbook of Innovation Management*. Oxford: Oxford University Press, pp. 625–47.

Davies, A. and Brady, T. (2000). "Organisational capabilities and learning in complex product systems: Towards repeatable solutions," *Research Policy*, 29: 931–53.

Davies, A. and Brady, T. (2016). "Explicating the dynamics of project capabilities," *International Journal of Project Management*, 34(2): 314–27.

Davies, A., Dodgson, M., and Gann, D. M. (2016). "Dynamic capabilities for a complex project: The case of London Heathrow Terminal 5," *Project Management Journal, Special*

Issue: Innovation and Project Management: Bridging Contemporary Trends in Theory and Practice, 47(2): 26–46.

Davies, A. and Frederiksen, L. (2010). "Project modes of innovation: The world after Woodward," Research in the Sociology of Organizations, Special Issue: Technology and Organization: Essays in Honour of Joan Woodward, 29: 177–215.

Davies, A., Gann, D. M., and Douglas, T. (2009). "Innovation in megaprojects: Systems integration at London Heathrow Terminal 5," California Management Review, 51(2): 101–25.

Davies, A., MacAulay, S., Debarro, T., and Thurston, M. (2014). "Making innovation happen in a megaproject: The case of London's Crossrail," Project Management Journal, 45(6): 25–37.

Davies, A. and Mackenzie, I. (2014). "Project complexity and systems integration: Constructing the London 2012 Olympics and Paralympics Games," International Journal of Project Management, 32: 773–90.

De Meyer, A., Loch, C. H., and Pich, M. T. (2002). "Managing project uncertainty," Sloan Management Review, 43(2): 6–67.

Dodgson, M., Gann, D. M., MacAulay, S., and Davies, A. (2015). "Innovation strategy in new transportation systems: The case of Crossrail," Transportation Research Part A: Policy and Practice, 77: 261–75.

Dodgson, M., Gann, D. M., and Phillips, N. (2014). "Perspectives on innovation management," in The Oxford Handbook of Innovation Management. Oxford: Oxford University Press, pp. 3–25.

Dvir, D. and Shenhar, A. (2011). "What great projects have in common," MIT Sloan Management Review, 52(3): 19–21.

Edkins, A., Geraldi, J., Morris, P., and Smith, A. (2013). "Exploring the front-end of project management," Engineering Project Organization Journal, 3(2): 66–85.

Edmondson, A. (2012a). Teaming: How Organizations Learn, Innovate, and Compete in the Knowledge Economy. San Francisco: Wiley.

Edmondson, A. (2012a). "Teamwork on the fly," Harvard Business Review, April: 72–80.

Egan, J. (1998). Rethinking Construction: The Report of the Construction Industry Task Force. Department of Transport, Environment and Regions.

Eisenhardt, K. M. and Tabrizi, B. N. (1995). "Accelerating adaptive processes: Product innovation in the global computer industry," Administrative Science Quarterly, 40: 84–110.

Eisenhardt, K. M. and Martin, J. A. (2000). "Dynamic capabilities: What are they?" Strategic Management Journal, 21: 1105–21.

Eisenhardt, K. M. and Sull, D.N. 2001. Strategy as simple rules, Harvard Business Review, January 2001: 107–116.

Eisenhardt, K. M., Furr, N. R., and Bingham, C. B. (2010). "Microfoundations of performance: Balancing efficiency and flexibility in dynamic environments," Organization Science, 21(6): 1263–73.

Engwall, M. (2003). "No project is an island: Linking projects to history and context," Research Policy, 32: 798–808.

Ethiraj, S. K., Kale, P., Krishnan, M. S., and Singh, J. V. (2005). "Where do capabilities come from and how do they matter? A study in the software services industry," Strategic Management Journal, 26: 25–45.

Floricel, S. and Miller, R. (2001). "Strategizing for anticipated risks and turbulence in large-scale engineering projects," International Journal of Project Management, 19: 445–55.

Flyvbjerg, B. (2014). "What you should know about megaprojects and why: An overview," Project Management Journal, 45(2): 6–19.

Flyvbjerg, B., Bruzelius, N., and Rothengatter, W. (2003). *Megaprojects and Risk: An Anatomy of Ambition*. Cambridge: Cambridge University Press.

Flyvbjerg, B., Garbuio, M., and Lovallo, D. (2009). "Delusion and deception in large infrastructure projects: Two models for explaining and preventive executive disaster," *California Management Review*, 52(2): 170–93.

Gann, D. M. and Salter, A. (2000). "Innovation in project-based, service-enhanced firms: The construction of complex products and systems," *Research Policy*, 29: 955–72.

Geraldi, J., Lee-Kelley, L., and Kutsch, E. (2010). "The Titanic sunk, so what? Project manager response to unexpected events," *International Journal of Project Management*, 28: 547–58.

Gil, N. (2009). "Developing cooperative project-client relationships: How much to expect from relational contracts," *California Management Review*, 51(2): 144–69.

Gil, N. and Tether, B. (2011). "Project risk management and design flexibility: Analysing a case and conditions of complementarity," *Research Policy*, 40: 415–28.

Grabher, G. and Thiel, J. (2015). "Projects, people, professions: Trajectories of learning through a mega-event (the London 2012 case)," *Geoforum*, 65: 328–37.

Helfat, C. E. (2000). "Guest editor's introduction to the special issue: The evolution of firm capabilities," *Strategic Management Journal*, 21: 955–9.

Helfat, C. E. and Peteraf, M. A. (2003). "The dynamic resource-based view: Capability lifecycles," *Strategic Management Journal*, 24: 997–1010.

Hirschman, A. O. (1967). *Development Projects Observed*. Washington, DC: The Brookings Institution.

Johnson, S. B. (2002). *The Secret of Apollo: Systems Management in American and European Space Programs*. Baltimore and London: John Hopkins University Press.

Jones, C. and Lichtenstein, B. (2008). "Temporary inter-organizational projects: How temporal and social embeddedness enhance coordination and manage uncertainty," in S. Cropper, M. Ebers, C. Huxman, and P. Smith Ring (eds.), *The Oxford Handbook of Inter-Organizational Relations*. Oxford: Oxford University Press, pp. 231–55.

Lavallo, D. and Kahneman, D. (2003). "Delusions of success: How optimism undermines executive's decisions," *Harvard Business Review*, July: 56–63.

Latham, M. (1994). *Constructing the Team*. London: HMSO.

Lenfle, S. (2011). "The strategy of parallel approaches in projects with unforeseeable uncertainty: The Manhattan case in retrospect," *International Journal of Project Management*, 29: 359–73.

Lenfle, S. and Loch, C. (2010). "Lost roots: How project management came to emphasize control over flexibility and novelty," *Californian Management Review*, 53(1): 32–55.

Loch, C., De Meyer, A., and Pich, M. (2006). *Managing the Unknown: A New Approach to Managing High Uncertainty and Risk in Projects*. Hoboken, NJ: Wiley.

Merrow, E. W. (2011). *Industrial Megaprojects: Concepts, Strategies, and Practices for Success*. Hoboken, NJ: Wiley.

Michaud, P. and Lessard, D. (2000). "Transforming institutions," in R. Miller and D. R. Lessard (eds.), *The Strategic Management of Large Engineering Projects: Shaping Institutions, Risks, and Governance*. Cambridge, MA: MIT Press, pp. 151–63.

Miller, R. and Lessard, D. (2000). *The Strategic Management of Large Engineering Projects: Shaping Institutions, Risks, and Governance*. Cambridge, MA: MIT Press.

Miller, R. and Lessard, D. (2001). "Understanding and managing risk in large engineering projects," *International Journal of Project Management*, 19: 437–43.

Mintzberg, H. (1983). *Structures in Fives: Designing Effective Organizations*. Upper Saddle River, NJ: Prentice Hall.

Morris, P. W. G. and Hough, G. H. (1987). *The Anatomy of Major Projects*. Chichester: Wiley.

Morris, P. W. G. (1994). *The Management of Projects*. London: Thomas Telford.

Morris, P. W. G. (2013). *Reconstructing Project Management*. Chichester: Wiley.

National Audit Office (2005). *Case Studies: Improving Public Services through Better Construction*. London: National Audit Office.

O'Reilly, C. A. and Tushman, M. L. (2008). "Ambidexterity as a dynamic capability: Resolving the innovator's dilemma," *Research in Organizational Behavior*, 28: 185–206.

Perminova, O., Gustafsson, M., and Wikström, K. (2008). "Defining uncertainty in projects: A new perspective," *International Journal of Project Management*, 26: 73–9.

Pich, M. T., Loch, C. H., and De Meyer, A. (2002). "On uncertainty, ambiguity and complexity in project management," *Management Science*, 48(8): 1008–23.

Royal Academy of Engineering. (2014). *Public Projects and Procurement in the UK: Sharing Experiences and Changing Practice*.

Sapolsky, H. M. (1972). *The Polaris System Development: Bureaucratic and Programmatic Success in Government*, Cambridge, MA: Harvard University Press.

Sayles, L. and Chandler, M. K. (1971). *Managing Large Systems*. New York: The Free Press.

Scott, R. W. Levitt, R. E., and Orr, R. J. (2011). *Global Projects: Institutional and Political Challenges*. Cambridge: Cambridge University Press.

Shenhar, A. J. (1993). "From low to high-tech project management," *R&D Management*, 23(3): 199–214.

Shenhar, A. J. (2001). "One size does not fit all projects: Exploring classical contingency domains," *Management Science*, 47(3): 394–414.

Shenhar, A. J. and Dvir, D. (1996). "Toward a typological theory of project management," *Research Policy*, 25: 607–32.

Shenhar, A. J. and Dvir, D. (2007). *Reinventing Project Management: The Diamond Approach to Successful Growth and Innovation*. Boston, MA: Harvard Business School.

Söderholm, A. (2008). "Project management of unexpected events," *International Journal of Project Management*, 26(1): 80–96.

Söderlund, J. and Tell, F. (2009). "The P-form organization and the dynamics of project competence: Project epochs in Asea/ABB, 1950–2000," *International Journal of Project Management*, 27: 101–12.

Stinchcombe, A. L. and Heimer, C. (1985). *Organizational Theory and Project Management: Administering Uncertainty in Norwegian Offshore Oil*. Oslo: Norwegian University Press.

Teece, D., Pisano, G., and Shuen, A. (1997). "The dynamic capabilities and strategic management," *Strategic Management Journal*, 18(7): 509–33.

Teece, D. (2007). "Explicating dynamic capabilities: That nature and microfoundations of (sustainable) enterprise performance," *Strategic Management Journal*, 28(13): 1319–50.

Teece, D. (2010). "Alfred Chandler and 'capabilities' theories of strategy and management," *Industrial and Corporate Change*, 19(2): 297–316.

Teece, D. (2012). "Dynamic capabilities: Routines versus entrepreneurial action." *Journal of Management Studies*, 49(8): 1395–401.

Thompson, J. D. (1967). *Organizations in Action: Social Science Bases of Administrative Theory*. New Brunswick, NJ: Transactions Publishing.

Van Marrewijk, A., Clegg, S. R., Pitsis, T., and Veenswijk, M. (2008). "Managing public–private megaprojects: Paradoxes, complexity and project design," *International Journal of Project Management*, 26: 591–600.

Ward, S. and Chapman, C. (2003). "Transforming project risk management into project uncertainty management," *International Journal of Project Management*, 21: 97–105.

Williamson, O. E. (1985). *The Economic Institutions of Capitalism: Firms, Markets, Relational Contracting*. New York: Macmillian.

Williams, T. and Samset, K. (2010). "Issues in front-end decision making on projects," *Project Management Journal*, 41(2): 38–49.

Winch, G. (2014). "Three domains of project organising," *International Journal of Project Management*, 32: 721–31.

Winch, G. and Leiringer, R. (2016). "Owner project capabilities for infrastructure development: A review and development of the 'strong owner' concept," *International Journal of Project Management*, 34(2): 271–81.

Winter, S. G. (2000). "The satisficing principle in capability learning," *Strategic Management Journal*, 21: 981–96.

Winter, S. G. (2003). "Understanding dynamic capabilities," *Strategic Management Journal*, 49(8): 1402–6.

Winter, S. G. (2012). "Capabilities: Their origins and ancestry," *Journal of Management Studies*, 24: 991–5.

Wolstenholme, A., Fugeman, I., and Hammond, F. (2008). "Heathrow Terminal 5: Delivery strategy," *Proceedings of the Institution of Civil Engineers: Civil Engineering*, 161(5): 10–15.

Zollo, M. and Winter, S. G. (2002). "Deliberate learning and the evolution of dynamic capabilities," *Organization Science*, 13(3): 339–51.

....

CHAPTER 15

MEGAPROJECT STAKEHOLDER MANAGEMENT

....

GRAHAM WINCH

INTRODUCTION

....

IN order to provide a forum for stakeholder voice on the TAURUS project to automate back-office settlement for the London Stock Exchange, the Securities Industry Steering Committee on TAURUS (SISCOT) was established with representation from the key players. At TAURUS' heart was the compulsory dematerialization (replacing paper share certificates with an electronic register of stock ownership) which threatened the perceived interests of brokers acting for private clients who were supported by the industry regulator. This committee included these brokers and provided significant input to the requirements for the TAURUS system, with each stakeholder trying to shape those requirements to meet their particular interests. The result was unmanageable scope creep leading to budget and schedule escalation, and finally to cancellation of the project after £80 million (in prices of the day) had been wasted. To those trying to deliver the project, SISCOT became known as the "Mad Hatter's Tea Party" (Drummond 1996).

The challenges that the TAURUS project team faced in managing their project's stakeholders were immense, and the CREST project that replaced it could only be a success due to a change in project scope that reduced the interest of the regulatory stakeholder and thereby reduced the power of opponents to TAURUS. The aim of this paper is to explore these types of challenges and to propose a research agenda on how stakeholders on megaprojects can be most appropriately managed by balancing the differing and often conflicting claims of various stakeholder groups. We will start by briefly reviewing the development of the managerial literature on stakeholder management over the last fifty years before examining more closely some of the recent research contributions to project stakeholder management. We will then turn to two other intellectual traditions which have generated significant insights into project stakeholder management: actor–network theory and institutional theory. We will conclude by suggesting some new directions for research and practice in project stakeholder management on the theme of *megaprojects and society* and the ethical considerations that follow.

15.1 STAKEHOLDERS IN STRATEGIC MANAGEMENT RESEARCH

The concept of a corporation's stakeholders in distinction to its share or stockholders who are its legal owners emerged at the Stanford Research Institute during the early 1960s as part of work on strategic planning (Freeman 1984). These ideas were rapidly picked up in work on strategic management (Ansoff 1968), project management (Cleland and King 1968), and elsewhere. For Ansoff, and Cleland and King, stakeholders were part of the corporate "environment" that had to be taken into account in pursuit of its objectives. Freeman developed these insights into a seminal contribution (1984; see also Parmar et al. 2010) on strategic management from which the current literature flows. Freeman argued that strategic management needed to move beyond a production function view, and even a managerial view that takes into account the interests of stockholders and employees, towards a stakeholder view of the firm which takes into account actors such as governments, non-governmental organizations, local communities, suppliers, and customers. He also emphasized that the stakeholder "map" of a particular corporation was contingent and could only be described empirically rather than categorically. On this basis, Freeman provided the widely accepted definition of a stakeholder in the literature (1984: 46):

> A stakeholder in an organization is (by definition) any group or individual who can affect or is affected by the achievement of the organization's objectives.

As the research inspired by Freeman evolved (Laplume et al. 2008), it developed four main lines of enquiry, which we will use to structure our review of the research in project stakeholder management. These lines of enquiry are as follows:

- *Stakeholder definition and salience* develops concepts and techniques for identifying who the stakeholders are and their relative importance for the successful pursuit of the firm's objectives. Mitchell et al. (1997) made a seminal contribution to this line of enquiry, arguing that stakeholder salience is a function of those stakeholders who are relatively powerful, are deemed to be legitimate, and have urgent claims.
- *Stakeholder actions and responses* investigates how stakeholders influence the behavior of the firm. Frooman (1999) argued that stakeholders use direct strategies when they hold resources upon which the firm depends, and more indirect strategies when they do not. Indirect strategies can include campaigning, forming coalitions and networks, and regulatory action.

- *Firm actions and responses* is an area to which Freeman (1984) devoted much effort, and can include corporate social responsibility activities, lobbying government and regulators, and collaborative relationship building.
- *Firm performance* investigates the returns to the firm for investment in stakeholder management capability. Generally, the return is shown to be positive, but the evidence is rather indirect, and not yet convincing.

Laplume and his colleagues (2008) note another trend in the literature with a shift from Freeman's original conception of stakeholder management as an essential part of rational strategic planning towards a view of stakeholder management as an ethical imperative (Gibson 2000). Yet this imperative poses new challenges because the criteria for evaluating the relative merits of different stakeholders become unclear once the Smithian moral imperative for the firm to make a profit is occluded. Gibson (2000) argues that this problem can be addressed by deploying notions of partiality and reciprocity, so long as stakeholders are identifiable and coherent social groups. However, there are those who advocate the inclusion of natural environment in the stakeholder map as the primordial stakeholder (Driscoll and Starik 2004). This is a radical extension to Freeman's definition, yet the natural environment is both clearly affected by (for example, pollution, global warming) and affects (such as depletion of exploitable natural resources, natural disasters) the firm in the pursuit of its objectives. Driscoll and Starik proposed an extension of the stakeholder saliency framework (Mitchell et al. 1997) to include "proximity" to take the natural environment into account.

Stakeholder management as part of strategic management has come a long way since the early sixties, but it does appear to have come to something of an impasse. It is notable that an earlier Oxford Handbook on Strategic Management (Faulkner and Campbell 2003) does not contain a chapter on stakeholder management and only passing reference in the text. Research interest in the strategic management field has moved on, and it is now strongest in the field of business ethics (Laplume et al. 2008). Another field in which there is growing interest in the concept is project and program management to which we now turn.

15.2 Stakeholders in Project and Program Management Research

Researchers in project and program management very soon realized the importance of the concept of stakeholder management (Cleland and King 1968), but this realization did not stimulate a significant research activity. Rather, the topic became a standard chapter in project management handbooks and guides such as Calvert (1995), Cleland (1998), McElroy and Mills (2000), Winch (2004) and, indeed, this current handbook. It has also generated a stand-alone text in Chinyio and Olomolaiye (2010). Recent literature reviews of research on project stakeholder management (Achterkamp and Vos 2008; Littau et al. 2010; Mok et al. 2015) show that research interest in the topic began to take off around 2005 and has gained momentum since; the latter review is particularly helpful, as it is focused on megaprojects. The three reviews together provide a good coverage of the journal-published research literature, but their reliance on bibliographic databases rather than a deeper understanding of the literature and its principal contributions has generated some gaps. So our review here will focus on more recent journal-published papers, but also cover earlier contributions published in books. We will structure our review using the categories developed by Laplume and his colleagues (2008).

15.2.1 Stakeholder Definition and Salience

Miller and Lessard (2000) provide thoughtful insight into the process of "project shaping" on megaprojects whereby the coalition of interests around the front end definition of a megaproject including sponsors, funders, governments, and key suppliers is configured and reconfigured until a viable project concept is defined and gathers sufficient momentum to move into execution. Flyvbjerg et al. (2003) further show how the dynamic of relationships between the sponsors of the megaproject and the financiers can create the "megaproject paradox" through the deliberate underestimation of costs and overestimation of benefits; that is, strategic misrepresentation of the investment case for the megaproject. Sallinen et al. (2011) analyse the salience of national government as regulator on a Finnish civil nuclear project. They show how the nuclear regulator has both power and legitimacy. It is the guardian of the safety of nuclear installations which gives it both considerable power (its technical requirements must be met) and legitimacy (civil nuclear would be politically unacceptable without its oversight). These combine to give it urgency as challenges in meeting its requirements are on the project's critical path. Yang et al. (2014) conducted a survey of projects managers to understand their perceptions of salience. They report that power is most important, followed by urgency and proximity, while legitimacy had little salience for these project managers.

15.2.2 Stakeholder Actions and Responses

Hughes reported the dynamics of stakeholder engagement on the Boston Central Artery/Tunnel and the aims of representatives of community stakeholders in "delivering some chunk of mastodon meat back to the tribe" (1998: 221). McAdam et al. (2011) further analyze the factors which generate opposition to pipeline projects in developing countries, distinguishing between legal opposition within existing institutional frameworks and political opposition outside those frameworks. Sallinen et al. (2011) show how the actions of the government's agent—the nuclear safety regulator—shape the management of the project. Mazur et al. (2014) show that the emotional intelligence of project managers is important for the development of internal and external stakeholder relationships in the defense sector; Vrhovec et al. (2015) explore resistance to IT-enabled organizational change by stakeholders. Turning to construction projects, Collinge and Harty (2014) and Heravi et al. (2015) demonstrate how stakeholder involvement varies by phase of the project. Law and Callon (1992) and Missonier and Loufrani-Fedida (2014) show how the network of stakeholders evolved over time on a jet fighter and IT project respectively.

15.2.3 Firm Actions and Responses

Winch (2004) shows how reducing the scope of the project (but not the mission) removed the interest of the regulator and thereby significantly reduced the power of one group of opponents to the project mission. Chang et al. (2013) study defense acquisition projects, stressing the importance of value cocreation with suppliers. De Schepper et al. (2014) further show how the use of private finance for public infrastructure projects significantly increases the complexity of project stakeholder relationships. Greiman (2013) shows how the project management team on the Boston Central Artery/Tunnel addressed communication with, and mitigation of, stakeholders. Yang et al. (2014) report that project managers tended to compromise with, or make concessions, to powerful stakeholders, while they tended to use a hold (do nothing) or compromise strategy for urgent stakeholders. Proximate stakeholders tended to be treated more gently. Eskerod and Vaagaasar (2014) show how the owner project management team works through the project life cycle to build up trusting relationships with both the senior sponsors of the project and the principal supplier to the project. Beringer et al. (2013) turn attention to portfolio management, and show the importance of internal stakeholders for effective project portfolio management.

15.2.4 Firm Performance

Project performance has traditionally been defined in relation to the Barnes (1988) triangle of achievement of time, cost, and quality objectives. Most of the literature on project stakeholder management reviewed here and covered in earlier reviews adopts this definition, if only implicitly, in terms of stakeholders as groups to be managed so that they do not disrupt progress of the project. Thus Greiman (2013) suggests that providing stakeholder mitigations on the Boston Central Artery/Tunnel added 30% to the total cost. However, if we turn to the project performance literature we can see that the debate there has moved on from this narrow definition to consider the different performance criteria espoused by different stakeholders. Taking the perspective of the owner and operator, Merrow (2011) presents regression analyses showing that high "team integration" leads to high project performance where representation of operators in the early phase project team is one of the more importance parameters constituting the team integration index. Authors such as Davis (2014) and Turner and Zolin (2012) show how stakeholders such as suppliers, users, and the project team will probably have differing and often incompatible perceptions of project performance.

15.2.4 Overview

This review demonstrates that empirical research on project stakeholders is a vibrant area with growing activity which will support megaproject management practice. Not all research reviewed above is on megaprojects, but even that which is not has relevance for megaproject management. As it developed, the project management field espoused a somewhat narrower definition of stakeholder than that proposed by Freeman (1984), perhaps influenced by Cleland (1986). It is clear from Littau et al. (2010: table A2) that project management researchers typically restricted the definition to those *interested in* the project rather than those *affected by* the project, implying a higher level of cognition from the stakeholder for inclusion in the analysis. This distinction is important because the former formulation excludes by definition the primordial stakeholder.

Most of the research reviewed here, and that covered in the three earlier research reviews upon which this review builds, is therefore clearly "instrumental" (Donaldson and Preston 1995) in that its premise is that effective engagement with stakeholder interests through either or both communication and mitigation is essential to the successful delivery of the project mission. The balance of the research reviewed which is focused on the project front end of defining the project mission is more "descriptive" (Donaldson and Preston 1995) in that it empirically explores the processes of megaproject front end shaping processes. Donaldson and Preston (1995) conclude their review by arguing that stakeholder management theory cannot rely on either a descriptive or instrumental perspective; rather, it needs a "normative" perspective. This is a point to which we will return.

Before we do this, we discuss some limitations to project stakeholder management research. One is conceptual, while the others concern the scope of research on megaproject stakeholder management. The conceptual issue is the problem of the absent stockholder. The fundamental premise of stakeholder theory (Freeman 1984) is that stakeholders are distinguished from stockholders who have a fiduciary claim on the focal organization; the analogous group for public organizations is taxpayers. So, who are the stockholders in a project? Most obviously, they are the financiers of the project. Where the project is financed by the owner organization from internal funds, then the project stockholders are the conventionally defined stockholders in the owner organizations, be they holders of equity or taxpayers. However, many owner organizations seek non-recourse finance for their megaprojects, and so the project stockholder may have a direct claim on the asset being created by the project and the associated cash flows its exploitation generates (Morrison 2012). Such arrangements on public projects are called public–private partnerships (Winch and Schmidt 2106). However, as we will see later, it is more helpful analytically to treat financiers of projects as a special type of stakeholder rather than a contrasting stockholder in project stakeholder management.

A related issue is the precise definition of the focal organization for the stakeholder analysis. As Davis (2014) demonstrates, some studies include the project manager or project team in the analysis, while others include the owner, client, or top management. For Freeman (1984), the "focal organization" is the firm, although he notes that this presumes consensus within that organization. He therefore recommends a pragmatic approach to focal organization definition depending on the details of the situation. By analogy, the focal organization would be the owner organization as defined by Winch (2014) which raises the capital for the investment in the project, "owns" the asset generated by the project, and goes on to exploit it for beneficial use to provide a return to the investors. However, this is counterintuitive from a project management point of view; surely the focal organization should be the temporary project organization? Yet the temporary project organization is a diverse coalition of interests (Winch 2014), and consensus certainly cannot be assumed, so much analytic power would be lost by this definition. An additional problem is that during front-end definition there is often not a project organization as such, and its formal establishment is an *outcome* of the shaping process by stakeholders; Cochrane et al. (2002), Cusin and Passebois-Ducros (2015), and Hughes (1998) all show how projects emerge from interactions between urban elites and are profoundly shaped before an "owner" organization is identified to manage the project.

We propose, therefore, to shift to a slightly more abstract level of definition and suggest that the *project mission* (Winch and Bonke 2002) be the focal point of stakeholder analysis, where the project mission is defined as the overall intent of the megaproject as a value proposition. This is distinguished from the project scope which is that total set of activities required to achieve the project mission. While this is a development from Freeman's definition, it has two advantages. It allows stakeholder analysis during the project shaping phase when there may not be a focal organization as such but there is a clearly emerging mission, and it is future-oriented in that the focal point of concern for stakeholders, including financiers, is often something that may not physically exist for many years hence. We therefore propose the following definition of a project stakeholder:

> A project stakeholder is any group or individual who can affect or is affected by the achievement of the project mission.

A second observation from this review is the complete absence of attention paid to the primordial stakeholder. Even Zeng et al. (2015), in their review of "social responsibility" on megaprojects, mention environmental concerns only in passing, yet for many stakeholder groups environmental concerns are the principal issue with megaprojects. Indeed, Gellert and Lynch (2003: 16) define megaprojects as "projects which transform landscape rapidly, intentionally, and profoundly," and analyse the ensuing primary and secondary "displacements" for both the natural and social environment. Driscoll and Starik (2004) see the natural environment as truly primordial, but we suggest here that the definition can be usefully relaxed to include those pre-existing artefacts valued by society typically captured by the word "heritage," such as ancient buildings and archaeo-logical remains.

Our third observation is that remarkably little attention has been given in the research on project stakeholder management to the distinctive characteristics of government, particularly national government, as stakeholder. Government is easily defined as highly salient, and its actions can have profound consequences for the progress of projects (King and Crewe 2013); indeed, few megaprojects can proceed without the formal approval of government. Yet at best, it lurks in the background of most analyses of project stakehold-ers. Eskerod and Vaagaasar (2014) mention in passing that the signaling project they studied was more favored by politicians than by the owners of the rail network who were actually making the investment, and that this gave the project team relative autonomy from senior management; but they do not pursue this line of enquiry further. Similarly, Chang et al. (2013) argue that suppliers advocated a nationalistic procurement policy, but do not analyse the political dynamics of implementing such a policy.

Only Sallinen et al. (2011) take the role of national government seriously in their analysis in focusing on a particularly important type of stakeholder: regulators. Indeed Merrow et al. (1981) argued that regulators are the principal source of budget overruns on megaprojects. Regulators for land use are a major factor in shaping all projects which consume spatial resources (Stringer 1995). Economic regulators for utility companies such as in the United Kingdom's Regulated Asset Base (Helm 2009) model act at the project portfolio level by agreeing a capital investment plan over the regulatory period—typically five years—consisting of multiple projects and programs.

Finally, we can observe that there are at least two applications of project stakeholder management concepts in the research literature. The first is descriptive and is interested in the front-end shaping of megaprojects and how the coalitions of stakeholders are assembled in terms of both incentivizing those who could benefit from the megaproject investment and mitigating the impact on those who could lose from it. The second fol-lows Cleland (1986) and is instrumental in being more concerned with the efficiency and effectiveness of project execution and mitigating the potential for stakeholders to disrupt that. Broadly, but with exceptions, the research journal literature tends to focus on the second problem while the extended case studies presented in the book-length lit-erature tends to focus on the former problem. We argue that we need both contributions in order to fully understand and hence manage stakeholders on megaprojects.

15.3 EXTENDING PROJECT STAKEHOLDER MANAGEMENT THEORY

These considerations suggest that some considerable effort needs to be put into extend-ing project stakeholder management theory for megaprojects both empirically and the-oretically. We now turn, therefore, to two theoretical approaches from sociology, which, we suggest, can help us in this enterprise. The first is actor–network theory; the second is institutional theory.

15.3.1   Actor–Network Theory and the Primordial Stakeholder

In his seminal study of attempts to regenerate the scallops of St Brieuc Bay, Callon (1986) argues for a sociology of translation in which human (fishermen and researchers) and non-human (scallops) actors are given conceptual equality in the analysis. Callon's concern is with the sociology of science and so he concentrates analytic attention on the researchers attempting to regenerate the scallop population of the Bay so that fishermen can continue to ply their profitable trade. Actor-network theory (Latour 2005) has thereby inspired those concerned with the relationship between the natural world and construction projects to adopt this distinctive—and controversial (Hacking 1999)—theoretical approach to analysis (Sage et al. 2011; 2014; Tryggestad et al. 2013) and to thereby conceptualize various types of fauna as project stakeholders. For instance, Tryggestad et al. (2013) show how the discovery of breeding ponds for a protected species of frog led to a significant reshaping of a housing development project involving considerable interaction between the developers, local government, and environmental campaigners.

Actor–network theory has at its core the analysis of technology as a social construct (Latour 2005), and so analysis could well be extended to other primordial stakeholders (in our extension) in the form of historically embedded technologies such as heritage artefacts. Indeed, the theoretical scope can be extended even further because Harvey and Knox (2015) identify the importance of the mountain itself as a stakeholder in a road-building project. This was recognized by the project management team who performed rituals to honour the mountain, including the hiring of shamans, and the widespread belief that the excavations on the mountain demanded human sacrifice in the form of site accidents and death. It has also been used for the analysis of the dynamics of information systems projects to insightful effect (see, for example, Missonier and Loufrani-Fedida 2014; Pollack et al. 2013). In particular, Law and Callon (1992) analyze the evolving stakeholder network around a failed UK jet fighter project. They argue that the relationship between the global network of external stakeholders and the local network of internal stakeholders needs to be managed with the project management team as the "obligatory point of passage" between the two. The inability of the project team to do this in their case led to schedule and budget escalation and hence cancellation of the project.

15.3.2   Institutional Theory and the Government Stakeholder

One of the classic contributions to institutional theory (Selznick 2011) is a case study of a megaproject: the development of the US Tennessee Valley, through a program of development of hydroelectric dams and farm effectiveness improvement born in the 1930s

New Deal era. Selznick shows how existing institutions shape the program through "informal coöptation," while the Tennessee Valley Authority (the government agency charged with the megaproject) used "formal coöptation" of the customers for its electricity by setting up distribution cooperatives. Its aim always was to ensure stability for its program in coping with its "institutional environment." While earlier work (often dubbed "old institutionalism") focused on the persistence of institutional structures, later work (often dubbed "new institutionalism") focuses more on agency and how institutional structures change and has become the predominant approach in organization theory (Greenwood et al. 2008). Despite this predominance, institutional theory has had relatively little influence in project management research in general and stakeholder management in particular, although there are currently some important lines of development.

The first line is concerned with transnational megaprojects; that is, megaprojects which have significant inputs from outside the country within which they are executed. Different nation-states have different institutional systems, and these have profound effects in shaping megaprojects executed within their territorial jurisdiction (Scott 2011). In general terms, the national business system (Whitley 1992; Winch 2000) shapes the execution of megaprojects, while differences in the specifics of regulatory systems can trip the unwary supplier, causing schedule and budget problems (Sallinen et al. 2011; Syben 1996). Normative and cultural differences can also have profound effects on project shaping and execution (Fellows and Liu 2016; Winch et al. 2000). Scott (2011) analyzes the three distinctive "organizational fields" of potential international stakeholders which have evolved around transnational megaprojects consisting of "global infrastructure players," including funding agencies such as the World Bank, international nongovernmental organizations such as Greenpeace, standards organizations such as ISO, and legal firms in London and New York. He contrasts this with the "host community" organizational field in-country around the particular project, and the organizational field generated by the members of the project organization.

A second body of work has applied institutional theory to public sector IT megaprojects (Currie and Guah 2007; Currie 2012). They define the "organizational field" as the sector which provides the context of the megaproject—in their case, the UK healthcare system. They analyze the tendencies toward "institutional isomorphism" among the various organizations that make up the organizational field, and also the activities of particular groups—particularly healthcare professionals—which attempt to resist such processes. This leads to an analysis of the "institutional logics" within the field associated with professionalism and managerialism and how these interact to shape the megaproject. They then show how the failure to fully involve particular groups—in particular, healthcare professionals—generated significant delays. From a stakeholder management perspective, the various organizations and groups (such as the Health Ministry, hospitals, general practitioners, and IT suppliers) that populate the organizational field are the stakeholders, and they express their various interests in the project in terms of institutional logics to which they adhere.

15.3.3 Megaproject Stakeholder Management Theory

We have shown how both actor–network theory and institutional theory can fill gaps in project stakeholder management theory and practice by enabling more trenchant analysis of different groups of stakeholders—primordial ones for actor–network theory and those associated with government for institutional theory. Of course, both theoretical perspectives make much broader claims to contribute to organization theory than these modest contributions, but there is no space to discuss those in this chapter. It should also be noted that that actor–network theory and institutional theory embody rather different ontological claims which, we suggest, cannot be syncretically combined; we need to choose between them.

Perhaps the major difference between the two perspectives is how the social is constructed. Actor–network theory sees the construction of the social as being generated through associations between actors either directly or mediated through non-human "actants" (Latour 2005). It is this concern to give the non-human equal status in the analysis to the human that the most striking contribution of actor–network theory lies, and is the source of its attraction for those wishing to include the primordial stakeholder in the analysis. Actor–network theory also insists that the actors in the network are constituted through those associations and do not have a prior definition which is brought to the interactions. Institutional theory, in strong contrast, analyses how pre-existing social relationships—be they regulative, normative or cultural (Scott 2008)—shape current social relationships. While there is increasing attention being paid in institutional theory to how institutions change through processes concepts such as "institutional entrepreneurship" and "institutional work," the focus remains on change in some pre-existing social formation. Thus actor–network theory emphasizes ahistorical agency and largely denies structural entities, while institutional theory reinforces the role of the historical structures and has only recently shifted research attention to agency in how those structures change.

From the point of view of stakeholder management theory, a fundamental premise is that stakeholders come to the firm with some sort of prior claim or interest, if only not to be adversely affected by the pursuit of the firm's objectives (Freeman 1984). So for this reason, actor–network theory would appear to be inappropriate for the development of theory in megaproject stakeholder management. If this argument is accepted, then is there any way that we can retain the important insights that actor–network theory brings to the analysis of the primordial stakeholder? Yes, there is. In all of the empirical contributions the fauna of concern are given voice by human agents. In these cases, the flora and fauna are only "unruly" because campaigning groups advocate their purported interests. Otherwise, they would simply be obliterated, as happens on projects such as the Three Gorges Dam (New and Xie 2008). On the other hand, institutional theory—complemented by social movement theory (McAdam 2011)—does provide conceptual tools for analyzing how the claims of particular primordial stakeholders are mobilized and how the claims of others are not.

The analysis of the local and global networks on a project (Law and Callon 1992) has notable similarities to the analysis of the three organizational fields in Scott's (2011) contribution, though in the latter case the focus on transnational projects means that the global network is split into two elements: the national network in the host country and the truly global network of transnational infrastructure players. Where the actor–network theory approach provides additional insight is in the mapping of the evolution of the relationships between the local and global networks (Law and Callon 1992; Missonier and Loufrani-Fedida 2014), and the importance of the centrality in the network of the project management team as the "obligatory point of passage" (Law and Callon: 31) between the local and global networks. In their analysis, it was the failure of the prime contractor to establish this position of network broker that played a profound role in the escalation and ensuing cancellation of the project. However, institutional theory can also provide subtle analysis of the evolution of stakeholder relationships, as Selznick (2011) shows, and the broker role between subnetworks of stakeholders plays an important part in social network analysis (Burt 2005).

We therefore conclude that institutional theory provides a valuable foundation for megaproject stakeholder management. To date, much of the research in the field has been theoretically eclectic, if not theoretically naive. Just as stakeholder management theory challenged theories of the firm derived from neoclassical economics which see management purely as the agents of stockholders, institutional theory developed from the analysis of government intervention in economic development during a period of weakened belief in market-based solutions in the 1930s (Selznick 2011). Others have also made the link between institutional theory and stakeholder management (Campbell 2007). However, organization theory cannot be simply applied to enable managerial action; theories are mediated through tools (Cabantous and Gond 2011). We therefore now turn to evaluating the various tools available for project stakeholder management.

15.4 TOOLS FOR MANAGING STAKEHOLDERS

Yang (2014) provides a valuable overview of some of the tools that can be used for stakeholder analysis, concentrating particularly on stakeholder mapping and social network analysis. We will follow this lead by also concentrating on these tools. Freeman (1984) advocated descriptive mapping of stakeholders. Bonke (1996) provided a more analytic approach in his pioneering mapping of project stakeholders, drawing on concepts from research on the social construction of technology (Pinch and Bijker 1987), which was one of the influences on the development of actor–network theory (Latour 2005). Later combined (Winch and Bonke 2002) with the power/interest matrix (Johnson and Scholes 2002), this mapping approach has a number of advantages. In addition to identifying potential stakeholders and characterizing their relative positions as proponents or opponents of the project mission, it also identifies their interests in the project mission and the potential ways in which their interests in that mission might be aligned positively. Olander and Landin (2005) and Winch (2004) show how this approach can be used to map changing stakeholder relationships through time. A recent development is to apply Covey's (1989) concepts of circle of influence and circle of concern to identify those stakeholders amenable to action by the project team, and those that are not.

The Stakeholder Circle tool (Bourne and Walker 2005; Bourne and Weaver 2010) consists of an attractive graphical presentation generated by proprietary software support by various templates for developing identification of the stakeholders and assessing their perceived relationship to the project. It is recommended that the mapping exercise is repeated more than once during the life cycle of the project to ensure the continuing alignment of the identified stakeholders. Many will find the formality of the analysis helpful, but the method does not appear to encourage investigating the motivations behind the various stakeholders' interests in the project, and in practice it appears to focus largely on internal stakeholders. It would also appear to be more an execution phase tool than one for understanding stakeholders during project shaping.

Drawing on their extensive experience with group decision support systems for strategizing, Ackermann and Eden (2011) report on stakeholder mapping workshops organized for a variety of clients over a number of years. A particular advantage of the paper is the attention paid to the mapping process, which is left largely undescribed in the approaches summarized so far. Following work with paper and post-its, the maps are developed using causal mapping software to capture both the identification of stakeholders and their relative power and interest with respect to the project. The causal mapping software also captures the motivations of various stakeholders, and the potential connections between them. One issue with causal mapping software is that its output can be rather difficult to interpret, but not too much should be made of this. As one participant in a workshop said: "I learned most from the argument about where to put them [the stakeholders on the grid]; the output itself was not much help" (Ackermann and Eden 2011: 188).

Following the lead of Rowley (1997), researchers concerned with project stakeholder management have applied social network analysis (SNA) to analysing stakeholder relationships. Yang et al. (2011) use SNA's measure of "status centrality" to determine the importance of stakeholders in the network. Yang (2014) compares SNA with the stakeholder circle approach reported above, finding that both are useful for project stakeholder analysis, with the former stronger on identifying relationships between stakeholders, and the latter for prioritizing their interests. By far the most sophisticated application of stakeholder management to stakeholder management on construction projects is the work of Pryke (2012) showing how the various "networks" (such as contractual, instruction and control) on the project overlap and reinforce each other. However, his work is limited to the local network of stakeholders who form the "project coalition" of those organizations which are in a contractual relationship with each other.

This review suggests that the stakeholder circle and SNA tools—which as Yang (2014) shows are complementary—are more appropriate for instrumental analysis of the project stakeholder network during execution. This is because they rely on complete identification of the stakeholder network and the collection of empirical data regarding their aspirations. Another issue with SNA is that a stakeholder showing as an outlier on the network might well be a powerful stakeholder who is being ignored by the project team, such as health practitioners on Connecting for Health, and a highly central stakeholder might be one that is being listened to far too much, such as the members of SISCOT on TAURUS. On the other hand, the stakeholder mapping approach, particularly when underpinned by causal mapping, is more appropriate for the descriptive analysis of the organizational and institutional processes of shaping the front end of megaprojects.

15.5 The Future for Research on Megaproject Stakeholders: Megaprojects and Society

Our discussion of project stakeholder management has been descriptive and instrumental in Donaldson and Preston's (1995) terms, but we promised to turn to the normative aspects. Steurer (2006) argues that stakeholder management research in the strategy literature has been largely replaced by a broader concern for research on business and society. We suggest that the next step for project stakeholder management research is also to develop a *megaprojects and society* line of enquiry to complement the existing descriptive and instrumental approaches. One theme along these lines is the research on "projectification" (Lundin et al. 2015) investigating the ways in which social and economic action is increasingly organized in projects, while Van Marrewick (2015) explores cross-cultural aspects. However, there is a much broader set of social concerns around megaprojects that almost by definition, have profound effects on the society around them.

A first set of concerns is *political*. Megaprojects are often—but not always—the outcome of political processes. Although there is a rationalistic justification for the project rooted in cost–benefit analysis, the real drivers behind the project are political initiatives to which the cost benefit analyses are shaped. For instance, policy initiatives by government are often implemented through IT megaprojects (King and Crewe 2013). The policy intent is a reform of some aspect of government activity, which often makes inaccurate assumptions regarding both the potential for developing new IT systems embedded within larger legacy systems, and time and effort required to develop those systems. In the UK case, we have discussed Connecting for Health; the latest of these highly ambitious policy-change driven projects in the United Kingdom to run into considerable difficulties is Universal Credit (National Audit Office 2013, 2014a). We need much more research into how policy-change-driven megaprojects are shaped through policy processes before they emerge as large-scale programs and hence as something to be managed as a project.

The work of Harvey and Knox (2015) exposes the influence of another aspect of the politics of megaprojects: systemic corruption at national and regional level in shaping the project both around whether the project would go ahead at all, and around its budget and schedule. They thereby introduce the much broader topic of what might be called the *stakeholders of the shadows* around megaprojects which has been largely ignored in the literature. Corruption is defined by the Global Infrastructure Anticorruption Centre as criminal acts of "bribery, extortion, fraud, cartels, abuse of power, embezzlement, and money laundering" (<http://www.giaccentre.org>). One egregious example of this is the Kariba Dam North Power Station project in Zambia (Morrell 1987). By their very nature, stakeholders of the shadows are very difficult to research, and the role of international campaigning organizations such as Transparency International is vital here.

Flyvbjerg and Molloy (2011) argue that strategic misrepresentation is a form of corruption; however, they are not suggesting that strategic misrepresentation is criminal, but unprofessional. We would argue that it is a matter of *governance* (Müller 2011); that is, it is about the relationship between the owner organization and its investment projects (Winch 2014), and more broadly, it is a problem of the relationship between centrally/nationally allocated budgets and devolved project promoters. Molloy and Chetty (2015) show how competition between cities in the context of lax budgetary controls generated a serious misallocation of scarce resources in a developing country: South Africa. Similarly, Reisner (1993) shows how competition between federal agencies generated investments in dams in the US West that were counterproductive both environmentally and economically. In both the public and private sectors, the response to these governance challenges has been the centralization of budgetary processes; one well-known public sector example is the Norwegian quality at entry process (Klakegg et al. 2016; Samset and Volden 2016). This is also happening in the UK public sector with the establishment of the Major Projects Authority in 2011 (National Audit Office 2014b).

A second set of concerns is *economic*. Development megaprojects—particularly for providing energy and transportation infrastructure—play a very important role in economic growth. Concern with this contribution has led to an interesting line of argument to the effect that project failures make a vital contribution to economic growth—what Hirschman calls the "hiding hand" (1995) of development projects where "entrepreneurial error" (Sawyer 1952) has serendipitous consequences. Such authors argue that development megaprojects are so daunting that a cool assessment of costs and benefits would not tempt anyone to go ahead with the project and so that it is only underestimation of costs complemented by *under*estimation of benefits which allows projects to go ahead and thereby yield their long-term benefits. This line of argument reaches its apogee in Hobsbawm's (1962: 57) argument:

> It is hard to deny a grudging admiration even to the most obvious crooks among the great railway builders. Henry Meiggs was by any standards a dishonest adventurer, leaving behind him a trail of unpaid bills, bribes and memories of luxurious spending along the entire western edge of the American continents, at home in the wide open centres of villainy and exploitation like San Francisco and Panama rather than among respectable businessmen. But can anyone who has ever seen the Peruvian Central Railway deny the grandeur of the concept and achievement of his romantic if rascally imagination?

Much the same could be said of the Canadian Pacific Railway (Cruise and Griffiths 1988), but Flyvbjerg and Sunstein (2016) are scathing about this line of argument and recommend better cost–benefit analysis (CBA). However, the argument for better CBA ignores the widespread critique of CBA for investment appraisal because of its inability to handle convincingly both negative and positive externalities to the direct investment case. Hirschman (1995) reviews some of the early debates, while later commentators have called CBA "nonsense on stilts" (Self 1970; see also Naess 2006). Even within the cost–benefit analysis research community, awareness is growing regarding its limitations for capturing all the benefits of megaproject investment (Vickerman 2007), while there also remain important issues on the cost side of the calculus—particularly the valuation of "natural capital" (Helm 2015).

All this means that megaproject investment evaluation and selection is a potentially rich area for research. To date, research has focused on technical improvements to the calculus. This is important, but is limited in scope. We do need to know much more about the behavioural aspects of CBA and project selection more generally. We need to understand better how CBA is used in practice, and the extent to which the analytic tools are "performative" (Cabantous and Gond 2011; Callon 1998); that is, how they socially shape the calculus rather than providing an objective means to calculate. We also need to understand more about how the power relationships within and between agencies shapes appraisal and selection in megaproject planning (Szyliowicz and Goetz 1995), and the broader set of power relations in the international construction industry (Linder 1994).

There is, therefore, much research to be done here, but in doing this research, we should be mindful of Keynes's argument as to why "animal spirits" are so important for initiating investment projects of all kinds, including megaprojects:

> If we speak frankly, we have to admit that our basis of knowledge for estimating the yield ten years hence of a railway, a copper mine, a textile factory, the goodwill of a patent medicine, an Atlantic liner, a building in the City of London amounts to little and sometimes nothing. (1961: 149)

In the light of this pervasive uncertainty, CBA is, arguably, no more than a structured way of making sense about the future rather than a refined project selection tool. While improvements can undoubtedly be made in CBA and investment appraisal tools more generally, megaprojects, in the end, will only actually be initiated if there is also a good dose of animal spirits in the mix, which inherently entail the risk of entrepreneurial error—be those entrepreneurs (promoters) in the public or private sectors.

Our final concern is *ethical*. One stakeholder that has not been mentioned in the literature surveyed is *future generations*, whose concerns, almost by definition, lack proximity, urgency, and power, even if they may be strong on perceived legitimacy. The United Nations Sustainable Development Goals of 2015 call, in Goal 9 (of 17), for the development of quality, reliable, sustainable, and resilient infrastructure, including regional and transborder infrastructure, to support economic development and human well-being, with a focus on affordable and equitable access for all (<http://www.un.org/sustainabledevelopment/infrastructure-industrialization/>).

Megaprojects will play a large part in achieving these goals. They build up the infrastructure of societies over long periods of time, and current generations benefit from the infrastructure investment decisions—be they wise or not—of earlier generations. Current infrastructure projects will be a legacy for future generations, but they will also, inevitably, entail the loss of natural capital. How should those trade-offs be made? Should today's stakeholders such as local residents whose quality of life will be negatively affected by the investment be allowed to deny future generations the benefits of the investment? Or should today's beneficiary stakeholders be allowed to deny the interests of the primordial stakeholders, which will generate a real natural capital loss for future generations. We need to engage in much more research about how these trade-offs *should* be made because the tools we presently have, such as CBA, often lack broad legitimacy and efficacy.

15.6 CONCLUDING THOUGHTS

In this chapter we have reviewed the stakeholder management literature from strategy research and its application to the field of project management. We have found that the project management research literature has been largely instrumental in its approach, epitomized by the restriction of the definition of stakeholder to those *interested in*, rather than the broader category of those *affected by* the delivery of the project mission. We also reviewed the more descriptive research on the front end of projects which provides the basis for a more thoughtful literature on the ways in which stakeholders shape the project mission itself. However, that literature failed to acknowledge the existence of the primordial stakeholder, so we reviewed the actor–network literature that has pioneered its analysis, but we noted that, in practice, the interests of the primordial stakeholder were only taken into account when social movements picked up their interests and so we recommended the merits of an institutional approach to megaproject stakeholder management. This would also enable researchers to analyze more easily the role of government in megaprojects.

Drawing on recent developments in strategy research, we argued for a more comprehensive perspective on megaproject stakeholder management, which we dubbed *megaprojects and society*. This perspective, we suggested, broadens out the analysis to include the *political issues* around corruption, governance, and the role of politics in the promotion and funding of megaprojects. It also includes *economic issues* and the role of the "hiding hand" and "entrepreneurial error" in megaproject funding. Better CBA can help to mitigate these challenges, but we also noted important limitations to the current state of the art in CBA as a megaproject selection technique.

Finally, we raised the *ethical issues* around megaprojects and the importance of seeing future generations as a key player within the megaprojects and society perspective.

Megaprojects are, in a very important sense, about short-term costs (say the ten-year horizon) for long-term benefits (say the fifty-year horizon). These costs are not only the capital cost of the investment but also include the possible loss of natural capital and the loss of amenity for local stakeholders. The path-dependency around large capital investments also implies that the opportunity costs associated with making the wrong investments are massive multiples of the simple sum of the capital foregone. Many nation-states and large corporations are struggling toward new ways of making these kind of intergenerational decisions, and so these inherently political processes are also an important part of the research field of megaprojects and society.

Acknowledgments

I am very grateful to Dr. Sandra Schmidt and to Dr. Natalya Sergeeva for their help in the preparation of this chapter.

References

Achterkamp, M. C. and Vos, J. F. (2008). "Investigating the use of the stakeholder notion in project management literature: A meta-analysis," *International Journal of Project Management*, 26: 749–57.

Ackermann, F. and Eden, C. (2011) "Strategic management of stakeholders: Theory and practice," *Long Range Planning*, 44: 179–96.

Ansoff, H. I. (1968). *Corporate Strategy.* Harmondsworth: Penguin.

Barnes, M. (1988). "Construction project management," *International Journal of Project Management*, 6: 69–79.

Beringer, C., Jonas, D., and Kock, A. (2013). "Behavior of internal stakeholders in project portfolio management and its impact on project success," *International Journal of Project Management*, 31: 830–46.

Bonke, S. (1998). "The Storebaelt fixed link: The fixing of multiplicity," London, Le Groupe Bagnolet Working Paper 14, <http://www.chantier.net/europe.html>.

Bourne, L. and Walker, D. H. (2005). "Visualising and mapping stakeholder influence," *Management Decision*, 43(5): 649–60.

Bourne, L. and Weaver, P. (2010). "Mapping stakeholders," in E. Chinyio and P. Olomolaiye (eds.), *Construction Stakeholder Management.* Oxford: Wiley Blackwell.

Burt, R. S. (2005), *Brokerage and Closure: An Introduction to Social Capital.* Oxford: Oxford University Press.

Cabantous, L. and Gond, J.-P. (2011). "Rational decision making as a performative praxis: Explaining rationality's eternal retour," *Organization Science*, 22: 573–86.

Callon, M. (1986). "Some elements of a sociology of translation: Domestication of the scallops and the fishermen of St. Brieuc Bay," in J. Law (ed.), *Power, Action, and Belief: A New Sociology of Knowledge.* London: Routledge, pp. 196–223.

Callon, M. (1998). "Introduction: the embeddedness of economic markets in economics." in M. Callon (ed.), *The Laws of the Markets.* Oxford: Blackwell, pp. 1–57.

Calvert, S. (1995). "Managing stakeholders," in J. R. Turner (ed.), *The Commercial Project Manager*. London: McGraw Hill, pp. 214–22.

Campbell, J. L. (2007). "Why would corporations behave in socially responsible ways? An institutional theory of corporate social responsibility," *Academy of Management Review*, 32(3): 946–67.

Chang, A., Chih, Y.-Y., Chew, E., and Pisarski, A. (2013). "Reconceptualising mega project success in Australian defence: Recognising the importance of value co-creation," *International Journal of Project Management*, 31: 1139–53.

Cleland, D. I. (1986). "Project stakeholder management," *Project Management Journal*, 17: 36–44.

Cleland, D. I. (1998). "Stakeholder management," in J. Pinto (ed.), *Project Management Handbook*. San Franciso, CA: Jossey-Bass, pp. 55–72.

Cleland, D. I. and King, W. R. (1968). *Systems Analysis and Project Management*. New York: McGraw-Hill.

Cochrane, A., Peck, J., and Tickell, A. (2002). "Olympic dreams: Visions of partnership," in J. Peck and K. Ward (eds.), *City of Revolution: Restructuring Manchester*. Manchester: Manchester University Press, pp. 95–115.

Collinge, W. H. and Harty, C. (2014). "Stakeholder interpretations of design: Semiotic insights into the briefing process," *Construction Management and Economics*, 32: 760–72.

Covey, S. R. (1989). *The 7 Habits of Highly Effective People*. London: Simon and Schuster.

Cruise, D. and Griffiths, A. (1988). *Lords of the Line: The Men Who Built the CPR*. Toronto: Penguin.

Currie, W. L. (2012). "Institutional isomorphism and change: The national programme for IT – 10 years on" *Journal of Information Technology*, 27: 236–48.

Currie, W. L. and Guah, M. W. (2007). "Conflicting institutional logics: A national programme for IT in the organisational field of healthcare," *Journal of Information Technology*, 22: 235–47.

Cusin, J. and Passebois-Ducros, J. (2015). "Appropriate persistence in a project: The case of the wine culture and tourism centre in Bordeaux," *European Management Journal*, 33: 341–53.

Davis, K. (2014). "Different stakeholder groups and their perceptions of project success," *International Journal of Project Management*, 32: 189–201.

De Schepper, S., Dooms, M., and Haezendonck, E. (2014). "Stakeholder dynamics and responsibilities in public–private partnerships: A mixed experience," *International Journal of Project Management*, 32: 1210–22.

Donaldson, T. and Preston, L. E. (1995). "The stakeholder theory of the corporation: Concepts, evidence, and implications," *Academy of Management Review*, 20(1): 65–91.

Driscoll, C. and Starik, M. (2004). "The primordial stakeholder: Advancing the conceptual consideration of stakeholder status for the natural environment," *Journal of Business Ethics*, 49: 55–73.

Drummond, H. (1996). *Escalation in Decision-making: The Tragedy of TAURUS*. Oxford: Oxford University Press.

Eskerod, P. and Vaagaaser, A. L. (2014). "Stakeholder management strategies and practices during a project course," *Project Management Journal*, 45: 71–85.

Faulkner, D. O. and Campbell, A. (eds.) (2003). *The Oxford Handbook of Strategy*. Oxford: Oxford University Press.

Fellows, R. and Liu, A. (2016). "Sensemaking in the cross-cultural contexts of projects," *International Journal of Project Management*, 34: 246–57.

Flyvbjerg, B., Bruzelius, N., and Rothengatter, W. (2003). *Megaprojects and Risk: An Anatomy of Ambition*. Cambridge: Cambridge University Press.

Flyvbjerg, B. and Molloy, E. (2011). "Delusion, deception and corruption in major infrastructure projects: Causes, consequences and cures," in S. Rose-Ackerman and T. Søreide (eds.), *International Handbook on the Economics of Corruption*, vol. 2. Cheltenham: Edward Elgar, pp. 81–107.

Flyvbjerg, B. and Sunstein, C. R. (2016). "The principle of the malevolent guiding hand: Or, the planning fallacy writ large," *Social Research*, 83: 979–1004.

Freeman, R. E. (1984). *Strategic Management: A Stakeholder Approach*. Cambridge: Cambridge University Press.

Frooman, J. (1999). "Stakeholder influence strategies," *Academy of Management Review*, 24: 191–205.

Gellert, P. K. and Lynch, B. D. (2003). "Mega-projects as displacements," *International Social Science Journal*, 55: 15–25.

Gibson, K. (2000). "The moral basis of stakeholder theory," *Journal of Business Ethics*, 26: 245–57.

Greiman, V. A. (2013). *Mega Project Management: Lessons on Risk and Projects Management from the Big Dig*. Hoboken, NJ: Wiley.

Greenwood, R., Oliver, C., Sahlin, K., and Suddaby, R. (eds.) (2008). *The Sage Handbook of Organizational Institutionalism*. London: Sage.

Hacking, I. (1999). *The Social Construction of What?* Cambridge, MA: Harvard University Press.

Harvey, P. and Knox, H. (2015). *Roads: An Anthropology of Infrastructure and Expertise*. Ithaca, NY: Cornell University Press.

Helm, D. (2009). "Infrastructure investment, the cost of capital, and regulation: An assessment," *Oxford Review of Economic Policy*, 25(3): 307–26.

Helm, D. (2015). *Natural Capital*. Princeton, NJ: Yale University Press.

Heravi, A., Coffey, V., and Trigunarsyah, B. (2015). "Evaluating the level of stakeholder involvement during the project planning processes of building projects," *International Journal of Project Management*, 33: 985–97.

Hirschman, A. O. (1995). *Development Projects Observed*. Washington, DC: The Brookings Institution.

Hobsbawm, E. J. (1962). *The Age of Capital 1848–1875*. London: Weidenfeld & Nicholson.

Hughes, T. P. (1998). *Rescuing Prometheus: Four Monumental Projects that Changed the Modern World*. New York: Vintage Books.

Johnson, G., and Scholes, K. (2002). *Exploring Corporate Strategy*, 6th edn. London: Prentice Hall.

Keynes, J. M. (1961). *The General Theory of Employment, Interest and Money*. London: Macmillan.

King, A. and Crewe, I. (2013). *The Blunders of Our Governments*. London: Oneworld.

Klakegg, O. J., Williams, T., and Shiferaw, A. T. (2016). "Taming the 'trolls': Major public projects in the making," *International Journal of Project Management*, 34: 282–96.

Laplume, A. O., Sonpar, K., and Litz, R. A. (2008). "Stakeholder theory: Reviewing a theory that moves us," *Journal of Management*, 34: 1152–89.

Latour, B. (2005). *Reassembling the Social: An Introduction to Actor-Network Theory*. Cambridge: Cambridge University Press.

Law, J. and Callon, M. (1992). "The life and death of an aircraft: A network analysis of technical change," in W. E. Bijker and J. Law (eds.), *Shaping Technology/Building Society*. Cambridge, MA: MIT Press, pp. 21–52.

Linder, M. (1994) *Projecting Capitalism: A History of the Internationalization of the Construction Industry.* Westport, CT: Greenwood Press.

Littau, P., Jujagiri, N. J., and Adlbrecht, G. (2010). "25 years of stakeholder theory in project management literature (1984–2009)," *Project Management Journal*, 41: 17–29.

Lundin, R. A., Arvidsson, N., Brady, T., Ekstedt, E., Midler, C., and Sydow, J. (2015). *Managing and Working in Project Society: Institutional Challenges of Temporary Organizations.* Cambridge: Cambridge University Press.

Mazur, A., Pisarski, A., Chang, A., and Ashkanasy, N. M. (2014). "Rating defence major project success: The role of personal attributes and stakeholder relationships," *International Journal of Project Management*, 32: 944–57.

McAdam, D. (2011) "Social movements and the growth in opposition to global projects," in W. R. Scott, R. E. Levitt, and R. J. Orr. (eds.), *Global Projects: Institutional and Political Challenges.* Cambridge: Cambridge University Press, pp. 86–110.

McAdam, D., Boudet, H. S., Davis, J., Orr, R. J., Scott, W. R., and Levitt, R. E. (2011). "'Site Fights': Explaining opposition to pipeline projects in the developing world," in W. R. Scott, R. E. Levitt, and R. J. Orr. (eds.) *Global Projects: Institutional and Political Challenges.* Cambridge, Cambridge University Press, pp. 279–309.

McElroy, B. and Mills, C. (2000). "Managing stakeholders," *Gower Handbook of Project Management*, Routledge Taylor and Francis Group, pp. 757–75.

Merrow, E. W. (2011). *Industrial Megaprojects: Concepts, Strategies and Practices for Success.* Hoboken, NJ: Wiley.

Merrow, E. W., Phillips, K. E., and Myers, C. W. (1981). *Understanding Cost Growth and Performance Shortfalls in Pioneer Process Plants.* Santa Monica, CA: RAND Corporation.

Miller, R. and Lessard, D. R. (2000). *The Strategic Management of Large Engineering Projects: Shaping Institutions, Risks, and Governance.* Cambridge, MA: MIT Press.

Missonier, S. and Loufrani-Fedida, S. (2014). "Stakeholder analysis and engagement in projects: From stakeholder relational perspective to stakeholder relational ontology." *International Journal of Project Management*, 32: 1108–22.

Mitchell, R. K., Agle, B. R., and Wood, D. J. (1997). "Toward a theory of stakeholder identification and salience: Defining the principle of who and what really counts," *Academy of Management Review*, 22: 853–86.

Mok, K. Y., Shen, G. Q., and Yang, J. (2015). "Stakeholder management studies in mega construction projects: A review and future directions," *International Journal of Project Management*, 33: 446–57.

Molloy, E. and Chetty, T. (2015). "The rocky road to legacy: Lessons from the 2010 FIFA World Cup South Africa stadium programme," *Project Management Journal*, 46: 88–107.

Morrell, D. (1987) *Indictment: Power and Politics in the Construction Industry.* London: Faber and Faber.

Morrison, R. (ed.) (2012). *The Principles of Project Finance.* Farnham: Gower.

Müller, R. (2011). "Project governance," in P. W. G. Morris, J. K. Pinto, and J. Soderlund (eds.), *The Oxford Handbook of Project Management.* Oxford: Oxford University Press, pp. 297–320.

Naess, P. (2006). "Cost-benefit analyses of transportation investments: Neither critical nor realistic," *Journal of Critical Realism*, 5: 32–60.

National Audit Office. (2013). *Universal Credit: Early Progress.* London: National Audit Office.

National Audit Office. (2014a). *Universal Credit: Progress Update.* London: National Audit Office.

National Audit Office. (2014b). *Major Projects Authority Annual Report 2012–13 and Government Project Assurance*. London: National Audit Office.

New, T. and Xie, Z. (2008). "Impacts of large dams on riparian vegetation: Applying global experience to the case of China's Three Gorges Dam," *Biodiversity and Conservation*, 17: 3149–63.

Olander, S. and Landin, A. (2005). "Evaluation of stakeholder influence in the implementation of construction projects," *International Journal of Project Management*, 23(4): 321–8.

Parmar, B. L., Freeman, R. E., Harrison, J. S., Wicks, A. C., Purnell, L., and De Colle, S. (2010). "Stakeholder theory: The state of the art," *The Academy of Management Annals*, 4: 403–45.

Pinch, T. J. and Bijker, W. E. (1987). "The social construction of facts and artefacts: Or how the sociology of science and the sociology of technology might benefit each other," in W. E. Bijker, T. P. Hughes, and T. J. Pinch (eds.), *The Social Construction of Large Technological Systems*. Cambridge, MA: MIT Press, pp. 17–50.

Pollack, J., Costello, K., and Sankaran, S. (2013). "Applying actor-network theory as a sense-making framework for complex organisational change programs," *International Journal of Project Management*, 31: 1118–28.

Pryke, S. (2012). *Social Network Analysis in Construction*. Oxford: Wiley Blackwell.

Reisner, M. (1993). *Cadillac Desert: The American West and Its Disappearing Water*. New York: Penguin.

Rowley, T. J. (1997). "Moving beyond dyadic ties: A network theory of stakeholder influences," *Academy of Management Review*, 22(4): 887–910.

Sage, D., Dainty, A., and Brookes, N. (2011). "How actor-network theories can help in understanding project complexities," *International Journal of Managing Projects in Business*, 4(2): 274–93.

Sage, D., Dainty, A., Tryggestad, K., Justesen, L., and Mouritsen, J. (2014). "Building with wildlife: Project geographies and cosmopolitics in infrastructure construction," *Construction Management and Economics*, 32(7–8): 773–86.

Sallinen, L., Ahola, T., and Ruuska, I. (2011). "Governmental stakeholder and project owner's views on the regulative framework in nuclear projects," *Project Management Journal*, 42: 33–47.

Samset, K. and Volden, G. H. (2016). "Front-end definition of projects: Ten paradoxes and some reflections regarding project management and project governance," *International Journal of Project Management*, 34: 297–313.

Sawyer, J. E. (1952). "Entrepreneurial error and economic growth," *Explorations in Entrepreneurial History*, 4: 199–204.

Scott, W. R. (2008). *Institutions and Organizations: Ideas and Interests*. Los Angeles, CA: Sage.

Scott, W. R. (2011). "The institutional environment of global projects," in W. R. Scott, R. E. Levitt, and R. J. Orr. (eds.), *Global Projects: Institutional and Political Challenges*. Cambridge: Cambridge University Press, pp. 52–85.

Self, P. (1970) "Nonsense on stilts": Cost–benefit analysis and the Roskill Commission," *The Political Quarterly*, 4: 249–60.

Selznick, P. (2011). *Leadership in Administration: A Sociological Interpretation*. New Orleans, LA: Quid Pro Books.

Steurer, R. (2006) "Mapping stakeholder theory anew: From the 'stakeholder theory of the firm' to three perspectives on business–society relations," *Business Strategy and the Environment*, 15: 55–69.

Stringer, J. (1995). "The planning enquiry process," in J. R. Turner (ed.), *The Commercial Project Manager*. London: McGraw-Hill.

Syben, G. (1996). *Learning the Rules of the Game Abroad: The Case of Friedrichstadtpassagen 207*. Le Groupe Bagnolet Working Paper 15, <http://www.chantier.net/europe.html>.

Szyliowicz, J. S. and Goetz, A. R. (1995). "Getting realistic about megaproject planning: The case of the Denver International Airport," *Policy Sciences*, 28: 347–67.

Tryggestad, K., Justesen, L., and Mouritsen, J. (2013). "Project temporalities: How frogs can become stakeholders," *International Journal of Managing Projects in Business*, 6(1): 69–87.

Turner, R. J. and Zolin, R. (2012). "Forecasting success on large projects: Developing reliable scales to predict multiple perspectives by multiple stakeholders over multiple time frames," *Project Management Journal*, 43: 87–99.

Van Marrewijk, A. (ed.) (2015). *Inside Megaprojects: Understanding Cultural Practices in Project Management*. Copenhagen: CBS Press.

Vickerman, R. (2007). "Cost–benefit analysis and large-scale infrastructure projects: State of the art and challenges," *Environment and Planning B: Planning and Design*, 34: 598.

Vrhovec, S. L. R., Hovelja, T., Vavpotič, D., and Krisper M. (2015). "Diagnosing organizational risks in software projects: Stakeholder resistance," *International Journal of Project Management*, 33: 1262–73.

Whitley, R. (1992). *Business Systems in East Asia: Firms, Markets, and Societies*. London: Sage.

Winch, G. M. (2000). "Construction business systems in the European Union: Editorial introduction," *Building Research and Information*, 28: 88–97.

Winch, G. M. (2004). "Managing project stakeholders," in P. W. G. Morris and J. K. Pinto (eds.), *The Wiley Guide to Managing Projects*. New York: Wiley, pp. 321–39.

Winch, G. M. (2014). "Three domains of project organising," *International Journal of Project Management*, 32: 721–31.

Winch, G. M. and Bonke, S. (2002). "Project stakeholder mapping: Analyzing the interests of project stakeholders," in D. P. Slevin, D. I. Cleland, and J. K. Pinto, *The Frontiers of Project Management Research*. Newtown Square, PA: Project Management Institute, pp. 385–403.

Winch, G. M., Clifton, N, and Millar, C. J. M. (2000). "Organisation and management in an Anglo-French consortium: The case of Transmanche Link," *Journal of Management Studies*, 37: 663–85.

Winch, G. M. and Schmidt, S. E. (2016). "Public–private partnerships: A review of the UK private finance initiative," in M. C. Jefferies and S. Rowlinson (eds.), *New Forms of Procurement: Public Private Partnerships and Relational Contracting in the 21st Century*. London: Taylor and Francis, pp. 35–50.

Yang, J., Shen, G. Q., Ho, M., Drew, D. S., and Xue, X. (2011). "Stakeholder management in construction: An empirical study to address research gaps in previous studies," *International Journal of Project Management*, 29: 900–10.

Yang, R. J. (2014). "An investigation of stakeholder analysis in urban development projects: Empirical or rationalistic perspectives," *International Journal of Project Management*, 32: 838–49.

Yang, R. J., Wang, Y., and Jin, X.-H. (2014). "Stakeholder attributes behaviors, and decision-making strategies on construction projects: Importance and correlations in practice," *Project Management Journal*, 45: 74–90.

Zeng, S. X., Ma, H. Y., Lin, H., Zeng, R. C., and Tam, V. W. Y. (2015). "Social responsibility of major infrastructure project in China," *International Journal of Project Management*, 33: 537–48.

CHAPTER 16

....

PRIVATE FINANCE

What Problems Does It Solve, and How Well?

....

GRAEME HODGE AND CARSTEN GREVE

16.1 INTRODUCTION: THE ROLE OF PRIVATE FINANCE IN MEGAPROJECTS

PUBLIC–PRIVATE partnerships (PPPs) in infrastructure have been viewed in a wide variety of ways, from narrow definitions to broader conceptions. The OECD, for example, defines PPPs as "long term contractual arrangements between the government and a private partner whereby the latter delivers and funds public services using a capital asset, sharing the associated risk" (2012: 18). The World Bank sees PPPs more broadly as "a long term contract between a private party and a government entity for providing a public asset or service in which the private party bears significant risks and management responsibility and remuneration is linked to performance" (2015). What is beyond doubt here is that the idea of infrastructure PPPs is now well established around the globe.[1] There is also a general agreement all over the world that private finance plays a significant role in the long-term infrastructure contracts being entered. Furthermore, PPP is now well established as one of our favorite mechanisms of procurement for public infrastructure projects (Hodge et al. 2010). Private finance was part of the PPP idea from the beginning. The UK is often credited with starting the PPP wave of projects by naming their public policy program "The Private Finance Initiative" (PFI) (Terry 1996). In 2012 the UK government revisited the policy and after a lengthy deliberation came up with "PF2"—a modernized version of using private finance for public infrastructure projects (HM Treasury 2012). PPPs have also played an important part of what Flyvbjerg (2014) defines as megaprojects. After the global financial crisis in 2008–2009, PPPs came under pressure (Greve and Hodge 2013). Private finance for infrastructure projects came under fire. Private finance dried up for certain projects, and bankruptcies occurred. While there has been much debate about the use of private finance, there are few overviews of what private finance can do and how much the policy of private finance in infrastructure has accomplished. The purpose of this chapter is therefore to take stock of the role of private finance in PPPs.

This chapter therefore asks: what problems do private finance and the PPP long-term infrastructure contract technology solve in megaprojects, and how well? The first argument posed is that the reasons for wanting private finance in megaprojects have varied between countries and changed over time, but have essentially been related to two primary formal rationales. The second argument is that there is increasing academic evidence about how well private finance does, but that, despite the loud and often colorful debates, the verdict is still out because the evidence is not all one way.

The chapter reviews the current literature on private finance in PPPs and examines some of the key contributions to the discussion on private finance. It is structured in the following way. The first section discusses the PPP phenomenon briefly; the second section discusses the reasons given for the use of private finance; the third section examines the evidence on how well private finance solves problems; and the fourth section offers a discussion and conclusion.

16.2 A Brief History of Private Finance in Public–Private Partnerships

This section describes the evolution of using private finance as part of PPP infrastructure projects. The possibility of using private finance for infrastructure projects such as toll roads goes back thousands of years. In more recent times, de Vries (2013: 11) describes the place of cofinancing and private financing throughout the seventeenth and eighteenth centuries for the case of canals, land reclamation, and transport projects in the Netherlands and the United Kingdom. Likewise, France has for centuries employed private financing for public infrastructure, with the French concession model for water supply being refined during the 1800s. There is clearly a rich history of public–private mixing through time, and the idea of marrying private to public efforts is hardly new, as Wettenhall (2005: 2010) has said. Recent decades, however, have seen a renewed realization that no sector alone is likely to be capable of solving society's complex problems moving forward.

The modern rebirth of the PPP idea came from the United Kingdom in the early 1990s.[2] It was at this time that the option of using private finance in delivering public infrastructure was turned into a modern policy preference for a jurisdiction.[3] In 1992 the Conservative government led by John Major proposed the Private Finance Initiative. The main reason was that the Conservative Government was unable or unwilling to finance public infrastructure the traditional way through public-sector investment. The public funding of new infrastructure risked exceeding the national Public Sector

Borrowing Requirement (PSBR), so the Conservative government launched the idea that new infrastructure should be initially financed by private-sector sources. The public sector would gain in that it acquired new infrastructure. The private sector would gain because it acquired new investment opportunities and was able to earn a profit if the projects came in on time and on budget. It was also then seen as continuing an earlier trend to privatize the activities of government—a policy at which the Conservative government had already excelled.

The trend was picked up by other governments around the world. Australia was one of the first countries to be inspired by the UK experience. The state of Victoria, in particular, had been experimenting with private-sector financing through the late 1980s and early 1990s, alongside substantial budget difficulties and severe borrowing limits (PAEC 2006: 55). Following the success of the early CityLink road project and various prison projects during the mid- to late 1990s, it launched the Partnerships Victoria policy in 2000 to inject private finance as a preference for major public infrastructure projects. Canada followed in the early 2000s in many of its provinces. Quebec was also an early mover, and British Columbia developed one of the most ambitious and consistent PPP programs in Canada and indeed the world.

In 1997 the United Kingdom got a new government as power shifted from the Conservatives to New Labour. There were doubts whether the PFI scheme would be axed or whether it would be allowed to continue. After all, it was a variant of a privatization program that the Conservatives had heralded, and that Labour when in opposition had railed against. Tony Blair and the New Labour government decided to hold on to the program. Researchers have since debated why that was the case (Flinders 2010; Hellowell 2010). There were three reasons for Tony Blair to continue the PFI policy. First, the New Labour government came into office with ambitious plans for investing and developing in public-sector infrastructure—particularly schools and hospitals—but needed the financing capability to deliver on these promises. Second, New Labour adopted PFI as a way to signal to the City of London that the government was not anti-business, but could be seen as a reliable business partner. Continuing with the PFI scheme was a solid way to send the signal of a pro-business agenda. Third, the UK government was already seen as a world leader in the area of PPP and public infrastructure innovation. New Labour wanted to keep and build on the cutting-edge global position that the PFI policy offered at the time. And so it came to be that the New Labour government continued the PFI policy of the previous Conservative government. Later evidence revealed that investment in public infrastructure actually increased during the New Labour years. New schools sprang up, new hospitals were constructed, and new transport infrastructure was delivered. New Labour was seen as a proactive government that cared about infrastructure and megaprojects.

The PFI scheme attracted the interest of many countries in a similar situation to the UK. Countries wanted to invest and establish new megaprojects, but either did not have the money themselves or were unwilling to finance these ambitions. There was room for the private sector to step in with private finance. Spain, Italy, France, and the Netherlands all embarked on PFI schemes, and much of the inspiration came from the

UK model. Even today, countries still cite the United Kingdom as the main inspiration. Mexico, when presenting to the OECD recently about its PPP plans, explicitly cited the UK as the main source of inspiration for the way the legislation and the PPP unit was set up. International organizations began to spread knowledge about the concept of private finance. The World Bank analyzed PPP as a way to bring private finance into infrastructure projects in the developing world. OECD (2008) published a thorough report on PPPs titled *In Pursuit of Value for Money and Risk Sharing*. There were now reviews and recommendations about bringing private finance into public-sector megaprojects. Some countries stuck to the more traditional state-owned enterprise model and fairly conventional public-sector investment policies. The Scandinavian countries, for example, have not thus far shown a particular interest in the PPP model. Denmark, for instance, constructed three megaprojects (the Great Belt Bridge, the Øresund Bridge, and the Copenhagen Metro) through a state-owned enterprise model, where the state obtained a loan or guaranteed the loan obtained by the state-owned enterprise. This was an alternative to the PPP model with private finance, albeit a more traditional one, and a model that depended on Denmark having a sound economy with an AAA rating.

The global financial crisis (GFC) put a temporary halt to the victorious parade of the private-finance idea in public-sector megaprojects. The GFC came as shock to the PPP world in 2008. Most PPP projects had been financed by bank loans and investments. Now the banks suddenly became much more conservative, and some banks could not afford to extend credit or provide finance to the PPP projects (Connolly and Wall 2013; Hellowell and Vecchi 2013). In the "leading" PPP country, the United Kingdom, the government even had to step in to save some of the PPP projects from bankruptcy.[4] The United Kingdom at the time came up with a revised model in which the UK Treasury would temporarily take over some of the investments from the banks. Looking back, the United Kingdom had in essence started a practice of a mixed model of finance. It has made a big effort in trying to portray this change as a temporary situation designed to overcome the credit crisis, but the point is that a sole bank-financed PPP deal was no longer the first option for a PPP project. The UK Treasury has since withdrawn again from some of the projects, but the government does advocate a more mixed-finance model today. The UK government also revised its whole PFI policy scheme for PPPs. The result was the document on *A New Approach to Public–Private Partnerships* of 2012, in which the government advocates mixed financing (HM Treasury 2012).

The GFC certainly came as a surprise to PPP supporters and rocked the intellectual foundations of private-finance believers. The risk-adjusted calculus of capital-asset pricing models, the efficient-market hypothesis, and the notion of self-steering markets were all challenged. For a period, it seemed that the PPP idea was doomed and only on life-support as governments struggled to keep afloat many projects.[5] A while after the banking crisis, the Basel III rules were laid down. These rules make it more difficult for banks to engage in deals that involve a high degree of risk, and they soon lost their appetite for financing PPP deals in a big way. The PPP market suffered from this new approach from the banks.

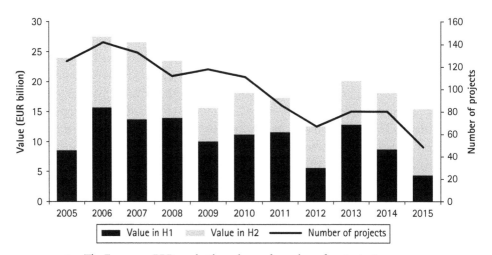

FIGURE 16.1 The European PPP market by value and number of projects since 2005.

A strong degree of interest in PPPs, however, continued to blossom, as shown in Figure 16.1. Here, it is evident that the high levels of interest in PPPs throughout Europe (at around €25 billion in deals each year) had trended down to around two thirds this level after 2010 (at around €15 billion annually.) Deal levels for both the first half-year (H1) and second half-year (H2) are indicated; European PPP Expertise Centre (2014).

This enduring interest in PPPs post-GFC came from a number of different sources. First, there continued to be a need and desire to invest in infrastructure and in mega-projects. The finance model is now not based only on private finance and on banks, but on mixed financing and financing from a wider variety of lenders. New players to the game include the pension funds, which have taken a more systematic interest in PPP deals. For the pension funds, the attraction lay in stable projects that often carried some form of government guarantee or political sponsorship, and the stable rate of return on investments that only governments could provide. Pension funds see megaprojects as desirable to their investment portfolio. Project risks are also being shared more evenly, with governments taking on a bigger proportion than was earlier the case. The second renewed interest came from international organizations that are now actively advising governments around the world, and especially in the developing world, about PPP projects. The World Bank and the IMF have been very active in this regard, and in 2015 the World Bank has launched a "PPP Knowledge Lab" that focuses on PPPs, including private financing. In some ways this might be viewed as a continuation and perhaps rebranding of a long-time interest in infrastructure provision from such organizations, but the partnership label and the appeal of seeking the best of both public-sector and private-sector capabilities remained powerful. The third renewed interest came from governments and regions in their active pursuit of industrial growth, and their desire to adopt the PPP policy brand and use private finance to help further growth policies. The European Union has recently taken such a step with the ambitious *An Investment Plan for Europe* (European Commission 2014). The European Commission is in the forefront of this policy, and has put forward the plan to raise for €315 billion of investments. The European Commission will only provide a small amount of the investment itself. Most of the investments sought are to come from the private sector in the form of private finance. The investments are targeted toward infrastructure projects in energy, transport, and digitalization. In some ways, the European Commission's plan can be characterized as PPPs on a grand scale. If realized, the Commission will spur many PPP projects in the coming years. Skepticism exists, however, as to whether the Commission can pull this plan off.

We might therefore summarize the evolution of arguments adopted by governments for using private finance for public projects in terms of three phases: the 1990s, after 2000, and after 2010. This is shown in Table 16.1.

Table 16.1 Three phases of arguments for using private finance in public projects

	Main features of private finance	Focus in research on private finance	Inspirational models
1990s	Private financed sourced from private investors via banks.	Private finance discussed mainly in crude terms and as a pragmatic way to obtain finance for projects, and examined and evaluated to see if there is an ideological/political perspective (Shaoul 2010).	UK PFI model.
2000s	Private finance sourced from private investors until GFC. Private finance "dries up" for a period from 2009 onward. Basel III means stricter rules for banks, which reduces the appetite of banks for PPPs.	Economists discuss private finance issues, including question of VfM versus total social costs, the cost of capital, and the role of the discount rate (Blanc-Brude et al. 2006; Boardman and Vining 2010; Vining and Boardman 2008). Individual private finance deals examined.	International experiences with private finance from Australia and Canada.
2010s	Institutional investors (pension funds) enter the market. Some government finance to supplement private finance lead to a mix of finance. Finance can now come from a variety sources.	More technical discussions on particular finance arrangements and models (de Bettignies and Ross 2010; de Vries and Yehoue 2013; Hellowell and Vecchi 2013).	Focus on use of private finance in a greater variety of countries, including the USA (with the municipal bonds market), developing countries, and China. World Bank and others give advice on the use of a wider range of alternative private finance options.

16.3 PRIVATE FINANCE AND THE PPP TECHNOLOGY: WHAT PROBLEMS DOES IT SOLVE?

This section considers the reasons given for using private finance for public infrastructure projects and megaprojects. There has been much debate in the literature over the years about the advantages and disadvantages of the use of private finance, and more broadly, the use of PPP technologies, in megaprojects. Contributions from fields such as public policy, public administration, political science, and accounting emphasize the extent to which private finance and PPP technologies such as long-term infrastructure agreements based on private-contract law may assist in the process of governing and in meeting both political and public policy goals.[6] Analysts from engineering, construction management, planning, and project finance emphasize the promise of better on-time and on-budget delivery, along with the probable mechanisms leading to these improvements. Those from economics, on the other hand, emphasize the possible theoretical advantages of privately financed long-term contracts along with the more modest degree to which our economic models have been calibrated to real world conditions (de Bettignies and Ross 2010; de Vries and Yehoue 2013). Our judgment on the main controversies is that there are two main sets of formal arguments for why private finance and PPP contract technology is attractive in megaprojects:

1. Private finance is needed because public finance is unavailable or politically unattractive in meeting government's ambition in infrastructure policy.
2. Private finance provides the private sector with an incentive to become engaged in public infrastructure projects and is a way of securing projects efficiently, as well as being delivered on time and on budget.

Both of these formal rationales[7] deserve discussion.

Private finance is needed because public finance is unavailable or politically unattractive in meeting government's ambition in infrastructure policy. Governments may have huge ambitions to develop new infrastructure, but do not have the means to finance these projects or are unwilling to take up loans themselves. Governments turn to the private sector to provide private finance. In the early days of PPPs in the 1990s, this mostly meant turning to the banks. Later governments have tried to court pension funds and convince them that they should invest in PPPs. Private finance, however, comes at a higher borrowing cost/higher interest rate than when governments try to borrow the money itself. If governments can get a much lower interest rate, why do they not just finance the deals themselves? Often, governments are not in a position where they can just borrow more money. In the European Union, for instance, government debt cannot currently be higher than 3% of GDP (OECD 2008: 45). So, some governments actually need the availability of private finance if ambitious infrastructure plans are to be carried out in real life. As we saw before, private banks were happy to lend to governments before the GFC. Capital was available; governments just had to ask. Complications arose later on the PPP policy development when the actual composition of the private-finance portfolio was dissected. In other instances, governments may not have the institutional arrangements readily in place to implement projects through SOEs and with public funding, and so may not consider these. In yet other instances, governments may wish to limit public sector debt as a policy aim, and hence prefer private-sector financing in principle. The use of private-sector financing as a policy preference, however, raises many issues as policy decisions are made, projects are evaluated, and contract arrangements are put in place. These issues include matters such as the risk profiles of the investments themselves, the rate of return gained by private investors relative to the risks taken, and the discount rate used when evaluating alternative delivery options. Such matters have occupied the literature on private finance deals for some time, and a fierce debate continues as to what kinds of deals government are getting into and their relative efficacy.

Private finance provides the private sector with an incentive to become engaged in public infrastructure projects and is a way of securing projects efficiently as well as being delivered on time and on budget. This second argument for the use of private finance is that it provides stronger incentives to have projects delivered on time and to the allocated budget, compared with traditional ways of delivering projects. The argument is that if private investors have put money in a project, they want to see a return on their investment, and they will be vitally interested in delivering the promised piece of infrastructure. When the private sector becomes engaged in financing, as well as delivering a PPP project, so the argument goes, they will provide greater discipline and focus on getting the job done efficiently and according to specification. The logic is that the private sector is more able and more capable of meeting a tighter project time schedule and a robust project organization.[8] As well, having signed up to a long-term legal contract, this will shield against unwanted political influence in project details. In short, these all ensure a greater focus on effective delivery. A crucial element in PPP delivery is also risk-sharing, as any text on PPPs emphasizes (OECD 2008). The provision of private finance not only encourages discussion about who is to take on what type of risk over the life of the project, but also clarity as to the precise agreement reached.

It could also be added that the private sector not only provides finance but also provides expertise and know-how from previous projects. PPPs therefore become a way for the public sector to tap into private sector expertise from early conception through to lifetime operation. Governments in a jurisdiction benefit from having a private-sector partner that has carried out many infrastructure projects in other parts of the world, and they can learn from experience elsewhere, from private-sector quality-assurance systems, and from projects in other countries.

We have now articulated the two primary sets of reasons why private finance and PPP technology is important to megaprojects. What has happened over time in the use of private finance? Again, there are competing views in the literature. It can certainly be said that private finance was needed in the first period of establishing PPPs in the United Kingdom, because the UK government simply did not have the means to finance the infrastructure projects initially desired by the Confederation of British Industries and supported by the government. This was even more apparent during Tony Blair's New Labour government when the ambition for the public sector was higher, yet the financial constraints remained substantial. So at the beginning of the modern PPP policy rebirth there simply was a need for access to capital. When banks became more interested in PPPs they started to court not only the UK government but many governments around the world, with loan opportunities in order to establish PPPs. UK banks also saw a market abroad as countries tried to emulate the UK experience. Later on, the argument was more about the private-sector discipline and risk sharing that came with accepting private finance. Governments and state-owned enterprises were not trusted, at least in the PPP adopting countries, to carry out ambitious infrastructure projects.

The degree to which private-sector discipline has led to achieving the goals sought has been hotly disputed. Many researchers and observers have claimed that the private sector has not in reality delivered efficient PPP deals, and that they continue to seek profit opportunities rather than thinking only about project development. Hodge (2004) warned early of the possibility that governments could use private finance as if it were a mega credit card, where the government buys big, overspends, but then clearly needs to pay the bill in the end. Careful attention to exactly how PPPs are financed has been given by Hellowell and Vecchi (2012, 2013) and Connolly and Wall (2013). The essence that these authors are trying to tease out is that the actual financial composition of the deals is highly important in the rest of the life of the PPP. Similarly, there is an argument about the use of a fair and correct discount rate. Researchers such as Boardman and Vining (2010) have disputed the choice of discount rates taken by many governments. Researchers such as Shaoul (2010) and Edwards et al. (2004) have been critical about the private sector's intentions and strategies in financing public infrastructure. And interestingly, the Scandinavian experience with government- and state-owned enterprise-run infrastructure projects has also shown to some extent that private finance is not necessarily a prerequisite for good project delivery.

16.4 Summing Up: What Problems Does Private Finance and PPP Solve?

Governments nowadays are likely to employ a mix of these formal rationales as justifications for PPPs. It is interesting to note that the European Commission's approach has to some extent pointed back to argument one again: the European Commission needs the actual private finance to get its ambitious *An Investment Plan for Europe* off the ground. The same trend can be observed in the developing countries where PPPs may be first and foremost a way to attract banks and especially pension funds to invest money in much needed infrastructure projects.

16.5 How Well Does Private Finance Work in Public–Private Partnerships?

We argued previously that private finance played a primary role in the PPP idea, and that, fundamentally, it aimed at solving two primary problems: the unavailability or unattractiveness of public finance; and the promise of better efficiency, timeliness, and expenditure accuracy. So, to what extent does private finance and the PPP technology succeed in solving these problems? And what does the evidence say about these debates? It is to these matters that we now turn.

There is little doubt on the first of these promises. The availability of private finance has always had the potential to assist governments in times of public-finance shortfalls. First, the possibility of adopting "user pays" schemes, whether through toll roads in past millennia or in more modern times, relieves governments of the need to even use public funds for major infrastructure projects, by definition. The degree to which infrastructure financing ought to come from the public budget (or be paid by users from their "private" budgets) is a matter for political judgment.

We noted earlier that the British government adopted private finance in the 1990s because it could not take out any further public-sector borrowing to meet its desire to provide new infrastructure. Prior to this time, though, many governments (like the business sector) had already experimented with operating leases so that infrastructure could be provided, but with public debt kept off the balancesheet. While of questionable legitimacy as far as financial clarity is concerned, there was nevertheless little doubt that at least for a while this "off-balance-sheet" tool enabled private infrastructure to be financed to deliver political infrastructure promises. The high-profile demise of the US company Enron, after its use of special off-balance-sheet vehicles to hide company debt, led to a renewed attention to debt honesty and balance-sheet accuracy. Today, it is little surprise that governments such as that of Victoria, Australia, include all privately financed infrastructure deals on the government balance sheet. And this practice is becoming increasingly prevalent. However, the practice of providing a government balance sheet itself according to internationally accepted accounting standards with the inclusion of PPP debt details on this balance sheet is not necessarily particularly common, internationally. Moreover, the continued existence of rules which constrain governments in their capacity to take out public borrowing also continues to make private-finance options attractive to governments.

The second of these private-finance/PPP widespread rationales deals with efficiency, timeliness, and expenditure accuracy, and has been viewed as the most legitimate. It has been the subject of much of the private finance/PPP research and investigation effort to date, because these values are central to the disciplines completing the work. This more technical rationale (and the associated debate on value-for-money, VfM) has been crucial to modern infrastructure discourse. And perhaps because of this, this rationale has arguably been the most heavily contested. In some ways, this strong contestation is not surprising. After all, disentangling the roles of many of the elements which today make up the PPP phenomenon is not necessarily a straightforward matter. The adoption of private finance to at least some degree is certainly a significant part of the PPP arrangement, but so too are many other matters. These include, for example, the existence of a single consortium; the bundling of contracts together; the detailed specification of services and performance standards; the type and size of commercial incentives; the sophistication of legal arrangements for taking on and rewarding risk taking; separating the institutional and contractual roles for financier, construction firm and client; strong professional skills on all sides; the employment of advanced construction techniques; and the quality of interrelationships between internal and external personnel. As well, of course, the legal, competitive, cultural, and governance environment in which a project delivery arrangement takes place can also be just as crucial as its internal commercial and institutional structures and cultures, to our minds.[9]

There is much written on these matters from a theoretical stance, at one extreme, but far less written calibrating such theoretical models to the real world and determining VfM or efficiency for real project alternatives. There is also much written advocating (and criticizing) project delivery alternatives such as those involving private finance on one side, but precious little rigorous and independent empirical work on the other, which again calibrates these ideas against our real-world experience. Indeed, it is our judgment that the knowledge base on PPP performance, even at the most fundamental levels, remains disappointingly low.

Viewing PPP success simply in terms of the VfM dimension, we have traced what can be learned from the performance evidence to date (Hodge and Greve 2009: 2013). The international review of Sarmento (2014) recently added to the field. Examples of some of the evaluation research included in these reviews are shown in Table 16.2. While not comprehensive, these examples give a fair flavor of the research findings to date.

The overwhelming lesson from empirical evidence to date is that despite the considerable experience with the PPP family of long-term infrastructure contract arrangements around the world, the polarized advocacy and criticism, and numerous professional glossy reports,[10] the VfM performance evidence is mixed and there are surprisingly few rigorous performance assessments in terms of the public interest. Independent rigorous assessments have been scarce. This has left our judgment as to the performance of PPPs worryingly open. Many assessments of PPP performance have of course been made covering either more general ground[11] or particular PPP concerns,[12] but most have analyzed business case projections rather than measurements of actual costs.[13] Most have also not been particularly rigorous from a statistical perspective, and have failed to employ control groups (Hodge 2010). The counterfactual of "traditional procurement" has also usually been vague as well, leaving such assessments unreliable. Hare (2013) said it well when he remarked that the available PPP evidence was "both weak and mixed."

Table 16.2 Selected PPP evaluations, 1998–2014

Study	Sample/cases	Country	Type of publication	Better VfM?	Comments/conclusions
Bloomfield et al. (1998)	A Massachusetts correctional facility	United States	Case study	No	7.4% more expensive through P3 lease purchasing; project was "wasteful and risky" with real risks to the public camouflaged
Arthur Anderson and LSE (2000)	Twenty-nine business cases analysed	United Kingdom	Initial evaluation	Yes	17% cost savings estimated against the PSC; risk transfer accounted for 61% of forecast savings
National Audit Office (2000)	Seven business cases from NAO (2000)	United Kingdom	Business cases	Yes	10–20% cost savings estimated
Walker and Walker (2000)	General observations of Australian cases	Australia	Literature review	No	PPP infrastructure financing deals seen as "misleading accounting trickery" with eroded accountability to Parliament and the public; private real rates of return up to ten times those expected for the public
Mott Macdonald (2002)	Thirty-nine traditional projects and eleven PFI projects selected	United Kingdom	Multiple cases reviewed	Yes	Traditional "public" infrastructure provision arrangements were on time and on budget 30% and 27% of the time, but PFI-type partnerships were on time and on budget 76% and 78% of the time, respectively
Pollitt (2002)	Ten major PFI cases	United Kingdom	Review of audit office cases	Yes	The best deal was probably obtained in every case, and good value for money was probably achieved in eight of the ten cases
Audit Commission (2003)	Ten traditional and eight PFI schools were compared	United Kingdom	Audit report	No	"We found no evidence that PFI projects delivered schools more quickly than projects funded in more conventional ways. The public sector comparator has lost the confidence of many people ..."

(continued)

Table 16.2 Continued

Study	Sample/cases	Country	Type of publication	Better VfM?	Comments/conclusions
Greve (2003)	Case study of Farum Municipality	Denmark	Case analysis	No	"The most spectacular scandal in the history of Danish public administration." It resulted in raised taxes for the citizens of Farum, higher debt for citizens, and a former mayor in prison
Fitzgerald (2004)	Eight PPP cases from Victoria	Australia	Report to government	Uncertain	PPP superiority over traditional delivery mechanisms was dependent on the discount rate adopted in the analysis; opposite conclusions were reached when using discount rates of 8.65% (where PPP was 9% cheaper) and 5.7% (where PPP was 6% more expensive)
Edwards et al. (2004)	Eight cases from roads and thirteen hospitals case studies	United Kingdom	Case reviews and interviews	No	Contracts reviewed three years in; "PFI is an expensive way of financing and delivering public services." "The chief beneficiaries are the providers of finance."
Grimsey and Lewis (2004)	Selected global observations across several sectors	Several countries	Literature review	Yes	"Preliminary evidence does seem to indicate strongly that PPPs offer one solution to the public procurement problem. There is not one 'model' of a PPP."
Pollitt (2005)	General observations of UK cases plus five cases	United Kingdom	Literature review	Yes	"It seems difficult to avoid a positive overall assessment."
Shaoul (2005)	General observations of UK cases	United Kingdom	Literature review	No	PFI has turned out to be very expensive with a lack of accountability; PFI policies "enrich the few at the expense of the majority."

(continued)

Table 16.2 Continued

Study	Sample/cases	Country	Type of publication	Better VfM?	Comments/conclusions
Boardman et al. (2005: 186)	Five roads, waste management, and water desalination cases	Canada and United States	Case reviews	No	Unless contracts both compensate the private sector for risks and then ensure that they actually bear it, "P3s will not improve allocative efficiency."
Auditor-General of New South Wales (2006)	Construction of nineteen schools in New South Wales	Australia	Audit report	Yes	Between 7% and 23% cheaper; auditor saw as "persuasive" the business case for these two PFI contracts
Pollock et al. (2007)	Reanalysis of Mott Macdonald and other reports	United Kingdom	Academic paper	No	"There is no evidence to support the Treasury cost and time overrun claims of improved efficiency in PFI" ... "[estimates being quoted are] not evidence based but biased to favor PFI ... Only one study compares PFI procurement performance, and all claims based on [this] are misleading."
Allen Consulting Group (2007)	Sample of twenty-one PPPs and thirty-three traditional projects	Australia	Consulting report	Yes	PPPs reported as being an 11% cheaper alternative to traditional projects measured from the point of contractual commitment (or 31% if taken from project inception); research project funded by Australia's peak infrastructure supply body
Blanc-Brude et al. (2006)	227 new road sections across fifteen EU countries, of which sixty-five were PPPs	European Union	Thirty-one regression analyses	Not tested	*Ex ante* PPP construction costs were 24% higher than traditional procurement; this is a similar magnitude to the traditional cost overruns; whether PPPs deliver lower overall life-cycle costs remains unknown

(continued)

Table 16.2 Continued

Study	Sample/cases	Country	Type of publication	Better VfM?	Comments/conclusions
Leviakangas (2007: 211)	A Finnish toll-road case study	Finland	Financial models	No	The hypothesis that private finance enabled welfare gains to be achieved was not confirmed
Vining and Boardman (2008)	Ten cases across several sectors	Canada	Public economics	Uncertain	In these ten case studies, exactly half were judged as economic "successes," while the other half were judged as "not successful"; those projects judged as not successful were generally bigger projects
Sarmento (2010)	"SCUT" highway project	Portugal	Economics	No	"If traditional procurement had been used, it would have been far less expensive … €2 billion or €3 billion less"; government judged as incapable of properly negotiating with private bidders
Vecchi et al. (2010)	Fourteen new and refurbished hospitals and support services	Italy	Finance	No	"Excess returns are being made by the investors in these projects … projected rates of returns … were very much higher than we would expect to find in a properly functioning and competitive market." A "very low level of systematic risk" was taken in PPP contracts by investors
Ball (2011)	Many projects	Australia and UK	Public management	No	In most cases, the risk transfer process provides PPP VfM
Boers et al. (2013: 470)	Reviewed forty-eight audit reports internationally	Twenty-one audit offices	Audit	No	"There is still no hard evidence to show that DBFM(O) projects represent the most efficient form of government procurement. There is no reason … to assume that [PPP] benefits will automatically accrue."

(continued)

Table 16.2 Continued

Study	Sample/cases	Country	Type of publication	Better VfM?	Comments/conclusions
Barlow et al. (2013)	Healthcare PPPs across nine countries	Europe	Health management	Uncertain	Mixed results were achieved with earlier PPPs which did not show VfM; newer PPPs promised more but were also harder to set up and manage
Regan (2014)	Review of international PPP experience	Several countries	Building and construction	Yes	The international evidence suggests that PPPs "are delivering better infrastructure services at lower cost than traditional procurement methods"

So, what do we see looking at the VfM results compared with traditional procurement? Reviews such as Hodge and Greve (2009) and Sarmento (2014) revealed three large groups of findings in the evaluation literature. The first group of evaluations shows superior PPP performance compared with traditional infrastructure delivery. Mainly through the risk-transfer calculus, these report lower cost estimates (of up to 31%) compared with traditional procurement. Examples of such assessments include the early report to the UK government of Arthur Andersen (2000) estimating costs savings amounting to 17%, and the Allen Consulting Group (2007) industry-funded report to the Australian government which looked at fifty-four public and private projects and concluded that "PPPs demonstrate clearly superior cost efficiency over traditional procurement" (of between 11% and 31%, depending on how this is measured). These have been supported by industry-linked research such as Regan (2014), and strengthened by practitioners who have confirmed good VfM for PPPs (Eadie et al. 2013). They have also been bolstered by studies estimating that PPPs were delivered on time more often (76% compared with 30% for traditional projects) and on budget (78% compared with 27% for traditional arrangements) (Mott-Macdonald 2002; National Audit Office 2002).

An opposing second group of studies, though, do not support a judgment of PPP superiority. Serious concerns here included excessive returns to investors (Vecchi et al. 2010), a biased VfM appraisal methodology in favor of policy expansion, and poor availability of information needed for project evaluation and scrutiny (Shaoul 2005). Even the UK Public Accounts Committee of Parliament labeled the public sector comparator (PSC) process as clearly "manipulation." Ball et al. (2007) noted "almost entirely subjective" risk analyses, and the UK Audit Commission (2003) "found no evidence that PFI projects delivered schools more quickly than projects funded in more conventional ways." As well, Pollock et al. (2007) criticized the Mott-Macdonald on-time and on-budget findings as having no solid evidence base, stating that "all claims based on [this] are misleading."[14] Some practitioners, too, remained skeptical of PPP VfM, ranking it seventeenth of twenty potential benefits, according to Umar et al. (2013), while policy critics saw PPPs as "fabulous deals—for all but taxpayers" (Davidson 2013) or else a "blueprint for bankruptcy" (Salzman 2014). Many Auditors General, as well, remained skeptical of PPPs. The Ontario (Canada) Auditor General, for example, reported bluntly that for seventy-four PPP projects, the tangible costs "were estimated to be nearly $8 billion higher than ... if the projects were contracted out and managed by the public sector" (OAGO 2014). Echoing concerns a decade earlier about risk valuation uncertainties, OAGO (2014) reported that the costing of risks tipped the projects in favor of PPP delivery, and yet "no empirical data support[ed] the valuation of the cost of the risks." On a more international scale, Boers et al. (2013: 470) reviewed forty-eight audit reports from twenty-one audit offices around the world, and concluded that "there is still no hard evidence to show that DBFM(O) projects represent the most efficient form of government procurement," and that while there are potential benefits to be gained from using PPPs, "there is no reason ... to assume that these benefits will automatically accrue."

A third large group of studies was also observed. These studies also doubted claims of PPP success, but the logic for this conclusion was that far greater analytical care was required before PPPs could be judged superior to traditional methods. Blanc-Brude et al. (2006), for example, conducted careful regression analyses across EU countries and found PPP roads were 24% more expensive initially than our expectations from traditional procurement—ironically, at about the same magnitude of traditional project cost overruns.[15] Fitzgerald (2004) argued that the size of costs savings claimed in his Australian PPP assessment was largely dependent on the discount rate used (with a lower discount rate suggesting a cost increase of 6% rather than the 9% cost saving estimated using the higher discount rate). Vining and Boardman (2008) judged only one half of the Canadian PPPs reviewed as successes, and Jupe (2009) viewed PPPs as "imperfect solutions" for transport in the United Kingdom.[16] Importantly, too, Hodge (2002) had already warned a decade earlier that while "the idea of risk transfer is all good in theory" there was in reality insufficient empirical work being done on the valuation and pricing of risks in PPPs, leaving us uncertain as to whether risks were being appropriately "shared" or being "shafted" back to taxpayers (cited in PAEC 2006: 158).

Overall, then, it is fair to say that the best reading of the PPP VfM evidence is that it is mixed. It is also fair to say that, as Sarmento and Renneboog (2014) put it, academics were generally skeptical that PPPs generated VfM, whereas governments were not.[17]

16.6 DISCUSSION AND CONCLUSION

This chapter has considered the use of private finance and PPP technologies in megaprojects, with the focus on what problems private finance solved, and how well. Several of the lessons here are clear. First, there is no doubt that private finance will continue to attract governments who are either unable or unwilling to publicly finance major public infrastructure projects. We need to acknowledge that the availability of private finance around the world has seen many megaprojects delivered when they would not otherwise have gone ahead. Equally, though, in the same way that a private credit card can be used with an inappropriately high interest rate to purchase today what is paid for tomorrow, so too can private finance amount to little more than a megacredit card for eager governments eyeing off a desirable, immediate, infrastructure transaction. Second, and on the more legitimate matter of delivery efficiency and value for money, it remains surprising how little we know about the effectiveness of PPP/private-finance techniques. At best, the evidence is mixed, and on average, little different compared with traditional project delivery techniques. At worst, though, private finance and PPP projects reward financial engineers and those involved in the transactions far more than users and citizens. The jury, though, remains out on this point. Third, it ought to be acknowledged that despite the VfM concerns and continuing debates around matters of governance and accountability,[18] the attraction and success of PPP as a "buy now, pay later" arrangement continues from the perspective of governments. There have, of course, been some failures and policy U-turns, but there continues to be clear attractions in the use of PPPs by many states. PPPs often meet the political needs, as distinct from economic needs of a jurisdiction, like a glove. Pragmatically, too, and fourth, there is a wide range of experience with PPPs. Practically, it can be concluded that the increased use of long-term legal contracts does shield against unwanted political influence in project definition and construction details. The commercial contract is a necessary discipline, and it seems to work. But it is equally true that there is no such thing as "the PPP model," and that because hundreds of variations are possible, learning reliable lessons from other jurisdictions remains fraught. It is easy to praise or criticize individual project successes or failures, but evaluating the policy effectiveness of the modern preference for privately financing major projects through techniques such as the DBFMO model remains a far more difficult task. Fifth, our modern focus on matters of on-time and on-budget project delivery has been understandable, but has also led to an environment where the importance of delivering "on time" and "on budget" has been overemphasized. The risk here is that the goalposts have changed over time, with the focus being taken off the more legitimate measure of unit costs of projects. To the degree that PPP projects are overpriced, this suggests that governments maybe willing to pay more than necessary in the pursuit of less political embarrassment in being associated with project time and cost overruns. Yet the reality here is also that there is much experience to indicate that the private-sector consortia do indeed usually take on real risks. Multiple projects in jurisdictions such as Australia have "failed" in the commercial sense because project risks such as construction difficulties (see the discussion on the Southern Cross Station in Hodge and Duffield 2010) or traffic figures were not adequately estimated (as in the case of the Sydney Cross City Tunnel). The commercial losses and bankruptcies experienced with these projects clearly show that the consortia have taken on huge commercial risks (which have not paid off). Australia's state governments have therefore not been exposed to the risks taken on by these consortia. But there is a dearth of clear efficiency evidence on average unit project costs overall, so that the average price that has been paid for the risks taken on by the private consortia is usually unclear. And yet the prices paid for the risks taken, as well as the unit costs of the infrastructure delivered, are perhaps the ultimate VfM and efficiency measures as far as citizens and users are concerned. There remains little published on this front. Such research gaps, amid the complex terrain of multiple PPP possibilities internationally will remain a priority for close examination.

Experience suggests that there is little doubt that private finance has played, and will continue to play, a pivotal role in megaprojects. The main challenge for a number of governments is how to ensure that the most efficient infrastructure deals are being pursued, and how to fund these projects in the long term. Private finance will in addition always provide a way to keep the private sector committed to public megaprojects and be happy to share risks, rather than government taking all the risks itself. The use of private finance through PPPs is also becoming more common in "new markets" such as the US PPP market, and this is probably a good thing insofar as increased competition in delivery methods and stronger transparency is encouraged (Department of Transport 2015; Sabol and Puentes 2014). In developing countries, too, the World Bank and IMF see private finance and PPP as a way to encourage investments in infrastructure that again would not otherwise occur. On the practice front, the United Kingdom's change toward its new "PF2" framework confirms that there was always room for improvement in their PFI model. So, while the jury remains out on the performance evidence for PPPs, much fundamental empirical research is yet to be done.

NOTES

1. While the language and the general notion of PPP is well established, it is equally important to acknowledge that there is in reality no such thing as "the PPP model" (Hodge 2013). It is more a phenomenon comprising hundreds (or perhaps thousands) of different types of arrangements around the globe. There are numerous decisions to be made when structuring a contract: the degree of finance from each sector; the project to be delivered; which party bears which risks; the strength of incentives for performance; and issues of transparency and the fabric to be applied to accountability and governance matters. So called leading PPP jurisdictions such as Canada and Australia neither share a common approach nor does each country have a single national model. Siemiatycki (2013), for instance, observes Canadian PPPs ranging from a majority of public finance to the opposite, conservative risk-transfer arrangements, and much variation in arrangements rather than a single national approach. And while Australian PPP guidelines suggest uniformity, the reality is that a wide range of different risk-transfer arrangements have been adopted along with different projects having quietly adopted different proportions of public and private funding at different times. More broadly, then, we might conclude that there are as many different ways of structuring infrastructure delivery arrangements as there are to write legal contracts.

2. Interestingly, Dewulf et al. (2012: 13) remark that the United Kingdom's PFI concession model "came out of the concession models already in use in Australia."

3. So, as Smith (1999) notes, while Hong Kong successfully delivered several huge (FDBO) road infrastructure projects over the period from the late 1960s to the late 1990s, and the Channel Tunnel project was given its initial blessing by Margaret Thatcher and Francois Mitterand in 1984, it was late in the 1990s when the UK government put the idea of private-sector financing for major projects "at the very heart of government's philosophy." In other words, the late 1990s saw the United Kingdom turning the PPP idea from a project delivery option into a public policy.

4. This also occurred, typically with no public visibility, in other countries such as Australia.

5. Indeed, after the GFC, commentators such as Konvitz (2012) announced loudly that "PPPs are dead! The PFI form of PPP is dead. Dead!" The authors of this chapter, however, disputed this belief, arguing that while times had certainly changed in the wake of the global financial crisis, a continuing political demand for privately financed long-term infrastructure contracts had more likely led to a need to rethink PPPs (Hodge and Greve 2013). The concept itself was being reshaped, and risk-sharing was being reconfigured rather than abandoned. To them, the PPP phenomenon was not dead, and the PPP brand was argued as being alive and well, albeit evolving under new forms. Others, such as Menard (2013), likewise concluded, around this time, that PPP were "going to stay with us."

6. Hodge and Greve (2013), for example, present two dozen goals for PPPs, and emphasize the small number that are explicit (rather than implied) and technical (rather than non-technical).

7. There is a third set of less visible and informal rationales that is also relevant here, to our minds. We have posited that PPPs (and thus PPP technologies such as private finance) appear to assist governments in many ways. PPP as either a policy or a project delivery tool may, for example, help governments by:

   - Putting infrastructure needs and priorities on the public agenda.
   - Emphasizing project delivery over planning concerns and "crashing through" megaprojects under private contract law.
   - Differentiating the government's policy position to that of an opposition party.
   - Moving any association with project risks away from government.
   - Improving the confidence of financial and business markets.
   - Strengthening links with relevant supporting groups.
   - Providing business or economic assistance in turbulent times, and enabling the sales of the nation's professional PPP/finance/construction services abroad.

   In short, then, PPP technologies may enhance a government's electoral prospects and ease the business of governing in a period in when democratic governance itself has become "more difficult" (Flinders 2014).

8. Of course, such arguments directly parallel the historical arguments supporting the privatization of state-owned enterprises two or three decades earlier (Hodge 2000).

9. Relevant matters on this score for a successful PPP encompass several assumptions that underpin all Western liberal economies. These include, for instance, assumptions as to the rule of law in a Western liberal democracy, including a range of cultural and historical factors such as a judicial system fiercely independent of and separate from both politics and the bureaucracy, legal systems that acknowledge that the government, private businesses, and individuals are all constrained under the law and are equal before the law, and a society in which formal legal contracts between parties and private property rights constitute fundamental building blocks of the economy. Moreover, Western economies usually assume a thriving mixed economy where a strong private sector, as well as a strong government, is

viewed as essential to economic growth, and well-developed competitive private markets to provide finance along with a range of professional services such as planning, project management, engineering construction, and design, finance, accounting, law, commercial dispute resolution, and so on. In addition, PPPs may assume strong regulators, both independent of political influence and uncorrupted by private wealth or personal connections, to underpin effective competition, and administrative decisions on tenders being driven by commercial criteria alone and not guided or influenced by political connections, family relationships, or personal links. Finally, Western economies may also typically assume that government and bureaucrats are accountable to citizens through multiple accountability mechanismsm, including a fierce media and a free press.

10. See, for example, KPMG (2014); OECD (2008); PricewaterhouseCoopers (2012, 2005); Ernst & Young (2013, 2007); Deloitte (2015, 2006).

11. See, for example, Hodge and Greve (2007); Berg et al. (2002); Bovaird (2004); Ghobadian et al. (2004); Edwards et al. (2004); Grimsey and Lewis (2004); Osborne (2001); Perrot and Chatelus (2000); Pollitt (2005); Savas (2000); Shaoul (2005); Vaillancourt-Rosenau (2000).

12. See Flinders (2005), Mott Macdonald (2002), National Audit Office (2000), Pollock et al. (2002), and National Audit Office (2009) for examples of PPP reviews taking a more specific focus.

13. Exceptions here include multiple studies by Shaoul (2005; 2010), as well as Fitzgerald (2004); Allen Consulting Group (2007); Leviakangas (2007); Blanc-Brude et al. (2006).

14. Difficulties in extracting these research data from behind government claims of "commercial-in-confidence" also amplified the concern that peer-review scrutiny was not welcomed because this well-publicized study lacked rigor.

15. This review rightly cautioned against making any further VfM conclusions, however, arguing that life-cycle costs over the longer term were still unknown.

16. At a personal level, our "most optimistic reading of the evidence thus far is that it is mixed" (Hodge and Greve 2009). We have for a decade and a half been concerned that PFI-type PPPs are "politically successful but financially dubious," or as the UK's House of Commons Committee of Public Accounts (2011) aptly expressed it a few years ago: "PFI deals look better value for the private sector than for the taxpayer." Bent Flyvbjerg (cited in Eldrup and Schutze 2013: 24, 105) appears to similarly have a mildly positive but ambiguous conclusion as to LTIC PPP success. He lists five project failures from Australian and US PFI-type PPP projects, as well as the massive London Underground maintenance firm Metronet in the United Kingdom and acknowledges that "robust empirical evidence is missing," but then concludes that "in sum, while several PPPs struggle to meet their goals, empirical evidence from academia and practice suggests that PPPs actually can deliver on their promises to improve project performance, to achieve innovation, and to transfer risks."

17. We ought note, as well, the additional concern about the ultimate affordability of PPP deals, which has been present for some time (Hellowell and Pollock 2007).

18. On the broad performance domain, *governance*, there has also been a range of illuminating commentaries. Indeed, questions of PPP governance and the legitimacy of PPPs as a governance tool have been just as controversial as matters of project efficiency and effectiveness. On the one hand, PPPs appear to have helped governments regain the capacity to steer the state as far as delivering new infrastructure projects go. On the other hand, however, multiple accusations have been leveled: ongoing analytical manipulation with public-sector comparisons lacking legitimacy and favoring private-finance delivery; decision-making arrangements lacking transparency; large, complex commercial deals

clearly being done with business partners rather than with citizens also as equal "partners"; traditional methods of gaining access to information and review through Freedom of Information or Administrative Law not now available to citizens under private law contracts; and governments lacking accountability amidst multiple conflicting roles. Little wonder that PFI type PPPs have been labeled "the illegitimate child" of the PPP family (Hodge 2006: 324). There are clearly continuing tensions in the PPP governance challenge. Likewise, public accountability challenges remain, though observers such as Willems and Van Doren (2011: 2012) argue that most PPP accountability concerns are overstated.

REFERENCES

Allen Consulting Group. (2007). *Performance of PPPs and Traditional Procurement in Australia*. Final Report to Infrastructure Partnerships Australia.

Arthur Anderson and LSE Enterprise. (2000). *Value for Money Drivers in the Private Finance Initiative*. Report commissioned by the UK Treasury Task Force on Public–Private Partnerships.

Audit Commission. (2003). *PFI in Schools*. London: Audit Commission.

Auditor General of New South Wales. (2006). The New Schools Privately Financed Project, Audit Office of NSW.

Ball, R., Heafey, M., and King, D. (2007). "The private finance initiative in the UK," *Public Management Review*, 9(2): 289–310.

Ball, R. (2011). "Provision of public service infrastructure: The use of PPPs in the UK and Australia: A comparative study," *International Journal of Public Sector Management*, 24(1): 5–22.

Barlow, J., Roehrich, J., and Wright, S. (2013). "Europe sees mixed results from public–private partnerships for building and managing health care facilities and services." *Health Affairs*, 32(1): 146–54.

Berg, S., Pollitt, M., and Tsuji, M. (eds.) (2002). *Private Initiatives in Infrastructure: Priorities, Incentives and Performance*. Aldershot: Edward Elgar.

Blanc-Brude, F., Goldsmith, H., and Valila, T. (2006). *Ex Ante Construction Costs in the European Road Sector: A Comparison of Public–Private Partnerships and Traditional Public Procurement*. Economic and Financial Report 2006/01, European Investment Bank.

Bloomfield, P., Westerling, D., and Carey, R. (1998). "Innovation and risks in a public–private partnership: Financing and construction of a capital project in Massachusetts." *Public Productivity and Review*, 21(4): 460–71.

Boardman, A., Poschmann, F., and Vining, A. (2005). "North American infrastructure P3s: Examples and lessons learned," in G. Hodge and C. Greve (eds.), *The Challenge of Public–Private Partnerships: Learning from International Experience*. Cheltenham: Edward Elgar.

Boardman, A. and Vining, A. (2010). "Assessing the economic worth of public–private partnerships," in G. Hodge, A. Boardman, and C. Greve, (eds.), *International Handbook on Public–Private Partnerships*. Cheltenham: Edward Elgar.

Boers, I., Hoek, F., van Montford, C., and Wieles, J. (2013). "Public–private partnerships: International audit findings," in P. de Vries and E. B. Yehoue (eds.), *The Routledge Companion to Public-Private Partnerships*. Oxford: Routledge.

Bovaird, T. (2004). "Public–private partnerships in Western Europe and the US: New growths from old roots," in A. Ghobadian, D. Gallear, N. O'Regan, and H. Viney (eds.), *Public–Private Partnerships: Policy and Experience*. Basingstoke: Palgrave Macmillan.

Connoly, C. and Wall, T. (2013). "The impact of the global financial crisis on public–private partnerships: A UK perspective," in C. Greve and G. Hodge (eds.), *Rethinking Public–Private Partnerships: Strategies for Turbulent Times*. Oxford: Routledge.

Davidson, K. (2013). "Some fabulous deals—for all but taxpayers," *The Age*, 29 July: 21.

de Bettignies, J.-E. and Ross, T. W. (2010). "The economics of public–private partnerships: Some theoretical contributions," in G. Hodge, A. Boardman, and C. Greve, (eds.), *International Handbook on Public–Private Partnerships*. Cheltenham: Edward Elgar.

Deloitte. (2006). *Closing the Infrastructure Gap: The Role of Public–Private Partnerships*. Deloitte Research Study.

Deloitte. (2015). *Trending P3: The Evolving Role of Value-for-Money Analysis in Supporting Project Delivery Selection*. Deloitte Research Study.

Department of Transport. (2015). *Expanding the Market for Infrastructure Public–Private Partnerships, Alternative Risk and Profit Sharing Approaches to Align Sponsor and Investor Interests*. Washington: US Department of the Treasury.

de Vries, P. (2013). "The modern public–private demarcation: History and trends in PPP," in P. de Vries and E. B. Yehoue (eds.), *The Routledge Companion to Public–Private Partnerships*. Oxford: Routledge.

de Vries, P. and E.B. Yehoue (eds.). (2013). *The Routledge Companion to Public-Private Partnerships*. Oxon: Routledge.

Dewulf, G., Blanken, A., and Bult-Spiering, M. (2012). *Strategic Issues in Public–Private Partnerships*, 2nd edn. Chichester: Wiley Blackwell.

Eadie, R., Millar, P., and Toner, L. (2013). "Public private partnerships, reevaluating value for money," *International Journal of Procurement Management*, 6(2): 152–69.

Edwards, P., Shaoul, J., Stafford, A., and Arblaster, L. (2004). *Evaluating the Operation of PFI in Roads and Hospitals*. London: Certified Accountants Education Trust.

Eldrup, A. and Schutze, P. (2013). *Organisation and Financing of Public Infrastructure Projects: A Path to Economic Development of the Danish Welfare Model*. Copenhagen: Offentligt-PrivatPartnerskab.

Ernst & Young. (2007). *The Road Ahead: Future of PPP in Australian Road Infrastructure*. Australia: Ernst & Young.

Ernst & Young. (2013). *Mayoral Position Paper on Public Private Partnerships*. Auckland: Ernst & Young.

European Commission. (2014). *An Investment Plan for Europe*, <http://ec.europa.eu/priorities/jobs-growth-investment/plan/index_en.htm>.

European PPP Expertise Centre. (2014). *Market Update: Review of the European PPP Market*, <http://www.eib.org/epec/resources/publications/epec_market_update_2015_h1_en.pdf>.

Fitzgerald, P. (2004). *Review of Partnerships Victoria Provided Infrastructure*. Melbourne: Growth Solutions Group.

Flinders, M. (2005). "The politics of public–private partnerships," *British Journal of Political and International Relations*, 7: 215–39.

Flinders, M. (2010). "Splintered logic and political debate," in G. Hodge, A. Boardman, and C. Greve (eds.), *International Handbook on Public–Private Partnerships*. Cheltenham: Edward Elgar.

Flinders, M. (2014). "Explaining democratic disaffection: Closing the expectations gap (commentary)," *Governance: An International Journal of Policy, Administration, and Institutions*, 27(1): 1–8.

Flyvbjerg, B. (2014). "What you should know about megaprojects and why," *Project Management Journal*, 45(2): 6–19.

Ghobadian, A., Gallear, D., O'Regan, N., and Viney, H. (eds.) (2004). *Public–Private Partnerships: Policy and Experience.* London: Palgrave Macmillan.

Greve, C. (2003). *When Public–Private Partnerships Fail. The Extreme Case of the NPM-Inspired Local Government of Farum in Denmark*, paper for the EGPA-conference, 3–6 September, Oerias, Portugal.

Greve, C. and Hodge, G. A. (2013). "Conclusions: Rethinking public–private partnerships," in C. Greve and G. Hodge (eds.), *Rethinking Public–Private Partnerships: Strategies for Turbulent Times.* Oxford: Routledge.

Grimsey, D. and Lewis, M. (2004). *Public–Private Partnerships: The Worldwide Revolution in Infrastructure Provision and Project Finance.* Cheltenham: Edward Elgar.

Hare, P. (2013). "PPP and PFI: The political economy of building public infrastructure and delivering services," *Oxford Review of Economic Policy*, 29(1): 95–112.

Hellowell, M. (2010). "The UK's private finance initiative: History, evaluation, prospects," in G. Hodge, A. Boardman, and C. Greve (eds.), *International Handbook on Public–Private Partnerships.* Cheltenham: Edward Elgar.

Hellowell, M. and Pollock, A. (2007). *Written Evidence to the National Assembly for Wales Finance Committee with Regards to Its Inquiry on Public Private Partnerships* <http://www.aog.ed.ac.uk/__data/assets/pdf_file/0009/96246/CIPHP_2007_Hellowell_EvidenceWelshFinanceCommittee.pdf>.

Hellowell, M. and Vecchi, V. (2012). "An evaluation of the projected returns to investors on 10 PFI projects commissioned by the National Health Service," *Financial Accountability and Management* 28(1): 77–100.

Hellowell, M. and Vecchi, V. (2013). "What return for risk? The price of equity capital in public–private Partnerships," in C. Greve and G. Hodge (eds.), *Rethinking Public–Private Partnerships: Strategies for Turbulent Times.* Oxford: Routledge.

HM Treasury. (2012). *A New Approach to Public–Private Partnerships.* London: HMSO.

Hodge, G. A. (2000). *Privatization: An International Review of Performance.* Boulder, CO: Perseus Books, Westview Press.

Hodge, G. A. (2002). "Evidence presented to the Public Accounts and Estimates Committee inquiry into private investment in public infrastructure," 30 April, Melbourne.

Hodge, G. A. (2004). "The trouble with public–private partnerships," *The Age*, 19 July.

Hodge, G. A. (2006). "Public–Private partnerships and legitimacy," *University of New South Wales Law Journal*, 29(3): 318–27.

Hodge, G. A. (2010). "Reviewing public–private partnerships: Some thoughts on evaluation," in G. A. Hodge, A. Boardman, and C. Greve (eds.), *International Handbook in Public–Private Partnerships.* Cheltenham: Edward Elgar.

Hodge, G. A. (2013). Public–private partnership: Ambiguous, complex, evolving and successful: Keynote address to global challenges in PPP: cross-sectoral and cross-disciplinary solutions?," Universiteit Antwerpen, City Campus, Hof Van Liere, 6–7 November.

Hodge, G., Boardman, A., and Greve, C. (eds.) (2010). *International Handbook on Public–Private Partnerships.* Cheltenham: Edward Elgar.

Hodge, G. A. and Duffield, C. (2010). "The Australian PPP experience: Observations and reflections," in G. A. Hodge, C. Greve, and A. Boardman (eds.), *International Handbook in Public–Private Partnerships.* Cheltenham: Edward Elgar.

Hodge, G. A. and Greve, C. (2007). "Public–orivate partnerships: An international performance review," *Public Administration Review*, 67(3): 545–58.

Hodge, G. A. and Greve, C. (2009). "PPPs: The passage of time permits a sober reflection," *Economic Affairs*, 29(1): 33–9.

Hodge, G. A. and Greve, C. (2013). "Introduction: Public–private partnership in turbulent times," in C. Greve and G. A. Hodge (eds.), *Rethinking Public–Private Partnerships: Strategies for Turbulent Times*. Oxford: Routledge.

House of Commons Committee of Public Accounts (2011). "Lessons from PFI and other projects," Forty-fourth Report of Session 2010–12, September.

Jupe, R. (2009). "New Labour, public–private partnerships and rail transport." *Economic Affairs*, 29(1): 20–5.

Konvitz, J. (2012). "Keynote address to the European Consortium for Political Research, Standing Group on Regulation and Governance," Exeter, June.

KPMG. (2014). *Public–Private Partnerships: Emerging Global Trends and the Implications for Future Infrastructure Development in Australia*, KPMG.

Leviakangas, P. (2007). *Private Finance of Transport Infrastructure Projects: Value and Risk Analysis of a Finnish Shadow Toll Road Project*, ESPOO, VTT Publications.

Menard, C. (2013). "Is public–private partnership obsolete? Assessing the obstacles and shortcomings of PPP," in P. de Vries, and E. Yehoue (eds.), *The Routledge Companion to Public–Private Partnerships*. Oxford: Routledge.

Mott Macdonald. (2002). *Review of Large Public Procurement in the UK*. London: Mott Macdonald.

National Audit Office. (2000). *Examining the Value for Money of Deals under the Private Finance Initiative*. London: The Stationery Office.

National Audit Office. (2002). *PFI: Construction Performance*. London: The Stationery Office.

National Audit Office. (2009). *Private Finance Projects*. A paper for the Lords Economic Affairs Committee.

OECD. (2008). *Public–Private Partnerships: In Pursuit of Risk Sharing and Value for Money*. Paris: OECD.

OECD. (2012). *Recommendation of the Council on Principles for Public Governance of Public–Private Partnerships*. Paris: OECD.

Office of the Auditor General of Ontario (OAGO). (2014). *Annual Report*, <http://www.auditor.on.ca/en/reports_en/en14/2014AR_en_web.pdf>.

Osborne, S. (ed.). 2001. *Public-Private Partnerships: Theory and Practice in International Perspective*. New York: Routledge.

Perrot, J.-Y. and Chatelus, G. (eds.) (2000). *Financing of Major Infrastructure and Public Service Projects: Public Private Partnerships, Lessons from French Experience Throughout the World*. Paris: Presses de l'ecolenationale des Ponts et Chaussees.

Pollitt, M. (2002). "The declining role of the state in infrastructure investment in the UK," in S. Berg, M. Pollitt, and M. Tsuji (eds.), *Private Initiatives in Infrastructure: Priorities, Incentives and Performance*. Aldershot: Edward Elgar.

Pollitt, M. (2005). "Learning from the UK Private Finance Initiative experience," in G. Hodge and C. Greve (eds.), *The Challenge of Public–Private Partnerships: Learning from International Experience*. Cheltenham: Edward Elgar.

Pollock, A., Price, D., and Playe, S. (2007). "An examination of the UK Treasury's evidence base for cost and time overrun data in UK value-for-money policy and appraisal," *Public Money and Management*, April: 127–33.

Pollock, A., Shaoul, J., and Vickers, N. (2002). "Private finance and value for money in NHS hospitals: A policy in search of a rationale?" *British Medical Journal*, 324: 1205–8.

PriceWaterhouseCoopers. (2005). *Delivering the PPP Promise. A Review of PPP Issues and Activities*, <http://www.pwc.com/gx/en/government-infrastructure/pdf/promise report.pdf>.

PriceWaterhouseCoopers. (2012). *Build and Beyond: Bridging the Gap, Meeting the Challenges of Healthcare Development in South East Asia*. KPMG, March.

Public Accounts and Estimates Committee. (PAEC) 2006. *Seventy-First Report to the Parliament, Report on Private Investment in Public Infrastructure*. Melbourne: Public Accounts and Estimates Committee.

Regan, M. (2014). "Value for money in project procurement," Faculty of Society and Design Publications, Paper 120. (Research Report for the Asian Development Bank 2013.) <http://epublications.bond.edu.au/fsd_papers/120>.

Sabol, P. and Puentes, R. (2014). *Private Capital, Public Good: Drivers of Successful Infrastructure Public–Private Partnerships*. Brookings Institute.

Salzman, R. (2014). *A Blueprint for Bankruptcy: Thinking Highways*, <http://www.truth-out.org/news/item/26848-a-blueprint-for-bankruptcy>.

Sarmento, J. M. (2010). "Do public–private partnerships create value for money for the public sector? The Portuguese experience," *OECD Journal on Budgeting*, 10(1): 93–119.

Sarmento, J. M. (2014). "Public–private partnerships," Doctoral thesis, Tilberg School of Economics and Management, University of Tilberg.

Sarmento, J. M, and Renneboog, L. D. R. (2014). *Public–Private Partnerships: Risk Allocation and Value for Money*. TILEC Discussion Paper, vol. 2014-017. Tilburg: TILEC.

Savas, E. S. (2000). *Privatization and Public–Private Partnerships*. New York: Chatham House and Seven Bridges.

Shaoul, J. (2005). "The private finance initiative or the public funding of private profit," in G. Hodge and C. Greve (eds.), *The Challenge of Public–Private Partnerships: Learning from International Experience*. Cheltenham: Edward Elgar.

Shaoul, J. (2010). "A review of transport public–private partnerships in the UK," in G. Hodge, A. Boardman, and C. Greve, (eds.). *International Handbook on Public–Private Partnerships*. Cheltenham: Edward Elgar.

Siemiatycki, M. (2013). "Is there a distinctive Canadian PPP model? Reflections on twenty years of practice," paper delivered to CBS–UBC–Monash International Workshop on PPPs, 13–14 June, Vancouver.

Smith, A. J. (1999). *Privatized Infrastructure: The Role of Government*. London: Thomas Telford.

Terry, F. (1996). "The private finance initiative: Overdue reform or policy breakthrough?" *Public Money and Management*, 16(1): 9–16.

Umar, A. A., Zawawi, N. A. W. A., Khamidi, M. F., and Idrus, A. (2013). "Stakeholder perceptions on achieved benefits of PFI strategy," *Modern Applied Science*, 7(4): 31–40.

Vaillancourt-Rosenau, P. (ed.) (2000). *Public–Private Policy Partnerships*. Cambridge, MA: MIT Press.

Vecchi, V., Hellowell, M., and Longo, F. (2010). "Are Italian healthcare organizations paying too much for their public–private partnerships?" *Public Money and Management*, 30(2): 125–32.

Vining, A. and Boardman, A. (2008). "Public–private partnerships in Canada: Theory and evidence," *Canadian Public Administration*, 51(1): 9–44.

Walker, B. and Walker, B. C. (2000). *Privatisation: Sell Off or Sell Out? The Australian Experience*. Sydney: ABC Books.

Wettenhall, R. (2005). The public–private interface: Surveying the history." in G. Hodge and C. Greve (eds.), *The Challenge of Public–Private Partnerships: Learning from International Experience*. Cheltenham: Edward Elgar.

Wettenhall, R. (2010). "Mixes and partnerships through time." in G. A. Hodge, C. Greve and A. Boardman (eds.), *International Handbook in Public–Private Partnerships*, Cheltenham: Edward Elgar.

Willems, T. and van Dooren, W. (2011). "Lost in diffusion? How collaborative arrangements lead to an accountability paradox," *International Review of Administrative Sciences*, 77(3): 506–30.

Willems, T. and van Dooren, W. (2012). "Coming to terms with accountability: Combining multiple forums and functions," *Public Management Review*, 14(7): 1011–36.

World Bank. (2015). *PPP Knowledge Lab*, <https://pppknowledgelab.org>.

CHAPTER 17

··

WIDER IMPACTS
OF MEGAPROJECTS

Curse or Cure?

··

ROGER VICKERMAN

17.1 INTRODUCTION

MEGAPROJECTS—projects that have the capacity to have transformative effects on economies and communities—have always been controversial. Throughout history, communities or individuals have been disrupted in the interest of what was often described as progress as armies or engineers (groups frequently indistinguishable) created roads or dams. Perhaps the best-documented cases of the historical megaprojects were the nineteenth-century railways. Since railway development either required parliamentary approval, as in the case of the largely privately financed railways of Britain, or was directly provided by governments, we have good historical evidence of the arguments put forward by both promoters and objectors. Although these have become more scientific over the past two centuries, the arguments remain essentially the same. Promoters of schemes claim transformational effects on people's lives and local economies. Objectors cite environmental degradation and the draining of local economies through increased centralization of activity in major centers. As decisions on megaprojects have become more dependent on increasingly sophisticated analysis, analysts have been expected to give more and more precise estimates of these effects, often stretching the techniques beyond their limits.

In this chapter we assess the state of the art in the evaluation of megaprojects with a particular focus on their wider impacts. We begin with an outline of what these wider impacts are and how they can be analyzed. We then look at some historical evidence before turning to the use of such impacts as a justification for projects today. The discussion is set against a background of increasing skepticism over the validity of using the wider-impacts argument to justify projects, as retrospective audits suggest that claimed benefits have frequently failed to be delivered. At the same time, governments are being urged to use megaprojects as a way of kick-starting economies emerging all too sluggishly from the recession triggered by the 2008 financial crisis.

17.2 WIDER IMPACTS

The traditional appraisal of transport projects has focused on the balance between user benefits and costs. User benefits derive principally from the savings in time which new facilities permit through faster travel, reduced congestion, the elimination of the need to change vehicles or modes, and so on. Effects on surrounding areas leading to increases in land values or rents are not additional to this, as they represent the capitalization of the increased journey benefits. This fear of double-counting benefits led to a general reluctance to consider any concept of wider economic benefits.

The problem with this approach is that it assumes, often implicitly, that all markets display the characteristics of perfect competition. Thus any change in the costs of transport because of new infrastructure will be perfectly reflected in the costs of users and hence in the prices they charge for their services using that transport. Prices of transport-intensive goods will fall, and the wages of commuters will also fall. Any attempt to include these changes would indeed double-count the original transport change.

But such markets are not always, or perhaps ever, perfect. In these circumstances, transport cost changes do not pass seamlessly into price changes in transport-using markets. Imperfectly competitive firms can use the effect of these changes in input prices on their margins to seek increased profit (no reduction in price) or increased market share (through lower prices and reduced margins). Thus the net effect of a change in transport costs could lead to total effects, which were either larger or smaller than the direct change in user costs might imply. Hence the need to consider wider impacts, which could be positive or negative, rather than assuming they would always be positive as implied by the use of "benefits."

While it was always understood that the perfect competition assumption provided a limiting case (Jara-Diaz 1986), the theoretical development underlying the wider impacts story derived from the development of the so-called new economic geography (NEG). Originating in the international trade literature, but rapidly applied to the case of cities and regions (Krugman 1991), NEG's main contribution was to show that in conditions of imperfect competition a fall in transport costs between two places could have unpredictable effects on their economies. This depended in part on their initial position. If one region were to be much larger in economic terms than that to which it enjoyed improved communication, then the scale economies and greater efficiency already enjoyed would make it easier for the large region to exploit the improved communications. Thus instead of better transport spreading economic welfare it may ultimately lead to greater concentration. At another, lower, level of transport costs, however, the same change in transport costs would lead to such costs no longer being a relevant consideration in the choice of location. If this also coincided with the growth of congestion and other negative externalities on the larger economy, the net effect could be deconcentration and the desired leveling of economic activity between regions. But it might also depend on the extent of the fall in transport costs. Marginal changes may simply enhance the process of concentration, but step changes in transport costs may have distinctly different effect, allowing a poor region to compete where previously it had not been able to do so, while the richer region might suffer from greater congestion costs. Such step changes are more likely to be associated with megaprojects.

The conclusion from this is essentially no conclusion; the impacts of change in transport supply could have differing effects according to the initial situation of the cities or regions involved, the degree of change in the transport offer, and also the ability of users to take advantage of that change. What it does imply, however, is that the impact will be case specific so that we need an effective way of identifying and measuring the probable effects. We cannot say a priori that improved transport will lead to either concentration or deconcentration of economic activity.

17.3 The Basis of Wider Economic Impacts

In the previous section we identified the underlying premise of there being wider impacts. In this section we go behind this in a little more detail to understand the theoretical basis of what generates such impacts. The key to understanding this is the impact of changing transport costs on productivity. There are three interrelated processes at work here: better labor market sorting, labor market thickening, and changes in competitive structure.

The simplest aspect of this is the way lower transport costs enable workers to access more suitable jobs, and employers to have access to better-qualified workers. This includes the extent to which reduced transport costs induce workers to enter the labor market. The direct effects of this are picked up in the induced travel user benefits, but the extra productivity from better sorting is not.

Labor market thickening occurs as the effective density of labor supply at a location increases with improved accessibility. This is a well-known phenomenon, usually studied in the aggregate as the way that productivity is systematically higher in larger urban areas. Venables (2007) has shown how not allowing for this would lead to a systematic underestimate of total benefits from a transport improvement. While the aggregate evidence and the theoretical justification give reasonable grounds for accepting the premise of an additional productivity link, more detailed disaggregated evidence of the impact on individual sectors from a specific transport improvement has been given by Graham (2007). This evidence was significant, as it was used as a justification for proceeding with the development of Crossrail—a megaproject to construct a new tunneled rail link across London. Without the clear evidence of positive wider impacts, the project would have struggled to generate overall positive net benefits.

What is being measured here is the way better accessibility will reduce the cost of access to jobs for workers and the size of the labor market catchment area for employers seeking workers. Thus the effective density or economic mass increases. The increased accessibility lowers the generalized cost of reaching a job, thus increasing the effective net real wage from that job. The increased real wage stimulates an increase in labor supply, and this leads to an increase in output as more workers are hired. Because of the lower cost of achieving this increase in output there is a rise in productivity associated with the increased employment that affects all workers. Hence the total net effect is not just the increased number of workers multiplied by average productivity levels, but it needs to reflect the enhanced productivity of all workers from being in the denser labor market (Venables 2007).

A further element of the potential wider impact is that on competition. Traditional methods of appraisal assume that there is perfect competition in the markets for activities that use transport. The implication of this assumption is that a given fall in transport generalized costs will have an equal impact on all firms in a particular sector and will be passed on by firms in the form of an equivalent reduction in the price of the activity. However, when firms have different mark-ups over marginal cost, as a result of imperfections in competition, the impact is no longer so straightforward. Here firms can use their differential mark-ups to absorb transport price changes into changes in profit or use them to gain a strategic advantage by lowering prices more than the reduction in transport costs. Hence more efficient firms can increase market share, and hence market power, at the expense of less efficient firms. This can affect different firms in one location, leading to change in local concentration of firms in different locations. If firms in one market have a higher level of productivity than those in another because of, for example, a larger initial market size, then they can exploit the change in transport costs more effectively than firms in another location, and this leads to differential growth in the two locations. This is the basis of the argument for increased concentration arising from lower transport costs stemming from the model of Krugman (1991) (and see Fujita et al. 1999; SACTRA 1999). From the point of view of wider impacts, the key question is the impact this has on output, but there is no a priori prediction, which will depend on the relative degree of imperfection in competition in the different markets and the extent to which firms can exploit the change in transport costs to increase market share or enter new markets.

17.4 Transport and Productivity

We have identified that changes in transport may have impacts on productivity and hence on economic growth and welfare. This is the crucial step in understanding the wider impacts argument, but it is also one that has produced the most controversy. Here we unpick the argument in a little more detail.

Transport as an agent of economic growth has a long history. Economic historians have for a long time attempted to identify the impact of major innovations in transport such as canals and railways as a factor in economic growth. These excursions into history have created great controversy such as that initiated by Fogel's work on American railways (Fogel 1964). The essence of this work was to identify the "social dividend" arising from the railways, the extent to which income per capita was higher at the end of the period by an amount that would not have been possible without the railways (Leunig 2006, 2010). The counter-argument is that the growth of the railways was a result rather than a cause of the economic growth. Transport in this view is permissive rather than instrumental in the higher growth.

The argument received renewed impetus from work designed to demonstrate that social infrastructure could have a positive impact on economic growth. Aschauer (1989) was concerned to demonstrate that instead of crowding out private investment, publicly provided infrastructure could raise the productivity of private investment. This was an attempt to negate the arguments for reducing public involvement in social capital advanced during the 1980s in the United States and the United Kingdom. The crowding-out argument suggested that investment in infrastructure by public-sector bodies potentially reduced the rate of return on private investment because public-sector bodies were able either to use increased tax revenues or lower borrowing costs to raise the effective cost of investment to the private sector. The Aschauer approach used an augmented aggregate production function that included various indicators of public infrastructure, including transport, to show a positive impact of such factors on economic performance. This implied that the rate of return on public infrastructure investment was sufficiently high to more than compensate for any crowding-out effect, and thus, in effect, provision of high-quality infrastructure could raise the productivity of private-sector firms by more than higher levels of investment by those firms.

Aschauer's work was controversial and provoked a large industry of attempts to reinforce or disprove the basic findings (see Gramlich 1994 for a valuable summary of the arguments). Defense of the work was not helped by various econometric problems with the original estimation, but on balance the subsequent research suggested that although the impact was probably rather smaller than Aschauer's original work suggested, the general premise was upheld that infrastructure investment had a broadly positive impact on productivity and growth.

At the core of the argument is the extent to which better transport enlarges market size, and hence agglomeration, which in turn enhances productivity and economic growth. The link between urban size and productivity had been explored for some time, again with mixed results (see Glaeser and Gottlieb 2009 for a discussion of the evidence). Generally, larger cities were found to be more productive, but there was no consistency in the implied elasticity either overall or sector by sector. Extending the argument, it was also presumed that if better transport could operate like any enhanced input, investing in that improvement could lead to lagging regions catching up more advanced regions. This argument was a potentially attractive one in that it implied a case for a policy of investment in transport as an instrument of regional convergence; if transport provision in different regions could be made more equal, then their economies would be likely to converge.

At the same time as Aschauer was developing the regional aggregate production function approach, a study for the European Commission (see Biehl 1991 for a useful summary) came to broadly similar conclusions, but with one significant difference. The Biehl study looked more carefully at the extent to which the various elements of the production function actually operated as constraints on output. This showed that, while there was a general association of higher productivity with higher levels of infrastructure provision, regions where the lack of transport was not a constraint would be less likely to benefit from additional investment in this area than those where it was a constraint. Thus concentrating investment just on infrastructure-poor areas would not provide overall benefits to growth in the European Union. Although there may be some benefit from such investment, if other constraints were not addressed there would be less benefit than might be expected. This raises the problem for policy makers of a choice between putting more infrastructure into leading regions to overcome the constraint that congestion puts on future development and attempting to redress the imbalance in poor regions by concentrating investment there.

The "new economic geography" approach pioneered by Krugman (1991) highlighted this problem of what has become known as the two-way road effect (SACTRA 1999). If transport between two regions is improved, the relative impact on the two regions is uncertain. It will depend on the initial relative economic status of the two regions, the initial level of transport generalized costs between the two regions, and the extent to which these costs fall as a result of the improvement. If the two regions are at very different stages of development, a core-periphery situation, and transport costs only fall by a relatively small amount, then the core region has the economic advantage of lower costs to exploit the reduced access costs at the expense of the peripheral region. Firms in the core can now supply markets in the periphery more cheaply and resources will be attracted to the core from the periphery. This is the argument often employed by those seeking to discredit the claim that peripheral regions will automatically benefit from lower access costs. Indeed it goes back to an argument advanced by Hotelling (1929) that small cities would be better at campaigning for more barriers to access than better access if they wished to avoid their markets being swamped by goods from larger cities.

But the key point of the Krugman analysis (see Fujita et al. 1999 for a fuller development) is that this is not a universal outcome. If the core city is already facing rising costs from congestion or if the fall in transport costs is sufficient to overcome the cost disadvantage of the smaller markets in the peripheral region, then the improvement in transport can lead to convergence. The final outcome is always case-specific and not generic.

What the "new economic geography" approach does make clear is that the aggregate modeling of these outcomes is unlikely to give accurate results. The impact of transport cost changes depends on reactions in individual markets, so a more disaggregated approach is required. Venables (2007) provided a simple model to show how traditional approaches that showed how falling transport costs would lead to increased city (labor market) size failed to capture how that increased size raised the productivity of all workers. Building on Venables model, Graham (2007) used data for the London metropolitan region to show how the building of a new rail line, Crossrail, would lead to the increasing effective density of local labor markets, generating an increase in productivity as a result of the increased agglomeration. The analysis was conducted at the sector level and it showed clearly how the impact differed by sector, with traditional manufacturing sectors showing much lower impacts than business or financial services. The much higher elasticities of these service sectors showed that in a large metropolitan region improved transport could be sufficiently productivity-enhancing to generate significant positive wider economic benefits. Graham's results enabled a more robust business case to be developed for the Crossrail project for which the direct user benefits were insufficient to justify the £16-billion cost of the project (Table 17.1).

Graham's later work has added significant caveats to any assumption that this has shown that positive wider impacts will always be present and sufficient to justify a marginal project. Graham et al. (2010) show how the distance decay of the impacts of improved transport is quite strong. Areas close to an access point such as a rail station will benefit, but this effect wears off rapidly so that 10 km away there is relatively little effect (see also Melo et al. 2012). Secondly, the results show potential instability and cannot be simply transferred between different projects (Graham and Van Dender 2011). Overall, however, there is a consistent body of evidence (see, for example, Melo et al. 2013), suggesting that for most large-scale transport investments there are wider economic impacts not captured in traditional appraisal methods that may account for an additional 10–20% of benefits, suggesting that rule-of-thumb mark-ups may not have been far wide of the mark.

Table 17.1 Benefits from Crossrail

Benefits	Welfare (£million)	GDP (£million)
Business time savings	4,487	4,847
Commuting time savings	4,152	
Leisure time savings	3,833	
Total transport user benefits	12,832	
Increase in labor force participation	3,094	872
People working longer	0	0
Move to more productive jobs	485	10,772
Agglomeration benefits	3,580	3,094
Increased competition		0
Imperfect competition		485
Exchequer consequences of increased GDP		
Addition to conventional appraisal	7,159	
Total (excluding financing, social and environmental costs and benefits)	19,991	20,069

Source: Department for Transport (2005)

17.5 THE LIMITATIONS OF WIDER BENEFITS

But are such positive wider impacts always there, and can the results of studies based largely on urban transport improvements be generalized to interurban projects? The main driver in the urban studies has been the increased effective density of labor markets leading to greater economic mass driving agglomeration-based increases in productivity. In the interurban context the core-periphery argument may be thought to be a stronger driver of the economic impact. In the case of the proposed HS2 high-speed rail line in the United Kingdom, applying the standard model as used in the case of Crossrail appeared to show much smaller wider benefits and a benefit–cost ratio (BCR) that could support the project without taking the wider benefits into account (Table 17.2). Here the wider benefits are only about 20% of the direct benefits as opposed to around 55% in the case of Crossrail. Graham and Melo (2011) studied this in more detail with an extension of the existing model, and although they found some additional wider benefits these were on a much smaller scale than might be expected from the case of Crossrail. It is also interesting to note that both the BCRs increase with network size and that the increment from adding the wider benefits also increases.

Table 17.2 The economic case for HS2

BCR components	Phase 1 (£billion)	Full network (£billion)
1 Transport user benefits		
Business	£16.9	£40.5
Other	£7.7	£19.3
2 Other quantifiable benefits	£0.4	£0.8
3 Loss to government of indirect taxes	−£1.2	−£2.9
4 Net transport benefits = (1) + (2) + (3)	£23.8	£57.7
5 Wider economic impacts (WEIs)	£4.3	£13.3
6 Net benefits including WEIs = (4) + (5)	£28.1	£71.0
7 Capital costs	£21.8	£40.5
8 Operating costs	£8.2	£22.1
9 Total costs = (7) + (8)	£29.9	£62.6
10 Revenues	£13.2	£31.1
11 Net costs to government = (9)–(10)	£16.7	£31.5
12 BCR without WEIs (ratio) = (4)/(11)	1.4	1.8
13 BCR with WEIs (ratio) = (6)/(11)	1.7	2.3

Source: Department for Transport (2013)

Most transport models, and hence the derivation of benefits from them, are based on the usual economist's assumption of marginal changes in continuous demand and cost functions. Megaprojects, however, almost by definition, lead to step changes in costs for which the behavioral responses are not always easy to predict (see Vickerman 2015a for a fuller discussion of this point). In such circumstances it is less appropriate to use models based on marginal changes. In the labor-market thickening case discussed previously, the question is what happens when two large labor markets are brought closer together rather than just the expansion of a single labor market. Does this result in a core-periphery-type response, in which the core labor market tends to gain at the expense of the more peripheral one, except in the case of very large changes in transport costs? Or can both labor markets benefit from the spillover effects? Venables (2013) has suggested that the effects may be stronger if, instead of the usual sector-by-sector approach to understanding agglomeration, we consider the agglomeration benefits to activities or skills. This may be the source of observations made in France following the introduction of TGV services between major cities that there was not a significant movement of firms either to or from Paris, but that within firms there was some movement of activities to benefit from agglomeration benefits at the skill/occupation level (Plassard and Cointet-Pinell 1986; Klein and Claisse 1997; Dornbusch 1997; Burmeister and Colletis-Wahl 1996).

While the impact on labor markets is the most direct and common way of identifying agglomeration effects, changes in business to business connectivity may provide an additional source of economic impact. Identifying such effects is less simple than the labor-market effects, and has proved to be more controversial. In work commissioned as part of the proposed HS2 high-speed rail line linking London with major cities in the Midlands and the north of England, KPMG (2013) claimed to have identified significantly larger wider economic impacts than suggested by adding business connectivity to the more conventional labor-market-based analysis. The left-hand column of Table 17.3 shows the maximum impacts based on assumed elasticities of productivity to

Table 17.3 Impacts of connectivity on GDP from HS2

| | GDP impact per year | |
	Initial estimates	Mode-share weighted estimates
Total impact for GB economy	£15 billion	£8 billion
Of which results from:		
Rail connectivity to businesses	£13 billion	£7.5 billion
Rail connectivity to labor	£1 billion	n/a
Car connectivity (to labor and businesses)	£0.2 billion	£0.3 billion

Source: KPMG (2013)

connectivity. In further sensitivity analysis, using a mode-share approach to weight the relative importance of connectivity for productivity, impacts of about 50% of these were estimated, but still a significant £8-billion uplift to the annual level of GDP.

This research used local area-based production functions to estimate the probable gains from increasing accessibility. The changes in connectivity were based on changes to generalized costs in a series of segmented transport markets. These estimates were then used to model the probable changes in business location as the relative accessibility of different locations changed. Critics of this work (see, for example, the evidence by Overman in House of Commons 2013) claimed that unrealistic elasticity values and methods of aggregating impacts from different modes were being used to obtain estimates of annual gains of up to £15 billion from completion of the project. Even halving these suggested benefits would yield a net figure well in excess of those produced by the accepted method of calculating wider economic impacts; contrast the estimate of around £70 billion over the whole appraisal period in Table 17.2 (Department for Transport 2014a). Similar attempts to calculate such overall benefits had been made relating to a series of projects designed to improve accessibility between northern cities in the United Kingdom (SERC, 2009). The comparison between these methods boils down to an argument about elasticities, or more generally to the behavioral assumptions it is appropriate to make in a case of a step-change in transport costs and accessibility (see the exchanges between Overman and KPMG in House of Commons Treasury Committee 2013).

While wider economic impacts have been seen as an important issue to address in getting accurate estimates of the total impact; for the majority of megaprojects total benefits are usually driven by direct user benefits. These tend to be dominated by the value of time savings. Megaprojects will typically tend to produce significant savings in time and/or increases in reliability, and thus accurate valuation of time savings will be critical. Moreover, these time savings will in most cases be dominated by savings in time for business travelers, and the valuation of these has also become the object of some criticism. Business time savings, for example, account for over 40% of the user benefits estimated for the HS2 high-speed rail project in the United Kingdom (Table 17.2). This is driven by such time savings on rail being valued at more than five times the value for leisure travel (Department for Transport 2014b). While the basis for these calculations is kept under review (see, for example, Wardman et al. 2013), concern for the potential overvaluation of such savings is based on a number of factors. Increasing criticism has focused on the assumption that time spent traveling is always a disbenefit such that business travelers' value of time depends on their productivity and wage rate. The counter-argument is that modern technology—email, wi-fi, and so on—that allows the business traveler to continue to work while in transit has changed this assumption; the business traveler can continue to be productive. Studies that have investigated the question of whether transport and communications are substitutes or complements tend toward the view that they are more likely to be complements (Mokhtarian 2003; Choo et al. 2007). The question then concerns how productive the environment is on a busy train? The business traveler may be able to continue with low-level activities such as email and keeping in touch with the office, so the value of time savings may be smaller than that indicated by the wage rate. But how much smaller? Presumably not as low as the leisure traveler's value of time savings; but we are in the area of speculation not based on observable quantities. This debate is relevant here because it may affect the relative importance of wider impacts that may become more significant if direct user benefits are valued downwards.

17.6 Using Wider Benefits as a Justification for Projects

We have shown here that there is a sound theoretical and empirical basis for justifying the inclusion of wider economic impacts in the appraisal of megaprojects. However, there is a danger that such benefits are only sought when a project is found to be marginal on the basis of its direct user benefits. In such a situation there will always be seen to be pressure to make these benefits as large as possible; the cure becomes a curse. What is needed is an objective way of determining first, when its wider impacts should be included, and second, an accepted method of their valuation.

The second of these is perhaps easier to deal with. Although there is potential for some elaborate modeling of the impacts on the wider economy through, for example, computable spatial general equilibrium models (Bröcker and Mercenier 2011), these are large, complex, and expensive to populate with data. A simpler and more ad hoc way of dealing with various elements has been used by the UK Department for Transport (2005; 2014a). This identifies four elements: agglomeration impacts; output change in imperfectly competitive markets; labor supply impacts; move to more or less productive jobs. Output and labor supply impacts are assessed for all projects of over £20 million. Agglomeration impacts are restricted to cases where the investment is close to a major employment center. Employment relocation is considered only if there is evidence from a detailed land-use–transport interaction model that such relocation is probable.

The labor-supply impact is a simple application of an elasticity to the change in the net wage, resulting from a reduction in transport costs. The change in labor supply is then multiplied by the productivity of an average worker to give the expected change in output. The imperfect competition effect—the impact on output changes in the implied mark-up as output increases but costs fall—is not modeled directly, but an arbitrary uplift of 10% is applied to the time-and-cost benefits for business and freight users. This is a topic requiring further research to identify both the variation in mark-up across areas with different accessibility and the market responses to changes in accessibility.

The agglomeration effect uses the method developed by Graham (2007), which estimates the change in effective density (economic mass) from a change in accessibility using disaggregated firm level data. The agglomeration effect is then given by applying the elasticity of productivity with respect to density to the change in effective density.

Clearly this involves a considerable effort in data collection and analysis, hence its restriction to projects where there are expected to be agglomeration impacts.

However, the theoretical analysis of the new economic geography leads us to believe that there is no a priori way of identifying where such effects could occur. Certainly it is not just a consequence of project size, as large changes in accessibility can arise from relatively small (in financial terms) projects if they, for example, unlock the potential of an area. Similarly, a megaproject defined simply by its value may have relatively small effects on the relative accessibility of different locations and thus on the change in agglomeration.

17.7 From Wider Benefits to Transformational Impacts

The argument has moved recently from a simple wish to ensure that any appraisal captures all the relevant benefits to one of providing a justification in terms of megaprojects having the potential to rebalance the spatial structure of the economy. The methodology developed by KPMG used in the case of the HS2 project is a move toward this even-wider-impacts argument. Interestingly, it also takes us full circle and back to the much earlier research into the impact of the railroad on US economic growth. In policy terms it moves the argument away from the purely economic appraisal of a project to justify the expenditure towards one of using investment in the megaproject as an instrument of wider economic policy objectives. From the point of view of the policy maker this makes for a simpler argument when justifying a project. It gives a clear rationale for a project in terms that affect the entire economy and are not dependent on detailed technical arguments about values of time savings or agglomeration economies. Although the overall outcome depends on these detailed calculations, when the results can be placed in the context of job creation and regional development it makes for a simpler message. But is it reasonable to place this burden of transforming the economy on a single project, however large. Laird et al. (2014) have argued that an approach based on cost–benefit analysis is likely to remain the most effective way of appraising major transport infrastructures, but that more needs to be done to understand the differences that arise between calculations of benefit–cost ratios and the changes in Gross Value Added that characterize economic transformation.

Transformational impacts create the impression of enormous changes in the economy and its regional distribution. Connection to a new major infrastructure can, on a much smaller scale, be transformational for individual cities. By creating new connections that previously did not exist, development opportunities can be unlocked. However, simply creating such opportunities does not imply that they will be realized, and many smaller cities have failed to benefit from the creation of high-speed rail links (see Garmendia et al. 2012; Vickerman 2015b), although others have been able to identify some benefits

(Ahlfeldt and Feddersen 2010, 2015). Once again we can see the lack of an a priori case for guaranteed wider benefits.

17.8 SOME CONCLUSIONS AND POINTERS FOR THE FUTURE

The principal argument in this chapter has been that there exists both a theoretical and an empirical case for the existence of wider economic impacts from large-scale transport infrastructure projects. Methods exist to estimate these and the consensus is that, where they exist, they typically account for an additional 10–20% of benefits. Such positive wider impacts are not guaranteed from every project, however. And where they do exist for some regions there could also be negative impacts on others, which reduces the aggregate effect. As the theoretical case suggests, the empirical outcome is dependent on a series of conditions relating to economic structure, the level of transport costs, and the extent of changes in these occasioned by the investment in question.

The danger is in assuming that wider benefits will always come to the rescue of a project which is proving to be marginal on the basis of the direct user impacts in a standard transport cost–benefit analysis. The basis of a business case for any project starts with the direct impacts; it is likely only to be very particular cases where the wider benefits will rescue a project. The Crossrail case in the United Kingdom has become the main example of a project where not only were large potential wider benefits identified, but these became a deciding factor in the decision to go ahead with the project. The peculiarities of this project are that it is creating significant changes in accessibility for sectors with high agglomeration elasticities, but the results cannot simply be assumed to be transferable to other projects. Relying on wider impacts is likely to be a curse, but it also encourages skepticism about their existence in all cases. The House of Lords (2015) was persuaded to be highly skeptical of such benefits in the case of the HS2 high-speed rail line in the United Kingdom. Some essentially may regard the supposed alchemy of wider benefits to be a way of countering the impact of adjustments for optimism bias in the guidance on project appraisal (HM Treasury 2013).

Wider impacts were never intended to be a cure for all investment appraisals, especially marginal ones, but, as argued by Venables et al. (2014), part of the process of ensuring completeness in any appraisal. The problem is that there are still gaps in the underlying research base that have prevented the development of an unequivocal standard methodology incorporating all the relevant elements, until these are resolved the wider-impacts argument is likely to continue. Moreover, it is still suggested by some that wider impacts as currently measured are a mirage essentially involving double counting of direct benefits (Crozet 2015).

So what are the requirements of a method to ensure the correct treatment of wider impacts? They start with a clear statement of the rationale for a project. Much of the confusion surrounding the case for HS2 came from its being perceived, first as a case for improving accessibility through time savings, then as means of increasing rail capacity, and finally as an agent for rebalancing the UK economy between south and north. While much of this was in perception, the absence of a clear justification on the basis of all these points from the start gave hope to objectors that the case was being changed to react to objections. Describing simply and clearly what a major transport investment is designed to achieve is the first step in a robust appraisal.

Secondly, a preliminary assessment of the potential for wider economic impacts—sometimes called an economic impact report—is needed. This needs to assess the baseline economic situation of the areas likely to be affected by the project. Relevant factors include the economic structure, the relative importance of transport costs in local industries, the degree of self-containment of labor markets, and the relative mobility of industries (that is, how easily they could relocate as a result of changing accessibility). The precursor to this assessment is, however, the choice of the relevant study area. Too frequently, the proposers of projects focus on too narrow a geographical area to assess economic impacts. This ignores the potential for both negative and positive spillovers, and not just with adjoining areas. With megaprojects there is a likelihood that there will be impacts at a national scale, and thus to assess the overall net impact a national framework for analysis is needed. However, this does not mean that a standard national model can be used for all projects. Different projects will have differential effects on each activity and hence on each area or region, given the variation in responsiveness to changes in accessibility and in distance decay, both by activity and mode.

Thirdly, there is a need for more research on the relevant responses to changes in accessibility/transport costs. Venables (2013) has suggested that agglomeration may work more at the level of activities and skills than at the level of industries or sectors. Traditional estimation of elasticities depends on a model of marginal changes, not the sort of step changes associated with megaprojects. This suggests a need for more behavioral research on such responses (see Vickerman 2015b for further discussion of this point). This research also needs to examine more closely individual behavior in response to changes in accessibility to address the issue concerning how travelers—business travelers in particular—use time savings, and hence the appropriate value when time spent traveling can also be used for work.

The problem often faced is that advances in much of this research are only conducted within the context of a particular project with particular needs. In the United Kingdom we have seen how the estimation of agglomeration effects was a response to the needs of Crossrail and attempts to produce a new approach to overall economic impacts at a regional level by the needs of the Northern Way initiative and then HS2. The problem with this is that the methods adopted are viewed as being special pleading for the project, as the research is usually funded by the project promoter. Although subsequent analysis is often undertaken centrally as part of the need to update appraisal guidance—as in the case of the official guidance on wider economic impacts by the UK Department for Transport—it is difficult to get away from the special pleading implication (and the Department is often the ultimate promoter of megaprojects as the holder of the key public budget).

The assessment of wider economic impacts has been shown to be a vital element in any megaproject appraisal. Methods for the robust estimation of all the dimensions of such effects on labor markets, on competition, on productivity, and ultimately on national output, have developed significantly in the last ten years. However, wider acceptance of the implications remains less well developed, and wider impacts remain the subject of much skepticism.

REFERENCES

Ahlfeldt, G. M. and Feddersen, A. (2010). "From periphery to core: Measuring economic adjustments to high speed rail," London School of Economics and University of Hamburg, <http://eprints.lse.ac.uk/29430/>

Ahlfeldt, G. M. and Feddersen, A. (2015). "From periphery to core: Measuring agglomeration effects using high speed rail," Spatial Economics Research Centre Discussion Paper 172, London School of Economics, <http://www.spatialeconomics.ac.uk/textonly/SERC/publications/download/sercdp0172.pdf>.

Aschauer, D. (1989). "Is public expenditure productive?" *Journal of Monetary Economics*, 23: 177–200.

Biehl, D. (1991). "The role of infrastructure in regional development," in R. W. Vickerman (ed.), *Infrastructure and Regional Development: European Research in Regional Science*, vol. 1. London: Pion, pp. 9–35.

Bröcker J. and Mercenier, J. (2011). "General equilibrium models for transportation economics," in A. de Palma, R. Lindsey, E. Quinet, and R. Vickerman (eds.), *A Handbook of Transport Economics*. Cheltenham, UK and Northampton, MA: Edward Elgar.

Burmeister, A. and Colletis-Wahl, K. (1996). "TGV et fonctions tertiaires: grand vitesse et entreprises de service à Lille et Valenciennes," *Transports Urbains*, issue 93.

Choo, S., Lee, T., and Mokhtarian, P. L. (2007), "Do transportation and communications tend to be substitutes, complements, or neither? The US consumer expenditures perspective, 1984–2002," *Transportation Research Record*, 2010: 121–32.

Crozet, Y. (2015). "High speed rail and urban dynamics: Wider or targeted economic effects? Paper to seminar on high-speed rail and the city: Urban dynamics and tourism," Paris-East University, January.

Department for Transport. (2005). "Transport, wider economic benefits, and impacts on GDP," Technical Paper.

Department for Transport. (2005). *Transport, Wider Economic Benefits, and Impacts on GDP*, Technical Paper.

Department for Transport. (2013). *The Economic Case for HS2*. London: HS2 Ltd.

Department for Transport. (2014a). *WebTAG: TAG unit A2-1 wider impacts*, <https://www.gov.uk/government/publications/webtag-tag-unit-a2-1-wider-impacts>.

Department for Transport. (2014b). *WebTAG: TAG unit A1-3 user and provider impacts*, <https://www.gov.uk/government/publications/webtag-tag-unit-a1-3-user-and-provider-impacts-november-2014>.

Dornbusch, J. (1997). "Nantes, sept ans après l'arrivée du TGV Atlantique," *Notes de Synthese du SES*, Mai–Juin.

Fogel, R. M. (1964). *Railroads and American Economic Growth: Essays in Economic History*. Baltimore, MD: Johns Hopkins University Press.

Fujita, M., Krugman, P. R., and Venables. A. J. (1999). *The Spatial Economy: Cities, Regions and International Trade*. Cambridge, MA: MIT Press.

Garmendia, M., Romero, V., de Ureña, J. M., Coronado, J. M., and Vickerman, R. W. (2012). "High-speed rail opportunities around metropolitan regions: The cases of Madrid and London," *Journal of Infrastructure Systems*, 18: 305–13.

Glaeser, E. L. and Gottlieb, J. D. (2009). "The wealth of cities: Agglomeration economies and spatial equilibrium in the United States," *Journal of Economic Literature*, 47: 983–1028.

Graham D. J. (2007). "Agglomeration, productivity and transport investment," *Journal of Transport Economics And Policy*, 41: 317–43.

Graham D., Gibbons, S., and Martin, R. (2010). *The Spatial Decay of Agglomeration Economies: Estimates for Use in Tansport Appraisal*, Report for Department of Transport.

Graham D. J. and Melo P. C. (2011). "Assessment of wider economic impacts of high-speed rail for Great Britain," *Transportation Research Record*, 2261: 15–24.

Graham D. J. and Van Dender, K. (2011). "Estimating the agglomeration benefits of transport investments: Some tests for stability," *Transportation*, 38: 409–26.

Gramlich, E. M. (1994). "Infrastructure investment: A review," *Journal of Economic Literature*, 32: 1176–96.

HM Treasury. (2013). *The Green Book: Appraisal and Evaluation in Central Government*, <https://www.gov.uk/government/uploads/system/uploads/attachment_data/file/220541/green_book_complete.pdf>.

Hotelling H. (1929). "Stability in competition," *The Economic Journal*, 39: 41–57.

House of Commons Treasury Committee. (2013). *The Economics of HS2*, oral evidence, 5 November 2013, <http://data.parliament.uk/writtenevidence/committeeevidence.svc/evidencedocument/treasury-committee/the-economics-of-hs2/oral/3472.html>.

House of Lords Economic Affairs Committee. (2015). *The Economics of High Speed 2*. First Report of Session 2014–15, HL Paper 134. London: The Stationery Office.

Jara-Diaz S. R. (1986). "On the relationships between users' benefits and the economic effects of transportation activities," *Journal of Regional Science*, 26: 379–91.

Klein, O. and Claisse, G. (1997). *Le TGV-Atlantique: entre recession et concurrence*. Lyon: LET.

KPMG (2013). *HS2 Regional Economic Impacts*, HS2 074, High Speed Two (HS2) Limited.

Krugman, P. (1991). "Increasing returns to scale and economic geography," *Journal of Political Economy*, 99: 483–99.

Laird J., Nash C., and Mackie P. (2014). "Transformational transport infrastructure: Cost–benefit analysis challenges," *Town Planning Review*, 85: 709–30.

Leunig T. (2006). "Time is money: A reassessment of the passenger social savings from Victorian British railways," *The Journal of Economic History*, 66: 635–73.

Leunig T. (2010). "Social savings," *Journal of Economic Surveys*, 24: 775–800.

Melo, P. C., Graham, D. J., and Brage-Ardao, R. (2013). "The productivity of transport infrastructure investment: A meta-analysis of empirical evidence," *Regional Science And Urban Economics*, 43: 695–706

Melo P. C., Graham, D. J., and Noland, R. B. (2012). "The effect of labour market spatial structure on commuting in England and Wales," *Journal Of Economic Geography*, 12: 717–37.

Mokhtarian, P. L. (2003). "Telecommunications and travel: The case for complementarity," *Journal of Industrial Ecology*, 6: 43–57.

Plassard, F. and Cointet-Pinell, O. (1986). *Les effets socio-économique du TGV en Bourgogne et Rhônes Alpes*, DATAR, INRETS, OEST, SNCF.

SACTRA (Standing Advisory Committee on Trunk Road Assessment). (1999). *Transport and the Economy*. London: The Stationery Office.

SERC (Spatial Economics Research Centre). (2009). *Strengthening Economic Linkages between Leeds and Manchester: Feasibility and Implications*, Report to the Northern Way, <http://www.spatialeconomics.ac.uk/textonly/SERC/publications/download/Northern_Way_Project_Technical_Report.pdf>.

Venables, A. J. (2007). "Evaluating urban transport improvement: Cost–benefit analysis in the presence of agglomeration and income taxation," *Journal of Transport Economics and Policy*, 41: 173–88.

Venables, A. J. (2013). "Expanding cities and connecting cities: The wider benefits of better communications," unpublished draft, Oxford.

Venables, A. J., Laird, J., and Overman, H. (2014). *Transport Investment and Economic Performance: Implications for Project Appraisal*, paper commissioned by the UK Department for Transport.

Vickerman, R. W. (2015a). "High-speed rail and regional development: The case of intermediate stations," *Journal of Transport Geography*, 42: 157–65.

Vickerman, R. W. (2015b). "Economic impacts of transport policy," in C. A. Nash (ed.), *Handbook of Research Methods and Applications in Transport Economics and Policy*. Cheltenham: Edward Elgar, pp. 389–402.

Wardman, M., Batley, R., Laird, J., Mackie, P., Fowkes, A. S., Lyons, G., Bates, J., and Eliasson, J. (2013). *Valuation of Time Savings for Business Travellers*, Institute for Transport Studies, University of Leeds.

CHAPTER 18

QUALITY ASSURANCE IN MEGAPROJECT MANAGEMENT

The Norwegian Way

GRO HOLST VOLDEN AND KNUT SAMSET

18.1 INTRODUCTION

PUBLIC investment projects do not always meet the expectations of different stakeholders. Cost overruns are apparently the most common failure reported in the media. In studying more than 4,000 large government funded projects, Morris and Hough (1991) found that cost overruns were typically between 40% and 200%. Flyvbjerg et al. (2003) analyzed 258 infrastructure projects in twenty countries over a sixty-year period and concluded that nine of ten projects had cost overruns. Further, Pinto and Slevin (2006) claim that a culture has developed (in the United States) whereby decision makers no longer see any reason to give credence to figures presented in the early phase of projects and instead acknowledge already at that stage that cost overruns will occur.

Another serious type of problem associated with projects is that they may not be able to produce the anticipated effect, rendering public resources wasted.

The three levels of project success, all of which are important, can be defined as follows (Samset 2008):

1. Operational success: the project is delivered as promised with both time and cost efficiency.
2. Tactical success: the project produces the maximum utility/benefit for users at the lowest possible cost.

3. Strategic success: the project contributes to the desired societal development (as intended within its long-term objective) at the lowest possible cost and in a financially sustainable manner.

These three levels are in accordance with the three levels of achievement identified in the project management literature: (1) the outputs, (2) the outcome (first-order effects for users), and (3) the long-term effects for society.

In practice, the focus is primarily on operational success. However, as major public investments typically have a broader impact on society, an assessment of a project's tactical and strategic performance should be a vital aspect of the overall assessment of its success.

Public megaprojects are devised from needs that are politically expressed through dialogue between various stakeholders. The process of devising such projects typically involves government at various administrative levels, local government, political institutions, the public, the media, and contractors and consultants in the private sector. Such processes are often complex, disclosed, and unpredictable, as described and analyzed in an in-depth study by Miller and Lessard (2000) of sixty major projects focused on the reconciliation of uncertainty and feasibility in the front-end phase. They can also be affected by deception and irresponsibility if stakeholders pursue hidden agendas rather than strive for openness and social responsibility, as discussed by Miller and Hobbs (2005) and Flyvbjerg et al. (2003).

In the field of project management, research has focused on the project itself and the improvement of the involved processes and procedures rather than on the governance framework that could or should provide direction and help improve the outcome of these processes. Project governance has become an issue of importance in the project management community only recently; see, for example, Müller (2009). Governance regimes for major investment projects comprise the processes and systems that the financing party must implement to ensure a successful investment. Such a regime typically includes a regulatory framework to ensure adequate quality at entry, compliance with agreed objectives, and management and resolution of issues that may arise during a project, among others. It may also include an external quality review of key governance documents. However, the government, as represented by the responsible ministry, would have neither the necessary competence nor the need to interfere in the design and management of a project at the operational level. It would have a tactical and strategic perspective, and it should have a restricted role in facilitating structured, responsible, and efficient preparation and implementation.

Flyvbjerg et al. (2003) discusses the ambitions, risks, and effects related to megaprojects based on a large sample of projects. The authors conclude that the problems with such projects mainly concern negligence regarding risks and a lack of accountability among project promoters, whose primarily aim is to develop projects for private economic or political gain rather than for public benefit. To resolve the megaproject paradox, they suggest that (1) risk and accountability should be much more centrally placed in decision making regarding megaprojects, (2) regulations should be in place to ensure that risk analysis and risk management are carried out, and (3) the role of government should be shifted to reduce its involvement in promoting projects, maintain an arm's length distance, and restrict its involvement in forming and auditing the public interest objectives of megaprojects. Also that (4) four basic instruments should be employed to ensure accountability in decision making by (a) ensuring transparency, (b) specifying performance requirements, (c) devising explicit rules to regulate project construction and operations, and (d) involving risk capital from private investors, where the assumption is that private investors' willingness to invest would initially provide an effective indication of the viability of a project.

18.2 FRONT-END GOVERNANCE OF MEGAPROJECTS IN NORWAY

In 1997 the Norwegian government initiated a study to review the systems for planning, implementing, and monitoring large public investment projects because of a series of negative experiences with cost overruns, delays, and low project success in general. The study reviewed eleven project cases in the transport, defense, and construction sectors, and focused on (1) whether the documentation that provided the basis for decisions was adequate when the project was approved and (2) whether project implementation was satisfactory. The study (Berg et al. 1999) found that of the eleven projects, only three were completed within the original budget; cost overruns for the other eight were as high as 84%. Moreover, the underlying documentation was deficient in a number of projects. The study ultimately concluded that failures in the initial phase of projects prior to the decision to proceed were generally the main cause of the low success rate for projects.

Further, a challenge with public investment projects in Norway has been that planning processes are often sectoral and locally based. The front-end phase has typically been a bottom-up process where ideas are generated locally by those who benefit from the project, and there may be strong incentives to overestimate utility and underestimate costs. Such incentives, referred to as "perverse incentives" in Samset et al. (2014), create

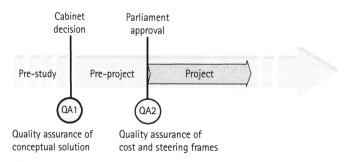

FIGURE 18.1 The Norwegian quality-at-entry regime for major public investment projects.

a classic principal-agent problem. Broader economic analysis is typically conducted at a later stage when the conceptual solution has already been selected.

In 2000 the Norwegian Ministry of Finance introduced a mandatory Quality-at-Entry regime (Figure 18.1) to address the challenges described above. Initially, the aim of the regime was to reduce the problems with cost overruns; that is, to ensure operational success. In 2005 the regime was expanded to include quality assurance of the choice of conceptual solution in order to ensure that the right projects are started and that unviable projects are rejected; that is, to improve tactical and strategic success. The regime was designed to improve analysis and decision making in the front-end phase—particularly the interplay between analysis and decision making. It was based on the notion that the necessary rules for decision making were already in place; however, there were no binding rules to ensure quality and consistency of analysis and decisions.[1]

To accommodate the needs and practices of different ministries and agencies, the scheme is devised to avoid being strict and overly comprehensive. Thus it establishes requirements for the type of documentation that must exist, but it does not require that public agencies use specific tools, formats, and so forth, and does not interfere with project implementation as such. Rather, the aim of the scheme is (1) to ensure political control with fundamental go/no-go decisions, (2) to ensure an adequate basis for decisions, where the focus is on essential matters rather than on the details, and (3) to establish a distinct set of milestones and decision gates that would apply to investment projects in all sectors. To fulfill these aims, the scheme was devised (1) to anchor the most essential decisions in the Cabinet itself, (2) to introduce a system for quality assurance that is independent of government and sufficiently competent to overrule analysts, and (3) to ensure that the governance regime is compatible with the procedures and practices of the affected ministries and agencies.

Under the Norwegian Quality-at-Entry regime, highly skilled external consultants, prequalified by the Ministry of Finance, are now assigned to perform quality assurance of the decision documents in all public investment projects with a total budget exceeding NOK750 million (approximately €80 million). During the first four years, such quality assurance was performed in some fifty projects, where cost estimates and decision documents were scrutinized prior to funds appropriation by Parliament. The involved consultants had expertise within project management and cost engineering. Based on this initial experience, the regime was then expanded, and it now involves two separate quality assurance processes to ensure the basis for decision making regarding (1) the choice of conceptual solution (QA1) and (2) the budget, management structure, and contract strategy for the chosen project alternative (QA2). For QA1, broader competence, including competence in social science and economics, is required.

The review process is fairly similar in both QA1 and QA2. The reviewer first receives documentation from the sectoral ministry and its subordinate agency, and then examines the documentation to check whether it provides a sufficient basis for decision making. If the documentation is insufficient, additional information may be requested. The reviewer also conducts independent analyses and calculations (an uncertainty analysis and, in QA1, a cost–benefit analysis). Finally, the reviewer writes a report and presents it to the sectoral ministry and the Ministry of Finance. The report is generally then made public.

QA1 is a qualifying step for QA2, and QA2 is a qualifying step for submission to the budget process. Having QA1 performed on a project does not guarantee that QA2 will be performed, and having QA2 performed on a project does not guarantee that the project will be prioritized by Parliament. The QA1 process begins with a decision in the sectoral ministry responsible for the project and the participation of the Ministry of Finance as a quality body. When the external reviewer submits his report, the case is evaluated by the Ministry of Finance and presented to the Cabinet, which then decides whether to proceed with the project. The sectoral ministry may also decide to stop the process after QA1. If a decision is made to continue with a pre-project, the resulting document will be subjected to external review (QA2). After the QA2 report is delivered, the Cabinet still has two options: either stop the project or allow it to enter into the budget process, but without any guarantee that it will be prioritized (Christensen 2011).

18.3 THE DATA

After fifteen years of operation (by 2015), nearly two hundred projects have been subjected to QA2 reviews, and about eighty of these are completed and in the operational phase. The QA1 scheme has been in operation for ten years, and about seventy projects have so far been through a Conceptual Appraisal (CA) followed be an external QA1 review. However, none of these projects have been finalized thus far. To date, only eleven of the projects have undergone both QA1 and QA2.

With few exceptions, the projects subjected to QA1 and QA2 represent major public investments with an expected investment cost above the threshold value of approximately €80 million. For most of the projects, the cost estimates range from €70 million to €300 million, although some of them have a much higher cost estimate. For example, the acquisition of new fighter aircrafts is estimated to cost about €7 billion.

About half of the projects fall under the purview of the Ministry of Transport (mainly road and rail), and the other half are mostly projects under the Ministry of Defense, and construction and ICT projects in different parts of government. The agency for the construction of public buildings (Statsbygg) under the Ministry of Local Government and Modernization is also involved, as is the Ministry of Finance in its role as the manager of the QA scheme.

Since its inception, the involved parties have gained considerable experience with the QA scheme. A trailing research program funded by the Ministry of Finance continuously collects data on the projects and the QA process and thus contributes to the learning process. However, information on the effects of the scheme is only now becoming available, as it takes time to plan and implement large investment projects. Indeed, the process to conduct CA and QA1 reviews before the Cabinet's decision typically takes two–four years. Most of the projects then enter the pre-project phase, which ends with a

QA2 review and Parliament's approval, and if approved they proceed to an engineering and construction phase, which typically takes two–five, and in exceptional cases up to ten years. Only after this point can the final cost, time, and quality of delivery—in other words, indicators of the project's operational success—be registered. In order to observe the long-term effects for users and society, one has to wait even longer, until the project has been in operation for some years.

The present study is based on information from the QA1 and QA2 reports, CA reports and, other project documents that provided the basis for the external quality reviews, parliamentary propositions including cost and steering frames, as well as final reports and evaluations from ministries and agencies and other documents regarding project delivery and effects.

Data were collected between 2010 and 2015. Agencies and ministries responsible for the projects have provided support in data collection and quality control of figures. Approved cost frames and steering frames were collected from parliamentary propositions and resolutions. For the completed projects, the final costs were based on project accounts produced by the responsible agencies and reported to their respective ministries. These are public figures that are presented to Parliament and signed off by the Auditor General each year. There may be some weaknesses regarding the quality of these cost data, as will be explained. However, it should be noted that the researchers have been through a quite thorough process of verification, including reviews of accounts and interviews with responsible officers, to clarify issues, obtain details about price indexes used, and so on. Aass (2013) and Welde (2014) provide a more detailed account of the data and the researchers' analyses to ensure validity of information. It should also be noted that the projects we are dealing with here are the country's very large ones, which receive special attention from both agencies, ministries, and politicians, with strict requirements for analysis up front and external quality assurance. The projects are therefore well documented and monitored as compared with other projects outside the QA scheme.[2]

We reserve the right of inaccuracies related to the following errors:

- Final costs for completed projects could be somewhat incomplete. So far, there is no evidence that agencies were trying to "hide" project costs, but the researchers' possibilities to verify if all real project costs were included in the accounts were of course limited.
- In some cases, cost figures may only be available long after the project is finalized, due to ongoing judicial conflicts with suppliers regarding compensation for changes and additions.
- Agencies' reporting of the final costs may be incomplete. The agencies have varying practices for registering the final cost. This study includes all projects for which we had access to the final cost, which might create a bias towards agencies that provide researchers with timely and accurate data, such as the Norwegian Public Roads Administration. The proportion of road projects in the study is 58%, whereas that in the overall population of quality assured road projects is 48%. We regard this

discrepancy as acceptable, and it should be noted that it is only a matter of delay, not of missing data as such. One should, however, also be aware that the relatively limited number and the predominance of road projects limit the accuracy and strength of any statistical analysis in the study. The composition of projects in several different sectors also implies that conclusions are not representative of projects in individual sectors.

- Calculation of price adjustment and use of indexes may cause some inaccuracy. The agencies' methods and practices regarding price adjustment vary somewhat. Road projects are price-regulated with the official index for road construction. In other projects, the agencies' own price adjustments are applied. The largest agencies have established their own cost indexes and procedures for adjusting the cost and steering frames on the basis of real cost development in their sectors. In the period covered in this study, all such indexes have increased above the Consumer Price Index (CPI).
- Correspondence between project scope and cost accounting may be somewhat divergent.

In relative terms, however, any discrepancies between the reported and the actual final cost are presumably small and constitute at most no more than a few percentages of the total cost. For example, as the implementation phase in most projects is limited to a few years, the choice of price index is not expected to have a significant effect on the level of cost compliance or on differences between sectors.

These data on final costs include all sixty-seven projects that had been completed at the time of study. With a few exceptions (outlined later), these projects constitute the whole population of QA2 projects where the final cost had been established and reported. To our knowledge, fourteen additional projects that underwent QA2 are completed, but their final costs have not yet been established. These projects are not discarded but only temporarily suspended, and will be included when cost figures are available. Rather than relying on forecasts for the final costs, we prefer to wait until reliable data are available. Our study is updated annually based on a steadily increasing number of projects.

Only four projects have been excluded from the study. Three are PPP projects on account that their final cost will not be available because of a non-disclosure agreement between the concessionaries. One road project is not eligible, since it underwent considerable changes in scope throughout its implementation so that meaningful comparisons between budget and cost border on the pointless.

To determine the effect of the QA1 scheme is another issue altogether. We would have to wait until investment projects were three–five years into the operational phase before their effects could be evaluated in a tactical and strategic perspective. The current situation (in 2015) is that none of the projects subjected to QA1 has yet been completed; thus it will take time before the effect of this more fundamental and comprehensive intervention can be evaluated. So far, a total of eleven of the first QA2 projects have been evaluated *ex post* in terms of their effects on users and society, nine by external evaluators, and two by our own researchers. This has provided us with valuable information, however, since they have not been through QA1; they will serve only as a control group for subsequent evaluations of the impact of QA1 projects.

18.4 QUALITY ASSURANCE OF THE CHOICE OF CONCEPTUAL SOLUTION (QA1)

The current procedure during the QA1 phase is for the responsible Ministry to prepare a Conceptual Appraisal (CA) report or pre-feasibility study of the investment case. This report should include the following documents:

1. *Needs analysis*. In this document, all stakeholders and affected parties are identi-fied, and the relevance of the anticipated investment in relation to their needs and priorities is assessed.
2. *Overall strategy*. Based on the prior analysis, consistent, realistic, and verifiable immediate and long-term objectives are specified in this document.
3. *Overall requirements*. This document identifies all the requirements, such as func-tional, aesthetic, physical, operational, and economic requirements, that need to be fulfilled.
4. *Possibilities study*. With the "opportunity space" delimited by the needs, objectives, and requirements, this document provides the limits to what is possible, and iden-tifies realistic alternative conceptual solutions.
5. *Alternatives analysis*. At least two alternatives and the so-called zero alternative (no project) are analyzed to specify their operational objectives, essential uncer-tainties, cost estimates, and so forth, and the alternatives are subjected to a full cost–benefit analysis that is reported in this document.
6. *Guidelines for the pre-project phase*. This document includes a suggested imple-mentation strategy for the preferred alternative.

The CA report is now being scrutinized by external reviewers (QA1). Also, they per-form a complete cost–benefit analysis of the alternatives based on guidelines from the Ministry of Finance. The reviewers present their findings in a report containing their assessment and advice regarding the following:

- Uncertainties likely to affect the project.
- The anticipated economic benefits and costs of the concepts analyzed.
- The ranking of the alternatives.
- The management strategy.

The purpose of QA1 is to assist the Ministry in ensuring that the decision regarding the choice of conceptual solution has been subjected to a fair and rational political process.

Ultimately, of course, the concept is selected through a political process in which external reviewers play no role. The reviewers' role is limited to controlling the professional quality of the underlying documents that provide the basis for the decision. As a fundamental requirement, at least two viable alternative concepts in addition to the zero alternative should be reviewed.

The Ministry now analyses the documents and presents the case to the political level. As the project owner, the state must determine how to best solve the underlying problem that triggered the project and the associated societal needs. The Cabinet now makes the decision regarding the choice of conceptual solution and decides whether to proceed with the pre-project phase.

18.5 LESSONS RELATED TO QA1

Ten years after the first QA1 report was produced, it is still too early to evaluate the effects of the scheme. Our knowledge is limited by the type of projects that have undergone QA1, the quality of CA and QA1 reports, and the resulting decisions. Indirectly, one can also infer some of the spin-off effects in government, industry, and academia after the introduction of the scheme.

As of 2015, approximately seventy projects have undergone CA and QA1. There is little doubt that the quality of the CA reports has improved steadily over time and that there is a convergence toward a common best practice. The same trend can be observed with the QA1 reports—quality assurers have gained years of experience and shown a positive learning curve (Samset and Volden 2013). Some reviews in the literature have already examined the performance of the CA/QA1 process in the transport sector and stakeholders' experience with the scheme; see, for example, Rasmussen et al. (2010); Statens vegvesen (2012); and Bjertnaes (2012). These studies suggest that the CA/QA1 process may consume time and resources, but overall, agencies seem to benefit from the scheme. In particular, the scheme provides a more systematic approach to the early identification of project ideas than the prior system. Rather than going straight to selecting road sections and determining a technical solution, planners are forced to take a broader perspective and to discuss societal aspects, which allows ideas to mature and stimulates creativity in the agencies. The process in the scheme also increases the likelihood that the most effective option will be included in the analysis.

The QA1 scheme allows the ministries and Cabinet to have a more direct influence in the early stages of the process in comparison to local stakeholders, who have traditionally had a significant influence, especially in road projects. However, there is still room for improvement. One in-depth study of seventeen projects (Samset et al. 2013) specifically examines how the opportunity space is defined and utilized in CA reports. A recurrent problem is that the conceptual solution has already been selected before the CA process, either because of path dependency in the agencies or political constraints and limitations. Another study (Statens vegvesen 2012) suggests that quality assurers give disproportionate attention to economic considerations and that they should balance economic impacts with the achievement of various political objectives. Finally, some ministries and agencies have drawn attention to the futility of undergoing the full CA/QA1 process in cases where, in their opinion, there are simply no alternatives apart from one feasible conceptual solution.

In studying the CA and QA1 recommendations and the resulting decisions for the first seventy QA1 projects, trailing researchers have found that quality assurers agree with the sectoral ministry on the ranking of concepts in one third of the cases. In the remaining two thirds of the cases, the quality assurer and the sectoral ministry disagree on the ranking of concepts. The QA1 reports more often recommend the zero alternative or a more economically feasible concept. In the QA1 report, the quality assurer often criticizes the sectoral ministry for its failure to explore the entire opportunity space, particularly with respect to less expensive concepts, during the CA process. Most of the seventy projects have now been through political treatment by the Cabinet, and almost 80% of them have entered into the pre-project phase with one (or sometimes more than one) concept. In only 6% of the cases, the Cabinet has rejected the project altogether, normally in accordance with the QA1 recommendations. Not surprisingly, we observe that when the quality assurer approves the CA recommendation in the QA1 report, the Cabinet normally follows the recommendation. The QA1 process thus increases the confidence that the proposed concept is the most efficient and effective alternative. However, when the recommendations diverge, the outcome is less predictable. In such cases, the Cabinet follows the recommendation by the sectoral ministry more often than the QA1 recommendation, but in some cases, project proposals are withdrawn or sent back to the sectoral ministry for new CA appraisal, or the Cabinet chooses a completely different concept (Grindvoll 2015). The results indicate that the Cabinet is now more informed about the consequences of projects—mostly the economic consequences—and that they take QA1 recommendations seriously. However, the choice of a project concept clearly remains a political decision.

Notably, there is no tradition in Norway of prioritizing public investment projects according to their anticipated economic viability, and this is particularly the case with road projects (Welde et al. 2013). This lack of prioritization according to viability applies to both politicians and government agencies. The QA1 scheme can ensure only that decision makers are well informed about both alternatives and their economic implications. Over time, however, it may become more difficult to select conceptual solutions that are obviously ineffective and that are clearly inferior to other alternatives. Evidence also suggests that an independent QA1 report showing that an investment is poorly justified may be influential and thus essential for the Cabinet to make a sound decision in a controversial case. One example is the proposal by sports enthusiasts and local communities to hold the Winter Olympics in Norway in 2018 and later in 2022; the proposal was for the state to guarantee the investment cost. In both cases, the Cabinet rejected the proposal, though only after the QA1 report indicated that the benefits were overestimated and that the costs were underestimated.

One noticeable impact of the CA/QA1 scheme is that the ministries' opportunity space has been broadened during the appraisal process, owing to the advice from quality assurers, as they play a role not only as controllers but also as advisers. In several cases, the CA documents were rejected by the external reviewers, resulting in a second round in the appraisal process, with new conceptual alternatives. In addition, there is reason to believe—though it is difficult to prove—that many of the most poorly conceived investment proposals are now screened out before they even reach the CA/QA1 stage. Such proposals can be rejected early because of the improved processes and procedures in the involved ministries and agencies, which probably constitutes the most important beneficial effect of the QA1 scheme.

18.6 QUALITY ASSURANCE OF THE CHOSEN PROJECT AND ITS BUDGET (QA2)

QA2 is performed at the end of the pre-project phase, and the aim is to provide the responsible ministry with an independent review of its overall management document before it is submitted to Parliament for approval and funds appropriation. This review constitutes not only a final control measure to ensure that the budget is realistic and reasonable, but also a forward-looking exercise to identify managerial challenges ahead. The analysis should help substantiate the final decision regarding the project's funding, and it should be useful during and after implementation as a reference for control.

As inputs to the quality assurance review, the agency is obliged to provide the following:

(1) The overall management document (steering document).
(2) A complete base estimate for costs and, if relevant, income/revenue.
(3) An assessment of at least two alternative contract strategies.

The quality assurer reviews and verifies these documents and conducts a separate analysis of success factors/pitfalls and the overall uncertainty scenario. The cost uncertainty analysis should be based on the base estimate, and it should stipulate the expected additions in order to establish the expected costs and associated uncertainties. The quality assurer gives recommendations regarding (1) the proposed cost frame, including necessary contingency reserves and the agency's steering frame, and (2) the appropriate strategy for managing the project in order to keep within the cost frame, including the management and authorization of contingency reserves.

The proposed cost frame is established by using standard procedures for stochastic (probability-based) cost estimation, based on either mathematical–analytical methods or simulation tools. The result is a cumulative probability distribution of the investment cost, as will be shown. The proposed cost frame is normally P85 with deductions for possible simplifications and reductions (the so-called reduction list) that can be implemented during the project if there is a danger that the cost frame will be exceeded.

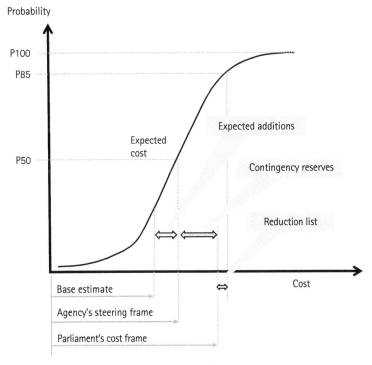

FIGURE 18.2 Stochastic cost estimation: definition of key terms.

The agency's steering frame is lower—normally at the P50 level—in order to avoid incentives to use contingency reserves; see Figure 18.2.

Parliament and the responsible ministry are naturally not required to follow these recommendations. The final overall cost frame for the project is decided by Parliament, and the ministry will then determine the steering frame for the executing agency. In professional terms, the QA2 review heavily relies on project management expertise; that is, how to ensure that the project outputs are delivered on time, with the agreed quality and within the cost frames. Contract strategy is an important part of the exercise, as are elements of economics, including incentive theory, transaction-cost theory, and organization theory more generally. Quality assurers are expected to have expertise in all these areas.

18.7 LESSONS RELATED TO QA2

Although QA2 recommendations regarding cost and steering frames are only advisory, we find that in about 70% of the projects the approved cost frame is identical to the QA2 recommendation, and in the remaining 30% of the projects, there are only minor deviations. Further, the final steering frame is identical to the QA2 recommendation in 54% of the projects, and with two exceptions, the deviations are within ±10% (Samset and

Volden 2013). These results indicate that the QA2 process and the stochastic cost estimation techniques used during this process are trusted as a basis for determining the budgets of major public investment projects.

The first analysis of cost compliance was presented in 2013 based on all QA2 projects completed by the end of 2012, with an established final investment cost (Samset
and Volden 2013, 2014). In all, there were forty such projects at that time, and the results
were promising.[3] As many as thirty-two of the forty projects—80%—were completed
within or below the cost frame. Moreover, some of the projects had significant savings,
totaling about €500 million (mostly road projects). The total net savings for the projects
taken as a whole were more than €300 million, or about 7% of the total investment. This
is an exceptionally good result in comparison with what one could expect based on past
experience and findings from a number of studies in other countries.

A total of seventy-eight projects submitted to QA2 review have now been completed
(2015), and the final cost has been established for sixty-seven of these (84%). The results
from the update of the previous analysis where these projects are included (Welde
2015) are presented below.

18.7.1 Final Cost Relative to the Approved Cost Frame

Figure 18.3 shows the difference between the final cost and the cost frame approved by
Parliament, where the latter largely corresponds to the P85 estimate. The data show that

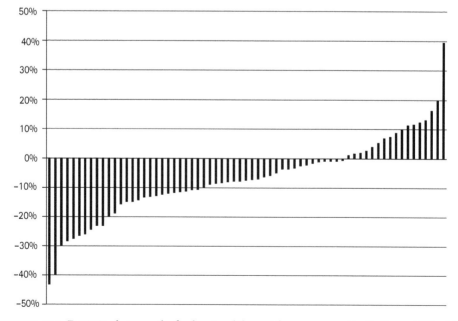

FIGURE 18.3 Deviation between the final cost and the cost frame approved by Parliament (N = 67).

fifty-three of the sixty-seven projects—79%—were completed within or below the cost frame. The total net savings for the projects taken as a whole was almost €600 million, or about 7% of the total investment.

18.7.2 Cost Deviation by Sector

Figure 18.4 shows the extent to which projects in different sectors complied with their approved cost frames. The number of projects is still too small to draw any firm conclusions, but the defense sector notably has had no projects with cost overruns. The railroad sector also performed above average, with only 14% of the projects with cost overruns.

18.7.3 Cost Deviation by Date

Another factor that may influence the problem of cost compliance is the date on which the project was commissioned. Indeed, the outcome of a project may be positively affected by learning effects, or positively or negative affected by economic cycles, in the sense that price changes may be greater or lesser than the variation captured by the uncertainty analysis.

Figure 18.5 shows the difference between the final cost and the approved cost frame for the projects, which are now sorted by time of inception, commissioned through 2000–2012. We find a vague tendency for cost overruns to have occurred in the middle part of the period, 2004–2008. On average, the projects in this period had final costs that were relatively equal to their cost frames (0% deviation), whereas the mean deviation for projects commissioned before and after this period was 13%; that is, considerable cost savings. The difference between the two means is statistically significant at

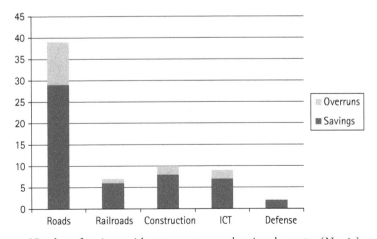

FIGURE 18.4 Number of projects with cost overruns and savings by sector ($N = 67$).

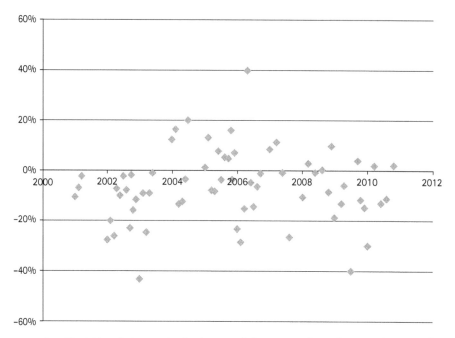

FIGURE 18.5 Deviations between the final cost and the approved cost frame at the time of commissioning for the project ($N = 67$).

the 0.05 level. This vague tendency may be due to strong cost increases in the construction industry that occurred in this period. Alternatively, the subsequent Global Financial Crisis of 2007–2008 may have had unforeseen consequences. Beyond these explanations it is difficult to determine any cause of the vague tendency observed.

18.7.4 Final Cost in Relation to the Agency's Steering Frame

As mentioned previously, the steering frame for the executing agency largely coincides with the estimated median (P50). Given the uncertainty associated with project implementation, one must not only expect deviations but also accept them. With steering frames at P50, we should expect equal numbers of overruns and underruns, and with a sufficiently large portfolio, the average for the whole portfolio should be close to the median.

The differences between the final cost and the steering frames are illustrated in Figure 18.6, and the results are as expected. The differences are almost symmetrically distributed around the median, indicating that cost control at the portfolio level is good. The distribution is slightly skewed to the right, however, with 48% of the projects below and 52% above the steering frame. There is an average positive deviation of 2.8%. Ideally, the deviation should be zero.

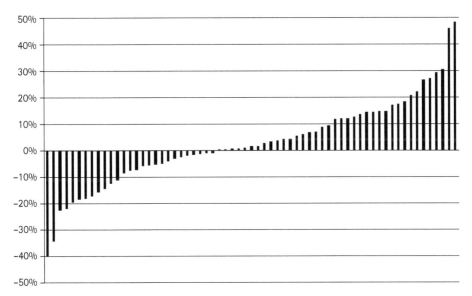

FIGURE 18.6 Deviation between the final cost and the agreed steering frame for the project ($N = 65$).

As mentioned, researchers are now in the process of performing more extensive *ex post* evaluations of projects that have undergone QA2 and are now in their operational phase where benefits for users and society may be measured. The results for the first eleven projects evaluated indicate that, overall, their rate of operational success is high, but not only in financial terms. Only two of eleven projects exceeded their cost frames, whereas five exceeded their steering frames. Furthermore, only two experienced delays, and four had (insignificant) shortcomings related to quality and functionality. The projects were essentially well organized and executed. Most risk factors that do indeed materialize were identified in the QA2 reports. However, notably, in one of the projects, expensive adjustments and upgrading were necessary in the first few years after it opened. This finding shows the importance of focusing on the life-cycle cost, not exclusively the investment cost.

The results from the first projects that have undergone QA2 show that the majority have been completed within the cost frame. Further, the deviation between the final cost and the steering frame is almost symmetrically distributed around the median. These results indicate that at the portfolio level the Norwegian state is now effectively controlling costs in major public investment projects. Moreover, as the deviations are both positive and negative to almost the same extent, there is no incentive to spend contingency reserves when unnecessary. This result is likely due to the practice of establishing a lower steering frame for the executing agency (typically at the P50 level).

The data reveal a tendency for overruns to have occurred in the middle part of the period (that is, projects started in 2004–2008). Monitoring how the results develop over time and in different sectors is thus important. The first set of completed projects may be somewhat biased in the sense that these projects were implemented in a time-efficient manner. Road projects are somewhat prevalent among the first completed projects, and many of them were rather uncomplicated. By contrast, a number of defense and ICT projects that started many years ago remain unfinished, and we are still waiting for their results.

18.8 Discussion

Considering the results that have been discussed, QA2 seems to have helped improve cost management and ensure cost control in major public projects in Norway. The situation in the 1990s was that major cost overruns were the norm rather than the exception, in both Norway and other countries. International research (Flyvbjerg et al. 2003) has shown that the situation has neither improved nor worsened over the past seventy years. However, caution should be made when comparing the results to the situation in the 1990s and in other countries. What QA2 ensures is that projects are now more mature when they are approved by Parliament, that the cost estimate is realistic, and that it includes necessary contingency reserves (corresponding to P85 level minus a reduction list). An important part of the picture is that the projects are normally approved (and the cost frame set) at a later stage in the planning process today than in the 1990s. Previously, the cost frame was often based on earlier and less realistic estimates and did not always include provisions for uncertainty.

Generally speaking, the encouraging results concerning cost compliance could be interpreted in two ways—either that investments projects that have undergone QA2 are now implemented at a lower cost than before, or that the cost frame is established later based on more mature and therefore more realistic estimates. While projects in the 1990s experienced large overruns in relation to their budget, we see today that projects may have overruns compared to "very early estimates" (Welde et al. 2014). What QA2 cannot prevent is an increase in the project content, scope, and cost during the process that *precedes* QA2. Before the cost frame is set, projects have often undergone a long front-end phase where user groups and stakeholders have great expectations. When the project is presented to Parliament it may be too late to reject the proposal, even in cases where the project scope has grown beyond what is considered an efficient solution to the societal needs. It is at the QA1 stage where the cost estimate is compared with expected benefits to determine whether the project is worth implementing. However, if the cost estimate increases between QA1 and QA2, the assessment of the project's tactical and strategic success from the QA1 stage will no longer be valid. Only now can we observe the first projects that have been subjected to both QA1 and QA2, and the researchers examining the effects of the QA scheme will expand their focus accordingly. If an increase in scope between QA1 and QA2 is a prevalent problem, a solution could be to change the QA scheme in the future so that the cost estimate at QA1 is binding for the subsequent pre-project phase (the so-called design to cost principle).

The issue of selection bias always needs to be investigated. A relevant question is whether the magnitudes of overruns have changed not only between the large projects but overall across all projects. In such a situation it may be difficult to conclude that the implementation of quality assurance for large projects alone was the major cause of the differences in the magnitudes of cost overruns among large projects. Odeck et al. (2015) tested for this issue of selection bias in a similar study. They found that while cost overruns in small road projects had remained constant, large road projects under the QA2 scheme had experienced significant reduction in the magnitudes of overruns during the same period.[4]

The Norwegian Quality-at-Entry regime is essentially a top-down regulatory scheme that was introduced to enforce a qualitative change in government practice and to improve quality at entry for major investments. It does not interfere with current procedures in the involved ministries and agencies, but merely aims to improve existing documents that provide an essential basis for political decision making. Naturally, the regime was initially somewhat controversial, as it entailed the involvement of external experts in matters handled by the ministries and agencies, as well as an additional cost and time delay. In reality, however, it has essentially received constructive responses from the ministries and agencies, that have adapted their practices to meet the new quality requirements and, in some cases, also adopted the scheme as a self-regulatory procedure.

A recent study (Kvalheim et al. 2015) examines whether the Norwegian government is better informed when making decisions about major public investment projects today compared with the period before the QA scheme was introduced. Based on a sample of projects from before and after the QA scheme was introduced, as well as interviews with twenty-four public planners and leaders, the study shows:

1. The quality of the decision documents has improved considerably.
2. The essential factors for the choice of conceptual solution are covered in the CA/QA1 analyses.
3. The premises for making a decision are well documented.
4. Recommendations are clear and transparent.
5. The projects are sufficiently mature and ready for parliamentary approval after QA2.

A significant feature of the Norwegian QA scheme is the spin-off effects that it seems to have had on both the government and the private sector. In the period after the scheme was introduced, we find a clear trend of improved practices in the areas of cost estimation and budgeting, risk assessment, and strategic planning. Moreover, there is growing awareness in the government regarding the need to improve the quality of decision documents, broaden the scope of analyses to include alternative concepts, and avoid making overly detailed analyses at an early stage. Such awareness has also proliferated into the consulting and construction industries, which have clearly responded positively to the new procedures and requirements in these areas in their role as suppliers to the public. We can also see that front-end management has become an issue within the community of professionals in project management, and training courses are now being offered by a number of institutions and consultants. Improved practices have also been adopted and institutionalized by various government agencies. Sectors not subjected to the QA scheme—notably, health authorities (Myrbostad et al. 2010), electric utilities (St. Meld. Nr. 14 2011–2012), and the Oslo municipal authority (Oslo Kommune 2011)—have voluntarily introduced variants of the scheme. Other countries have also shown interest in the scheme. For example, in Sweden a variant of the CA report, directly inspired by the Norwegian scheme, was introduced in 2013 as a new step in early planning. The Province of Quebec, Canada, has also introduced a similar scheme.

As mentioned, one fundamental aspect of the governance regime is that at least three alternative conceptual solutions should be analyzed at an early stage, when options are still open. The alternatives should be analyzed to the same degree of specification to ensure that the assessment of the alternatives is fair. This requirement has triggered a debate regarding what defines a conceptual solution. For instance, should conceptual solutions constitute different technical solutions to the same problem (for example, a bridge versus a tunnel in an infrastructure project for crossing a fjord), or should conceptual solutions be determined based on differences in the combined effects of different projects in the broadest sense? Whatever the answer, as the regime has put this issue on the public agenda, it has had a notable effect on analysts, politicians, and the public. This issue, and the emphasis on economic analysis, might prove significant in the aim to identify relevant alternative concepts and select the most viable project alternative.

18.9 CONCLUSION

In this chapter we have discussed the necessity of governance regimes in securing the interests of the financing party in public investment projects—that is, in improving the overall decision making and success of public projects—from both an operational and a tactical and strategic perspective. We have presented and discussed the Norwegian Quality-at-Entry regime, which requires two external quality assurance interventions before project implementation. In this top-down regulatory regime, major decisions are anchored at the political rather than the administrative level of government. The approach of limiting interference in existing practices and procedures inherent in the scheme seems to be effective, and it may facilitate the development of self-regulatory schemes, which may ultimately make central top-down interventions unnecessary. Openness and transparency seem to be essential for improving the governance of public investments.

Lessons so far indicate that projects subjected to budgetary quality assurance (QA2) are now largely completed within their cost frames. Hence, at the portfolio level, the state is able to more effectively control the cost of major investment projects. Perhaps the most intriguing aspect of this study, as compared to other studies of cost compliance in projects, is that our figures are consistent, based on the same principle and methodology for all projects, and therefore comparable. The good results concerning cost compliance should, however, not be confused with evidence that Norway implements its major projects more cost-efficiently than other countries. What QA2 cannot prevent is an increase in the project content, scope, and cost during the process that *precedes* QA2. It should be a topic for future research to investigate whether this is a prevalent problem.

It is too early to determine whether quality assurance of the choice of conceptual solution (QA1) has increased the tactical and strategic success of projects, but it is clear that the systematic appraisal of the choice of conceptual solution is considered useful.

The Norwegian QA regime is a novel and simple approach to improving project governance. With a few exceptions—most notably, the lack of requirement for risk capital from those who initiate and benefit from the project—the scheme is in line with Flyvbjerg et al.'s (2003) recommendations. It ensures that the projects are mature and well-defined when presented to Parliament, it requires the use of stochastic cost-estimation methodology, and it contains incentives for the agency not to use the whole cost frame. So far, the scheme seems to work well in a Norwegian context. However, this does not imply that it will be preferable in any context. Other countries with different institutional contexts, specific types of projects, and major, long-lasting projects, may require other approaches.

Project governance has become an issue in the project management community only recently. To move forward in this field, numerous questions need to be answered. What procedures are applied in different countries and agencies, and what are their effects? What would it take to develop more effective governance regimes at the international, government, or corporate level in order to ensure maximum utility and return on investment for society and investors? What is the optimal mix of regulations, economic means, and information in improved governance regimes for major investment projects? A challenge for the project management community will be to shift the focus beyond the delivery of the project itself to the broader issues of the project's utility and effects. A recent study compared governance schemes for major public investment projects in Norway and five other countries (Samset et al. 2015). There are many similarities between the schemes, but also differences regarding, for example, the number of project phases, decision points, and interventions, and who performs quality assurance. All schemes are of a fairly recent date, and it is too early to explore their effects and compare their success, but this would be an interesting topic for future studies. An increased understanding and sensitivity in this area could be of mutual benefit to both the financing and the implementing parties.

NOTES

1. A parallel here would be private financial institutions, where investment projects are assessed almost exclusively based on a review of the investors' credibility and collateral available, with little regard to the substantive issues related to or characteristic of the investment project as such.

2. All agencies are obligated to keep accounts according to the Regulations for State Financial Management (Finansdepartementet 2013). The accounts provide a basis for control over the allocation of appropriations and the basis for analysis of activities, including final costs in individual projects. Final costs cannot be tampered without compromising the accounts. The Auditor General audits agency accounts annually.

3. The accrued expenses in the projects are collected annually through the agencies' accounting systems and followed up as part of the agencies' internal control systems. During the construction phase, the agencies report accrued expenses to the responsible ministry and provide forecasts for final costs. Upon completion, total annual costs are adjusted to a common price level using the appropriate indexes and used internally as part of the agencies' internal evaluation systems. The data are owned by the responsible agencies, but are publicly available for research and other purposes.

4. We do not have access to data on the final costs of smaller projects from agencies other than the Norwegian Public Roads Administration, so we cannot conclude with certainty that quality assurance alone is the main reason for changes in the magnitudes of overruns, but the study by Odeck et al. (2015) concluded that quality assurance has led to a reduction in cost overruns among road projects which make up a majority of the projects in our study.

REFERENCES

Aass, T. (2013). *Kostnadskontroll i prosjekter som har vært underlagt ekstern kvalitetssikring KS2.* Concept working paper.

Berg, P., Østby, L.-E., Lilleby, S., Styrvold, S., Holand, K., Korsnes, U., Rønning, K., and Johansen, F. (1999). *Styring av statlige investeringer: Sluttrapport fra styringsgruppen.* Ministry of Finance.

Bjertnaes, A. M. (2012). *Konseptvalgutredninger: intensjon og forbedringer.* Master's thesis, NTNU.

Christensen, T. (2011). "The Norwegian front-end governance regime of major public projects: A theoretically based analysis and evaluation," *International Journal of Managing Projects in Business,* 4(2): 221.

Finansdepartementet (Ministry of Finance). (2013). *Reglement for økonomistyring i staten Bestemmelser om økonomistyring i staten.* Oslo: Finansdepartementet.

Flyvbjerg, B., Bruzelius, N., and Rothengatter, W. (2003). *Megaprojects and Risk: An Anatomy of Ambition.* Cambridge: Cambridge University Press.

Grindvoll, I. L. (2015). *Hva har skjedd med KS1-prosjektene?: Status per mars 2015.* Concept working paper.

Kvalheim, E. V., Christensen, T., Samset, K., and Volden, G. H. (2015). *Har regjeringen fått et bedre beslutningsunderlag? Om effekten av å innføre konseptvalgutredning (KVU) og ekstern kvalitetssikring (KS1 og KS2) for store statlige investeringsprosjekter.* Concept working paper.

Miller, R. and Hobbs, B. (2005). *Governance Regimes for Large Complex Projects,* paper for the EURAM 2005 conference, University of Montreal.

Miller, R. and Lessard, D. R. (2000). *The Strategic Management of Large Engineering Projects: Shaping Institutions, Risk and Governance.* Cambridge, MA: MIT Press.

Morris, P. W. G. and Hough, G. H. (1991). *The Anatomy of Major Projects: A Study of the Reality of Project Management.* Chichester: Wiley.

Müller, R. (2009). *Project Governance.* Farnham: Gower.

Myrbostad, A., Rohde, T., Martinussen, P., and Lauvsnes, M. (2010). "Regime for planlegging og beslutning i sykehusprosjekter." Concept Report no. 25.

Odeck, J., Welde, M., and Volden. G. H. (2015). "The impact of external quality assurance of costs estimates on cost overruns: Empirical evidence from the Norwegian road sector," *European Journal of Transport and Infrastructure Research*, 15(3): 286–303.

Osol Kommune (2011). *Konseptvalgutredning (KVU) i Oslo kommune. Krav og veiledning.*

Pinto, J. K. and Slevin, D. P. (2006). *Organizational Governance and Project Success: Lessons from Boston's Big Dig.* Concept Symposium 2006, NTNU, Trondheim.

Rasmussen, I., Heldal, N., Homleid, T., Ibenholt, K., Skjelvik, J. M., and Vennemo, H. (2010). "På vei til kvalitet?: Evaluering av KS1 i transportsektoren." *Vista Analyse Report.*

Samset, K. (2008). *Prosjekt i tidligfasen: Valg av konsept* Tapir Akademisk forlag

Samset, K., Andersen, B., and Austeng, K. (2013). "Mulighetsrommet: En studie om konseptutredninger og konseptvalg," Concept Report no. 34. Norway: Ex Ante Academic Publisher.

Samset, K. and Volden, G. H. (2013). "Investing for impact. Lessons with the Norwegian State project model and the first investment projects that have been subjected to external quality assurance," Concept Report no. 36. Norway: Ex Ante Academic Publisher.

Samset, K. and Volden, G. H. (2014): "Front end governance of major public projects: Lessons with a Norwegian Quality Assurance scheme," *International Journal of Architecture, Engineering and Construction*, 3(2): 110–19.

Samset, K., Volden, G. H., Olsson, N. and Kvalheim, E. V. (2015). "Styringsregimer for store offentlige prosjekter: En sammenliknende studie av prinsipper og praksis i seks land. [Governance schemes for major public investment projects: A comparative study of principles and practices in six countries]." Concept Report no. 46. Norway: Ex Ante Academic Publisher.

Samset, K., Volden, G. H., Welde, M., and Bull-Berg, H. (2014). "Mot sin hensikt: Perverse incentiver—om offentlige investeringsprosjekter som ikke forplikter," Concept Report no. 40. Norway: Ex Ante Academic Publisher.

Statens Vegvesen (Norwegian Public Roads Administration). (2012). *Evaluering av KVU/KS1. Færre og bedre KVU-er.*

St. Meld. Nr. 14. (2011–2012). *Vi bygger Norge: om utbygging av strømnettet.*

Welde, M. (2014). *Oppdaterte sluttkostnader: prosjekter som har vært underlagt KS2 per mai 2014.* Concept working paper.

Welde, M. (2015). *Oppdaterte sluttkostnader. Prosjekter som har vært underlagt KS2 per september 2015.* Concept working paper.

Welde, M., Eliasson, J., Odeck, J., and Börjesson, M. (2013). "Planprosesser, beregningsverktøy og bruk av nytte-kostnadsanalyser i vegsektor: En sammenligning av praksis av Norge og Sverige," Concept Report no. 33. Norway: Ex Ante Academic Publisher.

Welde, M., Samset, K., Andersen, B., and Austeng, K. (2014). "Lav prising, store valg: En studie av underestimering av kostnader i prosjekters tidligfase. [Low estimates, high stakes: A study of underestimation of costs in projects' earliest phase]." Concept Report no. 39. Norway: Ex Ante Academic Publisher.

CHAPTER 19

··

THE GOOD MEGADAM
Does It Exist, All Things Considered?

··

THAYER SCUDDER

19.1 INTRODUCTION

RIVER basins, some of the world's largest dams, and dam project-affected people have been my laboratory in Africa, the Middle East, and Asia for the past sixty years. Let me be clear from the start that this chapter is not an attempt to demonstrate ways in which megadam benefits can be improved and adverse impacts avoided by such means as better siting and environmental flows, and by adequate environmental, sociocultural, and health impact studies as part of a participatory options assessment process.

Since 1956 I have spent a lifetime trying to reduce the destructive impacts of large dams on river basin ecosystems and on the people and communities who live in and are dependent on those ecosystems. While my colleagues and I can claim that our efforts have resulted in many project-affected people becoming less poor than would otherwise be the case, my major accomplishment to date has been to lead a research team that stopped a multipurpose megaproject. That was the Government of Botswana's Southern Okavango Integrated Water Development Project that the government suspended in late May 1992, just before our team presented in a public lecture a final report that initiated a process that resulted in the Okavango Delta becoming a World Heritage Site in 2014.

In what follows, my intention is to explain why large dams are a poor—indeed unacceptable—investment for the future. While covering a range of topics in a single chapter requires a high level of generalization, it is essential for the reader to understand not only that each dam is responsible for creating its own history but that each history is influenced by the encompassing environmental and national/international context. In other words, large dams are not built within a vacuum. Incorporation of an occasional case history is intended to emphasize the critical importance of that point.

19.2 THE POLITICAL ECONOMY
OF LARGE DAMS

Large dams continue to be a key part of a no longer functional, yet still dominant, global political economy that continues to be favored by International Financial Institutions, the World Trade Organization, Bilateral Official Development Assistance, most nation-states, professional associations such as the International Hydrological Association and the International Commission on Large Dams, and leading macro-economists. All such institutions and individuals not only favor consumption-based increased Gross Domestic Product (GDP) as the key measure of growth, but assess the consumption of such irreplaceable natural capital as free-flowing rivers as income (Daly 1994).

The 2008 Growth Report: Strategies for Sustained Growth and Inclusive Development chaired by Nobel Prize–winning economist Michael Spence and published by the World Bank for the Commission on Growth and Development, while realizing that "the global economy has outrun our capacity to manage it" (Commission on Growth and Development 2008: 203), still advocates significantly increasing GDP rates, as illustrated by their emphasis on thirteen economies that "have grown at an average rate of 7% a year or more for 25 years or longer. At that pace of expansion, an economy almost doubles in size every decade. This report is about sustained, high growth of this kind" (1).

My conclusions about megadams overlap with James C. Scott's analysis in *Seeing Like A State: How Certain Schemes to Improve the Human Condition Have Failed*, in which he argues that disastrous examples of large-scale "state initiated social engineering," including megadams, involve four elements. The first is the state's "administrative ordering of nature and society." The second is a high-modernist ideology, which Scott argues "typifies the current emphasis on sustained increases in national GDP at the expense of the World's environment." Scott's third element requires the ability of an authoritarian state to use its power to implement its schemes, while the fourth requires a prostrate civil society.

Where I part with Scott is that his third and fourth elements can apply to any powerful nation. Where megadams are involved, for example, democratic India and the United States should also be included. An important Indian example would be the Sardar Sarovar Dam on India's most holy Narmada River, while megadams on the Missouri River would be good US examples of destructive projects. In both the Sardar Sarovar and Missouri River cases, as elsewhere, Scott's prostrate civil society was dominated by the poor, including indigenous communities.

It is relevant that proponents of such projects tend to be major political figures. Egypt's Nasser equated the Aswan High Dam with the pyramids, while Ghana's first president saw the Volta Dam as symbolic of Ghana's forthcoming industrialization, with a commemorative stamp showing him with the dam in the background (David Brokensha, verbal communication). India's Prime Minister Nehru compared the

Bhakra Dam with the Hindu temples of the past, and years later laid the corner stone for Sardar Sarovar. In the United States, President Roosevelt "fathered" the Tennessee Valley Authority. More recently, Narendra Modi, who previously had been the Chief Minister of the state most favored by Sardar Sarovar, within three weeks of becoming India's current Prime Minister, pushed his new government to approve the building of gates to heighten the dam by 17 meters, in spite of the fact that thousands of people had still to be adequately resettled at the dam's prior height (Report of the Central Fact Finding Team, 2015).

19.3 Economic and Financial Costs

19.3.1 Introduction

With most of the best sites already dammed in the OECD countries, dam construction has shifted to China, India, Brazil, and newly industrializing countries in the tropics and subtropics. In lower-income countries, as in South East Asia and throughout most of Africa (which in the past often were unable to repay loans from international financial institutions), a new system of financing has emerged whereby an internationally operating private or state-owned engineering company acquires the finance to build, own, operate, and transfer a dam to the host country after a twenty-five-year or longer period. As the largest rather than the only shareholder, the company may take on partners, including the host country.

19.3.2 Flaws in Economic and Financial Analysis: Megadams Are Not Cost Effective

Throughout my career, those who have agreed with me that environmental and social costs of completed large dams were too high, nonetheless insisted that economic benefits significantly exceeded economic costs. That argument has been irrefutably undermined since the publication of Ansar, Flyvbjerg, Budzier, and Lunn's "Should we build more large dams? The actual cost of hydropower megaproject development" (2014).

Based on a statistical analysis of 245 large dams in Africa, Asia, Europe, Latin America, and North America built between 1934 and 2007, the authors concluded that "even before accounting for negative impacts on human society and environment, the actual construction costs of large dams are too high to yield a positive return" (2014: 2). High costs were not just associated with unanticipated problems and mistakes that occur during long construction periods averaging 8.6 years for large dams (another reason why large dams are a poor option for dealing with time-dependent development issues), but also because "Actual costs were on average 96% higher than estimated costs," (6), while "projects that take longer have greater cost overruns: bigger projects take longer" (1).

Furthermore, the "evidence is overwhelming that costs are systematically biased toward underestimation." Two complementary explanations are involved. First, the authors argue that the experts and lay persons involved, according to relevant psychological research, are "systematically and predictably too optimistic about the time, costs, and benefits of a decision." Second, "optimistic judgments are often exacerbated by deception, i.e. strategic misrepresentation by project promoters" (2).

19.3.3 The Current Build, Own, Operate, and Transfer (BOOT) Approach to Large Dam Construction

In the lead-up to the formation of the World Commission on Dams (WCD) under the International Union for Conservation and Nature (IUCN) and the World Bank, the two sponsors organized a workshop in 1997 at IUCN headquarters in Gland, Switzerland. A Reference Group of thirty-eight participants was invited (thirty-five attended) that represented principal actors (aside from project-affected river-basin inhabitants themselves) in the large dam debate. To provide them with some common background, five overview papers were presented.

The senior author of the paper on "Engineering and economic aspects of planning, design, operation and construction of large dam projects" was Engelbertus Oud, head of the Water Power and Land Development Department of Lahmeyer International GmbH, which was Germany's largest consulting engineering company. In his paper, coauthored with Terence C. Muir, Oud wrote: "The trend toward private sector financing will inevitably lead to a reduced focus on economic optimality and greater focus on financial viability" (1997: 23). In addition there will be "externalization of the indirect costs associated with the project to the maximum extent possible" and "off-loading as much risk as possible onto other parties, particularly onto the government" (p. 21).

19.3.4 Flaws in a Politically Biased Options Assessment Process

Free-flowing rivers in which megadams are built (and which are frequently national or international heartlands), and their flora, fauna, and human inhabitants, seldom figure prominently in evaluation criteria for generalizing about macroeconomic development and the role of large dams in that development.

Indeed, during my research on large dams, I have never come across an adequate options assessment process—"adequate" being defined as assessment of a number of ways, of which a dam is only one, for meeting specific goals. More often, the decision to build a large dam has already been made by national or state political leaders, with options assessment restricted to deciding which dam site to select.

> Comprehensive options assessment should commence at the beginning of the decision-making process for water resource development and continue throughout the operation of whatever programme or project is selected. All relevant stakeholders and categories of concerned people should be involved. Economic, financial, and technical issues should be complemented by equal consideration of environmental, institutional, and social issues. (Scudder 2005)

19.3.5 Discount Rates Are Too High

When involved in major infrastructure projects, discount rates used by international financial institutions tend to run between 10% and 12%. That means that environmental, river basin societal and dam repair and decommissioning costs that occur more than a decade beyond a dam's completion are ignored, as are costs for delta and flood-plain restoration as currently underway in Europe and the United States.

In effect, as Oud and Muir (1997) state, "High discount rates do not support sustainable development, as the long-term damages or costs associated with a project are simply discounted away" (23). For that reason, the authors favor a discount rate of 0%–3% annually, as has been used in "several environmental studies ... dealing with global warming" (23).

19.3.6 Emergency Repair and Decommissioning Costs

19.3.6.1 *Emergency Repair: The Kariba Case*

Commissioned in 1960, the Kariba Dam created what is still the world's largest artificial reservoir, with four times the storage capacity of the United States' Lake Mead backed up behind the Hoover Dam. By 2015, engineers expressed concern that the plunge pool, excavated at the base of the 128-meter dam when water was released from one or more of Kariba's gates, could eventually undermine the dam's foundations. Currently, the plunge pool has deepened to 90 meters, with the Zambezi River Authority (ZRA) and reputable international engineers agreeing that without major rehabilitation works on the plunge pool and the flood release gates, the dam could collapse in two to three years. Collapse would not only risk the downstream destruction of Mozambique's large Cahora Bassa Dam but also risk the lives of up to 3 million people within the Lower Zambezi River Basin.

As rumors began to circulate in 2014 that a possible collapse might be imminent, Zambia and Zimbabwe's Zambezi River Authority requested immediate assistance from international financial institutions and national governments. Following a World Bank assessment, three international groups and the Swedish Government agreed to provide

$270 million in grants and loans at a signing ceremony in February 2015. Counting ZRA's $19.2 million, such high costs were certainly not included in the original cost–benefit analysis for Kariba.

19.3.6.2 *Decommissioning and Dam Removal: Glines Canyon and Elwha Dams*

In the United States more than a thousand dams have been removed (O'Connor et al. 2015). Although most of those dams are small, included is the world's largest, and presumably most expensive, dam removal project to date. Involved were two dams on the Elwha River in Washington State. One was the 64-meter-high Glines Canyon Dam, which was removed in 2014, and the other the 33-meter-high Elwha Dam, which was removed in 2012. The combined cost of the two removals was $351 million.

Although $351million was not easily acquired, adverse impacts had previously cost downstream users much more in terms of destruction of fisheries, loss of livelihood for impacted Native Americans, and major erosion problems. Because of sediment back-up behind the lower Elwha Dam, the delta beaches and marshes had been seriously eroded. Most adversely affected has been a 3-mile spit, formed to the east by Elwha River sediment that protects the harbor of the City of Port Angeles. Erosion control with rip-rap along the outer edge had been expensive, costing the Army Corps of Engineers "approximately $100,000 annually" (<https://en.wikipedia.org/wiki/Elwha_Ecosystem_Restoration>). Erosion had also reduced the size of the reservation of a Native American society, although far more serious were the adverse impacts of the dam on eight species of salmon, two of trout, and clam beds important to Native American livelihood.

Fortunate for scientific research on the restoration process following removal of the dams is that 83% of the river basin lies in the Federal Government's Olympic National Park, which has joined with the Bureau of Reclamation and the Native American tribe to plan, manage, and research river restoration. Even before the upstream dam had been removed, pre-dam ecosystem restoration was under way:

> [B]irds, bugs, and mammals are feasting on salmon eggs and carcasses as fish once again nourish the watershed ... The river is hard at work with its restored natural flow, rebuilding its plunge pools, log jams and gravel bars ... Revegetation ... is unfolding dramatically. Already, terraced banks of the former lakes are burgeoning with alder and cottonwood ... (Mapes 2014)

... hence reinforcing research on dam removals elsewhere in the United States "that rivers are resilient, with many responding quickly to dam removal. Most river channels stabilize within months or years, not decades, particularly when dams are removed rapidly ... The rapid physical response is driven by the strong upstream/downstream coupling intrinsic to river systems" (O'Connor et al. 2015).

19.3.7 Inadequate Political Will, Budget, and Staff Capacity on the Part of Governments and Project Authorities

These deficiencies are especially prominent where community resettlement is involved. According to a statistical analysis of fifty dams, "a major lack of planning capacity occurred in 27 (66%) of 41 cases with adequate data" (Scudder 2012), while the authors of the World Bank's 1994 *Bankwide Review* of all Bank-assisted projects involving resettlement concluded that the "timely availability of adequate funds ... may be the single most powerful explanatory operational variable behind the failure to implement resettlement operations well" (Section 6: 11). As for political will, the *Bankwide Review* found that to be a recurring deficiency.

19.3.8 Monitoring and Evaluation (M&E) Are Weak

One of the most disturbing findings of the World Commission on Dams was "the lack of monitoring of the impacts of dams and the complete failure to conduct proper *ex post* evaluations of performance and impacts" (WCD 2000: 184). The extensive knowledge base of the World Commission on Dams "shows that historically, few comprehensive post-project evaluations have taken place after the commissioning of large dams. This applies to virtually all regions and countries. With few exceptions, there has been little or no monitoring of the physical, social and environmental effects of dams, a necessary input for such evaluations" (WCD 2000: 226–7). "That such large investments have been rarely evaluated once they have been in operation for a significant period suggests little obligation on the part of powerful centralized agencies and donors to account for the costs and benefits incurred. Perhaps more critically it signals a failure to actively engage in learning from experience in both the adaptive management of existing facilities and in the design and appraisal of new dams" (184).

On *ex post* audits, Asit Biswas (Stockholm Water Prize winner, 2006), though a critic of the World Commission on Dams and the Commission's final report, states: "One of the major reasons why the current non-productive debate on dams has thrived is the absence of objective and detailed *ex post* analyses of the physical, economic, social and environmental impacts of large dams" (Tortajada, Altinbilek, and Biswas 2012).

A more specific M&E problem in all the dams that I have studied is the inadequacy of pre-project benchmark studies which are so necessary both for an adequate options assessment process and for adequate monitoring for adaptive management purposes and subsequent evaluation. What pre-project assessments are done have been too late in the planning process, with the result that project-affected people have already suffered significant but unrecorded negative impacts. Examples include government regulations that resettlers cease building new houses, extending farm land and/or opening new businesses that would subsequently be flooded, and/or governments cease providing or upgrading services (agriculture extension, health clinics, and schools especially) that continue in surrounding unaffected areas.

19.3.9 Corruption

For the ten projects on which I have spent the most time in years and number of visits, corruption has been noted for at least five, including the three noted in what follows. It ranges from large-scale corruption at the top, involving national leaders and engineering companies, to local officials responsible for compensation and development projects for affected people.

In Lesotho, several prominent companies were blacklisted by the World Bank when found to have paid bribes during competition for contracts for the Highlands Water Project, while in China the government reported that in 2000 "corrupt officials had embezzled $60 million ... from resettlement funds for the Three Gorges Dam project" (WCD 2000: 187, box 6.9). In connection with Kariba Dam resettlement, my colleagues and I have documented not-infrequent cases where local officials such as chiefs and headmen allocate for cash or other personal benefits high-value (for irrigation, tourist lodges, and so forth) customary land to outsiders.

Much more extensive and diversified corruption has been associated with the Sardar Sarovar Project in the Indian States of Gujarat, Madya Pradesh, and (to a lesser extent) Maharastra. Much of that corruption pertains to the resettlement process, with officials lying to the Courts about having completed resettlement requirements for thousands of families so that they could further heighten the dam (Report of the Central Fact Finding Team 2015).

19.4 ECOLOGICAL AND ENVIRONMENTAL COSTS

19.4.1 Free-Flowing Rivers, Large Dams, and Engineers

> Human impacts on the hydrologic environment have increased on the order of ninefold since 1950 ... Only a portion of this impact stems from withdrawals of water ... Most of it stems from human manipulation of natural flow patterns through the construction and operation of dams, reservoirs, dikes, and levees. (Postel and Richter 2003)

More recently, Grill et al. (2015), based on innovative research dealing with river fragmentation and flow regulation, "found that prolonged and prolific dam building has resulted in large-scale deterioration of the majority of global river basins, with at times heavy to severe impacts." Also in 2015, Beard, a former Commissioner of the US Bureau of Reclamation, wrote in *Deadbeat Dams* not only that "we should remove unnecessary and environmentally destructive dams to restore our rivers and streams" (Beard 2015: 63), but also should abolish the Bureau of Reclamation.

The negative ecosystem and environmental impacts associated with dams are increased because companies responsible for building dams and sponsoring governments seldom have employees with sufficient oversight knowledge. That is especially true of the engineers in charge of both construction and overall project management. While serving on the World Commission on Dams, my closest colleague was Jan Veltrop, who prior to his retirement had been Chief Engineer and a member of the Board of Directors of Harza Engineering Company. A member of the US National Academy of Engineering, he was also Honorary President of the International Commission on Large Dams. Traveling together on field trips, we also arranged to precede the Commission's arrival in Brazil in order to make a several-day visit to the Tucurui Dam in the Amazon Basin to examine environmental and resettlement issues. I remember clearly Veltrop telling me that throughout his thirty-seven-year career at Harza, his engineering responsibilities were so great that he had no time to become aware of, let alone think about, associated environmental and sociocultural costs and issues when he was involved with such large dams as Yacyreta (Argentina), Tarbela (Pakistan), and Ertan (China).

On various occasions during my career, engineers-in-charge and other officials have tried—unsuccessfully I might add—to restrict my work as a consultant or adviser by such means as restricting my access, requiring project officials to accompany me, and warning community leaders to ensure that community members are discreet in what they tell me. At worst, a small minority of those in charge see resettlers as "people in the way," with one chief engineer telling me that what the indigenous people in his project needed was "sterilization."

19.4.2 Evaluation and Research on Free-Flowing Rivers

Recent research and improved research tools further point up the value of free-flowing rivers as natural capital. In 1997, Costanza et al. published in *Nature* an article on "The value of the world's ecosystem services and natural capital." Of seventeen categories of ecosystem services examined in sixteen biomes, the highest benefits in dollars per hectare came first from estuaries and second from freshwater swamps and river flood-plains. Yet the functions and financial values of free-flowing rivers have been generally ignored in development discourse and especially in options assessment and cost–benefit analyses for megadams and other infrastructure that obstruct river flows.

Grill et al.'s (2015) recent research is leading to more detailed and precise analysis on how large dams adversely affect the ecological and financial value of free-flowing rivers. Also important is increased use of remote sensing, which has improved assessment of environmental changes within river basins (Petit et al. 2001) and the distribution of impacts on human communities and livelihoods within river basins (Richter et al. 2010).

19.4.3 Floodplain and River Restoration

The restoration movement got underway in the 1970s with an emphasis on what came to be called "environmental flows" from dams primarily to benefit certain species of fish. Although I have not researched the broadening of the environmental flows concept, unknowingly I may have helped pioneer its application in 1980 by linking "regularization of drawdown within the reservoir behind the [Kariba] dam, synchronized with simulation of a downstream flood. Properly executed it would increase significantly the production of crops, livestock, and fish by lake-basin and downstream residents. It would also have the advantages of increased social equity and reduced environmental impact" (Scudder 1980).

Today, restoration has broadened to include removal of dams, levees, and other obstructions to free-flowing rivers in order to restore to the extent possible natural flood regimes based on increasing knowledge of former wetlands and riparian forest cover. Although much of the research and restoration has occurred in Europe and North America, there are scattered examples elsewhere. Postel and Richter (2003) provide a Sampling of River Restoration Efforts including Type of Flow Restoration and Ecological Purpose (Table 4.1), and various examples. Richards and Hughes (2008) cover "Floodplains in Europe," while Hughes, Moss, and Richards (2009) deal with "Uncertainty in riparian and floodplain restoration," with both chapters in Darby and Sears (2008). Looking to the future, I suspect the main problems facing restoration will be property rights, competition over scarce water supplies, and finance.

19.4.4 Climate Change

Climate change is an excellent example of the type of unexpected events that often have unfavorable impacts on large projects such as megadams that require long-duration construction phases. Such events tend to be environmental (dam-induced or other earthquakes, for example) or related to changes in a nation's governance or political economy. They were coded as major in more than half of the forty-four cases with sufficient data in Scudder and Jay's fifty-dam statistical analysis (Scudder 2012).

Those supporting large dams tend to ignore the increasing risks and uncertainty that climate change presents owing to expected increases in such extreme events as drought and floods. According to Ebinger and Vergara (2011), "heavy reliance on hydropower creates significant vulnerability to climate change and is a feature that many low- and middle-income countries have in common," and where hydropower impacts are summarized as "reduced firm energy, increased variability, and increased uncertainty." Moreover, "long-lifespan infrastructure, such as hydropower plants, is generally less adaptable to changes in actual facilities whereas a short-lifespan infrastructure can be replaced in the long term as the climate changes."

Although one needs to be careful about attributing to climate change a specific drought that decreases availability of reservoir water for irrigation and generation of hydropower, drought is already affecting generating capacity in California. Power output by May 2015 had been reduced by about one third from the Shasta Dam, which backs up the largest reservoir in California, while electricity production at other dams in the state is "expected to be less than 20% of normal because of low water levels" (Xia 2015). In Ghana, drought periodically has reduced hydropower generation from the Volta Dam at Akosombo to the extent that in 1977 income from fisheries actually exceeded that from hydropower. Climate change can also be expected to influence reservoir evaporation rates, which already amount to about 10% in large reservoirs such as Lake Powell (USA), Kariba, and Lake Nasser (Egypt).

Recent severe dam-induced downstream flooding caused by sudden release of reservoir waters to avoid overtopping is also suggestive of an increasing frequency of destructive events owing to climate change. Extreme downstream floods were released from the Kariba and Cahora Bassa Dams in 1987, 1989, 1997, 2001, 2005, and 2008 (Beilfuss 2012). In Nigeria, 1999 releases from the Kainji Dam on the Niger River caused serious downstream damage, while releases from the Tiga and Challawa Gorge Dams on the Hadejia-Nguru system in 2001 inundated 350 downstream communities and farm lands. In the latter case initial reports referred to more than a hundred deaths (Scudder 2005: 226).

19.4.5   Associated Environmental Degradation: Environmental Costs Associated with Fragmentation of Either a Free-Flowing River or a Portion of a River Basin

19.4.5.1 *Immediate Upstream Areas*

Dam-related roads in upstream areas risk opening up catchments to legal and illegal timber extraction and mining at the risk of increasing reservoir siltation and pollution. The risk is especially great in the remaining tropical forests in South East Asia, where local and transboundary wildlife poaching also continues to be a major problem.

19.4.5.2 *Reservoir Basins, Greenhouse Gas Emissions, and Sedimentation*

Now that increasing construction of large dams has shifted to the tropics and subtropics, an increase in greenhouse gases (especially methane and CO_2) following reservoir formation can be expected. That is especially the case where heavily vegetated, relatively shallow basins are only partially cleared or where clearance only of valuable timber does not remove leaves, vines, and other debris, the decay of which favors the production of greenhouse gasses (see especially articles by P. M. Fearnside on the Brazilian Amazon and the World Commission on Dams' *Dams and Development* on Brazil's Tucurui Dam). Far more pre-dam and post-dam research is needed, however, since undammed natural habitats may also release greenhouse gases; hence "a floodplain tropical forest in Amazonia may emit methane from soils, and, at the same time, absorb carbon dioxide in leaves" (World Commission on Dams 2000: 76).

Decaying vegetation through the agency of bacteria can also produce methylmercury—a serious toxin of the central nervous system, which I first encountered when Robert Goodland and I joined Canadian colleagues to evaluate (and reject) Hydro-Quebec's proposed Grande Baleine Dam on the James Bay Peninsula. Especially at risk from the toxin where dams had been built were pregnant women who consumed carnivorous fish at the end of the food chain in which methylmercury had become concentrated.

Especially in the tropics and subtropics, the inundation of the riverine forest fringe can adversely affect the livelihood of local communities. After the Kariba reservoir filled, the Gwembe Tonga, for example, lost access to timber for making dugout canoes, to wildlife, and to a wide range of non-timber forest products including edible and medicinal plants.

Eventually, reservoir siltation (averaging 0.5–1% per annum for large dams) will reduce each large dam's utility.

19.4.5.3 *Downstream Flows and Fisheries*

The erosion capacity of silt-free waters below large dams tends to broaden rivers by undercutting banks, toppling the riverine forest fringe, and undercutting bridge abutments and other structures. On the other hand, channelization of river flows by regularizing dam releases, or building levees and barriers to control outflows, have had a very adverse effect on flood plains and highly productive wetlands.

In regard to fauna, downstream fisheries in particular are adversely affected. According to the World Commission on Dams, "the blockages of sediment and nutrients, the re-regularization of streamflow, and elimination of the natural flood regime can all have significant, negative effects on downstream fisheries" (2000: 84). Anadromous fish, like temperate zone salmon that breed in fresh water and mature in the ocean before returning to the same river to breed, are especially adversely affected and have become extinct in some dammed river systems.

19.4.5.4 *Negative Impacts on Delta Ecosystems*

Significant impacts of large dams on deltas, which are highly productive ecosystems, "have yet to be built into the water resource and energy development options assessment process and, more specifically, into feasibility studies for large dams" (Scudder 2005: 229). A wide variety of dam impacts are largely negative. For example, the delta-building process temporarily stops when dammed river flows periodically fail to reach the delta, which occurs, for example, on the Colorado, Indus, and Yellow Rivers.

Elsewhere, delta size and topography is irreparably changed, as is the case today with the Nile Delta. Mohammad Kassas may have been the first scientist who warned that the Aswan High Dam's completion in 1967 had "brought the delta building process to a halt" (Kassas 1972: 179), "with coastal retreat ... actively taking place now at the alarming rate of several meters per year" (186). Twenty-one years later, Stanley and Warne (1993) wrote:

> Changes in the natural cycle of Nile flow and sediment discharge had profound consequences, including: accelerated erosion along parts of the delta coastline [Smith and Abdel-Kader 1988; Frihy et al. 1991; Frihy 1992]; marine incursion onto low-lying

northern delta plain sectors [Stanley 1988, 1990]; curtailment of flood silt deposition that had formerly served as natural fertilizer and had offset land subsidence [Shalash 1982]; increased salinization of cultivated land, as natural flooding no longer flushed out evaporitic salts [Shata and El Fayoumy 1970; Kashaf 1983]; sharp decline in fish populations, both in lagoons and seaward of the delta, as a result of decreased nutrients carried to the coast [Aleem 1972]; and choking of canals and waterways by water hyacinth (*Nymphaea*). This last effect increased water loss through evapotranspiration and fostered schistosomiasis [Waterbury 1979].

Densely populated, as well as being Egypt's agricultural heart land, the Nile Delta is one of three global deltas most threatened by sea-level rise (Climate Change 2007). Aware of the many reasons why physical barriers would not be a solution to Mediterranean intrusion, by the end of the 1980s the Egyptian Government was planning the "voluntary" resettlement of the first million delta inhabitants to the High Dam's Lake Nasser Basin (Adaptation Fund 2011: 8; Government of Egypt 1988), at the expense of 48,000 resettled Nubians and their descendants who continue to claim to successive Egyptian governments their "Right to Return" to Old Nubia (Scudder 2016: 40–1).

The Nile Delta is an extreme case, as is the erosion of the Mississippi Delta in the United States. Nonetheless, delta erosion has become a global problem. So too is saline intrusion, not just into deltas but also affecting the lower reaches of major rivers like the Yangtze because of the elimination of natural flood regimes by upstream dams. Loss of biodiversity is yet another major cost. Owing primarily to the construction of the Kariba and Cahora Bassa Dams, "the Zambezi Delta—the largest and most valuable on Africa's East Coast—has slowly been drying out" (Scudder 2005: 230).

When I overflew the Zambezi Delta in 1996, biologist Brian Davies pointed out the extent to which mangroves—invaluable as breeding and feeding areas for wildlife, including oceanic fish and shrimp—were being destroyed. Beilfuss and colleagues (2000) note that savannah woodland is encroaching on open delta floodplains, making it easier for poachers to gain access, with Tinley (1994) reporting a reduction of large mammals by 95% or more.

19.5 RESERVOIR BASIN COMMUNITY RESETTLEMENT

19.5.1 Introduction

Although dam resettlement planning guidelines had improved until recently, my colleague John Gay and I "found no significant evidence of changes in implementation outcomes over time" during our statistical analysis of fifty large dams (Scudder 2012: 52). Furthermore, the management of the World Bank (the institution that in the 1980s pioneered resettlement and nine other safeguard policies for large dams) was, at the time of writing, seeking support from its Board to hand over safeguard planning and implementation to its borrowers—few of which have the capacity, budget, and political will to implement them. At the same time, the International Hydropower Association (whose senior most influential sponsors include China's Three Gorges Project Corporation and Electricité de France) has, through its 2010 Hydropower Sustainability Assessment Protocol, seriously weakened the 2000 Guidelines for Good Practice of the World Commission on Dams.

19.5.2 Resettlement Outcomes

Experts as varied in their backgrounds as Asit Biswas and Robert Goodland (former Chief Environmental Adviser of the World Bank Group) both consider dam resettlement "to be the most contentious issue associated with large dams" (Scudder 2012: 37). To date, outcomes of the resettlement process in connection with the small number of large dams that have been adequately studied has left the majority worse off economically, socially, and culturally. According to Scudder and Gay's analysis, in thirty-six (82%) of the forty-four cases with adequate information, living standards of the majority were worsened, with no improvement in more recent projects (Scudder 2012: 46). Living standards were restored in five cases (11%) and improved in only three cases (7%).

19.5.3 The Magnitude of Dam-Related Community Resettlement

In 2000, the World Commission on Dams estimated that 40–80 million people had been relocated because of dam construction. The variation in estimates not only illustrates resettlement's magnitude, but also the extent to which accurate resettler counts have been ignored during dam planning and implementation.

19.5.4 Evaluation and Research

Although the words *models* and *theory* have been used lightly in describing the results of research on the resettlement process in connection with dams, highways, urban renewal, and other development projects, the phrase *frameworks for further analysis* would be a more accurate description of research progress to date. The main problem, even with dam resettlement, which has been the most researched, continues to be the lack of long-term studies to test what hypotheses and frameworks exist. In the meantime, the best, but inadequate, approach is to combine the existing analytical frameworks.

The most useful analysis of existing frameworks resulted from the School of Advanced Research's Advanced Seminar on "Rethinking Frameworks, Methodologies and the Role of Anthropology in Development-Induced Displacement and Resettlement" in September 2005 (Oliver-Smith, 2009). Four frameworks received particular attention. The first in time, with support from Elizabeth Colson, was Scudder's Four Stage Framework for explaining the process of successful dam resettlement in the few cases where it had occurred (Scudder and Colson 1982).

More interested in development-induced resettlement failure, Cernea (1997) developed, in the 1990s, his Impoverishment Risks and Reconstruction framework. Downing has emphasized resettlement-related human rights issues (Downing 1996), while Downing and Garcia-Downing (2009) emphasize how resettlement forces people to re-examine such primary cultural questions as "Who are we? Where are we?" De Wet (2006), based on his own long-term research on forced community resettlement initiated during South Africa's Apartheid era, concludes that the many complex and unpredictable issues that characterize resettlement create a type of complexity that is just not amenable to the type of rational approach that characterizes Cernea's Impoverishment Risks and Reconstruction framework.

I find De Wet's concerns relevant simply because social scientists have yet to explain an even more basic question: just what kind of a system is a sociocultural system? Influenced by the natural sciences, there was a time when anthropologists considered sociocultural systems as equilibrium systems, as did economists in reference to traditional societies. Colson's research and my ongoing long-term research on the Kariba resettlers indicate that immediately following resettlement one could argue that in trying to adapt, Gwembe Tonga—during Stage Two—reacted as if a sociocultural system were an equilibrium system. But during Stage Three's development, their sociocultural system could be best explained as an open-ended coping system.

Of the four frameworks, only the first attempts to delineate the process in a series of four stages whereby a majority of resettlers in eight analyzed projects either maintain or improve their living standards into the second generation. Stage 1 deals with the dam-planning process, which is rarely shorter than five years. During that period, the living standards of the majority can be expected to decline because governments will not provide additional services during the dam planning and construction process, while those to be resettled are warned (or should be warned) not to build new houses, start new businesses, or clear new gardens prior to their removal.

Stage two involves the multidimensional stress that characterizes involuntary resettlement during a several-year period immediately following a community's physical removal. I hypothesize that during that time a majority of resettlers cling to the familiar while trying to regain household self-sufficiency. Multidimensional stress is hypothesized because at least in some cases mortality and morbidity increase, resettlers (women in particular) grieve for their lost homes, worry about the future, and cling to the familiar to the extent possible, which results in a reduction of cultural inventory.

Stage Three is the most interesting because, having regained household self-sufficiency and adjusted to a new habitat (including increased government oversight), a majority begin operating as if a sociocultural system is an open-ended one. Resettlers at the household level begin to diversify their production systems, educating their children and rebuilding their communities. As for the fourth and last stage, that involves the project authorities handing over institutional and livelihood development responsibilities to local government and to the resettlers whose second generation has now developed the capacity not only to take over leadership from the first generation, but also to compete for their share of government services. Analysis of the resettlement process tends to stop at that point because it becomes increasingly difficult to isolate and analyze resettlement impacts in a community's ongoing history.

19.5.5 Dam Resettlers are Incorporated into a National/International Political Economy; Hence the Importance of Education

The large majority of those resettled in connection with large dams are low-income rural people. Where dams are built in isolated areas, which is often the case, a majority of resettlers may be indigenous people, as with the Kinzua Dam in New York and the Grand Coulee Dam in the State of Washington.

Roads constructed to the dam site are often the first to penetrate the future reservoir area. Since, to date, resettlers have preferred, generally speaking, to rebuild their communities as close to former homes as possible, roads and tracks are built to planned resettlement sites in the future resettlement basin, as well as for other purposes such as bush clearance. Such road building plays a major role in opening up the project area to the outside world, as do immigrant dam laborers, since few resettlers have the necessary skills.

The record to date is that such incorporation has failed resettlers to even maintain the majority's prior living standards and quality of life, for four major reasons. The first reason is that reservoir flooding removes the best arable land along river banks and in tributary deltas, the riverine fringe of trees, and the more valuable non-timber forest products and invaluable dry-season grazing.

The second reason is that, in most cases, the less productive inland soils that remain must be shared with the host population that can be expected to inhabit potential resettlement areas. Problems with hosts generally relate to access to arable land and political and religious control over whatever resettlement areas governments have set aside for resettled communities. Physical conflict or lawsuits may result, especially where arable land becomes inadequate for the host population and resettler children.

The third reason involves immigrants who arrive seeking new opportunities associated with dam construction and reservoir creation. If fishers, they tend to be more experienced than resettlers and hosts, while whose seeking prime land for vacation housing, tourist mainland and island resorts and game reserves, and irrigation of cash crops, tend to be better educated, endowed with capital, and politically connected. They are also more apt to corrupt local leaders in order to acquire prime resettlement areas for their ventures. In Scudder and Jay's statistical analysis of fifty-dam resettlement outcomes, resettler inability to compete with immigrants was mentioned in twenty (43%) of forty-seven cases, versus inability to compete and integrate with hosts, which was mentioned in fourteen (32%) of forty-four cases.

Fourth, no dam project, with the possible exception of the Aswan High Dam resettlement, has provided sufficient education and training to enable previously isolated resettlers to become nationally competitive.

For a minority of resettlers, however, incorporation within a wider political economy can have major advantages, especially where resettlement policies provide, for the first time, vocational training and primary and secondary schools. The provision of schools in connection with the Kariba Dam led to the formation of a Gwembe Tonga elite in what was formerly an homogeneous classless society (Scudder and Colson 1980).

The value of a secondary school education will vary according to differing national contexts. At the very least it will enable graduates to staff village schools and clinics in the resettlement area and to become local leaders. In the Kariba Case, the first five hundred students graduated at the time when Zambia became independent, so that even secondary school graduates were needed to fill positions vacated by colonial civil servants or to be further educated. (With a PhD from MIT, Gwembe Tonga resettler Mwiindace Siamwiza subsequently became Zambia's leading scientist.)

There is a tendency for planners and dam project authorities to downplay the potential of low-income resettlers as potential innovators and for their capacity for education. When I first lived in the small Gwembe Tonga village of Mazulu in 1956–1957, while Kariba was being constructed more than 100 km downstream, there were only 156 residents living in round, windowless thatched huts. Following resettlement in 1958, demand for education in the two newly built primary schools, within a short walk, had begun to increase, with more and more graduates (including a slowly increasing number of girls) applying to the small number of secondary schools.

When schooling expenses (especially for travel, tuition, and boarding) had become a major problem for the first secondary-school graduates who desired further education, my wife and I began to cover the tuition of any Mazulu student accepted for tertiary education. To date, we have funded tuition for more than forty boys and girls who are the children and grandchildren of the 156 Mazulu villagers in 1956. Some have graduated from the University of Zambia or have received further education overseas. Others have taken three-year courses in teacher training colleges, as well as in agriculture and natural resources institutions or during short vocational training courses.

That potential for education, I believe, exists in every dam resettlement project. Yet even today in the best planned dam projects, far too little emphasis is placed on the affordable education that is necessary if a viable resettlement process is to be handed over to the second generation of resettlers.

19.5.6 Health

Three major types of health problems are associated with the resettlement process. The first type is the risk of increased mortality and morbidity associated with the physiological and psychological stress that is hypothesized to accompany involuntary dam-related community resettlement. With the exception of Egyptian Nubians resettled in connection with the Aswan High Dam and Gwembe Tonga resettlement in connection with the Kariba Dam, there are, however, still few data on resettlement-related higher death rates. As for psychological stress, Colson's *The Social Consequences of Resettlement* makes it very clear that women in particular suffered serious psychological stress during and after being moved.

The second type of health problems are due to inadequate planning and implementation during the resettlement process. Most serious are the lack of proper benchmark studies of the health of future relocatees, the provision of inadequate domestic water supplies following removal, and the crowding of resettlers in communities that are larger and closer together. The water situation is especially ironic granted the fact that those relocated previously lived besides free-flowing rivers. Even in the best cases where boreholes for every five households are drilled and equipped with pumps, water resources too frequently dry up, and/or equipment breaks down and is not fixed because of inadequate maintenance, budgets, or lack of spare parts. Crowding is associated with government policies to consolidate resettlers in larger communities (hence risking inadequate land being available for economic development) for the provision of improved education, development-oriented extension services, and health facilities, as well as for increased administrative control.

The third type of health problems are those specific to the new physical environment and social surroundings in which the first and subsequent generations of resettlers find themselves. Useful as an example are qualitative data collected over a sixty-year period on Kariba resettlement. On the Zimbabwe side of the Kariba Lake Basin, a hushed-up epidemic of human trypanosomiasis broke out in a number of communities resettled back in the bush at the base of the escarpment. On the Zambian side, most noteworthy were the unexplained deaths of fifty-six women and children in several villages that had been relocated below the dam. The probable cause was the consumption of poisonous tubers collected in an unfamiliar environment as relish to accompany the evening meal.

Among 1,600 Gwembe Tonga moved to the adjacent plateau, forty-one children died of dysentery over a three-month period during the first two years. Malaria and schistosomiasis increased within villages relocated close to the reservoir, while increased crowding in villages was associated with higher rates of dysentery and, since the 1980s, of cholera, which had previously been rare in rural Zambia. On the other hand, it would be risky to associate very high death rates from HIV/AIDS that were common throughout the Gwembe Valley in the 1990s with the Kariba Dam and resettlement, since the Gwembe Tonga had high labor migration rates among males before the dam was constructed. However, the arrival of immigrants to fish the reservoir after 1964 most certainly was responsible for specific cases of HIV/AIDS among village women who came to the fish camps to acquire fish and sell local produce.

19.6 DOWNSTREAM COMMUNITY IMPACTS

Now that dam construction has shifted to newly developing countries in Africa, South Asia, South East Asia, East Asia, and Latin America, the numbers of dam-affected downstream communities and households has multiplied. In 2010, Richter et al., using remote sensing to estimate populations living within 10 km of affected rivers, reached a conservative estimate of 472 million people who were "potentially affected ... to experience negative effects on their livelihoods by altered river flows" caused by upriver dams. That estimate "exceeds by six to twelve times the number directly displaced" (Richter 2010: 16) by resettlement, as estimated by the World Commission on Dams.

The main reason for experiencing possible negative effects was livelihood dependence on the natural flood regime of what had formerly been a free-flowing river. In each of the abovementioned regions, livelihood dependence included, to varying degrees, flood recession agriculture of a variety of dry season food and cash crops that complemented rainy season agriculture, grazing for livestock during the dry months when hinterland grazing and fodder were scarce, fishing for income and a major source of protein, and processing and trade of riverside and aquatic products. In addition to permanent residents, people dependent on such resources included, for example, pastoralists who migrated from inland areas to riverside pastures during the dry season, and fishers who seasonally shifted between downriver and upriver locations. In some cases, as below the Bakalori Dam in Nigeria (Adams 1993) and the Volta Dam in Ghana (Hilton and Kowu Tsi 1973), residents were so dependent on a free-flowing river that significant numbers of households had to leave their homes after dam construction occurred.

The Isaacmans, in their *Dams, Displacement, and the Delusion of Development*, provide one of the few detailed descriptions of the chaos that a large dam—in this case, Cahora Bassa in Mozambique—caused to hundreds of thousands of people:

> Cahora Bassa not only changed the Zambezi forever, but it also affected the lives of every individual—male and female, old and young, peasant and fisherman—who lived adjacent to the harnessed waters. Its consequences, which continue unabated, were catastrophic for over half a million people who depended on the river for their livelihoods ... In this way, the hydroelectric project radically altered livelihood strategies, endangered food security, and transformed residential patterns downstream. (Isaacman and Isaacman 2013: 135)

19.7 HANDING OVER

Responsible handing over by a project authority should occur as soon as the government has the capacity and the budget at least to maintain a successful development process for project-affected communities. Most complex is the further handing over of a successful resettlement process to resettled communities. To date, handing over ongoing planning, implementation, and monitoring responsibilities is one of the least satisfactory results associated with large dams, simply because it occurs before the government and the resettlers have had the capacity to continue a satisfactory resettlement process.

The main reason for this unacceptable situation is that the engineering firms involved, as well as the governments, tend to see a project as completed as soon as the newly constructed dam is operational. That conclusion also applies to the international financial institutions; hence the World Bank's *Doing a Dam Better: The Lao People's Democratic Republic and the Story of Nam Theun 2* was published in 2011, while six years later, the unfinished Resettlement Implementation Process was still ongoing.

Handing over is best dealt with where an informed requirement, in a Concession Agreement or other legally binding document, is signed by both the project author-ity and the government. Also essential is some form of benefit-sharing that involves financing and improving government capacity to facilitate further handing over of responsibility to resettlement communities. Successful examples of benefit shar-ing include either the availability of project revenue, as is made available to affected communities in Norway, becoming a partner in the project as pioneered in Canada between a government parastatal and Native American communities, or receiv-ing their own major irrigation project, as in Egypt in connection with the Aswan High Dam.

19.8 CONCLUSION

When Elizabeth Colson asked me, in 1956, to join her in a one-year pre-relocation study of 57,000 Gwembe Tonga before their removal in connection with the Kariba Dam on the Zambezi River, I knew virtually nothing about involuntary resettlement or the damming of free-flowing rivers. Ten years later, more experienced after a fur-ther one-year Kariba restudy and research and consultancies dealing with the Aswan High Dam in Egypt and the Kainji Dam in Nigeria, I not only had concluded that large dams provided an exceptional opportunity for integrated river-basin development, but I had also emphasized my views at various international conferences and in follow-up publications.

On the other hand, I was also becoming a concerned advocate for more attention to be paid to the environmental and social costs throughout the river basins associated with dam construction. Although my concern increased over the years, in 1998, my selection as a commissioner on the World Commission on Dams was due to my experi-ence with environmental and social issues and to my apparent neutrality between the anti- and pro-dam factions.

In fact, I was becoming increasingly anti-dam; but Jacques Leslie, in his *Deep Water* (2005), characterized me as the Commissioner still looking for "One Good Dam." Leslie found the answer to that paradox when he wrote in an August 2014 *New York Times* Opinion that "Thayer Scudder … has changed his mind about dams … he has concluded that large dams not only aren't worth their costs, but that many currently under con-struction 'will have disastrous environmental and socioeconomic consequences.'" So, my answer to the title of this chapter—"The Good Megadam: Does It Exist, All Things Considered?"—is *No, the good megadam does not exist!*

ACKNOWLEDGMENTS

Useful comments on an earlier draft of this chapter were received from Elizabeth Colson, Deborah Moore, John Gay, Peter Bosshard, Jacques Leslie, Sandra Postel, and David McDowell.

REFERENCES

Adams, W. M. (1993). "Development's deaf ear: Downstream users and water releases from the Bakalori Dam, Nigeria," *World Development*, 21(9): 1405–16.

Adaptation Fund. (2011). Proposal for Egypt, 31 August.

Aleem, A. A. (1972). "Effect of river outflow management on marine life," *Marine Biology*, 15: 200.

Ansar, A., Flyvbjerg, B., Budzier, A., and Lunn, D. (2014). "Should we build more large dams? The actual cost of hydropower megaproject development," *Energy Policy*, March: 1–17, <http://dx.doi.org/10.1016/j.enpol.2013.10.069>.

Beard, D. P. (2015). *Deadbeat Dams: Why we Should Abolish the U.S. Bureau of Reclamation and Tear Down Glen Canyon Dam*. Boulder, CO: Johnson Books.

Beilfuss, R. D. (2012). *A Risky Climate for Southern African Hydro: Assessing Hydrological Risks and Consequences for Zambezi River Basin Dams*. Berkeley, CA: International Rivers.

Beilfuss, R. D., Dutton, P., and Moore, D. (2000). "Land cover and land use changes in the Zambezi Delta," in J. Timberlake (ed.), *Biodiversity of the Zambezi Basin Wetlands. Vol. III: Land Use Change and Human Impacts*. Bulawayo: Biodiversity Foundation for Africa and Harare/The Zambezi Society. Consultancy Report for IUCN ROSA.

Cernea, M. M (1997). "The risks and reconstruction model for resettling displaced populations," *World Development*, 25(10): 1569–88.

Climate Change. (2007). Impacts, *Adaptation and Vulnerability. Assessment Report of the Intergovernmental Panel on Climate Change*, <https://www.ipcc.ch/pdf/assessment-report/ar4/wg2/ar4-wg2-chapter6.pdf>.

Colson, E. (1971). *The Social Consequences of Resettlement: The Impact of the Kariba Resettlement on the Gwembe Tonga*. Manchester: Manchester University Press, Institute for African Studies, University of Zambia.

Commission on Growth and Development. (2008). *The Growth Report: Strategies for Sustained Growth and Inclusive Development*. Washington, DC: World Bank.

Costanza, R., d'Arge, R., de Groot, R., et al. (1997). "The value of the world's ecosystem services and natural capital." *Nature*, 387: 253–60.

Daly, Herman. (1994). "Farewell speech": 1–7, <http://www.whirledbank.org/ourwords/daly.html>.

Darby, S. and Sears, D. (eds.). (2008). *River Restoration: Managing the Uncertainty in Restoring Physical Habitat*. Chichester: Wiley.

De Wet, C. (2006). "Risk, complexity and local initiative in forced resettlement outcomes," in C. De Wet (ed.), *Development-Induced Displacement: Problems, Policies and People*. Oxford and New York: Berghahn Books, pp. 180–202.

Downing, T. E. (1996). "Mitigating social impoverishment when people are involuntarily displaced," in C. McDowell (ed.), *Understanding Impoverishment: The Consequences of Development-Induced Displacement*. Oxford and New York: Berghahn Books, pp. 33–48.

Downing, T. E. and Garcia-Downing, C. (2009). "Routine and dissonant culture: A theory about the psycho-socio-cultural disruptions of involuntary displacement and ways to mitigate them without inflicting even more damage," in A. Oliver-Smith (ed.), *Development and Dispossession: The Anthropology of Displacement and Resettlement*. Santa Fe, CA: School for Advanced Research Press.

Ebinger, J. and Vergara, W. (2011). *Climate Impacts on Energy Systems: Key Issues for Energy Sector Adaptation*. Washington, DC: World Bank. World Bank Energy Sector Management Assistant Program.

Frihy, O. E. (1992). "Sea-level rise and shoreline retreat of the Nile Delta promontories, Egypt," *Natural Hazards*, 5: 65–81.

Frihy, O. E., Fanos, A. M., Khafagy, A. A., and Komar, P. D. (1991). "Nearshore sediment transport patterns along the Nile Delta, Egypt," *Journal of Coastal Engineering*, 15: 409–29.

Government of Egypt. (2010). Presidential Decree no. 476.

Grill, G., Lehner, B., Lumsdon, A. E., et al. (2015). "An index-based framework for assessing patterns and trends in river fragmentation and flow regulation by global dams at multiple scales." *Environmental Research Letters*, 10 015001: 1–29.

Hilton, T. E. and Kowu-Tsri, J. Y. (1973). "The impact of the Volta scheme of the Lower Volta floodplains," *Journal of Tropical Geography*, 30: 29–37.

Hughes, F. M. R., Moss. T., and Richards, K. S. (2009). "Uncertainty in riparian and floodplain restoration," in S. Darby and D. Sears (eds.), *River Restoration: Managing the Uncertainty in Restoring Physical Habitat*. Chichester: Wiley, pp. 79–104.

Isaacman, A. F. and Isaacman, B. S. (2013). *Dams, Displacement and the Delusion of Development: Cahora Bassa and Its Legacies in Mozambique, 1965–2007*. Athens. OH: Ohio University Press.

Kashaf, A. A. I. (1983). "Salt-water intrusion in the Nile Delta," *Groundwater*, 21(2): 160–7.

Kassas, M. (1972). "Impact of river control schemes in the shoreline of the Nile Delta," in M. T. Farvar and J. P. Milton (eds.), *The Careless Technology: Ecology and International Development*. Garden City, NY: Natural History Press.

Leslie, J. (2005). *Deep Water: The Epic Struggle Over Dams, Displaced People, and the Environment*. New York: Farrar, Straus and Giroux.

Leslie, J. (2014). "Large dams just aren't worth the cost," *New York Times, Sunday Review* Opinion, 24 August.

Mapes, L. V. (2014). "Elwha runs free," *Seattle Times*, 17 August: A15.

O'Connor, J. E., Duda, J. D., and Grant, G. E. (2015). "1000 dams down and counting," *Science*, 348(6234): 496–7.

Oud, E. and Muir, T. (1997). "Engineering and economic aspects of planning, design, construction and operation of large dam projects," in *Large Dams: Learning from the Past, Looking at the Future*. Gland, Switzerland: IUCN–World Bank, pp. 17–39.

Petit, C., Scudder, T., and Lambin, E. (2001). "Quantifying processes of land-cover change by remote sensing: resettlement and rapid land-cover changes in south-eastern Zambia," *International Journal of Remote Sensing*, 22(17): 3435–56.

Porter, I. C. and Shivakmar, J. (eds.). (2011). *Doing a Dam Better: The Lao People's Democratic Republic and the Story of Nam Theun 2*. Washington, DC: World Bank.

Postel, S. and Richter, B. (2003). *Rivers for Life: Managing Water for People and Nature*. Washington, DC: Covelo; London: Island Press.

Report of the Central Fact Finding Team. (2015). "Drowning a valley: Destroying a civilization," 10 May.

Richards, K. and Hughes, F. M. R. (2008) "Floodplains in Europe: The case for restoration," in S. Darby and D. Sears, *River Restoration: Managing the Uncertainty in Restoring Physical Habitat*. Chichester: Wiley, pp. 16–44.

Richter, B. D., Postel, S., Ravenga, C., et al. (2010). "Lost in development's shadow: The downstream human consequences of dams," *River Alternatives*, 3(2): 14–42.

Scott, J. C. (1998). *Seeing Like a State: How Certain Schemes to Improve the Human Condition Have Failed*. New Haven and London: Yale University Press.

Scudder, T. (1980). "River-basin development and local initiative in African savanna environments," in D. R. Harris (ed.), *Human Ecology in Savanna Environments*. London: Academic Press, pp. 383–405.

Scudder, T. (2005). *The Future of Large Dams: Dealing with Social, Environmental, Institutional and Political Costs*. Sterling, VA, and London: Earthscan.

Scudder, T. (2012). "Resettlement outcomes of large dams," in C. Tortajada, D. Altinbilek, and A. K. Biswas (eds.), *Impacts of Large Dams: A Global Assessment*. Berlin and Heidelberg: Springer, pp. 37–67.

Scudder, T. (2016). *Aswan High Dam Resettlement of Egyptian Nubians*. SpringerBriefs on Case Studies of Sustainable Development. Singapore: Springer.

Scudder, T. and Colson. E. (1980). *Secondary Education and the Formation of an Elite: The Impact of Education on Gwembe District, Zambia*. London: Academic Press.

Scudder, T. and Colson, E. (1982). "From welfare to development: A conceptual framework for the analysis of dislocated people," in A. Hansen, A. and A. Oliver-Smith (eds.), *Involuntary Migration and Resettlement*. Boulder, CO: Westview Press, pp. 267–88.

Shalash, S. (1982). "Effects of sedimentation on the storage capacity of the High Aswan Dam reservoir," *Hydrobiologia*, 92: 623–39.

Shata, A. and El Fayoumy, I. (1970). "Remarks on the hydrogeology of the Nile Delta, UAR," in *Hydrology of Deltas: Proceedings of the Bucharest Symposium, 1969*, vol. 2, pp. 385–96.

Smith, S. E. and Abdel-Kadar, J. (1988). "Coastal erosion along the Egyptian delta," *Journal of Coastal Research*, 4: 245–55.

Stanley, D. J. (1988). "Subsidence in the northeastern Nile Delta: Rapid rates, possible causes, and consequences," *Science*, 240: 497–500.

Stanley, D. J. (1990). "Recent subsidence and northeast tilting of the Nile Delta, Egypt," *Marine Geology*, 94: 147–54.

Stanley, D. J. and Warne, A. G. (1993). "Nile Delta: Recent geological evolution and human impact," *Science*, 260: 628–34.

Tinley, K. (1994). *Description of Gorongosa–Marrameu Natural Resource Management Area, Section 2: Ecological Profile of the Region (Form, Content, Process)*. Harare: IUCN ROSA.

Tortajada, C., Altinbilek, D., and Biswas, A. K. (eds.) (2012). *Impact of Large Dams: A Global Assessment*. Berlin and Heidelberg: Springer.

Waterbury, J. (1979). *Hydropolitics of the Nile Valley*. Syracuse, NY: Syracuse University Press.

World Bank. (1994). *Resettlement and Development: The Bankwide Review of Projects Involving Involuntary Resettlement 1986–1993*. Washington, DC: Environment Department, World Bank: Section 6:11.

World Commission On Dams. (2000). *Dams and Development: A New Framework for Decision-Making*. The Report of the World Commission on Dams. London: Earthscan.

Xia, R. (2015). "It's also a watt shortage: Lack of rain is cutting power production at California dams," *Los Angeles Times*, 17 May: B1 and B5.

PART IV

CASES

....

CHAPTER 20

CRACKING THE CODE OF MEGAPROJECT INNOVATION

The Case of Boeing's 787

....

VERED HOLZMANN, AARON SHENHAR,
YAO ZHAO, AND BENJAMIN MELAMED

20.1 INTRODUCTION

ON 26 September 2011, Boeing Corporation publicly announced the delivery of its first 787 Dreamliner transporter to All Nippon Airways.[1] That event took place almost forty months later than originally planned, and after a long series of unexpected delays. The actual development cost of the program was estimated at about $40 billion and was "well more than twice the original estimate" (Mecham 2011). Adding to the trouble was the discovery of a malfunction, a year later, in a lithium battery of one plane, which caught fire after take-off, and some structural problems in another one. These problems led to several months of grounding ordered by the Federal Aviation Administration (FAA) on the entire Dreamliner fleet already in service.

The Dreamliner was designed to be the most advanced commercial aircraft ever built and the most efficient to operate. However, its late delivery and early service problems were particularly troubling for a leading company, which is considered one of the world's most experienced manufacturers of commercial aircraft. Boeing's experience fits a typical pattern seen in many megaprojects, which was dubbed by Flyvbjerg (2014) the "Iron Law" of "over time, over budget, over and over again." Based on decades of studies, Flyvbjerg's assessment of megaprojects' performance suggests that "the conventional way of managing such projects has reached a 'tension point,' where tradition is challenged and reform is emerging."

In the context of Flyvbjerg's quest for better a understanding of megaprojects, this chapter can be seen as a modest contribution. By taking an "inside out" approach, we analyze Boeing's internal experience with the Dreamliner, while describing the chain of events and analyzing why they happened. Furthermore, we go one step further and retrospectively offer possible ways to avoid similar problems in the future.

Boeing 787 was not a public infrastructure project funded by a national or local government. As a purely commercial enterprise it was undertaken to enhance the strategic position of a leading company in the fast, competitive, and dynamic market of commercial flight services. However, the most unique aspect of the Dreamliner was the degree of innovation attempted by it. The Boeing 787 integrated a significant collection of new practices, involving new technologies, new business and incentive models, and a new organizational setting to deal with its traditional supply chain. Thus, to better understand the uniqueness of this megaproject, we adopt in this chapter an innovation management perspective, based on recent developments in the theory and practice of innovation.

Our conclusion is simple. Boeing's delays and other problems *could have been minimized, if not prevented*. More importantly, a careful early analysis of the project's *innovation* challenges and potential difficulties might have anticipated many of the problems that followed, might have led to a more realistic plan, and might have avoided some of its losses, as well as its reputational damage.

We start by describing the backdrop to Boeing's decision to launch the Dreamliner megaproject. We next outline the new challenges and their resultant difficulties, and describe the development history as well as the actions taken in response to delays. We then use a collection of recently developed frameworks to analyze the project's degree and extent of innovation, leading to a discussion on how these problems could have been mitigated or even avoided. We conclude with a list of lessons that may be applied when facing similar challenges in future highly innovative megaprojects.

20.2 THE BOEING 787 DREAMLINER MEGAPROJECT

20.2.1 Boeing's History of Commercial Aircraft Building

Boeing started its commercial jet era with the 707-model line that rolled into service in 1957, followed by the 727, 747 families, and later, 737, 757, and 767, which collectively dominated airline markets for almost six decades. Eventually, Boeing's most successful plane, the 777, was introduced in 1995 and has established new standards in aircraft design and construction. When the Dreamliner was conceived, Boeing was highly confident that it was well positioned for another huge success. However, from its inception, the program's development process turned out to be quite turbulent.

20.2.2 The 787 Vision

Boeing's concerns in the early 2000s were driven by the need for lowering fuel costs, achieving acceptable noise levels, mounting demand for point-to-point direct connections, and financing structures that would cover the huge costs involved in building a carrier for the twenty-first century. The Dreamliner project was initiated as a response and as a strategic pre-emptive move to counter Airbus's 380 program.

The project was approved in April 2004, with a delivery date set for mid-2008. Soon thereafter, Boeing received a record order from All Nippon Airways, followed by additional orders from fifty-five other customers, for a total backlog of 850 airplanes at an estimated sales value of $140 billion.

20.2.3 Dreamliner's Innovation Challenges and Resulting Difficulties

The Dreamliner was a revolutionary plane in many aspects: physical characteristics, technology, management style, financing, engineering, design management, quality control, assurance procedures, and assembly processes. Many of these challenges were undertaken deliberately as strategic opportunities to take advantage of new developments in aviation technology and to speed up design and development cycles. However, as we will show, only a few of the steps needed to address these challenges were taken upfront.

20.2.4 Technology Innovations

Boeing planned the Dreamliner to provide rapid long-haul transportation, at 20% lower cost. The new aircraft was therefore made of lightweight composite materials, which consisted of 50% of its weight (and 80% of its volume) (Teresko 2007; Ye et al. 2005; Slayton and Spinardi 2015). However, this technology presented several new structural challenges for designing such big fuselage sections, which in turn led to prototype failures during the testing stage, thus adding to the project's cost and delaying its schedule (Holmes 2006).

The Dreamliner was designed to use a "fly-by-wire" technology for signal control using electric power, rather than mechanical controls. These innovative technologies were also new to commercial aircraft design, and resulted in added delays owing to extended periods of wiring, installation, and integration processes (Ye et al. 2005; Holmes 2006).

20.2.5 Business Model Innovation

To speed up the design process, Boeing decided to outsource an unprecedented proportion of the design, engineering, manufacturing, and production to a global network of seven hundred local and foreign suppliers (Pritchard and MacPherson 2004; MacPherson and Pritchard 2005). This decision turned a traditional supply chain into a "development chain," where subcontractors are involved early on and are required to

Table 20.1   Boeing 787 build-to-performance model

Scope	Contractual arrangement/responsibility
System design and architecture	Boeing as main contractor
Detailed part design	Suppliers
Interface design	Boeing defines interfaces; suppliers provide detailed designs, and Boeing serves as referee
Selecting and managing Tier-2 suppliers	Tier-1 suppliers
Intellectual property	Owned by suppliers
Non-recurring development costs	Amortized costs paid by suppliers from 787 revenue
Time of payments to suppliers	When 787 is certified and delivered to customers

perform not only the manufacturing and assembly work, but also the design and development (Tang et al. 2009).

In addition to the huge outsourcing program, Boeing introduced a new incentive model called *Build-to-Performance*. Under this model, a new risk and revenue sharing contract was created, where suppliers bear the non-recurring R&D cost up front, own the intellectual property of their design work, and acquire a share of the revenues from future airplane sales. Table 20.1 summarizes 787's Build-to-Performance development model.

With the Build-to-Performance model, suppliers became strategic partners who share risks and rewards, and consequently have a long-term interest in the project and its outcomes (Sodhi and Tang 2012). However, every subcontractor was also asked to integrate its own subsystems and ship the preassembled subsystems to a central integration site operated directly by Boeing (Turner 2013). Unfortunately, many of these subcontractors were not able to meet the desired quality requirements, delivery schedules, and appropriate documentation.

20.3   THE DREAMLINER'S DEVELOPMENT HISTORY

20.3.1   Comparing Project's Events to the Original Plan

According the original plan, by June 2007, all subassemblies were supposed to have been completed and delivered. The maiden flight was planned for August 2007, and the first delivery to take place in May 2008. In accordance with this plan, a rollout ceremony was held on 8 July 2007, for the first 787 (Norris and Wagner 2009). However, the aircraft's major systems had not yet been installed, and many parts were only attached with temporary non-aerospace fasteners (Trimble 2007). This was the first in a series of delays, which occurred prior to the first test flight nearly a year and a half later than planned (Cohan 2009; Kotha and Srikanth 2013). Table 20.2 displays the detailed sequence of events.

Table 20.2 787 Dreamliner sequence of main events

Year	Month	Events
2002	December	Responding to airlines' calls for more fuel efficiency rather than extra speed, Boeing drops its "Sonic Cruiser" concept. Much of the Sonic Cruiser's composite materials, avionics, and engine technology will reappear in the 787.
2003	December	Everett, WA, is chosen as the first assembly plant.
2004	April	Boeing board of directors gave formal approval to the 787 Dreamliner program.
2004	July	ANA places a fifty-aircraft order.
2005	September	Main features of the 787 aircraft design are complete, and detailed design work is sent to Boeing's global partners.
	December	288 orders by the end of 2005.
2007	June	A 0.3-inch gap was found at the joint between the nose–cockpit section and fuselage section, made by different suppliers. Engineers fixed it by disconnecting and reconnecting internal parts.
	July	The first assembled 787 is rolled out at Everett, but unknown to the viewers, it is a hollow shell.
	September	**1st delay**: three months, owing to a shortage of fasteners and incomplete software.
	October	**2nd delay**: six months for first deliveries and three months for test flight, owing to unfinished work passed along by global partners and delays in finalizing the flight control software; Mike Bair, 787 program head, is replaced by Pat Shanahan.
	December	346 orders by the end of 2007.
2008	January	**3rd delay**: three months for test flight, owing to unnamed suppliers and slow assembly progress at the Everett plant.
	April	**4th delay**: six months, again for test flight; total of fifteen months behind the original schedule for first deliveries, owing to continuing problems with unfinished work from suppliers.
	September	A second machinists' strike begins at Boeing, lasting 57 days; the company struggles for a month afterward to get production back on track.

(continued)

Table 20.2 Continued

Year	Month	Events
	November	News emerges of a new, embarrassing, and serious problem: about 3% of the fasteners put into the five test aircraft under construction in Everett were installed incorrectly and had to be removed and reinstalled.
	December	**5th delay**: six months; Shanahan is put in charge of commercial-aircraft programs, and Scott Fancher takes day-to-day operations lead on the 787 project; more than 900 orders by the end of 2008.
2009	January–February	Middle East leasing company LCAL and Russian airline S7 group cancel thirty-seven orders.
	June	**6th delay**: test flight is postponed indefinitely, owing to a structural flaw at the wing–body joint
		Australian carrier Qantas cancels fifteen orders.
		Boeing writes off $2.5 billion because the first three aircraft are unsellable and suitable only for flight tests.
	July	Boeing announces that it will acquire the 787 rear fuselage assembly plant in Charleston, SC, buying out its partner Vought for about $1 billion.
	October	An additional ten orders are canceled; the total number of order reduces to 840.
		Intensive talks between Boeing and the Machinists' Union end in acrimonious failure; Boeing announces the choice of Charleston, SC, as the second final assembly plant.
	November	Boeing mechanics complete the wing–body joint fix; engineers repeat the wing stress test, and the Dreamliner gets the green light to fly.
2010	August	**7th delay**: Boeing delays delivery of the first aircraft by three months because of engine failure and availability issues.
	November	Boeing halts Dreamliner tests after an onboard fire.
	December	**8th delay**: Boeing delays delivery **indefinitely;** no delivery date given.
2011	September	First aircraft is delivered; forty months total delay.
2013	January	Entire 787 fleet in service is grounded for months by the FAA because of battery problems.

20.3.2 Development Difficulties

The new technology of composite materials used in the Dreamliner required redesigning of the main fuselage and its fasteners, and reassembly of incorrect installation, which had created extensive delays and cost overruns (McInnes 2008). For example, fuselage design changes required altering joints between sections after barrel mating demonstration, and the outboard wing required a revised wing design to strengthen it, resulting in an 8-ton increase in maximal take-off weight (Domke 2008). Similarly, insufficient supplies of various components, such as frames, clips, brackets, and floor beams, as well as sleeve fasteners, extended these delays further. In one case, the delivery of the highly specialized fasteners was delayed by sixty weeks (Lunsford and Glader 2007). Furthermore, some fasteners, which had to connect titanium structures to carbon-fiber, were installed incorrectly, causing even more delay (Gates 2008). Finally, since suppliers failed to meet expectations, a major segment of the work was passed back to Boeing's final assembly line (FAL), which resulted in at least fifteen months of additional delays and an unexpected volume of "traveled work" back and forth to the FAL.

20.3.3 Boeing's Reaction to the Unexpected Delays and Challenges

The challenges in the Dreamliner megaproject, including redesign needs, part short-ages, incorrect installation of fasteners, software development difficulties, and even a union strike, required Boeing to take corrective actions in order to "stop the bleeding" and put the project back on track.

A Production Operation Center was established in Boeing's Everett plant in December 2008, to handle the unexpected flow of challenges and relevant data. The new center's mission was to "monitor global production of Boeing's suppliers, solve problems quickly, and keep the program advancing" (James 2009). It aimed to pro-mote better coordination and communication with three levels of suppliers. The Center had acquired access to translators in twenty-eight different languages, and employed mechanical engineers, procurement agents, supplier management work-ers, global logistics experts, and numerous controllers from the company's quality group.

Testing procedures were redefined in order to start testing the Dreamliner's compo-nents and modules as soon as possible, at the original manufacturer site, before being shipped out to the next assembler. The reordering of these testings enabled Boeing to identify flaws and solve problems early on in the production process, thereby saving rework and costs.

Boeing's least reliable supplier turned out to be Vought, which was responsible for 23% of the airplane's entire fuselage structure. To better control Vought's work, Boeing decided to acquire Vought's entire Dreamliner operations in South Carolina for $580 million (Kotha and Srikanth 2013).

20.3.4 Analyzing the 787 Project's Innovation Challenges

Currently available theory and frameworks regarding innovation management and its connection to complex project management offer insights into the genesis of Dreamliner's events. Such a connection is still not fully developed since most studies have often focused on small-scale product innovations, with a few exceptions, such as Altfeld (2010); Biedenbach and Müller (2012); Bosch-Rekveldt et al. (2011); Davies et al. (2009); Davies and Mackenzie (2014); Shenhar and Dvir (2007); Geraldi et al. (2011); Lenfle and Midler (2009); and Pich et al. (2002).

20.3.5 Contingency Theory in Highly Innovative Megaprojects

Structural contingency theory—which first emerged in the 1960s—suggests that in order to succeed, organizations should be aligned with their environment (Burns and Stalker 1961; Drazin and Van de Ven 1985; Pennings 1992; Thompson 1967; Galbraith 1982; Burgelman 1983). It was only a question of time before it was realized that projects can be viewed as "temporary organizations within organizations" (Lundin and Soderholm 1995), whence one can apply contingency theory to projects as well (Pich et al. 2002; Turner and Cochrane 1993; Shenhar 2001). The essence of these ideas is that "*there is no one best way*," and "*one size does not fit all*" (Henderson and Clark 1990; Eisenhardt and Tabrizi 1995; Balachandra and Friar 1997; Souder and Song 1997; Shenhar and Dvir 2007; Sauser et al. 2009).

Contingency theory has recently been combined with complexity theory in studies of highly complex projects. For example, Geraldi et al. (2011) suggest an umbrella typology of five different dimensions of complexity—structural, uncertainty, dynamics, pace, and sociopolitical. Howell et al. (2010) present uncertainty as the most common research theme in project contingency theory (PCT), followed by complexity, team empowerment, criticality, and urgency, while Bosch-Rekveldt et al. (2011) demonstrate the elements that contribute to project complexity by introducing a technical, organizational, and environmental (TOE) framework for complexities.

20.3.6 How Innovative was the Dreamliner?

Applying a contingency approach to the Dreamliner megaproject suggests that some of the difficulties could have been mitigated or averted via an appropriate management approach. Boeing incorrectly assumed that the 777's previous successful approach would extend to the 787 project. Aiming to complete this megaproject in record time in order to reap the profits from the expected demand for a highly efficient plane, the company applied its well-familiar previous management practices. However, the 787 project encountered a set of new challenges, which the company did not experience in any of its earlier programs. As the following analysis will demonstrate, it seems that failing to address these challenges in time was the main reason for the project's delays and cost overruns.

The first major new challenge that Boeing faced was using the new technology of composite materials in its fuselage construction instead of a traditional aluminum body.

The new technology caused Boeing to underestimate the effort and time needed to manage program uncertainties before the airplane was approved for flight. When initial prototypes failed in ground testing, the company had to add more design–build–test cycles to its original plan, thereby extending the development schedule and increasing costs. The new electronic controls and fly-by-wire technologies only added to the challenge.

The second innovation that deviated from traditional practices was Boeing's decision to outsource much of the design and development work to dozens of subcontractors worldwide. The intention was to save costs and speed up the development effort. However, once again, the company underestimated the difficulty of implementing such a wide-ranging outsourcing plan. Not only did many of these subcontractors lack the advanced state-of-the-art design experience needed for such an ambitious task; the company failed to institute proper vendor training and coordination and control processes, as well as setting the policy and guidelines needed to coordinate such a complex network. Consequently, many of these vendors failed to complete their tasks, leaving the company with much additional work back home.

20.3.7 The Diamond of Innovation Analysis

To analyze the Dreamliner megaproject innovative challenges, we used the *Diamond of Innovation* model, which provides a framework for project classification and adaptation of management to the best approach for each case (Shenhar and Dvir 2007). Projects are

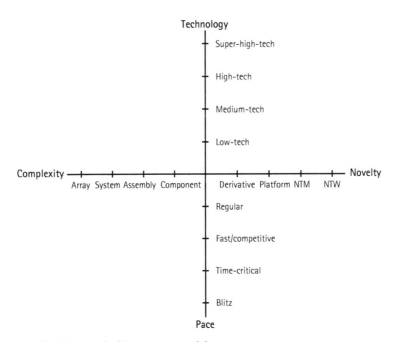

FIGURE 20.1 The Diamond of Innovation model.

classified based on a universal set of at least four dimensions: *novelty, technology, complexity*, and *pace*, where each dimension consists of four possible categories. Selecting a category in each dimension creates a unique diamond shape graphic, which serves as a project classifier. Once a classification is selected, the model specifies its unique impact and recommends a specific style of project or program management. The Diamond of Innovation model is depicted in Figure 20.1, and its dimensions and their impact on a project are summarized in Table 20.3.

Table 20.3 Diamond of Innovation model: definitions, dimensions, and project types

Novelty Market Innovation: how new is the product to the market, users, and customers. Novelty level impacts market-related activities and the time and effort needed to define and freeze requirements (a higher novelty would delay this freeze).	*Derivative* Improvements in an existing product (e.g., a new color option in an MP3 player; the addition of a search feature in a software program) *Platform* A new generation on an existing product line (e.g., new automobile model; new commercial aircraft) *New-to-the-market* Adapting a product from one market to another (e.g., first PC; consumer's microwave oven) *New-to-the-world* A product that no one has ever seen before (e.g., the first post-it note)
Technology Technological Innovation: the extent of new technology used. It impacts product design, development, testing, and the requisite technical skills (a higher technological level requires additional design cycles and results in a later design freeze).	*Low-tech* No new technology is used (e.g., house; city street) *Medium-tech* Some new technology is used (e.g., automobile; appliances) *High-tech* All or mostly new, but existing, technologies (e.g., satellite; fighter jet) *Super high-tech* Critical technologies do not exist (e.g., the first Apollo moon landing)
Complexity Level of System Innovation: represented by the complexity of the product or the organization. Complexity impacts the degree of formality and coordination needed to effectively manage the project.	*Component/Material* The product is a discrete component within a larger product, or a material. *Assembly* Subsystem performing a single function (e.g., CD player; cordless phone) *System* Collection of subsystems, multiple functions (e.g., aircraft; car, computer) *Array* Widely dispersed collection of systems with a common mission (e.g., city transit system, air traffic control, and Internet)
Pace Urgency of the Innovation: how critical is your time frame? It impacts the time management and autonomy of the project management team.	*Regular* Delays are not critical (e.g., community center) *Fast-competitive* Time to market is important for the business (e.g., satellite radio; plasma television) *Time-critical* Completion time is crucial for success by exploiting a window of opportunity (e.g., mission to Mars; Y2K) *Blitz* Crisis project; immediate solution is necessary (e.g., Apollo 13; September 11)

20.3.8 The Dreamliner's Novelty, Technology, Complexity, and Pace

The Diamond of Innovation model suggests that the Dreamliner megaproject would be classified as follows:

- **Novelty.** From the customers' perspective the Dreamliner is another generation in an existing line of previous commercial aircraft built by Boeing, and is therefore considered a *Platform*. However, for the company's subcontractors (who may be seen as "users"), the Build-to-Performance business model constituted an unknown experience. That would place the novelty at the *new-to-the-market* level, which suggests that the new business model would require pilot testing and iterative model modifications until the final version is established and fully understood.
- **Technology.** The Dreamliner took advantage of several innovative, recently developed technologies. The technology of composite materials was relatively new to the commercial aircraft industry, and no prior experience existed on how to design and integrate it into a large wide body such as 787. In addition, Boeing used the related technology of electronic controls (fly-by-wire) for the first time in a commercial aircraft. The innovative nature of these new technologies placed the Dreamliner in the category of a *High-Tech* innovation on the technology dimension. These new technologies called for additional time, more testing, and additional design–build–test cycles, as well as more prototyping.
- **Complexity.** A typical aircraft development program could be considered a *system*, since its subsystems are built by several functional areas or subcontractors and then integrated in a single location. However, the exceptional amount of design and development work that was outsourced to hundreds of subcontractors worldwide required enormous amounts of coordination and clear rules in work procedures, as well as documentation. Such unprecedented complexity pushed the Dreamliner's complexity from the *system* level to the *array* domain. The higher level of complexity required an innovative and more developed organizational structure.
- **Pace.** The Dreamliner was a *fast competitive* project, aiming to get the plane to market in record time so as to benefit from the growing demand for an environmentally friendly aircraft with reduced airframe maintenance requirements.

Based on these observations, the classification of the Dreamliner would be *platform/new-to-the-market, high-tech, array*, and *fast competitive*. This specific classification calls for a unique style of management. However, a careful analysis of the Dreamliner's actual management style shows that Boeing adopted a style that differed from the attributes of novelty, technology, and complexity. Accordingly, the actual approach chosen for managing novelty was that of a *platform* with a mere next-generation introduction, without taking into consideration the *new-to-the-market* nature of the new business incentive model. Similarly, the project's management approach to technology was closer to *medium tech* approach, rather than the requisite *high-tech* level,

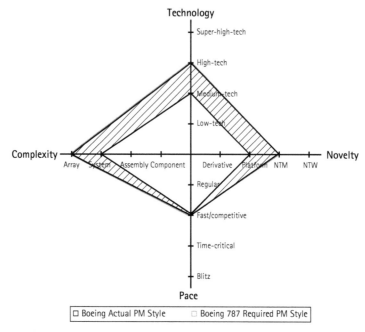

FIGURE 20.2 The Dreamliner's Diamond of Innovation.

while the one chosen to manage complexity was in the category of *system* rather than *array*. Figure 20.2 depicts the discrepancies between the required management style (bold diamond) and its actually adopted counterpart (dashed diamond). This shaded area represents the *Management Shortfall*—a concept coined by Bent Flyvbjerg to visually describe the difference between the required and actual management styles.

The Diamond of Innovation may not be the only way to analyze the Dreamliner's challenges. Additional frameworks may be further used (for example, Pich et al. 2002; Geraldi et al. 2011), as we show next.

20.3.9 Categories of Project Learning

Pich et al. (2002) characterizes projects based on the degree of information available upfront to the project teams. Each of their three types of projects calls for a different project management strategy, as described in what follows:

- An *instructionist* **project** is a project where most of the information needed for planning is available and the project team has good understanding of the "best policy" to be implemented. This project typically involves optimization that is focused on common methods such as critical path and risk management.
- A *selectionist* **project** does not have enough information to define an optimal policy. Consequently, the team is faced with a higher level of uncertainty and cannot

accurately anticipate the results of its actions. Rather than exploit existing knowledge, the team is encouraged to explore, by planning multiple trials and prototypes, and executing them simultaneously, until the best performing solution is selected.

- A *learning* **project** is susceptible to unforeseen events that might influence its course. In this environment there is little benefit in detailed planning of the entire project, as the unforeseen events might alter the course and require repeated readjustments.

In the 787 the new technologies of composite materials called for comprehensive uncertainty analyses with sufficient time for testing and redesign cycles. Similarly, the extensive outsourcing of design and the new business model called for a slower pace of adaptation. It appears that Boeing employed an instructionist strategy based on assumed low-level uncertainty, where activities, times, and costs are essentially predictable, and no surprises are expected. In reality this project called for a selectionist style of management, which would ensure sufficient resources for repetitive design, intense prototyping, and a comprehensive program for subcontractor training and certification.

20.3.10 Typology of Complexity

Geraldi et al. (2011) identify five dimensions of a project complexity: structural complexity, uncertainty, dynamics, pace, and sociopolitical complexity.

- **Structural complexity** relates to a large number of distinct and interdependent elements, impacted by size, variety, and interdependence of elements.
- **Uncertainty** represents the gaps between the amounts of available and required information to make a decision. Uncertainty has an intrinsic relationship with risks (Turner and Cochrane 1993).
- **Dynamics** refers to changes in factors such as goals or specifications. Changes that are not well communicated or assimilated by the team lead to disorder, rework, or inefficiency.
- **Pace** relates to the temporal aspects of a project. It represents the urgency and criticality of time goals.
- **Sociopolitical complexity** relates to the problems involved in managing stakeholders, lack of commitment, or problematic relationships among stakeholders or team members, and differences in language, culture, and discipline.

Geraldi et al. (2011) indicate that complexity dimensions are frequently interdependent. These interdependencies were clearly evident in the Dreamliner case. The significant number of changes required to get the project back on track increased the extent of dynamics as compared with the original intent. It also brought about several changes in leadership during the development period.

Finally, Boeing's decision to outsource design to a large network of subcontractors, while using the new Build-to-Performance incentives model gave rise to a high level of sociopolitical complexity. In retrospect, it seems that the project should have been better prepared for these kinds of complexities. Such preparations would require intense sub-contractor education, followed by a tight system of coaching, reviewing, and controlling.

20.4 DISCUSSION

20.4.1 What Was Done? What Could Have Been Done?

It seems that Boeing had underestimated the managerial consequences of utilizing significant technological and other innovations. The Dreamliner's immature technologies needed time, more testing, additional design-build-test cycles, and more prototyping. Failing to incorporate these additional steps into its original plan gave rise to failures in prototype testing, and subsequently forced the company to rework the design, again and again. Had the company taken into account these uncertainties up front and allowed for all these added-on processes, it would have eventually saved part of the final cost.

By outsourcing an unprecedented amount of design and development to hundreds of subcontractors, Boeing significantly increased the level of project complexity. This increase called for a different kind of organization and new managerial processes, including structural changes. Working with many subcontractors worldwide turned out to be ineffective due to the lack of vendor education, training, and verification.

Under the Build-to-Performance risk-and-revenue-sharing contract, a delivery delay by a supplier would immediately cascade to downstream suppliers, with dire consequences to the project. Conversely, if a supplier delivers fast and well, it would benefit others but increase that supplier's costs. Thus, once a supplier realizes that it may not lose (or gain) much if it does less (or more) work, traveled work inevitably ensues when some partners are slower than others. Critical link theory tells us that the worst delays are transferred to delays in integration, and eventually to substantial delays in testing and delivery. In summary, system integration under the Build-to-Performance model may take longer and require more iterations.

The implementation of the new business model and attendant incentives was new to Boeing and its partners, requiring additional attention and longer learning periods, as well as testing, to better understand the complications inherent in this model.

20.4.2 A Scenario of an Alternative Plan

In retrospect, it stands to reason that the Dreamliner project would have yielded far better outcomes had it been planned and managed differently. Based on the above discussion, we present a scenario of an alternative plan and attendant events under a management approach properly aligned with the identified innovation challenges (see Table 20.4).

Table 20.4 Comparison of the Dreamliner's actual events to a proposed
alternative plan

Year	Actual event	Proposed simulated alternative
2003	Program approved	Program approved
2004	Program launched; original first delivery date planned for 2008	Program launched; first delivery planned for 2009
2005	Final configuration selected	Assessment of potential program challenges, uncertainty, complexity, and their impact on the plan and its resources
2006	Subsystem design starts	Final configuration selected Detailed subsystem design with extensive policy and control guidelines prepared; vendor selection criteria and training program prepared
2007	Gap found between cockpit and fuselage First delay announced Unplanned redesign added; suppliers' crisis causes work to be taken back	Extensive training and certification of subcontractors Performing three planned design cycles; close work with suppliers; extensive integration and prototype testing
2008	Backlog reaches 900 orders	
2009	Additional unplanned redesign cycles	First delivery; this is a more realistic plan, extending only eighteen month beyond the original date
2010	Eighth delay announced; indefinite delay Fifty orders cancelled	
2011	First delivery forty months later than scheduled	

The alternative scenario demonstrates that the original plan was unrealistic. A more realistic plan, taking into consideration the additional aspects of innovation, uncertainty, and complexity would have resulted in a longer schedule than originally envisioned, but still much shorter than the one that actually materialized, thus saving about eighteen months and around 40% of the costs.

20.5 CONCLUSIONS

Our "inside-out" look at the Dreamliner project could give rise to far-reaching lessons, extending beyond aerospace to a wide range of domains. The Dreamliner project was unique in many ways. It adopted a bold strategic approach to using recent innovations in technology and business models in order to sustain Boeing's leading position. While these decisions were indeed strategically justified, their implementation fell far short. Embarking on its past successes, Boeing underestimated the impact of innovation on its execution strategy.

Still, as an ambitious megaproject adopting a novel but untried strategy, the Dreamliner project has generated important lessons that may benefit future aerospace programs and beyond. In the comments that follow, we present some immediate lessons for aerospace, followed by wider implications for future megaprojects. We conclude with a list of potential pitfalls for projects involving large-scale innovation, and how to avoid them.

20.6 THE DREAMLINER'S LESSONS FOR AEROSPACE

The high degree of novelty in the Dreamliner's technological innovations called for a much higher level of expertise, allocation of time, and other resources than originally planned for. An established framework and criteria for assessing and managing such innovative technologies would help to estimate more accurately the time and number design cycles, needed prototypes, and degree of testing. An early understanding of the levels of technology is thus needed to address such challenges in advance.

In a similar vein, the Dreamliner's requisite development effort was far more complex from an organizational standpoint than in Boeing's previous programs. The lesson here is that as compared with just outsourcing manufacturing, the outsourcing of much of the design and development calls for an infrastructure of appropriate supporting and coordinating systems. From a strategic standpoint, the company was not ready to fully manage the innovative business model of Build-to-Performance. This kind of business model innovation calls for a systematic and thoughtful procedure for controlling strategic outsourcing, supplier selection, contracting, monitoring, testing, and quality control. In addition, open communication and well-planned monitoring and controlling of supplier processes could reduce traveled work, as well as help detect early problems. Finally, a different risk-revenue sharing contract is needed, which provides mid-course financial incentives for suppliers to work faster and better while penalizing laggards for delays and unnecessary traveled work.

20.6.1 What Could the Dreamliner Teach Us about Megaproject Innovation

Innovation is clearly one of the major drivers of economic growth; yet it is a risky business, and often ends up in disappointing results or failure. Dreamliner's difficulties were clearly due to a high degree of innovation introduced by this project and the failure to deal with this innovation early on. However, just like many megaprojects, the Dreamliner also involved an extensive level of complexity on a scale and timeline never tried before in the aerospace industry. Indeed, many other megaprojects today involve substantial complexities owing to a large number of components and technologies, involvement of numerous organizations, and widely dispersed teams.

So what does all this lead to? Perhaps the 787 experience provides the key to "cracking the code" of megaprojects. When it comes to innovation, the challenge is even bigger, leading to higher risk, which often requires adapting specific management processes during the development project. And yet management of innovation in megaprojects is still not fully understood and is much less studied at this time.

20.7 "Cracking the Code": Adapting to Challenge

Flyvbjerg's (2014) hope for "light at the end of the tunnel" may be partially realized via the lessons discussed. The Boeing alternative scenario described previously suggests that there *was* a way to manage this megaproject better. Had the company realized earlier that the degree of challenge undertaken by the Dreamliner was much higher than in previous programs, it would have put in place different processes, organizational designs, and additional resources. In this case the challenge was based on higher levels of uncertainty, technology, structure, and business models. But challenges may also be due to other reasons, based on political, environmental, and economical risks, to mention a few.

So what exactly is the challenge in a megaproject, and how is it related to innovation? To answer this question, let us return to the meaning of *innovation. Innovation* means successfully getting new ideas to market. When markets run at a faster technological pace, and become more demanding, more competitive, and more complex, there is a clear need for more and better ideas of getting to market successfully. Similarly, the appetite for megaprojects grows with every big initiative, political ambitions, or new technologies, but naturally, new ideas of getting to market can be tested only through projects or programs. The previous discussion suggests that the appetite for innovation in megaprojects is getting bigger than ever, and unless companies depart from the "management as usual" trend, megaproject costs will keep rising, with overruns growing ever bigger.

The "adaptive approach" to managing projects was illustrated in the Dreamliner case via the Diamond of Innovation as a possible framework for analyzing the innovation challenge in megaprojects. Classifying a project using the Diamond dimensions leads to specific decisions based on each dimension.

We may be standing at the gates of a new era in project and megaproject management—an era that will acknowledge formally that "one size does not fit all projects" and that every project has its own challenges and difficulties (Shenhar 2001). Past experience should provide guidance, but it is always the *unknown* that may trip a project. Accepting this fact may be a first step in successful planning of megaprojects. Developing an "adaptive approach" to managing projects may be the next key that could "crack the code" by avoiding the vicious cycle of overruns and disappointments. Of course, this calls for a major change in mindset and extensive development of new techniques, frameworks, and tools. While we are still not there, the writers of this article believe it is possible.

Since no comprehensive management system exists as a guide on how to plan and manage arbitrary megaprojects, we nevertheless employ our insights to conclude this chapter by suggesting a list of guidelines and recommendations for future leaders and decision makers in large and challenging megaprojects.

20.8 How Can Innovation Challenge Pitfalls Be Avoided in Future Programs?

1. "Past performance does not guarantee future success." This well-known adage clearly applies to innovation. Although experience counts, overconfidence achieved by past success may sometimes be a disadvantage. Known–unknowns, and particularly unknown–unknowns, are potential pitfalls that may get you.

2. Do not assume that careful risk management is sufficient. Boeing was well familiar with classical risk management; in the Dreamliner case, it was simply not sufficient. There was a clear need for analyzing or even recognizing the magnitude of the innovation challenge involved. Classical risk management is essentially assessing "what could go wrong," but as we have seen, assessing the degree of innovation means estimating "how long will it take it to get right." That part was apparently missing during the Dreamliner's planning phase.

3. Do not rush to execution. Research has shown that the most successful and great projects spent a long time up front in fully defining the project, identifying potential difficulties, selecting the right approach to your specific project, and obtaining full commitment from all parties, before proceeding to execution (Dvir and Shenhar 2011).

4. Carefully analyze your experience. Assess all your capabilities and make a list of things with which you are familiar and have done before. When embarking on a new program, however, carefully identify all needed activities; then distinguish between the familiar and unfamiliar parts, which require new skills or practices. The latter type will be considered the *innovation group*.

5. A well-known and classic tool is the Work Breakdown Structure, which defines all project activities in a tree-type structure. When using this tool, carefully assess all actions and activities needed in the new program. You may find out that even

the most innovative projects can use familiar elements that had been done before, while others are new to you or your company. Distinguish all the new activities from the rest, and treat them differently (Orhof et al. 2013).

6. Use a framework to analyze the new and unknown parts. Treat the unknown parts as "long lead items" and complete them earlier than you actually need them. You may want to build several small-scale prototypes to design, build, and test the unknown elements. Based on the level of innovation and anticipated uncertainty, you should determine the number of cycles you might need for each new part.

7. Even the most careful plan may not identify all needed activities up front. In some cases you may find out later on that you need to add previously unanticipated activities to your original plan. Thus your original WBS may be updated to reflect the newly identified work packages. These "unknown–unknowns" must rely on a reserve of unallocated resources (see next).

8. Leave sufficient slack resources for "unknown–unknowns." Remember that the classic and typical planning cycles are often approved by finance executives who often require you to plan everything up front. However, in the uncertain world of innovation and highly complex projects, this is simply impossible. Therefore, leave sufficient contingency resources based on assessment of levels of innovation and challenges. Such resources may be tapped when needed.

9. To make things easier for financial executives you may also offer incentives to your managers and teams if they do not use all contingency resources. First, you should not penalize them when they are using all those resources, and second, you would reward them for leaving the unused ones on the table. Treat slacks as "insurance" against unknown challenges, and be ready to accept a degree of overruns when they happen.

In sum, effective management of innovation challenges in megaprojects is possible. It calls for a careful assessment of each innovative component, anticipating the proper managerial implications, and leaving adequate buffer resources to cope with unknowns.

20.9 Epilog

At the end, and to its credit, Boeing "got it right." The Dreamliner program moved on from development to manufacturing, eventually realizing its expected economic benefits. With a good initial record of service and demand, it seems that the Dreamliner is set to become a most successful plane—a delight for travelers, and a source of pride for Boeing, the airlines using it, and the aerospace industry at large. Above all, it is an economic success that will generate sustainable revenues and profits for many years to come, and ultimately, be remembered as a success story. However, the lessons from its late debut should not be forgotten. They should serve as a warning sign to forthcoming innovative megaprojects, and hopefully help future projects avoid similar pitfalls.

Note

1. The original paper that now forms this chapter was not funded by Boeing Cooperation and was not officially presented to the company. It represents solely the authors' opinion.

References

Altfeld, H. H. (2010). *Commercial Aircraft Projects: Managing the Development of Highly Complex Products*. Farnham: Ashgate.

Balachandra, R. and Friar, J. H. (1997). "Factors for success in R&D project and new product innovation: A contextual framework," *IEEE Transactions on Engineering Management*, 44: 276–87.

Biedenbach, T. and Müller, R. (2012). "Absorptive, innovative, and adaptive capabilities and their impact on project and project portfolio performance," *International Journal of Project Management*, 30(5): 621–35.

Bosch-Rekveldt, M., Jongkind, Y., Mooi, H., Bakker, H., and Verbraeck, A. (2011). "Grasping project complexity in large engineering projects: The TOE (Technical, Organizational, and Environmental) framework," *International Journal of Project Management*, 29(6): 728–39.

Burgelman, R. A. (1983). "A process model of internal corporate venturing in the diversified major firm," *Administrative Science Quarterly*, 28: 223–44.

Burns, T. and Stalker, G. (1961). *The Management of Innovation*. London: Tavistock.

Cohan, P. (2009). "Boeing's 787 Dreamliner faces another nightmare engineering delay." *Daily Finance*, 13 November 2009, <http://www.aol.com/article/2009/11/13/boeings-787-dreamliner-faces-another-nightmare-engineering-dela/19236308/?gen=1>.

Davies, A., Gann, D., and Douglas, T. (2009). "Innovation in megaprojects: Systems integration at London Heathrow Terminal 5," *California Management Review*, 51(2): 105–26.

Davies, A. and Mackenzie, I. (2014). "Project complexity and systems integration: Constructing the London 2012 Olympics and Paralympics Games," *International Journal of Project Management*, 32(5): 773–90.

Domke, B. (2008). *Boeing 787 Lessons Learnt*. EIXDI: Ref. PR0813399 (Issue 2), <http://www.planebusiness.com/buzz/airbus2.pdf>.

Drazin, R. and Van de Ven, A. H. (1985). "Alternatives forms of fit in contingency theory," *Administrative Science Quarterly*, 30: 514–39.

Dvir, D. and Shenhar, A. (2011). "What great projects have in common," *MIT Sloan Management Review*, 52(3): 19–21.

Eisenhardt, K. M. and Tabrizi, B. N. (1995). "Accelerating adaptive processes: Product innovation in the global computer industry," *Administrative Science Quarterly*, 40: 84–110.

Flyvbjerg, B. (2014). "What you should know about megaprojects and why: An overview." *Project Management Journal*, 45(2): 6–19.

Galbraith, J. R. (1982). "Designing the innovating organization," *Organizational Dynamics*, Winter: 5–25.

Gates, D. (2008). "Boeing 787 fastener problems caused by Boeing engineers," *The Seattle Times*, 1 December.

Geraldi, J., Maylor, H., and Williams, T. (2011). "Now, let's make it really complex (complicated): A systematic review of the complexities of projects," *International Journal of Operations and Production Management*, 31(9): 966–90.

Henderson, R. M. and Clark, K. B. (1990). "Architectural innovation: The reconfiguration of existing product technologies and the failure of established firms," *Administrative Science Quarterly*, 35: 9–30.

Holmes, S. (2006). "The 787 encounters turbulence: Technical glitches and manufacturing woes could delay Boeing's breakthrough," *Business Week*, 19 June: 38–40.

Howell, D., Windahl, C., and Seidel, R. (2010). "A project contingency framework based on uncertainty and its consequences," *International Journal of Project Management*, 28(3): 256–64.

James, A. (2009). "Boeing's 787 production is mission-controlled, *SeattlePi*, 30 April, <http://www.seattlepi.com/business/405751_boeing29.html>.

Kock, A., Heising, W., and Gemünden, H. G. (2014). "How ideation portfolio management influences front-end success," *Journal of Product Innovation Management*, 32(4): 539–55.

Kotha, S. and Srikanth, K. (2013). "Managing a global partnership model: Lessons from the Boeing 787 'Dreamliner' program," *Global Strategy Journal*, 3(1): 41–66.

Lenfle, M. and Midler, C. (2009). "The launch of innovative product related services: Lessons from automotive telematics," *Research Policy*, 38 (1): 156–69.

Lundin, R. A. and Söderholm, A. (1995). "A theory of the temporary organization," *Scandinavian Journal of Management*, 11(4): 437–55.

Lunsford, J. L. and Glader, P. (2007). "Boeing's nuts-and-bolts problem: Shortage of fasteners tests ability to finish Dreamliner," *Wall Street Journal*, 19 June.

MacPherson, A. D. and Pritchard, D. J. (2005). "Boeing's diffusion of commercial aircraft design and manufacturing technology to Japan: Surrendering the US aircraft industry for foreign financial support," *Canada–United States Trade Center Occasional Paper No. 30*. Buffalo: State University of New York.

Mecham, M. (2011). "787: the century's first jet to fly; 787's impact will likely be remembered long after its tardiness is forgotten," *Aviation Week and Space Technology*, 26 September.

McInnes, I. (2008). "A 787 supply chain nightmare," *Aerospace-technology.com*, 25 March, <http://www.aerospace-technology.com/features/feature1690/>.

Norris, G. and Wagner, M. (2009). *Boeing 787 Dreamliner*. Minneapolis, MN: Zenith Press, MBI Publishing Company.

Orhof, O., Shenhar, A., and Dori, D. (2013). "A model-based approach to unifying disparate project management tools for project classification and customized management," in *Proceedings of the 2013 INCOSE-IS Annual Conference, June 2013, Philadelphia*.

Pennings, J. M. (1992). "Structural contingency theory: A reappraisal," *Research in Organizational Behavior*, 14: 267–309.

Pich, M. T., Loch, C. H., and De Meyer, A. (2002). "On uncertainty, ambiguity and complexity in project management," *Management Science*, 48(8): 1008–23.

Pritchard, D. J. and MacPherson, A. D. (2004). "Industrial subsidies and politics of World Trade: The case of the Boeing 7e7," *The Industrial Geographer*, 1(2): 57–73.

Sauser, B. S., Reilly, R. R., and Shenhar, A. J. (2009). "Why projects fail? How contingency theory can provide new insights: A comparative analysis of NASA's Mars Climate Orbiter loss," *International Journal of Project Management*, 27(7): 665–79.

Slayton, R., and Spinardi, G. (2015). "Radical innovation in scaling up: Boeing's Dreamliner and the challenge of socio-technical transitions," *Technovation*, 47: 47–58.

Sodhi, M. S. and Tang, C. S. (2012). *Managing Supply Chain Risk*, vol. 172. New York: Springer.

Souder, W. E. and Song, X. M. (1997). "Contingent product design and marketing strategies influencing new product success and failure in US and Japanese electronics firms," *Journal of Product Innovation Management*, 14: 21–34.

Shenhar, A. J. (2001) "One size does not fit all projects: Exploring classical contingency domains," *Management Science*, 47(3): 379–414.

Shenhar, A. J., and Dvir, D. (2007). *Reinventing Project Management: The Diamond Approach to Successful Growth and Innovation*. Boston: Harvard Business Press.

Tang, C. S., Zimmerman, J. D., Nelson, M. S., and James, I. (2009). "Managing new product development and supply chain risks: The Boeing 787 case," *Supply Chain Forum: An International Journal*, 10(1): 74–86.

Teresko, J. (2007). "The Boeing 787: A matter of materials. Special Report: anatomy of a supply chain," *Industry Week*, <http://www.industryweek.com/forward/emailref?path=node/12343>.

Thompson, J. D. (1967). *Organizations in Action*. New York: McGraw-Hill.

Trimble, S. (2007). "Boeing 787 first flight suffers two-month delay." *Flight International*, 10 September 2007, <http://www.flightglobal.com/news/articles/boeing-787-first-flight-suffers-two-month-delay-216664/>.

Turner, E. (2013). *The Birth of The 787 Dreamliner*. Kansas, MO: Andrews McMeel Publishing.

Turner, J. R. and Cochrane, R. A. (1993). "Goals-and-methods matrix: Coping with projects with ill defined goals and/or methods of achieving them," *International Journal of Project Management*, 11(2): 93–102.

Ye, L., Lu, Y., Su, Z., and Meng, G. (2005). "Functionalized composite structures for new generation airframes: A review," *Composites Science and Technology*, 65: 1436–46.

....

CHAPTER 21

THE POWER OF SYSTEMS INTEGRATION

Lessons from London 2012

....

ANDREW DAVIES

21.1 INTRODUCTION

....

A megaproject is a large temporary organization and process established to design, produce, and integrate complex products, systems, and services that cost US$1 billion or more (Flyvbjerg 2014), such as oil and gas platforms, airports, motorways, hospitals, new generations of aircraft, and major sporting events. Scholars have identified some of the dimensions that make megaprojects so challenging and difficult to manage, including their scale, urgency, uncertainty, institutional structure, and involvement of multiple public and private stakeholders (Morris and Hough 1987; Miller and Lessard 2001; Altshuler and Luberoff 2003; Flyvbjerg, Bruzelius, and Rothengatter 2003; Van Marrewijk 2007; Van Marrewijk, Clegg, Pitsis, and Veenswijk 2008; Scott, Levitt, and Orr 2011; Merrow 2011; Sanderson 2012; Flyvbjerg 2014).

In these and other studies, megaprojects are often described as complex without defining or clarifying what causes complexity (for example, Van Marrewijk, Clegg, Pitsis, and Veenswijk 2008). Until recently (Davies, Gann, and Douglas 2009; Davies and Mackenzie 2014; Brady and Davies 2014), the challenge of dealing with complexity has been largely neglected in megaproject research. This is surprising, because megaprojects require an exceptional level of technical and managerial capability because of their complexity. Several studies suggest that project organizations deal with complexity by developing capabilities in systems integration (Prencipe, Davies, and Hobday 2003; Hobday, Davies, and Prencipe 2005; Shenhar and Dvir 2007). A systems integrator is the organization responsible for integrating components into a complete system, defining interfaces and managing interdependencies among its various parts, and coordinating the network of contractors involved in each project. Systems integration techniques and processes originally developed to design and integrate complex weapons and space exploration projects (Morris 1994, 2013; Johnson 1997, 2003; Hughes 1998, 2004) are now widely used to manage megaprojects across military and civil sectors of the economy.

This chapter presents an in-depth case study of the construction of the London 2012 Olympic and Paralympic Games. The approach to systems integration used to deliver London 2012 addressed the two levels of complexity associated with this megaproject. Prime contractors were appointed to manage each individual system as separate project (such as the Olympic Stadium and Velodrome), and the task of integrating the entire collection of systems and engaging with multiple stakeholders was performed jointly by the client and its delivery partner. The chapter is divided into the following sections. Section 21.2 frames our study in a brief review of the systems integration and project management literature. Sections 21.3 and 21.4 discuss the research methods and introduce the case study. Section 21.5 on research findings identifies the layered structure of systems integration used to manage the London 2012 project. Section 21.6 discusses what we can learn from our case about the wider role of systems integration in megaproject management, and the chapter concludes with Section 21.7 by suggesting some promising avenues for future research.

21.2 Background Literature

Several studies offer a definition of project complexity and identify some of the management challenges involved in dealing with it (Shenhar 1993; Shenhar and Dvir 1996; Hobday 1998; Gholz 2003). They suggest that the project can be conceptualized as a system because the structure of a project organization reflects the complexity of the system it produces (Williams 1999; Shenhar 1993, 1996; Shenhar 2001; Shenhar and Dvir 2007). The product or outcome of each project involves numerous interconnected parts, components, subsystems, and entire systems. Project outcomes often include physical artefacts (such as hardware and software) and intangible services (such as logistics, maintenance, and operations). Increasing complexity calls for more elaborate forms of organization and formal processes to cope with the challenge of integrating multiple components, managing interfaces between subprojects, and dealing with numerous interdependencies (Shenhar and Dvir 2007).

Informed by this approach, we can suggest that megaprojects involve the two highest levels of complexity (see Table 21.1). First, some megaprojects produce individual systems consisting of components with multiple functions that together meet a specific operational requirement, such as the development of the Airbus A380 or a national air traffic control computer system. In a "system project" a single organization (a client or prime contractor) usually establishes a central project or program office to coordinate the technical efforts of a large network of in-house functional groups and external subcontractors. Second, a more complex type of megaprojects produces a large collection of systems, each serving their own specific purpose, that work together to achieve a

Table 21.1 Levels of complexity in megaprojects

	System	System of systems
Definition	Integrate various components and subsystems, jointly performing multiple functions into an entire system or platform to meet a specific operational requirement	Integrate a dispersed and large-scale array of platforms and systems, each with a specific purpose, to achieve a common goal
Project complexity	System, platform	System of systems, array
Examples	Aircraft, weapon system, communications network, or single building construction	Airport, urban development, mass transit system, the English Channel Tunnel or a national missile defense system

common goal, such as the Channel Tunnel rail system connecting the United Kingdom and France, or Hong Kong International Airport. In a "system of systems" or "array project" a large temporary organization (a stand-alone project organization, joint venture, or separate company) is responsible for contracting and coordinating many individual projects (dedicated to delivering a specific system) that make up the array and deals with a financial, legal, and political issues.

Systems integration first emerged in the 1950s and 1960s deal with the complexity involved in the design and integration of weapons systems projects (such as Atlas, Titan, and Polaris ballistic missiles) and Apollo moon-landing missions (Sayles and Chandler 1971; Sapolsky 1972, 2003; Morris 1994; Hughes 1998, 2004; Gholz 2003) and is now used across many public and private sectors (Prencipe et al. 2003). Systems integration may be undertaken in-house by a client organization or a prime contractor, or be subcontracted to a specialized firm. This organization understands how components fit together in a whole system. Although it rarely produces individual components, the systems integrator must "nurture the in-house capability ... to know more about the total effort than any of the contracting parties" (Sayles and Chandler 1971: 319). It coordinates the large network of contracting parties involved in the design, production, integration, test, commission, and handover of a fully operational system. It manages the interfaces between subprojects, deals with component suppliers through separate contracts, and is accountable for meeting time, cost, and quality performance goals. The systems integrator relies on formal contracts, shared collaborative goals, and other forms of persuasion to encourage the parties involved to identify and solve unexpected problems that may arise when components are joined together.

With a few exceptions (Gholz 2003), research on systems integration has largely focused on individuals systems (Hobday et al. 2005), and some authors claim that more complex system of systems projects "involve much less of an integration problem" (Shenhar and Dvir 2007: 109). Building on recent research by the author and colleagues, this chapter challenges this assumption by identifying how systems integration is accomplished in an in-depth case study of a large array project: the construction of the London 2012 Olympics (Mackenzie and Davies 2011; Davies and Mackenzie 2014).

21.3 RESEARCH AIMS AND METHODS

Undertaking a single case study provides a theoretically sound way of studying the process and context of organizational change (Pettigrew 1990). As long as it is carefully chosen, a case can be used to develop generalizations about how things work which may be appropriate and valid for a larger number of samples. We wanted to explore how organizations responsible for delivering megaprojects cope with complexity. When we began our research in December 2010 we saw the London 2012 project as a critical case (Flyvbjerg 2006), allowing us to produce an in-depth understanding of the action-oriented processes and structures developed and applied on a megaproject to integrate a large collection of systems. We classified the construction of the Olympics as the most complex type of project (system of systems/array) and examined the structure and processes used to integrate the overall system and each individual system, and coordinate the interdependencies between them.

Since its completion, however, there is evidence to suggest that London 2012 is being held up as a new delivery model whose lessons should be applied on other publicly procured megaprojects megaprojects in the United Kingdom (Armitt 2013; Royal Academy of Engineering 2014). This suggests that the project is becoming a paradigmatic case (Flyvbjerg 2006) because of its role as an exemplar of how systems integration might be performed on other megaprojects.

Interviews were undertaken in two phases to explore how systems integration tasks were performed at different levels of complexity in the project. For a fuller description of the methods employed, see Davies and Mackenzie (2014). Working with our interviewees we identified two main levels: the system of systems (the program level) and individual systems contracts (the project level).

In the first phase of interviewing, we focused on the organizational structure and processes involved in managing the overall program. Interviews were conducted with the Olympic Delivery Authority (ODA) which acted as the client for the program and CLM—the temporary joint venture between CH2MHill, Laing O'Rourke, and Mace—which was formed specifically to act as the ODA's "delivery partner." The interviews focused on how the ODA and CLM worked together as a systems integrator to oversee, coordinate, and integrate each project within the overall program.

In a second phase of interviewing, our focus shifted to five specific projects identified by key interviewees to address the complexity of different systems in the array: the Olympic Stadium, the Velodrome, the Aquatics Centre, the Athletes Village, the International Broadcast Centre/Media Press Centre, and largely temporary structures (Basketball, Handball, and Eton Manor). Interviews with the ODA project sponsor and the CLM project manager were complemented with interviews with the relevant principal contractor (project director). The interviews addressed the ways in which each individual project fitted within the overall program, while being tailored to meet specific needs and circumstances of each system.

21.4 RESEARCH SETTING: CONSTRUCTING LONDON 2012

London was awarded the 2012 Olympic and Paralympic Games on 6 July 2005. The promise of creating a lasting legacy for London was key to winning the bid, and influenced the approach used to design and construct the venues and connecting infrastructure. The ODA was set up in 2006 as a temporary client and public-sector organization to oversee the design and construction of the Olympic Park infrastructure, venues, Olympic Village, and transport systems. It was responsible for handing over the Olympic venues to the London Organizing Committee of the Olympic Games and Paralympic Games (LOCOG)—the private sector organization responsible for staging the Games.

21.4.1 Project Life Cycle

The pace, planning, and scheduling of the London Olympics program was dictated by an "immoveable deadline." The project was time-critical because the games had to open on 27 July 2012. The ODA recognized that although the construction schedule could not be manipulated, a realistic budget and secure contingency was needed to cope with the risks and uncertainties surrounding the project. But the original budget of £4.2 billion submitted with the bid document in 2005 severely underestimated the costs of constructing and hosting the games. The final budget was announced in Parliament in March 2007. It was set at £9.3 billion and included a contingency of £1.2 billion. The ODA's budget for construction was £8.1 billion. The CLM strategic planning team established a baseline definition of the detailed scope, budget, schedule, risk, and interfaces of the program which was published as the 500-page "Yellow Book" in November 2007. This document was revised and published as the "Blue Book" in November 2009 to account for the numerous changes in scope that had occurred since the original publication.

The baseline documents became the main point of reference for scheduling the work and monitoring how the budget was spent during construction. The project life cycle was divided into six phases:

- Year 1 (2006–2007): this phase handed over the 600-acre Stratford site to the ODA.
- Year 2 (to Beijing 2008): the "demolish, dig, and design" phase prepared the site for the "big build" phases.
- Year 3 (to 27 July 2009): the "big build" (foundations) phase prepared for the construction of Olympic Park infrastructure and venues.
- Year 4 (to 27 July 2010): the "big build" phase (structures).

- Year 5 (to 27 July 2011): the "big build" phase (completion).
- Year 6 (to 2012): the phase was a year of testing in the run-up to the Games.

Planning permission for the Olympic Park was secured in October 2007, and construction started in May 2008. The construction program was divided into four yearly phases, with milestones published for each year. Building most of the venues ahead of schedule introduced some temporal contingency into the program. Annual phases were translated into more specific target objectives and milestones for the individual systems, setting out clearly how each project was expected to perform against the overall program schedule. Deadlines published online and therefore subject to public scrutiny provided an added incentive to avoid schedule slippages.

21.4.2 Project Organization

The construction program consisted of more than seventy projects (planned, approved, and managed by principal contractors), including fourteen temporary and permanent buildings, 20 km of roads, twenty-six bridges, 13 km of tunnels, 80 hectares of parkland, and new utilities infrastructure. The major venue projects were clustered on the Olympic Park (Olympic Stadium, Aquatics Centre, Velodrome, International Broad Centre/Media Press Centre, and Athletes Village), many of which were individually large, high-cost, and complex. As an indication of the scale of task, 12,635 people worked on the Olympic Park and Olympic Village during the peak period of construction at the end of March 2011. A summary of the permanent and temporary venues which we studied in our research is provided in Table 21.2.

Construction of the Olympics broke down into many individual projects and was managed as a program. A program refers to the managerial approaches used by organizations to achieve a strategy, vision, or defined goal by coordinating a diverse array of interrelated projects (Maylor, Brady, Cooke-Davies, and Hodgson 2006; Pellegrinelli, Partington, and Geraldi 2011). While we refer to London 2012 as a project, the word *program* is used specifically to refer to the processes established to manage the interrelated set of projects. We use the term *system project* to designate specific projects within the overall array, such as the Olympic Stadium project and Velodrome project. Each principal contractor was responsible for managing its own chain of subcontractors. The rest of this section provides an in-depth analysis of the structure and process established to construct the London Olympics.

21.4.3 Project Outcome

Construction of London 2012 was completed on time in July 2011, thirteen months before the games started on 27 July 2012, providing sufficient time to test the venues

Table 21.2 Major systems within the Olympics Park

Major systems	Principal contractor	Suite of contracts	Key characteristics
Permanent structures			
Olympic Stadium	McAlpine	Target Cost New Engineering Contractor (NEC3 Option C)	Construction of the 80,000-capacity stadium was completed in March 2011 safely, on time, and within budget.
Aquatics Centre	Balfour Beatty	Target Cost (NEC3 Option C)	Completed in July 2011, this iconic building housing two swimming pools was designed by architect Zaha Hadid, with two temporary "wings" to provide 17,500 capacity during the games and 2,500 capacity in legacy.
Velodrome	ISG	Target Cost (NEC3 Option C)	Construction of the cycling track was completed in February 2011.
Athletes Village	Lend Lease	Changed from Construction Management (CM) to mix of CM and Design & Build (fixed price NEC3 Option A)	Completed in December 2011, it provided accommodation for 17,000 athletes and officials and 2,818 new homes in legacy.
International Broadcast Centre and Main Press Centre	Carillion	Design & Build (fixed price NEC Option A)	Completed in July 2011, this venue supported 20,000 broadcasters and journalists during the games.
Largely temporary structures			
Eton Manor	Mansell Construction Services	Managed Packaged Strategy	Aquatics training venue with three Olympic-size temporary swimming pools during the Games. Dismantled and transformed to host wheelchair tennis during Paralympics. After the Games, turned into multipurpose sports centre.
Basketball Arena	CLM	Managed Packaged Strategy	Construction of the 12,000-capacity venue was completed in June 2011. Dismantled after the Games and reused at other UK and overseas events.
Water Polo	CLM	Managed Packaged Strategy	5,000-capacity temporary venue completed. Components dismantled and reused elsewhere in the UK.

and use the feedback from the trials to prepare for the Games. While the final cost of £6.8 billion (2011) was within the £8.1 billion allocated for construction, the project was significantly over budget when compared with the original baseline in the bid document.

A number of contextual factors shaped the program, such as status of the project, pressures to succeed, and the economic crisis of 2008, which called for new approaches to funding and the allocation of risk. As Sir John Armitt, the ODA's Chair, emphasized, the "Olympic project is the most high profile that you could imagine" (Kortekaas 2012), and a significant factor facilitating the overall progress of the program was the so-called Olympics effect (Mackenzie and Davies 2011). A desire not to avoid the poor performance of recent public projects—such as the heavily over budget and delayed Wembley football stadium—and the fact that the Olympics was the world's most prestigious sporting event, fostered a widespread attitude that this was "a once in a lifetime opportunity, so you don't want to get it wrong, because if you do, it'll be apparent to everyone in the industry. That's quite a motivator" (CLM interview).

21.5 RESEARCH FINDINGS

This section identifies how systems integration was undertaken to construct the Olympics venues and infrastructure. Our findings suggest that the structure and process of integration was arranged in a layered structure to match overall the complexity of the project (see Table 21.3). In the London 2012 project, the task of integrating the system of systems was undertaken jointly by the client and delivery partner. Performing the role of client, the ODA established the goals of the program, worked closely with the delivery partner to plan the program, monitored progress against those goals, and provided a single interface between the overall system and its external environment. CLM was appointed as delivery partner and integrator for the program and interfaces with individual projects. Principal contractors involved in London 2012 were responsible for integrating and delivering each system project (such as venues and infrastructure) against time, cost, quality, and other strategic objectives, and assisting in the coordination of interfaces with adjacent systems.

21.5.1 System of Systems

At the level of the system of systems, a structure and process was established with capabilities to understand the total system, manage external interfaces with multiple stakeholders, coordinate the progress of the overall program, and help manage individual system projects (see Figure 21.1).

Table 21.3 Systems integration on the London Olympics 2012

Level of complexity	Task	Organization	Examples from London 2012
System of systems (array project and external environment)	Wider tasks involved in managing multiple stakeholders and internal focus on monitoring the overall progress of the program	Client	Public sector client organization (220 staff) manages interface with sponsor, defines the scope and budget, and coordinates with delivery partner Responsible for managing "upward" to diverse external stakeholders (international, national, and local), single government interface, and minimizing "noise" to shield CLM from external interventions ODA–CLM colocated during planning to build team and align objectives
System of systems (program of interrelated system projects)	Managerial task to coordinate the integration of an interrelated set of system projects internally focused on managing the program	Delivery partner	Private sector delivery partner (500 staff) manages the program, principal contractors, and communication with ODA Combines specialized capabilities and complementary assets of CH2MHill, LOR, and Mace Professional services contract with ODA to bring "highest skills"
Individual system (system project)	Technical task to integrate a single system project	Prime contractor	Contractors with capabilities and prior experience in specific systems (e.g. stadia and roof structures) Suite of contracts (ranging from risk-sharing to fixed-price) with principal contractors tailored to complexity of each project CLM co-located with principal contractors and ODA representative on site in integrated project teams during construction

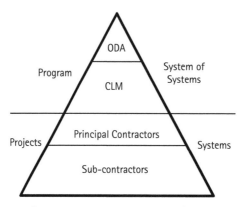

FIGURE 21.1 London 2012 Olympics: program, projects, and systems.

21.5.1.1 *Organizational Structure: Client and Delivery Partner*

After winning the Olympics bid, the ODA faced the challenge of integrating a large-scale and complex system of systems involve multiple stakeholders in a densely populated part of a major city. The Olympic Park had to be constructed and available for use by a fixed date across a constrained site involving multiple systems which became increasingly interconnected as more venues were constructed. At the same time, the ODA had to engage with many stakeholders and institutional interests associated with the program such as government, local authorities, railway authorities, and local community groups involved in shaping the programs and defining its outcomes.

As the client responsible for delivering the program, the ODA could have assumed responsibility for overall systems integration, but soon recognized the difficulties it would face in attempting to attract people with the experience, skills, and knowledge needed to manage such a challenging program. The ODA considered appointing a large prime contractor (such as Bechtel) for program management and multiple contractors for project management, but after some consideration decided that a new joint-venture organization established as a "clean sheet of paper" was required to deal with the complexities involved in delivering the construction program, whereas it was felt that a prime contractor might be unwilling to change, explore alternatives, or abandon its established routines. David Higgins, the ODA's chief executive, believed that the delivery partner should encompass the broad-based systems integration capabilities required to manage the program and interfaces between individual system projects.

CLM was selected as the preferred international consortium and delivery partner for the program, because it brought together three firms with a track record in the successful delivery of large and complex programs and projects (Hone, Higgins, Galloway, and Kintrea 2011: 7). Each partner brought distinctive capabilities, experience, and complementary assets. The US firm CH2M Hill had a track record as a program manager and an ability to integrate component parts of complex projects, including previous Olympic construction projects. Laing O'Rourke and Mace successfully worked together as major contractors on the £4.3-billion Heathrow Terminal 5—one of the largest and complex recent UK projects. Laing O'Rourke had strong capabilities in construction, and Mace was renowned for its expertise in project management. Ian Galloway—recruited from Bechtel to lead CLM—was the only CLM employee; all other CLM staff were contractually connected to their parent companies. By appointing CLM, the ODA could tap into the skills and expertise found in three large firms which it needed to manage different phases of the project. At its peak, CLM employed around 500 staff. If the 220 ODA staff are included, the overall program management cost around 10% of the program expenditure.

The task of systems integration across the overall program was divided between the ODA and CLM. The ODA concentrated on dealing "upward" by establishing a single interface between the overall project and the often conflicting interests of around 750 stakeholders, including London's Mayor, sporting bodies, LOCOG, the Greater London Authority, five London boroughs, the International Olympic Committee, and the British Olympic Association. CLM was responsible for keeping the ODA fully informed about the progress of the project measured against the schedule, managing "downward" across the overall program and acting as project manager in collaboration with principal contractors on each major construction project.

A "layered structure" was created to manage the different levels of systems integration across the program. As one manager explained:

> Make sure you have the ability to manage integration. Integration is a huge huge …
> This is about management and integration, and flexing all the different layers. So,
> you had this layer cake of how we would approach the whole project program. So,
> it's really about how you structure—it's all about structuring and how you're going to
> deliver things. (CLM interview)

The ODA and its assurance team participated in media and parliamentary enquiries, obtained financial support, and sought government approval for any significant proposed changes in scope. Under the ODA's leadership, the delivery partner and principal contractors were driven by the time and cost objectives of the program, but expected to achieve a number of secondary objectives published as six priority themes, such as sustainability, legacy, and health and safety. The ODA published a strategy for each of them, including specific objectives and principles applied across the program, cascading down from CLM to principal contractors and beyond.

This division of tasks allowed the ODA to provide oversight and assurance for the program and gave the CLM the autonomy needed to manage the program and projects. The ODA acted as a buffer protecting its delivery partner from outside "interference" added to the system by external stakeholders that could make integration more difficult. CLM worked as a "consultant" for the ODA, with incentives to meet various milestones and targets. This dual structure forged a clear alignment of objectives between the ODA and CLM, and between CLM and the principal contractors (for example, CLM and Lend Lease on the Athletes Village project).

The ODA and CLM had to find a way of working collaboratively and openly as virtu-ally integrated organization during the planning, design, construction, and handover of the venues to LOCOG. The relationship between the two organizations adjusted over time to address the changing requirements and different phases of the program. Joint review meetings held throughout the program served to align their organizational mod-els, capabilities, and resources (Hone et al. 2011: 7).

In the start-up planning phase when the ODA and CLM were first established, they were colocated in an off-site location to build a team between the client and delivery partner and align their strategic objectives, processes, and culture. CLM directors formed part of the ODA's executive management team. Forging a relationship based on trust and openness was facilitated by holding joint team events and social activities. When the program moved from planning into design and construction, a decision was made not to colocate ODA and CLM organizations. The core ODA team continued to work at the planning head office in Canary Wharf, whereas the CLM team moved to the various construction offices on site at Stratford. When CLM colocated with each princi-pal contractor, the core organizational linkage shifted to the CLM and contractor levels of the system. This geographical separation of the central ODA organization and CLM teams reflected the new division of tasks. The ODA performed the role of client and project sponsor, and CLM worked to achieve overall program outcomes and ensure that each project was delivered against defined goals.

21.5.1.2 *Integration Process: Program Management*

The ODA and CLM worked together to coordinate the integration of multiple systems, minimize unexpected interactions, and respond flexibly to deal with problems that might hinder progress of each individual project and the overall program. Those elements that could be firmly fixed at the beginning were forced by the program's deadline, funding constraints, the physical requirements of site, and capacity of systems. Carefully prepared plans, schedules, and deadlines guided the performance of the delivery partner and prin-cipal contractors, and helped to anticipate risks in advance and mitigate them when they occurred. Program management processes were designed to ensure that tasks performed in one part of the project were predictable and consistent with those undertaken by orga-nizations working in other parts. Emergent events, interface problems, and unfolding situations that could not be foreseen in advance depended on the capabilities of the collab-orating organizations involved to respond flexibly and rapidly. As one manager clarified:

> I always tell my guys is, anybody can manage the steady state; when things go wrong, it's about how we solve problems together—contractually, commercially, co-operationally. (CLM interview)

The ODA established a monitoring and assurance process to ensure that each proj-ect provided detailed, regular, and accurate information on progress in terms of budget, scheduling, and performance. This process helped to increase the visibility of unexpected problems, ill-defined interfaces, or changes in specifications. Monthly reports provided information to measure progress, forecast costs, and changes in schedule, scope, or budget using an early warning "traffic light" tracking system to identify issues in order of importance. Issues flagged as red or amber were identified in monthly meetings by the program team, but were dealt with at the project level. When emergent issues were identified, the project teams would estimate the additional costs and time needed to solve them. An assurance process was established to avoid schedule slippages associated with the introduction of change. Monthly trend reviews involving the ODA and CLM allowed senior managers to identify trends which might not be apparent at lower levels.

Acting as the client's program and project manager, CLM managed each individual contract, administered the change control process, and provided assurance that each principal contractor was achieving its targets and keeping pace with the program. As one interviewee explained, the main challenge was to establish a structure to manage the complexity of the integration process:

> If you take the components we have on the Olympic park individually, there's probably nothing overly complex; if you put them all together, that's where the complexity is. That's really meant that we've had to focus a lot of our time and effort, on integration. (CLM interview)

Different phases of integration were managed during the life of the program, including design, construction, and operational handover. Digital technologies and software tools were established to coordinate each phase of integration (such as Project Wise and Project Documentation Management System). In the design phase, CLM had to manage interdependencies between adjacent projects. A "Design Interface Schedule" system showed how a design change in one part such as a venue impacted on other parts of the program. In the construction phase, CLM attempted to simplify the integration process by dividing the management of systems into relatively self-contained "vertical" buildings (the permanent and temporary venues) and interconnected "horizontal" infrastructure (utilities, roads, and bridges). In the operational handover phase, CLM was "pulling the whole thing together to make sure it operates as one" (CLM interview).

A highly structured change control process was established to uncover, report, and document problems hindering progress, provide vital information about integration problems and poorly performing or neglected parts of the system, and make the changes required to keep the program on track. Any significant change proposed by the principal contractor had to be approved by the ODA. At the end of each month, project teams reported any changes to the "Change Control Board" chaired by the ODA chief executive. During the early phase of the program, as many as forty-five people in a room would discuss monthly reports. This number gradually reduced to as few as six people as the program reached completion. This change control process "flushed things up to the surface quickly so you could address and deal with them" (ODA interview).

Dealing with unforeseen problems depended on intense collaboration among the contracting parties and "an organizational culture that was highly-action oriented" (Hone et al. 2011: 8):

> I think it was really the dynamic of having enough, you know, good people, excellent people with a real attitude of, you know, rapid assessment and decision making, be able to see issues, discuss them, make decisions and move on. (ODA interview)

The ODA and CLM "wanted to work by persuasion and by consensus, but from a position of strength" (ODA interview). The use of workshops and informal meetings to build consensus around problems and solutions helped to achieve and maintain a close alignment of ODA and CLM over time.

21.5.2 Individual Systems

At the level of individual systems, each project was managed as a self-contained organization and process with clearly defined interfaces with other systems in the overall array (see Figure 21.1).

21.5.2.1 *Organizational Structure: Prime Contractor*

The integration of each individual system project (such as the Velodrome and Olympic Stadium) was planned and managed independently by a prime contractor, known as the "principal contractor" on London 2012. The ODA used a variety of risk-sharing and fixed-price contracts with the principal contractors to address the specific requirements, challenges, and complexity of each project. This suite of contracts was designed to support clearly defined procedures and forge the collaborative relationships between the ODA, CLM, and principal contractors required to deal with unpredictable, ill-defined interfaces, and changing conditions found within and between each project. Contracts for individual venues were held by the ODA and managed by CLM. Project delivery was finalized when the accepted program was agreed with the principal contractor responsible for individual systems, including the work breakdown structure, schedule, milestones, and risk allocation.

Principal contractors were encouraged to exploit their own distinctive systems integration capabilities and prior experience to create solutions tailored to the requirements of specific venues and infrastructure:

> We were given the freedom to determine how we were going to deliver the targets that the ODA were setting. And we all do things slightly differently because of the circumstances we found ourselves in, it's largely driven by the nature of the venue and program issues and suppliers and so on. (Principal contractor interview)

Principal contractors were expected to find their own way of meeting individual targets and schedules for their project, and implementing the ODA's Priority Themes such as the Health and Security theme. Risks were reduced by appointing principal contractors and coalitions of subcontractors with tried and tested capabilities developed while working together on previous projects.

Individual system projects largely corresponded to a single venue such as the Velodrome or a part of the system-wide infrastructure (such as utilities). The projects ranged in complexity from the iconic Aquatics Centre with its unique roof design, to the relatively standardized, modular, and reusable systems used to build the Athletes Village and temporary venues. For example, whereas on the Athletes Village the project team preformed "one thing 3,000 times," on the Aquatics Centre there were few opportunities for standardization, because the team did "3,000 things once" (Stimpson 2011). The most complex projects (Aquatics Centre, Velodrome, and Olympics Stadium) were procured using a risk-sharing contract (target price with pain/gain) to promote collaboration and the flexibility to expose issues and face known risks, deal with unexpected situations, and explore opportunities to improve performance.

Each project had its own contingency fund, and contractors were incentivized to deliver projects within agreed target costs. Venue projects based on less complex designs and standardized reusable components (such as the International Broadcast Centre/Media Press Centre) were procured using more traditional fixed-price Design and Build contracts. The procurement strategy for the Athletes Village eventually used a combination of Construction Management and Design and Build contracts. A "managed package" was appropriate for the temporary venues (basketball, water polo, and Eton Manor) given that their unusual requirements were less attractive to conventional contractors used to building venues, but not dismantling them. CLM assumed the roles of principal contractor and project manager for the temporary venues, and let the work out as packages to a list of framework contractors for engineering, construction, modular buildings, temporary seating, and fit-out.

21.5.2.2 *Integration Process: Project Management*

The process of integrating individual system projects into the overall array had to be carefully managed. The independence and autonomy of principal contractors had to be preserved while encouraging the collaboration and responsiveness needed to deal with interdependencies with adjacent venues and common infrastructure. As one of the principal contractors explained:

> We're an island site but there are still interfaces. For example, the bridges contracts were really tricky for CLM and the contractor and they were really tricky for us because we had some awkward interfaces at the end of the bridges. We had literally one man working on bridges interfaces for a year, and that was closely interfaced with the CLM design managers. So there were certain areas where we interfaced closely, where the external technical review teams had to do their stuff. We interfaced closely on that. (Principal contractor interview)

Dealing with interdependencies of this kind could not be addressed by one organization alone. It required the continuous interaction and penetration of all collaborating parties. The ODA and CLM appointed representatives to work closely on site as part of colocated, integrated project teams with principal contractors. The pairing of an ODA executive (project sponsor) and CLM executive (project manager) applied across all the system projects (and bundles of smaller projects). The ODA project sponsor was responsible for defining the project goal, securing approval for the project business case, and managing stakeholders. The ODA sponsor worked with the CLM delivery partner manager, who was responsible for working with the principal contractor to deliver the project against program objectives.

CLM established standardized processes, reporting procedures, and documentation tools to coordinate the interdependencies between individual system projects. Vertical procurement of the buildings created a buffer around each system project, which helped to define and limit the number of interfaces with other systems and infrastructure. As one manger put it: "So you drop a cylinder over it and say everything inside that cylinder belongs to the PC [principal contractor]," whereas "infrastructure has all been procured horizontally" (CLM interview). Each contractor could focus on its task of designing and integrating specific systems because "In venues they get their own area—so you can make your contractor king of their island, if you like, though not many of them are islands" (CLM interview). The Olympic Park surrounding these islands was divided into four zones, and teams of engineers and managers were responsible for understanding:

> How each of the areas of the park would be integrated together ... there's all the integration that goes around making the park work ... But then you sit at the end of it with a massive kit of parts, and it creates a huge integration problem. (CLM interview)

With so many system projects occurring simultaneously and in sequence on a constrained site, the most frequently occurring situations and problems from start to finish were associated with "integration" (Hansford 2010). The interdependency between systems was about

> ... the complexity of inputs and the complexity and the understanding of the interrelationship between those inputs. And what is one contractors' input is another contractor's output. It's a system approach. (CLM interview)

Despite efforts to limit the number of interactions and minimize interface problems, all of the systems were interconnected, and some projects such as infrastructure works had interfaces with every other part of the park. The ODA and CLM established an integration process to manage the park as a complete system, with interfaces between fifteen to twenty contractors working at any particular time. CLM established a "program integration" group and organized "integration committees" to identify how slippages or changes in one venue or connecting infrastructure (such as water and energy supplies) impacted others. The CLM integration group originally functioned as a central organization with the oversight required to understand how all the components fitted together. As the London 2012 project moved toward completion, the group operated in a more decentralized way as construction progressed to deal with issues at the individual project level.

While the London 2012 emphasized the importance of using tried and tested processes and technologies, each individual system project was encouraged to innovate and adapt its processes if there was a significant opportunity to improve performance. Working in close proximity in colocated project teams over an extended period of time fostered the shared understanding, trust, and openness required to identify emergent problems at an early stage and strive collaboratively to find innovative solutions:

> Management action has been very much about how we make a decision, right or wrong. It might all sound simple, this, but the complexity of what we're working with has been very changeable. So, that's worked well. It's getting the visibility. (CLM interview)

Two examples help to illustrate how the parties involved in the system projects identified problems together, adjusted their plans, and responded flexibly to new opportunities and unexpected situations. First, ISG, the principal contractor responsible for the Velodrome, identified an opportunity to reduce costs and save time by changing the roof design from a steel to a "cable net" roof. After some consideration, CLM agreed to this radical change to the original design, including incurring the risk of purchasing 13,500 metres of cables before the design was finalized. The ODA provided time to evaluate the proposal and ultimately accepted the change even though it exacerbated short-term time pressures. In an attempt to shift the risk to the principal contractor, the ISG's contract was changed from target price with pain/gain to fixed price. The cable net roof took only nine weeks to construct rather than the six months for the steel roof.

Second, as a result of the economic downturn in late 2008, private funding was no longer available to pay for the Athletes Village. The ODA's decision to switch to public funding triggered a reappraisal of design and encouraged the principal contractors and CLM to develop lower-cost schemes. In the original plan, for example, the Athletes Village would have been built by the private sector and leased to LOCOG for the Games. The ODA solved the problem by using contingency money and other savings on the program to fund construction of the Village and recover the money by selling the development after the Games. The ODA renegotiated Lend Lease's contract, and most of the buildings were procured with the principal contractor using a lump sum, Design and Build contract.

21.6 DISCUSSION

Our study of London 2012 identified a layered structure of systems integration, corresponding to the two levels of complexity associated with this megaproject. At the systems level, the integration task was performed jointly by the client and delivery partner. Davies and Mackenzie (2014) introduced the term "meta systems integration" to describe this task because it depends on the ability to preside over, look across, and understand the entire collection of systems well enough to make trade-offs and reach decisions in the interests of overall system goals. At the system level, the project was decomposed into a large number of individual system projects. In each system project, a single prime contractor coordinated and integrated the technical efforts of its subcontractors.

Whereas integrating a single system is primarily a technical engineering challenge (Shenhar and Dvir 2007), our study suggest that dealing with a system of systems calls for wider strategic capabilities and skills to manage the overall program and multiple stakeholders affected by the project. In our case, the client was primarily occupied with monitoring overall progress against the project goals and dealing with legal, political, and financial issues. It dealt with all external interfaces between the system and the external environment. One of the biggest challenges is that a megaproject crosses so many boundaries between organizations, including sponsors, external stakeholders, and contractors with strong independent identities, motivations, and priorities. The systems integration task is, therefore, strongly affected by the actions of multiple stakeholders, with diverging concerns and conflicting interests, in the external environment within which the system is developed and delivered. In the London 2012 project, the client dealt with this by establishing a buffer to insulate the delivery partner and contractors from endless changes in scope and "noise" emanating from frequent and potentially disruptive interventions from external parties.

Whereas the focus of the client's attention was "upward" and outward to external stakeholders, the delivery partner managed "downward" and across the program of interrelated system projects. The delivery partner represented the interests of the client and was responsible for coordinating the overall program, achieving the project's strategic priorities and dealing with interdependencies between each system project.

A form of tight–loose management was established to manage the program and individual projects within it (Mackenzie and Davies 2011; Davies and Mackenzie 2014). Whereas the delivery partner established consistent and standardized processes and clearly defined budgets and schedules to keep the overall program on track, flexible contractual arrangements encouraged principal contractors to find their own routes to achieving specific project goals and devise processes tailored to the requirements and complexity of each system. Each principal contractor was encouraged to exploit its own distinctive capabilities, work with trusted partners and subcontractors, and create bespoke project execution strategies. The delivery partner and client representative participated in colocated integrated project teams with principal contractors to coordinate interfaces with adjacent or affected systems and ensure that the progress of each system project was aligned to the system-wide goals of the program.

As an early study of the Apollo space program recognized, in "complex projects managers learn to expect the unexpected, that what looks good today may be in deep trouble tomorrow" (Sayles and Chandler 1971: 311–12). Carefully planned processes and schedules which serve to freeze components of a system into a given position may have to be unlocked to introduce change and adapt to unexpected situations. In the London 2012 case, the client created a budget and contingency to address possible risks and opportunities. Planning to achieve deadlines ahead of time created a temporal buffer to prevent overall progress from being held back by poorly performing systems. The ODA and CLM established integration processes and worked collaboratively with principal contractors to uncover and solve interface problems. The client also managed a highly structured change control process to promote innovation when opportunities arose to improve performance.

So what generalized principles can we learn from our case study of London 2012 that will apply to other megaprojects? As early studies of complex projects recognized, there are "no magical management system cures" (Sapolsky 1972: 253) and no "single predictable managerial strategy" (Sayles and Chandler 1971: 317). But it is clear that the organization responsible for delivering a megaproject must develop a systems integration structure and process to match the complexity of the system it produces. However, it faces a number of choices about how to establish capabilities in systems integration. These can be developed by a large client, experienced prime contractor, or joint-venture delivery partner established on a temporary basis and disbanded on completion of the project. The increasing scale and complexity of megaprojects (Flyvjberg 2014) would suggest that few organizations (clients or prime contractors) have the capabilities in-house to address all aspects of systems integration. In the United Kingdom, the dual structure of a client and delivery partner created for London 2012 is becoming more frequent and is receiving increasing attention around the world as a possible model for integrating complex megaprojects. For example, a version of this approach is being used to program-manage the United Kingdom's £14.8-billion Crossrail high-capacity suburban railway project connecting the east and west of London.

Our findings are limited to a single case of temporary client organization under public ownership, and more research is clearly needed to understand how systems integration capabilities may be created for megaprojects delivered by other organizations, including permanent or repeat clients, and under different forms of public and private ownership. For example, BAA (formerly British Airports Authority), the privately owned client organization responsible for the Heathrow Terminal 5 project, adopted the strategy of building systems integration capabilities in-house, because as a repeat client, it had a strong incentive to develop capabilities that could be used on subsequent megaprojects (Davies et al. 2009).

21.7 CONCLUSION

This chapter began by suggesting that an organization responsible for delivering a megaproject must in some way mirror the complexity of the system it produces. Our research underlines the importance of developing a broad set of systems integration capabilities to manage the most complex type of system megaproject. In addition to the technical and managerial capabilities required to design and integrate individual systems (Shenhar and Dvir 2007), we identified the wider role of systems integration in managing the interfaces between multiple systems within a program, and between the system as a whole and the external environment within which it is conceived, developed, and delivered. A layered structure was created for the London 2012 project. Each level of the overall system was integrated by a separate type of organization: a prime contractor for each system, a delivery partner coordinated the interrelated projects within the program, and a client established the goals of the overall project, monitored its progress, and managed the numerous stakeholders affected by it. Although difficult to undertake because of the long duration and resources needed, future research on megaprojects could benefit from comparative studies exploring the relevance of some of our initial propositions about complexity and the lessons of systems integration.

References

Altshuler, A. and Luberoff, D. (2003). *Mega-Projects: The Changing Politics of Urban Public Investment*. Washington, DC: The Brookings Institution.

Armitt, J. (2013). *The Armitt Review: An Independent Review of Long Term Infrastructure Planning Commissioned for Labour's Policy Review*. London: Labour Party.

Brady, T. and Davies, A. (2014). "Managing structural and dynamic complexity: A tale of two projects," *Project Management Journal*, 45(2): 21–38.

Davies, A., Gann, D., and Douglas, T. (2009). "Innovation in megaprojects: Systems integration at Heathrow Terminal 5," *California Management Review*, 51(2): 101–25.

Davies, A. and Mackenzie, I. (2014). "Project complexity and systems integration: Constructing the London 2012 Olympics and Paralympics Games," *International Journal of Project Management*, 32: 773–90.

Flyvbjerg, B. (2006). "Five misunderstandings about case-study research," *Qualitative Inquiry*, 12(2): 219–45.

Flyvbjerg, B. (2014). "What you should know about megaprojects and why: An overview," *Project Management Journal*, 45(2): 6–19.

Flyvbjerg, B., Bruzelius, N., and Rothengatter, W. (2003). *Megaprojects and Risk: An Anatomy of Ambition*. Cambridge: Cambridge University Press.

Gholz, E. (2003). "Systems integration in the US Defense Industry," in A. Prencipe, A. Davies, and M. Hobday, *The Business of Systems Integration*. Oxford: Oxford University Press, pp. 279–332.

Hansford, M. (2010). "Race to the finish," *New Civil Engineer*, 22–29 July.

Hobday, M. (1998). "Product complexity, innovation and industrial organization," *Research Policy*, 26: 689–710.

Hobday, M., Davies, A., and Prencipe, A. (2005). "Systems integration: A core capability of the modern corporation," *Industrial and Corporate Change*, 14:1109–43.

Hone, D., Higgins, D., Galloway, I., and Kintrea, K. (2011). "Delivering London 2012: Organization and programme," *Proceedings of the ICE: Civil Engineering*, 164(5): 5–12.

Hughes, T. P. (1998). *Rescuing Prometheus*. New York: Pantheon Books.

Hughes, T. P. (2004). *Human-Built world: How to Think about Technology and Culture*. Chicago: University of Chicago Press.

Johnson, S. B. (1997). "Three approaches to big technology: Operations research, systems engineering and project management," *Technology and Culture*, 38(4): 891–919.

Johnson, S. B. (2003). "Systems integration and the social solution of technical problems in complex systems," in A. Prencipe, A. Davies, and M. Hobday (2003). *The Business of Systems Integration*. Oxford: Oxford University Press, pp. 35–55.

Kortekaas, V. (2012). "Olympics contractors build on experience," *Financial Times*, 15 February.

Mackenzie, I. and Davies, A. (2011). "Lessons learned from the London 2012 Games construction project," *London Olympics Learning Legacy*, ODA 2011/269, <http://www.london2012.com/learninglegacy>.

Maylor, H., Brady, T. B., Cooke-Davies, T., and Hodgson, D. (2006). "From projectification to programmification," *International Journal of Project Management*, 24: 663–72.

Merrow, E. W. (2011). *Industrial Megaprojects: Concepts, Strategies, and Practices for Auccess*. Hoboken, NJ: Wiley.

Miller, R. and Lessard, D. R. (2000). *The Strategic Management of Large Engineering Projects: Shaping Institutions, Risks, and Governance*. Cambridge, MA: MIT Press.

Morris, P. W. G. and Hough, G. H. (1987). *The Anatomy of Major Projects: A Study of the Reality of Project Management*. Chichester: Wiley.

Morris, P. W. G. (1994). *The Management of Projects*. London: Thomas Telford.

Morris, P. W. G. (2013). *Reconstructing Project Management*. Chichester: Wiley-Blackwell.

Pellegrinelli, S., Partington, D., and Geraldi, J. A. (2011). "Program management: An emerging opportunity for research and scholarship," in P. W. G. Morris, J. K. Pinto, and J. Söderlund, J. (eds.), *The Oxford Handbook of Project Management*. Oxford: Oxford University Press, ch. 10.

Pettigrew, A. (1990). "Longitudinal field research on change; Theory and practice," *Organization Science*, 1(3): 267–92.

Prencipe, A., Davies, A., and Hobday, M. (2003). *The Business of Systems Integration*. Oxford: Oxford University Press.

Royal Academy of Engineering. (2014). "Public projects and procurement in the UK: Sharing experiences and changing practice."

Sanderson, J. (2012). "Risk, uncertainty and governance in megaprojects: A critical discussion of alternative explanations," *International Journal of Project Management*, 30: 432–43.

Sapolsky, H. M. (1972). *The Polaris System Development: Bureaucratic and Programmatic Success in Government*. Cambridge, MA: Harvard University Press.

Sapolsky, H. M. (2003). "Inventing systems integration," in A. Prencipe, A. Davies, and M. Hobday (2003). *The Business of Systems Integration*. Oxford: Oxford University Press, pp. 15–34.

Sayles, L. R. and Chandler, M. K. (1971). *Managing Large Systems: Organizations for the Future*, New Brunswick, NJ: Transaction Publications.

Scott, W. R., Levitt, R. E., and Orr, R. J. (2011). *Global Projects: Institutional and Political Challenges*. Cambridge: Cambridge University Press.

Shenhar, A. J. (1993). "From low- to high-tech project management," *R&D Management*, 23(3): 199–214.

Shenhar, A. J. (2001). "One size does not fit all projects: Exploring classical contingency domains," *Management Science*, 47(3): 394–414.

Shenhar, A. J. and Dvir, D. (1996). "Toward a typological theory of project management," *Research Policy*, 25: 607–32.

Shenhar, A. J. and Dvir, D. (2007). *Reinventing Project Management: The Diamond Approach to Successful Growth and Innovation.* Boston: Harvard Business School Press.

Stimpson, J. (2011). "Vital venues delivered to order," *New Civil Engineer,* Major Project Report: Delivering the UK Games, February.

Van Marrewijk, A. (2007). "Managing project culture: The case of Environ megaproject," *International Journal of Project Management,* 25: 290–9.

Van Marrewijk, A., Clegg, S. R., Pitsis, T., and Veenswijk, M. (2008). Managing public–private megaprojects: Paradoxes, complexity and project design," *International Journal of Project Management,* 26: 591–600.

Williams, T. M. (1999). "The need for new paradigms of complex projects," *International Journal of Project Management,* 17(5): 269–73.

CHAPTER 22

....

ICONIC URBAN MEGAPROJECTS IN A GLOBAL CONTEXT
Revisiting Bilbao

....

GERARDO DEL CERRO SANTAMARÍA

22.1 INTRODUCTION

THE planning and construction of iconic urban megaprojects (IUMPs) has grown into a standard policy choice by urban and regional elites in globalizing cities. Politicians, business leaders, and others in local and regional growth machines fulfil their personal and professional ambitions by investing in and promoting IUMPs, aspiring to reach global status and positive economic change for their cities. Many urban elites worldwide have been greatly influenced by the so-called Bilbao effect—the perception that the Guggenheim Museum Bilbao resulted in a "Cinderella transformation" of the northern Spanish city and economic capital of the Basque Country. In the dominant discourse concerning architecture's surrender to capitalism's commercial goals, the Guggenheim Bilbao has been and remains to be mistakenly and repeatedly portrayed as the "catalyst" for the city's radically successful transformation from industrial powerhouse to regional service center. However, the key to understanding the intensification and spreading of the belief by many urban elites worldwide that iconic architecture alone can revitalize an urban economy is to be found not in the financial feasibility and economic impacts of IUMPs, but rather in the force of iconic architecture to transform a city's image (del Cerro Santamaria 2007). In fact, the Guggenheim Bilbao enhanced the relevance of the debate about commodification, commercialization, and replicability of IUMPs as urban elites across five continents actively sought to have a Frank Gehry Guggenheim constructed in their own cities. With a focus on the Bilbao case, this chapter shows how iconic architecture plays a fundamental role in the deployment of contemporary globalized urbanization and the increased desire of urban elites to surrender to the promise—and discontents—of IUMPs.

22.2 FROM INDUSTRIAL POWERHOUSE TO REGIONAL SERVICE CENTER

The last forty years of global capitalist development have featured both a shift in urban governance from managerialism to entrepreneurialism (Harvey 1989) and a widely shared perception of cities as nodes within a global network of relationships and exchanges. In a context of relentless globalization, political and business elites have come to expect improved urban and regional economic performance from linkages to the global economy. As a result, city and regional planning schemes in the past thirty years have focused on the implementation of regeneration and revitalization policies designed to achieve global visibility for cities and the attraction of visitors and investments. The city of Bilbao in northern Spain was no exception. Bilbao underwent dramatic economic restructuring during the 1970s and 1980s—initially through global industrial changes that contributed to the elimination of approximately 40% of industrial jobs in the area over a single decade. Following this traumatic development, Bilbao undertook its own revitalization program in an attempt to turn the city into a modern, competitive metropolis capable of meeting the challenges of the twenty-first century. Using strategies common in other revitalized cities in Europe, the program proposed the following:

- Transforming the city-center waterfront, Abandoibarra, into a business, commercial and cultural epicenter (including the 1997 Guggenheim Museum Bilbao).
- Developing port and airport capacity.
- Building a new subway system.
- Constructing new highways and railroad paths, a new downtown, and an intermodal transit station.
- Developing a new convention center.
- Establishing a new technology park, which includes the headquarters of the European Software Institute.

Five key features stood out in this planning program. First, it was a state-led revitalization project funded almost entirely by Basque and Spanish institutions. The estimated US$2-billion budget amounts to a significant portion of the Basque GDP in 1996. Furthermore, it was a significant investment in a metropolitan region occupying 5.7% of the Basque Country's land area in which nearly half of the Basque population resides. Second, and as a result of its scale, the revitalization project was a long-term program spanning over two decades. Most, though not all, of the infrastructure projects were completed in 2015. Third, the program specifically sought to diversify the local economy. By combining production and consumption-oriented revitalization strategies, the program aimed at attracting large and small firm investment in different sectors of the economy, including high-tech steel production and innovative shipbuilding as well as the convention and tourism businesses. Fourth, considerable emphasis was placed upon the city's internationalization, which in practice meant fostering foreign trade flows and attracting cultural tourism. Fifth, most of the new buildings and other facilities to mark Bilbao's revitalization were commissioned not to local architects but rather to "starchitects" with a very high standing in the global architectural profession, including Santiago Calatrava, Norman Foster, Robert A. M. Stern, Frank Gehry, Cesar Pelli, Rafael Moneo, and Alvaro Siza.

The centerpiece of the revitalization scheme was Abandoibarra, an old industrial riverfront area in downtown Bilbao planned to become the new Central Business District and iconic mile in the city. The enlargement of the Super Port, in addition to transferring the sea containers away from the Nervión River, freed up Abandoibarra for new architectural icons such as:

- Norman Foster's New Subway System (1995)
- Frank Gehry's Guggenheim Museum (1997).
- Santiago Calatrava's Zubizuri Bridge (1997)
- Javier Manterola's Euskalduna Bridge (1997)
- F. Soriano and D. Palacios's Euskalduna Convention Center (1999).
- Juan Francisco Paz's Maritime Museum (2001).
- Ricardo Legorreta's Meliá Bilbao Hotel (2003)
- Robert A. M. Stern's Zubiarte Shopping Mall (2004).
- Arata Isozaki's Isozaki Gate (2008)
- Rafael Moneo's University of Deusto Library (2010).
- Alvaro's Siza's Auditorium of the Basque Public University, UPV-EHU (2010).
- César Pelli's Iberdrola Tower (2011).
- NYC Balmori Associates's Plaza Euskadi (2011).
- Zaha Hadid Architects Zorrotzaure Bridges (under construction in 2017)

The most visually stunning and successful project within Abandoibarra is the Guggenheim Museum Bilbao which, paradoxically, was not initially included in the revitalization plan. The Guggenheim came to symbolize Bilbao's historic transformation, and the radical image change that put the city "on the map of world consciousness," according to Peter Hall (2001). The project was widely acclaimed as a successful enterprise that transformed Bilbao into a major city player in the avant-garde of world architecture. An exemplar urban icon, the Guggenheim Museum Bilbao poses intriguing questions about the role of iconic architecture and IUMPs in urban revitalization, the significance of culture and tourism for urban economies, and the ability of local and regional administrations to actually yield economic development for their citizens.

22.3 THE GUGGENHEIM MUSEUM: A GLOBAL VENTURE FOR BILBAO

One of the most dramatically attractive features of the Guggenheim project was, for Basque officials, that it constituted a global venture. The entire Guggenheim Bilbao project was carried out by former Guggenheim Foundation Director Thomas Krens as a global expansion project. For Basque negotiators, it was a foreign investment project. The Basque officials saw themselves as representatives of a sovereign nation conducting international affairs. The Basques had to persuade Krens that investing in the Basque Country was a good opportunity, except that the entire investment would come from local money. Coinciding interests and similar views about the type of project they were handling contributed greatly to the signing of an agreement. Krens, the fundraiser and entrepreneur, had mainly a circumstantial relationship with the city of Bilbao. Gehry, the artist, fell in love with the city's "incredible toughness" immediately: "I am attracted to industrial hardness in the midst of a green valley" (Gehry 2001). Indeed, Gehry managed to achieve the Basque aspirations for an emblematic building with a great market potential as well as Krens's vision for a construction analogous to that of Chartres Cathedral in the fourteenth and fifteenth centuries (Jodidio 2001). His creation was one of what Giovannini described as "the stellar buildings which will help to define the cultural pecking order in a unified Europe where cities are becoming increasingly more important as nations are receding" (Giovannini 2001). The same critic offered the picture of world cities emerging in the global economy "powered by world-class architecture" in a 2001 article that he appropriately titled "The Bilbao Effect":

> The rust belt city, Spain's Pittsburgh, needed a postcard image comparable to the Eiffel Tower and the Sydney Opera House to symbolize its emergence as a player on the chessboard of a united Europe and a globalized economy. It needed a monument. One building and $110 million later, Bilbao is now a contender as a world city, and many of the world's second- and third-tier cities have called Mr. Gehry's office, hoping for a comparable Cinderella transformation. (Giovannini 2001)

22.4 Frank Gehry's Architecture

Giovannini's central thesis about the emergence of city-states to the detriment of nation-states is still only conjectural, fourteen years after it was published. However, his comments about the importance of architecture in remaking a city's image have not lost relevance. The Guggenheim Bilbao's instant and lasting worldwide success was first of all the success of an architectural icon, and this would prove critical in making the museum both a symbol and a magnet for the city of Bilbao. What are the factors that determined the almost unanimous acclaim of Frank Gehry's design in 1997 and thereafter? One finds that architectural and non-architectural factors answer this question.

Among the former, we have to consider both Gehry's high standing in the architectural profession and, in particular, the absolute originality of his design for Bilbao. According to leading American architectural theorist Anthony Vidler, former Dean and Professor at the prestigious Cooper Union for the Advancement of Science and Art in Manhattan, the design is "refreshingly unconventional vis-à-vis for example the rather stiff Getty" (Vidler 2002). Although Gehry was already a well-established architect when he created his design for Bilbao, the new Guggenheim in the Basque capital arguably made him a truly global architect.

Among non-architectural factors, one must consider the novelty of Krens's idea of global museum franchises. Moreover, for American observers and other outsiders, the agreement between a prestigious American cultural foundation in financial difficulties and a declining city with a reputation for political conflict and terrorism was an unconventional one:

> The story of events in Bilbao turned out to be journalistically viable; in fact, it was a good story. Drawn to Bilbao by reports of an extraordinary building, journalists found numerous other elements of narrative interest: a down-and-out city attempting a comeback; a volatile political situation; a multinational museum ... (Raouen 2001)

The whole project thus had the potential to attract press attention, but it is Gehry's design that has been attracting millions of people to Bilbao since the museum opened in 1997. Gehry himself said about the wishes of the Basques:

> They were very explicit. They wanted a Sydney Opera House. They wanted the thing to bring people to Bilbao and put the place on the map. I tried to do it. (Gehry 2010)

Critic Mildred Friedman told Sydney Pollack in the Director's 2005 documentary, *Sketches of Frank Gehry*:

> He [Gehry] began to delve into all these ideas that he'd been beginning to work with and just went the whole way there. I don't think there is a building that comes anywhere near it in this period of art history. (Friedman 2010)

Former Guggenheim Foundation Thomas Krens argued that:

> Bilbao has been the watershed thing for Frank. He was an interesting architect until Bilbao opened. After that, he became a transcendent architect. (Krens 2010)

Arguably, Frank Gehry knew how to visually and spatially convey a new era for museums, which no longer serve as "cabinets of curiosities," but instead as "cultural theme parks," as Victoria Newhouse discussed in her book *Toward a New Museum* (1998), which includes a chapter on the Guggenheim Bilbao. Similarly, critic Jayne Merkel explained these new functions of museums:

> The goal of much museum architecture today is to stun ... museums are no longer just repositories of treasures [...] they have become objects in their own right ... museums today do not merely conserve; they entertain, feed patrons, sell wares, host parties, and make displays. (Merkel 2002)

According to critic Martin Pops, one way to aesthetically establish this new era for the museum and make an extraordinary impact is to present a building which is a fluid enactment of process, rather than a stylization of it:

> "How could a building be made to look like it's in process?" asked Gehry to himself in 1985. A literal way, of course, is to "unfinish" it, as Gehry "unfinished" the tower, its exterior partially clad, its skeletal structure exposed. [Another way] is by introducing a metaphor of natural process ... For the Guggenheim he designed the metallic flower ... Gehry's curves may seem private inventions but, according to Charles Jencks, they "certainly come from nature, and are close to the lessons of chaos and catastrophe theories." (Pops 2000)

Another factor that explains the attractiveness of Gehry's Bilbao building, in both aesthetic and experiential terms, has to do with the architect's ability to infuse both local and global discourses. As Judith Bell put it:

> With his building in Bilbao, the language that once seemed idiosyncratic has taken on a new, universal meaning [...] Flowing and at times vertiginous, this explosion of undulating spaces crafted of titanium and glass [...] speaks not only to and of its immediate surroundings and this particular moment, but of the future and the shape of things to come. (Bell 1998)

It has been argued that the building's perceived responsiveness to the city derived from Gehry's appreciation for Bilbao's industrial past, and his evocation of such past with a building shape that has been compared to that of a vessel. Art critic Paul Goldberger explicitly stated that:

> Gehry's genius has been to create buildings that seem to be arbitrary and irrational but in fact are deeply responsive to their surroundings and to the need of their users. (Goldberger 1997)

And Gehry himself said about the urban context of his creation:

> There's a river, there's a huge bridge. There's a nineteenth century city [sic], and it's at a higher level than the river. The city has a green valley surrounding all this, which makes it all kind of palatable. I was fascinated with the big bridge and the dynamics of the city, which was vibrant in terms of traffic, energy, and everything going on ... I had so many elements to resolve: how to make a connection to a nineteenth-century city, how to bring people down to the river's edge, how to engage the bridge, how to deal with the Basque culture, their interests, their roots. (Gehry 2010)

The international press generally portrayed the construction of the museum from the viewpoint of the architect, implicitly assuming that the building owed exclusively to Gehry's design. There is, however, an alternative perspective to explore from the Basque side that concerns the actual construction of the museum following Gehry's design. It was uncertain whether the design was even buildable until Gehry's use of CATIA—a specialized software package originally developed for the aerospace industry—presented the design in three dimensions, and the Basques confirmed they could build it.

> The complexity of the construction task, though even more difficult than anticipated, grows into a welcome challenge. It becomes a dare to be met in the Basque Country, which has a "culture of metal" … and "contractors who are proud of their work." (Stein 1997)

The complex process of construction did not require professional expertise from the United States, nor from elsewhere; a Basque engineering and construction company accomplished it, with Basque capital, engineers, architects, and workers. The company was IDOM, and it participated in the project meetings that occurred every six weeks during the design phase. IDOM designed the steel shell that provided the building's skeleton. They made an essential creative decision—to modify a stone mill machine to make it work with undulated metallic surfaces. Gehry himself has modestly acknowledged:

> I believe that the true miracle is not to design buildings, because I can have some talent and all; the miracle is to get them built. But I don't think people truly realize the revolution this building represents in the construction sector. (Gehry 1997)

Oxford Professor Bent Flyvbjerg has compared project efficiency between the Guggenheim Bilbao and Sydney Opera House (Flyvbjerg 2005). According to Flyvbjerg, the Bilbao project was very successful because Frank Gehry ensured that what he calls "the organization of the artist" prevailed during construction. The goal is to prevent political and business interests from interfering with design, "to arrive at an outcome as close as possible to the original design drawings." On the contrary, the organization of the artist was not implemented in Sydney, where political and business interests seized control of the construction process almost from the beginning. Flyvbjerg explains:

> By enforcing "the organization of the artist," by accurate budgeting and cost control, and by using advanced computing technology, Bilbao gained a building that works as an art museum, as a work of art in its own right, as a business, as a much-needed development vehicle for the Basque region, and as a source of inspiration for lovers of good architecture and good city and regional planning everywhere. Sydney, by doing the opposite on all counts, got an opera house unsuited for opera. The part of the building that Utzon got to finish—the outside—is as iconic, to be sure, as the museum in Bilbao. The shells in Sydney Harbor have placed Australia on the global map like nothing else. But given the costs involved—the destruction of the career and oeuvre of an undisputed master of 20th-century architecture—Sydney provides a lesson in what not to do. (Flyvbjerg 2005)

22.5 THE "GUGGENHEIM EFFECT" IN BILBAO

The Bilbao public's response to the museum in 1997 was overwhelming, according to a poll conducted by Bilbao newspaper El Correo during the first two days after inauguration in 1997. "Surprising," "magnificent," "impacting," and "expensive" were among the most common adjectives used by local visitors to describe the building (El Correo 1997). 4,502 people waited in line to enter the building on opening day. One visitor noted: "You need an open mind to acknowledge some of the things exhibited as works of art." Others thought it was expensive to pay 700 pesetas (US$5) to see the museum and its art collection. Visitors accustomed to attending art exhibits were uncomfortable with the continuous warnings from the museum's personnel about the appropriate distance to be kept while viewing the paintings. Long lines continue to be a common feature of the Guggenheim today.

Foreign visitors seemed to have a more positive opinion of the building than locals. According to the poll, 97% of Basque residents and 100% of foreign tourists thought positively about Gehry's building. However, only 54% of Basque respondents and 78% of foreign tourists believed that the works of art in the museum were "interesting." Most respondents said they would come back (El Correo 1997). Many among the public questioned the artistic value of the exhibited works and the cost of the museum, though they showed an appreciation for the building's design and its potential ability to project a positive image of the city. Regardless of personal taste and keen appreciation for the art exhibited in the museum, however, the fascinating impact of the building is almost instantaneous, as this author experienced in 1997 and thereafter. The temptation is to remain outside the museum, walk around, and admire the building as a gargantuan and magnificent sculpture. Once inside, the focus is on the "architecture of the jumping universe" (Jencks 1997)—the stunning, complex, and apparently chaotic mix of unexpected shapes and volumes in the building's unique rooms and galleries.

Critic J. E. Kaufman reflected on the Guggenheim's possible success:

> Will the Guggenheim Museum Bilbao prove a success? A 1992 study projected annual income of $14 million, about half from private sources, and annual attendance of more than a half a million, about half from the region and the rest from Spain and elsewhere. It estimated the economic impact to reach $35 million per year, generating $4 million in taxes. Critics doubt the validity of the projections, citing the region's underdeveloped art resources and audience, Spain's lack of a tradition of private support, and the city's poor tourist appeal. When the Guggenheim recently sent sample shows of twentieth-century art from its collection to venues in Bilbao (the SRGF received $1 million each for two shows), the surveys drew a total of barely 100,000 visitors, which may be an indication of the difficult road ahead. But the Basques are banking on the Gehry masterpiece and the prestigious Guggenheim name pulling in the crowds. In the management contract signed in 1994, they precluded the Guggenheim Foundation's opening any other museum in Europe without Basque consent, except an Austrian proposal which was pending at the time. (Kaufman 1997)

Kaufman's skepticism was justified. In the literature on IUMPs, most commentators argue that iconic megaprojects can effectively transform a city's image, but are often not financially feasible. A widely shared perception is that the Guggenheim Bilbao has refuted this major premise. However, an examination of the data reveals a more complex picture. A 1999 study by consulting firm KPMG Peat Marwick showed that 5,383,062 people visited the Bilbao Guggenheim from October 1997 to October 2002, and 83% of them (4,467,941 people) went to Bilbao exclusively to see the museum, or extended their stay in order to see it. Visitors spent around US$556 million in the five-year period, of which 35% was spent in restaurants, bars, and cafeterias, 26% was spent in local stores, 23% in hotels, and almost 6% in transportation. The study estimated the impact on the Basque economy to be worth US$445 million, suggested that approximately 4,000 jobs were directly or indirectly created or maintained, and noted that the Basque Treasury had collected about US$84 million in value-added taxes, corporate taxes, and income taxes (KPMG Peat Marwick 1999).

Beatriz Plaza, a Basque researcher, calculated the impact the Guggenheim was having in attracting tourism to the Basque Country (Plaza 2000). She stressed that tourism existed in Bilbao prior to the Guggenheim. Leisure tourism constituted 8% of the total tourist flows in 1996, whereas business travelers constituted 60% of the total. Plaza's intent was to find out how much *additional* tourism could be attributed to the museum following its opening in 1997. She argued that tourist growth in the Basque Country

> … may be a result of the worldwide growth in tourism, the favorable business cycle, the dynamism of the International Fair Center of Bilbao, the increasing attractiveness of San Sebastian (previously the main leisure tourism destination in the Basque Country), or even the cease-fire declared by ETA in September 1998, which ended in December 1999. We must delimit the Guggenheim Museum Bilbao effect. (Plaza 2000)

Plaza countered KPMG's results and offered significantly different figures. While KPMG argued that the museum had attracted 97,525 visitors in June and July 1998, Plaza's figure is just 35,655—a third of the KPMG estimation. According to her, the Guggenheim factor explained the arrival of 1,069,650 visitors in the period 1997–2002, rather than the 4,317,190 estimated by the consultants. Plaza showed that occupancy in top, luxury hotels had been considerably higher than occupancy in other hotels (85 vs. 46%) from 1997 to 2002. She interpreted these figures as an indication that business travel, rather than the Guggenheim, would explain a proportion of the growth in visitors to the city (Plaza 2000). Although this interpretation does not seem conclusive based on her data, the idea is accurate that the Guggenheim did not represent the beginnings of the hospitality industry in Bilbao.

Data from 2014 demonstrate the museum's recent contributions to the local economy. Visitors during that year totaled 1,011,363, with two thirds coming from outside Spain. Lowest attendance was in 2002 with 851,628 visitors, which was considered to be a good result following the terrorist attacks in New York and Washington on 11 September 2001. The year of highest attendance remains 1998, with 1,307,200 visitors (see Table 22.1). Museum officials estimated that the economic impact on the local economy during 2014

Table 22.1 Basque Country and Biscay GDP growth, and visitors to Guggenheim, Biscay, and Basque Country, 1992–2015

	GDP growth Basque Country[1]	GDP growth Biscay[2]	Visitors Basque Country[3]	Visitors Biscay[4]	Visitors Guggenheim[5]			Opening of iconic buildings
					Total	% from Spain[6]	% from abroad	
1992	6.4	7.0	858,173	316,199	N/A	N/A	N/A	
1993	3.4	3.5	862,410	296,354	N/A	N/A	N/A	
1994	7.3	6.9	968,551	323,211	N/A	N/A	N/A	
1995	8.3	7.4	1,018,011	331,484	N/A	N/A	N/A	
1996	6.9	6.3	1,054,322	355,279	N/A	N/A	N/A	
1997	7.2	6.8	1,129,720	391,703	259,234	89	11	Guggenheim Museum
1998	9.1	8.4	1,439,724	570,298	1,307,200	73	27	
1999	8.3	8.8	1,536,064	609,158	1,060,000	55	45	Euskalduna Convention Center
2000	8.0	8.3	1,515,621	590,677	975,000	54	46	
2001	5.3	5.4	1,432,869	553,071	930,000	52	48	Maritime Museum
2002	5.0	5.7	1,559,804	609,448	851,628	46	54	
2003	6.2	7.2	1,638,420	650,564	874,807	41	59	
2004	7.8	7.7	1,809,254	770,998	909,144	37	63	Zubiarte Shopping Mall

Year	[1]	[3]	[2]	[4]	[5]			
2005	7	1,887,260	7.9	843,102	965,082	40	60	
2006	7.1	2,076,958	6.6	971,239	1,008,774	40	60	
2007	6.7	2,164,130	6.9	1,036,225	1,002,963	33	67	
2008	1.8	2,088,183	2.4	1,002,484	951,369	34	66	
2009	-5.4	2,059,911	-4.4	987,238	905,048	40	60	
2010	1.9	2,314,552	2.8	1,098,041	956,417	38	62	Deusto Library, Basque Public University
2011	0.4	2,420,997	-0.2	1,179,323	962,358	38	62	Iberdrola Tower, Plaza Euskadi
2012	-2.0	2,420,107	-2.1	1,174,627	1,014,104	36	64	
2013	-1.1	2,368,080	-1	1,145,054	931,015	35	65	
2014	1.9	2,424,832	1.9	1,140,832	1,011,363	36	64	
2015	2.45[7]	N/A	2.35[7]	N/A	914,500[8]	35	65	

[1] Percent variation over previous year. (Source: Eustat.)
[2] Percent variation over previous year. (Source: Eustat.)
[3] Number of people staying in hotels. (Source: Eustat.)
[4] Number of people staying in hotels. (Source: Eustat.)
[5] Head count. (Source: Guggenheim Museum.)
[6] Including the Basque Country.
[7] Up to 30 June 2015.
[8] As of 15 October 2015.

was worth approximately US$330 million, including retail, hotels, leisure, transportation, and restaurants. The Guggenheim generated approximately US$50 million for the Basque treasury in taxes, and contributed to the direct and indirect creation or maintenance of 6,375 jobs (a probably optimistic figure). Visitors spent US$28.5 million (8.6% of the total) inside the museum (tickets, guided visits, store, and special events), US$255 million (68%) on accommodations and catering, US$46 million (14%) on shopping in retail businesses, US$44 million (13%) on leisure, and US$15.5 million (5%) on transportation (GMB 2014). These are good figures, but they represent only 0.85% of Metro Bilbao's GDP, which was around US$38.5 billion in 2014, and about 2.2% of the city's US$15 billion GDP the same year (GMM 2014). In sum, the museum does not contribute significantly to the urban economy, although it is a positive addition.

The museum compares well in financial terms to similar cultural institutions elsewhere. In the first years after its opening, the Guggenheim Bilbao self-financed at 75%, and the initial investment of US$100 million by the Basque government was quickly recouped. However, taken in a broader context it is not easy to see the "miracle" in economic terms that many have proclaimed. The only local presence of international capital is the firm that built the Zubiarte Shopping Mall in Abandoibarra, and the Sheraton chain, which built a hotel in the same area, only to sell it a few years later to the Spanish company Meliá after disappointing profits. The annual number of visitors has remained stable around 1 million, and the powerful magnet of the Guggenheim icon has influenced the increased number of visitors to other amenities in the Basque Country. However, no clear correlation can be established between the growth of the Basque tourist industry and the evolution of the Basque GDP (see Table 22.1).

Additional positive externalities of the museum need to be examined in terms of the consequences of image change for the Basque Country and Bilbao (the Basque administration has saved a large sum in free worldwide media exposure). Such consequences, however, are difficult to measure directly, even if eighteen years after the opening of the Guggenheim in 1997, the effects are patent. The media impact of the new museum allowed Basque officials to present Bilbao as a competitive metropolis of innovative ideas looking to the future, far beyond the cultural realm, and to transform the city into a global convention center. The museum's instant and worldwide media impact put Bilbao on the map; the sustained flow of convention delegates, tourists, gourmets, journalists, and others to the city in the past eighteen years has contributed to steadily fostering a positive change in the international image of the Basque capital.

22.6 The "Bilbao Effect" in the World

Sustained media attention keeps the museum and the city of Bilbao attached to multiple global discourses:

> While the material processes of Bilbao's revitalization plan make the space of flows visible insofar as they document the shift to a new economic model as well as the

construction of an infrastructure to support it, it is the press coverage of events in Bilbao that position Bilbao within an international flow of consciousness. (Raouen 2001)

The Bilbao effect transcended the discursive realm into the material world, since many officials in cities around the world considered it possible to effect local transformations similar to Bilbao's by simply building a Guggenheim Museum. The Guggenheim Foundation itself was able to openly advertise itself as a global art organization with a new, successful vision for the museum of the twenty-first century. The Foundation advertised this project in a 2002 exhibition entitled "The Global Guggenheim: Selections from the Extended Collection":

> With locations in New York, Venice, Bilbao, Berlin, and Las Vegas, the Solomon R. Guggenheim Foundation has come to define the concept of "global museum" … This concept of the "extended collection" is a logical progression from the museum's early history and subsequent development … From the beginning … the Guggenheim has placed great importance on reaching beyond local audiences in order to share its collection with a broader public … Under Krens's direction, the Guggenheim Museum Bilbao opened to wide acclaim in 1997. Since then, the New York museum has greatly benefited from this stunning architectural arena in which to bring its collection and special exhibitions to new European audiences … by forging worldwide alliances, the Guggenheim has redefined the parameters of acquisition and ownership previously inscribed in the concept of the museum collection … this approach has generated a cutting-edge program of special exhibitions, breathing new life into the contemporary concept of the museum by putting fashion, design, multimedia, and non-Western art into dialogue with key works in the traditional Modernist canon. (Alsdorf 2002)

Critic Paul Klebnikov explained Krens's explicit and forceful global approach to museum management after Bilbao:

> In 1988, when the then-42-year-old Krens came to the Guggenheim, the museum consisted of the famous Frank Lloyd Wright spiral on Fifth Avenue in Manhattan and a small subsidiary collection in Venice. Today the Guggenheim boasts a branch in New York's SoHo district, a gallery in Berlin and the wildly successful new museum in Bilbao, Spain. Construction is under way for two Guggenheim branches in Las Vegas, Nevada [already open in 2002, and closed again in 2003]. Approval has been given for another, bigger museum in Venice. Two museums in Brazil—in Rio de Janeiro and in an unspecified city in the northeast of the country—are undergoing feasibility studies. A global strategic partnership with Russia's venerable Hermitage may produce a Guggenheim on Palace Square in St. Petersburg. And now Krens has the approval of New York's mayor Rudolph Giuliani for a 700 million megamuseum in lower Manhattan, south of the Brooklyn Bridge [the plan was abandoned in the wake of 11 September 2001] … Krens ticks off the places he would like to install Guggenheims: "Two or three institutions in South America [including Brazil], East Asia, South Asia, the Middle East, Africa." (Klebnikov 2001)

Many urban officials contacted the Guggenheim Foundation with firm plans, though just a handful went beyond the initial conversations—Rio de Janeiro, Vilnius, Salzburg, Guadalajara, and Taichung—only to see negotiations end before reaching an agreement. The Foundation planned for a large Guggenheim museum on the waterfront in lower Manhattan, and it engaged Frank Gehry as the architect. His essentially complete designs for the building were showcased in 2001 at the Fifth Avenue museum, but these plans were disrupted by the economic downturn of the early 2000s and the 11 September 2001 attacks, which prompted reconsideration of any plans in New York. Two outposts of the Guggenheim opened in Berlin (1997–2012) and Las Vegas (2001–2008), but they did not achieve much success and had to close. Abu Dhabi and Helsinki have been successful contenders. The Guggenheim Abu Dhabi (designed by Frank Gehry) is expected to open in 2017, after several delays, and the Guggenheim Helsinki project unveiled the winning design in June 2015, following an international competition. Plans are completed or near completion for new cultural hubs centered on museums in Saudi Arabia (Mecca), Australia (Perth), Albania (Tirana), and Brazil (Belo Horizonte). What became Eastern Europe's largest museum—the Mystetskyi Arsenal, with 50,000 square metres (540,000 square feet) of exhibition space—opened fully in Kiev, Ukraine, in 2011.

The Bilbao effect was utilized to explain events whose causal relationship with the success of Gehry's building is not easy to prove. For instance, the success of the Bilbao museum has been credited with the increased wave of museum construction, extension, and reform in the United States in the past fifteen years. Critic L. A. Wilson argued that the museum in Bilbao "was widely credited with having sparked an economic boom in northern [sic] Spain" (Wilson 2001), which other cities aimed to replicate. She quoted architecture critic Robert A. Ivy, editor-in-chief of Architectural Record, who proclaimed that "Gehry's Bilbao has conflated cultural, economic, and political interests, alerting all to what a dazzling object in the cityscape can accomplish" (Ivy 2001). The Guggenheim building in the Basque capital was also perceived as the beginning of a new era in which museums are thought of as monumental sculptures, potentially becoming the most important work in an institution's collection. Museum plans developed all over the United States, including New York (a new Guggenheim by Gehry and the Whitney extension by Rem Koolhaas), Philadelphia by Tadao Ando, Hartford (Connecticut), Boston, Bellevue (Washington), San Francisco, Denver, Saint Louis, Milwaukee, Cincinnati, Savannah, Kansas City, Atlanta, Austin, and Charlotte (North Carolina). The mayor of Denver was quoted as predicting that the jumble of metal-clad, faceted geometric forms that made up architect Daniel Liebeskind's design (open in 2006) would "put us on the map as a world-class destination city" (Webb 2001)—a still unrealized wish.

Two examples illustrate the interest sparked worldwide. In 2002, Taichung, a Taiwanese city, invited Thomas Krens to consider a future Guggenheim there, after the museum's overtures to other Asian cities such as Tokyo, Hong Kong, and Singapore had failed. The mayor of Taichung drew frequent comparisons to Bilbao and hoped that a local branch of the Guggenheim would help revitalize the local economy. The local press noted Krens' comments that smaller cities often stood a better chance of winning bigger projects due to available incentives and resources, while larger cities often had their investments and plans already set. However, the Guggenheim Director added that a big project such as a new museum "would have to surmount a daunting number of non-artistic hurdles, including adequate financial backing" (Krens 2002). A group of local officials, scholars, and architects had prepared a detailed proposal for Krens, who remained uncommitted. Following Krens' movements closely, the press noted with disappointment that "the director reportedly skipped planned meetings with Taichung city councilors and a group of Taipei architects, opting to visit the National Palace Museum in Taipei instead" (Habecker 2002).

Geelong—the capital of the province of Victoria, Australia, about 50 miles southwest of Melbourne—also made a bid for a Guggenheim branch. Predictably, the potential impact of the yet-to-be-built museum was compared to Sydney Opera House, despite no draft design of it. A local reporter stated that "while critics abound, the announcement of a pre-feasibility study this evening shows that Geelong is serious about chasing its dream to establish a Guggenheim museum" (Bunworth 2002). He interviewed the chairman of the Guggenheim bid, for whom inspiration came from Bilbao, "once considered a dying rustbelt town with no prospects of rejuvenation" (Cousins 2002). The article gathered opinions from other prominent local residents who had joined the bidding effort. The group, including professors and scholars, believed that a Guggenheim museum would be "a big blockbuster business" for Geelong. According to a professor from the Royal Melbourne Institute of Technology, the city ought to be "constructing these buildings by famous architects, having big shows, moving around the world between them, and [we would get] large numbers of people through the doors" (van Schiak 2002). Acknowledging that Bilbao may be different from Geelong, he continued: "Within an hour's flying time of Bilbao you have many millions of people. Within a couple of hours flying time you have over 100 million people. You've also got Bilbao well on the routes, the tourist routes" (van Schiak 2002). However, they remained confident, asserting that "the only way we would be out trumped now is if someone came along with US$200 million and said, 'here you are, let's go'" (Cousins 2002). In September 2002, Geelong's bid seemed to intensify, with local plans to commission an extensive feasibility study practically approved (Bunworth 2002). Not too surprisingly, thirteen years later the Geelong project has yet to materialize.

The Bilbao effect became commonplace in academic circles. Some used it to illustrate larger philosophical points. Leading American architect Peter Eisenman, a former Professor at The Cooper Union for the Advancement of Science and Art in Manhattan, used the Bilbao effect as a confirmation of his aesthetic viewpoint. According to Eisenman, people have forgotten how to experience and appreciate the present in the contemporary media-mediated society: "The 'Bilbao effect' has reminded people that architecture has the potential to elicit unchoreographed responses that reconnect the mind, the body, and the eye. That is the role architecture traditionally played" (Eisenman 1999). He declared that architects should aim at capturing the "energy of the moment" in their designs: "It's not the style of a building or the place where it's located that matters. What matters is that there are moments in time which can live in the present, carried through literature, through art, through film and also through architecture" (Eisenman 1999).

22.7 The Fading Away of
the Bilbao Effect?

> The truth is, the Bilbao effect is largely a myth. Frank Gehry's museum alone didn't turn around that city. It capped decades of civic renewal. Flashy, even brilliant buildings rarely rejuvenate neighborhoods or guarantee crowds and cash just by virtue of their design [...] Sadly, museums, like cities, have squandered fortunes praying to this false idol. They still do. (Kimmelman 2012)

The example of the new Ordos Art Museum in Inner Mongolia—beautifully designed by MAD, a prestigious firm of Beijing architects—suggests (not too surprisingly) that just building a terrific museum is not enough to ensure success. The city of Ordos has sprung up fast and is relatively wealthy, thanks to discoveries of oil and gas, but the museum has no collections and precious few plans for exhibitions. No wonder it is devoid of visitors.

The Guggenheim in Abu Dhabi, scheduled to open in 2017, will be twice the size of the museum in Bilbao, and twelve times the size of the Frank Lloyd Wright Guggenheim in New York. Carol Vogel in *The New York Times* refers to this Gehry design as "a graceful tumble of giant plaster building blocks and translucent blue cones" (Vogel 2014). The outcome of the Guggenheim Helsinki's international competition was known in June 2015, with the winning project going to the Paris-based firm Moreau Kusunoki Architectes. Even before actual construction, these two projects have attracted significant criticism; the projects could be questioned along three main lines: (1) iconic architecture is no longer the hegemonic visual discourse in urban revitalization; (2) the franchise model imposed by the Guggenheim means that local officials have no autonomy to make major decisions on matters from exhibition calendars, to budgets and investments; and (3) local cultural identities are usually neglected under a foreign global arts model. In addition, the environmental impacts of the projects may not be negligible. The Abu Dhabi project has also been controversial around issues of workers's rights and labor conditions. In spite of mounting criticism, if the new Guggenheim Museums in Finland and the United Arab Emirates result in even half the impact of that of Bilbao's, the term *Bilbao effect* will continue to carry weight on both sides of the debate.

The Bilbao effect faced significant criticism and skepticism among numerous architecture and art connoisseurs. *Chicago Tribune* critic Blair Kamin (2002) noted that the rise of "starchitects" poses a broad set of questions about the impact of globalization on an art that is ultimately local:

> Should 15 or 20 starchitects be designing all the world's great buildings? What does it mean if every city has its Gehry, its Koolhaas, its Calatrava? Are the backers of these buildings simply seeking known commodities rather than taking genuine artistic

risks? Can the stars tailor their style to a vast, cross-cultural array of functions and places? (Kamin 2002)

The critic located the beginning of the trend in the 1976 Houston Pennzoil Place, dubbed by the residents "the milk cartoons." He noted that the fashion spread to other cities such as Chicago in the 1980s, where architects were put in charge to

> design eye-catching creations that would enhance a building's marketability […] There is something […] to be gleaned from starchitects, but only if they are willing to look deeply at [a city] and to adapt their work to the city's essence and its economics. (Kamin 2002)

Architectural critic Witold Rybczynski asked whether the cities commissioning new museums by starchitects can become the next Bilbao in terms of visitors. He noted that attendance at the Experience Music Project in Seattle, designed by Frank Gehry for Paul Allen in 1996, decreased by a third eighteen months after the museum opened, while the number of visitors to the local art museum increased by more than a third during the same period. Recently, a portion of the building was converted into a science-fiction museum. Despite its unusual architecture, consisting of colorful, rounded forms said to be inspired by electric guitars, the museum of rock music and Jimi Hendrix memorabilia, the Experience Music Project has not proven to be a success. Rybczynski was "skeptical that designing in the full glare of public competitions encourages architects to produce better buildings. The charged atmosphere promotes flamboyance rather than careful thought, and favors the glib and obvious over the subtle and nuanced" (Rybczynski 2002).

> The Pulitzer Foundation for the Arts [designed in Saint Louis by Japanese architect Tadao Ando, opened in 2001, and defined by its promoters as the "unmuseum"] is a small building that was not meant to attract a vast public. Yet it would be nice to think that the building signals at least an alternative, if not an end, to the Bilbao effect. The chief aim of architecture should not be to entertain, titillate, or shock viewers. After the third example of swirling titanium and colliding prisms, the effect begins to wear thin. Le Corbusier understood this, which is why he did not repeat the sculptural effects of Ronchamp in other buildings. Once was enough … The "wow" factor may excite the visitor and the journalist, but it is a shaky foundation on which to build lasting value. (Rybczynski 2002)

More recently, Rybczynski (2008) has argued that "perhaps the Bilbao effect should be called the Bilbao anomaly," since "the iconic chemistry between the design of a building, its image and the public turns out to be quite rare, and somewhat mysterious."

> Herzog & de Meuron's design for Beijing's Olympic Stadium is ingenious, for example, but instead of the complex engineering, it was the widely perceived image of a "bird's nest," a nickname that did not originate with the architects, that cemented the

building's international iconic status. The woven steel wrapper seemed to symbolize both China's ancient traditions and its rush to modernization. However, for every bird's nest there are scores of building failures that are not only costly, but fail to spark the public's imagination. Failed icons do not disappear though, which is indeed problematic. Since the Bilbao effect mistakenly teaches that unconventional architecture is a prerequisite for iconic status, clients have encouraged their architects to go to greater lengths to design buildings that are unusual, surprising and even shocking. The shock, however, will inevitably wear off, and 100 years from now most aspiring iconic constructions will resemble a cross between a theme park and the Las Vegas strip. (Rybczynski 2008)

Despite the media success of the Bilbao Guggenheim, the Bilbao effect has proven to be difficult to replicate in most places, even for Frank Gehry. On the other hand, some architectural icons, such as Gehry's Stata Center at MIT, work well with no Bilbao effect; most MIT scientists working in the building praise its playful and inventive feel (Campbell 2007). Cooper Union alumnus Daniel Libeskind's jagged edges, sharp angles, and complex geometries (the extension to the Denver Art Museum, the Royal Ontario Museum in Toronto, or the Danish Jewish Museum in Copenhagen) have not had the universal acclaim of his Jewish Museum Berlin—an illustration that success, impact, and visitor attraction are not necessarily a function of a building's spectacular design. Many works by Shigeru Ban or Tadao Ando are excellent examples of highly admired and successful architecture in the antipodes of iconic buildings designed to stun.

The jury is still out in 2017 regarding Gehry's highly anticipated Guggenheim Abu Dhabi and the massive West Kowloon Cultural District (WKCD) in Hong Kong, which stand among the most prominent cultural megaprojects in recent years. The WKCD is a project of such scale and ambition that it could "define the nature of the public realm in the 21st century," according to a rather hyperbolic statement by Rem Koolhaas (2013). The WKCD has met significant criticism from the planning to the sconstruction phases. Although a Guggenheim is not part of the project, the WKCD replicates all the expected controversies associated with IUMPs, including cost overruns, negative environmental impacts, gentrification risks, drawbacks of top-down cultural engineering, neglect of local cultural identities, and uncertain economic success (del Cerro Santamaria et al. 2013). None of these externalities bode well for cities that are counting on instant icons to salvage them during times of economic malaise.

22.8 CONCLUSIONS

UMPs often rely on iconic architecture to succeed. Iconic UMPs (IUMPs) have come to play a central role in the standard urban policies designed to gain global visibility and attract visitors and investments to cities. Widely considered a successful case of image reconstruction via iconic architecture, however, the Guggenheim Bilbao presents lights and shadows when the focus of the analysis is on economic and cultural impacts. The Guggenheim Bilbao triggered an immediate and lasting worldwide interest among tourists, artistic circles, the architectural profession, journalists, and the educated public, based on the iconic architectural style of the building, as well as local, contextual, economic, and political conditions. Far from being the trigger for, and prime mover of, revitalization, the museum postdated it. Up to now it has not generated substantial foreign investment in the Basque city, nor significant positive outcomes in the job market.

Bilbao's economic performance after the opening of the Guggenheim broadly follows the ups and downs of economic cycles, a clear indication of both the embeddedness of cities—and IUMPs—in multiple scales of socioeconomic action and the limited power of architectural icons to explain urban economic change. In the hypothetical case in which the star of the Bilbao Guggenheim begins to dim and visitors cease to arrive in Bilbao in large numbers, the consequences for the Basque city would not amount to significant economic decline, as the museum represents just 2.2% of the Bilbao economy. Cities are complex formations, and a spectacular building alone, even if projected by experts and the media on a worldwide scale, is not usually capable of shifting their fortunes in fundamental ways.

In addition, urban leaders, managers, and entrepreneurs in cities worldwide ought to remember that it was not the local government but the regional Basque government that backed a Guggenheim Foundation in financial trouble, with substantial resources of its own and with complete discretion to make decisions about the use of their funds. Furthermore, not every city is well positioned to be "put on the map"—especially second- or third-tier cities that are comparable to Bilbao in terms of size but are located off main routes and flows of people and commerce. Bilbao is located in one of the top three tourist destinations in the world (Spain), which has been a factor in the museum's spectacular ability to attract visitors. Spain receives about 65 million visitors annually, of which approximately 2.5 million tour the Basque Country, with around 1 million visiting the Guggenheim Museum in Bilbao.

The visual appeal and media success of Frank Gehry's building strengthened the leverage of the Guggenheim Foundation, which after Bilbao negotiated only in places with obvious locational and financial advantages. Such advantages are more common in larger, first-tier cities that are already on the map and therefore less interested in getting a Guggenheim. The Foundation had its share of failures, but even when agreements materialize, as they did in Abu Dhabi and Helsinki, it is not certain that tourists will visit those cities in annual numbers equivalent to the population of their metropolitan areas, as in the case of Bilbao. Institutional contexts, specific policy instruments, and territorially grounded social dynamics give rise to distinct patterns of IUMP development and help explain the degree to which IUMP succeed or fail.

To be sure, cities should not expect to be able to replicate the success of Bilbao just by implementing fashionable urban policy and global media discourses. Each city has a local history, a region within which it develops, and a specific political make-up that influences local decision-making processes. Cities and regions around the world partially adhere to their own specific logic of development. Each city shows particular features that contribute to explaining decline, and each may need localized strategies for redevelopment. Applying the standard elements in the revitalization mix, including IUMPs, to cities around the world may be unavoidable owing to rapid and acritical adoption of policy discourses from center to periphery. However, expecting to replicate a city's success by merely adopting such strategy often is a recipe for disappointment.

Overall, the place of Bilbao on the world stage has irreversibly changed after the Guggenheim, which unequivocally shows the power of IUMPs to transform a city's image in times of globalization. Moreover, the worldwide media impact of the Guggenheim Bilbao represented a turning point that significantly enhanced the debate about commodification, commercialization, and replicability of IUMPs in large-scale redevelopment schemes. As a result, the post-Bilbao dramatic increase in the interest by urban elites to surrender to the promise—and discontents—of IUMPs has become one of the keys to explaining prominent aspects in the deployment of contemporary globalized urbanization. In this context, the traditionally overlooked synergies between research-based evidence, management, and governance of IUMPs in globalizing cities ought to become a priority area for urban and regional policy makers to address.

References

Alsdorf, B. (2002). "The Global Guggenheim: Selections from the Extended Collection," <https://www.guggenheim.org/exhibition/the-global-guggenheim-selections-from-the-extended-collection>.

Bell, J. (1998). "Architecture with a twist," *The World and I*, July.

Bunworth, M. (2002). "Geelong dreams of a Guggenheim gallery," ABC Online, 22 April, <http://www.abc.net.au/7.30/content/2002/s537640.htm>.

Campbell, R. (2007), "Does Gehry's Stata Center really work?" *Bloomberg Business*, 19 June, <http://www.bloomberg.com/bw/stories/2007-06-19/does-gehrys-stata-center-really-work-businessweek-business-news-stock-market-and-financial-advice>.

Cousins, J. (2002). "Geelong dreams of a Guggenheim gallery," ABC Online, 22 April, quoted in N. Bunworth, <http://www.abc.net.au/7.30/content/2002/s537640.htm>.

del Cerro Santamaria, G. (2007). *Bilbao: Basque Pathways to Globalization*. London: Elsevier.

del Cerro Santamaria, G. et al. (ed.). (2013). *Urban Megaprojects: A Worldwide View*. London: Emerald.

Eisenman, P. (1999). Quoted by Diane Manuel in Stanford News Service, October, <http://news.stanford.edu/pr/99/991006preslec.html>.

El Correo. (1997). Guggenheim Museo Bilbao, November, <http://servicios.elcorreo.com/guggenheim/museo/mu.htm>.

Flyvbjerg, B. (2005). "Design by deception: The politics of megaproject approval," *Harvard Design Magazine*, no. 22, Spring/Summer, pp. 50–9.

Friedmann, M. (2010). Quoted in M. Tyrnauer, "Architecture in the age of Gehry," *Vanity Fair*, <http://www.vanityfair.com/culture/2010/08/architecture-survey-201008>

Gehry, F. (1997). Quoted in C. Caicoya, "From project to construction," *Arquitectura Viva* 55: VII–VIII.

Gehry, F. (2001). Quoted in J. Zulaika, "Tough beauty: Bilbao as ruin, architecture and alle-gory," J. R. Resina (ed.), Iberian Cities. New York and London: Routledge.

Gehry, F. (2010). Quoted in M. Tyrnauer, "Architecture in the age of Gehry," Vanity Fair, <http://www.vanityfair.com/culture/2010/08/architecture-survey-201008>.

Giovannini, J. (2001)."The Bilbao effect," Red Herring, 12 February, <http://georgemaciunas. com/exhibitions/fluxus-as-architecture-2/fluxhousefluxcity-prefabricatedmodular-build-ing-system/fluxhouse-fluxcities/articles/red-herring-magazine-the-bilbao-effect-by-joseph-giovannini/>.

GMB (Guggenheim Museum Bilbao). (2014). Estudio del Impacto Económico generado por la actividad del Museo Guggenheim Bilbao, internal report.

GMM (Global Metro Monitor). (2014). Brookings Institution, <http://www.brookings.edu/ research/reports2/2015/01/22-global-metro-monitor>.

Goldberger, P. (1997). "The politics of building," The New Yorker, 13 October, 73 (31): 48–53.

Habecker, W. (2002). "Museum official says Taichung has long way to go," Taipei Times, 6 June, <http://www.taipeitimes.com/News/biz/archives/2002/06/06/0000139235>.

Hall, P. (2001). "Global city-regions in the twenty-first century," in A. Scott (ed.), Global City-Regions: Trends Theory, Policy. Oxford: Oxford University Press.

Harvey, D. (1989). "From managerialism to entrepreneurialism: The transformation in urban governance in late capitalism," Geografiska Annaler, B 71: 3–17.

Ivy, R. (2001). Quoted in A, Wilson Lloyd (2001), "Architecture for art's sake," Atlantic Monthly 287: 85–8.

Jencks, C. (1997). The Architecture of the Jumping Universe: A Polemic: How Complexity Science is Changing Architecture and Culture. New York: Academy Press.

Jodidio, P. (2001). "Un nouvel imperialisme?" Connaisance des Arts, 545: 7.

Kamin, B. (2002). "How stellar are 'starchitects'?" Chicago Tribune, 27 January, <http://articles. chicagotribune.com/2002-01-27/news/0201270415_1_new-dorm-starchitects-new-york-city-designer>.

Klebnikov, A. (2001). Museums Inc. Forbes, 8 January.

Kimmelman, M. (2012)."Why is this museum shaped like a tub?" The New York Times, Art and Design Section, 23 December, <http://www.nytimes.com/2012/12/24/arts/design/amster-dams-new-stedelijk-museum.html?_r=0>.

Koolhaas, R. (2013). Quoted in E. Dunham-Jones, "The irrational exuberance of Rem Koolhaas," Places Journal, April, <https://placesjournal.org/article/the-irrational-exuberance-of-rem-koolhaas/>.

KPMG Peat Marwick. (1998). Estudio de impacto economico del Museo Guggenheim Bilbao, report.

Krens, T. (2002). Quoted in W. Habecker (2002), "Museum official says Taichung has long way to go," Taipei Times, 6 June.

Krens, T. (2010). Quoted in M. Tyrnauer, "Architecture in the age of Gehry," Vanity Fair.

Merkel, J. (2002). "The museum as artifact," The Wilson Quarterly, 26 (1): 66–79.

Newhouse, V. (1998). Towards a New Museum. New York: Monacelli Press.

Plaza, B. (2000). "Evaluating the influence of a large cultural artifact in the attraction of tour-ism: The Guggenheim Museum Bilbao case," Urban Affairs Review, 36(2): 264–74.

Pops, M. (2000). "Gehry's Guggenheim in Bilbao," Salmagundi, 124/125: 17–49.

Raouen, M. (2001). "Reflections on the space of flows: The Guggenheim Museum Bilbao," Journal of Arts Management, Law and Society, 30 (4): 283–300.

Rybczynski, W. (2002). "The Bilbao effect," Atlantic Monthly, 290(2): 138–42.

Rybczynski, W. (2008). "When buildings try too hard," *Wall Street Journal*, 22 November, <http://www.wsj.com/articles/SB122731149503149341>.

Stein, K. (1997). "Guggenheim Museum Bilbao," *Architectural Record*, October: 77–8.

van Schiak, L. (2002). Quoted in M. Bunworth (2002), "Geelong dreams of a Guggenheim gallery," ABC Online, 22 April.

Vidler, A. (2002). Dean and Professor of Architecture, The Cooper Union for the Advancement of Science and Art, New York. Personal communication, October.

Vogel, C. (2014). "A new art capital, finding its own voice: Inside Frank Gehry's Guggenheim Abu Dhabi, *The New York Times*, 4 December, <http://www.nytimes.com/2014/12/07/arts/design/inside-frank-gehrys-guggenheim-abu-dhabi.html?_r=0>.

Webb, W. (2001). Quoted in A. Wilson Lloyd, "Architecture for art's sake," *Atlantic Monthly*, 287: 85–8.

CHAPTER 23

....

PRIVATE PROVISION OF PUBLIC SERVICES

The Case of Australia's Motorways

....

DEMI CHUNG

23.1 BACKGROUND: THE PUBLIC–PRIVATE PARTNERSHIP PROCUREMENT METHOD

PUBLIC–PRIVATE partnerships (PPPs)[1] have increasingly become a popular procurement method of deploying private provision in delivering public services. They involve the private sector providing infrastructure-based services that have been historically regarded as the responsibility of government (Broadbent and Laughlin 2004: 4). The partnership concept differs from other forms of private provision such as contracting out and privatization in the dimensions of risks and rewards sharing and the greater private involvement in finance arrangements (Hodge 2005). The relationships within a PPP are established by a concession contract which enables a commercial organization to design, build, finance and operate an asset for an agreed period; hence they are also known as DBFOs.[2] The principal rationale is that PPPs facilitate risk transfer to the party that has the greatest capacity to manage that risk (Partnership Victoria 2000; HM Treasury 2006; WWG 2006).

In the DBFO framework the private sector is contracted to supply a bundled product that comprises two distinct elements: the creation of an asset and the whole-of-life asset management (WWG 2006: 8). The public sector, on the other hand, purchases a service instead of an asset, with predefined payment levels, which are payable only when the service meets required standards (Debande 2002: 359). The payment mechanism is linked to the requirements set out in the output specification and the results of the risk assessment (Akbiyikli et al. 2006: 72), and is embedded with the conditions of penalizing poor performance (English and Baxter 2008). The objectives of the payment structure are to provide private proponents with a number of incentives to deliver value for money. Since the recoupment of costs and future profit rely on a flow of suitable quality services from the asset, PPPs encourage the private proponent to build the required asset on cost, and to use efficient technology (Debande 2002: 360). Further, the revenue receipts flow to the private operator only when the construction of the asset has been completed and the service is fully operational, thus it also motivates the private consortium to finish the construction element sooner. Evidence suggests that the PPP contractual mechanism has better facilitated the integration between the asset creation and its ongoing management compared with contracts delivered under the traditional procurement method (NAO 2003).

The role that the private sector plays in the second element of this bundled product varies between social infrastructure projects and economic infrastructure projects. Social infrastructure projects, such as hospitals, schools, and prisons, where government retains demand risk (NSW Treasury 2007: 1) are normally funded from state revenue (English and Guthrie 2003: 503). Service purchase payments include a direct government subsidization to the private sector partner for the availability of the facility (English 2005a), and a revenue stream directly pays for service provision (English 2006).

In economic infrastructure projects such as motorways, the private sector is usually contracted to bear the market risk, and they are funded by user charges (English and Guthrie 2003: 503) rather than from consolidated funds.[3] In these capital-intensive projects, the creation of assets is likely to dominate. In DBFO roads, after the construction is complete, the provision of the associated service (for example, toll collection, roadwork, and lighting maintenance) is a relatively minor component of the arrangement (Walker 2005). The public sector's involvement is limited to monitoring adherence to the contract, and renegotiation of changes to services supplied (Debande 2002: 367) or other contractual elements such as financing (VAGO 2007). In exchange, the private operator negotiates a concession right with the government for a period that warrants an agreed rate of return to private equity (Arndt 1998; English 2005b; Glaister et al. 2000). In addition to financial contributions, governments can exercise their regulatory power to underwrite direct and indirect financial returns to private investment through a number of variables inherent in the toll model, such as the concession term, toll escalation options, and traffic demand management measures (Chung 2009).

In some cases the economic PPP model offers the private proponent substantial financial and non-financial values in various forms: (i) government guarantees of borrowing or government loan, (ii) the right to charge motorists, (iii) the right to negotiate for term variations and toll variations, and (iv) the right to negotiate with government to change existing traffic arrangements (such as road closures or to construct a new ramp diverting traffic to the DBFO road) or to influence future infrastructure planning. Recent developments reveal that these concessions also deliver substantial financial values to government in different forms, such as receipts of concession fees: for example, Sydney's M2 and Melbourne CityLink; up-front receipts of Business Consideration Fees, such as Sydney's Cross City Tunnel and Lance Cove Tunnel; no net cost to government, such as Cross City Tunnel; no ongoing government contributions in return for the ownership of some sections of a new road, such as Melbourne EastLink (VAGO 2005: 191, 193).

Motorways have been one of the most active economic PPP markets in Australia. Over the years, PPP motorways have evolved to a stage where greater benefit is being delivered to the public sector. Brown (2005: 437) succinctly describes the status quo of the Australian market of private motorways:

> The structure of early toll road agreements seemed to be tilted in favour of the private sector, with the existence of [material adverse events] clauses and the ability to significantly delay rent payments to the government. In more recent examples the private sector assumes more of the downside traffic risk while the government shares in excess toll revenue.

New South Wales (NSW) is an Australian state that shows the strongest preference for PPP schemes in motorways, both in terms of number and the financial sums involved. Projects include the Sydney Harbour Tunnel (SHT), the Eastern Distributor (ED), the Hills M2 Motorway (M2), the M4 Motorway (M4), the M5 South-West Motorway (M5), the Westlink M7 (M7), the Cross City Tunnel (CCT), and the Lane Cove Tunnel (LCT). Projects developed in the other states of Australia include the North–South Bypass Tunnel in the State of Queensland, Melbourne CityLink (MCL), EastLink and Peninsula Link in the State of Victoria.

It has been more than two decades since the first private motorway in Australia—the SHT—was open to traffic, yet no comprehensive evaluation of PPPs in the road transport sector has been sighted. It is the intention of this chapter to fill this gap. This study evaluates the extent to which the rationale of risk allocation—that is, risk is transferred to the party that is best capable of managing it—has facilitated the delivery of value for money through private provision.

In the next section, the chapter will unfold the evolution of PPPs in road transport and present a number of cases in Australia. The final section (23.3) concludes the chapter and offers suggestions for future research.

23.2 RISK ALLOCATION AND PERFORMANCE OF DBFO TOLLWAYS: CASE STUDIES

Risk transfer to concessionaires had been absent in early DBFO motorways. Some early experiments, such as the SHT and the M2, are indeed risk-free investments to private proponents. More recent projects experienced a substantial reduction in the scale of the guarantees provided. Yet there still exist implicit promises to protect the private sector against downward demand risk and to warrant return on private equity.

In many instances, risks of design and construction have been satisfactorily transferred to the private sector (Mills 1991; VAGO 1996a; Arndt 1998; NAO 2003). In particular, road projects that involve the highest proportion of construction component compared with operation and maintenance (O&M) costs generate the greatest VFM (Debande 2002). However, the haziness as to who should be the bearer of the remaining risks makes it difficult to disentangle the lines of responsibility. PPPs have also given rise to a host of new dimensions of risks regarding public accountability, governance, and reputation. The remainder of the section presents a number of case studies to analyze the evolution of risk-sharing arrangements in DBFO motorways. Contractual and financial details of these cases are summarized in Appendix A (Table 23.1).

23.2.1 Sydney Harbour Tunnel (Contract Executed in 1987)

This contract was entered into by the Department of Main Roads NSW (the DMR) with the Sydney Harbour Tunnel Company (SHTC). One of the project criteria was that the tunnel to be financed, constructed, and operated "as a private venture facilitated by a lease of public property for a fixed period" (NSWAGO 1994: 250).

The central financing instruments were the AU$223 million interest-free loan (the Net Bridge Revenue Loan) provided by the DMR (NSWAGO 2003: 217) and the AU$497 million thirty-year inflation-indexed bonds issued to the market by the SHTC (NSWAGO 1994: 263). Interest forgone on the state loan was estimated at a minimum to be AU$1,150 million (1994 dollars) (NSWAGO 1994: 251). The repayment of the RTA's loan is due in 2022 and is subordinated to all other obligations of the SHTC (NSWAGO 2003: 217). The continuously declining toll collections and rising operational expenses have impinged on the company's ability to repay the authority. The DMR has underwritten the principal outstanding on the bonds for a price of AU$3.5 million, irrespective of the actual usage of the tunnel (NSWAGO 1994: 251; Arndt 1998: 22). The net present value of this underwriting liability was estimated at AU$345 million as of 30 June 2006 (NSWAGO 2006b: 128).

Few DBFO projects did not transfer risk of cost overruns on construction, but SHT is a prime example. The entire toll revenue of both the Sydney Harbour Bridge and the Tunnel were used to support the tunnel's construction (Mills 1991: 282). Possible delay in tunnel opening would not defer revenue flowing to the SHTC, because revenue was guaranteed to the company starting from a fixed date—10 October 1992—irrespective of whether the tunnel was in use by that time (SHTA 1987: Schedule 5). Not only did the state government contribute to the cost of construction; it has also underwritten the revenue stream[4] for the SHTC. The Ensured Revenue Stream (ERS) obligates the government to top up these payments in the event that actual toll receipts fall below the predetermined level, as it has agreed to make payments to "enable the operator to meet financial obligations in connection with the operation of the Tunnel and the payment of principal and interest upon moneys borrowed by it for the design, construction and operation of the Tunnel" (SHTA 1987: Schedule 5). As a result of the continuously widening gap between toll collections and operating expenses incurred by SHTC, the ERS paid by the authority has amounted to AU$176.7 million (nominal value) for the four-year period 2004–2007 (NSWAGO 2007).

One of the adverse effects of government guarantee was that it offset the benefits of packaging the construction and O&M of the asset into one bundle. The concessionaire had few incentives to perform efficiently in the post-construction phase because risk of O&M, such as road conditions and slow clearance of vehicle breakdowns, did not constitute a threat to SHTC's cash flows, as revenues are independent of tunnel toll receipts. The absence of performance-based payment incentivized the company to minimize the level of expenditure on maintaining the tunnel's condition (Mills 1991: 287).

The financial package offered by the NSW government was rated as "unusually attractive" by international investors (Tiong 1995). The project expected a real IRR of 15.75% per annum (NSWAGO 1994: 263). The private equity investors only contributed AU$7 million—equivalent to 1% of the project's value (Mills 1991). The government-underwritten bonds had a maturity longer than the usual maturity of 10–20 years in the Australian capital market (Tiong 1995: 187); meanwhile, the risk-free inflation-indexed yield to private investors was as high as 6.8% (NSWAGO 1994: 263). The 6.8% estimate on the risk-free return does not include the state's liability to cover the private proponent's tax payable to the Australian Taxation Office (ATO). In 2003, a AU$24-million liability was added to the state's bill (NSWAGO 2003: 209). The liability covers SHTC's past and future taxes as the result of DMR's failure to successfully negotiate with the ATO for an allowance for the depreciation deduction by the SHTC.

In an "extraordinary" finding, the state audit office discovered that the whole contract had been packaged to fulfill a concealed strategic objective (NSWAGO 1994). At the time the contract was negotiated, state governments were subject to the "global limits" of borrowing set by the loan council.[5] The private firm SHTC was in substance a financing vehicle through which the DMR was able to remove the *visible* risk of "overborrowing" from its balance sheet:

> The arrangements were consistent with intentions to avoid Loan Council restrictions and they suggest the Authority did not wish these arrangements to be known to Members of Parliament and the public which ultimately bore the risks by the Authority. (NSWAGO 1994: 293)

The lesson learnt from the SHT seemed to have exerted some influence in later developments. Subsequent DBFO motorways, such as the M2 and the ED, have set financial rewards that were commensurate with traffic volume risk.

23.2.2 M2 Motorway (Contract Executed in 1994)

The M2 set a precedent in the Australian privately financed motorway market. The contract demanded a land rent[6] payable by the concessionaire for the right to levy tolls. The amount represents the value of the right perceived by the market. The present value of this rent payable was estimated at AU$1.1 million in 1995 (NSWAGO 1995: 13). It is questionable that this value is realizable, since it was agreed by both contracting parties that cash payments would not commence until 2028 (NSWAGO 1995: 86), or may not commence at all during the entire length of the concession if returns to private equity fall short of an agreed threshold return.

The M2 project contains several favorable features for the private proponent, such as a safe return in a highly risky investment that is enabled by rent payment deferrals, free use of land owned by the Road and Traffic Authority (the RTA), indemnity from the RTA against any future increases in cost, and an exemption from state land tax. It is, however, a marginal improvement over the SHT, as the private operator has no recourse to the state when toll revenue falls below projections.

The Hills Motorway Limited (Hills)[7] was chosen as the finalist on the basis that the proponent was the only one offering to undertake the project "without any requirement for RTA's *direct* financial contribution or any RTA underwriting" (NSWAGO 1995: 49; emphasis added). Generous terms were offered to Hills to ensure that this criterion was adhered to. The concession is of forty-five years length, after which the ownership of the motorway transfers to the government at no cost. It can be ended as early as thirty-six years if the motorway returns private investors a post-tax annual benefit of 16.5% (NSWAGO 1995: 22). At financial close, the annual pre-tax cash return to equity was estimated at 18.5% per annum vis-à-vis 6%[8] return to the RTA (NSWAGO 1995: 12).

The value of rent payable by the Hills was equivalent to AU$887.4 million (in nominal dollars; see NSWAGO 1995: 86). Until the project has realized a real post-tax return of 12.25% per annum, Hills has the discretion to pay rent in either cash or non-interest-bearing promissory notes which are subordinated to all other debts of the project. Until then, the RTA has no right to present any of the notes for cash payment. Although Hills requires no financial support from the RTA, the government has contributed to the project AU$120 million in land acquisition and AU$66.5 million in upfront capital payment (NSWAGO 1995: 49; Walker and Walker 2000: 218; NSWIIG 2005: appendix 2). The forgone benefit arising from deferment in cash receipts adds another bill of AU$28.4 million (net present value estimated by the NSW Auditor-General's Office; see NSWAGO 1995: 86) to NSW taxpayers, topping the price up to AU$215 million.

To make high return to equity plus rentals to RTA appears possible, Hills' financial model had to be built on a number of risky assumptions. Its traffic projections are substantially greater than the maximum flow identified in the Environmental Impact Statements (EISs). The revenue estimates assume a AU$2.00 toll compared with a AU$0.70 toll in the EISs (NSWAGO 1995: 12). These assumptions signify the exposure to high market risk and the reduced likelihood of obtaining the required rate of return. The expensive toll evidences that the cost of assuming market risk has been priced into the toll, thereby passing the risk to motorists.

In spite of the overly optimistic expected rate of return, an interesting piece of information discloses that the forecasted real rate of return after tax given in the Base Case

Model will never exceed 11.78% (NSWAGO 2000). Contract documents also reveal that Hills expected AU$408.6 million financial contribution from the government in the form of RTA promissory notes to be issued between 1998 and 2025 (Walker and Walker 2000: 217). Knowingly, the RTA entered into the contract, notwithstanding the possibility of receiving cash returns from the M2 is near zero. The source of revenue to Hills comes from toll collections. The poor traffic performance suggests that the government would never be able to redeem these notes. The actual Annual Average Daily Traffic (AADT) in 2004 was 72,944 (NSWIIG 2005), barely reaching 85% of the 85,094 forecast estimated in the Base Case Model (NSWAGO 2000).[9] The net present value of these promissory notes, as of 30 June 2007, was AU$4.276 million (RTA 2007: 129). There appears to be an incentive rent payable to the RTA (NSWAGO 1995: 89), but the circumstances under which the incentive component can be realized are unclear.

Risk allocation was asymmetric. While risks of inflating costs to Hills are very well-considered and corresponding government concessions have been sought in agreements, there is no provision for sharing upside benefits between the two parties (NSWAGO 1995: 36). In 1999, Hills restructured the M2 debt facilities, resulting in more funds being available for early equity distribution (NSWAGO 2000), but yet there was no renegotiation for the early cash repayment of promissory notes. In the absence of obligations requiring negotiation to return government better outcomes in circumstances favorable to Hills, RTA must indemnify Hills for any future increases in state and commonwealth taxes, and council and water rates (NSWAGO 1995: 66). The project was camouflaged as if Hills would carry all down-side traffic risk,[10] but it is highly unlikely that the state can escape the risk, given that the demand for traffic is a vital component of land rent receipts. A significant proportion of O&M risk rests with the RTA, only the risk of major repairs is shifted to the Hills (NSWAGO 1995: 44, Table 1). Hills is protected against network risk in two dimensions (NSWAGO 1995: 41). One is to inflate the expected risk-adjusted rate of return by increasing tolls from planned levels, so private ownership has resulted in a higher toll for motorists than would under public ownership. The second dimension is to seek restoration under the Material Adverse Event (MAE) regime: if the government modifies the public transport network in the Northwest Region of Sydney that would adversely affect Hills' capacity to collect tolls, the state is required to repay all debts owed by the company and is liable for financial compensation to equity investors for the notional return (NSWAGO 1995: 67). These contractual conditions and the rhetoric of "non-recourse to the government" have exposed the government to potentially unlimited financial risk.

This leaves the only project benefit to NSW citizens being improved traffic conditions in the Northwest region. In this light, Hodge described the NSW government as "prone to making bad business deals for the sake of delivering conspicuous infrastructure projects" (Hodge 2005: 323). The greater value arising from better traffic flows began to be realized after the recent roadwork connection bridging the M2 with the LCT. The two connecting urban DBFO motorways together bring the state government a step closer to achieving an integrated road network in Sydney. It is difficult, however, to conclude that this benefit has outweighed the risk exposed to state citizens.

23.2.3 Melbourne CityLink (Contract Executed in 1995)

The MCL is the first private motorway in the state of Victoria. In 1995, with no publicly available economic and financial evaluation having been undertaken prior to the project's commencement (Brown 2003), the Transurban consortium comprising Transfield Holdings Pty Ltd and Obayashi Corporation successfully bid to undertake the AU\$2.1-billion MCL project in conjunction with the State of Victoria. The project involved the expansion and connections of three of Melbourne's major freeways—the Tullamarine, West Gate, and Monash. The private road links Melbourne Airport, major port facilities, the industrial centers southeast and west of the city, and by-passing the central business district (VAGO 2007). CityLink was incorporated to act as the project vehicle for the development.

Under the established arrangements, Transurban is expected to operate the MCL for a period of thirty-four years. The concession term can be terminated as early as in twenty-five years and six months, or be extended to warrant Transurban a post-tax real rate of return of 17.5% (VAGO 1996a). The tolls were set to maximize revenue (Lay and Daley 2002). As a condition to reduce traffic risk for Transurban, the Victorian government agreed to implement certain traffic management measures involving specific changes to the existing road network in the vicinity of the MCL (known as *Agreed Traffic Management Measures*). Removals of any of these agreed measures would trigger renegotiation under the MAE regime because Transurban has based its traffic and revenue projections on the assumption that these measures will be implemented (VAGO 1996b). The government must ensure that future transport policies will not jeopardize MCL being the central part of Melbourne's transport network (VAGO 1996a). Such a condition hamstrings the government's flexibility for network redevelopment. This is manifested in the ongoing AU\$37-million MAE claim lodged by the private operator alleging that developments in the Docklands area on which parts of the link is constructed have resulted in the loss of revenue (Hodge and Bowman 2004; Brown 2005).

The concession deed confers on CityLink the right to design, construct, commission, operate, maintain, repair, and impose tolls for the use of the facility in exchange for the payment of concession fees of AU\$141.8 million. These payments are required to be made in three tranches (see Appendix A, Table 23.1). Payment options are attached with high degrees of flexibility.

First, the obligation to pay the concession fees can be discharged by the issue of non-interest-bearing concession notes to the state (CityLink 1995). Concession notes must be redeemed at the end of the concession period. Provision for their early redemption is subject to the realization of an annual post-tax real return to private equity of 10%

provided it does not mar CityLink's ability to repay senior debt (CityLink 1995). This deferment option, which was estimated to have a value of AU$780 million in Brown (2003), has significantly enhanced returns to private equity.

Second, in 2005 and 2006, the Victorian government struck two concession-note buy-backs with Transurban in order to source funds to upgrade two public roads connecting the MCL. In June 2005, VicRoads (the Victorian road authority) and Transurban agreed to encash a number of the concession notes with a face value of AU$305.3 million for AU$151 million cash (VAGO 2007: 24). The proceeds were used to fund the upgrade of the Tullamarine–Calder Interchange and to share extra revenue associated with the road works, including AU$11 million up-front payment to VicRoads. In May 2006, VicRoads further agreed with Transurban to encash its remaining interest in the concession notes (which have a face value of AU$2.884 billion; see VAGO 2007: 25), and to use the proceeds to partly fund the upgrade of the West Gate and Monash freeways. As part of this deal, Transurban also agreed to upgrade the Southern Link section of MCL, located in the middle of the freeway corridor, at an estimated cost of AU$166 million. Extra revenue generated by the road works will be shared between VicRoads and Transurban (VAGO 2007).

The decision on two encashment transactions was justified by VicRoads on the basis that they would minimize risks of a decline in value of the concession notes over time. The benefits arising from these two risk-mitigating encashment deals were confirmed by the Victorian Auditor-General's Office (VAGO 2007: 26). However, in the absence of comparative studies performed by the government and documented risk assessment, the VAGO was unable to draw conclusions on whether the encashment options were the best alternative to fund the two upgrade projects.

Although substantial commercial risks have been transferred to Transurban, other risks that are beyond the control of both the government and the private sector are to be shared between Transurban and users of the link (VAGO 1996a). A risk regarding public governance surfaced. At the time of the proposal, the MCL was highly controversial because the DBFO motorway replaced two existing untolled freeways (Lay and Daley 2002). The Kennett government exercised its legal power to "crash through" this road project with the enactment of *Agreement for the Melbourne City Link Act* (Hodge 2005: 320). While there was no separate provision for the protection of consumers, the concession term can be extended to fifty-four years in an effort to ensure profitability for the consortium (Hodge 2005).

Nevertheless, the MCL has become a milestone in Australian PPP tollways. It is the first fully electronic tolled road in the country, and it has established that there is a growing acceptance that tolling could be used for congestion management and the potential for a wider road pricing application. The replacement of toll booths by an automated tolling system and variable tolling scheme to better manage traffic congestion have been extended to subsequent motorway developments, including the M7 and the MEL. Despite the criticism, the MCL is a "success" in terms of achieving its transport objectives and take-up by the community (Lay and Daley 2002).

23.2.4 Cross City Tunnel (Contract Executed in 2002)

The Cross City Tunnel is unique in its own right because essentially the project was a "forced" solution by urban planners. It was intended to be an urban design solution to reduce traffic on city streets and to improve urban amenities along William Street.

Originally, the concept of the CCT was a short tunnel with portals on the western side of the Kings Cross Tunnel and underneath the Australian Museum. But soon the objective changed to a longer tunnel that would improve William Street and the surrounding areas. Subsequently, the private bidder Baulderstone (a member of the winning consortium—the CrossCity Motorway or the CCM) submitted a revised, non-compliant bid in which the portals were extended to the eastern side of the Kings Cross Tunnel, and an extra lane was added to feed onto the Harbour Bridge. This concept had changed the project to a longer and more costly tunnel. The government had to lift the toll cap twice to allow for the additional works to be funded for (NSWAGO 2006a). The first was to change the toll escalation formula (originally toll variation was linked to Consumer Price Index increases), which would have an impact on the toll, being 35% greater than originally planned by 2018. The second change allowed CCM to raise the base toll by 15 cents (30 cents for heavy vehicles). The combined effect of these two deals resulted in an increase of up to 51 cents to the toll on tunnel opening (NSWAGO 2006a: 6). The impacts of these two deals on tolls are summarized in Appendix B (Table 23.2).

The DBFO contract was awarded to the CCM in 2002 not only because its design would provide a better urban solution, but also because it met the government's policy at the time that these projects had to be built at no net cost to the government. The CCM offered the RTA the highest up-front payment, while other bidders sought a payment from the RTA (NSWAGO 2006a: 24). To showcase its capacity to earn greater revenue sooner, and to offer the upfront payment (JSCCCT 2006b: 81), the CCM modeled unusually optimistic traffic forecasts that exceeded the ceiling capacities in its competitors' and the RTA's estimates (NSWAGO 2006a: 5). Against the RTA's advice, CCM insisted on these numbers because it felt that the longer tunnel would provide better benefits, hence attracting greater traffic.

The two agreements between the RTA and the CCM to lift the toll cap enable the government to adhere to the rhetoric of "no net cost to government" by passing on the project's financial risk to motorists. Ferocious public resistance to the expensive toll and associated road closures resulted in low patronage. The tunnel was placed in receivership in December 2006—a year after its opening—owing to poor patronage. It was sold to another private consortium in 2007 for AU$700 million. By that time, actual patronage had been under a third of the CCM's estimates (Clegg and Poljak 2007). The tunnel was sold the second time on 26 June 2014 for AU$475 million to Transurban—again because of poor traffic volume. Resistance to excessive tolls and road changes signaled strong public disapproval of the CCT.

The government argued that the patronage risk and therefore revenue risk had been allocated out too, as reflected in the drastic devaluation of AU$102 million in CCT's holding by CKI (the equity holder of CCT) in 2006 (JSCCCT 2006a: 67). But the government had not realized at the time that the risk of choosing an inexperienced operator would tarnish its reputation and distort the PPP policy framework. As a consequence, the government backed down from its support for the project. Extensive media exposure about the tension between the government and the CCM brought the two parties into disrepute. Considerable public resources were spent on a number of parliamentary inquiries and an independent report commissioned by the government (known as the Richmond Report) to re-evaluate the merit of the PPP policy framework.

The CCT "fiasco" has raised a new dimension of concern over the financing of a road infrastructure that was intended for purposes beyond a simple transport task. It is questionable whether the "user pays" principle should be extended to finance a road infrastructure that is intended for future urban design planning, and of which a substantial proportion of benefit does not accrue to motorists.

23.3 CONCLUSION AND THE WAY FORWARD

After over two decades of development, private provision in road infrastructure has progressively evolved into a more risk-balanced approach. And yet based on the overall empirical experience, which has too often not been favorable from the perspective of taxpayers, it is doubtful whether to date DBFO roads have delivered true VFM to the public.

In the cases studied, risk allocation and associated payment and pricing mechanisms were formulated to attain specific political objectives and to maximize revenue to the private operators. The concept of bundling asset creation with the whole-of-life asset management has failed to deliver the proposed outcome of maximizing VFM through cost savings to taxpayers over the asset's life cycle. The sophistication of the incentive payment mechanism has yet to motivate risk undertaking by the private sector. This is because the design of financial mechanisms does not contemplate optimal risk allocation but is tailored to the interests of the contracting parties. The concept of sharing cost and risk with the private sector has been "rationalized" by passing on risks and costs to motorists and the community. Private provision has conveniently provided governments with "strategic flexibility" to escape parliamentary and public scrutiny (NSWAGO 1994: 292–3; Hodge 2005).

As seen above, erroneous traffic forecast is the norm across projects and time. It has been documented elsewhere that traffic forecasts are produced to justify a course of action which has been already been chosen for political reasons (Wachs 1990). Traffic projections are a derived effort by both sectors with the view of getting the contract awarded and fulfilling the strategic objective of the public-sector agency. Ample evidence indicates that forecasts have been fabricated not to show the most likely outcomes, but to satisfy political intent (Flyvbjerg et al. 2006) and/or to deceive investors in order to raise finance from the market (Flyvbjerg et al. 2005). These have translated into poor VFM to both the community and private equity investors who have suffered from the loss in value in these megaprojects. Original investors of the CCT received only 20% of their original investment when the concession was sold to another consortium (Clegg and Poljack 2007).

The objectives of the responsible public agency brought to these contracts may have distorted the assessments on traffic volume predictions. There is a strong link between the capacity of a proponent to offer a least-cost deal to the responsible public agency and the traffic predictions underlying a proposal. For example, the consideration of no recourse to government in Sydney's M2 has taken precedence over other criteria (NSWAGO 1995: 49). In some cases, the tendering process which provides poor incentive to private companies—who would be induced to be overoptimistic in predicting traffic growth in order to win the concession—further compounded the effect leading to erroneous traffic forecasts. The CCT tendering model invited all bidders to bid on either the development cost or the BCF (JSCCCT 2006b: 73). It was taken as providing "a perverse incentive to bid on high patronage" (NSWAGO 2006a: 61). A typical *ex post* solution has been the reversal of volume risk back to the public sector, either through concession-period extension or by permission to lift the toll cap.

DBFO motorways make up pieces of an integrated network jigsaw. It is inevitable that their scope can be extended beyond a simple road solution. As recent experience suggests, they can be a useful device to congestion management that is based on the "user pays" principle, and can be a solution to town planning issues. It is important that governments understand risks associated with the intended project objectives and are therefore able to negotiate appropriate and equitable risk-sharing arrangements with private partners. To this extent, the present risk-shifting approach has proven inadequate. A proactive risk management paradigm that adheres to the rational of risk allocation—as opposed to risk shifting—is in need for a sustainable DBFO regime.

Table 23.1 DBFO motorways in New South Wales and Victoria

	NSW								Victoria	
	Sydney Harbour Tunnel (SHT)	M4 (two sections)	M5 (two stages)	Hills M2 Motorway (M2)	Eastern Distributor M1 (ED)	Cross City Tunnel (CCT)	Westlink M7 (M7)	Lane Cove Tunnel (LCT)	CityLink (MCL)	EastLink (MEL)
Actual opening date to traffic										
	Sep 1992	15 May 1992	Aug 1992/Sept 1994	May 1997	Dec 1999	Aug 2005	Dec 2005	Mar 2007	Aug 1999	29 Jun 2008
Planned date for opening to traffic										
	Oct 1992	15 Feb 1993	28 Feb 1995/Sept 1994	30 Dec 1997	18 Aug 2000	18 Oct 2005	13 Aug 2006	10 May 2007	Jul 2000	Nov 2008
Projected date for handover										
	Sep 2022	Feb 2010	Sep 2023	May 2042	Jul 2048	Dec 2035	Feb 2037	Jan 2037	Jan 2034	Dec 2043
Concession period										
	30 years	20 years	31 years	36–45 years	48 years	30 years	30 years	30 years	25–54 years	35 years
Capital cost [a]										
	AU$683 million	AU$246 million	AU$382 million	AU$616 million	AU$684 million	AU$680 million	AU$2,230 million	AU$1,684.8 million	AU$2,100 million	AU$3,800 million
Upfront payment by (−ve)/to (+ve) government agency										
	−AU$223 million (state loan); +3.5 million	Nil	Nil	−AU$66.5 million (capital payment)	+AU$10.2 million[b]	+AU$96.8 million + gst (RDF + BCF)	+AU$193 million+ gst (RDF + BCF)[c]	+AU$79 million + gst (RDF + BCF)	Nil	+AU$15 million (compensate the state for movements in interest rates between the bid period and the financial close); +AU$20 million (land licenses and freeway leases for the state land and works valued at AU$318 million)

(Continued)

Table 23.1 Continued

	NSW								Victoria	
	Sydney Harbour Tunnel (SHT)	M4 (two sections)	M5 (two stages)	Hills M2 Motorway (M2)	Eastern Distributor M1 (ED)	Cross City Tunnel (CCT)	Westlink M7 (M7)	Lane Cove Tunnel (LCT)	CityLink (MCL)	EastLink (MEL)
Financial contribution by (−ve)/to (+ve) government agency										
−Revenue top-up by ERS	+Land lease: AU$46.6 million paid in advance[d]	+Land loan AU$22 million;[d] cash loan AU$85 million; construction payment AU$10 million	+Land rent: (basic + incentive); AU$215 million (see text)	−$25 million; +land rent (basic AU$1 + BCF AU$15 million p.a.)[e]	+Land rent (basic AU$1 + incentive)	+Land rent (basic AU$1 + incentive)	+Land rent (basic AU$1 + incentive)	−AU$266 million; +annual concession fees in three tranches; +incentive rent[f]	+incentive rent payable in relevant periods where actual revenue is greater than projected revenue[g]
Annual average daily traffic: actual [h]										
	88,000 as of 2011	115,000 as of Q4, 2009	121,000 as of Q2, 2014	107,000 as of Q2, 2014	52,000 as of Q2, 2014	33,000 as of Q2, 2014	154,000 as of Q2, 2014	76,000 as of Q2, 2014	791,000 as of Q2, 2014	194,000 as of Q3, 2011
Annual average daily traffic: projected [h]										
						87,088		104,800		300,000
Present toll (full length car trip, as of January 2016)										
	AU$4.00 peak hours and AU$3.00 non-peak hours week day for all types of vehicles; south-bound direction only	Toll-free since February 2010 when concession reverted back to the state government	AU$4.49 (cars) AU$12.07 (trucks); both directions	AU$6.61 (cars) AU$19.83 (trucks) for the full length	AU$6.68 (cars) and AU$13.36 (trucks); north-bound direction only	Full tunnel: AU$5.31 (cars) and AU$10.62 (trucks); SJYC exit: AU$2.50 (cars) and AU$5.01 (trucks); both directions	Distance-based variable tolls, 38.73 cents/km capped at AU$7.75 (cars); 81.74 cents/km capped at AU$16.35; one way; both directions	AU$3.17 (cars) AU$8.11 (trucks) for the full length and AU$1.59 (cars) AU$4.05 (trucks) for Military Road e-ramp; both directions	Distance and time-based variable tolls, capped at AU$8.57 for cars and AU$11.42 for trucks; one way; both directions	Distance-based variable tolls, with discounts on weekends and public holidays, capped at AU$5.94 for cars and AU$15.74 for trucks; one way; both directions

Consortium partners (major equity holders)

Transfield Pty Ltd, Kumagai Gumi Corporation	SWR partners, Macquarie Infrastructure (MIG)	MIG, M5 Holdings, Cogent Nominees	Transfield from June 2005; previously Abigroup, Obayashi Corporation	MIG; previously Infrastructure Trust of Australia, Leighton Motorway Investment	ABN Amro, Leighton Holdings from June 2007; previously CKI, Bilfinger Berger, SAS Trustee Corporation, J.P. Morgan Nominees Australia	MIG, Transurban, Abigroup, Leighton Holdings	CKI and Li Ka Shing Foundation from July 2004; previously ABN Amro Australia	Transfield Holdings Pty Ltd, Obayashi Corporation Transurban	Macquarie Bank (financier), Thiess and John Holland (construction), Sociedad Iberica de Construcciones Electricas, S.A. (tolling system and integration of roadside equipment), Transfield Services Australia Pty Ltd (operations and maintenance services)

Operator

Sydney Harbour Tunnel Company	SWR Operations	Interlink Roads	Tollaust subcontracting to The Hills Motorway	Airport Motorway Ltd (AML)	CrossCity Motorway subcontracting to Baulderstone Hornibrok	Westlink Motorway	Lane Cove Tunnel Co subcontracting to Transfield Services	Transurban	ConnectEast

[a] Details of the capital cost for each project are as follows:

SHT: AU$683 million (1986 price), including construction cost of AU$554 million (NSWAGO 1994; NSWIIG 2005).

M4: includes the Western Section missing link; Mays Hill–Prospect and the Eastern Section widening; James Ruse Drive and Silverwater Road east of Parramatta. AU$246 million (1988 price) which consists of construction cost of AU$110 million for both sections, with the remaining value including interest, maintenance, and taxation (NSWAGO 1994).

M5: includes Stage 1 (Beverly Hills–Moorebank) and Stage 2 (Moorebank–Prestons). AU$382 million (1991 price), which is made up of two components: (i) M5 main link cost of AU$317 million; cost of land acquisition AU$22 million paid by the RTA and construction cost of AU$295 million that is funded by Interlink (CBA loan AU$250 million) and the RTA (AU$35 million loan and AU$10 million construction payment); (ii) M5 Western extension; construction cost of AU$65 million funded by the RTA loan (AU$50 million) and Interlink (CBA loan AU$15 million); the RTA's loans to Interlink (some of which are at concessional interest rates) are subordinated to Interlink's other debt and are not repayable until the end of the project term (NSWAGO 1994).

M2: AU$616 million (1994 price), which consists of design and construction cost (AU$369 million), project establishment cost (AU$26 million), overhead expenditure (AU$6 million), distributions to investors (AU$47 million), net project finance costs including interest earned (AU$33 million), debt service reserve (AU$15 million), all are funded by private debt and equity; plus AU$120 million land acquisition paid by the RTA (Hills 1994; NSWAGO 1995).

ED: AU$684 million (1997 price), which consists of cost of financing, development, design, construction, fitout, and commissioning (NSWAGO 1997).

CCT: AU$680 million (nominal price), which consists of cost of development, design, construction, fitout, and commissioning (NSWAGO 2006).

(Continued)

M7: AU$2,230 million (nominal price), which represents the total cost of the project including the cost of connecting roadworks and financing costs, the cost of design and construction for the motorway is AU$1.54 billion (Westlink M7 2005).

LCT: AU$1,684.8 million (1999 price), which consists of the cost of development, design, and construction, fitout and commissioning that is funded by AU$542.8 million of equity investments, and AU$1,142 million of debt finance; the estimated cost of the project was AU$815 million (JSCCT 2006c).

MCL: AU$2,100 million (1996 price), which consists of AU$1,800 million contribution from Transurban to cover the cost of design, finance, construction and operation of the project, and AU$256 million financial cost of the state government to finance associated works, including property acquisition, the widening of the Tullamarine Freeway from Moreland Road to Bulla Road, and the implementation of certain agreed traffic management measures (VAGO 1996a).

MEL: AU$3,800 million (2005 price), which consists of the fixed contract price of the project's design and construction, AU$2,500 million; the remaining value includes capital and financial costs (VAGO 2005: 194).

[b] AU$10.2 million paid by the private operator comprises two cash payments of the concession fee: AU$2.2 million in February 1998; AU$8 million in August 2000.

[c] The federal government contributed AU$356 million towards the M7 project (NSWAGO 2006b).

[d] Land lease of AU$46.6 million (being a total of seventeen years' rent for the land on which the motorway was built) was paid by SWR in two tranches: the sum of AU$22,094,340.11 on or before the commencement date; and the sum of AU$24,521,348.11 on 31 May 1991 (NSWAGO 1994, p.357). RTA land loan was repaid by Interlink in 1997. These two payments are treated as prepayments of the remaining lease over the concession period. They are recorded as liabilities–"unearned revenue" in RTA's book and amortised annually (RTA 2007: 142). Note that the nature of these land leases differs from those in later projects. Land leases of M4 and M5 are the rents charged for the land on which the motorways were built. Land rent in later projects was the price concessionaires paid for the right to charge tolls and retain them for their own benefit.

[e] RTA's financial contribution: AU$5 million for the transfer of risk of interest rate movements between the announcement of the preferred proponent and financial close, including the risk associated with the issue of indexed bonds by the private proponent; and AU$20 million construction cost to compensate AML for modifications added to the original project proposal, half of which was to ensure the construction of the Sydney Art Gallery landscaped canopy. Up to 65% of the land rent can be made in promissory notes, which can be redeemed only after an annual real after–tax return of 10% to equity has been earned.

[f] AU$266 million, includes AU$107 million expended towards the acquisition of land; AU$10 million towards the construction of a separate emergency tunnel by Transurban in accordance with the State Works Agreement; and costs associated with works financed by the government (VAGO 1996b). Three tranches of annual concession fees payable semiannually: AU$95.6 million for the first twenty-five years, AU$45.2 million for years 26–34, and AU$1 million for the remaining years, all payable in non-interest-bearing promissory notes if the cumulative real/post-inflation rate of return on equity is less than 10% per year and the total dollar amount of promissory notes redeemed in any financial year exceeds 30% of the distributable cash flow of the preceding financial year (VAGO 2007: 23); incentive rent payable in relevant periods when actual post-tax real return to private equity is greater than projected return (CityLink 1995).

[g] The concessionaire ConnectEast is not obliged to pay concession fees to the state for the right to operate the motorway. In return for the concession right, ConnectEast will build two sections of the new road (a 2-km enhanced bypass of Ringwood and a new 4.75-km bypass of Dandenong) that are non-tolled, and hand them over to the Victorian government at no cost once construction is complete (VAGO 2005: 193).

[h] Data obtained from <http://chartingtransport.com/2012/03/03/traffic-volumes-on-australian-toll-roads/>

Source: CityLink (1995); EastLink (2004); JSCCT (2006a, 2006b); Hodge (2005); NSWIIG (2005); NSWAGO (various years); RTA (Contract Summary, various years); RTA (2007); SHTA (1987); VAGO (1996a, 1996b, 2005) Westlink M7 (2005).

APPENDIX B

Table 23.2 Changes to the toll compared with the original project concept

Toll component	Original project concept	After the change	Reason for change
Toll escalation formula	CPI adjusted toll escalation	Opening Dec 2011[a]: Greater of 4% and CPI Jan 2012–Dec 2017[a]: Greater of 3% and CPI After Dec 2017[a, b]: Greater of CPI and 0%	To avoid the RTA paying an extra AU$75 million costs following the Supplementary EIS and associated additional Conditions of Approval
Base toll level	Cars: AU$2.50 for main tunnel AU$1.10 for exit at SJYC[c] Heavy vehicles: AU$5.00 for main tunnel AU$2.20 exit at SJYC	Cars: AU$2.65 for main tunnel AU$1.25 for exit at SJYC Heavy vehicles: AU$5.30 for main tunnel AU$2.50 for exit at SJYC	Allowed in return for CCM carrying out AU$35 million of additional work identified for the RTA

[a] Quarterly adjusted. Effectively, the adjustment is greater than 4%. If the CPI were treated as an annual figure, then the toll charged at 31 December 2005 would have been AU$3.45, not AU$3.56.

[b] If CPI is negative during any quarter, the toll will remain at the same level until the CPI is positive.

[c] Sir John Young Crescent.

Source: NSWAGO (2006a); JSCCT (2006a).

NOTES

1. PPPs are also termed Privately Financed Projects (PFPs) in the procurement policy of NSW–WWG 2006. The early generation of the British equivalent is named Private Finance Initiative (PFI). In this chapter, the terms are interchangeable, while PFIs refer specifically to projects undertaken in the United Kingdom.
2. The use of terminology varies between countries. In the United Kingdom, DBFO in transport involves the transfer of ownership at the end of concession period (Glaister et al. 2000), while the similar arrangement in Australia is termed BOOT (Debande 2002: 380).
3. An exception is the shadow toll program used in the UK in which the private operator is directly compensated by the Highways Agency.
4. During the contract negotiation it was evident to all parties that user tolls would not be sufficient to cover the costs of the tunnel. Accordingly, the DMR agreed to pay an Ensured Revenue Stream to meet all SHTC's risk exposure and to provide SHTC with financial returns irrespective of actual toll levels or actual tunnel users (NSWAGO 1994: 265).
5. Readers are referred to Walker and Walker (2000) for a full history of the "global limits" of borrowing.

6. The term *rent* is not to be misinterpreted as the payment for leasing the land on which the motorway is running; it pays for the right to levy tolls. To avoid confusion, when discussing payment/value of the right to toll, this chapter uses the term adopted by the RTA and calls it "land rent" or "rent," whereas "land lease" refers to payments for leasing the land from the government.

7. In 2005, Hills was acquired by Transurban, which now owns and runs the M2.

8. The 6% return has not considered the value of land contributed by the RTA (NSWAGO 1995: 88). The inclusion of the land value will of course further deteriorate the return to the RTA.

9. Patronage seems to be improving since the opening of Lane Cove Tunnel. The AADT of M2 presented in Appendix A was the latest figure reported by the new equity owner, Transurban. It appears that the actual AADT has exceeded the original forecast of 90,200. It is unclear whether this will trigger the cash redemption of the promissory notes.

10. When the 1995 Audit Report asserted that the RTA was the cobearer of traffic risk, the RTA disputed the assertion and argued that the Hills had confirmed its status as the sole bearer as evidenced in the Project Prospectus issued by the company: "The Company carries the risk that traffic volumes and revenue are lower than those projected" (NSWAGO 1995: 19).

REFERENCES

Akbiyikli, R., Eaton, D., and Turner, A. (2006). "Project finance and the private finance initiative (PFI)," *Journal of Structured Finance*, 12(2): 67–75.

Arndt, R. H. (1998). "Risk allocation in the Melbourne CityLink Project," *Journal of Project Finance*, 4(3): 11–24.

Broadbent, J. and Laughlin, R. (2004). "PPPs: Nature, development and unanswered questions," *Australian Accounting Review*, 14(2): 4–10.

Brown, C. (2003). "Transurban City Link: Hindsight view," *Finance and Treasury Professional*, August: 18–20.

Brown, C. (2005). "Financing transport infrastructure: For whom the road tolls," *Australian Economic Review*, 38 (4): 431–8.

Chung, D. (2009). "Private provision of road infrastructure: Unveiling the inconvenient truth in New South Wales, Australia," *Road and Transport Research* 18(1): 68–85.

CityLink (1995). *Agreement for the Melbourne City Link (Act No. 107/1995)*. Victorian Government.

Clegg, B. and Poljak, V. (2007). "Sold: $700m Cross City Tunnel." *Australian Financial Review*, Wednesday, Sydney, 20 June, pp. 1, 52.

Debande, O. (2002). "Private financing of transport infrastructure," *Journal of Transport Economics and Policy*, 36(3): 355–87.

EastLink (2004). *Mitcham–Frankston Freeway: Concession Deed*. Victorian Government.

English, L. (2005a). "Using Public Private Partnerships to achieve value for money in the delivery of healthcare in Australia," *International Journal of Public Policy*, 1(1–2): 91–121.

English, L. (2005b). "Evaluation and monitoring of Public Private Partnerships," *Submission to the Legislative Assembly Public Accounts Committee Inquiry into Public Private Partnerships*, Sydney, Sub. No. 4.

English, L. (2006). 'Public Private Partnerships in Australia: An overview of their nature, purpose, incidence and oversight," *University of New South Wales Law Journal*, 29(3): 250–62.

English, L. and Baxter, J. (2008). "Using contracts to govern hybrid public–private partnerships: A case study of Australian prisons," *AFAANZ/IAAER Conference*, Sydney, Australia, 6–8 July 2008.

English, L. and Guthrie, J. (2003). "Driving privately financed projects in Australia: What makes them tick?" *Accounting, Auditing and Accountability Journal*, 16(3): 493–511.

Flyvbjerg, B., Holm, M. S., and Buhl, S. L. (2005). "How (in)accurate are demand forecasts in public works projects? The case of transportation," *Journal of the American Planning Association*, 71(2): 131–46.

Flyvbjerg, B., Holm, M. S., and Buhl, S. L. (2006). "Inaccuracy in traffic forecasts," *Transport Reviews*, 26(1): 1–24.

Glaister, S., Scanlon, R., and Travers, T. (2000). "Getting Public Private Partnerships going in transport," *Public Policy and Administration*, 15(4): 49–70.

HM Treasury. (2006). *PFI: Strengthening Long-Term Partnerships*. London: HM Treasury.

Hodge, G. (2005). "Public–private partnerships: The Australasian experience with physical infrastructure," in G. Hodge and C. Greve (eds.), *The Challenge of Public–Private Partnerships: Learning from International Experience*. Cheltenham: Edward Elgar, pp. 305–31.

Hodge, G. and Bowman, D. M. (2004). "PPP contractual issues: Big promises and unfinished business," in A. Ghobadian, O. R. Gallear, and N. V. Howard (eds.), *Public–Private Partnerships: Policy and Experience*. Houndmills: Palgrave Macmillan, pp. 201–18.

JSCCCT (Joint Select Committee on the Cross City Tunnel). (2006a). *Cross City Tunnel and Public Private Partnerships: Second Report*. Parliament of New South Wales.

JSCCCT (Joint Select Committee on the Cross City Tunnel). (2006b). *Cross City Tunnel: First Report*. Parliament of New South Wales.

JSCCCT (Joint Select Committee on the Cross City Tunnel). (2006c). *Third Report: Lane Cove Tunnel*. Parliament of New South Wales.

Lay, M. G. and Daley, K. F. (2002). "The Melbourne CityLink project," *Transport Policy*, 9(3): 261–7.

Mills, G. (1991). "Commercial funding of transport infrastructure," *Journal of Transport Economics and Policy*, 25(3): 279–98.

NAO (National Audit Office). (2003). *PFI: Construction Performance*. London Report by the Comptroller and Auditor General, HC 371, Session 2002–03.

NSWAGO (New South Wales Auditor-General's Office). (1994). *Private Participation in the Provision of Public Infrastructure: The Roads and Traffic Authority*. New South Wales Government, Sydney Report No. 13,

NSWAGO (New South Wales Auditor-General's Office). (1995). *Performance Audit Report: Roads and Traffic Authority: The M2 Motorway*. New South Wales Government, Sydney Report No. 16.

NSWAGO (New South Wales Auditor-General's Office). (2000). *Review of M2 Motorway Documentation (Reported in Auditor-General's Report to Parliament 2000, Volume 3)*. The Audit Office of New South Wales, Sydney.

NSWAGO (New South Wales Auditor-General's Office). (2003). *Roads and Traffic Authority of New South Wales (Reported in Volume 5 of the Auditor-General's 2003 Report to Parliament)*. The Audit Office of New South Wales, Sydney, pp. 209–18.

NSWAGO (New South Wales Auditor-General's Office). (2006a). *Performance Audit: The Cross City Tunnel Project*. The Audit Office of New South Wales, Sydney.

NSWAGO (New South Wales Auditor-General's Office). (2006b). *Roads and Traffic Authority of New South Wales (Reported in Volume 4 of the Auditor-General's 2006 Report to Parliament)*. The Audit Office of New South Wales, Sydney, pp. 121–9.

NSWAGO (New South Wales Auditor-General's Office). (2007). *Roads and Traffic Authority of New South Wales, Sydney (Auditor-General's Report to Parliament 2007 Volume 6)*. The Audit Office of New South Wales, Sydney, pp. 69–74.

NSWIIG (New South Wales Infrastructure Implementation Group). (2005). *Review of Future Provision of Motorways in NSW*. The Premier's Department, Sydney.

NSW Treasury. (2007). *State Infrastructure Strategy: New South Wales 2006–07 to 2015–16*. Office of Financial Management, Sydney.

Partnerships Victoria. (2000). Department of Treasury and Finance Victoria, Australia.

RTA. (2007). *RTA Annual Report 2007*. Roads and Traffic Authority.

SHTA. (1987). *Sydney Harbour Tunnel (Private Joint Venture) Act 1987*. New South Wales Government.

Tiong, R. L. K. (1995). "Risks and guarantees in BOT tender," *Journal of Construction Engineering and Management*, 121(2): 183–8.

VAGO (Victorian Auditor-General's Office). (1996a). *Report of the Auditor-General on the Statement of Financial Operations, 1995–96*. Victorian Auditor-General's Office.

VAGO (Victorian Auditor-General's Office). (1996b). *Report on Ministerial Portfolios, May 1996*. Victorian Auditor-General's Office.

VAGO (Victorian Auditor-General's Office). (2005). *Auditor-General's Report: Results of 30 June 2005, Financial Statement and Other Audits, Report No. 2005:17*. Victorian Government.

VAGO (Victorian Auditor-General's Office). (2007). *Funding and Delivery of Two Freeway Upgrade Projects, PP No 69, Session 2006–07*. Victorian Government.

VicRoads. (2006). *Environmental Management Guidelines*. Roads Corporation, Victorian Government.

Wachs, M. (1990). "Ethics and advocacy in forecasting for public policy," *Business Professional Ethics Journal*, 9(1/2): 141–57.

Walker, B. (2005). "5 things that Auditors-General should be doing about PPPs," *Dissent*, 18: 50–3.

Walker, B. and Walker, B. (2000). *Privatisation Sell Off or Sell Out? The Australian Experience*. Sydney, NSW: ABC Books.

West, M. (2008). "Roads to nowhere," *Sydney Morning Herald*, 16 July <http://business.smh.com.au/business/roads-to-nowhere-20080716-3fna.html?page=fullpage#con>

Westlink M7. (2005). *Summary of First Deed of Variation*.

WWG. (2006). *Working with Government: Guidelines for Privately Financed Projects*. New South Wales Government.

CHAPTER 24

MEGAPROJECTS AS POLITICAL SYMBOLS

South Africa's Gautrain

JANIS VAN DER WESTHUIZEN

24.1 INTRODUCTION

MEGAEVENTS like the Olympics, the World Cup, or Expos are short-term, high-profile events associated with high levels of tourism and other economic impacts. Proponents of urban and infrastructure develop and quickly adopt megaevents as strategies for long-term economic development and job creation. Yet given the sheer costs involved, the infrastructure requirements, and need for political stability, megaevents have typically been hosted in the advanced industrial world. More recently, however, newly industrializing and emerging economies in the developing world have also sought to host major events, and with them, launch massive new infrastructure projects.

While the literature on urban development and megaevents is extensive, the literature on megaevents and transport systems as a type of megaproject is not explicitly tied together. One explanation may be transport's relative peripheral position in relation to the tourism–destination–management literature generally, possibly because travel to and from an event is temporary. Yet, the impacts of travel are "concentrated in time and have the potential to cause significant short-term problems for destination areas, such as congestion and pollution" (Robbins, Dickinson, and Calver 2007: 303).

Megaprojects are physical, very expensive, and public; and involve the creation of structures, equipment, and/or prepared development sites that are generally either wholly or in part publicly financed (Althshuler and Luberoff 2003: 2). Besides transportation projects, other examples include power plants, water projects, information technology, and aerospace initiatives. In fact, megaprojects can be categorized into four different types of megaproject: infrastructure (such as dams, ports, and railroads), extraction (such as minerals, oil, and gas), production (for example, massive military hardware such as fighter aircraft, chemical plants, and manufacturing parks), and consumption (such as tourist installations, malls, and theme parks). In the past two decades, the number of megaprojects has exploded, particularly in the developing world. Merrill Lynch estimates spending on infrastructure in emerging markets to be US$2.25 trillion annually between 2009 and 2012 (Kardes et al. 2013: 906). As a more critical literature on the political economy of megaprojects has emerged, their sustainability in terms of economic cost, environmental impact, and public support is increasingly being scrutinized. Not unlike debates around the suitability of megaevents and their long-term impact, critical analysts frequently lament the fact that megaprojects typically incur budget overruns, overestimate long-term employment opportunities, minimize environmental impact projections, and limit public-consultation processes (Flyvbjerg, Bruzelius, and Rothengatter 2003). In South Africa, the Gautrain has emerged as a particularly interesting case study of a megaproject that was initially closely identified with the country's bid to host the 2010 soccer World Cup. To illustrate these similarities, this article focuses on three dimensions: firstly, public consultation and the role of special interest groups; secondly, the issue of cost and passenger forecasts; and thridly, the intangible, "mythical" discourses that often surround megaprojects. "Mythical" in this context simply refers to the way in which symbols, images, and metaphors are the products of symbolic processes, with images serving as "a proxy for a set of unstated assumptions [obscuring alternatives] that do not usually have the courtesy to parade themselves in rank order on the drill ground of the imagination" (Boulding 1956). These three dimensions are significant, as they constitute the discursive field upon which both opponents and proponents of megaprojects contest the need for a megaproject. Precisely because of the huge costs involved in megaprojects they are inherently political issues, since they usually make considerable fiscal claims, prompting debates about costs and benefits. However, as this chapter will illustrate, the discursive contests between supporters and opponents are not only based on material claims, but equally, the symbolic role of megatransport projects as identity signifiers. In developing-world contexts these are often related to status projections. It is therefore not coincidental that Gautrain's proponents tried to link completion of the Gautrain to South Africa's successful hosting of the 2010 World Cup—another status signifier of South Africa's "emerging power" role.

24.2 TRANSPORT: THE POLITICAL ECONOMIC CONTEXT

By 2011, 12.2 million people lived in Gauteng, South Africa's smallest but also most densely populated region, with 25% of the South African population and generating nearly 34% of the country's GDP and 10% of the GDP of the entire African continent. South Africa has the largest number of cars per 1,000 people in Africa (followed by Nigeria and thereafter Liberia), with one in five South Africans owning a car. In global terms, South Africa ranks at 86th place (just after Jordan), whereas Gauteng accounts for nearly 40% of all cars driven in the country (Cars per Capita in Africa 2014). With car traffic on the corridor between Johannesburg and Tshwane (Pretoria) increasing by 7% per year, and endemic congestion and regular gridlock traffic, the primary purpose of the Gautrain is "to attract motorcar users to a public transport mode; something which could not be achieved in South Africa before now [and] requires a fast, comfortable, safe, secure and predictable alternative" (Van der Merwe 2002: 23).

In a country with abysmally poor public transport, access to, and ownership of, a motor vehicle implies not only greater convenience but confers status and an identity of unrivaled upward mobility. Car ownership is a culturally deeply ingrained part of South African life: well over R200 billion is spent on personal transport—approximately 15% of GDP. In contrast, the United States—one of the world's most motorized countries—spent about 13% of GDP on cars (Mostert 2005: 1). In fact, the psychology of car ownership is so deeply rooted that the sheer act of walking inspires apprehension. Historically, South African writers

> lament the inability to perambulate the streets of Johannesburg in a manner that is inconspicuous, safe and convenient. Seemingly, their insights follow on from *Tant Sannie's* earlier declaration in *The Story of an African Farm*, that "men who walk are thieves, liars, murderers, Rome's priests, seducers." Olive Schreiner is one of the first to highlight how walking is positioned in the white imagination: it is an act that inspires apprehension and so warrants suspicion in the South African context, setting us apart from 19th century Europeans who took to the streets in droves. (Moonsamy: 2014)

Transport remains one of the most enduring features of the social stratification processes generated by apartheid. For the poor and working classes, public transport—certainly in comparison to the developed world—is not only underresourced and unreliable, but also consumes a larger proportion of income than for the middle class, which has access to private cars. Hence, the minibus–taxi industry emerged and has historically grown in reaction to the sheer inadequacy of public transport. As Moonsamy (2014) writes:

> The taxi industry has become hardened by its own history of exclusion; during apartheid, it sought to provide informal public transport for black citizens who had none. It was, literally, a transport system at the margins—a defiant symbol of resistance. Today, reaching speeds to match the Gautrain, the taxi still stands as an audacious pronouncement of itself—it remains resistant to law and attempts at formalization.

It therefore comes as little surprise that when a multibillion-rand public transport project—with a budget larger than the entire national transport budget (for all forms of transportation)—was announced, the project was steeped in controversy.

The debate about the Gautrain as a megaproject also needs to be contextualized within the significance of transport infrastructure to South Africa's position in the global political economy. Given South Africa's difficulty in pursuing a low-wage, mass-manufacturing development path based on "flexible" labor, while massive and fundamental skill deficiencies in key sectors forestall adoption of a relatively productive but high-wage value-added trajectory, one strategy is to develop, and more importantly *project*, South Africa and especially Johannesburg as the pivotal center of African transport, logistics, telecommunications, and related services.

24.3 THE GAUTRAIN NETWORK

In February 2000, former Premier of Gauteng province, Mbhazima Shilowa, announced a rapid-rail system linking Pretoria, Johannesburg, and OR Tambo International Airport as one of ten spatial development initiatives (SDIs) under the aegis of the Gauteng Provincial Government's Blue IQ program (Rogerson 2004). The network consists of two lines: one linking Johannesburg and Pretoria, and the other linking Sandton to OR Tambo International Airport, with two anchor stations at Pretoria Station and Johannesburg Park Station, and seven other stations in Hatfield, Centurion, Midrand, Marlboro, Sandton, Rosebank, and Kempton Park (Rhodesfield). Traveling at up to 160 km per hour, commuters are able to travel from Pretoria to Johannesburg in only 35 minutes, and between Sandton and OR Tambo Airport within 15 minutes. The section from Marlboro to OR Tambo Airport is 13 km long and has three stations. Completed on 7 June 2012 with the opening of the final section between Rosebank and Johannesburg Park Station, the line is 80 km long, with ten stations, 11 km of tunnels, and 7.5 km of bridges. By the end of May 2008, more than a third of the tunneling was completed. The megaproject was touted to create more than 83,000 direct and indirect jobs, and "has the potential to increase the provincial Gross Domestic Product (GDP) growth rate by a further 0.6–0.9%" (Van der Merwe 2002: 23).

The significance of a public–private partnership (PPP) has been heavily touted as central to the success of the Gautrain. Public-sector funding for the project came from three sources: the Gauteng provincial budget, provincial borrowing from national government, and a conditional grant from the National Treasury via the National Department of Transport. Bombela—the private-sector investment consortium—would invest approximately R3.9 billion towards capital costs. The consortium which won the bid in July 2005 consists of Borbardier Transportation (Canadian), Bouygeus Travaux Publics (French), and the South African companies Murray & Roberts, RATP International, the SPG Group, Loliwe Rail Contractors/Rail Express, Standard Bank, Rand Merchant Bank, and ABSA Bank.

During parliamentary testimony, government contended that "private lenders tended to play a strong oversight role when their finance was being used in a project. They monitored the use of their money far more effectively than government could. Indeed, private lenders had a debt service recovery ratio which they would not allow to be breached" (Transport Portfolio Committee 2005a: 7). The rhetorical attraction of a PPP in the case of the Gautrain reinforces Siemiatycki's (2005a: 71) observation:

The public–private partnership appears to adopt an enabling quality fitting into a narrative that celebrates cooperation between diverse shareholders as a means of achieving more than any one party could on its own. In this narrative, the private sector becomes a valued part of the team, willing to stand shoulder to shoulder with the public sector and assume a degree of risk in order to deliver the infrastructure.

Bombela is responsible for the construction and operational aspects of the project (the latter for at least fifteen years), while the provincial government covers the shortfall if the patronage forecasts are not met and the preferred bidder "did not receive the minimum required total revenue," although limitations were set on what provincial government would cover (Transport Portfolio Committee 2005a: 7). For the period 2011–2012, the Gauteng Department of Roads and Transport allocated R259 million to cover the patronage guarantee, yet during the planning stages of the project, Deputy Minister of Transport, Jeremy Cronin indicated that no precise figures were discussed: "We were never told at what level they were guaranteeing … We certainly asked that question a great deal" (Thomas 2013b: 148). In May 2013 it was announced by the GMA that as a result of increased ridership, the patronage guarantee government pays to Bombela dropped from between R80 million to R85 million a month in 2012 to between R70 million and R75 million a month in 2013 (Venter 2013a).

24.4 PUBLIC CONSULTATION AND SPECIAL INTEREST GROUPS

Comparative research suggests that megaproject proponents typically sequence public consultation at the end of the decision-making process, after substantive project specifications have been finalized, and approval of the project is a fait accompli (Siemiatycki 2005b). In South Africa it was only after the Minister of Finance announced in Parliament at the end of October 2005 that the Gautrain was a national project, that parliamentary hearings could be scheduled. Cabinet was set to make a decision about the project in early December 2005. This meant that the Transport Portfolio Committee (TPC) in Parliament had only two weeks of the remaining parliamentary session to examine the project, the implication being "that Parliament will have a few hours in which to assess what will be (if the project goes ahead) the largest-ever budgetary allocation, by a considerable amount, to a public transportation project" (Transport Portfolio Committee 2005b). Concluding its deliberations—with considerable apprehension about the project—the TPC cited nearly eighteen issues of concern, and warned that

> if real connectivity, that begins to overcome the divide between first and second economies, indeed proves to be possible, then it will certainly enhance the social value of the project. We cannot assess the prospects of a revised project without much more information being available, but we are concerned that hurried attempts

in this regard might result merely in a retro-fit, while not adding anything serious to existing transport challenges. (Transport Portfolio Committee 2005b)

Questioning the desirability of a high-speed train when its accessibility to the poor and working class is very unlikely, the Congress of South African Trade Unions (Cosatu) called for the project to be put on hold until a comprehensive transport system had been developed, and threatened to call a strike against the project if talks with the government stalled (Chibba 2006). That the Gautrain elicited strong public interest and reaction is evident from the fact that—according to Gautrain advocates—nearly 147 Environmental Assessment Investigations and meetings had been held, including legal action by some affected residents to modify its routing (Donaldson 2006). However, it would seem as if so much time had been consumed by these processes that timeframes came under fire—with the project's connection to 2010 making it all the more potentially calamitous. During his parliamentary submission, Gautrain CEO Jack van der Merwe emphasized that South Africa had a "moral and legal duty" to begin construction of the train by 2006, and hinted at the possibility that South Africa could lose the right to host the event if the Gautrain were not completed on time. However, during the course of his testimony the TPC established that South Africa's Bid Book had made no reference to the Gautrain (Transport Portfolio Committee 2005b). Subsequently, Gautrain proponents explicitly sought to delink the Gautrain from 2010, noting that the decision to build a Gautrain had already been taken in 1997 and that it was primarily intended for Gauteng commuters, not the soccer tournament (*Africa Research Bulletin* 2006/07). While it is generally acknowledged that megaprojects are touted by particular interest groups, comparative analysis reveals that rail transit is particularly prone to such processes. Rail transit projects elicit support on the basis of their supposed "spillover" potential such as the revitalization of neglected urban precincts from businesses in downtown/central business district (CBD) areas, construction companies, construction and transit labor unions, environmentalists, advocates for the poor, and many others who see transit as a means of overcoming developmental and amenity challenges (Altshuler and Luberoff 2003: 217). As such, proponents are fond of demonstrating rail projects as a public good in order to enhance mass appeal. Because the Gautrain had so often been criticized as an "elitist project" by opponents, at the launch of construction Minister of Transport Jeff Radebe was at pains to note that "this is not about elite public transport but [rather] about creating a mass transit system that caters for workers and business people, civil servants and scholars, shoppers and leisure seekers to get them where they want to be—safely, securely and affordably" (Radebe 2006).

Given the extent to which Gautrain had been perceived as a project for the middle class, allegations of equity interest by Cabinet members in the Gautrain investment consortium hardly warmed the South African public to the necessity of the project. According to the *Sunday Times*, former Home Affairs Minister Nosiviwe Mapisa Nqakula, Education Minister Naledi Pandor, former Deputy Health Minister Nozizwe Madlala-Routledge, and former Parliamentary Speaker Baleka Mbete, all stand to benefit from the Gautrain via various equity interests (*Sunday Times* 2006). Although

Mapisa-Nqakula admitted that she sat in a Cabinet meeting that approved the project in December 2005, she "was unaware at the time that Dyambu Holdings, in which she owns shares, was part of the Gautrain consortium" (*Sunday Times* 2006). Pandor reiterated that she was an ordinary member of one of the bidding companies, with no decision-making capacity within the company, and had acquired a "minute ownership" long before she came into government (*Mail & Guardian* 2006). Prompt dismissal of these allegations by the relevant ministers and other government leaders, as well as by former President Mbeki himself, however, seems to have forestalled the demands by the opposition Democratic Alliance for an investigation into the Gautrain by the Auditor-General. Nevertheless, what this instance reveals is that the Gautrain—like so many other megaprojects—remains vulnerable to the problem of clearly identifying (or separating) the public interest from the private interest, and "the creation of a dual role for government as both a project promoter and the guardian of interest issues" (Siemiatycki 2005b: 262). Given these dynamics, the issue of costs and forecasts became an important part of the debate.

24.5 Costs and Forecasts

Transport infrastructure budgets—as a rule—notoriously underestimate costs. In one of the largest samples of its kind, comparing statistical costs of 258 projects in twenty countries, Flyvbjerg et al. found that compared to road, fixed links (bridges and tunnels), and rail, average cost escalation on rail was highest at 45%, and that "high-speed rail tops the list of cost escalation at an average of 52%, followed by urban rail with 45% and conventional rail with 30%" (Flyvbjerg et al. 2003: 80). Moreover, in geographical terms, cost escalation for rail projects in the developing world were considerably higher than in Europe or North America, and they warn that "the evidence shows that it is sound advice for policy and decision makers as well as investors, bankers, media, and the public to take any estimate of construction costs with a grain of salt, and especially for rail projects and fixed links" (Flyvbjerg et al. 2003: 80).

Cost is the single most controversial aspect of the Gautrain megaproject. In 2004–2005, the total national budget for all public transportation modes amounted to R4.67 billion. In contrast, the budget for the Gautrain alone increased from R7 billion in 2001 to R12 billion in 2002, and by October 2005 it stood at R20–25 billion. (These figures refer to projected overall budget estimates.) This, while South Africa's existing urban passenger rail service, Metrorail, remains in dire need of replacement. Major efforts to recapitalize the country's aging and dilapidated passenger trains were only mooted in President Mbeki's State of the Natione address in 2007. With only 3,600 of 4,600 coaches in working condition, being on average forty years old, and with technology dating from 1956, there were huge problems with overcrowding as well as enormous delays, according to the CEO of South African Rail Commuter Corporation (SARCC), Mr Lucky Montana. While the Gautrain Management Agency (GMA) reiterated that the total cost of R25.2 billion was "a fixed price, fixed scope and fixed period contract," inflationary pressures in early 2008 meant that "for every percentage-point rise in the CPIX, construction costs will increase by about R250 million a year" (Khuyzwayo 2008). By 2013, some suggested that costs had crept up to more than R30 billion, despite the fact that in 2008 Jeremy Cronin, then chairman of the Transport Portfolio Committee, lamented the cost creeping up to R35 billion "quietly and below the radar," while MPs "were told hand on heart that the written-in-stone absolute upper limit was R20 bn" (Louw 2014). At the same time, the 2012/13 provincial budget contains cuts in infrastructure spending from R36 billion in the previous budget to R30 billion, with a representative from the Gauteng finance department confirming that the Gautrain was one of the reasons for this drop in funding for other infrastructure projects in the province (Thomas 2013a: 86).

The sustainability of the Gautrain stands or falls on passenger figures. The more people use them, the more affordable high-speed rail links will become. Yet skeptics and proponents often project different figures. The GMA projected an estimate of 45,000 initial one-way daily passengers, increasing to 120,000 daily passengers by 2010, while a figure of 70,000 passengers per day was considered "well over the international norm for the introduction of new rail services" (Del Mistro and Roodt 2001: 3). Indeed, the attainment of the 70,000 daily passenger figure would result in the reduction of approximately 20% of private vehicles on the N1 corridor between Tshwane and Johannesburg (Del Mistro 2002: 22). However, projected passenger figures generated in 2001 estimated these to be 12,400 morning peak-hour journeys, increasing to 23,000 morning peak-hour journeys by 2016 (Brocklebank, Burnett, Rand, and van der Walt 2001). Both Mostert and Del Mistro in 2005 and 2006 estimated initial passenger figures of approximately 20,000 per day (Mostert 2005). By August 2011 the average number of train passengers *per month* using the Gautrain from June 2010 to June 2011 was 235,163, based on figures provided by the Minister of Transport in the National Assembly. However, there is no general consensus of actual figures, with media reports varying between 39,000 to 40,000 and 45,000 to 47,000 passenger journeys per weekday (Batwell 2013; Burmeister 2012). By March 2013 it was reported that weekday ridership had increased to about 48,000, "stabilizing at a relatively consistent level of 14,000 to 16,000 passengers a day." However, the increased demand "placed severe strain on the train system during peak periods, with demand already approaching levels only predicted in year ten of the concession period," according to a Bombela spokesperson (Venter 2013b). Complicating operations is the asymmetrical ridership pattern, with the morning peak from Pretoria to Johannesburg extremely busy and the reverse much less so, as well as low demand during the middle of the day. Moreover, by late 2014 it was reported that owing to the increased costs related to the Gauteng e-toll system coming into operation, average weekday passenger trips increased to 52,400 train users and 21,000 bus users (Venter 2014). In terms of demographics, a 2012 survey revealed that about 35% of passengers were black; 12% Asian; 45% white; and 8% "coloured," with female passengers dominating. The largest group of passengers—35%—fall in the 35–49-year-old age group, while about 20% of passengers are younger than 24 (Most Gautrain Passengers Women 2012).

Gautrain management also contended that from an environmental point of view, the train would have distinct environmental advantages over other forms of transport. The 2002 Environmental Impact Assessment (EIA) concluded that "since the Gautrain rail corridor passes through an already largely urbanized area, most identified impacts pertain to the socioeconomic environment. Potential impacts on the biophysical environment are relatively few" (Thomas 2013a: 82). The GMA stresses the possibility of decreased carbon emissions from fewer vehicles on the road and less air pollution in the province: "….it is anticipated that Gautrain will reduce CO_2 emissions by about 70 tons." Yet, as Thomas (2013a: 83) notes, this assessment fails to consider that power-station emissions will nevertheless increase in order to provide electricity to Gautrain—a particular problem in the South African case given the country's high level of dependence on coal-generated power stations. In fact, the EIA concludes that "no net gain or decrease in overall emissions can be observed after comparisons are made between the overall increase (power station) and decrease (from regional decrease in vehicle numbers) in calculated emissions" (Thomas 2013a: 83).

One specific environmental problem that has bogged operations of the network has been tunnel water-ingress between Johannesburg Park station and section E2 and the section between the Rosebank station and the Marlboro portal. A longstanding issue between the GMA and government—delaying opening of the Park Station–Rosebank segment by nearly four months in 2011—an arbitration tribunal ruled in November 2013 in favor of the provincial government, ordering Bombela to undertake remedial work to stem the inflow of water into the tunnel between Johannesburg Park Station and the E2 station. It was also found that the section between the Rosebank station and the Marlboro portal had not been built according to contract specifications. However, the extent of the water ingress did not affect train operations in any way (Venter 2015).

By 2012, Gautrain management claimed that 33,100 jobs were created for South Africans, of which 86% went to historically disadvantaged individuals, 59% were youth, (over a fifty-four-month period), women 10%, and people with disabilities 0.6% (Van der Merwe et al. 2012: 651). The women's training program, introduced in 2007, led to 121 women participating in a learnership and mentoring program, while another skills development initiative by Bombardier was the assembly of the Gautrain's rolling stock of rail cars in Derby (UK), to where seventeen South African Bombardier employees were sent to work on the assembly of the first fifteen cars. The remaining eighty-one cars were assembled in South Africa at a mirror plant, to ensure a higher degree of skills transfer. However, it needs to be kept in mind that most of the parts required to assemble the trains are not manufactured locally and need to be imported from abroad (Thomas 2013a: 82). As with ridership figures, estimates vary as to how many jobs were created. The Bombela Consortium claims that in total, 92,900 direct, indirect, and induced jobs were created by the end of May 2009, and the Gauteng Minister for Local Government, Qedani Dorothy Mahlangu, announced in March 2009 that roughly 11,700 jobs were created. The vast majority of these jobs were, however, only temporary during construction, and roughly 2,700 permanent position were required to operate and manage the Gautrain (Thomas 2013a: 81).

Nevertheless, as Flyvbjerg et al. caution:

> ... cost-underestimation and escalation indeed appear to be intentional and part of power games [being] played by project promoters and forecasters, aimed at getting projects started. Cost-underestimation is used strategically to make projects appear less expensive than they really are, in order to gain approval from decision makers to build the projects. Such behaviour best explains why cost escalations are so consistent over time, space, and project type. (Flyvbjerg et al. 2003: 84)

In sum, forecasting accurate passenger figures for transportation megaprojects is as complex and elusive as forecasting the impact of hosting megaevents upon a country's gross domestic product (GDP). In both cases, the issue of risk remains. However, megaprojects differ from megaevents in one crucial respect: the debate about alternatives. In the case of the Gautrain, this debate revolves around the use of high-speed buses.

24.6 "Trains are Sexy, Buses are Not"

As is the case with many other transportation megaprojects, the debate about the feasibility of the Gautrain has also raged between advocates for more investment in system-wide improvements to bus networks, and those in favor of massive fixed rail-based rapid-transit systems. Del Mistro and Roodt, for example, have proposed a high-quality bus-based system with a dedicated public transport line along the median of the freeway, with terminals at the end of the route operating at a minimum frequency of 5 minutes in the peak period, and 15 minutes during the off-peak period (Del Mistro and Roodt 2001: 5). However, the Ben Schoeman highway constitutes less than half of the total Gautrain route length, and problems arise on those parts of the route that are highly congested, subject to intersections and other impediments. Overcoming these obstacles would be costly, "even comparable to the Gautrain cost," and it would be more difficult to connect stations as directly as through the Gautrain (Van der Merwe 2002: 23). However, in terms of capital cost, the Gautrain is much more costly—estimated at R776.45 million per passenger, compared with R65.6 million per passenger on a bus service. The Gautrain is, therefore, effectively three times more costly than the road-based alternative. Another plus, however, is that the high-speed rail option is likely to use approximately 5% less energy than the bus service, and rail has greater carrying capacity (Del Mistro 2008: 22–3). Some transport experts have also argued that passengers traveling via bus on dedicated bus lanes could potentially travel between Pretoria and Johannesburg in 69 minutes compared with 60 minutes on the Gautrain but at considerably lower costs. Others have also lamented the fact that the Gautrain lacks integration with the existing transportation system in the province, including the Metrorail, buses, and mini-taxis. As transportation academic Vaughan Mostert contends:

> There is no holistic transport system in Gauteng or for that matter, anywhere in South Africa. Formal public transport is fragmented, inadequate in terms of both route coverage and frequency, and has failed to develop in keeping with urban expansion. There is no integrated ticketing, scheduling, marketing or branding. Different operators offer different services under different sets of rules. Users do not perceive formal public transport to be a coherent product. (Thomas 2013a: 88)

Exceptions to this trend, however, are the Rea Vaya Bus Rapid Transit (BRT) system in Gauteng and MyCiTi bus network in Cape Town, both of which connect both affluent and less wealthy parts of the city, and are much less expensive than a rapid rail network and more affordable for travelers. Yet as Thomas (2013a: 88) argues, the BRT was designed and implemented once the Gautrain was already a *fait accompli*, during which, "[P]lanners did not engage in deliberation and debate in advance of constructing the Gautrain, but rather built it as a stand-alone project without considering how it might integrate with other modes of transportation, such as a BRT system" (Thomas, 2013a: 88). Yet the Gautrain has its own bus network that transfers commuters to and from Gautrain stations. Although the operating company Bombela wants the luxury buses to transport between 14,000 and 15,000 passengers per day, only 30% of Gautrain passengers make use of the bus system. While a Bombela spokesperson notes that the 30% is "above the global average for other similar systems," some media reports lament the extent to which the buses run without any passengers, especially during the off-peak hours of 09h to 15h (Burmeister 2012). That a series of Gautrain bus-driver strikes over transport allowances in 2011 and 2012 meant that the service came to a complete halt on various occasions, did not install a great deal of public confidence, and by Bombela's own admission may have resulted in a 10% drop in passengers (Burmeister 2012).

Beyond these cost–benefit calculations, however, grasping the attraction of rail over bus services requires reaching into the realm of mythology and the images associated with different transportation modes. The significance of megaprojects, and transport networks in particular, is not only confined to tangible goods; nor are the debates about public transport merely utilitarian in nature. As Siemiatycki (2005b) remarks:

> At a time when our conception of modernity and progress is driven by a paradigm that emphasizes the corrective powers of science, rationality and technology, megaprojects present an imagery of possibility that transcends their tangible benefits. Instead, they create a metanarrative of hope, reflecting an optimism that "big-bang" solutions may be able to solve some of the most pressing problems of our time.

Indeed, a growing literature suggests that the promotion of rail projects relies crucially upon symbolic imagery to acquire public acceptability (Richmond 1998). For it is through the combination of both tangible and intangible factors in the construction of aspiring images "that the promotion of public transit merges function with form, becoming the intersection of mass mobility and mass/popular culture" (Siemiatycki 2006: 278). Tying major infrastructural projects discursively to megaevents enables project advocates to infuse both notions of national identity, and to underline the necessity of conforming to the demands of "competiveness" as dictated by the pressures of globalization. In short, issues of identity and megaprojects as "signifiers" appear as part and parcel of a set of intangible, near-mythical factors. The temptation by Gautrain's promoters to portray South Africa's right to host the soccer World Cup as being dependent upon the construction of the high-speed rail network is a clear demonstration of these dynamics. Similarly, upon receipt of the first four-car set of the train handed over to Gauteng Premier at the time, Mbhazima Shilowa, in Derby on 8 July 2008, the Gautrain was noted as being "ready to bear the pride of the South African nation" (Gautrain Ready to Bear the Pride of the Nation 2008). With the commissioning of the Gautrain tunnel-boring machine, the provincial premier noted the tradition of giving names to such machines, and christened it Imbokodo, in reference to the women who, on 9 August 1956, marched to the Union Buildings in Pretoria, chanting "Wathinta abafazi, wathinta imbokodo" ("You touch a woman, you strike a rock") (Shilowa 2007). During the first trip aboard the Gautrain, with 150 guests from government and the media, on 3 February 2009, Gauteng Premier Paul Mashatile noted: "Our golden train is now finally where it belongs. And although Gautrain's physical home is here in Gauteng, her real home is in the heart and minds of all South Africans." Amid pelting rain, the premier referred to the wet weather as a good omen, much like a rainy African wedding, commenting that "we are truly blessed" (African Blessing 2009). The symbolic significance of infrastructure to the globalization process should not be underestimated. In fact, along with consumption and production, infrastructure is "the great space-shrinker, and power, wealth and status increasingly belong to those who know how to shrink space, or know how to benefit from space being shrunk" (Flyvbjerg, Mette, Skamris, and Buhl 2003: 77). Richmond (1998: 13) aptly describes high-speed trains as "technological sex symbols on steel rails," and once these are also powerfully imbued with representations of national identity, other transportation alternatives which cannot capture the public imagination with equal élan fall by the wayside. In his fascinating examination of the politics surrounding Los Angeles' adoption of a rail transit system, Richmond demonstrated the powerful role of myth and its construction through symbolic processes in getting decision makers to adopt high-speed rail over bus services, even though the former is less suited to the low-density and widespread distribution of population and economic activity in Southern California, which "generates a dispersed and complex pattern of transportation demands among a myriad origins and destinations" (Richmond 1998: 4). Nevertheless, interviewees noted, for example, that rail "is something you can relate to. I don't know how many people get terribly excited about a bus that's running on a freeway" (Richmond 1998: 15). Even when decision makers were confronted with analytical research supporting the suitability of bus over rail, these would be rejected. If images of speed and sophistication are compelling in the established industrial democracies, they would seem all the more alluring to the aspiring economies of the developing world such as South Africa or India. The New Delhi metro, for example, is seen as becoming "a vehicle to promote the bright future of Delhi as a high-tech, rationally planned, competitive city; a vision which itself draws heavily upon the experiences and imagery of cities around the world" (Siemiatycki 2006: 285). Likewise, in South Africa, Gautrain CEO Jack van der Merwe described the Gautrain not only as "sexy," but as "a new energy that has come to life—a golden thread that connects Africa to the world, bringing jobs to people and people to jobs" (Van der Merwe 2008). Similarly, in February 2009, Van der Merwe noted the significance of the train's nose: "It gives the perception of speed. We know this train had to be 'perceived' as fast. This really is an African beauty I think we can be proud of." Gauteng MEC for transport, Ignatius Jacobs, described the first trip on the Gautrain as a "victory" and a "dream on wheels" (*Mail & Guardian* 2009).

That the Gautrain has been so closely associated with the preparations for 2010 and the pre-eminence of the linkage to Africa's biggest and busiest international airport are significant demonstrations of the external face of the country's marketing power. Notions of speed, connectivity, and above all, modernity perform a highly strategic discursive role, not only in terms of urban-boosterism but also as a demonstration of South Africa being a part of the African continent because it constitutes the gateway to the global economy and the splendors which the process of globalization can provide. High-modernity constitutes the abiding *leitmotiv* throughout these descriptions. Anchored in the conviction of scientific and technical progress associated with the industrial revolution in Western Europe and North America from the 1830s until the First World War, it has strongly informed notions of state development, though as a faith it was shared across a wide spectrum of political ideologies (Scott 1998: 88). Promoted by the *avant-garde* among planners, engineers, technocrats, architects, scientists, and high-level administrators:

> The temporal emphasis of high-modernism is almost exclusively on the future. Although any ideology with a large altar dedicated to progress is bound to privilege the future, high modernism carries this to great lengths. The past is an impediment, a history that must be transcended; the present is the platform for launching plans for a better future. A key characteristic of discourses of high-modernism and of the public pronouncements of those states that have embraced it is a heavy reliance on visual images of heroic progress toward a totally transformed future ... To the degree that the future is known and achievable—a belief that the faith in progress encourages—the less future benefits are discounted for uncertainty. The practical effect is to convince most high-modernists that the certainty of a better future justifies the many short-term sacrifices required to get there. (Scott 1998: 95)

In an analysis of blog posts about the Gautrain's readiness for the 2010 FIFA World Cup, Pritchard and Du Plessis (2010: 63) cite the following verbatim quotes from blog posts:

> We now have a world-class public transport system that we can be proud of.
>
>   Regardless of our petty games, the Gautrain is a must-do for anyone living in Joburg–Pretoria–Midrand (eventually)—I believe everyone should experience it, even if it's for a short trip ... everyone needs to feel, smell, touch, and live the Gautrain for just one stop ... it's an incredible thing and it makes me so proud to be a South African and better yet, a Joburgerian!

>   Our breath was taken away, and we all felt extremely proud to be sharing in the
>   dream of what the Gautrain is.
>   What a superb experience ... the sort of infrastructure that assures we have the
>   potential to become a world-class city!

In many ways, the Gautrain represents a symbolic demonstration of the kind of advances that globalization and technological prowess set in motion, and fulfils a fundamental role in signaling South Africa's ascendance and that of Gauteng in the semiperiphery of the world economy in particular. Gautrain's proponents are fond of comparing it with other train networks in the developed world. At the launch of the Gautrain project on 28 September 2006, Mbhazima Shilowa (2006) noted that a dedicated service for local and international passengers will be created

> with decentralized check-in facilities available at Sandton Station, *as is the case in London and Stockholm*. The price of an air ticket will be able to include a train trip to and from Sandton, and passengers will be able to check in baggage at Sandton. An air ticket will, therefore, also be able to stipulate, for example, London to Sandton or Sandton to Cape Town. The airport connection service will bring Gauteng in line with many major cities in the world, where it is becoming common practice to link cities and international airports by rail.

It is also striking that Gautrain management in 2014 similarly invoked the London Undergound (and not another emerging city in the South) as a comparative example to justify the Gautrain's patronage guarantee:

> Imagine shutting down the London Underground simply because its revenue does not cover its operating costs. London would grind to a halt in hours, as would its economy, and shortly after that, the economy of the entire subregion. On the contrary, the London Underground is an essential enabler of the regional economy. It is not a profit centre in its own right and no thinking person expects it to be. Everyone does, however, expect that it must be operated efficiently and cost-effectively. The same applies to the Gautrain. (Braithwaite 2015)

24.7 CONCLUSION

Given the enormous costs involved in megaproject construction and especially transportation projects, and the impacts such projects have on the public fiscus, these projects are inherently political affairs. However, the political economy of megatransport projects reveal that both material and ideational dimensions shape the field upon which both proponents and opponents contest the need for a megaproject. In the case of the Gautrain, the debate about material considerations centered essentially on cost–benefit concerns. In this regard, public ridership figures became an essential tool of contestation. Opponents contend that these figures are insufficient to sustain the project without a government-backed patronage guarantee, while proponents argue that over time, these figures will increase or simply produce different figures. Whereas opponents argue for a better bus service, proponents contend that trains can deal with greater volumes. Opponents highlight cost underestimation, while proponents argue for job creation. In these debates, the extent to which public consultation occurred and the degree of inclusivity these processes facilitated are an integral part of the politics of megaproject construction. While these material considerations are important, intangible issues relating to questions about identity, image, and symbolism also appear to be significant in explaining the decision by state and corporate elites to embark on an infrastructural project of such magnitude. In the South African case, the Gautrain appears to be seen as a status symbol by its supporters. Hence Johannesburg, "like London and Stockholm," also has a high-speed airport link, which is, after all, much more sexy than having an airport bus service. Moreover, as a marketing tool as the first high-speed rail project in Africa, the Gautrain also projects South Africa's aspirational role as a hub for regional if not continental transport infrastructure. Hence, given both these material and ideational considerations, and despite continued concerns as to the Gautrain's financial sustainability, reports suggest that the network may in the near future be extended. Possible extensions being considered include a link from the existing Park Station to Westgate, a link from the existing Rhodesfield station to Boksburg, a rapid-rail link from Naledi in Soweto to Mamelodi, and a link from the existing Sandton Station to Randburg (Venter 2014).

References

African Blessing as Gautrain Makes Sleek Debut. (2009). *Mail and Guardian Online*, <http://www.mg.co.za/article/2009-02-03-african-blessing-as-gautrain-makes-sleek-debut>.

Africa Research Bulletin. (2006/07). December 2006 and January 2007.

Altshuler, A. and Luberoff, D. (2003). *Mega-Projects: The Changing Politics of Urban Public Investment*. Washington, DC, and Cambridge, MA: Brookings Institution Press and Lincoln Institute of Land Policy.

Batwell, J. (2013). "South Africa's Gautrain missing ridership targets," *International Railway Journal*, February 28, <http://www.railjournal.com/index.php/africa/south-africas-gautrain-missing-ridership-targets.html>

Boulding, K. E. (1956). *The Image, Knowledge and Life in Society*. Ann Arbor: University of Michigan Press.

Braithwaite, E. (2014). "In defence of the Gautrain," *Business Day*, 20 July, <http://www.bdlive.co.za/opinion/2014/07/20/in-defence-of-the-gautrain>.

Brocklebank, P., Burnett, S. L., Ras, N., and Van der Walt, G. (2001). "Gautrain: Demand and revenue forecast" (unpublished paper).

Burmeister B., (2012). "Gautrain ghost buses," <http://www.focusontransport.co.za/index.php/regulars/focus-on-bus-and-coach/bus-and-coach/1169-gautrain-ghost-buses.html>.

Cars per Capita in Africa: Which Country has the Most Cars on the Road? (2014). *Be Forward*, <http://blog.beforward.jp/regional-topics/africa/cars-capita-africa-country-cars-road.html>.

Chibba, R. (2006). "Cosatu rails against the Gautrain," *Mail and Guardian Online*, 30 March, <http://mg.co.za/article/2006-03-30-cosatu-rails-against-gautrain/>.

Del Mistro, R. (2002). "Taking a spin on the Gautrain," *Civil Engineering: Magazine of the South African Institute of Civil Engineers*, 10: 22–6.

Del Mistro, R. (2008). "Rapid rail project in Gauteng," presentation slides, South African Cities Network Seminar on Public Transport, University of Cape Town.

Del Mistro R. and Roodt, L. (2001). "Alternative-based public transport between Johannesburg and Pretoria," (unpublished paper).

Donaldson, R. (2006). "Mass rapid rail development in South Africa's metropolitan core," *Land Use Policy*, 23: 344–52.

Flyvbjerg, B., Bruzelius, N., and Rothengatter, W. (2003). *Megaprojects and Risk: An Anatomy of Ambition*. Cambridge: Cambridge University Press.

Flyvbjerg, B., Mette K., Skamris H., and Buhl S. L. (2003). "How common and how large are cost overruns in transport infrastructure projects?" *Transport Reviews*, 23: 71–88.

Gautrain Ready to Bear the Pride of the Nation. (2008). 8 July, <http://www.gautrain.co.za/index.php?pid=1693&ct=1&fi d=7&click=0>.

Kardes, I., Ozturk, A., Cavusgil, T., and Cavusgil, E. (2013). "Managing global megaprojects: Complexity and risk management," *International Business Review*, 22: 905–17.

Khuzwayo, W. (2008). "Gautrain denies rocketing costs," *Business Report*, 20 March, <http://www.busrep.co.za/general/print_article.php?fArticleId=4314292&fSectionId=5>.

Louw, L. (2014). "Gautrain trundles over needs of the poor," *Business Day*, 28 May, <http://www.bdlive.co.za/opinion/columnists/2014/05/28/gautrain-trundles-over-needs-of-the-poor>.

Mail & Guardian (2009). 3 July.

Mbeki: Stereotyping Behind Gautrain Saga (2006) *Mail & Guardian*, 8 December.

Moonsamy, N. (2014). "Efficient public transport still eludes working class citizens," *Business Day*, 8 September, <http://www.bdlive.co.za/opinion/2014/09/08/efficient-public-transport-still-eludes-working-class-citizens>.

Mostert, V. (2005). "Commentary on South African public transport policy, with emphasis on the Gautrain scheme," written Submission to Transport Portfolio Committee, Parliament, May 2005, <http://www.pmg.org.za/docs/2005/051116commentary.htm>.

Most Gautrain Passengers Women. (2012), <http://www.iol.co.za/news/south-africa/gauteng/most-gautrain-passengers-women-survey-1.1269801#.VOXnvuaUfts>.

No Guarantee Gautrain will be Ready for 2010. (2006). *Mail & Guardian*, 11 October.

Pritchard M. and Du Plessis C. (2010). "An exploratory analysis of citizen journalists as editorial gatewatchers: A case study of Gautrain blog posts vis-à-vis completion for the 2010 FIFA Soccer World Cup," *Communicare*, 29: 48–68.

Radebe, J. (2006). "Address at the launch of construction of Gautrain rapid rail link," Marlboro, 26 September, <http://www.gov.za/j-radebe-launch-construction-gautrain-rapid-rail-link>.

Richmond, J. E. D. (1998). "The mythical conception of rail transit in Los Angeles," *Journal of Architectural and Planning Research*, 15: 294–320.

Robbins, D., Dickinson, J., and Calver, S., (2007). "Planning transport for special events: A conceptual framework and future agenda for research," *International Journal of Tourism Research*, 9: 303–11.

Rogerson, C. M. (2004). "From spatial development initiative to Blue IQ: Subnational economic planning in Gauteng," *Urban Forum*, 15: 74–101.

Scott, J. C. (1998). *Seeing Like a State: How Certain Schemes to Improve the Human Condition Have Failed*. Binghampton, NY: Yale University Press.

Shilowa, M. (2006). "Speech by Gauteng Premier Mbhazima Shilowa at the launch of the Gautrain Project," 28 September, <http://www.gov.za/m-shilowa-launch-construction-gautrain-rapid-rail-link>.

Shilowa, M. (2007). "Speech by Gauteng Premier Mbhazima Shilowa at the commissioning of the Gautrain tunnel boring machine," 13 December, <http://www.gautrain.co.za/index.php?pid=1524&ct=1&fid=7&click=4>.

Siemiatycki, M. (2005a), "The making of a mega-project in the neo-liberal city: The case of mass rapid transit infrastructure investment in Vancouver, Canada," *City*, 9: 67–83.

Siemiatycki, M. (2005b). "Reviews: Risky business," *City*, 9: 261–3.

Siemiatycki, M. (2006). "Message in a metro: Building urban rail infrastructure and image in Delhi, India," *International Journal of Urban and Regional Research*, 30: 277–92.

Sunday Times. (2006). "Serious concerns over Gautrain's feasibility," 26 November.

Thomas, D. P. (2013a). "The Gautrain project in South Africa: A cautionary tale," *Journal of Contemporary African Studies*, 31: 77–94.

Thomas, D. P. (2013b). "Bombardier and the Gautrain project in South Africa: The political economy of Canadian investment in a rapid rail megaproject," *Studies in Political Economy*, 91: 137–57.

Transport Portfolio Committee (TPC). (2005a). "Gautrain Project: briefing," 8 November, <https://pmg.org.za/committee-meeting/5883/>.

Transport Portfolio Committee (TPC). (2005b). "Report of the Transport Portfolio Committee on Public Hearings on the proposed Gautrain Project," 16 November, <https://pmg.org.za/committee-meeting/5943/>.

Van der Merwe, C., van der Merwe, E., Van Zyl, O., and Negota, G. (2012). "Gautrain: successful implementation of socio-economic development objectives," *Abstracts of the 31st Southern African Transport Conference, 9-12 July*, <http://repository.up.ac.za/bitstream/handle/2263/20416/VanderMerwe_Gautrain%282012%29.pdf?sequence=3>.

Van der Merwe, J. (2002). "Taking the spin off Gautrain and putting issues in perspective," *Civil Engineering: Magazine of the South African Institute of Civil Engineers*, 10: 23–6.

Van der Merwe, J. (2008). "Gautrain: Acceptance of first trains', <http://www.gautrain.co.za/contents/train_acceptance/J%20vd%20Merwe.doc>.

Venter, I. (2013a). "Gauteng route extensions under review as ridership ramps up," *Engineering News*, 24 May, <http://www.engineeringnews.co.za/print-version/gautrain-2013-05-24>.

Venter, I. (2013b). "Gautrain 2012 ridership up 60%, placing 'severe strain' on capacity," *Engineering News*, 9 April, <http://www.engineeringnews.co.za/article/gautrain-2012-ridership-up-60-placing-severe-strain-on-capacity-2013-04-09/>.

Venter, I. (2014). "Gautrain ridership rises as e-tolls go live," *Engineering News*, <http://www.engineeringnews.co.za/print-version/gautrain-2014-01-17>

Venter, I. (2015). "Solutions still to be considered for Gautrain tunnel water-ingress problem," *Engineering News*, 30 January, <http://www.engineeringnews.co.za/article/gautrain-2015-01-30>.

CHAPTER 25

LARGE DAM DEVELOPMENT

From Trojan Horse to Pandora's Box

RHODANTE AHLERS,
MARGREET ZWARTEVEEN, AND KAREN BAKKER

25.1 INTRODUCTION

DAMS are back on the agenda and they are larger than ever. In 2014, 626 hydropower dams with capacity of over 1MW were under construction and another 3,071 were being planned (Zarfl et al. 2014). Benefits anticipated by proponents of large dams include enabling the expansion of irrigated land, improving drinking water supply, controlling floods, and producing hydropower. Studies—notably the World Commission on Dams (WCD) report *Dams and Development* (2000)—have documented that these benefits tend to be unevenly distributed and are produced at extremely high social and environmental costs. Large dams are generally justified with projections that are unattainable. Indeed, large dams have consistently been characterized by what World Bank evaluator Besant-Jones termed "pervasive appraisal optimism" (cited in Usher, 1997: 61)—an optimism that is characteristic of megaprojects in general and involves consistently erring on the risky side of planning by relying on overly positive assessments of future gains and benefits, while externalizing and underestimating environmental and social–cultural costs (Ansar et al. 2014; Flyvbjerg, Bruzelius, and Rothengatter 2003; Goldsmith and Hildyard 1984; Khagram 2003; Klingensmith 2007; Priemus, Flyvbjerg, and Wee 2008; Usher 1997; WCD 2000). Megaprojects, such as large dams, are also typically plagued by principal-agent problems and rent-seeking provoked by the enormous investments required (Flyvbjerg 2014).

The 45,000 large[1] dams constructed during the twentieth century drastically altered the world's rivers, causing tremendous and far-reaching socioecological transformations (McCully, 1996).[2] Growing opposition coupled with their disappointing performance resulted in a slowdown of large dam development toward the end of the twentieth century. Although none of these concerns have disappeared, large hydraulic infrastructure again figures prominently on development agendas (Zarfl et al. 2014; see also Pomeranz 2009;

International Rivers Network 2014). In the five years following the WCD (2000) report, no less than thirty-five very large dams (with crests over 150 meters) and three hundred dams with crests over 60 meters started construction (ICOLD 2006). In Africa, by 2010, nineteen large dams were under construction (International Rivers Network 2010). The largest, most costly (estimated to be $80 billion; Cole et al. 2014), and possibly most controversial dam complex proposed—the Grand Inga project in Democratic Republic of Congo—was approved by the World Bank in 2013 but has been delayed until 2017. Not only has the moratorium on dam construction been lifted, but the dams built are larger than ever before. Countries as diverse as China, Brazil, India, Loa PDR, Ethiopia, Rwanda, Mozambique, Turkey, and the Democratic Republic of Congo are constructing large dams or are planning to do so. Governments of these countries mobilize a "right to development" discourse to promote dams (Hirsch 2010; Islar 2012; Öktem 2002) for flood protection, hydropower production, desalinization, or a combination of these.

Increased recognition of climate variability has buttressed the popularity of large dams, as hydropower is framed as an important source of green energy in response to the global call for alternative, non-fossil energy sources (Ahlers et al. 2015; Imhof and Lanza 2010). The International Hydropower Association, for example, argues that hydropower's operating efficiency and flexibility make it the least-cost option of all clean energy options, and that its "unique characteristics place it at the center of our future clean energy systems" (International Hydropower Association 2014: 1). Their putative "greenness" is also mobilized by International Finance Institutions and institutional investors to actively support plans for new large hydraulic infrastructures. However, this interest is also driven by the 7–20% projected returns on investment as infrastructure is an increasingly important asset class in processes of financialization (Ahlers and Merme 2016; Hildyard 2012; Merme et al. 2014). Furthermore, hydropower projects present opportunities for economies that seek much needed foreign exchange. In sum, proponents present hydropower as a straightforward way to exploit the power potential trapped in uncontrolled rivers, thereby supplying electricity, reducing greenhouse gases, and attracting foreign currency for sustainable regional development.

The current boom in large infrastructure development, with dams that are much larger and far more costly than before, is happening in the absence of systematic empirical evidence on how dams affect poverty, environments, and livelihoods (Dufflo and Pande 2007). Alongside a general lack of comprehensive knowledge on the cumulative impacts of large dams (Lehner et al. 2011; Vörösmarty et al. 2010; Fletcher 2010), information on whether potential benefits outweigh the social and environmental costs incurred is sparse (Ansar et al. 2014). Particularly in the current global environment that is increasingly uncertain because of climate change, producing such evidence is fraught with considerable disagreement on how to best predict, assess, and value such impacts (WCD 2000; Cole et al. 2014). Assessments are always context- and concept-dependent, while the use of varying scalar (space and time) assumptions results in substantially different outcomes. This, coupled with the fact that those who experience the costs and risks of large hydraulic infrastructures are usually not the ones who enjoy the benefits and profits, makes it particularly difficult to achieve consensus about whether and where dams should be built. Indeed, the assessments and measurements themselves become part of what is contested in dam development.

With the exception of the references to climate change and green energy, the argu-ments used to justify contemporary dams resemble those of the previous century, with dams being depicted by proponents as a prerequisite for development, and as unrivaled suppliers of food, water, and energy security (Usher 1997; Bakker 1999; WCD 2000; Ledec and Quintero 2003; Scudder 2005; Briscoe 2010; Hirsch 2010). This chapter, how-ever, shows that the current century provides a very different context for dam develop-ment than the twentieth century. Dam projects today involve a more diverse set of actors with distinct and at times contradicting interests as the boundaries between public, pri-vate, and non-governmental sectors have blurred. In addition, the uncertainties of cli-mate change further complicate dam development. The proliferation of actors and the hazy relations between them in the context of climate variability have made the assess-ment of the costs, benefits, and risks of dam building increasingly difficult and conten-tious. Not only does this complicate transparency and democracy of dam governance, it makes it extremely urgent.

To explore how dam development is intrinsically political, we use a Lefebvrian anal-ysis of the "production of space" to define dams not as objects in space but as agents in spatial strategies and as sites of continued and dynamic struggles. These struggles happen through combined technological, discursive, and institutional means, and include disagreements about the nature and purpose of "development." A conceptual-ization of nature, technology, and society as mutually constituted informs this theoriza-tion, thereby shifting questions of dam design and development from the indisputable domains of nature, biology, or technology—domains only accessible by an exclusive group of experts—to the contingent domains of society and politics. This opens up these questions for debate and widens definitions of expertise, thereby also prompting the need to rethink to what extent large hydraulic infrastructures can best be regulated and controlled (Zwarteveen 2015).

We first elaborate our Lefebvrian theorization of the role of dams in producing partic-ular landscapes, and then proceed with a characterization of twentieth-century dams as Trojan Horses. Drawing in particular on the example of the Egyptian Aswan High Dam, we show how large dams, legitimized as bringers of economic development, were carriers of political and ideological spatial strategies. Dam development in the twenty-first cen-tury is a process better captured as a Pandora's Box, revealing complex financial flows and intricate networks of public and private actors seeking diverse objectives, as illustrated by an example from the Mekong. We conclude the chapter by carving out the contemporary landscape of dam development and the implications for democratic governance.

25.2 Dam Building as the Production of Space

Dams carry meaning in multiple ways. They demonstrate how unruly "nature" can be conquered and "idle" resources exploited to advance civilization; they render visible the great feats of engineering and the unlimited possibilities of technology; and they are landmarks on a nation's path to development. As Cullather (2002: 521) phrased it: "For Nehru, for Zahir Shah, for China today, the great blank wall of a dam was a screen on which they would project the future." Their impressive visual presence makes dams into excellent prestige projects to symbolize the might of ruling powers, and with it, create a national image of progress, prosperity, and strength (Kaika 2006; Swyngedouw 1999). From the moment they are conceived, dams set in motion a series of processes of social and biophysical reordering, whereby certain avenues for change are created and others foreclosed, none of which is fully predictable or controllable.

To make sense of the transformations that dams provoke, we draw on the work of Henri Lefebvre (1991) regarding the production of space. Lefebvre's ambition was to reveal and thus question the ideology and politics underlying urban design, illuminating how it is always historically rooted, riddled with contradictions, and continuously contested in everyday life (Goonewardena et al. 2008). Following Lefebvre, we conceptualize large hydraulic infrastructures as the production and transformation of particular sociospatial relations through perpetual, conflict-laden interactions among opposed spatial strategies (Brenner and Elder 2009: 367). In not ontologically separating the biophysical system from the social or technological system, this theorization positively resonates with that of other critical environmental scholars who aspire to rethink society–nature relations by understanding nature and society not as two distinct phenomena or domains, but as always already implied in each other. Such theorizations thus propose considering water, people, and infrastructure in their mutual interactions, positing that they exist and indeed "are" because of and through each other (Haraway 1991; Moore 2011), thereby collapsing "fields" that are usually apprehended separately (Swyngedouw 1999: 318). Water scholars have proposed terms such as "waterscapes" (Swyngedouw 1999; Baviskar 2007), "hydrosocial networks" (Bakker 2010), or "hydrosocial cycles" (Linton and Budds 2014) to express the notion that river or groundwater trajectories, as well as the resulting floods or scarcities, are not natural processes but the outcome of specific histories and practices of water resources exploitation or "development." Large dams have been central in the reconfiguration of landscapes by simultaneously redirecting flows (social and ecological) and reordering societies (institutionally, politically, economically, and culturally) (Harvey 1996; Meehan 2013; Scott 1998).

By questioning the nature–culture (or technology–society) divide, these ontologies also question the very foundations of scientific knowledge production. Conceptualizing dams as the contested production of space demystifies the possibility to see and know (the impacts of) large dams from an unidentified or objective position—what Haraway (1991) calls the god-trick: "the false vision promising transcendence of all limits and responsibility." This has important implications for ways of thinking about and organizing dam governance, or for institutionally regulating and containing the environmental and social impacts of dams. For one, the responsibility and authority for assessing such impacts cannot be simply relegated to scientific experts, as norms of scientific objectivity that are anchored in the possibility to separate nature from society (and science from politics) do not apply. Because any assessment of the social and environmental impacts of large dams is context- and concept-dependent, and a function of scalar and temporal assumptions used, experts' assessments can never be totally independent.

The impact of dams, whether positive or negative, reaches far beyond the (social, political, or biogeophysical) moment and location in which they were constructed. Already before dams are constructed and brought into operation, they are conceived and planned, the infrastructure designed, the material and financial needs gathered and applied, the political support assured, and a constituency arranged. A dam is conceived with a particular purpose and location in mind by particular actors with interests that may be social, economic, or political. Rather than an empty space void of practice, meaning, or ideals, this location is a river basin, where people live, fish swim, birds fly, and water flows. At the moment of construction, the scientists and engineers planning the hydraulic structure have already redesigned the landscape in their imagination and on their drawing tables: flowing water courses are conceived as potential volumetric quantities to be managed as inputs for hydropower generation or irrigated crop production. Through their visions and designs, they thus redefine the river as a bundle of potential resources lying idle, and wasted if not used.

This biophysical reordering is accompanied with an institutional reordering, often entailing the move of water rights and water decision-making powers from local organizations to new ones at basin, national, or regional scales. As people, roads, structures, flora, and fauna are moved or inundated, previously unconnected places now become part of an envisioned institutional construct called a river basin. Consequently, the landscape (or waterscape) takes on a different purpose and thereby a different meaning, while still carrying institutional and material legacies from the past, both in the form of more or less visible material or social manifestations and in the form of ideas or values (Lefebvre 1976; Kogan 2013). The redistribution of stakes, meanings, powers, and responsibilities that this transformation of the waterscape entails does not stop or stabilize after construction, but often continues through the politics of dam operation decisions. Rather than a mere technical or neutral mathematical equation or model, the operation of dams tends to become the playing ground of continued negotiations and bargaining about whose needs get recognized and whose demands are met, about land and water rights and competing sources of livelihood.

Common to large dam projects is that those most directly experiencing the effects and impacts have least influence on dam operation decisions, often because they already have been rendered relatively powerless and voiceless through the process of dam design and construction. Initial design choices tend to favor one or several uses of water over others. Dam construction, by literally pouring these choices into concrete, functions as a continuous and self-enforcing mechanism to iteratively endow the stakes of the initial decision makers. The degree of freedom for dam operation to absorb possible new stakes or adapt to a changed equilibrium of interests are severely limited because of the inflexible nature and sheer size of dams. Upon reaching the end of its operational utility, these structures demand decommissioning—an issue that is currently becoming more urgent given the age of many twentieth-century dams. The cost of decommissioning have generally been left out of many, if not all, original cost–benefit analyses, and the useful life of these structures is often much shorter than anticipated.[3] Some of these dams find themselves on arid riverbeds and have lost all possible utility, while others hold sediment and water loads that may be toxic or hazardous in other ways. Decommissioning may be as disruptive as the initial placement of the dam itself.

To conclude, we approach and conceptualize large hydraulic infrastructures as active agents in continuous and dynamic processes of space production. These are processes in which social practices and meanings interact with biophysical materialities, resulting in the emergence of new landscapes that carry crystallizations of the past. Embodying struggles over desired practices, ideals, and meaning, the outcomes are necessarily always and everywhere contested. Lefebvre emphasizes the relations between the material, mental, and social dimension of space, or in his words between a perceived, conceived, and lived landscape. This defies overtly structuralist notions of the production of space as being one of (capitalist) design, but also usefully rejects positivist notions of innocent "natural" rearrangements. Lefebvre argues that it is in the heterogeneity of everyday practices and experience that "lived space" is produced, with capital reproducing itself in contradictory and simultaneously contested ways. Lived space is therefore never a linear outcome of conceived space, which is one reason why it defies accurate forecasting. Large dams concretize the relational and dialectical nature of the triad as they are produced by and embedded in, and by their conception and construction influence sociopolitical and socioeconomic networks in contradictory ways. They mobilize networks of capital, knowledge, and (geo)politics, and are pivots in spatially huge landscape transformations, not only spanning the rural and urban landscape, but also intimately connecting them.

25.3 TWENTIETH-CENTURY DAM BUILDING: TROJAN HORSES

The twentieth century witnessed an explosion of dam construction. Where in the nineteenth and early twentieth century dams were developed primarily by private actors, this rapidly changed by the mid-1920s, when both the former Soviet Union and the United States began to pour public money into dams. The post-World War II era showed a particularly rapid increase owing to a rise in Asian dam building, post-colonial projects, and the availability of surplus US military dollars that sought investment. Figure 25.1 shows the proliferation of large dams over the century. In the 1950s, Nasser in Egypt spoke of dams as *pyramids for the living*,[4] and Nehru in India referred to dams as *temples of modern India*.[5] Both were in the midst of post-colonial nation-building, making it easy to read dams as a paradigmatic expression of the modernity that characterized the era: the drive toward controlling nature, the belief in technological solutions for social ills, and the promotion of a mimetic vision of Western society as the only image of civilization, with the nation-state as the privileged state form (Cullather

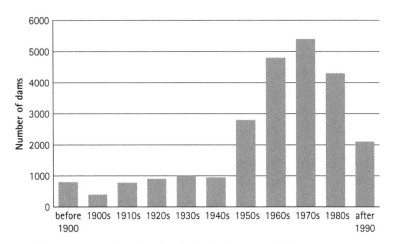

FIGURE 25.1 Construction of dams by decade during the twentieth century.

(From World Commission on Dams 2000.)

2002; Klingensmith 2007). Dams were allotted beneficial powers in solving a multi-tude of problems: "In a sense, it is indeed impossible for a country to have development without dams, as both are part of the same discourse" (Baghel and Nüsser 2010: 241, after Escobar 1995).

A more in-depth review of the historic trajectories of dam building in the twenti-eth century reveals that dam dynamics not only expressed and harnessed modernist and post-colonial energies, but were also importantly shaped by cold war geopolitical maneuvering, in addition to being influenced by global markets and regional politics (Ahlers et al. 2014; Tucker 2010). As large dams demand substantial capital, they were important sites of the accumulation and absorption of surplus capital, constituting what David Harvey termed spatiotemporal fixes of capital. Hence, the surge in dam building after World War II and in the 1970s can largely be explained by how it allowed absorb-ing accumulated US "war dollars" and the "petrodollars" from oil-producing nations that were sitting "idle" in Western banks. The investment of these large sums of capital, in what in the twentieth century were primarily public projects, demanded substantial involvement of the state, and with it, the aid industry. During the 1970s and 1980s, when dam building in developed countries had significantly slowed down or stopped alto-gether, dams were packaged as aid by most OECD countries.[6] This meant that they were not only accompanied by a series of conditionalities, but also generated new foreign markets for the increasingly redundant domestic dam industry (Usher 1997). Hence, dams facilitated the absorption of surplus capital, the expansion of the donor industries, and the increase of debt for the global South.

Characteristic of this period of dam development was that it was based on, and con-vincingly celebrated, the ability of engineers to harness natural resources for the benefit of development and civilization—a celebration that hinged on a representation of the landscape as a bundle of resources wasted if not brought under control. The proposed reordering of the landscape went accompanied with transformations in the relations of (re)production and consumption to better align them with purposes of capital accumulation and political control. This process of commensuration and crafting coherence forcefully ignored and subsequently reshaped existing sociocultural differences. Large dams were used to produce and showcase the unity and modernity of newborn or newly assembled nations, simultaneously legitimizing and consolidating the authority of the regime (Klingensmith 2007; Swyngedouw 2007; Westerman 2011). These large hydraulic structures thus were are an intrinsic part of profound national and international political projects to centralize and rescale control over water resources, and with it, advance a particular societal order. "Through this process, the symbolic richness and creative autonomy of daily life are progressively eviscerated and replaced by the homogenization and fragmentation of a technocratic rationality projected onto reality through the planned production of space" (Wilson 2011: 997–8). In sum, large dams as vehicles of development were very like Trojan horses, embodying far more than instruments for water storage.

The Aswan High Dam (AHD) in Egypt is a good example of twentieth-century dam development. Planned with the explicit purpose of enabling a shift from basin irrigation to perennial irrigation, and in the process altering agricultural relations of production from a smallholder system to one based on owner–tenant relations, its construction was finalized in 1970. New hydraulic structures, the extension of the area irrigated, and an increased cropping intensity (by extending the season through the control of flooding) were accompanied with the establishment of private property rights to land and water, creating a propertied class alongside a landless class dependent on wages (Smit forthcoming; Tignor 1966). The project clearly embodied a spatial project in which control over "nature" was accompanied by a vision of progress and a particular ordering of society. As Cromer noted in 1908 (cited in Tvedt 2004: 29): "When eventually the waters of the Nile, from the Lakes to the sea, are brought fully under control, it will be possible to boast that Man, in this case the Englishman, has turned the gifts of Nature to the best possible Advantage." When Egypt became independent in 1922, the dam was reinvented to serve Egypt's autonomy vis-à-vis Britain, which still controlled upstream Sudan and the upper White Nile. With a reservoir that could hold two years of Nile flow, upstream projects to store water for Egypt would become obsolete. The dam now symbolized the break from the colonial past, and served as a landmark for shifting control of the Nile toward Egypt (Mitchell 2002).

Internal political struggles, national uprisings in response to increasing food prices, and the militarization of the Suez Canal by the British in response to the war in Palestine triggered a chain of events that finally resulted in the replacement of the monarch by a military revolutionary command council. Along with the promise of the new and larger Aswan dam, the council introduced land reform and the nationalization of industries. The geopolitical context of upstream countries contesting British imperialism and the intensification of the Cold War encouraged the British and the United States to positively react to President Nasser's request for funding the AHD, as this would allow them to secure their influence in the region. Even though Nasser[7] agreed to the conditions

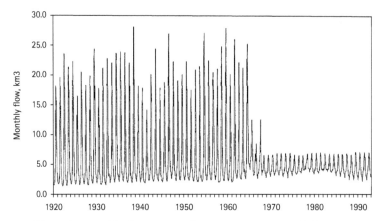

FIGURE 25.2 Change in monthly downstream flows owing to Aswan High Dam.

(From Sutcliffe et al. 1999.)

set by the World Bank, the United States finally withdrew, with the remark that "Egypt should get along for the time being with projects less monumental than the Aswan Dam" (Borzutzky and Berger 2010: 84). In response, Nasser nationalized the Suez Canal to use its revenues to construct the dam (Little 1965), and opened the doors to Soviet Union finance and engineers. After signing the agreement with the new military regime in Sudan, the construction of AHD could begin.

By creating a buffer against floods, drought, and upstream interference, the AHD materialized Egypt's claim. It simultaneously altered and regulated the river's regime (shown in Figure 25.2), and gave its government far-reaching means to control the river. Nevertheless, water logging and salinity plagued the delta, and the hydropower facility working at suboptimum levels produced energy primarily for the fertilizer industry. The resulting debt repayment drew Egypt into a severe financial crisis.

In sum, the AHD was mobilized in a variety of spatial strategies for territorial and hydraulic reordering[8] that favored and actively sought to produce a particular scientific, ideological, and political conception of the landscape. Central, and characteristic of the twentieth century, was the desire to extend state space and advance capitalist relations of production[9] through centrally managed irrigation systems, the accompanying nationalization and homogenization of land and water rights that transformed social relations of agricultural production, and the production of energy for industry and consumption. The case shows how the AHD represents a desired control over a landscape (biophysically, as well as socially), while simultaneously serving to visualize and enable this control (Warner 2013), with the nation-state as the privileged format of rule.[10] As the tangible material embodiment of political economic relations, the dam clearly reveals modernity's deeply geographical project: taming unruly nature and unruly people, establishing a particular organization of society, and legitimizing new social relations of production. The case also shows that the landscape is not so easily ruled and that the technology inserted into and merging with the historical conditions of the landscape produces new and, to a certain extent, unpredictable formations.

25.4 TWENTY-FIRST-CENTURY DAMS: PANDORA'S BOXES

The current conjuncture around dams is very different from that of the twentieth century, primarily because financialization and globalization have structurally transformed the relations between the social and the biogeophysical,[11] while advances in technology have compressed space and time (Harvey 1996; Smith 2006). The blurring boundaries between public and private actors in dam development, new processes of financialization, and increasing global unsettledness and uncertainties have together rendered the governance of dams both more urgent and more difficult than ever. We illustrate these with a case study of the Nam Theun 2 Dam in Laos.

The Nam Theun 2 Power Company (NTPC) involves the largest tributary dam in the Mekong Basin with an installed capacity of 1070MW. Completed in 2010, it is not only known as the most complex public–private partnership in the history of dam development (Wong 2010), but is also hailed for the collaboration between the World Bank and the Government of Laos on development objectives (Baird et al. 2015) and is an award-winning prototype for the best financial construction in the Asia–Pacific region (Merme et al. 2014). A Power Purchase Agreement signed between the power company and the electricity facilities determined that 95% of the energy produced is destined for Thailand and the remainder 5% for Laotian domestic consumption.

Since 2011, the company has been owned by three parties: the French EDF international, the Laotian State Enterprise, and the Thai Electricity Generating Public Company. Twenty-seven parties together financed the US$1.45-billion project, with a debt:equity ratio of around 70:30 (Ward 2010). Merme et al. (2014: 23) explain that the equity investors buy shares in the power company, and when enough equity is secured, debt financiers lend or secure the necessary remainder. The shareholders financed the equity package through loans, credits, and grants, while financial institutions, such as development banks and private commercial banks, finance and support the debt package with loans and guarantees. Figure 25.3 shows this construction of financial flows. The Laotian government eased labor regulations and provided investment incentives to attract international capital, such as extensive tax exemptions, and special import duty rates for materials, equipment, and supplies (Merme et al. 2014). Public-sector finance was limited but necessary for the guarantees that commercial investors demand and that Multilateral Development Banks (MDBs) and Export Credit Agencies (ECAs) provide. Under the Build–Own–Operate–Transfer (BOOT) arrangement, the consortium holding NTPC is allowed to develop, finance, construct, and operate the dam for a concession period of twenty-five years.

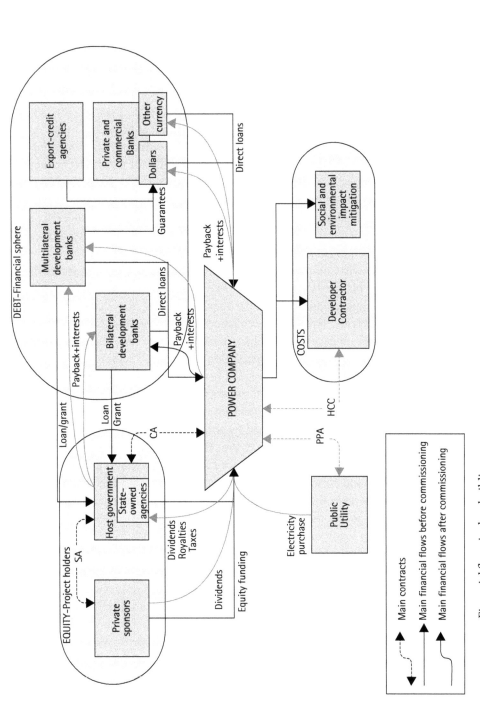

FIGURE 25.3 Financial flows in dam building.

(From Merme et al. 2014.)

The rights and obligations for both the government and the NTPC are specified in the Concession Agreement, which stipulates that NTPC controls all water management decisions related to NT2. Except for minimum water release obligations and restrictions, it has exclusive water rights over the flows of the Nam Theun and several other rivers. Even though the consortium is a public–private partnership, the full Concession Agreement is confidential. Full details of the transfer are not open to public scrutiny, such as the dam's operating cost, liabilities, or water management priorities, thus preventing public accountability (Probe International 2004). Potential social and environmental impacts, mitigation, compensation, and restoration measures have been identified,[12] but Mathews (2012) and International Rivers Network (2010) have reported a range of violations. Baird et al. (2015) show that the concession agreement does not obligate investors to pay the full costs of mitigation and compensation for downstream communities, and only a single one-time development intervention and minimal compensation were deemed sufficient to compensate for long-term ongoing impacts. In addition, the lifetime of the consortium is only twenty-five years. This means that the Laotian government is left to deal with the longer-term negative consequences of the dams, including the loss of fisheries, changing flood regimes, and the general disruption of socioeconomic and ecosystemic processes (Smits 2011; WCD 2000; Wong 2010).

It is difficult, if not impossible, to hold the dam financers and developers accountable for their actions, and they have no obligation to share information with the public. Under national and international commercial law, all contracts and related documents are confidential, with only the parties to the contract having full access to them. Hence, information concerning equity investments by the sponsors (core capital and loans) and private debt providers (ECA, banks, and other financial lenders) is not accessible. Only the documents concerning the host utility's involvement in dam building through loans and grants and the participation of public debt providers are publicly available.

The NT2 case is illustrative of how globally, in the past decade, large dams have increasingly been financed by private investors rather than the public sector (Briscoe 1999; Hildyard 2012; Hirsch 2010; Middleton 2009; Molle, Foran, and Käkönen 2009; Schultz 2002), facilitated by neoliberal reforms that since the 1980s have aimed to create competitive markets in the energy sector through corporatization, commercialization, and privatization. New global financial centers have developed (Shanghai, Singapore, Kuala Lumpur, and São Paulo), and regional economies have grown and consolidated, such as ASEAN and MERCOSUR. Combined with continuous (regional) economic growth during the last decade, this now makes the global South better placed to cofinance dams, facilitating the unilateral development of dams by accessing the required financial investments on the private market. In 2013, hydropower worth approximately US$35 billion in investment came on stream (Frankfurt School–UNEP Centre 2014).

In the Mekong, the US$760-million Nam Ngum 2 dam and the US$3.8-billion Xayaburi dam were fully financed by regional commercial banks and export credit agencies (Middleton 2009; BankTrack 2013; Matthews 2012). Merme et al. (2014) explain that compared to the high potential benefits and the conditions for investment facilitated by tax breaks, easing of trade rules, and obligations, the risks involved are limited. Not only do debt investments run over a relatively short period, but also risks are primarily borne by the national host, with IFIs, such as the WB and the ADB, providing political risk protection. Developers favor private investors because they carry fewer obligations in comparison with public or multilateral funding (Matthews 2012) that conditions their loans with social and environmental mitigation. Finally, the complexity of large infrastructure projects provides numerous possibilities for developing a myriad financial instruments that almost render the production of power to the sideline (Hildyard 2012; Lapavitsas 2013).

The NT2 dam is illustrative for contemporary dam development dynamics, and their incorporation in processes of financialization. Demands for renewable energy and targets set to reach these generate investment opportunities. Increasingly, diverse financial institutions are scanning strategic sectors, such as water, in which to lodge the surplus capital they control.[13] Which project to invest in, and via which financial instruments, is to a significant extent driven by the geography of resource capture and geopolitical relations. Increasing privatization and financialization of large-scale infrastructure has shifted dam planning, construction, ownership, and operation from the public to the private sphere. Consequently, this has decentered the role of the International Financial Institutions, the multilateral development banks, and the donor community, and with them their safeguards systems and environmental health-and-safety standards. Moreover, even though a large number of international standards have been put in place to ensure a series of safeguards, the system is far from foolproof and is easily eluded owing to a lack of transparency that undermines external accountability (Hildyard 2012; Matthews 2012; Merme, et al. 2014; Middleton 2009; Wright 2012).[14] The increased merging of the public and private, and the proliferation of stakeholders at multiple scales, are illustrative of the diffusion of governance characterizing dam-building coalitions in the twenty-first century. This leads to a situation where nobody oversees or understands the whole picture at any given point in time or location. While webs of agile and rapid financial flows and products thus rapidly produce megaspatial transformations with huge temporal impacts, their opacity and fragmentation effectively obfuscates possibilities for democratic decision making and accountability. This is problematic for three reasons. First, because financial interests do not necessarily or automatically align with the priorities of food security, access to water, or ecosystem integrity. Second, because decision-making institutions that govern dams and their impacts are disconnected in time and space. Third, the large investments required hijack national budgets over a long period of time, shifting public agency interest from public concerns to private gains.

This raises urgent questions of/for dam governance and democracy. What, for instance, is the level of public sector control over decisions shaping local livelihood security and environmental sustainability when these decisions are taken with minimal public involvement and in a context of dependency? How can effective forms of public accountability be institutionally regulated when the private-sector actors involved have a legal right to secrecy? In what follows, we offer some tentative answers to these questions.

25.5 Conclusion

We have shown how twentieth-century dams can be likened to Trojan Horses, legitimated as mechanisms of economic development while simultaneously operating as purveyors of political and ideological spatial strategies, reordering landscapes by taming unpredictable water flows as part of projects of expanding state space, and advancing capitalist relations of production. Dam building in the twentieth century thus facilitated "civilizing" and "normalizing" unruly communities, with society being reorganized through the thorough redefinition and delocalization of land and water rights. Precisely because dams both manifested and further established a concentration of political and economic powers able to redefine landscapes as homogenous and coherent (Lefebvre 1991: 352), contestation remained both geographically, as well as disciplinarily fragmented.

The actors driving dam development during the twentieth century were relatively easy to identify: public governance and financing organizations at national and international levels that used dams as the tangible material embodiment of their powers. Although difficult to challenge precisely because of these powers, they were conspicuously visible, and were usually embedded within or associated with the nation-state. In contrast, those responsible for contemporary dam development are much less easy to trace and find, as they are no longer primarily located in state agencies bound to some kind of accountability to a broader public. Indeed, dam building can now be characterized more as a Pandora's Box: it is the business of a multitude of actors and parties, with responsibilities for dam financing, building, and operation increasingly being assumed by private companies and financial agencies. The ever widening and globalizing dispersion of dam-building responsibilities and powers, coupled with a general absence of publicly available and reliable information, makes it difficult to unequivocally identify those responsible for dam construction and financing. This also makes it challenging to hold anyone accountable for the negative socioecological impacts of a dam, or to institutionally regulate accountability. Relying on ever more sophisticated "objective" information and participatory protocols to guarantee that dams are sustainable and socially beneficial will only partly fill this democratic void.

Hence, where the Trojan Horses were pivotal in ostentatiously visible geopolitical spatial strategies and tactics, the Pandora's Boxes represent a more complex conjuncture of spatial tactics that combine concealed motives of capital accumulation and financial speculation with open declarations of creating prosperity through economic development and adapting to climate change by harnessing green energy. Neoliberalization, accompanied by rapid technological advances, has radically altered both the dynamics of dam development, as well as the institutional possibilities for regulation and control. Financialization, climate variability, and uncertainties; a proliferation of private and quasi-private actors; and the blurring of the boundaries between public and private rights and responsibilities produce a governance setting that is more complex, opaque, and fragmented. It is certainly a setting and context in which dam development is much less public, because of the institutional room provided to protect private-sector compet-itiveness. Simultaneously, these larger-than-ever dams primarily geared for hydropower are confronted with a global community that is more than ever intimately connected. These connections facilitate the undemocratic processes of financialization that pro-duce uneven development, but also carry great potential for disrupting these by using their very speed and agility for new networks of contestation.

We contend that safeguarding sustainable and equitable hydropower development and more democratic forms of dam governance will depend importantly on creatively and strategically tapping into this potential to forge new practices of governance, including mechanisms of transparency and accountability. This demands the effec-tive organization of multiscalar alliances and coalitions between those experienc-ing and concerned about dam impacts. But it also requires active efforts to develop dam literacy and numeracy to allow wider distribution and discussion about what these impacts are, and educating those whose pension funds are invested in these projects. Here, sharing and mixing diverse sources of information and developing interdisciplinary knowledge is crucial, because the complexity and unpredictability of the socionatural dynamics provoked by dams defies straightforward predictions or assessments. The large distances in time and space between design and impact, and the disconnect between those who benefit from dam development and those who directly experience the consequences, make dam development a particularly wicked problem situation.

We argue that a Lefebvrian analysis of large dams and associated infrastructural development plans offer opportunities to think through these issues in a grounded and interdisciplinary manner. Lessons from the past show that dams are a particularly high-risk and high-cost affair, with benefits and costs unevenly and inequitable dis-tributed. However, equally important, we argue that analysis of spatial strategies (such as the conceptual triad of the lived, perceived, and conceived dimensions of space) can usefully complement analyses of the complex and contextual politics of specific dam projects.

Rather than developing objectified criteria for "good dams" as a way to contain neg-ative environmental effects, we call for more effort to be invested in creating "dam democracy": the development and distribution of analytical expertise on the full scope of costs and benefits of dams, both short-term and long-term. Unless forms of public accountability are effectively organized, and unless there are political possibilities for civil society groups to formulate and articulate alternative representations of the land-scape, the building of large dams should be put on hold. Dam development cannot con-tinue to be the monopoly of those who reap the short-term benefits, while others bear the costs—both now and in the future.

In short, this chapter has called for new ways of organizing "dissent" against large dams. To some degree, this may be thought of as the institutional organization (or channeling) of dissent, via which civil society may negotiate the distribution of costs and benefits of large dams on a more level playing field. This dissent should be viewed, we argue, as a normal and indeed useful and important part of the decision-making process regarding large dams. Our proposal thus calls for a more far-reaching governance transformation, beyond the (necessary but insufficient) development of globally valid and objectified criteria for "good dams." While useful, we argue that it is necessary and urgent to invest more effort in creating dam democracy—a concept that hinges on accepting the claim that dams will always be contested, and implies the necessity of embedding good governance practices within dam funding and development processes across multiple scales and jurisdictions. Dam democracy, as our analysis has suggested, requires simultaneous efforts to develop and enable dam numeracy and literacy in a context of transparency—which we suggest will lead to more equitable and sustainable outcomes for the future.

ACKNOWLEDGMENTS

Much of the work presented here is the result of research and discussions with Ineke Kleemans on twentieth-century dam development, with Vincent Merme on the Mekong and financialization, and with Ineke Kleemans and Hermen Smit on the Aswan High Dam.

NOTES

1. There is some disagreement about the definition of *large*. We follow the definition the World Commission of Dams applied and which comes from the International Commission on Large Dams. An overview of why such a classification is problematic is provided by Poff and Hart (2002).
2. For recent publications expressing these concerns, see for instance Fearnside (2005); Huber and Joshi (2015); Lehnder et al. (2009); Merme et al. (2014); Nilsson et al. (2005); Obosu-Mensah (1996); Öktem (2002); Showers (2009); WWF (2003); WWF (2013).
3. The accompanying faster and larger than anticipated loss in storage capacity, as Pomeranz (2009: 208) ironically points out for dams in the Himalaya region, is now used as an argument in itself for building more dams.
4. Fahim (1981: 233).
5. Nehru (1964); *The Hindu* (1957), in Klingensmith (2007: 254, 263).
6. The Organization for Economic Co-operation and Development. At the time of Usher's writing these were the original Member countries of the OECD; Austria, Belgium, Canada, Denmark, France, Germany, Greece, Iceland, Ireland, Italy, Luxembourg, the Netherlands, Norway, Portugal, Spain, Sweden, Switzerland, Turkey, the United Kingdom, and the United States. Plus the following countries that became members subsequently: Japan (1964), Finland (1969), Australia (1971), New Zealand (1973), Mexico (1994), the Czech Republic (1995), Hungary (1996), Poland (1996), and the Republic of Korea (1996).
7. Egypt had in the autumn of 1955 initially refused a Soviet offer as negotiations with the United States and the World Bank had reached an advanced stage by then (Biswas and Tortajada 2004).

8. Swyngedouw (1999) shows with far more detail how dams are used in similar spatial strate-gies in Franco's hydraulic plans in Spain. Another example is Frank Westerman's *Engineers of the Soul* (2011) for the hydraulic engineering in the Soviet Union.
9. For example, by introducing transferable land/water rights, the market as primary exchange, and agrarian industrial production.
10. This process is far from straightforward, historically specific and always contested as the case of Egypt shows. Even more so by the case of Afghanistan (Ahlers et al. 2014) where dam development by both the United States and the then Soviet Union were negotiated by a government seeking to unify a fragmented collection of ethnically diverse community into a nation-state.
11. For example, the possibilities of genetically modified organisms, the development of bio fuels, and the commodification and enclosure of remaining commons (such as forests, oceans, land/water rights, and so on).
12. The Environmental Assessment and Management Plan, the Resettlement Action Plan, and the Social and Environmental Management Framework and Operational Plan.
13. The April 2015 World Water Council/OECD report posits that the water sector should tap into the trillions of US$ that banks, pension funds, insurance firms, and sovereign wealth funds hold.
14. To mention but a few: the Equator Principles, Hydropower Sustainability Assessment Forum Protocol, United Nations Principles for Responsible Investment, WCD standards, International Finance Corporation Performance Standards, and WB safeguard policies.

REFERENCES

Ahlers, R., Brandimarte, L., Kleemans, I., and Sadat, S. (2014). "Ambitious development on fragile foundations: Criticalities of current large dam construction in Afghanistan," *Geoforum*, 54: 49–58.

Ahlers R., Budds, J., Joshi, D., Merme, V., and Zwarteveen, M. (2015). "Framing hydropower as green energy: Assessing drivers, risks and tensions in the Eastern Himalayas," *Earth Systems Dynamics*, 6: 195–204.

Ahlers, R. and Merme, V. (2016). "Financialisation, water governance and uneven develop-ment," *Wires Water*, 3: 766–74.

Ansar, A., Flyvbjerg, B., Budzier, A., and Lunn, D. (2014). "Should we build more large dams? The actual costs of hydropower megaproject development," *Energy Policy*, 69: 43–56.

Baghel, R. and Nüsser, M. (2010). "Discussing large dams in Asia after the World Commission on Dams: Is a political ecology approach the way forward?" *Water Alternatives*, 3(2): 231–48.

Baird, I., Shoemaker, B., and Manorom, K. (2015). "The people and their river, the World Bank and its Dam: Revisiting the Xe Bang Fai River in Laos," *Development and Change*, 46(5): 1080–105.

Bakker, K. (1999). "The politics of hydropower: Developing the Mekong," *Political Geography*, 18: 209–32.

Bakker, K. (2010). *Privatizing Water: Governance Failure and the World's Water Crisis*. Ithaca, NY: Cornell University Press.

BankTrack. (2013). *Dodgy Deal: Xayaburi Dam Project*, <http://www.banktrack.org/manage/ajax/ems_dodgydeals/createPDF/xayaburi_-dam_project>.

Baviskar, A. (ed.) (2007). *Waterscapes: The Cultural Politics of a Natural Resource.* Delhi: Permanent Black.

Biswas, A. (2004). "Dams: cornucopia or disaster?" *International Journal of Water Resources Development*, 20(1): 3–14.

Biswas, A. K. and Tortajada, C. (2004). *Hydropolitics and Impacts of the High Aswan Dam.* Cairo: Advisory Panel Project on Water Management, Ministry of Water Resources and Irrigation.

Borzutzky, S. and Berger, D. (2010). "Dammed if you do and dammed if you don't: The Eisenhower Administration and the Aswan Dam," *Middle East Journal*, 64(1): 84–102,

Brenner, N. and Elden, S. (2009). "Henri Lefebvre on state, space, territory," *International Political Sociology*, 3: 353–77.

Briscoe, J. (1999). "The financing of hydropower, irrigation and water supply infrastructure in developing countries," *International Journal of Water Resources Development*, 15(4): 459–91.

Briscoe, J. (2010). "Overreach and response: The politics of the WCD and its aftermath," *Water Alternatives*, 3(2): 399–415.

Cole, M. A., Elliot, R., and Strobl, E. (2014). "Climate change, hydro-dependency, and the African dam boom," *World Development*, 60: 84.

Cullather, N. (2002). "Damming Afghanistan: Modernization in a buffer state," *Journal of American History*, 89(2): 512–37.

Duflo, E. and Pande, R. (2007). "Dams," *Quarterly Journal of Economics*, 122(2): 601–46.

Escobar, A. (1995). *Encountering Development: The Making and Unmaking of the Third World.* Princeton: Princeton University Press.

Fahim, H. M. (1981). *Dams, People, and Development: The Aswan High Dam Case.* New York: Pergamon Press.

Fearnside, P. M. (2005). "Do hydroelectric dams mitigate global warming? The case of Brazil's Curuá-Una Dam," *Mitigation and Adaptation Strategies for Global Change*, 10(4): 675–91.

Fletcher, R. (2010). "When environmental issues coincide: Climate change and the shifting political ecology of hydroelectric power," *Peace Conflict Review*, 5: 1–15.

Flyvbjerg, B., Bruzelius, N., and Rothengatter, W. (2003). *Megaprojects and Risk: An Anatomy of Ambition.* Cambridge: Cambridge University Press.

Flyvbjerg, B. (2014). "What you should know about megaprojects and why: An overview," *Project Management Journal*, 45: 6–19.

Frankfurt School–UNEP Centre/BNEF (2014). *Global Trends in Renewable Energy Investment: Key Findings.* Frankfurt School of Finance and Management gGmbH, <http://fs-unep-centre.org/publications/gtr-2014>.

Goldsmith, E. and Hildyard, N. (1984). "The politics of damming," *Ecologist*, 14(5–6): 221–31.

Goonewardena, K., Kipfer, S., Milgrom, R., and Schmid, C. (2008). *Space, Difference, Everyday Life: Reading Henri Lefebvre.* New York and London: Routledge.

Haraway, D. (1991). *Simians, Cyborgs and Women: The Reinvention of Nature.* New York: Routledge.

Harvey, D. (1996). *Justice, Nature and the Geography of Difference.* Cambridge and Oxford: Blackwell.

Hildyard, N. (2012). *More than Bricks and Mortar. Infrastructure-as-Asset-Class: Financing Development or Developing Finance? A Critical Look at Private Equity Infrastructure Funds.* Dorset: The Corner House.

Hirsch, P. (2010). "The changing political dynamics of dam building on the Mekong." *Water Alternatives*, 3(2): 312–23.

Huber, A. and Joshi, D. (2015). "Hydropower, anti-politics, and the opening of new political spaces in the Eastern Himalayas," *World Development*, 76(c): 13–25. <http://econpapers. repec.org/article/eeewdevel/>.

ICOLD (2006). *The Role of Dams in the XXI Century*, <http://www.hydrocoop.org/publications/Role_of_Dams_new.pdf>.

International Hydropower Association. (2014). "Response of the International Hydropower Association to the publication *Should we Build more Large Dams? The Actual Costs of Hydropower Megaproject Development*, by Atif Ansar, Bent Flyvbjerg, Alexander Budzier, Daniel Lunn, <www.hydropower.org>.

Imhof, A. and Lanza, G. R. (2010). "Greenwashing hydropower," *World Watch*, 23(1): 8–14.

International Rivers Network. (2014). *World Rivers Review*, June, <http://www.international-rivers.org/node/8328>.

International Rivers Network. (2010). *African Dams Briefing*, <http://www.internationalrivers. org/files/attached-files/afrdamsbriefingjune2010.pdf>.

Islar, M. (2012). "Privatised hydropower development in Turkey: A case of water grabbing?" *Water Alternatives*, 5(2): 376–91.

Kaika, M. (2006). "Dams as symbols of modernization: The urbanization of nature between geographical imagination and materiality," *Annals of the Association of American Geographers*, 96(2): 276–301.

Khagram, S. (2003). Neither temples nor tombs: A global analysis of large dams. *Environment* 45(4): 28–37.

Klingensmith, D. (2007). *"One Valley and a Thousand": Dams, Nationalism and Development*. New Delhi: Oxford University Press.

Kogan, G. (2013). *The socio-environmental history of the floods in São Paulo 1887–1930*. Unpublished MSc thesis. Delft: UNESCO-IHE, <https://cosmopista.files.wordpress. com/2014/11/thesis_gabrielkogan.pdf>.

Lapavitsas, C. (2013). *Profiting Without Producing: How Finance Exploits Us All*. London: Verso.

Ledec, G. and Quintero, J. D. (2003). "Good dams and bad dams: Environmental criteria for site selection of hydroelectric projects," *Sustainable Development Working Paper No. 16*. Washington, DC: The World Bank, Latin America and Caribbean Region Environmentally and Socially Sustainable Development Department (LCSES).

Lefebvre, H. (1976). *The Survival of Capitalism*. London: Allison and Busby.

Lefebvre, H. (1991). *The Production of Space*. Oxford: Blackwell.

Lehner, B., Liermann, C., Revenga, C., Vörösmarty, C., Fekete, B., Crouzet, P., Döll, P., Endejan, M., Frenken, K., Magome, J., Nilsson, C. O., Robertson, J., Rödel, R., Sindorf, K., and Wisser, D. (2011). "High-resolution mapping of the world's reservoirs and dams for sustainable river-flow management," *Frontiers in the Ecology and Environment*, 9(9): 494–502, <doi:10.1890/100125>.

Linton, J. and Budds, J. (2014). "The hydrosocial cycle: Defining and mobilizing a relational–dialectical approach to water," *Geoforum*, 57: 170–80.

Little, T. (1965). *High Dam at Aswan: The Subjugation of the Nile*. New York: John Day.

Matthews, N. (2012). "Water grabbing in the Mekong Basin: An analysis of the winners and losers of Thailand's hydropower development in Lao PDR," *Water Alternatives*, 5(2): 392–411.

McCully, P. (1996). *Silenced Rivers: The Ecology and Politics of Large Dams*. London: Zed Books.

Meehan, K. (2013). "Tool-power: Water infrastructure as wellsprings of state power," *Geoforum*, 57: 215–24.

Merme, V., Ahlers, R., and Gupta, J. (2014). "Private equity, public affair: Hydropower financing in the Mekong Basin," *Global Environmental Change*, 24: 20–9.

Middleton, C. (2009). *Thailand's Commercial Bank's Role in Financing Dams in Laos and the Case for Sustainable Banking*, <https://www.internationalrivers.org/resources/thailand%E2%80%99s-commercial-banks%E2%80%99-role-in-financing-dams-in-laos-and-the-case-for-sustainable>.

Mitchel, T. (2002). *Rule of Experts: Egypt, Technopolitics, Modernity*. Berkeley: University of California Press.

Moore, J. W. (2011). "Transcending the metabolic rift: A theory of crises in the capitalist world-ecology," *Journal of Peasant Studies*, 38(1): 1–46.

Molle, F., Foran, T., and Käkönen, M. (2009). "Old and new hydropower players in the Mekong region: Agendas and strategies," in F. Molle, T. Foran, and M. Käkönen (eds.), *Contested Waterscapes in the Mekong Region: Hydropower, Livelihoods, and Governance*. London: Earthscan, pp. 23–45.

Nilsson, C., Reidy, C.A., Mats Dynesius, M., and Revenga C. (2005). "Fragmentation and flow regulation of the world's large river systems," *Science*, 308(5720): 405–8.

Obosu-Mensah, K., (1996). *Ghana's Volta Resettlement Scheme: The Long-Term Consequences of Post-Colonial State Planning*. San Francisco: International Scholars Publications.

Öktem, K. (2002). "When dams are built on shaky grounds: Policy choice and social performance of hydro-project based development in Turkey," *Erdkunde*, 56(3): 310–25.

Poff, N. L. and Hart, D. D. (2002). "How dams vary and why it matters for the emerging science of dam removal," *Bioscience*, 52: 659–738.

Pomeranz, K. (2009). "The great Himalayan watershed. Agrarian crisis, mega-dams and the environment," *New Left Review*, 58: 5–39.

Priemus, H., Flyvbjerg, B., and Wee, B. (2008). *Decision-Making on Mega-Projects: Cost–Benefit Analysis, Planning and Innovation*. Chletenham: Edward Elgar.

Probe International. (2004). *Ten Reasons Why the World Bank Should Not Finance the Nam Theun 2 Power Company in Lao PDR*, <http://journal.probeinternational.org/?s=Ten+reasons+why+the+World+Bank+should+not+finance+the+Nam+Theun+2+power+company+in+Lao+PDR>.

Scott, J. C. (1998). *Seeing Like a State: How Certain Schemes to Improve the Human Condition have Failed*. New Haven and London: Yale University Press.

Scudder, T. (2005). *The Future of Large Dams: Dealing with Social, Environmental, Institutional and Political Costs*. London: Earthscan.

Schultz, B. (2002). "Role of dams in irrigation, drainage and flood control," *International Journal of Water Resources Development*, 18(1): 147–62.

Showers, K. B. (2009). "Congo River's Grand Inga hydroelectricity scheme: Linking environmental history, policy and impact," *Water History*, 1(1): 31–58.

Smit, H. (forthcoming). "Increasing production, resource extraction and controlling territory through construction of large water infrastructure on the Eastern Nile 1820–2014."

Smith, N. (2006). "Nature as accumulation strategy," in L. Panitch and C. Leys (eds.), *Socialist Register 2007: Coming to Terms with Nature*. Monmouth: Merlin Press.

Smits, M. (2011). "Hydropower and the green economy in Laos: Sustainable developments?" unpublished paper presented at the *Conference on Planning for the Future: Decision Making on Energy Policy*, Kuala Lumpur, Malaysia.

Swyngedouw, E. (1999). "Modernity and hybridity: Nature, regeneracionismo, and the production of the Spanish waterscape, 1890–1930," *Annals of the Association of American Geographers*, 89(3): 443–65.

Swyngedouw, E. (2007). "Technonatural revolutions: The scalar politics of Franco's hydro-social dream for Spain, 1939–1975," *Transactions of the Institute of British Geographers*, 32(1): 9–28.

Tignor, R., (1966). *Modernization and British Colonial Rule in Egypt, 1882–1914*. Princeton. NJ: Princeton University Press.

Tvedt, T. (2004). *The River Nile in the Age of the British: Political Ecology and the Quest for Economic Power*. Cairo: American University in Cairo Press.

Tucker, R. P. (2010). "Containing communism by impounding rivers: American strategic interests and the global spread of high dams in the early Cold War," in J. R. McNeill and C. R. Unger (eds.), *Environmental Histories of the Cold War*. Washington, DC; New York; Cambridge: Cambridge University Press.

Usher, A. D. (ed.). (1997). *Dams as Aid: A Political Anatomy of Nordic Development Thinking*. London: Taylor & Francis.

Vörösmarty, C. J., McIntyre, P. B., Gessner, M. O, et al. (2010). "Global threats to human water security and river biodiversity," *Nature*, 467: 555–61.

Ward, M. (2010). *The Main Report of the Private Sector Investment Project*, <https://www.transparency-partnership.net/sites/default/files/2010_psi_ward_engaging_private_sector_capital_at_scale_in_financing_low_carbon_infrastructure.pdf>.

Warner, J. (2013). "The Toshka mirage in the Egyptian desert: River diversion as political diversion," *Environmental Science and Policy*, 30: 102–12.

Westerman, F. (2011). *Engineers of the Soul*. New York: Overlook Press.

Wilson, J. (2011). "Notes on the rural city: Henri Lefebvre and the transformation of everyday life in Chiapas, Mexico," *Environment and Planning D: Society and Space*, 29: 993–1009.

Wong, S. M. T. (2010). *Making the Mekong: Nature, Region, Postcoloniality*, PhD dissertation, Department of Geography, Ohio State University.

World Commission on Dams. (2000). *Dams and Development: A New framework for Decision-Making*. London: Earthscan.

Wright, C. (2012). "Global banks, the environment, and human rights: The impact of the equator principles on lending policies and practices," *Global Environmental Politics*, 12(1): 56–77.

WWC/OECD. "Water: fit to finance? Catalyzing national growth through investment in water security," *Report of the High Level Panel on Financing Infrastructure for a Water-Secure World*, April. Marseille: World Water Council.

WWF (2003). *Dam right! WWF's dam inititaive; An investor's guide to dams*, < http://awsassets.panda.org/downloads/investorsguidedams.pdf>.

WWF (2013). *The seven sins of dam building*. WWF International-Freshwater Programme and WWF-Germany, <http://awsassets.panda.org/downloads/wwf_seven_sins_of_dam_building.pdf>.

Zarfl, C., Lumsdon, A. E., Berlekamp, J., Tydecks, L., and Tockner, K. (2014). "A global boom in hydropower dam construction," *Aquatic Sciences*, <doi:10.1007/s00027-014-0377-0>.

Zwarteveen, M. (2015). "Regulating water, ordering society," Inaugural Lecture, University of Amsterdam, <http://www.oratiereeks.nl/upload/pdf/PDF-5940weboratie_Zwarteveen_-_DEF.pdf.>.

Index

Tables and figures are indicated by an italic *t* and *f* following the page number. Footnotes are indicated by 'n' followed by the footnote number if there is more than one footnote on the page.

Milton Keynes UK
Ingram Content Group UK Ltd
UKHW050655261024
450073UK00002B/1